BIG TOWN ☆ BIOGRAPHY

LIVES AND TIMES OF THE CENTURY'S CLASSIC NEW YORKERS

JAY MAEDER, Series Editor

Misha Erwitt, Daily News

DAILY NEWS BOOKS

DAILY ◉ NEWS

2000

BIG TOWN ★ BIOGRAPHY

LIVES AND TIMES OF THE CENTURY'S CLASSIC NEW YORKERS

Library of Congress
Catalog Card Number: 99-67788
ISBN: 1-58261-238-2

JAY MAEDER, Series Editor

ROBERT SHIELDS, Series Designer

LES GOODSTEIN, Executive Producer

PRINTED IN THE UNITED STATES

BIG TOWN ★ BIOGRAPHY

EDITOR'S NOTE

This volume collects most of the BIG TOWN BIOGRAPHY series that appeared in the New York Daily News between February and December 1999, and it is a companion to the previously issued BIG TOWN/BIG TIME, collecting the 1998 Daily News series of that name.

Most of the pieces herein appear as originally published. Some of them have been retouched to one degree or another. A few have been rewritten. One has been expanded from a single installment into a two-parter.

BIG TOWN/BIG TIME and BIG TOWN BIOGRAPHY were created by the Daily News in celebration of the City of New York on the occasion of the 20th Century's passage into the 21st. Both of these millennial observations were recipients of corporate funding that assured their runs. BIG TOWN BIOGRAPHY is grateful to P.C. Richard & Son and Consolidated Edison of New York for their sponsorship.

JAY MAEDER
New York Daily News
December 1999

Misha Erwitt, Daily News

BIG TOWN ★ BIOGRAPHY

LIVES AND TIMES OF THE CENTURY'S CLASSIC NEW YORKERS

TABLE OF CONTENTS

BIOGRAPHY 1
VIVIAN GORDON: Moth to the Flame...11

BIOGRAPHY 2
JOHNNY BRODERICK: True Detective...12

BIOGRAPHY 3
ARNOLD ROTHSTEIN: The Big Gray Rat...13

BIOGRAPHY 4
TEXAS GUINAN: Heart of Gold...14

BIOGRAPHY 5
GENE TUNNEY: Breaks of the Game...15

BIOGRAPHY 6
HENRY CLAY FRICK: American Sepulchral...16

BIOGRAPHY 7
THE DEAD END KIDS: East Side Story...17

BIOGRAPHY 8
KIP AND ALICE RHINELANDER: Social Error...18

BIOGRAPHY 9
ANNA LONERGAN: Silence of the Rose...19

BIOGRAPHY 10
ANTHONY COMSTOCK: Burning the Witch...20

BIOGRAPHY 11
DR. FREDERICK COOK: The Grail at the Top of the World...21

BIOGRAPHY 12
JOHN PURROY MITCHEL: The Boy Mayor...22
(Part one of two)

BIOGRAPHY 13
JOHN PURROY MITCHEL: The War Mayor...23
(Part two of two)

BIOGRAPHY 14
A. PHILIP RANDOLPH: Hammer and Tongs...24

BIOGRAPHY 15
JOHN D. ROCKEFELLER JR.: God's Gold...25

BIOGRAPHY 16
MOLLY GOLDBERG: Come Will and Come May...26

BIOGRAPHY 17
NATHAN HANDWERKER: Good Dog...27

BIOGRAPHY 18
FATHER DIVINE: Peace in the Valley...28

BIOGRAPHY 19
MAJOR BOWES: Around and Around...29

BIOGRAPHY 20
JACOB RUPPERT: The Old Ball Game...30

BIOGRAPHY 21
JAFSIE: Half-Dream...31

BIOGRAPHY 22
MAMMA LEONE: Un Piccolo Posticino...32

BIOGRAPHY 23
HETTY GREEN: Penny Saved, Penny Earned...33

BIOGRAPHY 24
BAT MASTERSON: Guns Off...34

BIOGRAPHY 25
CHARLES CHAPIN: The Good Earth...35

BIOGRAPHY 26
MONK EASTMAN: Our Lost Pal...36

BIOGRAPHY 27
KID DROPPER: Rites of Passage...37

BIOGRAPHY 28
NIKOLA TESLA: Stormbringer...38

BIOGRAPHY 29
ROBERT ELLIOTT: Good with Electricity...39

BIOGRAPHY 30
ARTHUR SCHOMBURG: The Frontiersman...40

BIG TOWN BIOGRAPHY

BIOGRAPHY 31
JOHN HAMMOND: White Cat...41

BIOGRAPHY 32
NATHAN STRAUS: Safe as Milk...42

BIOGRAPHY 33
RODMAN WANAMAKER: Dreamland...43

BIOGRAPHY 34
CLIFFORD HOLLAND: The Digger...44

BIOGRAPHY 35
MOCK DUCK: Red Flags...45
(Part one of three)

BIOGRAPHY 36
MOCK DUCK: Blood of the Flower...46
(Part two of three)

BIOGRAPHY 37
MOCK DUCK: Blood of the Rooster...47
(Part three of three)

BIOGRAPHY 38
SHIPWRECK KELLY: The Guy in the Sky...48

BIOGRAPHY 39
ALICE DIAMOND: Not the Kind to Bear a Grudge...49

BIOGRAPHY 40
ZELDA FITZGERALD: Awfully Happy...50

BIOGRAPHY 41
AL JOLSON: Faint Lavender...51

BIOGRAPHY 42
BIG TIM SULLIVAN: Damned Fine Irishman...52

BIOGRAPHY 43
R.F. OUTCAULT: Polychromous Effulgence...53

BIOGRAPHY 44
HARRY REICHENBACH: Packing the House...54

BIOGRAPHY 45
GEORGE AND IRA GERSHWIN: Out to Write Hits...55

BIOGRAPHY 46
ALAIN LOCKE: Forward on a Star...56

BIOGRAPHY 47
FRANKIE MANNING: At the Hop...57

BIOGRAPHY 48
CHARLES ATLAS: Clean Work...58

BIOGRAPHY 49
GEORGE V. DENNY JR.: Yes and No...59

BIOGRAPHY 50
EDWIN FRANKO GOLDMAN: On the Mall...60

BIOGRAPHY 51
TOSCANINI: Miracle of the Canaries...61

BIOGRAPHY 52
JOHN REED: The Free of Washington Square...62

BIOGRAPHY 53
SIDNEY HILLMAN: Constructive Cooperation...63

BIOGRAPHY 54
FATHER DUFFY: God and Country...64

BIOGRAPHY 55
SMOKY JOE MARTIN: Last of the Breed...65

BIG TOWN BIOGRAPHY

LIVES AND TIMES OF THE CENTURY'S CLASSIC NEW YORKERS

BIOGRAPHY 56
CONDÉ NAST: Golden Needles...66
(Part one of two)

BIOGRAPHY 57
CONDÉ NAST: Golden Needles...67
(Part two of two)

BIOGRAPHY 58
PHIL PAYNE: Cute Newspaper
Stuff...68
(Part one of two)

BIOGRAPHY 59
PHIL PAYNE: Cute Newspaper
Stuff...69
(Part two of two)

BIOGRAPHY 60
FRANCES GRAYSON: Still Small
Voice...70
(Part one of two)

BIOGRAPHY 61
FRANCES GRAYSON: Still Small Voice...71
(Part two of two)

BIOGRAPHY 62
GEORGE PALMER PUTNAM: Inventing Amelia...72

BIOGRAPHY 63
FLOYD BENNETT: The Isles Beyond the Ice...73

BIOGRAPHY 64
HELEN WALSH: Called by Angels...74

BIOGRAPHY 65
BERNARR MACFADDEN: Out Goes the Bad Air...75

BIOGRAPHY 66
BIG BILL DWYER: The Sporting Life...76

BIOGRAPHY 67
STANLEY WEYMAN: Not Wholly Symmetrical...77

BIOGRAPHY 68
RICHARD WHITNEY: Not Good
Enough...78

BIOGRAPHY 69
DIXIE DAVIS: Nice Boy...79

BIOGRAPHY 70
JOHNNY ROVENTINI: Smoke and
Mirrors...80

BIOGRAPHY 71
DICK MERRILL: Over the Trees...81

BIOGRAPHY 72
GERALD MacGUIRE: Conspiracy
Theory...82

BIOGRAPHY 73
JUAN TRIPPE: Chosen Instrument...83

BIOGRAPHY 74
BRIGID AND WILLIE HITLER: The In-Laws...84

BIOGRAPHY 75
GEN. ROBERT DANFORD: Under Arms, Sort Of...85

BIOGRAPHY 76
JOHN ROY CARLSON: The Joiner...86

BIOGRAPHY 77
MEYER LEVIN: The Bombardier...87

BIOGRAPHY 78
HARRY THE HIPSTER: Frantic...88

BIOGRAPHY 79
LEWIS VALENTINE: Many a Black Eye...89

BIOGRAPHY 80
RED BARBER: Another Country...90

BIG TOWN ★ BIOGRAPHY

BIOGRAPHY 81
SUGAR RAY ROBINSON: The Sweet Life...91

BIOGRAPHY 82
GENEROSO POPE: Good Soldier...92
(Part one of two)

BIOGRAPHY 83
GENEROSO POPE: Good Soldier...93
(Part two of two)

BIOGRAPHY 84
JOSEPH SCOTTORIGGIO: Rain on the Grave...94

BIOGRAPHY 85
JOE GOULD: The Duty of the Bohemian...95

BIOGRAPHY 86
ED AND PEGEEN FITZGERALD: For Better or for Worse...96

BIOGRAPHY 87
TOOTS SHOR: Prayers for the Dead...97

BIOGRAPHY 88
ROXY: Pleasant Dreams...98

BIOGRAPHY 89
DR. MARTIN COUNEY: All the World Loves a Baby...99

BIOGRAPHY 90
DAZZY VANCE: One and Only One...100

BIOGRAPHY 91
SAMUEL BATTLE: An Officer and a Gentleman...101

BIOGRAPHY 92
JOSEPH RYAN: Quiet Curses...102

BIOGRAPHY 93
WILLIE BRYANT: Something Big...103

BIOGRAPHY 94
MINNIE MARX: Mother's Day...104

BIOGRAPHY 95
BILLY STRAYHORN: Cracking the Code...105

BIOGRAPHY 96
HARRY SMITH: Perfecting the Self...106

BIOGRAPHY 97
MAD DOG COLL: Mayhem...107

BIOGRAPHY 98
GEORGE METESKY: Fair Play...108

BIOGRAPHY 99
VITO BATTISTA: Go Fight City Hall...109

BIOGRAPHY 100
FRED FRIENDLY: High Road...110

BIOGRAPHY 101
CHUCK McCANN: Absence of Restraint...111

BIOGRAPHY 102
STANFORD WHITE: All Things Gorgeous...112

BIOGRAPHY 103
SIME SILVERMAN: Mugging the Theater...113

BIOGRAPHY 104
HART CRANE: Falling Shadows...114

BIOGRAPHY 105
ANNE CHISARI: Human Interest Story...115

BIG TOWN BIOGRAPHY

LIVES AND TIMES OF THE CENTURY'S CLASSIC NEW YORKERS

BIOGRAPHY 106
OSCAR COLLAZO: Ni con Carcel, Ni con Balas...116

BIOGRAPHY 107
RALPH & ALICE KRAMDEN: Hitting the High Note...117

BIOGRAPHY 108
JUNIUS KELLOGG: The Unfixer...118

BIOGRAPHY 109
DR. WALLACE HOWELL: Stormy Weather...119

BIOGRAPHY 110
BOBBY THOMSON: Watching It Sail...120

BIOGRAPHY 111
RUDOLPH HALLEY: Streak of Light...121

BIOGRAPHY 112
THE HARLEM GLOBETROTTERS: Showtime in Jerusalem...122

BIOGRAPHY 113
AUSTIN TOBIN: The Port Authority...123

BIOGRAPHY 114
PAT WEAVER: Remembering the Future...124

BIOGRAPHY 115
BISHOP SHEEN: God Love You...125

BIOGRAPHY 116
BILL W.: Great White Light...126

BIOGRAPHY 117
SAM LeFRAK: Better Homes and Gardens...127

BIOGRAPHY 118
MICKEY MANTLE: So Young, So Strong...128

BIOGRAPHY 119
RUDOLF ABEL: The Spy Next Door...129

BIOGRAPHY 120
BILL SHEA: Piece of the Heart...130

BIOGRAPHY 121
CASEY STENGEL: The Baseball Angle...131

BIOGRAPHY 122
DION AND THE BELMONTS: Pure Bronx Soul...132

BIOGRAPHY 123
ED SULLIVAN: Sunday Night Story...133

BIOGRAPHY 124
J. RAYMOND JONES: Inside Outside...134

BIOGRAPHY 125
ROY COHN: No Fingerprints...135

BIOGRAPHY 126
ALLEN GINSBERG: Gone Dithyrambs...136

BIOGRAPHY 127
THE REV. JOHN GENSEL: Night Flock...137

BIOGRAPHY 128
GEORGE DELACORTE: Pharaoh in Wonderland...138

BIOGRAPHY 129
MOONDOG: Viking about Town...139

BIOGRAPHY 130
MARK RUDD: The Children's Crusade...140

BIG TOWN ★ BIOGRAPHY

BIOGRAPHY 131
THE SMOTHERS BROTHERS: Line of Responsibility...141

BIOGRAPHY 132
TINY TIM: The Voices Within...142

BIOGRAPHY 133
FREDDIE PRINZE: Everything in the World...143

BIOGRAPHY 134
JOE PAPP: The Torrent...144

BIOGRAPHY 135
SHIRLEY CHISHOLM: Riding Alone...145

BIOGRAPHY 136
JOE NAMATH: No Commandments...146

BIOGRAPHY 137
MARTIN HODAS: Naked City...147

BIOGRAPHY 138
FRANK SERPICO: Brothers in Blue...148

BIOGRAPHY 139
CRAZY JOEY GALLO: Dead Man Walking...149

BIOGRAPHY 140
THE KEKICHES AND THE PETERSONS: National
Pastime...150

BIOGRAPHY 141
JACQUELINE KENNEDY ONASSIS: Everyday
Things...151

BIOGRAPHY 142
ALBERTA HUNTER: Old Violins...152

BIOGRAPHY 143
MOTHER HALE: Amazing Grace...153

BIOGRAPHY 144
JONATHAN LARSON: La Vie Boheme...154

BIOGRAPHY 145
TONY BENNETT: Doing What You Do...155

BIOGRAPHY 146
AB CAHAN: Clean Noses...156

BIOGRAPHY 147
ARCHIE BUNKER: Change of Life...157

BIOGRAPHY 148
MADISON GRANT: All Along the Watchtower...158

**ALPHABETICAL LIST
OF BIOGRAPHIES**...159, 160

By JAY MAEDER
Daily News Staff Writer

*I'm a lady of the evening
And while youth and beauty last,
I never worry who will pay my rent.
For a while I'll be in clover,
And when easy days are over
I know I'll go the way that all
My predecessors went.*

THEY FOUND HER in a ditch in Van Cortlandt Park at daybreak, a pretty little frail gal with a rope knotted tight around her porcelain neck. Vivi admitted to 30; more likely she was 37ish or so; she still looked 19, one of those nature-blessed dolls time never touches, and she died beautiful, dressed in black cocktail velvet, one shoe off. Suddenly, on this Thursday the 26th of February 1931, the cops had a big problem here, strangled in the cold Bronx dawn. In her life, Vivian Gordon had been just another Broadway whore. In death, she was about to demolish the whole town.

HER SAD STORY went back to March of 1923, when Vivi — formerly one Bonnie Franklin of Michigan, now a broke and unemployed New York "fashion model," as they said, a young woman attempting to support a small daughter and make the daily ends meet — allowed herself to be picked up on W. 68th St. by a $20 john who turned out to be a vice cop named Andrew McLaughlin. Convicted of prostitution, she went to prison for three years; estranged ex-husband John Bischoff won custody of the daughter. Reporters found the child's heartbreaking letter as Vivi was hauled away: *Dear mama. I am very sorry you are sick. I hope you will be better soon. I miss you very much.*

By all accounts, Vivian Gordon went into the Bedford Reformatory a lambkin who was neither any better or worse than she should have been and came out a hardened criminal, determined to get hers in this life. Queen of the Courtesans, the papers started calling her after she died, a lass whose practice it had been to bed prominent gents and then threaten to make a lot of noise if they didn't pay up big. Vivi was no sweetie. This was understood. She was well known to Broadway. She was often seen with the racketeer Legs Diamond. She was soft enough to write poetry, but it wasn't the most sentimental stuff you ever read:

*I'm a lady of the evening
With a morning glory's beauty.
The payment for my raiment
I get in devious ways.
When some big and wealthy brute
Wants to love me 'cause I'm cute,
I admit that I submit
Because it pays.*

Broadway had seen her likes come and go. Some other strangled Vivi at some other moment would have been a single day's headline. But Vivian Gordon died on the eve of what was heralded to be her bombshell testimony before Judge Samuel Seabury's municipal corruption panel. The similarities between Vivi's sudden silencing and that of gambler Herman Rosenthal in 1912, as Rosenthal readied to sing out his guts to a grand jury, were more than apparent. In the Rosenthal case, a powerful police lieutenant had gone to the electric chair. Now Broadway trembled as the dead woman began to tell tales from her cold morgue slab.

THE SEABURY investigation had been smoldering since the previous summer, since about the time Supreme Court Justice Joseph Force Crater mysteriously vanished amid rumblings of various judicial irregularities, and it was not even yet in full fever. Eventually Mayor Beau James Walker would resign in disgrace; eventually Fiorello LaGuardia would come to City Hall in a

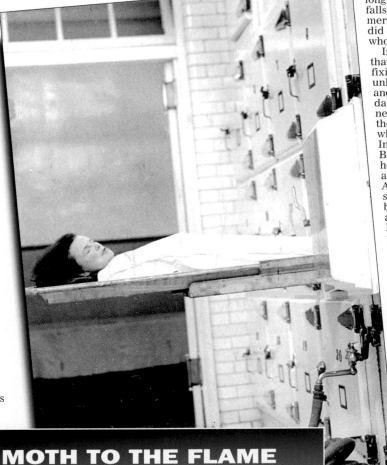

MOTH TO THE FLAME
Vivian Gordon

scalding bath of municipal reform; at the moment, in February 1931, Judge Seabury was still just sniffing at certain malodorous vice cops. Andrew McLaughlin was one of them, and these eight years later Vivi continued to harbor an old grudge. She was certain he had colluded with Bischoff to rob her of the daughter she was still fighting to win back. Vengefully she was ready to give up every dirty policeman and every grubby pol she had ever routinely met in her line of work. She had talked with Seabury once already, and she had another appointment. The judge felt she had the goods on a lot of important people.

Vivi had been perhaps a little given to hysteria. There was, it developed, no shred of evidence that either Bischoff or McLaughlin had any hand in her rubout. On the other hand, questions soon arose regarding the $2,000-a-year McLaughlin's mysterious ability to live well beyond his means. These questions then led to others, and presently McLaughlin was fired and indicted, just one of a

long parade of officers doomed to take falls as the Seabury probe burned mercilessly on. From her grave, Vivi did succeed in taking down the cop who had ruined her.

If it soon began to appear unlikely that Vivi's death was a case of witness fixing at all, by now what she had unleashed was out of control anyway, and fresh scandals kept breaking daily — particularly after the newspapers turned up the Queen of the Courtesans' Secret Diaries, which made nationwide headlines. In Audubon, N.J., 16-year-old Benita Bischoff followed every account of her mother's lurid life and death, and she wept every night. Apparently some schoolmates made some cruel remarks. Apparently a boy she liked withdrew his attentions. On Tuesday the 3rd of March, Benita stuffed towels into the kitchen doorjambs, walked to the range and turned on the gas.

THE OFFICIAL story, when it came out a couple of months later, was quite anticlimactically pedestrian. Vivi had been keeping company with a hood named Harry Stein, it was said, and it seemed he had developed a larcenous yen for her expensive mink coat. On the night of Feb. 25, so this yarn went, Stein and several confederates had lured Vivi from her E. 37th St. flat, put her into an automobile, choked the life out of her, divested her of the mink and dumped her in the Bronx. One Harry Schlitten confessed that he had been driving the death car and that he had watched the awful garroting in the rear-view mirror. On May 24, Mayor Walker and Police Commissioner Edward Mulrooney held a press conference to declare the Gordon case a simple matter of dishonor among thieves and to condemn the Seabury conspiratorialists who had been so quick to believe that cops had executed her.

For all that, there remained smart Broadway money figuring that a dope like Stein had to have been hired by some higher life form, and this line of argument was briefly introduced into Stein's trial, where it was hinted that Vivi knew too much about what had really become of the disappeared Judge Crater. In the end, this being New York City in 1931, Harry Stein was quickly acquitted of murder, and he seemed quite dumbfounded by the verdict.

*I'm a lady of the evening
Just like Cleopatra was.
The Queen of Sheba also
played my game.
Though by inches I am
dying,
There's not any use in crying.
I stay and play 'cause I'm
that way,
A moth that loves the flame.*

THE SEABURY PROBE would go on rattling the city to its basements for more than a year, but this was now the end of the sensational Vivian Gordon case. There has only been conjecture as to what Vivi might have really told Seabury had she lived another few days.

By JAY MAEDER
Daily News Staff Writer

HERE'S HOW Johnny Broderick handled ordinary smart guys. Here were three of them, standing outside a downtown restaurant, looking for trouble. Johnny smacked them around for a while, then he picked them up one by one and flung all three of them through the plate glass. Then he ran them in for malicious destruction of property, and the judge gave them 30 days and made them pay for the window.

Here's how Johnny Broderick handled racketeers like Vannie Higgins. Dapper Vannie would come around to Madison Square Garden for a sporting night out on the town, and Johnny would be waiting for him every time, and Johnny would send him crashing through a phone booth and make him leave. Vannie complained about this to the fixers on several occasions, but it never got him anywhere.

Here's how Johnny Broderick handled Legs Diamond, who blustered one night that he'd had enough of this Broderick and he was going to take the lousy copper for a ride. Word of this came to Johnny, who went out looking for a showdown and soon found Legs and his boys at Broadway and 46th. The boys fled at once. Legs gulped. Johnny dumped a trash bin over his head. Then he made him crawl away on his hands and knees as the whole Stem watched.

Here's how Johnny Broderick handled Two-Gun Crowley. Crowley was holed up at West End and 90th, fending off tear-gas bombs, challenging 300 cops outside to come and get him. Johnny stomped upstairs by himself, bashed down the door, ordered Crowley to come along and marched him out by the scruff of his neck.

Johnny was a good family man who spent his evenings around the piano at home in Jackson Heights with his wife and two daughters, and often he'd go back to St. Gabriel's parish in the old Gashouse District he'd grown up in and he'd sing "Mother Machree" in his beautiful tenor and all the old churchgoing ladies would nod and bawl. Then he'd go to his job, which was being the toughest, two-fistedest cop in New York City. Broadway Johnny, the papers called him, the One-Man Riot Squad. He broke his knuckles so many times that X-rays of his hands were literally used as medical school exhibits. Fellow cops called him Cemetery Bait, and they were all astonished when he actually lived long enough to finish 24 years on the job and retire.

JOHN JOSEPH BRODERICK came from E. 25th St., a turn-of-the-century Gashouse lad who quit school as a broth of a boy to go to

work driving brick trucks and coal wagons. As a young Teamster, he became labor leader Samuel Gompers' private bodyguard. For a while, he was a fireman. In January 1923 he joined the Police Department, and by April he made detective third grade, a jump that in those days a harness bull usually had to slave for about five years to accomplish. By March 1926 he was a detective first grade and running his own roving unit out of the Main Office Squad. It was, in fact, felt by no few of Detective Broderick's colleagues that he plainly had a Tammany angel somewhere in the city.

He was famous from the beginning for never bothering with a revolver or a nightstick. He used his fists, huge lethal pistons that could beat a man senseless in half a heartbeat. To "get brodericked" was recognized Broadwayese; it meant to be felled by a single piledriver punch. Dives would empty at the merest whisper that Johnny was coming around. Jack Dempsey always said he wouldn't fight Johnny for a million bucks.

At the same time, he was Broadway enough to wear tailored

TRUE DETECTIVE
Johnny Broderick

suits and monogrammed silk shirts — he admitted that he would have affected spats and a cane like his pal Mayor Jimmy Walker if he'd thought a $3,500-a-year cop could get away with it — and because he was charming and knew how to dress, he was usually appointed official escort when such VIPs as Queen Marie of Romania came to town. He was in trouble just once in his Roaring Twenties glory days, when, after police brawled with Communist fur strikers in 1926, he was accused of taking pay-offs from the fur companies. A court exonerated him. Otherwise, tirelessly mopping up the town with his longtime partner John Cordes, he was a public hero for years.

MAYOR WALKER'S fall from grace in late 1932 and the arrival of Fiorello LaGuardia's Fusion government a year later somewhat disrupted Broderick's career. As a

prominent symbol of Walker's New York, in early 1934 he abruptly found himself stripped of his grades, flopped back into uniform and sent out to pound a warehouse beat in Long Island City.

Somewhat mysteriously, this banishment didn't take: Just a few months later, LaGuardia's police commissioner, John O'Ryan, publicly called him a "model cop" and restored him to downtown detective status. Particularly after President Franklin Roosevelt personally requested his bodyguard services during a 1936 visit to the city, nobody in LaGuardia's administration ever troubled Johnny Broderick again.

BROADWAY Johnny had the satisfaction of finishing out his career on his own turf, in his middle age still a feared figure who prowled the Stem and its tributaries as a self-appointed demolisher of the clip joints that were fleecing just a few too many of the soldiers and sailors who were just a little too spellbound by the siren lights of Times Square. Through the war, a lot of boys had Johnny to thank for the beginnings of wisdom, as, meanwhile, a lot of sharpies got off the street fast, folding up their tents and clutching their bleeding noses.

Fifty years old, Johnny abruptly took retirement in July 1947. Something of a cloud darkened his departure; District Attorney Frank Hogan let it be known that Johnny was definitely under suspicion of having been entirely too friendly with certain underworld elements. Johnny addressed the whispers head-on; certainly he had visited gangster Owney Madden down in Hot Springs, he admitted; keeping up with the boys was his job. In any case, RKO was paying him a lot more than his $196-a-month pension for the film rights to his life story, and he could afford to retire anyway.

He tried to move into politics in 1949, but his bid for Tammany Hall's Times Square district leadership was unsuccessful. After that he settled into the life of a gentleman farmer outside Middletown, N.J. The RKO movie, which was supposed to have starred Robert Ryan, never got made. As late as 1959, there was still talk of a TV series or a Broadway musical or some other celebration of the life and times of New York's most legendary policeman, but nothing ever came of any of this either. On Jan. 16, 1966, Johnny died in his sleep at his home.

His obits still vividly remembered the One-Man Riot Squad of all those years earlier, and the Police Department took pains to make it clear that old Johnny was a dinosaur from another age, certainly no one who could ever fit into the enlightened modern 1960s. "He was a man of his time," reflected a veteran inspector who had known him for years. "Under the restrictions of today, he'd have a difficult time doing the things he did."

By JAY MAEDER
Daily News Staff Writer

THEY SAID OF Arnold Rothstein that he was the man who had fixed the 1919 World Series, though he was cleared of this charge in a court of law. It was, however, true that he had won $270,000 betting against the Chicago White Sox. And they said of Arnold Rothstein that he was the man behind Man o' War's only loss, and indeed he had cleaned up handsomely here as well. They said of Arnold Rothstein that he was the reason Gene Tunney took the heavyweight championship away from Jack Dempsey in September 1926, and, yes, it was the case that he had won $200,000 on that bout. There was perhaps a tendency among sporting men to imagine that when Arnold Rothstein bet on something, it had to be a sure thing. There were many things they said about Arnold Rothstein.

What they said about Arnold Rothstein that was demonstrably correct was that he was not always good about paying up when he lost. This has always been a lousy way for a professional gambler to run his business, and, when he was gut-shot inside the Park Central Hotel at Seventh Ave. and 54th St. on Sunday night the 4th of November 1928, it was widely agreed that his dishonorable ways had caught up with him at last. The papers all said pretty much the same thing: *Death. The only game he couldn't fix.*

He lingered until Tuesday morning. That very night, Al Smith lost the U.S. presidency to Herbert Hoover, and everybody said Arnold Rothstein would have won a good half million dollars.

THE KING OF 1920s Broadway was born a textile merchant's son on E. 47th St. in 1882. Never a lad much interested in day labor, by his early teens he was a capable pool shark, a habitué of the parlor run by New York Giants manager John McGraw; by century's turn he was a protégé of the gentleman gamblers Richard Canfield and Honest John Kelly, and in 1904 he opened his own faro house. After the 1912 Times Square murder of gambling kingpin Herman Rosenthal, Rothstein emerged as the principal financier of Broadway's floating crap games and other such enterprises. By the time of the '19 "Black Sox" scandal, he was the underworld's leading bailbondsman and was widely whispered to be the secret bankroll behind many rising criminal mobs.

The degree to which he had a hand in the Chicago fix was always murky; more likely he was just aware the fix was in and wagered accordingly; those more firmly implicated included his close associate Charles Stoneham, owner of the Giants. But it was the Series scandal that brought Rothstein to public attention, and thereafter he remained in the spotlight, a familiar high roller at the nation's racetracks and one of the more unassailable inhabitants of Mayor Jimmy Walker's roaring New York City, free to conduct his affairs as he pleased. A police commissioner who once denied Rothstein a gun permit got himself officially reprimanded.

For all the headlines, he was a man who lived in the shadows — like a rat in an alley, the criminal defense lawyer William Fallon said of him, "a big gray rat waiting for his cheese." Whatever the action was, the assumption went, Rothstein's fingers were sure to be in it somewhere.

HIS REPUTATION notwithstanding, the fact is that gamblers do drop bundles from time to time,

ARNOLD ROTHSTEIN SHOT

ROTHSTEIN FACES DEATH IN SILENCE
COAST GAMBLER, RAYMOND, TELLS ATTACKER'S NAME
Where Gambler Was Found

WOUND KILLS ROTHSTEIN; 3 BROADWAYITES HUNTED
Attended Stud Party's Gambler Welched
GIRL ATTACKER MOBBED
HIGH HONORS

THE BIG GRAY RAT
Arnold Rothstein

and through October 1928 all Broadway was abuzz with the story of the three-day stud game that had cost Rothstein somewhere between $300,000 and $800,000. The story went that once again he was stalling the payoff. The story went that his fellow players were most displeased.

On the night of Nov. 4, Rothstein dined with a showgirl at the Colony Club, then repaired to his regular table at Lindy's, on Broadway at 50th St., and held court until 10:20 p.m., when he took a phone call. On the line was one George McManus, a flamboyant Broadway character who had been present at the marathon stud game. There would be a brief creditors' conference in Room 349 of the nearby Park Central, McManus informed him. Rothstein appeared untroubled by the prospect. He declined someone's offer of a handgun, announced he'd be back shortly and strolled away whistling.

Forty minutes later, a hotel worker found him crumpling at the service entrance, his intestines and bladder demolished by a single bullet. Through his final agonized, gasping hours, he refused to utter a word to detectives at his hospital

bedside. Rothstein's death would cost a police commissioner and a district attorney their jobs and open municipal sewers to scrutiny that would ultimately force Jimmy Walker's resignation. The killing has not been solved to this day. In 1928, no one seriously expected that it ever would be.

EVEN AS the dead man went to his rest in Union Field Cemetery in Cypress Hills, there was already developing, as Daily News police reporter Frank Dolan noted, "a strange lassitude" in officialdom. Reports of the contents of Rothstein's vaults were rocking the town: millions of dollars' worth of stolen securities, ledgers proving him to be the moneyman behind numerous workers' strikes, notebooks establishing him as the nation's leading dope smuggler, documented links to top gangsters and respectable citizens alike. Rothstein was more than the monarch; he was nothing less than the octopus ("whose tentacles spread no man knows whither," reported the ever-lyrical Red Dolan). It was all plainly more than District Attorney Joab Banton really wanted to hear. Banton daily promised imminent arrests, but the stud players Rothstein was to have met were all released after questioning, and whenever Banton was pounced upon by the press he had, as Dolan put it, "nothing but fitful sobs to offer." Growled The News after some of the key vault evidence mysteriously disappeared: "This murder is making cynics out of a lot of people."

Indeed, months went by and nothing happened. By the summer of 1929, Police Commissioner Joseph Warren had been sacrificed. On-the-spot District Attorney Banton was on his way out too, ditched by Tammany Hall in favor of 69-year-old Thomas Crain, a more attractive candidate despite the fact that he was manifestly senile. In September, as Congressman Fiorello LaGuardia ran for mayor and made the unsolved killing a campaign issue, Banton angrily challenged him to name a single public official who had ever had any dealings with Rothstein, and LaGuardia immediately came up with evidence that a Tammany magistrate named Albert Vitale had borrowed nearly $20,000 from him. Amid this din, on the eve of Election Day, there was at last a murder indictment, against the gambler George McManus.

Once Walker was reelected, McManus went to trial and was immediately acquitted. It happened that there was no substantive evidence against him anyway, but on the other hand it was also true that he was the brother of a city police lieutenant.

THE ROTHSTEIN CASE, epitaphed The News, "will stand for many years to come as a classic example of how justice may be obstructed at every turn." Many documents from Rothstein's vault vanished forever. "If the Rothstein papers are ever made public," one lawyer who'd had an early glimpse at them said in 1929, "there are going to be a lot of suicides."

The sensational Vitale revelations, meanwhile, led directly to the Seabury probes that in 1932 forced Walker's resignation and paved the way for reformer LaGuardia's 1933 capture of City Hall.

In 1936, the Daily Mirror came up with suggestions that in fact Rothstein had never made it to Room 349 at all, that he had been gunned down in a stairwell by a drunken ex-con over an entirely separate financial disagreement. Whoever this shooter may have been, he rewrote 20th-century New York City's political history.

By JAY MAEDER
Daily News Staff Writer

TOWARD MIDNIGHT on Wednesday the 28th of June 1928, coincidentally enough the very night that New York Gov. Al Smith became the Democratic Party's presidential nominee and it was thus assured that Repeal would become a major election issue, raiding parties from President Calvin Coolidge's sternly Republican Department of Justice stormed through the Furnace Club, the Frivolity Club, the Jungle Room, the Beaux Arts, the Red Moon and several dozen more of Broadway's better joints and pinched 108 persons for alleged violations of the national Prohibition statutes. Among them, needless to say, was Mary Louise Guinan of the Salon Royale on W. 58th St., who, as perhaps the nation's foremost emblem of the everyday flouting of these statutes these nine dry years after the passage of the Volstead Act, was always getting hauled in for this and that and the other. These little local charges never stuck. New York's prim Committee of 14 kept branding Texas Guinan's various clubs "palaces of passion," but it was always the case, every time, that Tex's nubile showgirls, lasses such as young Barbara Stanwyck and 14-year-old Ruby Keeler, had their moms right there backstage monitoring them quite respectably. Nobody could say Tex didn't run a clean place. "Broadway is fairly crawling with tottering old ladies in lavender who are out chaperoning their hostess daughters," the Daily News observed. "Any young hostess can produce a mother. Two if necessary." Swell little game though all this had been for years, Texas Guinan was now in fact a federal case, and this was different.

In District Court in April 1929, Tex hitched up her sleeves to display her blinding bracelets and effortlessly made fools of her prosecutors. "The dry agents have testified that they saw many drunken people in the club," one inquisitor snapped. "Well, *they* were there," she purred. Tex was manifestly guilty of everything, and jurors took about half a minute to acquit her. "We're glad Miss

HEART OF GOLD
Texas Guinan

Guinan got off," The News editorialized. "A conviction would have been a victory for the Washington dry crowd which has baited and insulted New York City ever since the dry era began. Her acquittal in the face of all the evidence is a cheerfully hard-boiled answer, in the New York manner, to those tactics.

"It is more than that. If the dry snoopers don't change their present habits, Miss Guinan is the wealthiest defendant in a liquor case who will ever get to an actual jury trial in this city … How any jury can have the face to convict a penny-ante bootlegger after Miss Guinan's acquittal, we can't see. The little girl wasn't tried in vain."

The Justice Department fumed and stewed. All Broadway, meanwhile, danced and sang and made whoopee for days. About 50 U.S. senators, some of Tex's best customers, wired their congratulations.

THE STANDARD LINE about Tex was that she had a heart of gold and teeth to match. She really was a Texan, born in Waco in 1884, so proficient in trick riding and sharpshooting that she grew up on the Wild West roadshow circuit, the new Annie Oakley. After that, she landed in Hollywood and appeared in hundreds of silent oatburners. And after that, in the early 1920s, north of 35 by now,

she showed up in New York and fell in with Times Square racketeer Larry Fay, who was at this moment inventing the modern nightclub and who immediately decided that big, brassy, bob-haired, baubled Tex was exactly his idea of a hostess.

As Fay's El Fey Club became legendary, so too did Tex, queen of the storied Broadway night, lolling atop pianos, scratching drunks' ears, pouring oceans of overpriced gigglewater all around, merrily shouting "Hello, sucker!" at everyone who strolled into her clubs, pol and movie star and college boy alike. Subsequently Fay set her up in a few places of her own, and all through the Roaring '20s she was The Stem's most identifiable figure, a genially wisecracking broad full of quotable bons mots for the newspaper boys. "Success has killed more people than bullets!" "Nothing is more annoying than a husband!" "Men are like children and must be treated like children!" She was always easy pickings for the

moralists, who always gave her a laugh; they were the ones who most needed to visit her clubs, she said: "Then they would see what fools they are for not being happy."

Well, nobody loved the dry agents — "Uncle Sam's blue-snouted sleuths," The News jeered — and Tex always spotted them immediately when they showed up and turned the lights on them and called for applause. One night she had the band strike up "The Star-Spangled Banner" when the agents came in, and everybody successfully beat it out the back while the dopes stood at attention.

As things turned out, it was not the federals who finished Tex in New York. One of her bouncers did that, ill-advisedly ejecting one of Mayor Beau James Walker's well-connected pals one night. Late in 1929, correctly reading the handwriting on the wall as previously friendly local authorities became difficult, the lady moved to Chicago and set up shop anew.

THAT VENTURE lasted just a few months, until a shooting closed the club — "Money and women, they'll always cause trouble," Tex sighed — and in March 1930 she came back East. Through the summer she ran a place on Long Island. In September, she officially returned to Broadway, opening the Argonaut Club on W. 54th St. It burned down a few weeks later. "What's the matter?" The News inquired. "Hasn't Tex been kicking in?"

She tried taking 20 chorines and a jazz band on a European tour in May 1931, but France, Germany, Austria and Belgium refused them entry. "My name's getting me in plenty of trouble," she grumbled as papers around the globe headlined the spectacular journey to nowhere. Finally, Monte Carlo took the troupe in, and Tex left standing at the dock an Englishman who had offered to wed her so she could get working papers. SORRY COULD NOT MARRY YOU, she wired him. HAVE TOO MANY EXPENSES ALREADY.

Back in the U.S. by August, she opened a new hot spot in the Bronx, but that one shortly burned down too; by now, the Depression was making sucker money scarce anyway. In September, she took her girls on tour again — not glittering Europe this time, just the American burg circuit, starting with Bridgeport.

Somewhere in here, nearing 50, Tex found Jesus.

AIMEE SEMPLE McPherson was responsible for showing her the light. Not that evangelist McPherson herself was any mentor — she was mortified by Texas Guinan's attentions, actually — but Tex became obsessed with the idea of staging a dramatic production of McPherson's life story. "I'm becoming philosophical in my old age," she reflected. "I'm a good Catholic. I'll be a good evangelist. It's right up my alley. Once or twice, late at night sometimes, I've felt I could show people the way to happiness. You know what I mean. Not gin and jazz."

Still running her Gang of Twenty Beautiful Guinan Girls, now she was talking about opening her own tabernacle. "What an evangelist I'll make," she promised. "Lady Barker for the Lord. People will come from all over the world to see what the hell it's all about."

Instead, touring the Pacific Northwest in the fall of 1933, Tex fell gravely ill with amoebic dysentery. Rushed to a hospital in Vancouver, B.C., she died in a coma Sunday morning the 5th of November.

Two days later, Utah became the 36th state to ratify repeal of the 18th Amendment, and the times that had created Texas Guinan were over and done with.

TEX WAS BORNE back to New York by 18 of the 40 girls with whom she had left the city the previous January, and every sport on Broadway, from sugar daddies to bondsmen to cops to dips to good-time Charlies, showed up at the Gate of Heaven Cemetery in White Plains to pay their respects as she went to her rest. So did thousands of maddened housewives, who charged through police lines, climbed atop her vault and snatched up all the flowers as souvenirs. "Under the merciless spotlight," The News reported, "Tex seemed herself again."

By JAY MAEDER
Daily News Staff Writer

THE PRIDE OF Greenwich Village didn't even like the fight game very much. He was good at it, that's all; good enough, he recognized, to make a lot of money and leave the West Side docks far behind. It was purely a practical thing: efficient management of resources. Knocking a man down was something he knew how to do.

The fight game didn't like him very much either, and neither did the sportswriters or the fans. Gene Tunney didn't act like a fighter. Gene Tunney had airs. He spoke in complete sentences. He read Shakespeare, for God's sake. But it had to be granted that he was good. Between 1915 and 1928, he had 77 fights and lost just one of them, and only one man ever put him on the floor. Officially, he was down for nine. Unofficially, he was down for what felt to the whole world like eternity.

Years after the famous long-count fight, Tunney always insisted that he could have climbed to his feet any time he pleased. It was only that, down there on the mat, listening to the birdies tweet, lying there for another few seconds seemed the practical thing to do, particularly as long as the count was taking forever anyway.

The crowds roared in those days. Sometimes they still do. "Boxing has a romantic history that extends to the dawn of Christendom," said the well-read Tunney when he retired in August 1928. "It has actual drama. We see drama on a stage, but we realize that it is only a reflection of life. Boxing enfolds real drama." He was not unmindful of the poetry. He just didn't much like the game.

JAMES JOSEPH Tunney was born in May 1898, a longshoreman's son who grew up handy with his mitts around Greenwich and Christopher Sts. and went professional in 1915, easily beating all challengers. Shipped to France as a Marine, he became the light-heavyweight champ of first his regiment, then his camp, then the entire Corps. Then he met the American Expeditionary Forces champion and beat him too. Back home in 1919, he matter-of-factly told friends that someday he would be heavyweight champ of the world.

That same year, Jack Dempsey won that title when he bowled over Jess Willard and installed himself as a public hero in the golden age of prizefighting. The Pride of Greenwich Village was already breathing down his neck.

"THE FIGHTING MARINE" became America's light-heavyweight champ in January 1922 when he whipped Bat Levinsky at Madison Square Garden. A few months later, he lost the title to one Harry Greb, and most all the scribes wrote him off. At the Garden on Feb. 23, 1923, he made them eat their words when he slaughtered Greb and took the title back. Gene Tunney would never lose another fight.

On it went, and jaws began to drop: The man was a destroyer. At the Polo Grounds in July 1924, the referee stopped the fight when Georges Carpentier could no longer stand up. At the Polo Grounds in June 1925, Tunney annihilated Tom Gibbons, widely regarded as a leading contender for the heavyweight crown. By early 1926, the boxing world was reeling: Was this giant-killer going to be the one to challenge the legendary Dempsey?

The solons of the New York State Athletic

BREAKS OF THE GAME

Gene Tunney

On the floor, Sept. 22, 1927

Commission thought not; upstart Tunney, they said, could not even think about taking on the Manassa Mauler. In large disagreement was the boxing promoter Tex Rickard, who readily grasped what kind of gate Dempsey-Tunney would mean. In June, the commissioners flatly turned down Rickard's bid for a Dempsey-Tunney fight at Yankee Stadium. In July, Tunney handed the papers an astonishing public statement blistering commission chairman James Farley as a know-nothing political hack. It was a volcanic moment in ring circles. Fighters did not talk like that to the chairman. On Sept. 23, 1926, far from the commission's reach, Rickard defiantly staged the sensational Dempsey-Tunney bout at Sesquicentennial Stadium in Philadelphia.

The Mauler hadn't fought in three years. Even so, he was figured to take Tunney without breaking a sweat. It didn't happen. Tunney was simply the better fighter, and black-eyed Dempsey said so himself. "I have no alibis," he said. "I lost to a good man." Tunney, not otherwise known for graciousness, hailed the lion's heart of the fallen ex-champ.

And said he would be glad to give him a rematch any time.

THREE HUNDRED sixty-four days later, at Soldier Field in Chicago, before 150,000 screaming fans and a worldwide radio audience of 50 million, Tunney met Dempsey again in the fight no one has ever stopped talking about.

By Sept. 22, 1927, Tunney had plunged from popular favor. The public just didn't take to his standoffish, Shakespeare-reading ways. Not a lot

of people wanted him to stay champ. But Tunney, 29 years old and 189 pounds, remained the clearly superior ring general as Dempsey, a little older and a little heavier, made what one of the papers called "a dying man's effort to win." It was, indeed, noted that the Mauler fought plenty dirty, rabbit-punching Tunney again and again. Still, seven rounds into the thing, Tunney was giving Dempsey a beating.

Until, out of nowhere, two left hooks and a right cross knocked him off his feet for the first time in his life.

IT HAS ALWAYS been agreed that Tunney was on the floor for at least 14 seconds. But Dempsey stood dazed, failing to move at once to a neutral corner as required, and referee Dave Barry did not start the official count until the rest of the world had already counted five.

Tunney stirred at Barry's count of two — everyone else's seven.

Then, all things considered, he decided to stay down until Barry got to nine.

Whereupon, head cleared, he got up and proceeded to slug his way to a decision.

THE PLANET exploded. Even Tex Rickard shook his head and called Tunney the luckiest man who ever lived. Tunney conceded that the long count may have worked to his advantage. "But it wasn't my idea," he pointed out, not incorrectly.

"One of the breaks of the game," philosophically said Jack Dempsey, who would never fight again.

WOULD GENE Tunney have stayed champ without the long count? Who would ever really know? He fought just once more, at Yankee Stadium on July 26, 1928, against Tom (Hard Rock) Heeney, a man he shrugged off as "the best opponent that could be selected out of a very bad lot," and butchered him. The Stadium was only half full. Tex Rickard lost money.

A week later, worth $2 million, Tunney retired. "Professional boxing can offer me nothing further," he yawned. Two months after that, he married 21-year-old Polly Lauder, heiress to a steel fortune. The Pride of Greenwich Village had come a long way from the docks. The wedding story in the more formal papers identified the groom as "a son of Mrs. Lydon Tunney of Riverdale-on-Hudson."

The newlyweds honeymooned in Europe for a year. When they returned to New York in late 1929, Tunney had a British accent. "Gracious, I hope I haven't kept you waiting," he told reporters. Then he quoted Epicurus, used words like "ubiquitous" and asked a steward to fetch "a collation for these gentlemen."

Well, la-de-da, snorted the entire New York press corps. The man who had been heavyweight champion of the world didn't care. And he quietly disappeared into a life of country estates, yacht clubs and board directorships.

JACK DEMPSEY and Gene Tunney remained lifelong pals, not that they ever really saw each other very much. "Gene's always been around one class, and I've been around another," Dempsey observed in 1969. "I run a restaurant." That was another one of the breaks of the game.

When Tunney died in Greenwich, Conn., in November 1978, 83-year-old Dempsey cried like a baby.

By JAY MAEDER
Daily News Staff Writer

TO THE DEGREE that the steel magnate Henry Clay Frick ever thought much about irony, perhaps he found it amusing that the nation's coal miners were striking again on the very day of his death in December 1919 and that troops were readying to thrash them. It was otherwise his crusty satisfaction to note that he had outlived by several months his erstwhile friend and business partner Andrew Carnegie, who in his final days had sought a reconciliation that Frick took great pleasure in rebuffing. "Tell Carnegie," he snarled when the feeble old laird's olive branch was delivered to him, "that I will see him in Hell, where we are both going." No man to harbor illusions was Henry Frick. Neither, really, was Carnegie, who understood by that time that Frick lived in a much larger and finer house than he did.

Frick's astonishing mansion at Fifth Ave. and 70th St. survived him, as did Mrs. Adelaide Frick, upon whose eventual death, it was made known, the fabulous palazzo and the millions of dollars' worth of treasures therein would be deeded to the City of New York. Thereafter did everyone politely sit around waiting for Widow Frick to go on to her reward as well. Actually, she was still quite hale, and it took years yet. Old Adelaide lived on and on and on, and it was not until October 1931 that she finally gasped out her last, at age 72, somewhere in the bowels of her 90-room hideaway in Massachusetts. At this time, automatically, one of America's most important private art collections formally passed into the public realm.

But not without the all-but-eternal trusteeship of the late Mr. Frick's devoted daughter, a maiden lady named Helen, whose lifelong mission it would be to oversee the fortunes of the great Frick Collection and to ferociously and indefatigably preserve and protect her father's memory unto the moment of her own dying breath, which, even as had been her sturdy mother's, would be a long time coming.

FULLY A CENTURY later, one may reasonably regard Henry Clay Frick as having been really no more or less odious than many another practicing robber baron of his day. Granted, he might have personally caused the great Johnstown Flood that drowned thousands of unfortunates, but accidents happen, and the chronicles otherwise record him as having been among the 19th century's more notable industrial prophets, in his particular case the man who so early recognized that control of America's coalfields and coke ovens would render him so vital to the new steel industry that steelman Carnegie would essentially have no choice but to take him in as a partner. This pivotal amalgamation came to pass in Pittsburgh in 1882, and the relationship ended quite badly, literally in fisticuffs, but by then Frick was worth hundreds of millions of dollars.

By 1905, when Frick moved his family to New York City and took up residence in one of the world's great wonders, old William H. Vanderbilt's palatial mansion at Fifth Ave. and 51st St., which the Vanderbilts agreed to lease to him after they

The daughter

1 E. 70th St.

The father

discovered themselves to be financially pressed, he was resolved to spend many of those millions on the grandest art treasures of Europe. He was nothing but a parvenu, of course, just one more of these aspirants who for so many years had so peskily sought entry into the better classes ruled by Mrs. Astor and her Four Hundred. Good lord, there were still Vanderbilts who didn't get invitations, much less this Frick person. Well, anyone could have money. Anyone could live in a nice house. Anyone could hire men to plunder Europe's grand estates and ancient monasteries. Indeed, for some years it was hard to know whether it was Frick or J.P. Morgan who poured more incalculably bottomless buckets

AMERICAN SEPULCHRAL
Henry Clay Frick

of money into the oils and porcelains and tapestries and enamels in pursuit of which their agents ransacked the Continent.

Soon, Frick owned choice examples of practically everything: Rembrandt's 1658 self-portrait, Titian's portrait of Pietro Aretino, Holbein's Sir Thomas More, Velasquez's Philip IV, Bellini's "St. Francis in the Desert," three Vermeers, six Van Dycks, a Gainesborough and an Ingres and three Halses, the 14 Fragonard panels commissioned by Louis XV for Madame du Barry, dozens and dozens more. His collecting sensibilities were not without taste. Nor were they without passion. Nor, in truth, were they without genuine humility: "I can make money," he said at one point, not untouchingly. "I cannot make pictures."

Clouding this serenity of his autumnal years was the fact that the hated Andrew Carnegie had also moved to New York and had, at Fifth Ave. and 90th St., built a million-dollar house even more dazzling than the famous Vanderbilt showplace. This was not acceptable.

ACCORDINGLY, HENRY FRICK in 1913 began building a magnificent limestone temple 20 blocks to Carnegie's south. It cost $5 million, which showed Carnegie a thing or two, and it was never a home so much as it was a great vaulted hall suitable for the display of Frick's $50 million collection, a place that would endure forever, Frick's permanent testament to his own passage through this life, a monument for all the ages no less than Tutankhamen's tomb.

The Fricks actually lived in this grim mausoleum for a few years, which the old man spent wandering the cold and silent corridors, smoking a cigar, gazing

raptly at his priceless pieces for hours on end, and this is how he ended his time on this Earth.

The heiress Helen Clay Frick, who was 43 years old when her mother died and had long since pledged never to marry, now dedicated all her spinsterly days to the Frick Collection, which opened its doors to the public on Monday the 16th of December 1935 and was from the beginning so fustily conservative that it didn't acquire another piece for 25 years. Miss Frick was the sort of lady who, as late as World War II, was still being chauffeured about in a 1914 Pierce-Arrow. In 1948, she testily refused John D. Rockefeller Jr.'s offer of several Botticellis and Goyas on the grounds that they would "pollute" her father's legacy, and Rockefeller immediately resigned his Collection trusteeship in mortification.

ON AND ON AND ON lived Helen Clay Frick, who in 1965 was horrified to discover that a historian named Sylvester Stevens had written a less-than-flattering account of her sainted father's career. The coke king, Stevens reported, had mercilessly crushed his workers at every opportunity, forced them to slave in his mines, impassively watched them get shot down by guards during the coalfield strikes of 1892. All this was entirely true in every respect, and academics fretted as Miss Frick's indignant libel suit against Stevens became a landmark action that threatened to cripple the future of history-harvesting.

Miss Frick, bless her heart, in fact came to court as just a silly old woman; she had never read a biography of her father, she admitted; she could not dispute the facts of the matter; she merely thought that these were not nice things to say. Cumberland County, Pa., Common Pleas Court Judge Clinton Weidner had little patience with her. "It is not defamatory," he ruled in May 1967, "to say that a man built a monopoly in his business; that he was successful in beating down efforts at unionization; that he made extensive use of immigrant labor; that he cut wages; that he extracted the longest hours of work physically possible; that he broke the power of the union; that he was stern, brusque, autocratic." Indeed, Weidner speculated, Henry Clay Frick himself "would be proud" of everything Stevens had to say about him.

"At most," the judge concluded, "Miss Frick states that her feelings have been hurt."

Thus did Henry Clay Frick's gifts to mankind come to include not only his art collection but also case law establishing history's right to reflect upon the lives and times of such souls as he.

On and on and on lived his daughter, until November 1984, when she died at age 96.

By JAY MAEDER
Daily News Staff Writer

BY 1921, a generation or so past the best days of the Four Hundred and their fabulous million-dollar mansions, nobody who was anybody still cared to live on Fifth Ave. in the no-longer-fashionable 50s. Shops had moved in, for heaven's sake — smart shops, to be sure, but shops all the same — and the quality folks were all moving uptown as fast as they could. Except for Anne Harriman Vanderbilt, the recently widowed Mrs. W.K. Vanderbilt Sr. There were at least six or seven Mrs. Vanderbilts populating the society columns, but Mrs. W.K. Sr. was the only one who really mattered, at 60 the presiding matriarch of the Commodore's sprawling clan, and her decision upon old Willie K.'s death not to follow the northward migration produced many a gasp in your better circles.

Eastward turned Mrs. Vanderbilt instead, to the river's very edge, to the northeast corner of 57th St. and the old Avenue A, where 40 years earlier an entrepreneur named Effingham Sutton had built a house and proudly renamed the block after himself. Long ago this area had been called Cannon Point, a pastoral place of cliffs and orchards and walnut trees; by the grimy 1870s it was full of coalyards and breweries and slaughterhouses and fat-rendering plants, and Effingham Sutton's ambitious plans for its residential development accordingly proved less than visionary. After he went bust, the homes he had built had turned into the tawdriest of tenements, and by 1921, deep in the shadows of the Queensboro Bridge, this was still another place where nobody cared to live.

Except for Mrs. Vanderbilt, who for $50,000 bought old Effingham's house at 1 Sutton Place, rebuilt it as a modest four-story, 13-room Georgian cottage and then promptly induced several of her bestest girlfriends to put up fine new riverfront residences alongside hers, and ere long quite the exclusive little enclave was arising from the sooty heaps, little by little spreading down toward Beekman Place and over to Second Ave.

Sociologically speaking, there was now a colorful situation here: Mrs. Vanderbilt and her chums had moved into the neighborhood, but the ratty tenement poor had not moved out. By the early 1930s, the riverfront East 50s had become a strange otherworld — a place where frayed laundry hung on lines within sight of yacht slips, where young toughs baked potatoes in streetcorner garbage cans and scowled at the sports in their top hats and shiny roadsters, where tattered girls gazed dreamily at the bright windows of their befurred and bejewelled superiors, where there was nothing for any of them to do but stare into the maw of their own crushing poverty as formal gardens bloomed just feet away from them. It came to be called the Dead End.

Literally, that meant the streets stopped at the river's edge. Beyond that, it meant that no one here had a hope.

FEVERISHLY IDEALISTIC playwright Sidney Kingsley had won a Pulitzer Prize with his 1933 medical drama "Men in White"; now, two years later, he was returning with "Dead End," an unrelievedly grim portrait of daily life in the desperate streets abutting Sutton Place. The story revolved around a crippled tenement kid named Gimpy, who had grown up adoring a swell society girl from afar, knowing full well that her world could never be his, and a petty racketeer named Babyface Martin, who had come back to strut around his old neighborhood, and a gang of adolescent river rats who idolized the legendary Babyface and aspired to nothing more than someday going to reform school so they could be just like him. Kingsley was fundamentally a pamphleteer, and if his point, that mean streets

breed mean spirits, seemed an unsubtle one, theatergoing New York nevertheless seemed stunned by such a raw and profane revelation when "Dead End" premiered at the Belasco on Monday the 28th of October 1935. "Needless dirt," complained the Herald-Tribune critic Percy Hammond.

As, in polite society in 1935, indeed it was. And if "Dead End" was self-consciously a shocker in the first place, the production got more headlines yet as the morally authoritative kept clucking over the juvenile performers who had been cast as the neighborhood's roughneck troublemakers. They were a tough little bunch, certainly. Little wise guys, the lot of them, just street pups, sneering and spitting and shaking their fists. New York loved them; they ran away with the show from the

EAST SIDE STORY
The Dead End Kids

beginning and played it for two years. Their names were Billy Halop, Leo Gorcey, Huntz Hall, Bobby Jordan, Gabriel Dell and Bernard Punsley.

SAVE FOR MAYBE Huntz Hall, who really had grown up moderately two-fisted on E. 23rd St., the Dead End Kids were not particularly thugs at all. Gabe Dell had done "The Good Earth," Bobby Jordan, "Street Scene"; Billy Halop starred as radio's Western hero Bobby Benson. They were schooled performers; any one of them would have done Shakespeare had the opportunity come along. But Dead End Kidhood is what show business handed them, and it was this little-gutter-rodent ensemble that made them stars for a while; when "Dead End" went to film in 1937, playwright Kingsley insisted that the young Broadway troupe be retained for William Wyler's picture. Cast on the silver screen alongside Joel McCrea and Sylvia Sidney and an emerging heavy named Humphrey Bogart, they were suddenly big shots when the movie opened in August.

They were, moreover, the living embodiments of what the rest of America expected New York City punks to be, dese-and-dose little ruffians with short tempers and ready fists and hearts of gold, brats you'd never for a minute turn your back on

but would always be glad to have beside you in a brawl, and the Dead End Kids went on to play all this to the hilt as, after "Dead End," sans Punsley, who decided to leave show business, they kept reprising the roles in such dramas as "Angels With Dirty Faces" and "They Made Me a Criminal" and "Hell's Kitchen."

The Kids gleefully wrecked hotel rooms, scandalized interviewers, Bronx-cheered everything in sight. They were just terrible, the bad boys of Hollywood. Guys like Bogart and Jimmy Cagney and John Garfield regularly had to slap them around to teach them some manners.

EVEN AS MANY other kid stars have learned over the years, this couldn't last, and it didn't. The Dead End Kids were washed up in bigger-budget features by 1940 and began spinning off into subgroups — the East Side Kids, the Little Tough Guys, etc. — and it was always hard to know who exactly was a member of which outfit at any given moment. As they continued to crank out ever-cheaper second features, less and less were they damaged victims of social injustice and more and more were they just comic-relief smarties. Art-wise, their higher achievements were now the Saturday morning cliffhangers, such thriller-dillers as "Sea Raiders" and "Junior G-Men of the Air." By war's end, just Leo Gorcey and Huntz Hall were still seriously at work, starring as The Bowery Boys in dozens upon dozens of amiable B-movies that ran into the late '50s, until audiences began to weary of juvenile delinquents who were plainly about 40.

As early as 1944, Huntz Hall had confessed to columnist Hedda Hopper that he kind of regretted having been a Dead End Kid, that he thought the gang's antics over the years had probably encouraged a few lads to become vulgar bullies. Third Reich Germany, in fact, often showed Dead End Kid movies to its young people to show them what kind of hooligans Americans were. It was true you grew up a little rough at the edges sometimes when your neighbors were throwing gala garden parties and you were baking a potato in a garbage can on a streetcorner.

MRS. WILLIAM K. Vanderbilt Sr. died in 1940 at age 79. Poor people no longer particularly live in the immediate vicinity of Sutton Place.

By JAY MAEDER
Daily News Staff Writer

FROM GERMANY to the New World came the Rhinelanders in the year 1696, and here they settled New Rochelle and begat. They were quite meticulous about it. For 200 years, naught but the proudest blood streamed through the veins of old Philip Jacob Rhinelander's descendants as they amassed a real estate fortune second only to that of the Astors and assumed positions of importance at the most rarefied levels of New York and Newport society. True, there was a bit of clucking late in the 19th century when young Philip R. Rhinelander married a Kip. Still, the Kips were only slightly less distinguished. It was not as if young Rhinelander had married, for example, a Vanderbilt. Why, the Vanderbilts were nothing but Staten Island farmers.

In the year 1924, the last of the line was Philip's son, 21-year-old Leonard Kip Rhinelander, who happened to be something of a disappointment, a graceless and awkward lad who was in and out of sanitariums for treatment of assorted nervousnesses and who was regarded as perhaps a little feeble. For all that, he still belonged to the Sons of the Revolution and the Society of Colonial Wars and the Society of the War of 1812 and the Riding Club and the Badminton Club, and he was heir to $100 million, and accordingly he was one of high society's most eligible bachelors, fluttered at by the fairest of debutante flowers and even by a few hopeful widows. He was, after all, a Rhinelander.

But Kip's heart belonged to pretty Alice Jones, a common nursemaid and laundress, daughter of a New Rochelle busman, and on Oct. 14, 1924, he married his Cinderella in a civil ceremony so quiet that word did not get out into New York and Newport for several more weeks. Whereupon there erupted high society's most shocking public scandal in generations.

For Alice's father, English-born George Jones, was the son of a West Indian, and thus did West Indian blood stream through his own veins as well, and thus too did it stream through his daughter's.

Or, to put it another way, Alice Jones was a colored girl.

NEW YORK AND Newport were dumbstruck. In all the best clubs, at all the finest cotillions, there was talk of nothing but Kip Rhinelander and his dusky bride. Mortified Philip Rhinelander clapped his head in despair. He had tried his damnedest to stop this unthinkable thing. Kip had met Alice three years before, during one of his hospital stays; initially he was just dallying with a servant, as was an aristocrat's long-established privilege, but then affection had bloomed, and then everlasting true love. The father had sent the boy out west for two years to get over his foolheaded infatuation. But ardor did not subside. Now Kip had returned east, and he and Alice had eloped.

Reporters converged on New Rochelle and clamored around the modest Jones home on Pelham Road. "Is it true you've married the daughter of a colored man?" they shouted at Kip. "Yes," he snapped, "and we're very happy." It was true the newlyweds seemed devoted to one another, and Kip made it plain he didn't care what his father or the rest of high society thought. Man and wife took a small apartment, and every morning Kip climbed into his Packard roadster and drove to his family's Manhattan office, and every night he drove home again.

Until Nov. 20, when he drove into the city and did not come back.

Society reeled again when, on the day before Thanksgiving, Leonard Kip Rhinelander filed suit in Westchester Supreme Court, seeking to annul his

HIS COLORED BRIDE

DAILY NEWS

RHINELANDER'S BRIDE

SOCIAL ERROR

Kip and Alice Rhinelander

six-week marriage on grounds of fraud and deceit.
He'd never had the slightest idea, he contended, that his wife was not a white woman.

MANIFESTLY HAD the father and the family lawyers gone to work on Kip. "I'm certain my Leonard will return to me just as soon as he is able to free himself of those who are keeping him a prisoner," Alice told the papers. Amid recurring reports that she was refusing large amounts of Rhinelander money to just go away, she kept house for her husband for fully a year, sitting down at her window every evening, faithfully waiting for the Packard to drive up again. But it never did.

The sensational trial opened in White Plains on Monday the 9th of November 1925, and it was front-page news for weeks. On the first day, coffee-colored Alice acknowledged her Caribbean ancestry, confounding the Rhinelander lawyers who had spent months gathering mountains of documents to prove just that. Now their job was to paint her as a scheming gold-digger who had passed herself off as white to catch a weak-willed rich boy "on whom," declared barrister Isaac Mills, "no woman had ever smiled."

Day after day, Mills read into the record

hundreds of torrid letters Alice had written Kip, seeking to establish that she was not only a calculating siren but an irredeemably dissolute wanton as well. Day after day, Alice sobbed and covered her face; day after day, Kip trembled and shook and refused to look her in the eye. Increasingly it became clear that Kip himself had little hand in the wretched proceedings. Under cross-examination by Alice's lawyer, Lee Parsons Davis, he testified that his lawyers had stolen the letters from him and that he had not been able to prevent their being used as evidence.

"It wasn't in your power to control your own lawsuit?" Davis demanded.

Kip miserably shook his head.

"You were unwilling to have them used and powerless to prevent it?"

"Yes," Kip whispered.

The judge stopped the trial at several points, as it appeared Kip was on the verge of collapse. "The Rhinelander millions, not young Rhinelander, are behind this suit," Davis roared. "This is an effort to save an ancient name trailing back to the

Huguenots and to crush a humble New Rochelle family." Indeed, lawyer Mills put Alice's 63-year-old mother on the stand and quite irrelevantly forced her to confess that at age 18 she had borne a child out of wedlock.

Davis had a dramatic stunt of his own. On Monday the 23rd, he had Alice Jones Rhinelander disrobe in the judge's chambers. Weeping, clutching her mother's arm, she stood semi-naked for 10 minutes as jurors circled her and examined her dark body. However humiliating, Davis' tactic won the case for her. Jurors concluded that Kip could not possibly not have known his wife was not white.

DAVIS RESTED without putting her on the stand. "We are determined that this girl shall no longer be dragged in the mire," he told the jury. "The Rhinelanders have torn down the Jones' home over their heads. They have thrown this girl into the sewer and the slime. My God, how can the Rhinelanders ever forgive themselves?"

Lawyer Mills went on pleading for the "release" of "this schoolboy enamored of a sophisticated woman." In closing arguments, he devoted a full day to a diatribe against race-mixing. "There is not a mother among your wives who would not rather see her daughter with her white hands crossed on her shroud than see her locked in the embrace of a mulatto husband," he thundered at the jurymen. "There isn't a father among you who would not rather see his son in his casket than wed to a mulatto woman."

Softly replied Davis: "There's such a thing as race prejudice, but if you gentlemen are led by any passion or prejudice, race or otherwise, you will have done a great injustice." When the jurors returned their verdict, it was evident that Mills had thoroughly repulsed them all. Annulment was denied.

His lawyers swiftly hustled Kip out of the courtroom. It is not recorded that he and Alice ever saw one another again.

LATE IN 1929, Alice forlornly agreed to a divorce in exchange for a small monthly pension, and with the stroke of a pen, a Nevada judge erased Kip Rhinelander's social error. In February 1936, at age 33, Kip contracted pneumonia and died at his father's Long Island estate. "My lovely boy died of a broken heart," Alice told reporters. "I'll always love him." She was still wearing her wedding band.

By JAY MAEDER
Daily News Staff Writer

WILD BILL Lovett was not all that good with the sweet nothings. For all his everyday bravado, cracking stevedore skulls or shooting stevedores dead if it came to that, the boss of the murderous White Hand gang that ran the Brooklyn docks from Red Hook to Greenpoint could muster up no words when he came calling on Peg-Leg Lonergan's little sister, and Wild Bill's idea of courtship was mostly to sit mute all evening long in her family's parlor, stonily clutching his hat. The Irish Rose of the Waterfront did not find him particularly appealing in any case. *He kills fellers,* she protested to her father. *So does yer brudder,* pointed out the old man, who liked Wild Bill and approved of the match, and in the end there was nothing for fair Anna Lonergan to do but marry her Galahad after all.

Civil wedding vows were exchanged July 26, 1923. Proud Father Lonergan was not present, having in April been shot to death in his bicycle shop by Mother Lonergan in a dispute over his attentions to some neighborhood tramp. Peg-Leg had nobly sought to save his ma by swearing he did the job himself, but it was Mother Lonergan who went to trial, and the nuptials had to be deferred until after the acquittal came in. By this time, Wild Bill happened to be in the Raymond St. jail himself, facing a gun charge, but he managed to post bond and get over to Borough Hall for the ceremony with minutes to spare.

Now that he was a respectable married man, bride informed groom, he could consider himself out of the rackets. Wild Bill docilely agreed, and the newlyweds moved to Ridgefield Park, N.J. Save perhaps for the night Wild Bill pulled out a gun and shot off one of Anna's toes — "I want to see if you can take it," he explained — all was connubially blissful for several months, until one day in late October, when Wild Bill restlessly decided to run back to Brooklyn for a look-see into old business matters and was shortly thereafter located at the Dockloaders' Club at 25 Bridge St. with a balehook in his skull.

It was widely figured that Widow Lovett probably knew full well who had dispatched her notorious husband. For that matter, it was widely figured that she knew plenty about most of the day's dozens of dock murders, many of the victims her own friends and neighbors; often she was the one who went to the morgue to identify them. But she was not one for loose talk. In Irishtown, between Fulton Ferry and the Navy Yard, in the shadows of the Brooklyn and Manhattan bridges, there were three things that were universally despised. There were cops and there were Italians — neighborhood dogs bit both on sight — and then there were rats. Nothing on God's green Earth was lower than an informer.

Besides, Anna Lonergan Lovett was a deeply religious girl; all through childhood she had looked forward to being a nun, though that hadn't worked out. "Those who live by the gun, they die by the gun," she said piously. "It's in the hands of

SILENCE OF THE ROSE
Anna Lonergan

God." Forevermore could exasperated detectives count on the Rose of the Waterfront to hold her tongue, even when it came up her brother's turn to die and then her second husband's as well. Silent Anna, the newspapers called her, the woman who kept going to the morgue, again and again, wearing black.

THE WHITE HANDERS were New York's last old Irish gang, by the early 1920s firmly run by Wild Bill Lovett, a former war hero now regarded as one of the city's nastier extant customers, and the equally unpleasant Peg-Leg Lonergan, so called since the day he lost an argument with a Smith St. trolley car. There was much tribute to be exacted on the Brooklyn docks, from shippers and wharf owners and workingmen alike, and there was no good reason to give all this up merely because Bill Lovett had gone to his grave.

Accordingly, the late chieftain's 27-year-old brother-in-law, Peg-Leg Lonergan, assumed gang command, and Peg-Leg's sister, once she put a closure to her grieving, went on to take unto herself another White Hand husband, one Matthew Martin. And so the Irish Rose continued praying to St. Theresa for the safety of those engaged in what was essentially the family business.

St. Theresa had her hands full here, for there was no repelling the South Brooklyn Italians who, particularly once the fearsome Wild Bill was dead, daily became bolder in their Irishtown incursions. By Christmas Day 1925, hot-tempered Peg-Leg was extremely fed up with the lot of them. Late that night, very drunk and surly, he and two pals stormed into Italian territory, sat down at a table at the Adonis Social Club on 20th St. and then, three marauding micks well off their turf, began hurling slurs at every ginzo in sight.

This was quite spectacularly imprudent of the Irishtown boyos. Indeed, the lights quickly went out, mayhem thundered in the darkness and a few minutes later cops found all three of them dead of gunshot and cleaver injuries. Among the band of club patrons rounded up for questioning was one Alphonse Capone, formerly of Brooklyn, now of Illinois. He explained to cops that he was just visiting the old neighborhood for Christmas. Not all the newspapers immediately made him as the same Capone who was beginning to make a name for himself in the Chicago area.

ANNA LONERGAN Lovett Martin attempted to make a home with her new husband, but, what with one thing and another, as several of Peg-Leg's successors went on also to perish in the course of conducting their duties, it was simply the case that Matty Martin eventually came up for the leadership of what was left of the White Hand gang, which by 1930 wasn't much. The chronicles record that he was the last man to hold the position. By the time he was fatally ambushed in a DeKalb Ave. speakeasy in December 1931, it was generally agreed that the Italian gangsters, a modern new breed of them, men with names like Adonis and Mangano and Anastasia, were successfully taking over the administration of the docks and that the days of the old White Hand rule were done.

Dying in Cumberland Hospital, Matty refused to tell cops who had shot him. He whispered their names to his wife in his final moments, but she declined to pass along what he'd said. "I'm going to leave it in the hands of God," steadfastly declared the Irish Rose of the Brooklyn Waterfront.

SEVERAL YEARS later, the newspapers found her quietly in the employ of the city's Juvenile Aid Bureau, working to divert youngsters from the life that had killed most everyone who had ever loved her, and she asked them to please not write stories about her anymore or she might lose her job. The newspapers agreed that this would be the decent thing to do. She was never heard from again.

By JAY MAEDER
Daily News Staff Writer

"Godiva was equally guilty with Tom as soon as the peeping began. It was his eye, to be sure, but after all, it was her body."
— Heywood Broun, "Anthony Comstock, Roundsman of the Lord"

"In my heart I feel God approves."
— Anthony Comstock

TWENTY-FOUR years earlier it had been somehow less disturbing when elderly Madame Restell cut her throat in her bath rather than face charges for operating her fabled house of abortion at Fifth Ave. and 52nd St. "A bloody end to a bloody life!" the moral crusader Anthony Comstock had cried out in April 1878, proudly boasting that Madame was the 15th wicked soul he had personally driven to suicide.

In 1902, though, the matter of Miss Ida Craddock of W. 23rd St. gnawed at the belly. Miss Ida Craddock was a proper maiden lady who in her middle years had come to imagine that she was the chosen bride of Heaven's lustiest angel and had published a trembling fantasia called "The Wedding Night." For this celestial vision, she had been hauled into court by Anthony Comstock and convicted of purveying what was branded "indescribable obscenity," and the mortified Miss Craddock had gone home and turned on the gas. There was something unsettling about it. For all her fevered spinsterish silliness, really, Miss Craddock had seemed harmless enough.

By century's turn, Comstock was already on his way to becoming an old wheezer of a public joke, openly mocked by the less reverential journals, privately deplored by the leading citizens who had once been his champions. As recently as 1897, there had been Carnegie Hall testimonials to his indefatigably lifelong devotions to rectitude. Now, five years later, the lonesome death of Miss Ida Craddock was moving New Yorkers to reassess Anthony Comstock.

"I would not like to answer to God for what you have done," one prominent clergyman wrote him. Comstock cared not for the censure. He was, he declared, "stationed in a swamp at the mouth of a sewer," and there was work to be done.

WELL, OF COURSE, it had been a land of stern and wrathful and thoroughly unforgiving inquisitors from the beginning. That was the whole point of the New World. The original colonists were suspicious of basically everything, and the most pious of them had begun burning their witches almost the first minute they put down their miserable anchors, howling into their awful skies and beating their horrible drums, and soon enough everyone else moved out into the rest of the wilderness to found various other colonies. Much of New England remained the heart of darkness, and it hadn't changed much by March 1844, when Anthony Comstock was born in New Canaan, Conn.

He was directly descended from the ancient Puritans, and he grew up on his terrified knees before the grim bosom of the Congregationalist church. At 18, he plunged into his long and dour lifetime of good works by breaking into a general store in Winnipauk and smashing the liquor kegs. Late in the 1860s, he arrived in New York as a dry-goods clerk, and at once he sniffed the

BURNING THE WITCH
Anthony Comstock

prurient fumes of indecency wafting from the bookstalls and saw with his own eyes the ruin of those seduced. Moreover, he discerned, saloons often failed to observe the Sabbath. He began going to the police and preferring citizen's charges, and indeed before long he was successfully putting publishers and tavernkeepers out of business.

His campaigns won the support of the New York Tribune, whose reporters accompanied him as he made his rounds of the city's desperate quarters, and he came to the attention of the Young Men's Christian Association, which established a Committee for the Suppression of Vice and named him its chief. So YMCA-certified, he sought and got legislation against objectionable printed materials and the mailing thereof. By 1873, he was a nationally known figure.

That year, Congress commissioned him a special agent of the Post Office, and he broke from the YMCA and chartered himself independently as the Society for the Suppression of Vice. For decades to come, he fiercely stamped out salaciousness wherever it festered, dedicating himself to "protecting the young from the leprosy of this vile trash." Target lepers included Boccaccio, Walt Whitman and the authors of suffragette tracts. In 1893, discovering that it featured Egyptian belly dancers, Comstock attempted to indict the entire Chicago World's Fair.

HE PERFORMED some not-unuseful services;

among the things he found offensive were quack-medicine advertisements, and he significantly reduced their numbers. Otherwise, Comstock was a man who arrived in the 20th century demanding that department stores remove unclad mannequins from their windows, thundering against bridge games and Catholic Church raffles and arresting vendors who sold photographs of people dancing the tango.

He tried to prosecute the Art Students' League for issuing collections of figure studies. On one occasion, he brought obscenity charges against a woman for mailing a postcard upon which she had written that her husband was a "spitzbub."

Eventually, Comstock's disapproval got to be good as gold. In 1905, he tried unsuccessfully to block the New York production of a play called "Mrs. Warren's Profession," immediately made a hit of it and overnight established the reputation of its author, an "Irish smut dealer" named George Bernard Shaw. "Comstockery is the world's standing joke at the expense of the United States," Shaw said. "Europe likes to hear of such things. It confirms the deep-seated conviction of the Old World that America is a provincial place, a second-rate, country-town civilization."

In 1913, Comstock made a demure nude called "September Morn" the world's most famous painting when he ordered it out of a W. 46th St. gallery window and got prints of it banned from the mails; soon it was hanging everywhere. Judges were openly chuckling at him by now, and he took to shouting at them in court. The "hydra-headed monster" was everywhere, he fumed: "Decent people cannot be made to see or understand the necessity of doing anything."

BY THIS TIME, the society's directors were recognizing that Comstock was a doddering old nitwit and were grooming a young lawyer named John Sumner to assume his duties. Sadly grasping that he had been put out to pasture, Comstock went home and died in September 1915 at 71. Sumner himself put in 35 more years on the never-ending job; in his own vigilant career, he sought prosecutions against James Joyce, D.H. Lawrence, Mae West, radio programs, true-detective magazines and other outrages. By 1950, nobody was paying any attention to him either, and the Society for the Suppression of Vice was quietly dissolved.

"A case of sorts can be made out for censorship in any field, if you can imagine the job being administered by the wisest man in the world.... But no wise man would ever accept such a post. As things are constituted, it is pretty safe to assume that any given censor is a fool. The very fact that he is a censor indicates that."
— Heywood Broun

By JAY MAEDER
Daily News Staff Writer

UNDER SIEGE, his mighty triumph shockingly challenged, his grand claim to be the first man to behold the long-sought North Pole already in much dispute, Dr. Frederick Cook returned to the City of New York aboard a Danish liner on Sept. 21, 1909, and was met by jubilant thousands who threw a wreath about his neck and installed him at the head of a flag-draped, 200-car motorcade and serenaded him with a 1,000-voice choir. Brooklyn milkman turned physician turned world-famous explorer, 44-year-old Cook was driven through festooned streets, saluted by warships in the Hudson, cheered at gala banquets, wired warm congratulations by President William Howard Taft and the Pope. Over Willoughby Ave., proud Brooklynites built a victory arch in their hometown son's honor, inscribed in huge letters: WE BELIEVE IN YOU.

For a brief instant, nearly everyone believed in Dr. Frederick Cook. To this day, 90 years later, he still has champions who argue that he did what he said he did. Otherwise, he enjoyed just a moment of acclaim before all the world was reviling him as a liar and a scoundrel and a faker and a fraud, perpetrator of one of the fresh, forward-looking century's sorriest hoaxes, a man who brazenly broke the gentleman scientist's code to boast that he had gazed upon worlds that existed only in his dreams.

SCIENTIFICALLY speaking, the North Pole was pretty much worthless. The North Pole was nothing but ice; it was, after all, the North Pole. But the harsh business of getting there at all, identifying it by the stars, standing astride it — ah, there was the sport. Adventurers had tried for three centuries to cross the trackless wastes to the top of the world. Robert Peary of the United States Navy had spent nearly 20 obsessed years in search of the faraway frozen chalice. What anybody was actually going to do with the North Pole didn't matter. It was there to be found, conquered, claimed.

Cook and Peary had once been comrades: In 1891, when Peary was readying his second polar trek, he had advertised in the Brooklyn Standard-Union for volunteer shipmates and been answered by Cook, a recent graduate of New York University's School of Medicine who had no large practice yet and accordingly was happy to go along as surgeon. Things cooled a year later, when the unsuccessful party returned to New York and Peary, not a man to share limelight, forbade the young doctor from publishing any of his own observations of the northern wilds. By that time, Cook was an enthusiastic explorer himself: He made several Greenland forays on his own, and in 1897 he joined the great two-year expedition into the Belgian Antarctic, successfully winning every medal and trophy Belgium had to offer. In 1906, he stunned the world with his announcement that he had climbed Alaska's unclimbable Mount McKinley. By 1907, he was a great man, president of the Explorers Club in New York, a distinguished author, and now he and Peary were deadly rivals.

Early in 1907, as the aging Peary methodically prepared for one final, do-or-die, military-style assault upon the North Pole, a journey that would leave him either an immortal or a historical footnote, Cook quietly sailed for Greenland, traveling light, and the world didn't hear from him again until the first day of September 1909, when he cabled from the Shetland Islands that he had planted the U.S. flag at the North Pole on April 21, 1908, a year and a half earlier, and would shortly arrive in Copenhagen.

A thunderstruck world press converged on Denmark. There was no more colossal man on Earth than Dr. Frederick Cook, polar explorer, former Brooklyn milkman.

HE HAD MADE the polar dash with just two Eskimo companions, he said, and he had claimed

NEW YORK HERALD, SEPT. 15, 1909

THE GRAIL AT THE TOP OF THE WORLD
Dr. Frederick Cook

30,000 square miles of ice for the U.S. His long silence, he explained, was attributable to untold hardships suffered on the return to Greenland: The three of them had spent months living in a burrow; they had killed bears with knives to keep from starving; they had crawled hundreds of miles through savage storms.

The planet gasped at this fabulous tale of courage and daring. The University of Copenhagen showered Cook with scrolls. The New York Herald paid him $30,000 for his exclusive first-person story. On the night of Sept. 6, he was dining with King Frederick when an electrifying wire came in from Labrador:

Stars and Stripes nailed to North Pole. Peary.

COMMANDER PEARY, sponsored by the National Geographic Society and The New York Times, had left New York in July 1908 amid a rousing send-off. Far to the north in the spring of 1909, he learned that Cook was a full year ahead of him, and he was livid. He had devoted his life to finding the Pole, he had sacrificed eight frozen toes to the quest, his reputation was at stake; Cook was a mere interloper. From that moment, he dedicated every breath he drew to proving Cook's claim false.

Who was first to the Pole? Cook graciously congratulated Peary for his "rediscovery." But the matter of how far north Cook ever really got soon came to rest entirely upon his undocumented personal word of honor. He would not produce notebooks, astronomical data, any empirical proofs at all, anything but his red-blooded yarns of derring-do. Deeply suspicious London Daily Chronicle reporter Philip Gibbs swiftly branded them "wildly impossible" fairy tales. Back in New York, readers were treated to a clamorous war between two of the city's otherwise more

sobersided newspapers, as The Times daily published Peary's accounts of his adventures and The Herald published Cook's.

Returned to Brooklyn, the doctor embarked upon a profitable national lecture tour — as, meanwhile, Peary made it known that he had found Cook's two Eskimos and been assured that Cook had turned back far short of the Pole. At the same time, old whispers that Cook perhaps had fudged his Mount McKinley exploit now exploded as members of the party came forward with charges that he had never come close to the summit. Scientists became increasingly alarmed as Cook regularly promised to produce his hard polar data but never did. Cook's own lawyer gave up trying to defend him.

Everything fell apart four days before Christmas, when the University of Copenhagen read over the documents he finally provided and declared them "outrageously inadmissible." The university's president resigned in shame. Around the world, Cook was denounced as an "infamous wretch," a "monster of duplicity," "the North Pole swindler." Quietly, he disappeared from Brooklyn.

FOURTEEN YEARS later, he resurfaced as a Texas petroleum man, under federal indictment for mail fraud in a phony oil-lease scheme. He served five years in Leavenworth, then returned to the New York area to publish his prison memoirs and attempt to repair his tattered reputation. Through the 1930s, he still insisted he had been the first man to the Pole, unsuccessfully petitioned the American Geographic Society to reopen his case and at one point sought to sue the Encyclopedia Britannica for libel. On Aug. 5, 1940, three months after suffering an apoplectic seizure, he died in New Rochelle.

Modern scholars generally agree that Cook's polar assertions were in fact fanciful, or, to put it another way, bogus. On the other hand, it is also true that Peary's rival claims fell into serious dispute long before his own death in 1920. Debates continue. Many historians regard the great North Pole showdown of 1909 as a not altogether uncharming story of one hoaxer's collision with another.

By JAY MAEDER
Daily News Staff Writer

THROUGH THE summer and autumn of 1913, usually cunning Tammany Hall was determinedly committing two enormous professional blunders, turning against two of its own men who had proved less manageable than Tammany wished them to be, and, in so doing, demolishing itself, again, as it did from time to time.

In Brooklyn, Democratic boss Uncle John McCooey was leading a move to deny Tammany renomination to crustily unbossable Mayor William J. Gaynor and put up a more tractable candidate in his stead. In Manhattan, meanwhile, wigwam chieftain Silent Charlie Murphy, mightily aggrieved by Gov. William Sulzer's refusal to name a Murphy man to the state Highway Commission, spitefully ordered his Albany hatchets, Senate Majority Leader Robert Wagner and Assembly Majority Leader Al Smith, to engineer Sulzer's impeachment on trumped-up campaign-finance charges.

Both McCooey and Murphy were successful in their myopic endeavors. What they got as a direct result, on the 4th of November, was an anti-Tammany backlash that changed the face of New York City.

In re Sulzer: Perhaps they might have known better, but New York voters seemed genuinely startled to learn that Murphy was powerful enough to singlehandedly oust a popular and capable governor. They responded by bouncing out of office most every man who had voted to impeach, thus costing Tammany its control of the Legislature. For the rest of his life, Silent Charlie would admit that taking down Sulzer was as big a mistake as he'd ever made.

In re Gaynor: Dumped by Tammany, the beloved old mayor sought reelection as an independent, and perhaps he might even have defeated his colorless machine challenger, Public Service Commission chairman Edward McCall. Instead, in mid-campaign, a frail man since an assailant had shot him in the neck three years earlier, Gaynor died. His sudden disappearance opened the road for the candidate of the earnest Good Government goo-goos, a young reformer named John Purroy Mitchel, who trampled McCall on Election Day and, to Tammany's distress, immediately began giving the City of New York four of the most remarkably honest and administratively efficient years it has ever known.

JOHN PURROY MITCHEL first came to attention in 1907, when, as the city's 28-year-old Commissioner of Accounts, he led the formal investigation into charges of widespread contracting corruption brought by a citizens' group called the Bureau of Municipal Research. Mitchel's probe verified the reformers' allegations, and after his bombshell report was delivered to Gov. Charles Evans Hughes, the Tammany-puppet borough presidents of Manhattan, Queens and the Bronx were removed from office.

Another result of the scandal, in this unexpected new era of civic accountability, was Supreme Court Justice William Gaynor's ascension to the mayorship in 1909, once badly battered Tammany grasped the usefulness, at least in the short term, of supporting a man who did not openly appear to be a thief and a brigand. Power-brokering newspaper publisher William Randolph Hearst, his on-again, off-again alliance with Silent Charlie Murphy off again at the moment, was making his second run for mayor in 1909, and the Gaynor-Hearst contest was a noisy one. Amid the din, as Gaynor won the race, John Purroy Mitchel was elected president of the Board of Aldermen.

GAYNOR'S OTHERWISE honorable mayorship was sullied by the July 1912 murder of Broadway gambler Herman Rosenthal and the subsequent indictment of Police Lt. Charles Becker as the man who had ordered the killing. As revelations of the rogue cop's links to both Tammany and underworld elements shocked the town, it was Alderman Mitchel who ordered up major committee probes of New York's systemic police corruption. By mid-1913, he was the city's white knight, an obvious mayoral candidate despite his tender years.

Mitchel's campaign was warmly endorsed not only by the local goo-goo progressives but by such formidable national figures as President Woodrow Wilson and former President Theodore Roosevelt. He happened to be a Democrat, personally, but he was the nominee of both the Fusionists and the Republicans. Particularly once Gaynor was dead and gone, Tammany's McCall had little chance against the swashbuckling young reformer. On Election Day, he won office by a huge plurality. He was 34 years old.

WILLIAM RANDOLPH Hearst had the worst luck with assassins. In 1901, Hearst had been crucified for having whipped up the frenzy that many felt led to the Buffalo murder of President William McKinley; nine years later, his newspapers' attacks on Gaynor had been deemed responsible for a disturbed ex-city employee's attempt on Gaynor's life. Now, having helped to elect John Purroy Mitchel, only to have the Boy Mayor curtly show him the door one day, Hearst turned his papers loose on him. And on April 17, 1914, another deranged man who had come into possession of a gun took a shot at Mayor Mitchel.

Fortunately for Hearst, Mitchel was only grazed, freeing Hearst's sheets, the American and the Journal, to continue savaging him. Their paths would cross again, come another election season.

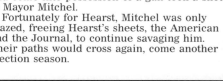

THE BOY MAYOR
John Purroy Mitchel
PART ONE OF TWO

MEANWHILE, MITCHEL was hard at work, sweeping changes across every level of city government. He flung hordes of Tammany hacks out of their jobs. He shook up the Police Department and embarked upon an ambitious program to modernize it. He cracked down on public-works waste and mismanagement. He ordered hospital reforms. He reinvigorated long-dormant plans for harbor improvements. He made traffic safety a priority, mandating that motor vehicles must carry red taillights. He presided over the implementation of the Dual Contracts that would join the IRT and the BRT into a unified city subway system-in-progress. He presided over the building of the great pipes that would bring Croton Reservoir water to the city.

And, from the Bureau of Municipal Research, to which he had always preserved close ties, Mitchel brought into city government an energetic young man to overhaul the entire sloth-friendly Civil Service system. His name was Robert Moses, and he would put his mark on New York for the next 44 years.

EUROPE EXPLODED, and war would reach across the sea to wound and infect John Purroy Mitchel's brightly idealistic public career. In the summer of 1914, barely six months in office, the Boy Mayor of New York City was already losing his grip on it, and he had less than four years left to live.

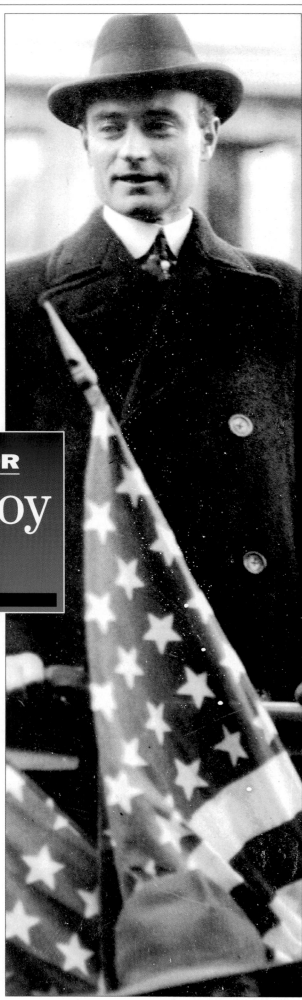

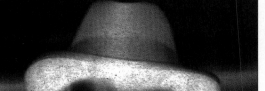
By JAY MAEDER
Daily News Staff Writer

EUROPE EXPLODED. The old empires convulsed. The old kingdoms fell. The old gods died. Across the sea in the City of New York, John Purroy Mitchel's City Hall was rattling as well.

The shining-knight Boy Mayor, swept into office in November 1913 in one of those paroxysms of municipal reform that New Yorkers periodically inflicted upon themselves, had swiftly proved a businesslike and incorruptible chief executive. Just a few months into his term, 34-year-old Mitchel was already being championed as a potential governor, and many were those who regarded him as fit for even loftier stations, America's first Irish Catholic capable of becoming a national political figure.

As mayor, though, Mitchel had history against him; New York sooner or later always wearied of its do-gooders. Beyond that, he was a socialite anyway, a silk-stocking sort, for all his visionary social ideals by no means a man of the people. That became clear when Europe exploded, and Mayor Mitchel took it upon himself to become a proudly chest-thumping militarist, urging U.S. intervention on behalf of Great Britain, calling on New Yorkers to demonstrate their true-blue loyalty. As it happened, very few Americans in 1914 were much interested in the faraway European War. Moreover, in 1914, two-thirds of the population of New York City was foreign-born. A good many of these people were Germans, who did not necessarily view Kaiser Wilhelm as the devil incarnate. And a good many of them were Irish, and did not necessarily love England so much. And most of them were voters.

THE WAR MAYOR
John Purroy Mitchel
PART TWO OF TWO

Mitchel did not appear to understand any of this. In all likelihood, his mayoralty began to dissolve on Aug. 6, when he issued a proclamation prohibiting the flying of any flag but the Stars and Stripes.

THE YOUNG PROGRESSIVE who had won City Hall pledging to end police corruption and municipal waste succeeded admirably in many of his forward-looking good works. This was a man who cracked down on inefficiencies inside, for example, the Department of Efficiency. Concerned about the public health, he oversaw pure-food legislation. Concerned about workplace safety in the wake of the Triangle Shirtwaist blaze, he enforced factory fire-drill requirements. Concerned about the cost of living, he sought to reduce food prices and municipalize the coal business. Concerned about unemployment, he sought city programs that would put the jobless to work building the subway system. He demanded maternity leaves for expectant schoolteachers. He appointed a black man to the Board of Education. He worked tirelessly to build vocational schools.

On the other hand, he had a real gift for irritating people. In July 1915, his warmongering temperament led him to order the perfectly harmless Organization of American Women for Strict Neutrality to take down its posters; the quarrel went to court, and the mayor lost. In the spring of 1916, he won the wrath of the Catholic Church when, amid a probe of apparent swindles inside the Department of Charities, he authorized police to wiretap several priests.

Catholic leaders on several occasions went to Gov. Charles Whitman, demanding Mitchel's ouster. Indeed, the city's original Committee of 100 was formed specifically to support the mayor as the Church laid siege to his administration. Hard feelings endured through the rest of his term.

There were large crises in the summer of 1916 — violent transit and garment workers' strikes, a polio epidemic that killed hordes of children. The mayor dealt with these matters, but increasingly his energies were devoted to New York's combat-readiness. He formed preparedness committees. He took two weeks of drilling at an upstate camp and invited all city employees to do the same. He urged compulsory military training in the public schools. He sought to build a system of coastal fortifications, to defend the city against European powers with which the U.S. was not in conflict.

The War Mayor, everyone was calling The Boy Mayor by now. Public sentiment turned somewhat in April 1917, when the U.S. did in fact join the war, and, for example, even William Randolph Hearst's Anglophobic New York American found it prudent to rename its popular Germanic "The Katzenjammer Kids" comic strip "The Shenanigan Kids." To whatever degree that Mitchel was validated, though, the fact was that this was already election season again, and Tammany Hall's long knives were already sharpened.

FOREVER ON AGAIN and off again, the wary alliance between Hearst and Tammany — "love feast," political observers liked to call the relationship — was on again in the spring of 1917. Hearst might have run for mayor yet again himself, this time even with Tammany chieftain Silent Charlie Murphy's personal blessing, but several of Murphy's top deputies, chiefly lower Manhattan boss Big Tom Foley and Foley's personal protégé Al Smith, wouldn't hear of it. And so Hearst and Murphy joined together to support the nomination of Brooklyn County Judge John F. Hylan.

Particularly as the notably empty-headed Tammany candidate had practically nothing on his mind at any given moment, he was personally rather irrelevant to what turned into one of the most viciously divisive elections in the city's history. The sole issue was Hearst, and after Mitchel dismissed Hylan as just a Hearst puppet barely worth discussing, he spent the campaign branding the publisher the Kaiser's man. Former President Theodore Roosevelt took the stump for Mitchel, agreeing that Hearst was a card-carrying Hun, or at the very least, the foremost German agent in America. Tammany's Albany boss, Sen. Robert Wagner, all but got labeled an enemy saboteur.

In the end, the chickens came home to roost. Along with the various other strikes against him, Mitchel had, with young Robert Moses of the Civil Service Commission, attempted to reform the city's hiring practices, and Tammany never lost an opportunity to remind the voters that this was the mayor who had tried to put 50,000 hardworking city employees out of their jobs. On Election Day, Mitchel went down to defeat by an even greater plurality than the one that had put him into office. This was the end of reform in New York City for a decade and a half.

JOHN PURROY MITCHEL walked out of City Hall on Jan. 1, 1918, and 11 days later he was commissioned a major in the U.S. Army Aviation Service. At Camp Gerstner in Louisiana on the 6th of July, two weeks before his 39th birthday, he was making his final qualification flight for air-war duty in France when his scout plane suddenly went into a dive. Mitchel was not properly belted, and the man many yet considered an attractive presidential prospect for 1920 pitched out of his seat and fell 500 feet to his death.

The old Mineola airfield on Long Island was renamed in his honor, and, for more than 30 years, veterans of the passionate old Fusion days held annual memorial services at his Woodlawn Cemetery tombstone, upon which is inscribed: *May His Angels Lead Thee Into Paradise, Which Is Thy Home, For In Israel There Is Corruption.*

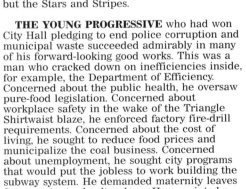

By JAY MAEDER
Daily News Staff Writer

THIRTY-FOUR years after Abraham Lincoln signed the Emancipation Proclamation, his son Robert Todd Lincoln became president of the Pullman Co., supplier to the nation's railroads of elegant sleeping cars and polite Negro porters to attend them. Old George Pullman, in his day, had liked to view himself as an enlightened employer who looked after his workers' comforts, and Lincoln, after Pullman's demise, maintained the benevolent paternalism. In the case of the emancipated porters, this meant they worked a mere 400 hours a month for about $6 a week, out of which wage they were required to buy their own uniforms and all their meals.

In the nation's Negro communities in the early 20th century, it was a badge of honor to be a Pullman porter. A man wasn't digging ditches. A man got to wear a jacket and fetch drinks and fresh bedlinen for high-class white folks who tipped him. Furthermore, by 1925 a man was earning $72.50 for his 400 hours. Accordingly, not every porter on the road was much interested when a Harlem firebrand named Asa Philip Randolph first began telling them how oppressed porters were.

Ten years later the International Brotherhood of Sleeping Car Porters won recognition as America's first black trade union, and A. Philip Randolph's role in one of the century's most pivotal labor struggles had earned him such stature that he would go on to back down two Presidents, force key civil-rights legislation and organize history's greatest march on Washington. And then he would die largely forgotten, dismissed as a fool old graybeard Uncle Tom by a fresh generation of firebrands who had barely heard of him.

FLORIDA-BORN in 1889, son of an African Methodist Episcopal preacher, Randolph came to New York as a young man, studied at City College by night and worked as sweeper, waiter and elevator operator by day. Deeply influenced by Karl Marx and the Socialist Party's visions of the nobility of the masses, he began trying to organize his co-workers and accordingly kept losing all his jobs. By 1917 he was editing a radical magazine called The Messenger, calling on black men to refuse military service and denouncing elder statesman W.E.B. DuBois as old and in the way. President Woodrow Wilson called him the most dangerous Negro in America.

Early on, he recognized the thousands of Pullman porters as a potentially powerful bloc. Never a porter himself, he became their formidable chief, winning wage increases, shorter hours and, in 1935, admission to the American Federation of Labor. Now, in the late 1930s, he was an unmistakably significant power broker, a man who controlled not only the porters' votes but also those of their families and friends.

Thus, in the spring of 1941, when Randolph announced that he would lead tens of thousands of his constituents in a protest march on the White House, President Franklin Roosevelt took due notice.

AT ISSUE WERE emerging defense-plant jobs, few of which seemed open to black workers.

(Circa 1946)

CULVER PICTURES

HAMMER AND TONGS
A. Philip Randolph

"Fellow Negro Americans, be not dismayed," Randolph declared. "You have power, great power…. Nothing counts but pressure, more pressure and still more pressure." By June, Randolph's porters had been joined by the Urban League and the NAACP, and black communities across America were astir. Increasingly distressed by this insurgency, Roosevelt asked New York Mayor Fiorello LaGuardia to sit down with Randolph and urge him to cancel the march. Randolph was unswayed. Then the President dispatched First Lady Eleanor Roosevelt to talk to him. Unswayed he remained. And now FDR summoned him directly to the Oval Office.

"Questions like this have sociological implications," Roosevelt patiently explained to his visitor. "They can't be gotten at with hammer and tongs. They can't be settled with marches."

Unswayed sat Randolph.

"You can't bring 100,000 Negroes to Washington," Roosevelt said. "We can't have that."

The President of the United States realized he was not getting through to the President of the Brotherhood of Sleeping Car Porters.

So Roosevelt sighed, picked up a pen and signed an order establishing the Fair Employment Practices Commission, possibly black Americans' single most important document since the 13th Amendment.

SEVEN YEARS LATER, Randolph took on Harry Truman over segregation of the military. Appearing before the Senate Armed Forces Committee in

April 1948, the witness announced that "Negroes are in no mood to shoulder a gun for democracy abroad so long as they are denied democracy here at home" and promised "mass civil disobedience." The senators threatened to indict him for sedition. Randolph dared them to do it. In July, Truman abolished military segregation, formally, in any case.

By 1958, when Ebony magazine pronounced him "the unquestioned No. 1 leader of the nation's 17 million Negroes," he was a powerful vice president of the lately merged AFL-CIO and a noisy crusader against discrimination in union locals. In 1959, he enraged AFL-CIO President George Meany when he railed publicly against "the second-class citizenship of the black laboring masses in the American labor movement." "Who the hell appointed you guardian of all the Negroes in America?" roared Meany, who apparently didn't read Ebony. In 1960, Randolph formed the breakaway Negro American Labor Council and called for workplace actions "as militant as the lunch counter sit-ins in the South." In 1961, the AFL-CIO voted to censure him, accusing him of creating "the gap that has developed between organized labor and the Negro community." Grumbled Meany: "We can only get moving on civil rights if he comes over to our side and stops throwing bricks at us. In the last two or three years, he's gotten close to these militant groups and he's given up cooperating for propaganda."

But in truth, "these militant groups" were already moving away from Randolph, who was 74 years old in July 1963 when a quarter of a million black and white Americans answered the call to march on Washington. "This civil rights revolution is not confined to the Negroes," he said there. "Our white allies know that they cannot be free while we are not." This did not sit well in less inclusionary quarters of the movement. A year later, when he denounced as racist a campaign by black activists to replace Puerto Rican workers in a 125th St. deli with blacks, he was openly jeered by younger radicals. Much, indeed, as he had openly jeered W.E.B. DuBois nearly 50 years earlier.

Appearing before Congress in December 1966, a key architect of President Lyndon Johnson's War on Poverty, he sadly admitted that for the first time in his life he was unable to communicate with "unreachable" young blacks. By late 1968 he feared a race war. "I want to see civil rights leaders take great care against overheating the ghettos," he said. "Throwing Molotov cocktails is not the answer to the problem of the Negro." It was pretty much the same thing FDR had said to him in 1941.

THE AGE OF railroads passed. The Pullman Co. ceased operations in 1969. The Brotherhood of Sleeping Car Porters quietly folded in 1978, a pointless dinosaur.

Randolph died in his Ninth Ave. home on May 18, 1979. He was 90. "No American did more for the cause of social equality and economic justice," said Vice President Walter Mondale. "A great warrior," said David Hyatt of the National Conference of Christians and Jews. "It's so sad," said Benjamin Hooks of the NAACP, "because there are so many young people today for whom that name means very little — and yet for more than 40 years he was a tower and beacon of strength and hope for the entire black community."

By JAY MAEDER
Daily News Staff Writer

"I am constantly concerned about how far short I may be falling of rendering the maximum service possible with the opportunities that have come to me. Every day, every night, I ask myself what I may be leaving undone which I ought to do."
— John D. Rockefeller Jr., June 1934

SOMETIMES A SINGLE obituary headline really does quite efficiently sum up a man's entire life and career. This was the case at the New York Daily News the morning after old John Davison Rockefeller Jr. expired on Wednesday the 11th of May 1960. **JOHN D. JR., 86, DIES,** the News reported. **HAD LOADS, GAVE LOADS AWAY.**

Which said pretty much what there was to say. Over a period of 50 years, Rockefeller had methodically dismantled an enormous private fortune and showered the world with hospitals and universities and public parks and anything else he deemed useful to its nourishment and enlightenment. Rockefeller money gave Fort Tryon Park and the Cloisters to New Yorkers, Rockefeller Center and the United Nations to their city's skyline, the Palisades Parkway to the forever unsullied bluffs across the river. At his death, it was calculated that about a billion Rockefeller dollars had passed in one fashion or another into the public realm.

He was the sole heir to the nation's most hated man, the richest old coot in all creation, John D. Rockefeller Sr. of Standard Oil. John D. Jr. had originally been expected to carry on in conventionally rapacious fashion. But sometimes a man just isn't much good at a particular job.

ROCKEFELLER SENIOR, son of a hawker who sold quack medicines at Midwestern county fairs, first prospered in his 20s by selling salt and pork to the Union Army during the War Between the States. Then he decided kerosene had a future. By the 1890s, his dreadnought Standard Oil trust, having swallowed every competitor in sight, was the largest and wealthiest company in the world. John D. Rockefeller Sr. lighted the lamps of China. The sun never set on his oceangoing fleet. He was called The Anaconda; trust-busting President Theodore Roosevelt declared war on him; even after the Supreme Court broke up Standard Oil into 33 companies, process servers dogged him for years. When his wife died in 1915, he had to leave her unburied for four months because armies of them were camped out at the cemetery.

For all his ruthless monopolism, which at the turn of the century was, after all, only good business, America's first billionaire was otherwise a simple and pious man who, even back in his $4-a-week apprentice bookkeeper days, had faithfully tithed to the Baptist church, to orphanages, to foreign missions. By the time his trust was dissolved, he had founded the University of Chicago and the Rockefeller Institute for Medical Research, and he was giving away millions and millions more at every turn. "It is every man's religious duty," he said, "to give all he can." The Rockefeller fortune, he announced in his old age, was not truly his. The gold belonged to God.

Into these philanthropies he enlisted as his primary agent his devoted son, who had grown up in a household in which, on the one hand, unimaginable sums of money were as taken for granted as the air that one breathed, and, on the other, strict daily prayer services and lessons in thrift hammered into him an unusually terrifying sense of mission. As long as he lived, it was all he ever knew.

The son 1920.

BORN IN 1874, Rockefeller Junior came to work fresh out of college at the Standard Oil building at 26 Broadway in New York City and quickly discovered that he had no stomach for his father's business. The boss's gentle-tempered son quite frankly had no talent at all for robber baronry; dispatched in 1914 to settle disorders at the family's Colorado iron mines, for example, he sided with the strikers instead, demanded improvements in their living conditions and began campaigning for the eight-hour day. It was not lost on Senior that Junior was the family almoner at heart. Increasingly out of the anaconda game by this point anyway, the father now turned

The father, 1933

flood relief, to a new medical school in Peking, to campaigns to eradicate yellow fever in Africa and South America. Scarce was there a good work left unperformed.

At the center of this fabulous flurry of gift-giving was unpretentious, sweet-souled John D. Jr., who still taught the Men's Bible Class at the Fifth Avenue Baptist Church on W. 46th St. and whose finger-waggling Sunday preachings, because he was a certified Great Man, often made the Monday papers, however essentially unremarkable. *Wealth brings responsibility. Haste makes waste. Idle hands are the devil's playground. Drive carefully. Shun tobacco and liquor.* For all that, he was tough enough to personally force the ouster of a Standard of Indiana executive who was marginally embroiled in the Teapot Dome oil-lease scandals; sternly championing business ethics, Rockefeller went before the Senate to blow the whistle on the Standard man and to express his mortification that Rockefeller interests were involved in the affair. By mid-1929, he was a figure of such uncompromising moral rectitude that reformers sought to run him as a New York mayoral candidate. A race between Rockefeller and the lesser principled incumbent Beau James Walker would have been high drama indeed, but John D. Jr. wasn't interested.

AT THE TIME of Senior's death at 97 in May 1937, when his son was 63, it was calculated that the two of them had given away $750 million or so. By now the family projects included John D. Jr.'s personal pet venture, the restoration of Colonial Williamsburg in Virginia, into which he happily put some $60 million. Meanwhile, the world's largest privately developed commercial project, Rockefeller Center in midtown Manhattan, continued to climb into the skies.

Rockefeller Center, built on property owned by Columbia University between 48th and 51st Sts. and Fifth and Sixth Aves., had initially been envisioned as the new home of the Metropolitan Opera and various other museums and institutes and whatnot as would make the Center the world's greatest cultural showplace. The stock market crash of '29 had put an end to most of that idea, and John D. Jr. was left stuck with a 99-year lease on the land. Construction bravely went ahead amid the depths of the Depression anyway, and there arrived in the city Radio City Music Hall, which was widely regarded as an opulent masterpiece, and an assemblage of office towers that were generally viewed as architectural nightmares. In November 1939, John D. Jr. personally drove the final rivet into the last of the Center's 14 buildings.

Ahead of him yet was what history would celebrate as his noblest gift of all, the $8.5 million parcel of land along the East River that, in 1946, became the site of the United Nations' permanent headquarters.

GOD'S GOLD
John D. Rockefeller Jr.

the fortune over to the son, named him chief of the Rockefeller Foundation and partnered with him in every man's religious duty.

Through the 1920s, John D. Jr.'s giveaways became regular newspaper fare. Here went $60,000 to the Princeton University Library, $200,000 to the American Academy in Rome, $1 million apiece to the Metropolitan Museum of Art, the American Museum of Natural History, Tuskegee Institute. Here went a million to restore the cathedral at Reims. Here went $1.6 million to help rebuild earthquake-stricken Tokyo, $2 million to the League of Nations in Geneva, $20,000 to Richard Byrd's 1926 North Pole expedition. In 1927 alone, father and son dispensed more than $11 million — to Mississippi

HAD LOADS, said the News, **GAVE LOADS AWAY.** "John D. Rockefeller Jr. was his father's memorial," added The New York Times — "unique the world over, among men of inherited great wealth, in dedicating his life to no other purpose than to promote the well-being of his fellow men." *Good, for you,* the Anaconda had told his only son on his 21st birthday, *is inseparably connected with the good you bring to others.*

By DAVID HINCKLEY
Daily News Staff Writer

"Vat's de matter, so late, Sammy? Let me look at your hands. Playing marbles, ha? A marble shooter you're gonna be? A beautiful business for a Jewish boy!"

— **Molly Goldberg**

FOR EVERY American who never lived in New York, and every New Yorker who never had a Jewish mother, not to worry: Molly Goldberg of Apartment 3-B, 1030 E. Tremont Ave., the Bronx, would fill you in.

America met Molly and her family on radio's Blue Network in November 1929, three weeks after Black Friday. Jake was the husband, a "cloak-and-suit operator." Sammy was the son, Rosalie the daughter. Uncle David and a dozen friends bobbed in and around the apartment. Mostly there was mother Molly, dispenser of exasperation, love and wisdom. Sammy would come home from school with a report card. Rosalie wanted to cut her hair. The point was Molly's response, usually some combination of bewilderment and loving concern.

"Come will and come may, I must face it," she would sigh.

Jake's role, where appropriate, might be to add, "You're breaking your father's heart."

By show's end, Sammy and Rosalie would have a lesson that they would one day dust off and pass along to their own Sammy and Rosalie.

That the lesson was modest — don't tell a lie, don't let your friends push you into mischief — was the point and the genius of Molly's alter ego Gertrude Berg, who created Molly, wrote all her lines, played her for two decades on radio and another five years on television and precisely defined the boundaries of her world. It wasn't the whole Bronx. It was her intersection, her market, her park, Mrs. Herman Across the Hall and Mrs. Bloom, as in *"Yoooooo hooooo, Mrs. Blooooooom."*

Through the worst of times — the Depression, the war — Gertrude Berg held Molly Goldberg's perimeter. Inside 1030 E. Tremont, a little chicken soup, literal or figurative, restored a measure of control.

The local club needed a show to raise money? Molly put on "Die Fledermaus." Jake working too hard? He should listen to Molly: "It's late, Jake, and time to expire."

Only come the bright days of the 1950s, ironically, did the outside world finally break into the place Gertrude Berg had built for Molly. And soon thereafter the Goldbergs' time had passed.

BUT SUCH A time it was. Long after Berg was an established writer and well-to-do star — she made $2,000 a week during the Depression — she would wander the peddlers' stalls of the lower East Side to stay fresh on the voices, the cadence of the conversation. She would make

COME WILL AND COME MAY

Molly Goldberg

scripts of this in her kitchen at 5 a.m., or in the reading room of the 42nd St. library.

She specialized in four-wall drama, a well-established staple of the Yiddish theater along lower Second Ave. Actors in Yiddish theater productions wrung their hands constantly over children assimilating and casting aside the old ways. Berg's winning move was to realize this had longer legs and broader appeal as comedy than as "The Jazz Singer."

In fact, laughter and trepidation were twins in Molly's world. Lost in Central Park once, Molly approached a mounted policeman: "Mr. Policeman, officer of the law, your honor, could you be so kindly if you would inform me of the location of where is 14th St.?" After he obliged, Molly was mostly relieved at not being arrested for violating some sort of rule she should have known about in this big scary new country.

But if Gertrude Berg understood the immigrant's terror, she did not live it.

Gertrude Edelstein was born in

the Jewish section of Harlem on Oct. 3, 1899. Her family owned the Catskills resort Fleischmann's, where as a teenager she wrote sketches for guests. When she was 14, she entertained a meeting of lawyers with skits about a character called Maltke Talnitzky, a woman with a "no-goodnik" husband.

As time passed, Maltke became Molly and Gertrude Edelstein became, at 19, Mrs. Lewis Berg, housewife and mother. In the mid-1920s she began submitting radio scripts. She could turn a one-liner — "If it's nobody, I'll call back"; "Give me a swallow, the glass" — and after several years of rejections, she was offered a one-month contract at $75 a week, from which she paid the cast of a show she called "The Rise of the Goldbergs."

Radio was exploding then, stations merging into networks, with fierce competition for new potential hits. But when Berg's show debuted, it was unsponsored because it was considered a rather daring experiment: a flagrantly Jewish drama, the first ever on network radio. It took 18 months of steadily rising ratings before a sponsor signed on — Pepsodent toothpaste — and by 1932 "The Goldbergs" was one of the two or three most popular shows on radio. In 1936, it moved from evenings to days.

It ended its radio run March 30, 1945, and while it would resurface four years later for a brief radio encore and five years of TV, 1945 was already far removed from 1929. "Better a crust of bread and enjoy it than a cake that gives you

indigestion" was good everyday wisdom during the Depression. In 1945, with the smell of prosperity in the air, it sounded like something grandma would say.

TO KEEP UP, Berg moved the Goldberg family to the suburb of Haverville. Rosalie joined the Girl Scouts and Jake ran for the town council, where he could no longer say things like, "I'm the father here, and I won't stand for any more of this shilly-shallying."

What he did say was what Berg wrote. "She ran the show with an iron fist," recalled Arnold Stang, who played neighbor Seymour Fingerhoof. "Very tyrannical in many ways. But she showed affection and had marvelous judgment. I learned more from her than any other director."

Producer Himan Brown wasn't so kind. "Berg was only in it for Berg," he said, and some saw the Goldbergs' one major off-camera drama as the real proof of that suggestion.

On CBS television from 1949 to 1951, as well as in a 1951 "Molly" film, Jake was played by Philip Loeb, a veteran actor with an affinity for left-wing causes that, in September 1950, landed his name in the Communist-hunting magazine Red Channels.

Loeb snorted that he was no Red and his membership in groups like the End Jim Crow in Baseball Committee simply endorsed what others agreed was the American thing to do.

Red Channels and its powerful political allies replied that Commies were equally happy with sympathizers or dupes. Loeb, like most colleagues, said he would neither apologize nor rat out his friends. In May 1951, General Foods announced it would no longer sponsor "The Goldbergs," for "business reasons." Seven tense months later, NBC said it would pick up "The Goldbergs," with Vitamin Corp. of America as its sponsor. NBC said it didn't know if Loeb would be in the cast. The president of Vitamin Corp. claimed he was not aware of any controversy.

Berg herself finally confirmed that Loeb was out. "There are 20 people depending on the show for a living, and their savings are dwindling," she said. "It's unfortunate that after doing what I did, waiting for the situation to clear, that I have to go along without him."

Actors Equity protested. Loeb got $85,000. It was three years before he found work again, Off-Broadway. On Aug. 31, 1955, he checked into room 507 at the Hotel Taft at 50th St. and Seventh Ave., hung a do-not-disturb sign on his door and swallowed several dozen sleeping pills.

POST-LOEB, another Jake in place, "The Goldbergs" continued on TV through October 1954. Berg would go on to write three Molly books. She estimated she wrote 10 million words on the Goldbergs over the years.

Outside the family, she won an acting Tony for "A Majority of One" in 1959, and she worked in films and theater right up until Sept. 10, 1966, when she left her Park Ave. duplex and checked into Doctors Hospital for heart tests. She died four days later, and millions of Americans mentally sat shiva, which, thanks to Molly Goldberg, they knew what it meant.

By JAY MAEDER
Daily News Staff Writer

TRUTH TO TELL, it has never been entirely clear exactly when it was that the enterprising German immigrant Charles Feltman first stuck a sausage in a bun and started peddling his "Frankfort roll" to the merrymaking Coney Island crowds. Some authorities have said 1864, some have said 1871, some have suggested various other years. For the sake of efficiency, Coney Island officially celebrated the 100th anniversary of the noble hot dog in 1967, which was probably close enough. For that matter, for a while there St. Louis was insisting that it was the rightful birthplace of the hot dog, not Coney Island, but of course nobody paid any attention to a burg like St. Louis.

What is known to be hard documented fact, at least according to Handwerker family legend, which is probably also close enough, is that one day in 1914 or thereabouts young Nathan Handwerker was working the counter at Feltman's dog emporium when a couple of his Boardwalk pals, these being a singing waiter named Eddie Cantor and a piano player named Jimmy Durante, happened to grumble to him that 10 cents was a lot of money to pay for a hot dog. And it happened that thrifty Nathan Handwerker absolutely agreed with them about this. So he scraped together $300, and in the spring of 1916, at the corner of Surf and Stillwell Aves., he opened up his own stand and started selling hot dogs for five cents, a price that included a root beer and a pickle.

Things come in this life and things go, but put it this way: Nathan Handwerker's hot dogs outlasted both Luna Park and Steeplechase.

HE HAD BEEN a shoemaker once. That was back in Belgium, to which as a lad he had moved from his birthplace, Galicia. In 1912, at age 20, along with tens of thousands of other such young men as himself, he arrived in New York City, where there were many shoemakers already, and he took a position as dishwasher and counterman at a lower Manhattan restaurant called Max's Busy Bee. Weekends he moonlighted at Feltman's German Gardens out on Coney Island, where the hot dog had been invented in 1864 or 1867 or 1871 or some other such year. Anyway, the hot dog had been around for a long time. As far back as the 1880s, there had been dozens of hot dog vendors working the Coney strip, and apparently once upon a time hot dogs had cost five cents, and apparently by 1914 they no longer did. Apparently Jimmy Durante and Eddie Cantor were reflecting upon the good old days when they visited their pal at the Feltman's counter.

Nathan Handwerker did two brilliant things shortly after he opened his stand:

One, he hired a smart young woman named Ida Greenwald to come to work for him and then had the good sense to marry her, and all the rest of his days he would always credit his Ida as being the real brains behind the operation, starting with the "secret special sauce" that distinguished Nathan's original red hots.

Two, after his 10-cent competitors started slipping word around that obviously a five-cent frank couldn't possibly be much good, he rounded up a crew of locals, slapped white coats and stethoscopes on them, had them mill around his stand eagerly gobbling up his hot dogs and then let it be publicly known that plainly his dogs were

GOOD DOG
Nathan Handwerker

good enough for the fine doctors at Coney Island Hospital, who ought to know from good. The hospital wasn't very happy about this little marketing adventure, but Nathan's place won its point, and it stayed very much in business after that.

Another thing that happened was that in 1923 the subway was extended to Coney Island, and enormous crowds began spilling out of the Stillwell Ave. station, all of them heading straight to Nathan's, and Nathan's stayed open 24 hours a day, all year long, as immutable a New York City institution as the Statue of Liberty.

LET US speak frankly: There is no epic pageantry to the life of Nathan Handwerker. The man sold hot dogs. This is what he did. But did he sell hot dogs. The chronicles record that every Broadway and Hollywood star you ever heard of, every mayor, every gangster, every visiting VIP, every Park Ave. socialite, all dined at Nathan's at one point or another, all of them eating standing up and wiping their mouths with napkins like anyone else, for years and years and years. In 1939, when President Franklin Roosevelt entertained King George VI and Queen Elizabeth of England at Hyde Park, he fed them Nathan's hot dogs. In the early 1940s, Nathan's stand at Surf and Stillwell launched an annual hot dog-eating contest that fast became firmly installed in the American culture, regularly celebrated in the newsreels. It came to be the case, as Nelson Rockefeller once observed, that no politician who had not first been photographed eating a dog at Nathan's could hope to win an election in New York State.

By late 1954, Nathan Handwerker was selling 6 million dogs a year and his son Murray was president of the Coney Island Chamber of Commerce, and they were both icons of Coney Island preservationism, profoundly at war with the indefatigable Robert Moses' grand plan to rebuild or rearrange everything in New York City. The dogs themselves, it was true, were 25 cents now. But they were still 8-inch dogs. "Moses has shrunk the amusement center of Coney Island considerably," Nathan said on one public

occasion.
"But never, and I mean never, will he shrink Nathan's frankfurters."

He was big business now, and regularly he was urged to think about expanding beyond Surf and Stillwell. "What for?" he always shrugged, gazing out at the beach and the boardwalk and the sun and the sea. "I got everything I need right here."

TIME PASSED, things changed, son Murray didn't share his father's view. In 1962, the old family business started opening other locations — on Long Island, in Yonkers, in Times Square, elsewhere. In 1968, the company went public. Within just a couple of years, the shareholders were complaining about management. Nathan's dogs were 40 cents now. That was hard to believe, but Nathan was philosophical in his old age. "If hot dogs were still selling for five cents," he mused in August 1970, "the country would be in bad shape."

He died in Florida at 83 on March 25, 1974, spared the heartbreak of having to watch his legendary Nathan's Famous fall apart. At the time of his death, the company was deep into franchising and there were several dozen Nathan's Famouses in the city and its environs. Many of them were poorly run; one of them in particular, at Eighth St. and Sixth Ave. in Manhattan, became the target of a Greenwich Village activist crusade in the late 1970s as it turned into a dope den given wide berth by neighborhood residents. It was finally thrown off the block, and in the early '80s the increasingly hard-pressed chain shut down 20 more of its metro stores. In December 1986, Nathan's Famous was sold off to a syndicate of investors for $17 million.

The more or less original Nathan's still stands at Surf and Stillwell on Coney Island, just where its founder put it, back when all the world was young and bright.

By JAY MAEDER
Daily News Staff Writer

"The individual is the personification of that which expresses personification. Therefore he comes to be personally the expression of that which was impersonal, and he is the personal expression of it and the personification of the pre-personification of God Almighty."

— **Father Divine**

IN THE BEGINNING was the Word, and the Word was with George Baker, and the Word was George Baker. And George Baker looked about him and saw that this was good, except for maybe the fact that a name like George Baker somehow failed to strike much awe into the hearts of the beasts of the Earth and the fishes of the sea. So he changed his name to God, which was much more impressive. Presently God came to the attention of Georgia authorities, who didn't much want to be bothered with some 5-foot-2 handyman who was calling himself God, and they informed God that either he could leave Valdosta on the next train or he could go to the state nuthouse. So it was that, around about 1914, God arrived in the City of New York.

There would arise a legend that he descended into Harlem in a cloud of smoke, and he never tried very hard to discourage anyone from believing this.

THERE HAVE in this forlorn vale of tears always been flocks desperately willing to entrust heart and soul to anyone who says he is God and speaks incomprehensibly enough to make the case, and soon enough did the silver-tongued deity collect into his shining Kingdom of Peace an army of angels to whom he promised everlasting celestial life and sometimes even jobs as waiters and maids on condition that they turn over to him their wages and do as he bade them do. By the late 1920s there were hundreds of faithful journeying every weekend to Heaven, which was located in Sayville, L.I., and they sang and danced and feasted and gave bald little Father Divine all their money, and Father Divine had, among other things, a fleet of limousines and his own private airplane.

Heaven was outfitted with loudspeakers through which God regularly proclaimed his godhood, and finally the Sayville neighbors started complaining about the racket. In June 1932, Father was convicted of maintaining a public nuisance and handed a year in jail. Four days later the sentencing judge keeled over dead. This retribution was now proof enough to all that God was truly in their midst — "I hated to do it," Father sighed — and, after the conviction was reversed and Father Divine abandoned Sayville and relocated Heaven to 20 W. 115th St. in Harlem, the hundreds soon became many thousands, and Father had himself a sure enough church.

Depression Harlem was full of storefront ministries dispensing succor for the soul; Father Divine, rather more usefully, dispensed hot meals. Through the mid-1930s his free kitchens and free boardinghouses offered momentary balm to countless transient unfortunates, and those who chose to join him in his mass cooperative remained assured of the creature comforts. "Pork chops are an important part of the theology," noted The New York Times. In return, Father's angels accepted strict conditions — no tobacco, no liquor, no gambling, no movies, no sex even between husband and wife — and happily went to work for nothing in his markets and barbershops and laundries and newspapers that reportedly gave him an income of $10,000 a week. "Thank you, Father!" they all cried out at every word he uttered. Many observers found these words rather baffling — "He rematerializates and he is rematerializable; he repersonificates and he repersonifitizes!" Father would say; "It is personifiable and repersonifiably metaphysicalzationally reproducible!" — but the flocks appeared to understand him perfectly. Asked by a reporter what the heck Father was talking about, one angel patiently explained: "The

PEACE IN THE VALLEY
Father Divine

abundance of the fullness."

Things went on serenely as Father kept building new Edens northward into the Hudson Valley farmlands. He liked to claim 30 million followers worldwide. More realistically, he might have had 10,000. Most were black women who took new angel names like Wonderful Wisdom and Glorious Illumination and Praise Grace and Thankful Kindness and Sunshine Bright. But he had many white followers as well: There was nothing ever racial about the Kingdom of Peace, where dwelt only harmony. Newspaper reporters who visited Father's communes marveled at the sight of the happiest bunch of people they'd ever seen, beaming devotees who spent their days thanking Father and chanting, "Peace, it's wonderful!" Child welfare authorities who occasionally looked in always found black and white children living and learning and playing together apparently quite pleasantly.

The papers were full of stories of people who insisted that Father had cured them of fatal illnesses, even raised them from the dead. Legions of former prostitutes, gamblers and dope fiends were forever joyously testifying to their reformations. There were those in officialdom who took due note. Said one magistrate: "He's doing something the police department and the mayor have been trying to do for a long time."

AS IS SO often the case with churches, ultimately there were backsliders. By late 1936, a number of disgruntled angels were taking Father to court, seeking redress of financial grievances. Large among these was a black woman called Faithful Mary, who had for years run the Harlem kitchens and served as Father's most emphatic public champion. Now she had concluded that Father wasn't God at all. "He's just a damned old man," she snapped. The apostasy rocked the Kingdom. The newspapers, of course, immediately redubbed her Unfaithful Mary.

At the same time, there was trouble with Father's chief deputy, a white man called John the Revelator, who stood accused of pressing affections upon an underage girl with his promise that their child would surely be the Redeemer. Meanwhile, reporters dug up Mother Divine, Father's long-abandoned wife, now near death in a nursing home, still a fanatically devoted angel despite

Father's refusal to pay her medical bills. "There will be no more prophets," she gasped at her end.

Finally, in April 1937, a mob of Father's defenders beat and stabbed a process server as he came to 115th St. and knocked on Heaven's door. Father Divine, charged with felonious assault in this incident, now fled the city.

POLICE TRAPPED the fugitive a few days later in a Connecticut basement. Father had always boasted that he could turn himself invisible when confronted by foes, but it turned out that this time the trick didn't work, and Father, once he realized that the cops could see him, came out from behind the furnace with his hands up. Back in New York, the assault charges didn't stick; Harlem shook with victory celebrations at Father's release, and prowl cars that thereafter ventured onto the Kingdom of Peace's block got pelted with bricks and bottles. The pelters often went to jail, shouting "The devil will get you!" at the judge.

None of this godly fervor quieted the aggrieved Faithful Mary, who had opened her own church by this time and was determined to put Father into receivership. Through the summer she testified before several grand juries that he was a tax-dodging crook who kept mountains of ready cash in secret treasure vaults. In August, besieged by lawsuits, Father disgustedly announced that he was going to leave his body and depart the Earth for 1,900 years.

ACTUALLY, HE ONLY went to Philadelphia, where in the early '40s he established Heaven anew. In 1946, past 80, he married a 21-year-old white woman who had been an angel since childhood — "spotless virgin bride," he always called her, and so she evidently remained — and who thereafter shared with him the front-office administration of the Kingdom of Peace. Through the 1950s and early '60s, Father's church ignored the civil rights movement altogether, blissfully oblivious to racial strife. Meanwhile, Father still had big cars and lots of diamonds. When he died in September 1965, age 100-something, thousands of pilgrims gathered at his coffin and waited for him to arise, which he didn't.

These years later, the conventional wisdom holds that Father Divine was perhaps less a divinity than a clever fellow who played the hand he was dealt. That said, there is no question that he fed some of the starving, clothed some of the ragged and brought salvation to some of the wicked. And the truth is that peace really *is* wonderful. George Baker, 5-foot-2 Georgia handyman, worked in, well, mysterious ways.

BIG TOWN ★ BIOGRAPHY

LIVES AND TIMES OF THE CENTURY'S CLASSIC NEW YORKERS

By JAY MAEDER
Daily News Staff Writer

"Well, if you won't let me go on, give me a buck."
— Unidentified entertainer at radio audition, 1935

THE BEST ESTIMATES from the relief agencies held that through most of 1935 there were probably about 300 simple souls arriving in the City of New York every week, by bus, by boxcar, by produce truck, whatever got them here, clutching their ukuleles and their accordions and their symphonic spoons and their talking dogs and their lovebirds that chirped out the marches of John Philip Sousa, migrating from every hamlet and valley toward their fateful moment on Major Edward Bowes' "Original Amateur Hour" radio program that would surely bring them stardom or at least steady $50-a-week road-show jobs. They were mostly hillbillies and dirt farmers and other such Depression-stricken unfortunates, ready to attempt anything that might put a meal in their empty bellies, but some of them were youngsters who had abandoned their schooling and some of them were nice old grannies who had sold their homes and everything else they owned. And not a one seemed to understand that Major Bowes got 10,000 letters a week from people just like them and that there was almost no chance they would even get preliminary auditions. The New York papers brimmed with sorrowful tales of the army of dreamers who never got close to Major Bowes' radio studio and who were now hopelessly stranded in the big town, sleeping on trains, begging for coins.

Major Bowes was sufficiently incautious on one occasion to let a reporter overhear him refer to the forlorn mobs shuffling outside Radio City Music Hall as "the poor boobs," but for the most part, when someone asked him if he felt personally accountable for all that human misery downstairs, he successfully managed to portray himself as a man offering only comfort in troubled times. "They are on fire with hope," he told The New Yorker in February 1936. "Isn't it all right to give them that chance, without accepting responsibility for their whole social and economic status? A big percentage of our applicants are on the relief rolls already. If we can get only a few of them off, we have accomplished a little something."

And perhaps there was a little something to be said for that. Over the two decades that he conducted what for a while was American radio's most popular program, Major Bowes provided the opportunities that pushed a number of his amateurs toward the big time — these included a skinny kid named Frank Sinatra, a thrush named Teresa Brewer, a young baritone named Robert Merrill and 7-year-old Beverly Sills — and he gave many hundreds more of them honest work in his traveling stage troupes. As for the rest of them, the thousands of never-weres huddled on the sidewalk outside, well, he said: "If they can't get back home again, I generally reflect that home was really no better for them than some other place."

AROUND AND AROUND
Major Bowes

CULVER PICTURES

THE MILITARY RANK was genuine, by way of the Army Reserve. Born in 1874, Edward Bowes was a San Francisco real estate man who made and lost several piles in the century's early years, wiped out by the earthquake one day, prospering again the next. After the World War, he showed up in New York and, with the impresario Roxy Rothafel, put up at Broadway and 51st St. a palatial theater called the Capitol. This, a few seasons later, came to the attention of exhibitor Marcus Loew, who took it over in a deal that left Bowes a well-to-do vice president of Loew's Metro-Goldwyn-Mayer film studio.

By this time, radio had arrived in the world, and Major Bowes had arrived on radio. The Capitol man, always looking to promote his showplace, was broadcasting variety acts from his stage on pioneer WHN as early as 1922; four years later, "The Capitol Family Hour" went national on NBC, and it stayed around into the early 1940s. Meanwhile, by the early '30s the Major was also managing WHN, where, it happened, there labored a producer named Perry Charles, who had for several years been fiddling with public competitions among amateur performers.

Later in his life, Major Bowes was notably reluctant to admit that Charles had done an amateur program before his own. As it happened, Charles had hardly invented the idea himself. The amateur night as a modern theatrical institution apparently originated in 19th-century English music halls, and it was an American vaudeville staple by 1900; audiences always roared and roared when some particularly awful aspirant or another got the hook or the seltzer-bottle treatment. This otherwise largely visual spectacle somehow translated quite well to radio several decades later. In late 1934, shortly after the Major

launched a local "Original Amateur Hour" on WHN, it was calculated that 90 percent of the New York radio audience regularly tuned in. By the spring of '35, when NBC picked him up, Major Bowes was a national sensation.

TEN THOUSAND applications a week, every week. No more than a couple hundred of these ever got as far as auditions, and no more than a few dozen of those got tagged to report to Radio City for Major Bowes' Sunday night broadcast. "Around and around she goes," cried the Major, spinning his Wheel of Fortune, "and where she stops, nobody knows." Cultural observers marveled at the fascinating cruelty of the thing; all but one or two or three of the contestants were just terrible, utterly ungifted, plainly nothing but comic relief — "little people who have suffered the dreadful wasp sting of the assumption of talent," as The New Yorker's Morris Markey put it, parades of hicks blatting at their clarinets, losing their places, giggling or weeping uncontrollably, often struck dumb altogether as their desperately awaited moment of attention finally arrived. Some of the hopefuls would no more start their routines before Major Bowes would whang his unforgiving gong and cry out, "All right, all right," thus permanently consigning them to whatever the rest of their lives were going to be. Audiences roared and roared. The Major kept a bouncer handy just in case some harmonica-playing cowboy who had spent weeks hitchhiking in from Montana didn't appreciate the gales of laughter.

"The Cinderella Hour," radio critics called Major Bowes' program. Hundreds of telephone operators and tabulators went to work at the end of every broadcast, tallying up the votes of 20,000 callers. Some of the night's winners weren't bad at all, and some got immediate wires from nightspot operators in Ohio and here and there. Quite a few others went straight into the Major's dozen or so traveling companies that serviced the nation's small-town theater circuits. Frank Sinatra, who in 1935 appeared on the Major's program as one-fourth of a singing group called the Hoboken Four, was one of those.

Lots more of them gave it up and quietly drifted back home, if they could even afford to do that, and in the bleak middle 1930s there were thousands who could not. Outside Radio City they shuffled about for weeks on end sometimes, clutching their ukuleles and talking dogs and begging for coins. Well, that was show business for you.

MAJOR BOWES moved to CBS in 1936, and his program remained one of radio's top 10 for some few years yet. But after a while the inherent charm of dueling trombonists and other such gladiators began to wear thin, and wartime phone restrictions killed off the call-in-vote novelty anyway, and the Major left the air in April 1945. He died at his home in Rumson, N.J., on June 13, 1946, the night before his 72nd birthday, after Francis Cardinal Spellman of New York rushed to his bedside to administer last rites, and he left $2.5 million to widows and orphans.

Under the auspices of one Ted Mack, who had worked for Major Bowes as a director of auditions, the "Original Amateur Hour" was reborn on network TV in 1948 and successfully ran on into the 1970s.

By JAY MAEDER
Daily News Staff Writer

THE BASEBALL boss who brought the mighty Babe Ruth to the New York Yankees in 1920 was also the man who quite cheerfully and without regret sent him on his way 15 years later, once The Bambino got to be fat and 40 and a pain in the neck. Babe Ruth had once earned $80,000 a year, and the best-paid man in baseball was none too pleased when his employer abruptly cut him to $70,000 late in 1931. "Never again will any player get that much a year," Col. Jacob Ruppert scowled. "The peak has been reached. Baseball is a business, and not even Yankee management can afford to pay such a salary."

The Babe settled for $75,000 for the 1932 season. A year later he settled for $55,000. Well, there was a Depression. In his final year as a Yankee, Babe was ordered to take $35,000 or leave it, and he took it. By February 1935, though, he'd had enough of The Colonel's bottom line, tough times or not, and out of New York he went at last, into his brilliant new career with the Boston Braves.

Ruppert was hardly distressed by the loss, and things continued ruthlessly. That same month, Lou Gehrig signed a one-year contract for $30,000, thus becoming the new best-paid man in baseball. At the same time, Ruppert was bringing in a brand-new Yankee, a promising teenager from the San Francisco Seals named Joe DiMaggio. Young Joe signed for practically nickels and dimes, and he was, by God, grateful.

JACOB RUPPERT was a very rich man who could afford to spend his life playing with his favorite toys, which included his brewery, his St. Bernards and the New York Yankees baseball club. His beer won gold medals. His dogs took blue ribbons. The Yankees, when he bought them in 1914, were miserable second-division waifs; at his death 25 years later, the team had claimed 10 American League pennants and seven World Series. "Everything he touched won first prize," eulogized Daily News sports editor Jimmy Powers. If some of his ballplayers thought him a skinflint, he seemed otherwise a noble enough soul: All through Prohibition he kept his brewery workers on his payroll, and his horses, after they retired, went to live out their days in comfort on his upstate farm.

Born in 1867 to a Bavarian brewer who in that year founded the celebrated firm that would slake New York City's great thirst for generations to come, Ruppert grew up every inch the prosperous businessman's son, the sort who started out as a humble barrel washer in the family firm and soon became general manager and vice president. His colonelcy was a real one, more or less: A private in the National Guard, 7th Regiment, one day he was named an aide to Gov. David Hill and suddenly promoted, and Colonel was thereafter how he liked to be addressed. In 1899, he was elected to Congress, where he served four terms. In 1911, by now president of the Jacob Ruppert Brewing Co. on Third Ave. at 90th St., his fancy turned to baseball. Again.

He had always liked the game; as a wealthy kid in Little Germany, he had financed a team of neighborhood urchins, buying them their

Spring training, 1934: With manager Joe McCarthy, infielder Lyn Larry, catcher Bill Dickey

THE OLD BALL GAME
Jacob Ruppert

equipment and uniforms. Since 1903 he'd been trying off and on to buy the New York Giants. Now, in 1912, he was being offered the Chicago Cubs, and he gave this some thought before deciding Chicago was too far from Broadway. About the only thing available locally was a dreadful little club called the Yankees.

The Yankees had once been the Baltimore Orioles. In 1903, they'd been bought by a couple of Broadway operators — Big Bill Devery, a former famously corrupt chief of police, and Frank Farrell, owner of one of the gambling houses Chief Devery had so faithfully protected — and brought to New York as the Highlanders. By 1914, rechristened the Yankees, haplessly and homelessly playing out of the Giants' Polo Grounds, they were definitely for sale.

This wasn't the most glorious opportunity that had ever come along, but The Colonel wanted a baseball team. In December, he and an associate, an ex-Army engineer wonderfully named Capt. Tillingham L'Hommedieu Huston, announced they would buy the terrible New York Yankees for $480,000.

NOTHING VERY spectacular happened until after the war, when Till Huston came home from France, now a full colonel himself and one-half of the partnership that New York would come to know as The Two Colonels, and, along with his partner the other colonel, changed the baseball landscape in the summer of 1919 by taking pitcher Carl Mays away from the Boston Red Sox in violation of a direct order by American League President Ban Johnson. When this matter went to court, it was The Two Colonels who won, and the fight directly resulted in the abolition of the old National Commission and the creation of the Office of Commissioner of Baseball.

After that, things began to turn around for the Yankees, particularly following the spectacular arrival of Babe Ruth. Suddenly, the club was

turning big profits and winning league pennants, although still losing championships to the Giants, and New York was beginning to look like it was going to be a Yankees town. At this point, Giants owner Charles Stoneham, at whose Polo Grounds the Yankees were still tenants, informed The Two Colonels that their rent had just skyrocketed. In reply, The Colonels bought land in the Bronx from the Astor family and, in May 1922, broke ground for the world's largest ballpark.

"Yankee Stadium is a mistake," Col. Ruppert chuckled. "Not mine. The Giants'."

TILL HUSTON, who had built railroads in the American Midwest and dredged harbors in Cuba, personally oversaw most every detail of the great park's construction, and he was there to accept his half of the cheers when it opened April 18, 1923. A month later, he was out; quarreling with Ruppert over Miller Huggins' managerial capabilities, he finally took a $1.25 million buyout, and that was the end of The Two Colonels in the city's sporting life.

The remaining colonel had other things to worry about — Prohibition, for example, which cut his brewery's annual production of 1.25 million barrels of real beer to 350,000 barrels of half-percent near-beer that nobody wanted to drink — but all through the '20s and all through the '30s, sole owner of the champion New York Yankees, he remained a fixture at his stadium, which he insisted on keeping so fanatically clean that sometimes he even swept it himself. The whole town loved and cherished The Colonel, even when he let Babe Ruth go.

And even when he refused a raise to rising star Joe DiMaggio, who by early 1938 was demanding $40,000 — "or else," as he testily put it. "If he means he will not play baseball this year," The Colonel said, "then we must accept his decision. He will play for $25,000 or not at all." DiMaggio played for $25,000, and got an unsympathetic response from most New Yorkers, who by and large, figured that 25 grand was plenty good enough for any ballplayer.

THEN, SUDDENLY, Ruppert fell feebly ill. He was able to attend just two games in the '38 season; in his sickbed, following his team via radio for the first time, he was so enchanted that he ordered all home games to be broadcast thenceforth. This was his last official act. On Friday morning, the 13th of January 1939, he died in his Fifth Ave. home.

Babe Ruth, reconciling their differences, had been his final visitor. "Colonel, you are going to snap out of this and you and I are going to the opening game of the season," Ruth promised him. The dying old man smiled, murmured a single word — "Babe" — and drifted off. He had always called him Ruth; he had never once ever called him Babe before. Babe stumbled out of the room, sobbing like a child.

IN JANUARY 1945, Jacob Ruppert's heirs and assigns, pressed for cash after having mismanaged the family fortune, sold the New York Yankees for not quite $3 million. Ten years later, the Jacob Ruppert Brewery Co. signed a deal to sponsor New York Giants broadcasts. The landmark firm went out of business in 1965, and its flagship Knickerbocker brand was sold to The Colonel's lifelong competitor, Rheingold.

BIG TOWN ☆ BIOGRAPHY

LIVES AND TIMES OF THE CENTURY'S CLASSIC NEW YORKERS

By JAY MAEDER
Daily News Staff Writer

SUCH A GROTESQUE carnival of improbable souls did the Lindbergh kidnapping case so swiftly become in its first mesmerizing weeks that even Dr. John F. Condon of the Bronx didn't seem especially strange.

Chicago gang boss Al Capone had pledged to find the stolen Lindbergh baby. So had a couple of Broadway racketeers named Bitz and Spitale. So had a prominent Virginia businessman, who claimed to be the abductors' appointed middleman and who had already led the revered American hero Charles Lindbergh on fruitless romps along the coast. So had whole daffy parades of seers and psychics. And now here, in the first week of April 1932, was Dr. John Condon, kindly old schoolmaster, all at once at the very heart of the terrible mystery.

In the many reassessments of the many years to come, after the elderly doctor had left the headlines, after he had stood up in court in Flemington, N.J., and doomed Bruno Richard Hauptmann with a single accusatory stab of his finger, it would come to be recognized how exceedingly odd he had been from the first: vague and shadowy and baffling, noted one magazine writer, not quite really there, "something out of a half-dream."

But in the spring of 1932, briefly, he had seemed to be the only man in the world who could bring Baby Lindbergh safely home again.

THE BRONX never had a prouder son than John Condon, who was born on E. 169th St. in 1860 and seldom strayed far. Everyone knew him. He was principal of Public School 12 on Westchester Square for 30 years. For decades he umpired every neighborhood ball game and marched in every civic parade. His poetry, stirring celebrations of his borough's noble history and bosky glens, regularly appeared in the Bronx Home News, which was fond of the old fellow and often sought out his opinions about this and that.

It was on the front page of the little Bronx paper on Monday the 8th of March 1932, one week after little Charles Lindbergh Jr. was reported missing from his Jersey crib, that Dr. Condon passionately declared that he would personally do anything in the world he could do "so a loving mother may again have her child."

And no doubt no one was more surprised than he when, the following evening, a letter was delivered to his home at 2974 Decatur Ave. *Dear Sir. If you are willing to act as go-between in Lindbergh cace pleace follow strictly insturciton.*

HAD THE WORLD'S most hunted criminals really made this unlikely man their conduit? In the desperate moment, Lindbergh elected to believe this, and he deputized Condon as his personal agent. Soon there began to appear a series of terse communications between the kidnap gang and a mysterious Jafsie — a code name derived from Condon's initials, J.F.C. — in the classifieds of the New York American. One evening, Condon sat alone in Woodlawn Cemetery and met a man called John to discuss ransom terms. Late on the night of Saturday the 2nd of

On the trail of the kidnap gang

April, Lindbergh drove him to St. Raymond's Cemetery and waited in the car as Jafsie delivered $50,000 in cash to a figure waiting among the gravestones.

But it was the cruelest of hoaxes. There was no baby at the designated pickup point. Within a few days, the Lone Eagle conceded that he had been swindled.

And now, as it became publicly known that Jafsie was Dr. John Condon of the Bronx, much suspicion began to fall on the old gentleman. *He had kept the $50,000 for himself, hadn't he? He was the sinister mastermind behind the whole affair, wasn't he? Why would a kidnap gang read the Bronx Home News anyway?* Jafsie indignantly protested this treatment, and indeed there were those who agreed that he was hardly a crimelord, merely something perhaps even worse. "Deluded old man," snorted the Daily News.

ON THE 12TH of May, a tiny corpse was found in the Jersey forests and identified by Charles Lindbergh as that of his lost son, and now Dr. John F. Condon, having no further purpose, was dismissed from the Lindbergh retinue as, meanwhile, the mad tale of the Crime of the Century turned more and more impenetrable, full of yarns within yarns, Chinese boxes of clues that led nowhere, hints of this, sniffs of that.

The Virginia businessman was unmasked as a mental case. The baby's nanny and her sailor boyfriend fleetingly became prime suspects. There were dark whispers that it was a deranged relative of Charles Lindbergh's wife, Anne Morrow Lindbergh, who had slain the child; a young maid in the Morrow household, one Violet Sharpe, abruptly swallowed poison and killed herself as Jersey police prepared to question her. The psychics and the seers went on swarming all around.

As for Condon, seeking to repair his blighted reputation, he spent two years detecting on his own, traveling the country, visiting police departments everywhere, pledging someday to find Cemetery John. Sometimes he went out on Long Island Sound in a rowboat, explaining to reporters that he was on his way to secret meetings with informants. On one occasion he swamped his boat and had to be rescued.

IN LATE 1934, a Bronx carpenter named Bruno Richard Hauptmann was charged with the kidnap and murder of the Lindbergh baby. He had been passing marked ransom money; in his garage were found thousands of identifiable dollars. Yes, he explained, he had been safekeeping the cash for his friend Isidor Fisch, who had gone to Germany and died. Everyone had a good laugh over this. *Fisch story,* they called it. From obscurity returned Jafsie, the only man who had ever seen Cemetery John, asked now to look at Hauptmann in a police lineup.

"I cannot positively identify him," Jafsie told the papers. "I cannot identify him at all."

This was not what authorities wanted to hear, and by the time Hauptmann stood trial in early 1935, Jafsie had reconsidered. "John is ... BRUNO RICHARD HAUPTMANN!" the doctor boomed from the witness stand, pointing at a blinking defendant who many modern investigators have concluded probably had little if anything to do with the Crime of the Century.

"Tell the mothers of the Bronx that they may leave their babies sleeping in their cribs," Condon grandly announced outside court, "and that my efforts for the return of the little golden-haired Lindbergh baby were directed for their protection and the safety of every child in the world."

AND NOW Jafsie's moment was over, though his name continued to bob up from time to time, somebody who had been a public figure once. He went on churning out heroic verse, such as the hymn he composed when the Bronx Chamber of Commerce feted him as a community pillar:
And when I am summoned to answer the call,
Just place me in Bronx verdant soil,
Where my generation fought and struggled on
As Bronxites and true sons of toil.
Late in his life he spent much of his time running a thrift shop on City Island. He died at 84 on Jan. 2, 1945, 10 years to the day after the Hauptmann trial opened.

SEVEN DECADES later, the old question of who or what Jafsie really was or was not continues to interest specialists in Lindbergh arcana. Still at hand is one ancient tale concerning one of the spiritualists who early insinuated himself into the kidnap case, a Rev. Peter Piritella, who ran a storefront church in Harlem. It was said that one member of his flock was Hauptmann's friend Isidor Fisch. It was said that another was Violet Sharpe, the suicided Morrow maid.

And a third, it was said, was Dr. John F. Condon, of 2974 Decatur Ave., the Bronx.

HALF-DREAM
Jafsie

By MARA BOVSUN
Special to The News

LONG before there was a tacky Theater District tourist trap called Mamma Leone's, there was a tiny Italian immigrant woman named Luisa, who wore her hair like a Gibson Girl and dreamed of *un bel di* when she could open a restaurant and serve the dishes her mother had taught her to make back home in Bazzana.

Papa said no. Gerome Leone was a prosperous wine merchant, too proud to have a working wife. Luisa's job was to raise the four boys — Joe, Gene, Celestine and Frank.

Besides, one of Papa's greatest joys was to invite homesick Italian singers from the nearby Metropolitan Opera to feast on his wife's cooking in his wine cellar on W. 38th St. A little vino and they'd be singing for their suppers. One regular freeloader was a big eater named Enrico Caruso. He liked Luisa's ravioli.

The family story went that it was Caruso who finally persuaded Gerome to let his wife have her dream. This happened at Luisa's 32nd birthday party on the second day of November in 1905. Papa provided the 60 guests. Luisa provided the food. Son Gene wrote later in his "Leone's Italian Cookbook" that his mother had to borrow a pushcart to lug all the ingredients home.

Sometime during the feast, after pounds of antipasto, ravioli and spaghetti and gallons of Chianti, Caruso asked Luisa when she was going to open *un piccolo posticino, solamenta per noi* — a little restaurant, just for us?

Greeting radio's Major Bowes and party

COURTESY OF YOLANDA LEONE

UN PICCOLO POSTICINO
Mamma Leone

Luisa pounced on the chance of a lifetime, dragging the stuffed tenor from his chair to the piano, where her wine-besotted husband was bellowing a quartet from "Rigoletto" with three singers from the Met.

"Gerolamo," beseeched Caruso, like the lovesick clown in "Pagliacci," "will you allow Luisa to open our little restaurant?"

Papa surrendered. The guests all shouted, "Bravo!" then raised their glorious voices in the drinking song from "La Traviata" until the walls of the little wine cellar shook. The merriment went on till dawn.

That is how Luisa Leone got her restaurant.

SHE DID NOT imagine that she was on the front line of a revolution that eventually would put pasta on every table in America and make Italian chefs the kitchen aristocracy of New York dining.

In 1905, hole-in-the-wall eateries offering the unfamiliar likes of cacciatore and piccata and scampi had only just begun springing up in the city. A Spring St. baker named Gennaro Lombardi that year served a strange new concoction of dough, tomatoes and cheese, reputedly America's first pizza. Luisa Leone's 20-seat bistro was a modest little joint when it opened in April 1906. But her first customer was Caruso.

The legendary tenor — said to have eaten in more places than George Washington had slept — dragged along so many buddies that the opening-night crowd had to sit on wine cases. From that night forward, Luisa's restaurant was never less than packed.

Her secret? The food was really good, and there was a lot of it. Fifty cents bought antipasto, minestrone, spaghetti and ravioli con ragout di manzo, roast chicken or scallopini piccata, cheese, homemade spumoni, caffe nero and a half bottle of wine.

In 1917, three years after Papa went to buy wine in California and never came back, leaving Luisa a widow at 40, the restaurant moved 10 blocks uptown, to 239 W. 48th St., in the heart of the Great White Way, and thereafter it grew into the largest all-Italian restaurant in the city — "possibly the largest anywhere," mused Daily News Broadway columnist Danton Walker. The place spilled over into adjacent buildings, with numerous private dining rooms, like the one for Ziegfeld Follies dancer Yvonne Shelton and her married gentleman friend, a state senator from Greenwich Village named Jimmy Walker, later to become mayor of the town. It was Walker who, somewhere between helpings of his favorite dishes — Vonnie and roast stuffed squab — first called Luisa "Mother Leone." It stuck. In time, everyone called her just Mamma.

MAMMA LEONE, with her ravioli and her 26 kinds of antipasto, was the toast of Broadway, pulling in an endless parade of the brightest from theater, sports, politics and commerce — Babe Ruth, George M. Cohan, Irving Berlin, Will Rogers, young Al Capone. W.C. Fields kept a special gallon goblet stashed behind the bar, bearing the inscription "For Milk Only." The Vagabond Lover, crooner Rudy Vallee, stopped by often, sometimes with the entire cast of his show, who performed for free in the open-air garden. Private rooms were set aside for cops, pols and newsmen, who would scribble their columns between meatballs and give a dime to a busboy to run them over to their papers.

The party went on for years. Gene and Celestine, reared in the business since they were old enough to carry plates, kept the customers happy up front. The brothers loaded the dining areas with paintings and statues and tapestries, built a massive wine cellar of Carrara marble and installed a gurgling stream in the main dining room so those who ordered the brook trout could fish for their supper themselves.

Mamma herself spent little time with the guests, concentrating instead on the kitchen; she began making sauces and soups early every morning and never stopped until midnight, after the last meal had been served and the next day's garlic peeled. Then she would eat.

Her home was an apartment over the restaurant, and she could look down at the main dining hall from her balcony. She rarely went to see any of her famous patrons on stage, screen or playing field. "What better place have I to be than my kitchen?" she shrugged. "I love my kitchen."

Badly cooked pasta was about the only thing that ever enraged her, and she was known to smack her employees with a long Italian bread if she found them inattentive. A cook named Angelino once let the spaghetti simmer too long, and an angry Mamma punished him by clipping three live lobsters to his butt.

SAVE FOR A few summer trips to the villa she bought back home in Bazzana, Mamma worked in her kitchen until a week before she died May 4, 1944.

Gene and Celestine Leone carried on together until Celestine moved to Florida a few years later and Gene took over the place himself, keeping it packed with celebrities by turning it into a carnival. He claimed to have swiped a 10-inch chunk of the Blarney Stone, which he put in the dining room wishing well. He built an on-premises stall for a donkey, an Italian good-luck charm. He brought in a truffle dog from Italy and had it take reporters on a lively and well-publicized romp through town, sniffing out truffles Gene had hidden. For a time, a forlorn swayback racehorse named Pounditout was kept tied to the bar, giving out hoofprint autographs.

When Gene hung up his apron in 1959 and sold out to Restaurant Associates, Mamma Leone's was often serving 6,000 dinners a night, usually including more than a ton of shrimp with Mamma's favorite sauce.

Not long after that, the celebrities stopped coming, and the storied old New York City institution was left to hordes of hayseed tourists; Mamma Leone's, with its singing waiters and strolling accordion players, was one of those must-visit guidebook places, like the Statue of Liberty, and so it remained for years. Most out-of-towners were sure that the tiny, white-haired woman who greeted them at the door was the matriarch who had started it all. She was, in fact, a hired Mamma impostor.

But everything eventually turned into a bad joke. By the time Mamma Leone's was mercifully closed in 1994, the Zagat Survey was calling it "a black hole of cuisine," serving "food like raw plastic."

There was no getting around it: Luisa Leone had left the kitchen.

By MARA BOVSUN
Special to The News

ONE WARM MAY day in 1908, there appeared at the luxurious Fifth Avenue beauty salon of Madame LeClaire a wrinkled old woman in a shabby black dress.

An elegant shopgirl took pity on the unfortunate and gave her a tour of the chandeliered rooms with blue silk walls and portraits of lovelies whose charms, so the story went, derived from beauty secrets given to Madame by a dying Austrian nun. The old woman asked many questions and curiously peered into the booths, where aging society matrons were smeared with Madame's miraculous black goo that would restore the glow of youth.

Then, to the shopgirl's astonishment, the old lady lifted her threadbare skirt and whipped out six $50 bills from the cash-stuffed pockets of her petticoat.

"I'll pay for this now," she announced, and started her rejuvenation at once.

This incident hit the newspapers a few days later, rocking the city: Henrietta Howland Robinson Green, the richest woman in America, the notorious Witch of Wall Street, was actually spending some of her money.

Hetty Green never let a nickel go. Sometimes she made $200,000 in a single day in the stock market, but her penny-pinching was legendary, followed by the papers for years. At her death in 1916, she was worth at least $100 million — more than $17 billion in modern dollars — yet she was famous for once having spent an entire day searching her home from top to bottom for a lost 2-cent stamp.

Eight decades after Hetty Green's death, she still easily made a listing of the 40 richest Americans of all time. She was the only woman on the list.

HETTY GREEN owned small railroads and prime real estate all over the country, but she moved from one seedy apartment to another to stay ahead of tax men and imaginary assassins. She did business on the floor of the Chemical National Bank, breakfasting on oatmeal she heated on the radiator, lunching on ham sandwiches she carried in her pockets. Chemical's officers were happy to let her camp out all day if she pleased.

Her miserliness might have been more understandable had she come up from poverty. But Hetty was heiress to a Massachusetts whaling fortune built by her grandfather and father, Edward Mott (Blubber) Robinson, and she had been fabulously wealthy since childhood — as well as canny and shrewd, thanks to her father's tutoring. She was reading the newspaper financial pages aloud to him at age 6.

Young Hetty was not unattractive, but suitors were put off by the rough mode of dress she came to prefer during her years of hanging around the whaling docks with papa. Blubber showered her with fine feminine gowns, hoping she might eventually appeal to some good society beau, but Hetty demonstrated no interest in the subject until after he died in 1865 and she inherited $6 million. Thereafter she married one Edward Henry Green, a Vermont merchant who had become a millionaire in Manila, and moved with

him to England, where she bore a son and a daughter.

Her tightwad ways were firmly established. Thanks to them, the boy, Edward Howland Robinson Green, or Ned, lost a leg at age 14. When he fell from a sled and cut a knee, Hetty refused to pay for a doctor, insisting upon home remedies even when the wound festered and the leg swelled. Finally she dressed in rags and took the boy to New York's Bellevue charity clinic, where doctors saw through the bogus poverty and demanded payment. Hetty bolted, going from one doctor to another, begging for free treatment. Ultimately, she was forced to pay to have Ned's leg cut off.

THE GREENS' marriage collapsed in the mid-1880s, along with the august firm of John J. Cisco & Son, at 59 Wall St., where the couple had

banked for years. As Cisco went belly-up, Hetty tried to pull out her money, about half a million in cash and $25 million in securities. But Cisco said no. Edward Green had taken out a $700,000 loan that he now could not repay. Until that debt was satisfied, Cisco insisted, Hetty could not have her money.

RICHEST WOMAN MAKES A SCENE, the New York World reported one morning in January 1885 when Hetty showed up at Cisco & Son. **CRYING FOR HER BONDS**, the Herald added. **SHE ROLLS ON THE FLOOR AND DEMANDS HER SECURITIES**. Day after day, Hetty screeched and wept and threw tantrums as the whole city watched. In the end, she had to give up and write out a check before Cisco surrendered her fortune, which she then stuffed into a cab and rushed over to Chemical National.

Soon after that, Edward Green moved into bachelor's quarters, never to return. When he died in 1902, Hetty bought a mourning veil and black dress, and all the rest of her days she wore little else.

That same year, she terrified New York's lawyers by getting a permit to carry a .44-caliber pistol. She had become convinced that attorneys had poisoned her father and husband and that she was next. **MRS. HETTY GREEN CARRIES A BIG REVOLVER**, the Herald announced. **BELIEVES LAWYERS WOULD SLAY HER**. Hetty assured reporters that she was a Quaker: "I would shoot not to kill but to disable." But everyone made a point of giving the Witch of Wall Street wide berth, all the same.

WITH AGE, she softened a bit, even began loosening the purse strings. Though she lived in a cold-water flat across the river in Hoboken, the historic beauty treatments of 1908 came along with a posh dinner party she threw at the Plaza Hotel. This was part of a campaign to marry off daughter Sylvia, who in 1909 did indeed wed an Astor.

Little by little, the world began to think more warmly of Hetty, and her birthdays were always celebrated by the papers. On her 78th, in 1913, a reporter who had apparently forgotten about Madame LeClaire, asked Hetty for the secret of her vitality and rosy cheeks. "That's not rouge and don't you think so for a minute!" she snapped. "That's because I always chew a baked onion."

The next day, the onion market went through the roof.

SHE DIED THREE years later after a stroke. By that time, the family fortune was being managed by son Ned, who had grown up to become a successful wooden-legged businessman. He inherited half of her unbelievable wealth and went on to blow much of it. At his death in 1936, he was one of New York's fastest-spending playboys and stage-door Johnnys.

Daughter Sylvia got the other half and lived on until 1951. Both she and Ned died childless. The fortune, what was left of it, got scattered to various charities and a few distant relatives.

PENNY SAVED, PENNY EARNED
Hetty Green

With daughter, Sylvia

By DICK SHERIDAN
Daily News Staff Writer

MANY ARE THOSE who come to New York to make names for themselves. Bat Masterson came to escape his.

He was 48 when he arrived in the city in 1902, seeking to put behind him a life spent roaming the American West as buffalo hunter, Indian fighter, gambler and one of the most famous lawmen of the wild frontier.

Things did not work out as the old gunfighter might have planned. Masterson's welcome to the city was a rude one. Shortly after first setting foot on New York's streets, he was arrested and charged with having conducted a crooked faro game on the train east.

Those who knew him were shocked. Though Bat was credited with killing more than a score of men, outright dishonesty was not particularly associated with the Masterson name. "He has always been considered 'square' when he sat down to a card table," reported The New York Times.

He seemed more upset that police confiscated his trusty old revolver than about being in custody. "It has often saved my life," he explained, ducking the question of how many men it had dispatched. One disappointed reporter noted that the gun had no notches on it.

The charges faded away when the complainant, a Mormon elder from Salt Lake City, bolted town without appearing in court. Once free, Masterson found himself a celebrity — and, though he had been planning to sail on to England, decided to stay on in New York for a while.

He would never leave. For the rest of his life, Bat Masterson was a New Yorker, one of the city's best-known newspapermen, a familiar bowler-hatted, cane-swinging figure in sporting circles, in high society, in Broadway's theaters and restaurants, forever mobbed by admiring tourists. Periodically, some backslapper always wanted to buy his historic revolver as a souvenir. From time to time he would reluctantly consent to part with it. He was always supplied with weapons he picked up cheap in pawnshops, and he was known to have sold the fabled "Gun That Won the West" at least six times.

NEW YORKERS had been breathlessly following the bloody adventures of Bat Masterson for two decades before he ever came to town.

It was a New York Sun correspondent who had made him famous, back in 1881. Visiting the boom town of Gunnison, Colo., in search of tales of Wild West mayhem in the heyday of the dime novel, the reporter began to hear stories about one William Barclay Masterson, a 27-year-old former peace officer who had supposedly killed 26 men, including seven practically all at once in a saloon shootout back when he'd been a Kansas sheriff. Another woolly yarn had him tracking down a pair of desperadoes, shooting them dead, then cutting off their heads and carrying them around in a sack as trophies.

All this and more the Sun man scribbled down without question. Bat Masterson got headlines in New York and across the nation, and readers

GUNS OFF
Bat Masterson

demanded more of his hair-raising adventures, and for years to come, the papers were more than happy to conjure them up, embellishing slim facts with great dollops of fantasy. Bat himself was no particular braggart, and he personally made few claims of gun-blazing heroics. But he was happy enough to let the papers write what they pleased. "They do it with such a recklessness and with such utter disregard of the truth that I make no kick," he told a friend. "I have concluded that they can't do me any harm."

The facts were that he'd been born in Canada in 1853, settled with his family in Kansas, and in 1871, just shy of 18, had struck out with his brother Ed to seek his fortune as a buffalo hunter. Subsequently the Masterson boys had signed on with the railroad, and in 1874 the Bat Masterson saga got its start when Bat was one of a small party of hunters who fought off several hundred Comanches and Kiowas at a place called Adobe Walls in the Texas Panhandle. Then he'd enlisted in the Army as a scout and survived much Plains combat, then drifted north to rough-and-tumble

Dodge City and put in several years as a lawman. After that he'd moved on to Denver. Through the 20 years he spent as the fast-draw hero of hundreds of vivid newspaper stories, he was working mostly as a gambler and boxing promoter, only occasionally taking on peacekeeping jobs, usually to help out such old friends as Wyatt Earp and Doc Holliday.

Between the facts and the fictions, he was a man of considerable reputation when he pulled up stakes in Denver and headed east to take up a new life as a New York City slicker. The old days were behind him. He was never known to mount a horse again. He didn't much like horses anyway. "Horses stink, at best," he said.

DURING HIS early days in the city, he worked as a boxing referee and spent time at the racetracks. Then he joined the staff of the New York Morning Telegraph, one of the city's breezier dailies, a paper concentrating mainly on sports and theatrical news, and his popular column, "Masterson's Views on Timely Topics," appeared three times a week. His friend, President Theodore Roosevelt, offered him a job as a U.S. marshal out West, but Masterson decided he liked newspapering better at this point. "If I were marshal," he wrote Roosevelt, "some youngster would try to put me out. ... I would be bait for a grownup kid who had fed on dime novels. No sense to that. I have taken my guns off, and I don't ever want to put them on again."

Though he did briefly accept a part-time appointment as deputy U.S. marshal for the southern district of New York, it was as a Telegraph man that he lived out the rest of his days. His newspaper pals included a young Louella Parsons, who would later become the celebrated Hollywood scandalmonger ("Just a kind-hearted old man," she would remember Bat), and a young Damon Runyon, who would eventually immortalize him in a short story that turned into Broadway's "Guys and Dolls."

On Tuesday morning, the 25th of October 1921, 67-year-old Bat Masterson breakfasted with his wife, Emma, a onetime Wild West dance-hall queen, in their apartment at 300 W. 49th St., then strolled to the Telegraph offices at Eighth Ave. and 50th St. and sat down at his desk to compose his column. *"There are many in this old world of ours who hold that things break about even for all of us,"* he wrote. *"I have observed, for example, that we all get about the same amount of ice. The rich get it in the summer — and the poor get it in the winter."*

Those were the tired old legend's last words. A few minutes later, a co-worker found him dead in his chair.

THE GOOD EARTH
Charles Chapin

By JOSEPH McNAMARA
Special to The News

COLD, RUTHLESS Charles Chapin thundered into New York in 1891 to run the city desk at Joseph Pulitzer's Evening World, and very soon he was the most hated man on Park Row. The Pirate, every newspaperman in the city called him. He delighted in humiliating his reporters in public. He was particularly fond of waiting till Christmas Eve to fire a man.

Chapin had learned his newspapering in brawling Chicago, where he grew up, and in St. Louis, where, at a Pulitzer sheet, he developed a knack for coming up with a sensational story on any listless day. This was a talent prized by Pulitzer, who nicknamed Chapin "Pinch" and sent him east to join the tooth-and-claw circulation wars between the World and New York's nine other big dailies. Park Row was an unforgiving street. Here, Chapin thrived.

By 1914, he was a legend. Moreover, he was rich. He was a nephew of Wall Street millionaire Russell Sage, a man he admired, and Chapin had been ushered into the world of stocks and bonds, which bought him a yacht, fancy automobiles, a racehorse and a summer home. At age 56, he enjoyed the good life. He and Nellie, his wife of 30 years, lived at The Plaza, drank the finest wines, frequented the choicest restaurants, wore the finest clothes.

Even his friends wished him nothing but grief and woe. And they got their wish.

CHAPIN HAD MADE a bundle in the pre-World War market, but then he began gambling on commodities. When the sugar market went bust, he went bust with it. Loans bailed him out of trouble, and, this time investing more wisely, he began to rebuild his fortune. But then the U.S. went to war with Germany. The stock market was torpedoed. Chapin was broke.

Now he and Nellie fell on cruel times. The Plaza evicted them for nonpayment of their bill; soon their new residence, the modest Hotel Cumberland, was pressing them for payment as well. Chapin's checks bounced all over town. His credit died. He borrowed. He scrounged. He decided there was nothing to do but kill himself.

On the night of Sept. 16, 1918, Chapin slipped a pistol from under his pillow, shot the sleeping Nellie once in the chest and readied to take his own life as well. But his wife wasn't dead yet. She lingered for two awful hours. And during that time he lost his resolve to put the second bullet into himself.

When Nellie finally died, Chapin dressed, went out and walked the streets in a daze. Hours later, a newspaper headline jolted him back to reality
— CHARLES CHAPIN WANTED FOR MURDER
— and he surrendered to the first policeman he saw.

CONVICTED OF second-degree murder and sentenced to 20 years to life, the man who had once been New York's most fearsomely powerful city editor arrived at Sing Sing on Jan. 7, 1919. Warden Lewis Lawes quickly offered him a job editing The Bulletin, the prison monthly, and soon Chapin was running a staff of convict reporters, all of whom complained that he was an impossible slave driver.

Budgetary shortfalls shut the paper down in 1922. The following spring, Chapin appeared in Lawes' office and asked if he could plant a few things in the prison yard. He didn't have much of a green thumb, he admitted, but he thought perhaps he could sow something. Lawes gave him the okay — and later Chapin came back, asking for permission to extend his small garden to the entire yard, to include benches and a fountain.

Recounted Lawes in his book, "20,000 Years In Sing Sing":

"I glanced over the yard…Nothing but dirt and stone and sand, trodden under countless feet for a hundred years…It was as barren to the eye as it was hopeless to the heart.

"Suddenly, I was ashamed. I turned to the slim man at my side and said, 'Tell you what, Charlie. Do the whole job. Put some life into this yard.' "

Chapin used his tobacco money to buy seed; the chaplain came up with a hoe, rake and shovel; 30 men went to work in the prison gardens. Soon there were rose bushes in profusion — within two years, 200 varieties of them — and five greenhouses. "The Rose Man of Sing Sing," the New York papers called the former World tyrant.

"I do not claim that flowers reform men, nor that the gardens reformed Chapin," Lawes wrote. "But they gave him a new perspective. And after all, is not that the aim of prison administration?

"Is there not hope for the most depraved? Is any heart hopeless?"

CHAPIN FELL SICK, his heart weak, his condition feeble. In the summer of 1930, a new drainage system was deemed necessary for the old Big House on the Hudson. The yard had to be ripped up — and with it, the gardens. Chapin, 72 years old, watched the destruction in silent sorrow. On Dec. 13, the warden was at his side in the prison hospital, holding his hand. "Is there anything you want, Charlie?" Lawes asked him. "Nothing," said the old man. "I am tired and I want to die."

And he did, and was buried beside his wife.

The following spring, Warden Lawes ordered the gardens replanted.

By MARA BOVSUN
Special to The News

DOCTORS AT THE New York National Guard recruiting station were aghast that day in October 1917 when one volunteer in the eager crowd stripped to reveal a body that looked like it had already faced down the Germans, and lost.

Razor, knife and bullet scars began at his ankles, ran up to his barrel chest and crisscrossed his neck and face. Decorating his belly were souvenirs of two slugs that had ripped through him years earlier, leaving wounds he had plugged with his fingers while dragging himself to the hospital. His nose had been mashed. On each side of his head, where most people have ears, dangled two shreds of flesh. What battles had this man been in? the doctors wondered.

"Oh, just a lot of little private wars around New York," William Delaney replied offhandedly.

Scars aside, the body looked pretty sturdy, so they let him sign up.

Thus began the soul cleansing of William Delaney, real name Edward Osterman, otherwise known as Monk Eastman, the terror of the lower East Side.

IN HIS GLORY, Monk had commanded an army of 1,200 of the city's meanest thugs, a grimy bunch of safecrackers, pickpockets and general ruffians from dangerous dives with names like the Flea Bag, the Bucket of Blood and Suicide Hall. The Eastman gang had turned the area between the Bowery and 14th St. into a no-man's-land, pocked by brawls with such rivals as the Yakey Yakes, the Red Onions and Paul Kelly's fearsome Five Pointers.

These gangs grew out of the dirt-poor Jewish, Italian and Irish immigrants who flooded into New York in the late 19th century, for whom a life of crime was often the only alternative to starvation. Monk himself, it happened, was the son of a prosperous Brooklyn deli man, and initially papa had tried hard to steer young Edward along a righteous path, setting him up as a dealer in puppies, pigeons and kitties. But the lad found different work for himself, dance hall bouncer, and a new name, the Monk, in honor of his simian ability to climb walls and swing through windows.

He never abandoned his pets. He was usually seen strolling about with a huge blue pigeon on his shoulder and a couple of cats tucked under his massive arms. Anyone he found being cruel to animals got a severe drubbing. "I like de kits and boids," Monk said.

Otherwise, what he carried were clubs, blackjacks and brass knuckles. Early in his career, he inflicted so many injuries that ambulance drivers dubbed Bellevue's accident ward the Eastman Pavilion. These talents were noticed by Tammany Hall, and soon Monk and his gang of Jewish toughs were Election Day fixtures, voting for their candidates two, three, four or more times and suggesting to other voters that perhaps it would be healthy for them to vote the same way.

Such a valuable man as Monk had powerful friends, and he was routinely released just as soon as he was arrested. This left him free to attend to the business of his hood-for-hire operation, which efficiently offered head whackings or ear chewings for $15, stabbings for $25 and more serious forms of mayhem for $100.

But, in the summer of 1903, the terrifying Battle of Rivington St. was too much even for Tammany. Three men died, as 100 gangsters, "in true Western style," the New York Herald reported, "fought through two miles of streets for five hours in defiance of the police until a square mile of territory was panic-stricken." When Monk was arrested again, in April 1904, after he fired a dozen shots at a Pinkerton detective, no Tammany lawyer showed up to help him, and off he went to Sing Sing for 10 years.

BY THE TIME he came out, most of his old gang was gone and there were no battles left for him to fight. Except for the World War.

At 44, he became a doughboy, fighting in the

OUR LOST PAL
Monk Eastman

fields of France with the 106th Infantry of the 27th Division, "O'Ryan's Roughnecks." There, in the trenches, the Monk was transformed. The hoodlum became a hero.

There were dozens of stories of his valor. Here was Monk, galloping across wasteland to rescue a wounded comrade. Here was Monk, leaping from crater to crater to wipe out nests of machine-gunners. Here was Monk, badly wounded, insisting upon leaving his hospital bed to rejoin his unit.

When he came home in April 1919, the men he had served with rallied behind him. The newspapers told of his redemption, holding him out as proof that even the most wretched can be saved. **MONK EASTMAN WINS NEW SOUL,** trumpeted the Tribune. **OFFICERS AND HUNDREDS OF SOLDIERS WHO FOUGHT WITH HIM ASK GOVERNOR TO MAKE HIM CITIZEN AGAIN.**

So it was that the Monk — citizenship restored, head high — marched on Fifth Ave. with other war heroes, cheered by the good people of New York who had once quaked at the mention of his name.

TWO DAYS AFTER Christmas 1920, the headline in the Daily News was **EX-CONVICT, WAR HERO, SHOT DEAD.** There were five bullets in Monk Eastman. A shady Prohibition agent named Jerry Bohan, who had been drinking with Monk in an East Side dive called the Blue Bird, was quickly charged with the killing. He claimed self-defense, and there was much press speculation as to how genuine Monk's celebrated rehabilitation had really been.

But the dead man's buddies from the 106th would hear none of this. Hank Miller and John Boland, two men who had fought alongside Monk, put up funds for a military burial. "Mr. Edward Eastman did more for America than Presidents and generals," Boland announced. "The public

does not reward its heroes. Now they are calling Mr. Eastman a gangster instead of praising him as one of those who saved America. But we'll do the right thing by this soldier and give him the funeral he deserves."

On an overcast, freezing morning three days before New Year's, 4,000 mourners — soldiers, women, children, blubbering old gangsters — showed up to send Monk off. Monk was dressed in full military regalia, wearing his service stripes and American Legion pin. On his shining black coffin was a silver plate inscribed *Our Lost Pal. Gone But Not Forgotten.*

After 12 hours of a whiskey-washed wake, the flag-draped coffin was borne on the shoulders of eight uniformed veterans to a waiting hearse at the Williamsburg Bridge Plaza. A double line of 24 buddies formed an honor guard. A procession of six polished black cars and 20 horse-drawn carriages joined the parade to the military plot at Brooklyn's Cypress Hills Cemetery. At graveside there was a 21-gun salute, and a bugler sounded taps as Monk's coffin was lowered into the ground.

A few days later, a grief-stricken crook named Edward Herberger journeyed in from Philadelphia to avenge his pal. With Bohan in jail, Herberger found no one to shoot, so he did the next best thing. He stuck up a gin mill and made off with $2,000. When Philly cops arrested him, they found, along with opium and safecracking tools, a photo of Monk Eastman draped in black.

By JAY MAEDER
Daily News Staff Writer

JOHNNY SPANISH and Kid Dropper had been pallies once, long ago, back when they were ambitious youngsters coming up in Paul Kelly's Five Points gang, sticking up messenger boys and Chatham Square storekeepers, but there had been a falling out. This occurred around about 1911, after Johnny Spanish, who always carried four revolvers, gained some notoriety when he came gunning for another mug and accidentally killed a small child instead and had to beat it out of town for a while. Upon his return, aggrieved to discover that his sweetie had in his absence taken up with Kid Dropper, he immediately confronted the faithless girl and shot her full of holes. It happened that her wounds proved nonfatal, and thereafter Johnny went to prison for seven years. At the same time, in an entirely separate matter, Kid Dropper went to prison for seven years himself. And so the both of them were removed from the City of New York until 1918.

By which time it was a different world altogether. Reemerged into sunlight, John Weyler and Nathan Kaplan found that reformers had taken a turn at running the town, and the familiar old plug-ugly gangs of yore — the Five Pointers, the Hudson Dusters, Monk Eastman's mob, all the other inelegant bonecrushers — were pretty much out of business. Both now discovered the marginally more sophisticated labor-goon dodge in this bright new day of postwar union solidarity.

Bosses wanted the union strikers crippled; the strikers wanted the scab workers maimed; there was plenty of goon work for everyone, actually, except that Johnny Spanish and Kid Dropper remained mortal foes and kept ferociously battling each other for the various lucrative contracts. The business dispute was settled July 29, 1919, amid a garment workers' walkout, when Johnny Spanish was shot down outside a lower Second Ave. restaurant and thus bequeathed the labor rackets to his old pally Kid Dropper, who, at age 28 now a leading figure in the city's underworld, proceeded to abandon his mongrel ways, put on a stiff collar and a flashy checkered suit and become a Broadway sport.

THE LOWER EAST Side was full of people who wore Nathan Kaplan's hideous scars on their faces. Kid Dropper liked to carve guys up, sometimes just for fun; modern times notwithstanding, he remained a Five Pointer by training and temperament and his instrument of choice was still a can opener. Among those he tattooed was one Jacob Orgen, better known as Little Augie, who in the early 1920s was getting

DROPPER, UNDER GUARD, SLAIN

GANG WAR — Surrounded by police and detectives as he was released from homicide charge in Essex Market Court yesterday, John Kaplan,

The slayer re-enacts the killing

Kid Dropper, victim of East Side gunmen's war, before arraignment in Essex Market Court.

Louis Cohen (left) manacled to Detective Otto Ransburg ... known as Kid Dropper, East Side gang leader, was killed by Louis Cohen, who said one or other had to die ...

DYING — At London home where she lies ill, hope was abandoned yesterday for ... Princess Anastasia of ...

WRECK — A Pennsylvania flier bringing wealthy summer ... Park, Deal and Long Branch, N.J. ... The locomotive dragged three ... cab was crush ...

RITES OF PASSAGE
Kid Dropper

into labor-gooning himself. Little Augie spent four months in the hospital after the Dropper ministered to him one day at Clinton and Broome Sts., and the two of them were never very friendly after that.

Indeed, relations grew even testier after Little Augie, not entirely ungallantly, rang up Kid Dropper one day and suggested that they work things out one-on-one with a gentlemanly duel on the Brooklyn waterfront, and the Dropper merely called the cops and informed them where they could find Augie with a loaded gun, and Augie then went to prison for a year on a Sullivan Law conviction.

Eventually, however, Little Augie regrouped, numbering among his employees two extremely efficient bruisers known to police and press at the time as Jacob Shapiro and Louis Buckhouse. Over the years to come, they would become more popularly known as Gurrah and Lepke. On Wednesday night, the 1st of August 1923, however, they were just a couple of Augie Orgen's gunners as Kid Dropper's Rough Riders gang and Little Augie's Little Augies, working opposite sides of a laundry strike, met each other for a blazing shootout on Essex St. between Broome and Delancey, and a couple of pedestrians were killed in the crossfire.

NEW YORK CITY was quite distressed by its

homicide statistics. There had been 260 murders in 1922, as compared to 17 in London, a city half-again larger. "Our system," bemoaned the Daily News, "is lacking in the three great essentials of law enforcement: Celerity, certainty and finality... . We shall be endangered and disgraced by the prevalence of crime until the apprehension and punishment of criminals are swift, certain and conclusive... . Politics is the most obvious source of inefficiency in law enforcement."

And, of course, it turned out there wasn't much the cops really had on the gangland czar Kid Dropper. At the Essex Market Court at Second Ave. and Second St. on the afternoon of Tuesday, the 28th of August, he was released, again, as he had been dozens of times before.

There was considerable police concern that assassins might be lying in wait for Nathan Kaplan at this very public moment in his career, and the newly freed man was surrounded by dozens of officers, including the legendary Capt. Cornelius Willemse, as he came out of the courthouse and stepped into a taxicab. Straight through police lines galloped a little man named Louis Cohen, who leaped onto the back of the car and, in as brazen an underworld execution as the city ever saw, fired four shots point-blank through the window.

Struck twice, Kid Dropper died on the spot. A detective sitting next to him was grazed. Willemse got a hole through his straw hat.

"I don't guess I'll get more than five years," Cohen boasted, plainly very pleased to be the big-timer who had dropped the Dropper.

ACTUALLY, TO his surprise, he got 20. His attorney was a state senator named James Walker, who argued that Cohen was merely a frightened laundryman the Dropper had menaced and that really he had done the city a great service by ridding it of a reptile. That part was true, but on the other hand, there was plenty of evidence that the 21-year-old shooter was one of Augie Orgen's boys, and at trial's end in December, General Sessions Judge Albert Talley blistered the jury for bringing in a murder-two verdict instead of murder one.

"The dignity and majesty of the law have been lost," Talley snapped. "This verdict will doubtless cause rejoicing among those of the defendant's type on the East Side tonight. Many a gun will be polished and slipped into a pocket by persons who put them away when Cohen was arrested. They get the idea from verdicts like this that you can't get juries to convict, so why worry?"

THROUGH THE 1920s there fell numerous men the papers liked to call the last of the ancient gangsters, and Kid Dropper was another one of these — "the most prominent link between the old-time gang history of New York and the shooting present," The News said. The same had been said about the skull-cracker Monk Eastman a few years earlier; it would be said about Joe "The Boss" Masseria a few years later, as the Italians began to displace Irishers and Jews in the city's underworld.

For the moment, Kid Dropper's successor in the labor rackets, Little Augie Orgen, was viewed as a modern. He would rule for four years before he, too, would become regarded as a dinosaur, standing in the way of progress, to be replaced in turn by Gurrah and Lepke, not the most loyal boys he ever hired.

Louis Cohen got out of prison in 1937. By that time, Kid Dropper's name was mostly long forgotten. But someone remembered. In January 1939, on Lewis St. between Broome and Grand, ambushers pumped Cohen full of slugs.

Cohen's trial lawyer, state Sen. Jimmy Walker, was elected mayor of the City of New York in November 1925.

BROWN BROTHERS

By JONATHAN LEWIN and JAY MAEDER
Daily News Staff Writers

"You may live to see man-made horrors beyond your comprehension."

— Nikola Tesla, 1898

THE MAIDS at the Hotel New Yorker avoided the shabby old gentleman in Room 3327. He was forever picking up sick pigeons and bringing them back to nurse them. And he mumbled about mad things: flowering deserts, giant power stations, death rays that could melt a city, radio signals from distant planets. Only his birds were there when he died in his bed on Thursday the 7th of January 1943, age 86, just another tired old man life had used up.

But because of Nikola Tesla, there were efficient electrical transmission systems in the world, and television and radar and remote control and neon lighting and everyday household appliances, and there were technological foundations for inventions yet unimagined. A quarter of a century earlier, fellow engineers had proclaimed him the father of the modern industrial revolution: *"Were we to eliminate from our industrial world the results of his work, the wheels of industry would cease to turn, our electric cars and trains would stop, our towns would be dark, our mills would be dead and idle."* By that time, 1917, Tesla was already an embittered hermit.

"For 40 years he lived and worked in a world of fantasy crackling with electric sparks, packed with strange towers to receive and emit energy and dreamy contrivances to give utopian man complete control of nature," The New York Times eulogized him. "It was the Jules Verne future that engrossed him . . . Communicating with Mars, plucking heat units out of the atmosphere to run engines, using the whole Earth as an electrical resonator so that a man in China could communicate wirelessly with another in South America, transmitting power through space — it was to such possibilities that he devoted the last 40 years of his long life.

"It was a lonely life."

ELECTRICITY WAS still a novelty in 1884, when 28-year-old Nikola Tesla, a Serbian

engineer who had been working for the Continental Edison Co. in France, arrived in New York and offered Thomas Edison an improvement upon the direct-current (DC) system. Tesla's far more efficient polyphase alternating-current (AC) system allowed much higher voltages than were possible with DC and enabled transmission over hundreds of miles, whereas DC required a power station every mile or two. Edison brushed him off. The great inventor had already committed himself to DC.

And so Tesla sold to Pittsburgh industrialist George Westinghouse the rights to his transformers and condensers and dynamos and coils. Westinghouse and Edison dueled for commercial electrical supremacy for several years. Tesla frequently gave spectacular demonstrations of AC's power, appearing before dazzled audiences silhouetted by flames as hundreds of thousands of volts coursed through his body. He was a great hit at Chicago's Colombian Exposition in 1893. Edison lost the war; it was Westinghouse who built the generators that harnessed Niagara Falls and birthed modern hydroelectric power. Before he died in 1931, Edison viewed as his largest mistake his failure to back AC.

STORMBRINGER
Nikola Tesla

BY THIS TIME, Tesla was deeply involved in experiments with wireless telegraphy. As early as 1890, he was beaming radio signals from his Houston St. laboratory to a boat on the Hudson River. In 1898, he astounded military observers at Madison Square Garden when he showed off a remotely controlled ship model and offhandedly predicted radio-guided torpedoes. That was three years before Guglielmo Marconi sent a demonstration SOS out to sea and became world famous as the "Father of Radio."

Much of what else Tesla was up to was always shrouded in secrecy. One night in August 1896 there was a terrific thunderclap that burst water mains and shattered windows across Little Italy. The ground rattled for 10 minutes as police converged on Tesla's laboratory. Inside, as the earthquake subsided, they found Tesla shutting down what he called a telegeodynamic oscillator. It created vibrations, he explained; it could easily shake apart the Brooklyn Bridge.

In the wake of this incident, Tesla found it necessary to move his mysterious lab to rural

Colorado. There he built a 200-foot transmitter and went to work simulating electrical storms, throwing his switches and spewing out great blasts and fireballs that rocked the night for miles around. Once he blacked out the entire town of Colorado Springs.

HE GOT BACK to New York in 1900, heavily in debt, having some years earlier chosen to release Westinghouse from the royalty agreements that would otherwise have made him rich. He was also under increasing attack from scientists who found him frankly disturbing; *practitioner of the black arts,* some were calling him. Still, he got J.P. Morgan's backing for a huge radio tower at Shoreham, L.I., from which he intended to beam signals around the entire world — and beyond.

But the Shoreham "world wireless station" did not long survive the emergence of Marconi — who had used a Tesla patent to send his 1901 SOS, and had indeed been backed by Thomas Edison. By 1903, as it became clear that Tesla had lost the radio race, Morgan stopped investing.

So ended Tesla's moment in the practical sciences. He retreated from the world and, as his financial woes mounted, mostly used his nightmarish machines to frighten away bill collectors.

MARCONI WON the Nobel Prize in 1909; Tesla sued for patent infringement; Marconi countersued; the court battle dragged on for decades. No longer able to afford a laboratory, Tesla pursued his experiments in cheap hotel rooms. He talked of wireless power transmission, harnessing the sun, turning deserts into verdant fields, lighting up the night sky so that ships and airplanes would never collide. In 1931, he said he was sending messages to Mars. In 1937, he said he was getting messages back.

Late in 1940, with Europe at war, he offered the U.S. government his death beam, based on "entirely new principles of physics that no one has ever dreamed about," a ray that could annihilate armies and destroy fleets of enemy aircraft. He proposed a network of transmitting plants that would send up a 50-million-volt defense wall no invader could penetrate. Officials declined.

"Again and again they jeered at me," he snapped late in his life, "and then years later saw that I was right."

WHEN HE DIED, surrounded by his pigeons, Tesla left behind more than 700 patents and an incalculable number of ideas never set to paper. To the end, he raged that Guglielmo Marconi was a common thief. Eight months after he died, the U.S. Supreme Court agreed, overturning Marconi's radio patents.

By GENE MUSTAIN
Daily News Staff Writer

ROBERT ELLIOTT once killed seven people in a week. Another time, he did four in a single night. He killed men and women, rich and poor, notables and nobodies — nearly 400 in all, more than anyone else in modern history, he always said.

Not that he was bragging.

"I am a mere tool of the state," explained New York's official executioner.

Except for his very first electrocution, which did not go so well, he was the right man for the job, and that began with his appearance — gaunt, gray, gangly and spectral, black eyes set deep in bony sockets, the very picture of death come knocking at the doors of the doomed. Inside the death chamber — apart from that admittedly unfortunate first time — Elliott comported himself like the reserved, competent electrician he was. He was so coolly professional about his work that few people knew he was personally against capital punishment because he felt it was about revenge, and revenge was God's business. But he was able to separate himself from the work, and he threw the switch without guilt.

"The decision that a man's life is to end has been made by the commonwealth that has selected me to do this job," he said. "Humaneness demands that it be done quickly and efficiently."

THROUGH HIS killing time, which ran from 1926 to 1939, he was an ordinary family man from Queens. He played bridge, fished in Long Island Sound, went to church every Sunday. He grew roses and glads. His six grandkids called him Bompa.

He was always good with electricity. Had been since he was an upstate farm boy growing up in the 1890s and one of the hands, a former telegraph operator, told him about the miraculous new invention. "It's going to be the most remarkable power that men ever worked with," the farmhand told young Elliott. "It's wonderful enough that we can send messages with it and it can be used for light. But that's only the beginning."

Enthralled by the new technology, Elliott quit a teachers' college at 19 and went to work for the local power company. Then, a few years later, he got an electrician's job in the Dannemora state prison's power plant.

And that's how he got into the execution business, in 1903, when state officials — thinking ahead to the time when then-executioner Edwin Davis would take retirement — sent him down to Sing Sing to learn how to strap a man into the electric chair and jolt him into eternity.

New York State had abolished hanging in favor of electrocution in 1889. The early chair was far from a perfect instrument; the first man to sit in the thing was basically roasted alive. As recently as a few months before Elliott showed up for training, the equipment was unreliable enough that one man somehow lived through his execution, as a surprised doctor discovered during autopsy.

Elliott had only a mild interest in these stories. He was interested in the workings of the chair, not the persons who sat in it. That first time out,

he made a mistake. He was attaching an electrode to the condemned man's leg — and looked up into his eyes, and saw the fear.

The electrician started to sweat. His legs shook, his hands trembled. Only by closing his eyes could he make his feet move. He staggered from the chair, toward the switch 10 feet away.

Witnesses in the chamber coughed nervously and shuffled their feet. Davis, the veteran executioner, came over to put a hand on Elliott's shoulder. "Steady," he murmured.

Elliott inhaled deeply. Then up went the switch that unleashed the new man-made lightning. The frightened man in the chair stiffened and slumped, quite dead.

Elliott never looked a prisoner in the eye again.

AS IT TURNED out, another man got Davis' job, and it wasn't until 23 years later that the prison system called on Elliott again. He was a private electrical contractor by that time, 52 years old and a grandfather. Execution was steady work. The job covered Massachusetts and New Jersey, as well as New York, and later Pennsylvania, Connecticut and Vermont. It paid $150 a pop.

And so he began bringing down the curtain on many famous cases. Elliott was the man who

pulled the switch on Ruth Snyder and Judd Gray, two-thirds of a sensational fatal love triangle. He was the man who dispatched Bruno Richard Hauptmann, the Bronx carpenter convicted of kidnapping and murdering Charles Lindbergh's baby son. He was the man who attended to Nicola Sacco and Bartolomeo Vanzetti.

He developed what became known as the Elliott Technique — one full shock of 2,000 volts; one lowering of current; another quick and heavy one; another lowering; and then a third big one to make certain. It always worked.

He tried to keep his new profession a secret, but eventually a mischievous reporter followed him home from Sing Sing to Queens one night and wrote a story about the executioner the papers had theretofore been calling "Mr. X."

"I'm just an ordinary human being," he said. "I'm no more responsible for killing these men than the judge and the jury."

The public disclosure had consequences. In 1928, a bomb blast ripped away the front of Elliott's Richmond Hill home. Sacco and Vanzetti sympathizers got the blame, and police built a permanent guard shack on his property. Thereafter he was never pleased when the press came around to visit.

"The less publicity I get in my business, the better," he grumbled. "I would rather shoot the juice into someone than talk to a newspaper reporter."

But it was a time of circuses in the public print, and Elliott recognized the lure of attractive, husband-murdering Snyder and her lover, Gray, when their time came.

"There was every element in the case to inflame the imagination of the newspaper-reading public that enjoys such sensations," he had to agree when he recalled the case later.

A morbid crowd gathered outside Sing Sing at the appointed hour on Jan. 12, 1928. More than 1,500 people had signed up to witness the demise of the first woman to die at the prison in the 20th century.

She was also the first woman Elliott would put to death. "It will be something new for me to throw the switch on a woman, and I don't like the job," Elliott told one of Snyder's lawyers a few days before the execution. The remark made the papers, contributing to the dramatic buildup.

But he had a job to do, and he did it. Snyder wept as she was placed in the chair. "Father, forgive them, for they know not what they do," she whispered. "Forgive me, Father, for I have sinned." The executioner, efficient and professional, focused on his work and did not look her in the eye. He never noticed that one of the witnesses had strapped to his ankle a camera that snapped a famous picture that would run the next morning in the Daily News.

BEFORE HIS DEATH in 1939, looking back, Elliott admitted that he often wondered whether he had ever executed an innocent man. Legal scholars who have studied New York's capital cases are certain that he did.

But Elliott could not permit himself to be troubled. He was merely a tool of the state. He was just the man who came to the death chamber to perform a function and to say nothing, ever, except these words, which he uttered every time, just before his long right arm reached for the switch:

"May God have mercy on your soul."

GOOD WITH ELECTRICITY
Robert Elliott

By RICHARD E. MOONEY
Special to The News

ARTHUR SCHOMBURG has been called the Sherlock Holmes of black history — a man with, as poet Claude McKay put it, a "bloodhound's nose" for tracking down rare books that shed light on an unknown past.

Born in Puerto Rico in 1874 of mixed parentage — his unmarried mother had African roots, his father German — Schomburg moved to New York at 17. Stung by the remark of a teacher who told him that "Negroes have no history," he dedicated his life to proving that teacher wrong.

Schomburg was not a scholar, but he shared the view of those who felt that the knowledge of history was the route to racial dignity. In a seminal 1925 essay, "The Negro Digs Up His Past," he wrote: "The American Negro must remake his past in order to make his future. History must restore what slavery took away."

To this end, he collected books, manuscripts, prints, photos, letters and any other evidence he could find. In 1926, his collection — 10,000 pieces at the time — was installed in the New York Public Library's 135th St. branch in Harlem, forming the core of what is now the renowned Schomburg Center for Research in Black Culture.

He was no J.P. Morgan. He did not collect just for the love of collecting, nor was he a millionaire. He collected to enlighten his fellow man, and he did it all while working in the mailroom at Bankers Trust Co.

Soft-spoken, endlessly energetic, he also was a co-founder of the Negro Society for Historical Research — "to show that the Negro race has a history which antedates that of the proud Anglo-Saxon race." He was grand secretary of the Masonic Prince Hall Grand Lodge, president of the American Negro Academy and a prolific writer and lecturer on subjects as varied as African flora and fauna and "Opportunities in Haiti for American Negroes." During the 1920s, his historic trove of poetry, prose and music was a valuable source of material for the creative writers and artists of the Harlem Renaissance — McKay, Langston Hughes and others.

Schomburg retired from Bankers Trust in 1930, spent a year curating the Negro Collection at Fisk University in Nashville, then returned to 135th St. as curator of his own collection. His very personal system for shelving his books was to arrange them by size and color, and when a newly hired librarian named Jean Blackwell Hutson rearranged them according to the standard Dewey decimal system, he fired her. Later rehired, she went on to run the center for many years.

COURTESY OF SCHOMBURG CENTER FOR RESEARCH IN BLACK CULTURE, NEW YORK PUBLIC LIBRARY

THE FRONTIERSMAN
Arthur Schomburg

FACTS OF Schomburg's early life are sketchy. Born Arturo Alfonso Schomburg in Santurce, Puerto Rico, he arrived in New York in 1891 and plunged into the Puerto Rican community's campaign for Puerto Rican and Cuban independence from Spain. He took work as a messenger for a large law firm, was soon promoted to clerk and considered becoming a lawyer himself. He married three times and fathered six sons and a daughter.

In Elinor DesVerney Sinette's biography, "Arthur Alfonso Schomburg: Black Bibliophile & Collector," one of the sons describes the state of the family rowhouse at 105 Kosciusko St. in Brooklyn: "There were books from the cellar to the top floor, in every room including the bathroom." Schomburg began lending some of his material to the library's 135th St. branch, helping librarian Ernestine Rose create a small collection of rare books about black people. It was the beginning of the main library's Division of Negro History, Literature and Prints — renamed the Schomburg Center in 1972.

The official version of the eventual transfer of the whole collection says that Schomburg approached the National Urban League, looking for a proper place to put everything. The league could not handle it, but sought out a $10,000 grant from the Carnegie Corp., which bought the lot and gave it to the library. The unofficial version is that Mrs. Schomburg gave her husband a choice — the books would go, or she would.

With $10,000 in the bank, Schomburg set off for Europe — and started buying more items for his collection.

THAT WAS HIS sole trip abroad. Mostly he acquired his treasures through dealers and traveling friends. On one occasion, the poet Langston Hughes sent him from the Soviet Union a photograph of the actor Ira Aldridge as Othello in a European production. Other friends got detailed requests, such as this one to a woman headed for Paris: "I wish you would go to the bookstore of Emile Neurry and ask for his catalogue ... There is an item No. 510 on page 52. The work is in six volumes ... See if you can obtain Volume 1."

"I have seen him approach an immense pile of apparently worthless material and unerringly find one or two treasures that would have been lost on a less inspired collector," said one colleague.

Among the Schomburg Center's gems are a first edition of the collected poems of Phillis Wheatley, the gifted African servant girl who lived in Boston in the 1700s; copies of the annual "Almanack" of Benjamin Banneker, the 18th-century mathematician and surveyor who helped design Washington, D.C.; collections of African tribal music; and a book of poems by Juan Latino, published in Spain in 1573 and believed to be the first printed book by a black person. Not overlooking the negative, Schomburg also collected Ku Klux Klan reports and titles like "The Negro, A Beast." Most of Schomburg's books carry his personal bookplate, with an engraving of a slave on his knees in chains.

ADDITIONS TO the collection since Schomburg's death in 1938 include Richard Wright's manuscript for "Native Son," hundreds of Duke Ellington 78s and 81 volumes of Gunnar Myrdal's notes for "An American Dilemma," his exhaustive discourse on race relations. Myrdal did research at the Schomburg Center, as did former Ghanaian president Kwame Nkrumah, when he was a college student in Pennsylvania, Spike Lee in preparation for his Malcolm X film and Alex Haley for "Roots."

The center was expanded in 1980 with construction of a large building around the corner on Malcolm X Blvd. and linked to the old branch. It is busy nowadays with community cultural activities, as well as a steady stream of the young and old, the black and brown and white, digging into its vast files, now grown to more than 5 million items.

In his final years, Schomburg showed disappointment in the outlook for American blacks. "I am becoming very doubtful of the Negro finding a place for himself in the next quarter of a century," he told a friend a year before he died at 64. At a memorial service, though, he was paid tribute as "wiser than we knew, a maker of scholars, a pioneer on the cultural frontier of a new race."

By DAVID HINCKLEY
Daily News Staff Writer

"Listen to boogie-woogie piano long enough, and it gets you — makes you want to show your teeth in an insane grin and drag somebody into a cave by her hair."
— Daily News critic John Chapman, reviewing John Hammond's "From Spirituals to Swing" concert at Carnegie Hall on Dec. 24, 1938

With Count Basie

IN EVERY FAMILY, it seems, even a family where Mother was the great-granddaughter of Commodore Vanderbilt and Father's father was Gen. Sherman's chief of staff and Father himself was a former deputy state attorney general who ran railroads and sat on the boards of 20 major corporations, there's always one.

In the John Henry Hammond family, it was John Henry Hammond Jr.

It wasn't that John Hammond ever completely spat out the silver spoon. Years after he left the family home at 9 E. 91st St., with its six floors, 16 bathrooms, two elevators and private ballroom, he returned for dinner weekly and brought his laundry. If it's true he was kicked out of the Social Register after his first marriage in 1941, he returned to grace in 1949 by marrying the well-bred Esme O'Brien, whose previous husband was the son of David Sarnoff.

John Hammond certainly never lost the assumption of the moneyed that, once he had determined how everyone should behave, it was his right — nay, his obligation — to direct them accordingly.

He simply envisioned a different world than did most of his family, or his class — a vision illustrated by the occasion in the spring of 1932, when Hammond was asked to find a band for a Saturday dance at the Mount Kisco Golf and Country Club.

The assumption was that he would locate something whose name ended in "Society Orchestra," which might lace a foxtrot or two into a tasteful selection of waltzes.

Instead, Hammond walked in with seven jazzmen, including Fats Waller, very likely the only person in the room who ever described himself as "300 pounds o' jam, jive and everything." Waller opened his first bottle of gin and played a 22-minute piano solo of "Bugle Call Rag."

It made for a night to remember at the stately Mount Kisco Club, whose president was John Henry Hammond Sr.

FOUR YEARS LATER, John Jr. joined an anti-Franco picket line outside the office of his uncle Ogden, a former ambassador to Spain. This was doubtless the reason that, in a 1939 society-page profile of Emily Vanderbilt Sloane Hammond, the sole note of son John was that he "is rumored to have voted the straight Communist ticket."

That's a line that would never have been written about Emily, a fervent Christian Scientist who, after her husband's death in 1949, donated the family's 277-acre Mount Kisco estate, Dellwood, to the church's Moral Rearmament movement.

Still, Emily knew by 1939 what she had in John Jr. While she was taking retreats to an arts camp in Georgia, accompanied by the likes of Mrs. Thomas Edison and the mother of President Franklin Roosevelt, her son's notion of travel was to drive to a new town, find the seediest after-hours club in the colored district and sit there all night, sipping lemonade and slapping his thigh to the beat of the band.

He stood out, this tall, well-dressed white fellow with the crew cut. But as for the Communist thing, he said no. The only party line he followed was good music. And so, although he did not sing, he did not dance and his instrumental career ended with viola lessons, it was in the music business that John Hammond wrote his story — discovering, promoting, even helping to shape

WHITE CAT
John Hammond

dozens of the most important musicians of the 20th century.

At age 22, he persuaded Columbia Records to let him produce Bessie Smith's last session and Billie Holiday's first. He cajoled Benny Goodman into recording his first swing session when Goodman was convinced swing would never sell. He found Count Basie in Kansas City and brought him to New York. He promoted Teddy Wilson, Lester Young, Fletcher Henderson and Charlie Christian.

No fan of bebop and no fan of Frank Sinatra pop, Hammond left Columbia after World War II to help direct several smaller labels, including Mercury, Majestic and the fledgling folk imprint Vanguard. Desperate to get hip, Columbia lured him back in the early 1960s, and this unreconstructed swing fan who still played 78s offered a contract to a strange young man who was called "Hammond's folly" before he became more widely known as Bob Dylan. Hammond also signed Aretha Franklin and Bruce Springsteen.

In fact, Hammond did as well at music as great-great-grandfather Cornelius did at commodoring, and with the same formula: patient groundwork, relentless obsession.

BORN IN 1910, Hammond discovered black music as a pre-teen. One story had him picking it up from the servants. Another had him so fascinated by "I'm Just Wild About Harry" that he conned his governess into taking him to see the show "Shuffle Along." Whatever the genesis, he spent his $1-a-week allowance during his prep school years at Hotchkiss on records and weekend trips to Harlem.

He dutifully enrolled at Yale, a family tradition, but 18 months later dropped out after coming into the first $12,000-a-year stipend of his inheritance. He took an apartment in the Village and parlayed small jobs — deejay, magazine writer — into the importance he wanted. He met musicians, he met executives, and soon he was a Columbia producer.

At the same time, his writing was raising his profile in both jazz and leftist circles. His reports for The Nation on the Scottsboro Boys trial in Tennessee remain models of advocacy journalism, though he occasionally would not allow facts to dilute the advocacy. Hammond was the source of the story, circulated for years, that Bessie Smith died because a white hospital turned her away

after a car crash. He doubtless saw this as a chance to make an important point. But in Bessie's case, it just wasn't true.

In any event, he used his newfound leverage to produce landmark events such as the 1938 "Spirituals to Swing" concert, which showcased black music previously unheard by the average Carnegie Hall patron. When John Henry Hammond Sr. attended the show, it also marked probably the only time the honorary chairman of the National Industrial Conference Board attended a benefit for the left-wing workers' publication New Masses.

It was also around this time that Hammond imported Basie, his all-time favorite bandleader — though his price for bringing the Count to New York was that Basie had to fire several of his own sidemen and use players Hammond preferred.

Hammond made mistakes. He turned down Ella Fitzgerald and loudly proclaimed that Louis Armstrong and Duke Ellington were wasting their talent. He implied more than once that he was the only white person in America who truly understood black music.

Nor did his struggle to rectify mistakes of the system always work out. In mid-1941, Hammond and author Richard Wright persuaded the governor of New Jersey to pardon Clinton Brewer, who was doing 20 to life in Trenton State Prison for murdering his wife. Illiterate when convicted, Brewer had taught himself to read and to write music, and his composition "Stampede in G Minor" had caught Hammond's ear. Upon Brewer's release, Hammond gave him a job arranging for Basie.

Then Brewer got a new girlfriend, whom he promptly stabbed to death and stuffed in a closet. Heading back to the big house for good, Clinton Brewer was heard writing another song.

BUT ON THE whole, things worked out for John Hammond. Political causes called Red in the 1930s — workers' rights, integration — became public policy. If his style was autocratic, his musical taste was superb, and music was the prize on which he kept his eye.

In the early '50s, it was widely believed that Hammond's social standing spared him the congressional scrutiny that ruined many of his ideological colleagues. His rejoinder was that politics just annoyed him and the real issues were social justice and music, which he believed to be intertwined.

Hammond died July 10, 1987, listening to a Billie Holiday record. Right up to the end, he said that of the things money could buy, he never found anything that beat a good jazz tune on a clean 78.

By BRIAN MOSS
Daily News Staff Writer

IF YOU'RE A native New Yorker, and your parents were native New Yorkers, and their parents were native New Yorkers before them — your family going back to the turn of the century in this city — you may well have Nathan Straus to thank for your very existence.

Profoundly shaken by the loss of his brother Isidor, who went down on the Titanic in 1912, merchant Nathan Straus retired from his family's great stores, R.H. Macy & Co. and Abraham & Straus, and devoted the rest of his life to giving away his considerable fortune. "What you give to charity in health is like gold," he would explain, paraphrasing a Hebrew saying: "What you give in sickness is silver and what you give in death is lead."

And if simply giving away money were all he did, it probably would have been enough to secure him a small place in history. But his humanitarian achievements were enormous. Nathan Straus saved babies' lives. Not just a few, or even a few hundred. Hundreds of thousands of them.

NATHAN STRAUS came to the United States from Bavaria as a 6-year-old in 1854. His family settled initially in rural Talbotton, Ga., where they attended the local Baptist church because there was no synagogue for hundreds of miles, and where Straus' father, Lazarus, was noted for being able to read the Bible in its original language.

After the Civil War, the Strauses moved to Philadelphia, then to New York, where they began to import china and glassware from Europe and opened a concession, selling those goods in R.H. Macy's department store. By 1888, they owned a half-interest in the store. Before 10 years had passed, they owned the store outright.

By that time, Nathan Straus was also the city's parks commissioner. And it was during this period that he began the crusade for which New York became exceedingly grateful.

It began with two events. The first was the death on a trip to Europe of one of Straus' six children, an infant named Sara. Her demise was attributed to bad milk, a common fact of life in those days before refrigeration and sanitary health regulations. Sometime later, Straus, whose Manhattan home was at 27 W. 72nd St., was raising milk cows for his family's use on property he owned upstate, and one day a seemingly healthy cow suddenly died. It turned out to have tuberculosis.

Straus was astonished. Although 30 years earlier Louis Pasteur had linked disease to milk, and the heating of milk to high temperatures — the process that came to be known as pasteurization — to the absence of microorganisms, it was only 10 years earlier that Robert Koch found the organism that caused tuberculosis. The connection between pasteurization and preventing illnesses from infected milk was not yet widely understood. Straus, though, decided that his children from

then on would drink only milk that had been pasteurized.

Moreover, he resolved, if pasteurization was crucial to the well-being of his own children, it should be important for all the children of his city as well.

HE BUILT A milk pasteurization laboratory and distribution center. Then he established depots around the city where the poor could have access to the healthy milk. The first, opened in 1893, was located on the East River Pier at Third St.

Straus thought it would be demeaning to give the milk away as charity, so he charged five cents for a day's supply. For those who did need charity, milk coupons were distributed throughout the city by doctors, the Board of Health, the Salvation Army and other agencies.

Not everyone was thrilled with Straus' campaign. Farmers in particular were unhappy that their unpasteurized product was being maligned as unsafe. In 1895, their political supporters managed to get Straus indicted on a charge of adulterating milk. He was convicted but given a suspended sentence, and he continued to establish milk stations at his own expense around the city.

Before he was finished nearly 30 years later — New York passed a law requiring milk to be pasteurized in 1914, but laws were being enacted around the country for years after that — he

established 297 milk stations in 36 cities, paying for them himself. Some 24,009,498 glasses and bottles of safe milk were dispensed during the 25-plus years of his project.

The result of this incredible philanthropy is priceless. But here is how it is measured in human lives: In 1891, 24% of babies born in New York City — nearly one in four — died before age 1. But of the 20,111 children fed pasteurized milk supplied by Straus over a four-year period, only six died. Nationally, as pasteurization became widespread, the death rate for children fell from 125.1 per thousand in 1891 to 15.8 in 1925. One historian determined that Nathan Straus directly saved the lives of 445,800 children.

In 1923, when the city celebrated the first 25 years of consolidation, a jubilee vote was held to honor the person who had done the most to benefit the public. The winner: Nathan Straus.

TO MATCH HIS fortune, Straus had enough energy for a dozen men, and his philanthropy extended far beyond his pasteurization campaign. During the financial panic of 1893, he reached deep into his own pockets to help his fellow New Yorkers. He used his milk stations to sell coal at the ridiculously low price of five cents for 25 pounds to those who could pay. Those who couldn't got coal for free. He opened lodging houses for 64,000 persons, who got a bed and breakfast for five cents, and separately funded 50,000 meals for a penny each.

He didn't wait for emergencies to institute ideas that would benefit his fellow citizens. Anonymously, he gave away thousands of turkeys. He built a recreational pier, the first of many that dotted the city's waterfront.

At Abraham & Straus, he noticed that two of his employees were starving themselves to save their wages to feed their families — then established what may have been the first subsidized company cafeteria.

In 1916, as a world war loomed, he sold his yacht Sisilina to the U.S. Coast Guard and used the proceeds to feed war orphans. Later, he would feed returning American servicemen at Battery Park.

And during his first trip to Jerusalem, in 1904, he became an ardent Zionist, establishing health facilities and soup kitchens in Palestine. The city of Netanya — Nathan in Hebrew — was named in his honor and the hope that he would favor it with his largesse.

He died in January 1931, having given away all but $1.5 million of his huge fortune, and thousands of New Yorkers lined the street outside Temple Emanu-El for his funeral. Twenty years before, at a dinner in his honor, he had given what could have been his own eulogy.

"I often think of the old saying, 'The world is my country, to do good is my religion,'" Straus had said. "This has often been an inspiration to me. I might say, 'Humanity is my kin, to save babies is my religion.' It is a religion I hope will have thousands of followers."

By JAY MAEDER
Daily News Staff Writer

With chiefs, 1913

CULVER PICTURES

DREAMLAND
Rodman Wanamaker

FOR DRYGOODSMEN, both father and son had unusual levels of poetry in their mercantile souls. Old John Wanamaker, in his day, had enjoyed funding Alaskan explorations when he wasn't busy running his department stores; Rodman Wanamaker, for his part, financed two attempts to fly across the Atlantic Ocean and otherwise devoted his life to the construction of heroic monuments all over New York City. It happened that most of the mighty memorials he envisioned never saw the light of day, including the one in the harbor that would have dwarfed the Statue of Liberty. For that matter, the ocean flights didn't work out either. Still, they were splendid dreams, and it is not every shopkeeper who dreams such things.

THE PATRIARCH, old John, had been among the 19th century's retail titans, the Philadelphia counterpart of New York's A.T. Stewart, whose stores had been famously serving the city's carriage trade for 50 years by the time old Wanamaker came to town in 1897, bought old Stewart's cast-iron marvel at Broadway and 10th St. and renamed it after himself. Thereafter was the John Wanamaker store off Astor Place one of the city's great institutions, a gracious public palace whose atrium and balconies swelled with the music of the store's pipe organ and sometimes even that of whole symphony orchestras. Here was where the well-to-do of Washington Square and Gramercy Park came to shop for motorcars as well as European finery. Here was where, one stupendous day in 1911, the first hot-air balloon ever to lift off from the top of a building sailed from the Wanamaker roof to New Jersey. Here was where an actual working wireless radio station received the first electrifying reports from sea that the unsinkable Titanic had gone down.

In 1913, Rodman Wanamaker was 50 years old, a civic pillar, confidant of mayors and governors and a man utterly consumed by two burning obsessions. One was aviation. The other was the American Indian and the noble native heritage thereof. In 1913, Wanamaker was simultaneously at work on two grandiose projects whose successful completion would have forever changed the course of the river of destiny.

Just three years after Glenn Curtiss daringly flew all the way from Albany to New York City, a Wanamaker aeroplane would now fly across a whole ocean. At the same time, from the heights of Staten Island there would arise a colossus, an enormous headdressed Indian chief, arm upstretched in peaceful greeting, an American beacon visible from miles at sea, long before the tired and poor and huddled would ever spot the speck called Lady Liberty.

THERE WERE those New Yorkers who frankly had a few doubts that the harbor really needed another majestic statue, but Rodman Wanamaker was proposing to pay for it himself, and in any case he had already persuaded Congress to pass legislation authorizing its construction on federal land atop Fort Tompkins. Up it was going to go.

The dedication of the National American Indian Memorial on Feb. 22, 1913, Washington's Birthday, was one of the more surreal events in the city's history. Outgoing President William Howard Taft himself turned to turn the first shovelful of earth. Solemnly present, as well, were 32 genuine Indian chiefs, elderly Apaches and Kiowas and Cheyennes and Chippewas and whatnot who had come to New York City by train and wagon and even horseback to witness what the program billed as "the union of the First Dwellers on the soil with the civilization of our day." Guns boomed. Bands played. The flag was raised. The chiefs gravely signed a document called the "Declaration of Allegiance to the United States."

And after that, the "Rodman Wanamaker Expedition of Citizenship to the North American Indian" went on a loudly trumpeted national tour, and for months the group visited dozens of reservations, added thousands of signatures to the Declaration of Allegiance and ceremonially played a recording made by the new president, Woodrow Wilson, offering all his Native American friends "distinguished recognition."

Things turned sour quite fast. There had been a fundamental misunderstanding. It seemed many of the Indians somehow had it in their heads that all this star-spangled fanfare meant that the U.S. government was granting them actual citizenship. As this was not the case at all, there began to arise some hard feelings once the Indians grasped that they still didn't have the vote. In short order, Rodman Wanamaker's plan to build the improbable statue was quietly abandoned.

MEANWHILE, BY THIS time, Glenn Curtiss had invented the amphibious seaplane and Wanamaker was commissioning him to cross the Atlantic. It wouldn't be until 1919 that fliers would finally make the hop, but that's because the World War came along in the meantime; certainly Curtiss seemed confident enough in 1913 that such a flight was already realizable, and he spent long months testing powerful new motors and giving his big flying boat, America, preliminary trials as Wanamaker put up the funds and arranged for the official sanction of the Aero Club of America.

The great adventure — "as important to aerial navigation as was the voyage of Columbus to transportation by water," Wanamaker proudly declared — was at last set for mid-July 1914. Whether the Wanamaker ship would have made it can never be known. In Sarajevo, an assassin's bullet ignited a European war; the flight was postponed, postponed again, finally canceled for the duration. Wanamaker gave the plane to the government. By now, credentialed as an aviation patron, he offered the New York Police Department a flying gunship in which officers could patrol the skies and search for German invaders. But the police really didn't want one.

AFTER THE WAR that had ended all wars, Wanamaker led the city's drives to honor the returning veterans and spent several years planning the construction of a magnificent memorial arch in Madison Square; hundreds of thousands of dollars were raised, but this was another Wanamaker monument that didn't get built. So was a second war memorial he tirelessly tried to put up in Central Park. In the end, the vets got an eternal flame.

He remained dedicated to the romance of the air — in 1925, Wanamaker's became the first store in the world to open an airplane department, offering Stout monoplanes for $25,000 each — and in 1926 he co-sponsored Richard Byrd's flight to the North Pole, then formed the America Trans-Oceanic Corp. and put up $1 million for Byrd's attempt to fly the Atlantic nonstop. Byrd made it, but not until June 1927, a few weeks after Charles Lindbergh did it first.

WANAMAKER DIED at 65 in March 1928, and for some years after that his nephew, also named Rodman Wanamaker, carried on the family ideals; Wanamaker the younger, a deputy police commissioner from the late '20s into the '40s, helped create a police department air wing, gave the force its first plane and later made New York the first city to put police helicopters into service.

The legendary old Wanamaker store on Broadway closed its doors the week before Christmas 1954. On July 14, 1956, the abandoned shell was destroyed by a blaze so spectacular that the fireman-flooded Astor Place subway tunnels shut down the IRT for a week.

By MICHAEL ARONSON
Special to The News

OPENING DAY, Nov. 13, 1927, was a Sunday, and people from all over used the day off to explore the new marvel. At one minute after midnight, more than 20,000 began to walk through the 1.6-mile twin-tube tunnel and another 51,748 began driving through it. To the east of the Hudson River, cars were backed up to the Brooklyn side of the Manhattan Bridge. On the Jersey side, the backup went through Jersey City all the way to Newark.

The Eighth Wonder of the World, it was called, and rockets lighted the sky, as they had when the Brooklyn Bridge was opened in 1883.

It wasn't the first tunnel from Manhattan, but it was the biggest, with a huge internal diameter of 30 feet — nearly twice the size of the subway tunnels — and it was the first designed for automobiles instead of trains. Here, at the top of the Roaring Twenties, Henry Ford and his competitors were mass-producing cars as fast as consumers could buy them — but Manhattan, which had suffered from traffic jams since the days of the horses, still relied on old trans-Hudson ferries to carry the modern vehicles to Jersey. The tunnel would change all that.

It would be the end of the congestion at the ferries. It promised, noted the Evening World, "to make motor car traffic between New York and Jersey City a matter of pleasure."

The man who had built the tunnel was just another professional engineer doing a job, and his name would have been little noted by the public at large had he not — like the bridge-building Roeblings, father and son, dead and crippled — sacrificed himself to his work. On opening day, three years after his death, the mighty new white-tiled monument beneath the river bore his name: Holland.

CLIFFORD MILBURN Holland was born in 1883 in Somerset, Mass., and trained as an engineer at Harvard, specializing in tunneling. On the day he graduated in 1906, he came to New York City and got a job as an assistant engineer on the construction of the IRT's first East River subway tube, which opened in 1908, connecting the Battery and Joralemon St. For the next round of four East River tunnels (the Seventh Ave.-Clark St. IRT tunnel and the BMT's tubes at Montague, 14th and 60th Sts.), he was the engineer in charge, and soon his reputation was that of the nation's leading tunneler.

The New Jersey Interstate Bridge and Tunnel Commission and the New York Bridge and Tunnel Commission had jointly discussed a trans-Hudson crossing since 1906. The two states wanted a fixed Hudson link to augment the total reliance on ferries, which were always subject to the vagaries of the weather, and, while horseless carriages were still a novelty in 1906, it was foreseen that motor traffic was coming soon.

A proposed tunnel — not a bridge, which might interfere with shipping in the bustling Port of New York — was approved in 1913. Clifford Holland, the foremost expert, was named chief engineer in 1919. Work began without fanfare in October 1920 on what was then called the Hudson

THE DIGGER
Clifford Holland

River Vehicular Tunnel.

Holland's quartet of East River subway tunnels had taught him all about the digging that his sandhogs had to do — but those tubes, as well as those of the Hudson & Manhattan Railroad and the Pennsylvania Railroad, carried electric trains. They didn't have to contend with the poisonous carbon monoxide of cars. The chief engineer's big job, then, was to figure out how to get rid of those exhaust fumes and replace them with good air.

Supervising experiments at Yale, the University of Illinois and the U.S. Bureau of Mines, Holland came up with an ingenious air-replacement system. Fumes were vented through the ceiling, while fresh air was pumped in along the roadway surface. Eighty-four giant fans provided that fresh air every 90 seconds. On each shore were two 10-story ventilation towers housing the fans and pumping 4 million cubic feet of air a minute. Holland's system would go on to be used in tunnels around the world.

But the strain of overseeing the mammoth project every day and every night for five years was too much for its commanding general. Holland suffered a nervous breakdown in the fall of 1924 and went to a Michigan sanitarium for a rest. There, he suffered a heart attack and died on Oct. 27, age 41.

His death came two days before the two digging crews, approaching from both east and west, were to meet. At the White House, President Calvin Coolidge was scheduled to press a button that would trigger the final blast for the "holing through." City and state officials from both sides of the river were readying for pomp and ceremony. Instead, the parties were canceled and the sandhogs quietly broke through without politicians present, and work continued. When they came together, the two tubes were off by less than three-quarters of an inch, a testament to Holland's precision.

IT HAPPENED that Milton Freeman, the new chief engineer, also died on the job, five months later, but by that time, officials had decided to rename the Hudson River Vehicular

Tunnel after Clifford Holland.

With a third engineer, Ole Singstad, on the job, the project was nearly completed by the summer of 1926, when the two governors dedicated the tunnel with a trans-Hudson handshake. But opening day was still more than a year away. Many management issues — tunnel policing, for example — remained unresolved. Moreover, there was uncertainty over the efficiency of the untried ventilation system.

In the fall of '27, an old jalopy was splashed with gasoline and set ablaze in mid-tunnel to test fire-control and emergency-evacuation procedures. Holland's ventilators worked as designed: Smoke from the burning car was quickly sucked into the ceiling and the fire was fast put out.

Finally, on Nov. 13, with all 3.1 million white wall tiles in place, the great Holland Tunnel opened. This time Coolidge did indeed press a White House button, to signal the beginning of the festivities.

Twenty lanes of cars narrowed into two and snaked into the tunnel all through the day, their drivers learning the regulations. The toll was 50 cents — it would remain 50 cents for more than 40 years — but motorists who stalled in mid-tunnel and had to be towed out were levied another dollar toll. Those who ran out of gas in mid-tunnel got charged a dollar a gallon.

On Dec. 5, the Holland recorded its half-millionth vehicle, a truck carrying Christmas trees. By the end of its first year of operations, 8.7 million vehicles had used it, 50 percent more than estimated. Money was coming in so fast that already there was talk that the $46 million in bonds used for construction could be paid back in 20 years. So great was the financial success that the two states started talking about building four more tunnels together.

At this point, however, the fledgling Port of New York Authority, which had built a pair of little-used Staten Island-New Jersey bridges and was in the midst of building another, as well as the George Washington Bridge, saw that the tunnel was a gold mine and successfully offered the states $50 million for this tube and the right to build more of them.

At the Manhattan entrance to his tunnel, there remains a small bust of Clifford Holland, fittingly hidden behind a Port Authority booth. Freeman, the second engineer, has a plaza named after him, also on the Manhattan side.

Second from left, Holland listens to questions about his tunnel.

BIG TOWN ★ BIOGRAPHY

By JAY MAEDER
Daily News Staff Writer

"The tong wars are excused by the more thoughtful Chinese as an unavoidable result of the trials of founding colonies in a strange land. Unless you are quick and mention it first, they will refer to six-shooter justice in the Old West, the Kentucky feuds and our Civil War. What, they argue, does a little tribute, a little violence amount to when a man knows at all times just where he stands with his friends and his enemies?"

— St. Clair McKelway
in The New Yorker, Dec. 30, 1933

EXECUTION WAS set for Saturday night the 28th of February 1932, on Mulberry St., across the river in Newark, and as the gentleman emerged from the headquarters of that city's Hip Sing tong, he was set upon by a shadow who pressed a gun straight to his throat and fired once. And this would surely have been the end of Mock Sai Wing, save for one immutable fact of life: It was an old joke, but it happened to be true, Chinese gunmen were absolutely the worst shots in the entire world, and at point-blank range, Mock Sai Wing had barely been grazed.

At police headquarters, the victim insisted he was merely a hardworking restaurant owner who had no enemies at all. "Mock Sai Wing me!" he kept jabbering politely, in the manner of Chinese who are being interrogated by white policemen. But a couple of old-timers dropped their jaws and recognized otherwise: "Mock Sai Wing"? This guy? Why, this was evil old Mock Duck himself, vanished from the Earth these many years, long ago reported to be in his grave. Here was the fearsome tong warrior who had terrorized New York City's Chinatown a generation earlier, the chain-mailed assassin who had sent rivers of blood flushing through old Mott and Pell and Doyers Sts. Here was none but Mock Duck.

And so Mock Duck arose from the dead. He was, the newspapers said, the national Hip Sing president and had been so for several years, perhaps the richest and most powerful Chinese in the United States. He gave his age as 54, which was about right, but many policemen refused to believe it, for the name of Mock Duck echoed far back into distant myth and memory. One veteran detective swore that Mock Duck had to be at least 109 years old.

RED FLAGS
Mock Duck
PART ONE OF THREE

IN THOSE frontier days, Chinatown had been populated by no more than a few thousand celestial souls, mostly Cantonese relatively recently arrived from the sorrows of the Western goldfields and railroad gangs, men who had brought with them deep allegiances to their tongs, or town halls, which were entirely New World inventions — "as American as chop suey," suggested Herbert Asbury in his 1927 "Gangs of New York" — that gave a man some measure of worth in what was otherwise his largely miserable lot. If the tongs administered opium, games of chance and women, they also administered food, housing, employment, justice and personal dignity. Or, to put it another way, the tongs provided to Chinese more or less exactly what Tammany Hall provided to many of the rest of the city's huddled masses.

In Chinatown at the turn of the century, as has always been the case since the dawn of time, the lot of some was less miserable than that of some others. Among the fortunate was Tom Lee, chief of the large and influential On Leong tong and a man genially known to Tammany and the city at large as the mayor of the tiny downtown sector

where tourists could eat exotic dinners and bargain for lovely jade statuettes and thrill-seekers could seek entry into what seemed hundreds of wonderfully dangerous fan tan and pi gow rooms. It was Tom Lee who presided over what prosperity there was. And it was young Mock Duck who seethed that Tom Lee was more fortunate than he.

Born Mock Sai Wing in San Francisco in the late 1870s, he came to New York in the late '90s, affiliated with the Hip Sing tong, far smaller and flimsier than Tom Lee's efficient organization. The On Leong membership was the merchant class; the Hip Sing claimed but laborers and seamen. When Mock Duck ambitiously demanded

a Hip Sing share of Chinatown's bounty, he got only indulgent chuckles in reply, for, since the dawn of time, there have always been foolish young men in the world.

Soon thereafter, an On Leong boardinghouse on Pell St. burned to the ground. And shortly after that, Hip Sing and On Leong warriors were regularly ambushing one another up and down Mott and Pell and at the blind "Bloody Angle" of dark and twisted Doyers St., in a war that would continue, off and on, for another three decades.

It was said of Mock Duck, probably apocryphally, that he was the man who first introduced the firearm to Chinatown, where matters theretofore had customarily been settled with the hatchet and the rope. He was, to be sure, as terrible a shooter as everyone else; his personal practice was to drop into a squat, point two guns in the general direction of whatever the target was, close his eyes tight, keep pulling the triggers until he ran out of bullets and then get up and run away. In the streets of Chinatown, it was impossible not to hit something or other, if only a stray tourist. Mock Duck, for his part, always wore body armor, and in dozens of savage shootouts that left uncounted numbers dead, he was known to be wounded only once.

IN THOSE frontier days, flags flew and posters went up on walls whenever new hostilities simmered, and therefore everyone except the imbecile barbarian round-eyes who lived beyond Mott and Pell and Doyers Sts. knew exactly when and where fresh eruptions would occur. This was not necessarily altogether uncivilized warfare. On the other hand, Tom Lee and the On Leong failed to consider one crucial point: The upstart Mock Duck was, in fact, American-born, and he understood the inscrutable mind of the white devil perhaps more keenly than did they.

There lived in the City of New York a distinguished Presbyterian churchman called the Rev. Charles Parkhurst. A decade earlier, he had been the man who singlehandedly brought about the legislative inquiries that briefly put Tammany out of influence and made Theodore Roosevelt the city's corruption-smashing police commissioner. Not that these goo-goo reforms had lasted very long, of course, but Parkhurst remained a civic pillar actively dedicated to the general betterment, and he was earnestly receptive when Mock Dock in 1904 presented himself to him as a preyed-upon workingman come with tales of the manifold On Leong wickednesses. In short order, the clucking reverend called down the New York Police Department on every On Leong gambling den in Chinatown, embarrassing Mayor Tom Lee a great deal. Whereupon the Hip Sing took the dens over, and crafty Mock Duck won great respect in Chinatown as a man of considerable substance, indeed a man who appeared to have the white man's law on his side.

MOCK DUCK'S coup brought the tong feuds to a boil, and for two years the red flags of war flew over Chinatown. City authorities did not otherwise make too large a point of interfering in Chinese affairs, but finally the carnage became too much; in 1906, one Judge Warren Foster of the Court of General Sessions consulted with the Chinese consul general, then called before him the top officials of both the On Leong and Hip Sing tongs, which, thanks to Mock Duck, were now by and large equals, and ordered a peace, period. Mott St. would be On Leong territory, Foster decreed; Pell would belong to the Hip Sing; Doyers would be neutral turf. Both sides agreed to abide by the court order.

And thus there was relative calm for several years.

Until the day a beautiful young woman called Sweet Flower arrived from California, and at this point, New York City's great tong wars were only beginning.

CORBIS

By JAY MAEDER
Daily News Staff Writer

SAVE FOR the occasional personal or commercial disagreement over this and that in the daily affairs of Chinatown, the 1906 tong truce insisted upon by New York's Chinese Consul General and Judge Warren Foster of the Court of General Sessions held generally fast until three years later, when the husband of the woman called Sweet Flower declined to honor a monetary claim pressed by his bride's former master.

Sweet Flower at 16 had been sold into the thrall of a high-ranking Hip Sing official in San Francisco, and all had been well in his house until California authorities intervened and forcibly disengaged her from service. Thereafter she had married a young man from the On Leong and traveled eastward to resettle in the City of New York. Great was the vexation of the deflowered property owner, who had paid good money for the girl and considered that he was due a refund. He had, after all, bargained for her in good faith. Surely it was no fault of his own that California law did not recognize the ancient wisdom of slavery.

Yet Sweet Flower's husband felt himself unobliged to make restitution. The matter, which was one of several thousand dollars, finally went before the tongs. A formal demand for settlement was made by the Hip Sing. The On Leong refused to pay up. Accordingly, on the night of Aug. 15, 1909, a Hip Sing assassin gained entry into the newlyweds' home, carved 21-year-old Sweet Flower into ribbons and cut off all her fingers.

War now exploded. Dynamite blasts rocked tiny Mott, Pell and Doyers Sts., bullets sprayed wildly in every direction, hatchets cleaved the air. It went on for several years. To the degree that accurate counts have ever been available, it is usually calculated that the Sweet Flower affair left 50 men dead and perhaps another 150 seriously injured.

THE CHINESE Theater on Doyers St. was a favorite killing field for both sides, and performances regularly stopped in mid-sentence as mayhem blew up somewhere in the audience and the theatergoers all ran shrieking for the doors. Things reached such a point that the popular stage comedian Ah Hoon frequently incorporated tong-war gags into his act. As Ah Hoon was himself an On Leong, his jests tended not to reflect very gloriously on the Hip Sing, and there were those of the Hip Sing who were affronted. Indeed, Ah Hoon was directly warned to find some new material. When he chose to ignore this counsel, posters went up across Chinatown, announcing that he would be slain onstage in full public view, at a stated time on a stated night in December 1909.

Quaking, Ah Hoon arrived at the Chinese Theater that particular evening surrounded by On Leong and New York Police Department bodyguards, and it turned out that no attempt on his life was made after all. And, even as his protectors escorted the threatened man to his home and stood guard outside his bolted door all through the night, word began to spread that the Hip Sing braggarts had lost much face.

In the morning, however, Ah Hoon was found murdered in his bed, somehow.

HIS DEMISE was, just a week or so later, followed by a theater slaughter that left a whole crowd of On Leong men dead in the aisles. Police picked up and questioned the Hip Sing chieftain, Mock Duck, as they always did whenever anything at all happened in Chinatown, and, as he always was, he was freed soon enough for lack of evidence.

Mock Duck was by now a figure much to be reckoned with. Long past were the days when he was but a usurper, rallying his ragtag Hip Sing against the vastly more influential On Leong. Long past were the days when he was the butt of public jokes, hooted at in the street as he trembled beneath the wrath of his shrew of a wife, a woman who was known to drag him home by his ear, cursing and cuffing and kicking him all the way. Mock Duck was now a warlord. When, in 1910, On Leong boss Tom Lee himself sought a truce, uneasily sensing that city authorities would not much longer tolerate the Chinatown carnage, Mock Duck could afford to sneer at him.

And so the tong wars continued. Typical was the flareup of Oct. 14, 1912, shortly after two Hip Sing gunmen were indicted for murder and three On Leong witnesses against them abruptly vanished from the face of the earth. On that afternoon, an army of On Leong men rampaged through Pell St., blindly firing at anything; half a dozen Chinese died in the hail of bullets, as did a random Irishman, a random Jew and a random horse, and the wounded included a police officer. It was a most embarrassing moment in an

die again. It is the contention of the Oriental calling himself Mock Sa an unknown assailant, is none other a generation ago.

OLD TONG CHIEF

...say, in ... street, ...content ...ear as ...p Sing ...al prof- ...assassin ...he Chi- ...leader. ...om the ...4 Mul- ...assail- ...hinese, ...ile and ...ark po- ...ck Sai ...al Ori- ...rs and ...d. As ...general ...g Pong ...Sings, ...ve had ...r debts.

...ck Duck.

He was rebuffed r ...efforts, but he stud ...ally inspiration can

BLOOD OF THE FLOWER
Mock Duck
PART TWO OF THREE

otherwise festive day for the city. President William Howard Taft was visiting, the U.S. Navy fleet was firing salutes on the Hudson and the New York Giants were playing the Boston Red Sox in the sixth game of the World Series at the Polo Grounds.

By May 1913, another truce was being forced upon the two warring groups, this one engineered by the Chinese minister in Washington and increasing numbers of distinguished Chinese merchants and educators who were not affiliated with either tong. The pact was signed and sealed, and one of the reasons for this was probably that, at this point, Mock Duck was no longer in the city. He had, surprisingly enough, actually gone to prison.

DURING A POLICE sweep, he had been found sitting in a room with two other men and what appeared to be gambling paraphernalia. As it happened, one of his companions was dead, freshly so, of a gunshot wound. For one reason or another, though, the corpse notwithstanding, a charge of selling policy slips was the only one prosecutors could make stick. Mock Duck did two years in Sing Sing.

When he got back to New York, he announced that his career as a tongman was over and moved from Chinatown to Brooklyn. Some years later, it was discovered that he had given up nothing and that pretty much everything the Hip Sing did through the 1920s bore Mock Duck's fingerprints. At the time, though,

appearances did suggest that he was retired from business. Indeed, around about 1918, an announcement of his death made the newspapers.

Perhaps this was merely one of those reportorial accidents. Still, Mock Duck saw no good reason to correct the misimpression. He reverted to the name given him at his birth, Mock Sai Wing, and no more thereafter did the name of the late Mock Duck particularly figure in any popular account of the ongoing life and times of Chinatown.

For Mock Duck was known to be dead and buried. Many were those who would later quite vividly remember having watched his funeral wagon roll by.

By JAY MAEDER
Daily News Staff Writer

SAVE FOR yet more of the occasional personal and commercial disagreements over this and that in the daily affairs of Chinatown, the 1913 tong truce held generally fast until the summer of 1922, by which time the venerable On Leong boss Tom Lee was dead and the famously bloody Hip Sing boss Mock Duck was also dead, or was said to be, and even the old Chinese Theater, where so much of the shooting had been done in days gone by, was long since closed, taken over by the New York Rescue Society. This was the usual bunch of salvation-bringing do-gooders, and most Chinese paid no attention to them, but it was still the case that in 1922 half a generation had passed without notably open combat in the streets.

July brought the death of Dr. Fong Foo Leung, the international Hip Sing president, credited with having maintained much of the long-standing peace. Then, a few weeks later, on the night of Aug. 7, one Ko Low, who ran a Doyers St. lodginghouse and was identified by the newspapers as a national Hip Sing officer, was gunned down as he left a restaurant at 24 Pell in the company of two white women.

Many law enforcement authorities, in New York and across the U.S., at once feared a fresh outbreak of formal tong hostilities. Others were more inclined to suspect that the killing was rooted in political unrest in China. Eventually, though, it began to appear that Ko Low had merely died amid tensions between the established New York Chinese and a wave of rougher-edged newcomers from the American West, the reason for this strife being the oldest one of all: the female of the species.

In New York City in the early 1920s, it was a sociological fact of life, acknowledged by Oriental and Occidental alike and commented upon in the public prints, that white women often found much to admire in Chinese men. The ungenerous of spirit sometimes suggested that opium was one reason for this, and that was in some cases no doubt so, but it was also true that many Chinese of the merchant and professional classes had taken perfectly respectable Caucasian wives and that a new generation of Chinese-American children was being born into the city. Word of this phenomenon spread westward, and to New York came floods of laboring classes, eagerly expecting to find willing round-eyed consorts of their own. What they found instead was that they were just raw country boys, of lesser social stature than the slicker New York Chinese, and greatly displeased

The funeral of Ko Low

BLOOD OF THE ROOSTER
Mock Duck
PART THREE OF THREE

were they to learn this.

Known to New York by now as the unofficial mayor of Chinatown was one Charlie Boston, who, significantly, was not affiliated with either tong and who, just as tellingly, made a large point of not being seen at Ko Low's extravagant funeral ceremonies. In a not unremarkable sign of changing times, Ko Low was buried by undertaker Charles Bacigalupo of Mulberry St., and Italian musicians played alongside Chinese as he went to his rest.

WHATEVER THE specific reason for Ko Low's dispatch, there was indeed a reignition of the old tong rivalries, on a national level. New truces were signed and quickly broken; gunfire felled Hip Sing and On Leong men across the land; by the summer of 1925, as the warfare became so fierce that both Cleveland and Boston proposed razing their Chinatowns outright to put an end to the ruckuses, the federal government at last stepped in.

In New York in early September, U.S. Attorney Emory Buckner teamed with local police and the

Secret Service to throw a cordon around all Chinatown. Every house on Pell, Mott and Doyers Sts., as well as the Bowery, East Bowery, Allen and Division Sts., was raided; patrons were ordered out of theaters; hundreds of Chinese who could not produce papers were hauled in and, under the moral-turpitude provisions of the 1924 Immigration Act, summarily put aboard China-bound boats.

Warned that the mass deportations would continue, the tongs quickly came to terms. On Sept. 14, a bird was ceremoniously slain and a peace compact signed at the Chinese Consulate on Astor Place. Buckner was not impressed. "If the Hip Sings and the On Leongs are going to get along without killing, well and good," he said. "But the immigration law is the immigration law, and the killing of a white rooster for peace purposes does not mean anything to us." Nor, for that matter, did it mean much to the tongs. Truces were still being signed four years later, when 30 national officials came to New York to pledge harmony forever, and they were still being signed a year after that.

It took, at last, the Japanese invader to put a stop to things. In February 1932, an emerging Chinatown leader named Eddie Gong, a Hip Sing who headed a group called the Patriotic League of Chinese, which had already raised $50,000 to send to the stricken homeland, declared the tong wars finished and proclaimed a new spirit of solidarity. "There are no tongs," he said. "We are all Chinese. Every man, woman and child feels that at any cost we must hold together as a people."

A few days later, Mock Sai Wing was shot outside Hip Sing headquarters in Newark, and the man who had once been the warlord Mock Duck returned to the world.

THROUGH THE 1930s, Chinatown was a principal staging ground for anti-Japanese rallies, boycotts of Japanese goods and fund drives. Through the 1930s, the tongs paraded side by side. Through the 1930s, the old "Yellow Peril" spawned by the early-century Boxer Rebellion gave way to a new popular image of a proud, brave, freedom-seeking people, one that the U.S. fighting forces would soon go to battle alongside. Some years later, to be sure, Mao Tse-tung's Reds would drive out the heroic Chiang Kai-shek, and Communist flags would fly high in Chinatown, and there would be some resumed unpleasantnesses. But that would be another cycle of history.

Of the mysterious Hip Sing leader Mock Duck, little more was publicly chronicled after The New Yorker in December 1933 warmly characterized him as a respected elder statesman, a man who had "done more than any other individual to make democracy reasonably safe for the Sino-American ... in the hodgepodge of idealism, irrationality and race prejudice which was, and is, American civilization." Mock Duck was subsequently reported to have died in Brooklyn in the early 1940s, age about 65. But then, he had died before.

By JAY MAEDER
Daily News Staff Writer

ONE OF THE things that was often said about Shipwreck Kelly was that he was called Shipwreck because he had survived the Titanic disaster, although in fact there seems to be no reason to believe that he ever came near the Titanic. It might have been some other Shipwreck Kelly who made this claim. There were a lot of Shipwreck Kellys running around during the Golden Age of Flagpole-Sitting in the 1920s, and there wasn't much Shipwreck could do about all these other flagpole-sitting Shipwrecks trading on his résumé, flagpole-sitting being basically a roustabout's game without much in the way of professional regulatory associations. For that matter, there were still Shipwreck Kellys on the loose for some years after the real Shipwreck died in 1952, not that by then there was so much call for flagpole sitters anymore.

But there certainly had been once upon a time, back in the dizzyingly goofy days when marathon dancers, six-day bicycle riders and championship goldfish swallowers were also some of the things that America found amusing, and Shipwreck was the best there was. You had a flagpole you wanted sat on, Shipwreck Kelly was your man. Over the course of nearly two decades, he calculated later, he had spent 20,613 hours sitting on flagpoles, 210 of them in subfreezing weather and 1,400 of them in the rain. He was in demand all over the country; he got big headlines wherever he went. In the summer of 1930, he made Atlantic City world-famous all by himself when he sat atop the Steel Pier's flagpole, 225 feet in the air, for 49 days and one hour.

That remains the modern record. Admittedly, the all-time perch-sitting championship is probably held by the Syrian ascetic St. Simeon Stylites, who sat upon a 48-cubit stone pillar for 37 years some 15 centuries ago and no doubt had his reasons. Flagpole-wise, though, Shipwreck Kelly is still the king, as it is not every Tom, Dick and Shipwreck who wants to try to spend more than 49 days sitting on a 10-inch ball.

HE WAS BORN Aloysius Kelly in Hell's Kitchen in 1893, an orphan at birth, his mother having died bearing him seven months after his rigger father fell to his death from a derrick, and he ran away to sea when he was 13 and later knocked around as a boxer, steelworker and steeplejack, eventually landing as a movie stuntman in Hollywood. It was there, in January 1924, that a theater owner looking for some publicity hired him to shinny up top the house flagpole and stay there for 13 hours. Los Angeles police had to send out reserves to control the popeyed crowds, and by the time he came down, he had similar offers flooding in from theaters all over the country and he was in a lucrative new line of work.

Over the next couple of years, he toured dozens of cities, drumming up crowds for theaters, department stores, banks, anything that had a flagpole. By now, though, he had spawned a whole industry, and there were flagpole-sitters

THE GUY IN THE SKY
Shipwreck Kelly

everywhere, and he began to recognize that what he needed was a specialty. Accordingly, he went into endurance flagpole-sitting. In New Orleans, he sat on a flagpole for 100 hours straight. At the St. Francis Hotel in Newark in June 1927, he sat for 312 hours. Two years later, in Baltimore, he stretched his record to 23 days.

He subsisted mostly on coffee and cigarettes. He had learned how to nap while sitting upright. He never had more than a simple leg strap securing him. "I don't take as many chances as a window cleaner," he always shrugged. Apparently he didn't find anything very unusual about his work. It was what he did. The newspapers were regularly full of pictures of Shipwreck Kelly, matter-of-factly brushing his teeth and shaving his face, hundreds of feet in the air. Back at home he had a perfectly normal family, a Mrs. Shipwreck and a little Shipwreck Jr., who always waved bye-bye whenever Dad went off to his job.

AFTER HIS astounding 1,177 hours atop the Atlantic City pole, there weren't a lot of challenges left. As it happened, the national flagpole-sitting craze had largely run its course by this time. The other thing was that police were taking an increasingly dim view of all the traffic jams he usually caused anyway, and as often as not, he got shooed down from his various roosts. In September 1935, when America's No. 1 Flagpole Sitter contracted with the University Heights Business Men's Association to climb a pole at Tremont and University Aves. in the Bronx and attempt to break his Atlantic City record, he was aloft for less than a day before a judge ordered his arrest as a public nuisance. For a

while, Shipwreck stood off the gathered cops, refusing to descend. But finally they threatened to chop him down, and he gave up.

There were one or two good headlines left. On Friday the 13th of October 1939, for example, 42nd St. was paralyzed by hordes of citizens goggling upward at Shipwreck Kelly, who, in celebration of National Doughnut Week, was eating doughnuts while doing headstands on a plank sticking out from the 54th floor of the Chanin Building. But Shipwreck's kind of work was pretty much drying up by this point. When war came, he went into the merchant marine and was heard from no more.

ON SATURDAY the 11th of October 1952, Shipwreck, who was 59 years old and living on home relief in a furnished room on W. 51st St., left his flat with a scrapbook full of his yellowed newspaper clippings under an arm and a minute or two later dropped dead in the street. Found among his belongings was a duffel still packed with his old flagpole-sitting gear, in case any fresh jobs came along.

Various of the inauthentic Shipwrecks, meanwhile, continued to make the papers for quite a while yet, including a Shipwreck who lived in New Rochelle and could always be counted on to climb something during festive civic events.

Atlantic City didn't forget Shipwreck Kelly. In 1976, as the shabby old community sought to revitalize itself by dedicating a New Steel Pier, officials launched a nationwide search for Shipwreck Kelly Jr., whom they hoped would be their guest of honor. It turned out, though, that Shipwreck Jr. had been dead three years — he was a Clyde Beatty Circus animal handler, and one day an elephant had stomped him to death — so they settled for Enzo Stuarti and the Bay City Rollers instead.

By JAY MAEDER
Daily News Staff Writer

LOUSE THAT he was to the very end, Legs Diamond actually left his endlessly patient wife sitting in the Albany speakeasy where they were celebrating his latest courtroom acquittal, promised to be back in an hour and headed straight for a midnight tryst with his longtime inamorata, the Ziegfeld showgirl Kiki Roberts. Four hours later, he decided he could use a little sleep and repaired back to his own hotel, and Legs was snoring away when underworld executioners slipped into the room and finally succeeded in dispatching him to the sweet bye and bye. Alice got the call about 5:45, at the speak, where she was still waiting.

This was the third time in 14 months such a call had come to her, and twice already had her husband been administered last rites, and twice had he miraculously come back from the abyss. But this time the rubout took; in the early morning hours of Friday the 18th of December 1931, Legs Diamond — the Clay Pigeon, the papers called him, the Human Sieve — was dead at last.

As a good gangland wife, Alice had always known it would come to this. "Goodbye, boy," she whispered in the rain at Mount Olivet Cemetery in Maspeth, Queens, as clumps of unconsecrated mud covered over his copper coffin, two days before Christmas.

JACK DIAMOND'S reign as New York's flashiest gangster-about-town was relatively brief, and it was not widely realized that there even was a Mrs. Diamond until his time here was already mostly used up. Alice Schiffer had married Jack in 1926, long before the papers ever started calling him Legs, but there'd never been a public sign of her — not when he got famously gunned down with Little Augie Orgen at Norfolk and Delancey Sts. in October 1927, not when he supposedly took over most of Arnold Rothstein's rackets after Rothstein got put on the spot in November 1928, not when he openly shot and killed a couple of mugs at the bar of his Hotsy Totsy Club in July 1929 and had to disappear from Broadway for eight months till five witnesses vanished and the heat went down. It was during this absence from things that rival mobs squeezed him out of his metropolitan operations and forced him to go into the beer business in the Catskills instead. Visiting the upstate Diamond farm, in the village of Acra in Greene County, a fortress of a place equipped with searchlights and machine-gun pillboxes, reporters finally turned up Mrs. Legs, the lady of the house.

Alice was a plump little thing, a deeply religious woman, devoted to Jack for all time, forever, come what may, prepared to forgive him anything, even glamorous Kiki Roberts. It was Kiki with whom Legs was dallying at a midtown hotel on Sunday the 12th of October 1930 when gunners showed up and shot him full of holes, and it was Alice who stayed at his hospital bedside for

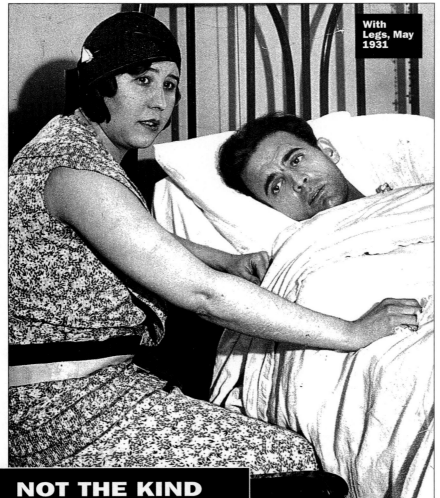

With Legs, May 1931

NOT THE KIND TO BEAR A GRUDGE
Alice Diamond

weeks as he fought off death. Alice was always telling reporters that she prayed for Legs day and night, and she just glared when they asked her what she knew about this Kiki doll. "She is not worth discussing," Alice sniffed.

And after that she nursed him back to health at the Acra compound, stuffing him with affection and good home cooking, until early in April, when Legs informed her that Kiki was moving in.

THIS UNUSUAL domestic situation made the New York papers right away. "The happy little threesome," snickered the Daily News. Actually, Alice soon moved out, and thereafter, Legs — who despite his elegant reputation was never more than a strong-arm thug — went about the business of muscling into the beer rackets of Greene, Ulster and Sullivan counties, Kiki often in tow. She was, in fact, in the car the night that Legs and his boys forced a local truck driver named Grover Parks off the road, tied him to a tree and set him afire.

Alas for Legs, Parks survived to name his assailants, and Gov. Franklin Roosevelt immediately sent racket smashers into Greene County, and so did the federals, and Legs got indicted for Prohibition violations even as outraged Acrans were forming vigilante squads to go after the handsome city slicker with pitchforks. Legs was jailed for two days. Two days after that, as he stood at the window of a country roadhouse, shotgun blasts from outside cut him down.

Kiki Roberts disappeared right away — indeed, while many figured that it was Acra farmers who had done the shooting, there were also those who thought Kiki might have set Legs up herself, that

the gunners were Legs' own disgruntled boys who didn't much like the way he slapped Kiki around — and to the hospital rushed faithful Alice Diamond, crashing past state policemen to be with the grievously wounded husband who had called for her.

"He didn't ask for any other woman?" she asked plaintively. A cop assured her that Legs had not, and she broke into sunbeams.

IN JUNE, the loyal Alice refused to testify before a grand jury convened by state Attorney General John Bennett to break up Legs' Catskills empire. In July, she was with Legs in court in Troy when a jury acquitted him of having assaulted Grover Parks. "You dear," she said, fondly patting his hand. And early in August she wailed bitterly as he was convicted of the federal liquor charges in Manhattan and sentenced to four years in prison, pending appeals.

In October, Kiki Roberts suddenly reappeared and surrendered to state authorities. There wasn't much against her, and soon she was back before the footlights on Broadway. By late November, as every tabloid newspaper reader in New York City knew, Kiki and Legs were an item again.

RETRIED IN TROY on a variant of the old Grover Parks charge — a flimsy state case at best, truth to tell — Legs was acquitted again at 8:30 p.m. on Thursday the 17th of December 1931, and Alice leaped over the chairs and hurled herself upon him, showering him with hugs and busses. Thereafter the Diamonds and a party of friends went into Albany to live it up for the evening.

About 1 a.m., Legs excused himself. He'd be back in an hour, he promised.

"HE LOVED HER and I loved him," Alice explained simply.

"Alice knew all about Kiki Roberts," her sister Mae said later. "But Alice wasn't the kind to bear a grudge. She recognized that Jack was so constituted that he could never be a faithful husband, and she knew she held in the hollow of her hand the best and finest part of his emotional side."

Within weeks of Legs' demise, Alice had put together a stage show — "to teach a moral lesson to young and old," she explained, "that crime is futile and that the old straight-and-narrow path is the only one to follow" — and for a few months she took the act through small vaudeville houses across New York, New Jersey and Pennsylvania, dressed in mourning. "The World's Most Talked-Of Woman," she billed herself. Kiki Roberts, meanwhile, was by now touring with a Legs show of her own. "I wish her all the luck in the world," Alice said. Kiki's production was rather the more successful of the two. By the summer of 1932, Alice was down to working the Coney Island freak tents, selling autographed photos, booked alongside the Armless Musician and the Twins from Peru.

LATE ON THE afternoon of Friday the 30th of June 1933, Legs Diamond's largely forgotten widow, age 32-ish, was found on the floor of her sparsely furnished room at 1641 Ocean Ave. in East Midwood, a bullet through her brain. There were three cups of coffee on the table, indicating that Alice had welcomed her callers, and Brooklyn cops let it be known that an expression of disbelief was frozen across her dead face.

It was theorized for a time that she might have been ready to come forward with information about Legs' death and accordingly been silenced. More probably, as it turned out, she had merely overheard too much about some unrelated neighborhood matter. There were suspects, but nothing was ever pinned on them.

Alice was buried with Legs at Mount Olivet, together with her boy for all the rest of time.

By DAVID HINCKLEY
Daily News Staff Writer

With Scott and Scottie

NOT FOR ZELDA Sayre of Montgomery, Ala., was the fate of the countless sparrows who, having conquered their small towns, flew to the big city intending the same, only to find theirs were now small dreams in a large nest and, after a time, to disappear without so much as a ripple in the breeze.

Zelda Sayre alighted in New York on April 2, 1920, and by noon April 3 had married F. Scott Fitzgerald, whose novel, "This Side of Paradise," had just made him the new swell of literary America.

She had long been the belle of the ball in Montgomery, the heartbreaker who gave her own heart to a Yankee, a young lieutenant from St. Paul by way of Princeton whom she met at a Montgomery Country Club dance in July 1918.

Zelda smoked and drank and had lots of beaus. She was smart, too, and she had big dreams, traits she shared with her charming soldier boy.

They married in St. Patrick's Cathedral, which served both their sense of grandeur and the concern of Zelda's family about their Episcopalian daughter marrying a Catholic in Montgomery. Scott took Suite 2109 at the Biltmore for the honeymoon, and when the newlyweds stepped onto the sidewalks of New York, there wasn't a cloud in the sky.

He was 23, marvelously handsome. She was 19, a classic pretty girl. They knew it. Scott was giddy that "This Side of Paradise," published just a week earlier, had sold out its first printing, and Zelda had bragged to Alabama school chums that New York was as good as hers. She would turn cartwheels in the lobbies of famous hotels, slide down their banisters.

The first time Dorothy Parker met her, Zelda was astride the hood of a taxicab, with Scott on the roof. Parker was unimpressed, saying Zelda had a "candy box face with a little bow mouth" and was prone to petulance.

This was not the last bad notice for Zelda.

THAT WAS NOT, at first, much of an issue. The literary world had gathered in New York in the heady opening hours of the Roaring Twenties, and the fashionable Fitzgeralds sat at its head table. They set up residence at the Commodore and were invited to every important party. "We felt like small children in a great, bright unexplored barn," wrote Scott years later.

But this sense of wonder came at a price: "After a few months, we had no idea who we were or what we were." To some, even friends, they were self-destructive alcoholics. By summer, Scott was getting no work done, so they took a house in Westport, Conn. — which simply lengthened their party commute. Scott and Zelda would take the train to the city and often be drunk on arrival. It made for spirited and highly public quarrels, a practice Zelda defended because she wanted to live "the life of an extravagant."

They returned to the city for the winter, setting up at The Plaza and reveling in the social whirl. But when the "Paradise" money was gone, Scott had to spend more time writing magazine stories, which left Zelda bored when nothing was up and unrestrained when something was. By 1921, they had begun hopping around the world — Paris, Long Island, the Riviera, London, St. Paul, Italy, Delaware — trying to keep the party fresh. She had their only child, Scottie, in 1922, and while they adored the baby, Zelda aborted a second one.

They remained regular visitors to New York, where they were revered as founding figures of the jazz age. In 1924, George and Ira Gershwin wrote a song called "Little Jazz Bird," about a bird that flutters into a cabaret and never wants to leave. A little jazz bird, the song concludes, is the only kind of bird to be.

ZELDA NEVER paid much mind to some of the wifely things Scott had hoped for, such as tending to his laundry. But she would engage him in discussion on anything, from literature to their friends to themselves, and in social situations she was his impetuous match. At a farewell dinner for Alexander Woollcott, she removed her black panties and tossed them to him, declaring he should be sent off with a tangible reminder of good fellowship.

At home, she kept meticulous scrapbooks of her life, and Scott's, both of which were turning out to be

AWFULLY HAPPY
Zelda Fitzgerald

just as noted as she knew they would be.

But Scott's 1925 novel "The Great Gatsby" sold poorly, intensifying his drinking and depression at a time when Zelda was pushing harder for a creative life of her own. Each had affairs. When Scott became friends with Ernest Hemingway, Zelda sneered that Hemingway was "phony as a rubber check." After reading Hemingway's "The Sun Also Rises," she cracked that it was about "bullfighting, bullslinging and bullshit."

The feeling was mutual. "If he could write a book as fine as 'The Great Gatsby,' I was sure he could write an even better one," Hemingway said of Scott years later. "I did not know Zelda yet, and so I did not know the terrible odds that were against him."

Come 1928, Zelda plunged obsessively into ballet, though at 27 she was hopelessly late and her 5-foot-2 frame ill resembled the lithe build of a ballerina. She also wrote magazine stories, but the catch was that because Scott had the reputation, they were published under both their names. For her story "A Millionaire's Girl," the Saturday Evening Post offered $4,000 with Scott's name or $500 with Zelda's. They took the four large.

In 1929, Zelda received an offer to join a ballet company in Naples — and declined it. By now, she was going for days without eating or speaking. In April 1930, she checked into a French clinic for treatment of a nervous breakdown. She was 29. She looked much older.

She would shuffle in and out of hospitals the rest of her life. She also would write a novel, "Save Me the Waltz," a respectable book that didn't sell much, and more stories. Her paintings were exhibited in the city in 1934, and she was chagrined that reviewers focused on her, not the art. Time magazine began by saying she was once "a more fabulous character" than Scott.

Eventually, neither was very fabulous, and during an extraordinary 1932 conversation, subsequently transcribed, Scott blamed everything on Zelda — saying he hadn't written a new novel in seven years because he wasted two years supporting her ballet career and three years tending to her illness.

"You are a third-rate writer and third-rate ballet dancer," he told her. He was "a professional writer with a huge following. I am the highest-paid short-story writer in the world. I have dominated — "

At this point, Zelda cut him off: "You are making a rather violent attack on a third-rate talent, then."

When Scott did finish that novel, his gloomy 1934 masterpiece "Tender Is the Night," he modeled the lead female character after Zelda and lifted passages almost verbatim from her letters.

But there was now more fragility than fight in Zelda. After one visit, she wrote, "It is a shame we should have met in harshness and coldness where there was once so much tenderness and so many dreams."

In kinder moments, Scott agreed. "We were the most envied couple in America in 1921," he said.

"We were awfully good showmen," Zelda replied.

"We were awfully happy," said Scott.

WHILE THEY LIVED together only sporadically after her illness, and not at all after 1934, he kept in contact and paid for her care. He also began living with Hollywood columnist Sheilah Graham and in bitter moments wrote that Zelda "never had the strength for the big stage. She thought she did, but she didn't."

Scott died Dec. 21, 1940, a great novelist many felt could have been greater.

Zelda did not attend his funeral, since she now ventured out only when she felt strong enough. When she came to New York, Scottie would take her window-shopping.

The Little Jazz Bird, now given to clutching a Bible and writing long letters about the apocalypse, died March 11, 1948, in a fire at Highland Hospital in North Carolina. She was buried next to the handsome young lieutenant she had met at the Montgomery Country Club on a summer night 30 years before.

Arriving at Grand Central, October 1938

By JAY MAEDER
Daily News Staff Writer

EVEN AS Al Jolson's triumphant comeback as a radio star was wowing everybody in the late '30s, one still usually spoke of the old duck in the past tense. "He was to popular show business what Dempsey was to the ring or Babe Ruth to baseball," wrote New York Daily News columnist Ed Sullivan in February 1938, respectfully enough, to be sure, but there it was: "Was." Jolson had announced his retirement half a dozen times already, grumbling about the youngsters and how the whole world had changed. But always he came back, again and again, because that's what troupers did when they could no longer bear the silences.

He was only in his early 50s. But he was old as the hills. The thing about Al Jolson was that he had always been an old-timer, as long as anybody could remember. His career went back to the Spanish-American War; by the time "The Jazz Singer" revolutionized moving pictures in 1927 with its single scratchy line of dialogue, the biggest of Broadway stars was already on his way to relicdom as a new generation of silky-voiced crooners came along to displace such ancient rafters-shaking shouters as himself. In his day, a man had to belt out a song just to make himself heard over the San Francisco Earthquake. These modern kids, Jolson sneered, they had to hang microphones on their tonsils.

For all that, the fact remained that he was an old-timer. "Once you slip," he had reflected once, "the descent is swift, and nothing can stop you."

He'd said that years earlier, back in 1931, backstage at the Winter Garden, and he hadn't had a show since.

BUT HADN'T HE been the hot cats once upon a time. He was born Asa Yoelson, son of a sixth-generation Russian cantor whose heart he broke when he kept running away to the bright lights of the New World; as a kid he sang for coins on the sidewalks of New York, and as a young man he toured for years with blackface vaudeville acts, and he was a seasoned professional minstrel by the time he got back to the city in 1911 and J.J. Shubert put him in a show called "La Belle Paree" at the new Winter Garden.

There at the Garden he headlined for years — in "Honeymoon Express" and "Dancing Around," in "Robinson Crusoe Jr." and in "Sinbad"; by 1922 he was the greatest star of the vaudeville stage, America's most popular entertainer, and his new

show, "Bombo," was playing in a 59th St. theater that bore his own name. All the nation sang his songs, mawkish, sentimental, heart-wrenching things that he fell to one knee to sob out as whole rooms sniffled and bawled. By 1924 he was making a new hit record every two weeks.

And then Hollywood called.

Later it would be popularly imagined that "The Jazz Singer," a treacly little tale of a cantor's son who broke his father's heart when he kept running away to the bright lights, was Jolson's life story. It wasn't — George Jessel had starred as Jackie Rabinowitz for two seasons on Broadway, and in fact Warner Bros. offered Jessel the film version first, and he turned it down — but it might as well have been. In October 1927, when "The Jazz Singer" premiered at the Warners' Theatre in New York, Jolson was in the audience and tears were streaming down his face as he watched himself sing the Kol Nidre, the Hebrew prayer of atonement.

SIGNING NOW with the Warners for a series of speakies, Jolson made "The Singing Fool" —

another tearjerker, the story of a driven entertainer who insisted upon going on with the show even as his small son lay dying — and its signature tune, "Sonny Boy," became the first American record to sell 3 million copies. In September 1928, two days after the picture opened, Jolson married Ruby Keeler, a 19-year-old dancer he had wooed away from a Broadway torpedo, and they sailed for Europe. On their return a month later, the newlyweds gave up New York and settled in California. And in January 1929, Jolson announced his retirement from the stage.

BUT HE COULDN'T stay away from Broadway. After making a few more pictures, he opened in "Wonder Bar" at the Bayes Theater in March 1931, his first show since "Big Boy" in 1925. "It was wonderful to see an audience again," he told reporters. "The old applause has been missing. I like to hear it again." There were indeed tremendous ovations, for a while, but then it became plain that the old slide-trombone voice wasn't there anymore, and the star quit the show after a couple of months and retired again. He had one more picture to make, he announced, and after that he'd spend his days at the track like a gentleman.

But this picture, released in February 1933, was Ben Hecht's "Hallelujah, I'm a Bum," which was successful enough that he was persuaded to sign on for a few more, including "Go Into Your

Dance," co-starring his wife, who was frankly a bigger draw than he was at this point. Jolson was a surprise radio hit by now, regularly a guest on the network variety hours, but his Hollywood star was fading fast. Late in 1939, his marriage to Ruby Keeler ended and he came back East. In September 1940, he tried one last show, "Hold on to Your Hat" at the Shubert; after a few months, pleading illness, he quit this one, too.

He was 55 now. He had no career left. All he had in front of him was the war, whose front lines he toured for a couple of years, singing for the soldiers, until he came down deathly sick. Flat on his back in a field hospital in the Far East, he overheard a nurse report that his temperature was 103. This brightened him considerably, and he sat up. "What's the record?" he inquired.

AFTER THE WAR, entertainment columnist Sidney Skolsky produced a film version of Al Jolson's life, "The Jolson Story," and Jolson himself sang all the old favorites — "Mammy," "Sonny Boy," "April Showers," "Avalon," "Carolina in the Morning," "Toot Toot Tootsie" — as actor Larry Parks lip-synched. The picture was a huge hit, and suddenly the old-timer had a new generation of fans — teenagers, for heaven's sake, unimaginably all rushing out to buy his records and sniff, as the Herald-Tribune put it, "the faint lavender odor of old times." Astonishingly, he was a recording star again. He was back on the radio, taking over the "Kraft Music Hall" after Bing Crosby's departure from that venerable institution. He was back on top.

All this lasted for just a couple of years. Late in 1948 he retired one more time. Producer Mike Todd tried to get him to do a nostalgia show at the Winter Garden, reprising his old glories, but he said no. He had seen too many old-timers trying to re-create their golden days, he said, "like old chunks of Camembert cheese. That's not for me." And out he went again, for good.

AND THEN BACK he came yet again, and this time it killed him. In September 1950 he persuaded President Harry Truman to let him go sing for the troops in Korea — "Oh, well, I can't get a job on radio or television," he joked to reporters — and the tour was grueling. On Monday night the 23rd of October, just back from the war zone, set to tape a segment of Crosby's radio program the next day, he was playing gin rummy with a couple of pals in a San Francisco hotel room when his trouper's heart suddenly stopped beating. "Well, this looks like the end," he said, and then the curtain fell.

THREE YEARS LATER, Danny Thomas remade "The Jazz Singer," and critics marveled that such a hoary, hokey, wheezing, whiskered story could ever have entertained anyone, even in a time long ago and a place far away.

By C.J. SULLIVAN
Special to the News

TIM SULLIVAN learned all about Tammany Hall charity in 1869, when he was a ragged 7-year-old from the crushing poverty of the Five Points slums. One cold day his teacher, Miss Murphy, took a look at his shabby shoes, kept him after school and quietly gave him a Tammany voucher for a new pair.

Three and four decades later, the powerful King of the Bowery still remembered Miss Murphy every Feb. 6. That was Shoe Day in New York. Social-welfare programs did not exist in the city at the turn of the century, and the poor relied on Tammany Hall, just as they always had, and Big Tim Sullivan always delivered. Every Feb. 6, personally, out of his own pocket, Big Tim gave away 7,000 pairs of shoes and socks to the needy.

Not that he was an easy touch. He made sure that the line was policed, that no one slipped back for a second pair. Big Tim was wise to such dodges. This was, after all, a man who as a kid bootblack years earlier had been known as Dry Dollar Sullivan because he would pull the revenue stamps off beer kegs, dry them on a stove and try to pass them off as dollar bills.

MORE ESTABLISHED New Yorkers despised the Irish when Tim Sullivan was a youngster. Irishmen had looted and plundered and murdered through the Draft Riots of 1863 and the Orange Day riots of 1871, and they were producing endless streams of children. Ireland had no snakes, the joke went, not because they'd been driven out by St. Patrick but because they'd all died after biting the Irish.

But by the 1880s, the Irish were 40 percent of New York's population, and Tammany Hall recognized that it would need the Irish vote to survive. Accordingly, young men like Tim Sullivan rose from destitution to positions of influence.

At 21, he had borrowed money to open a Bowery bar. Saloons doubled as Tammany clubhouses, and that made Sullivan a man who, at age 23, was electable to the New York State Assembly. In 1893, at 31, he went to the state Senate and became boss of the 6th Ward.

The 6th always went Democratic. A big, booming man, Sullivan regularly handed out money and favors to his constituents, who were Jews and Italians and blacks as well as Irish, and they were always happy to vote the straight Tammany ticket. Every summer, Big Tim held chowders for his good people, merry affairs overflowing with free food and beer. Whenever Big Tim walked past a crowd, he would always get a rousing chorus of, "Sullivan! Sullivan! He's a damned fine Irishman!"

At the same time, he was not entirely averse to lining his pockets with the windfall proceeds from gambling and liquor interests, and he made several fortunes. Notably, he had a talent for buying up cheap lots of city land that happened to get developed shortly thereafter. Moreover, beneficiaries of his largesse included his relatives and in-laws, many of whom found positions on the city payroll.

Still, by Tammany standards he was a relatively honest man, and the 6th Ward cherished him. "He made millions and gave away millions," it was affectionately said of Big Tim

DAMNED FINE IRISHMAN
Big Tim Sullivan

Sullivan.
By the late 1890s, he was Tammany's second-in-command under Boss Richard Croker.

Reform movements regularly sought to pitch Tammany Hall and men like Sullivan out of power. But Big Tim had patience. He knew that reformers were naught but gale-force winds knocking down trees, that Tammany was the forest itself, that Tammany had always still stood strong and sturdy after the winds died down. How many reformers ever got anyone a job? That's what Big Tim always asked at public rallies. Even so, late in 1901, Boss Croker himself could not survive a city cleanup and was forced to resign. At this point, Big Tim could have succeeded him as Tammany's chief.

He chose instead to keep running his own district and back his man, Silent Charlie Murphy, as New York's new boss. Murphy went on to run the show for the next quarter of a century. In 1902, meanwhile, Big Tim decided to run for Congress and see what kind of pickings there might be down in Washington.

AS IT TURNED out, he didn't like Washington very much. Congressmen were like hitching posts, he complained; people kept tying up their horses to him. After four years, he came back to the Bowery and reclaimed his state Senate job.

One of the most formidable men in state politics by now, unchallenged leader of a fiefdom, in 1911 he legislated two bills that still stand today. One designated Columbus Day a New York State holiday. The other was the Sullivan Law, making it a felony to carry a concealed weapon in New York City.

The day the Sullivan Law was put up for a vote, Big Tim gave what is regarded as his finest speech. "This bill," he cried, "will do more actual good and it will save more souls than all the preachers in the city for the next 10 years." He had the other senators in tears.

AFTER that, he began a slow slide into a physical and nervous breakdown. In January 1913, he was deemed incompetent, and his brother Patrick took him on a long tour of Europe to get "The Big Feller" out of public sight. He returned in July, looking pale and drawn, a fragile old man at 51. On Aug. 30, he wandered away from his nurses at his brother's home in Eastchester and, on railroad tracks not far away, was struck down by a train.

Sullivan's body lay unrecognized in a morgue for two weeks, as meanwhile the newspapers shouted the story of his mysterious disappearance. He was practically on his way to Potter's Field when a cop happened to look over his belongings and spotted his TDS cufflinks. "That's Big Tim Sullivan," the cop gasped.

All the Bowery turned out to mourn him. More than 25,000 people trooped to the Timothy D. Sullivan Clubhouse for his wake. His coffin was carried over the Williamsburg Bridge and driven up Kenmare St., named in honor of his mother's hometown in Ireland, and he was buried in Calvary Cemetery.

The man who had made millions and given millions away left an estate worth about $2 million. All of it went to his family. Not a cent was left to charity. Big Tim felt he had given enough.

By JAY MAEDER
Daily News Staff Writer

TOWARD THE END of the 19th century in Old New York, about half the city's people were foreign-born, and a great many of them lived crushed together in tenement squalor, and a lot of them were urchin kids who were essentially free as birds. Social workers clucked at their desperate lot; journalists gravely exposed the heartless evils that doomed them to their poverty. Newspaper and magazine cartoonists, on the other hand, generally found them to be pretty funny little folk, and there arose from the slums a sturdy school of humor revolving around the children of the gutters, high-spirited young ladies and gentlemen who reveled in their raggedness and gleefully grabbed apples off pushcarts and flung snowballs at the truant officer's hat and apparently didn't consider themselves particularly unfortunate creatures at all.

So it was that the laugh magazines of the 1890s, Judge and Puck and Life and the others, were full of slum youngsters and their hilarious antics, and so it was that these same rowdies came to populate the pages of The New York World's brightly colored Sunday newspaper feature section, the city's first. Swiftly running away with readers' hearts was one of them in particular, a hairless little mute who wore an oversized nightshirt and a simian grin. His name was Mickey Dugan. New Yorkers would come to know him as The Yellow Kid.

RICHARD FELTON Outcault's historic Yellow Kid was already vanished from the public prints by the time the 20th century dawned, and Outcault would go on to create a longer-lived and far more popular newspaper feature starring a lad named Buster Brown and a dog named Tige, but The Kid's legacy endures.

Scholars continue to debate to what technical degree "The Yellow Kid" itself was or was not America's first authentic comic strip — it was a single block cartoon, not a sequential series of panels — but The Kid's wild popularity, in first one paper and then another, as two rival publishers went to war over his services in a great splash of yellow ink, led directly to the immortal institution of the newspaper comic section. If R.F. Outcault was not the father of the comic strip per se, as historian Richard Marschall has observed, he was manifestly the father of the Sunday funnies.

OUTCAULT, OHIO-born in 1863, was in New York by the early '90s, working as a staff artist for Electrical World magazine and selling cartoons on the side to the humor weeklies. By 1895, his chief market was Joseph Pulitzer's New York World, the city's largest paper, nationally circulated. That same year, he occasionally began to drop into his slum-kid tableaux a little bald character who wore a nightshirt. That same year, a young Californian named William Randolph Hearst arrived in the

Self-portrait, with the Yellow Kid, 1905

R.F. Outcault

POLYCHROMOUS EFFULGENCE
R.F. Outcault

city, bought a feeble sheet called The Journal and resolved to knock the mighty Pulitzer off the newspaper hill. Among the first things he did in pursuit of this goal was, in early 1896, hire away from Pulitzer pretty much The World's entire Sunday department.

This brazen raid did not at first include Outcault, who, in a matter of a few months, had watched his Yellow Kid turn into a New York star, his face emblazoned across billboards and delivery wagons. Now The Kid's name was being licensed by manufacturers to sell candy and cigarettes and sheet music; by late summer, there was a Yellow Kid musical playing the Weber and Fields Broadway Music Hall. It was not that Hearst was blind to The Kid's popularity; the fact was that his Journal did not yet have color presses. The minute those presses were installed, that autumn of '96, Hearst launched his own Sunday color section — *Eight Pages of Polychromous Effulgence That Make the Rainbow Look Like a Lead Pipe!* — and suddenly Outcault's little slum rat, theretofore of The World, was running every Sunday in The Journal.

An epic circulation scrap ensued, with The Kid in the middle of it, as Pulitzer doggedly kept running a competing, post-Outcault version of his

prize feature (produced by World staff illustrator George Luks, who some years later would attain prominence as a member of the Ashcan School of New York artists). Readers, for their part, were glad enough to have two different Yellow Kids every Sunday; meanwhile, Hearst and Pulitzer sledgehammered away at each other on various other fronts, the headlines screaming ever louder, the crime yarns turning ever more breathlessly purple, the gentle Cuban people suffering ever more terribly at the hands of their barbaric Spanish masters. A century later, it is conventional wisdom that "yellow journalism" took its name from yellow-shirted Mickey Dugan. Actually, as historian Bill Blackbeard has noted in his definitive 1995 chronicle of The Kid's life and times, the term was in use before Outcault ever left Pulitzer.

Meanwhile, a great rush of new comic entertainments fast followed, as both Hearst and Pulitzer grasped that readers loved them, and the Sunday funnies were born. The better burghers of the community, the quality folks, were all properly horrified by such vulgar debasements, and here was still another reason neither The World nor The Journal was much welcome in more genteel households. The common everyday sort of soul, of course, always knew better. But it is said that to this day there are still several American newspapers that do not publish comic strips.

THE KID'S briefly glorious career ended in 1898, when Outcault quit Hearst and went to work for the much more respectable New York Herald. But the funny papers he had wrought went on exploding across the firmament, and in 1902, by which time the likes of "The Katzenjammer Kids" and "Foxy Grandpa" and "Happy Hooligan" had become Sunday institutions in every American parlor, Outcault came up with "Buster Brown" for The Herald.

No relation to Mickey Dugan at all, Buster was a snotty rich kid who lived in fashionable Murray Hill, not unlike the typical Herald reader, and what he did was perpetrate mayhem week after week, wrecking the family manse, tormenting the servants, sneering at established law and order while Tige shook his head sadly. Rendering all this morally instructive was the fact that week after week, unfailingly, Buster paid the price, getting himself good and spanked and then solemnly offering up resolutions as to what a very good boy he would be.

If "Buster Brown" might have seemed to have limited comic possibilities, the strip went on for 18 years — after 1906 in the New York American, once Hearst hired Outcault back again — and Buster became an even more valuable licensing property than The Yellow Kid had been, selling enough bread, chocolate, coffee, soap, clothing and shoes to make Outcault a wealthy man.

AFTER HE folded "Buster Brown" in 1920, R.F. Outcault retired to his home in Flushing, Queens, and devoted the rest of his life to painting. He died at 65 in 1928, by which time the Sunday visitors to America's homes had come to include Mutt and Jeff and Jiggs and Maggie and Winnie Winkle and Major Hoople and Skeezix Wallet and Moon Mullins and Andy Gump and Little Orphan Annie and Felix the Cat and dozens more four-color characters who all owed their existences to Mickey Dugan of Hogan's Alley.

By MARA BOVSUN
Special to The News

EVERYBODY LIKES a good practical joke now and then, but the tragic suicide of Miss O. Yuki in July 1920 didn't get a lot of laughs from city officials.

Police had been told the distraught Japanese girl had ended it all by drowning herself in Central Park. They dragged the lake near 73rd St. for two days, two days that grabbed gallons of newspaper ink but produced not a hair of Miss O. Yuki's comely head.

Miss O. Yuki finally did show up, a very much alive actress, star of a movie about a distraught Japanese girl who flings herself into a lake.

Enraged by still another outrageous film publicity stunt, District Attorney Edward Swann declared press agents a public menace and vowed to find the culprit. Leading the list of suspects was, of course, Publicity Enemy No. 1 — Harry Reichenbach.

Reichenbach was the first and greatest of moviedom's press agents, the P.T. Barnum of the fledgling film industry, the Silver King of Ballyhoo. He had once turned a no-name chorine into a star in a week just to win a bet with a drama critic. He claimed to have once overturned an entire South American government with a single newspaper ad.

Under Swann's third degree, Reichenbach admitted that, yes, he was the one who had dressed an orangutan in a tuxedo and checked him into the posh Knickerbocker Hotel, thus getting writeups for "Tarzan of the Apes." And yes, he had crammed a large lion into a piano case and smuggled it into the Hotel Belleclaire, causing a great panic, complete with fainting dowagers and screaming busboys, when a guest named Mr. T.R. Zann put in a room service order for 30 pounds of beef.

Yes, he said, he had paid a woman to go into convulsions during the Svengali closeup in "Trilby." She was rushed to Bellevue, where she awoke in time for the morning paper deadlines and started shrieking, "Those eyes! Those eyes! Take him away!" Doctors gravely warned of the movie's "catileptic stimulus," and theaters sold out.

And yes, he was the one who had pulled off the spectacular "Virgin of Stamboul" hoax just a few months earlier. The whole town was still talking about that one.

Meanwhile, he insisted, the Miss O. Yuki suicide stunt was not his. It was, he sniffed, "crude," hardly up to his standards. Indeed, Swann subsequently tracked down the responsible parties, who said they were very ashamed and promised never to do it again.

But Swann would never get such an assurance from Harry Reichenbach, unrepentant about gags so ingenious that, even when reporters guessed they were hoaxes, they often didn't let on that they knew.

"I can't see the harm a good fake does anybody," Reichenbach said as he left Swann's hot seat.

BORN IN 1882, Harry was a Maryland farm boy who at 13 ran away to join the circus after Wanda the Palm Reader peered deep into his future and uttered words that changed his life. "Listen, kid," Wanda said. "For every customer you get me, there's a nickel in it for you."

He gypsied around the country, spieling for the likes of Millie-Christine, the two-headed woman; Molly Grady, the Oriental Hula Rose of the Hareem; and Doc Crosby, who sold Wonder Tonic and Immortal Beverage. In time, he hooked up with Reynard the Great, the Fabulous Magician and Handcuff King, whom he made a hero everywhere they went. In Rutland, Vt., for example, the blindfolded wizard found a little lost girl in a shed miles from town. The real magician was Reichenbach, who had paid the tot's mother $50.

Reynard finally began to fancy himself a big-timer and insisted upon going to New York. But the town was too much for Reynard. He vanished. Reichenbach stayed. And eventually, he began to land theatrical assignments, usually concocting off-stage fictions to fill seats. Once he hired a woman to charge down center aisle at the Academy of Music on 14th St., bellowing "Marge, your baby is dying!" to a dancer on stage. Marge leaped over the footlights and dashed to the hospital, where photographers snapped her weeping at cribside.

The baby, naturally, was on Harry's payroll too.

REICHENBACH PULLED OFF his masterpiece in March 1920, when he was engaged to rescue a film called "Virgin of Stamboul," which was about an abducted Turkish beauty, and which reeked.

Off he went to Little Turkey, off Chatham Square, where he dug up six Turks — dishwashers, pastry cooks, lemonade vendors — and in two weeks transformed them into "Sheik Ali Ben Mohamed of Hedjaz" and his effendis and grand eunuchs. Fully costumed and rehearsed, the sheik and his entourage checked into the elegant Hotel Majestic. "We are the Turkish mission, which comes to your country on a very secret importance," Reichenbach informed hotel management. "Protect us please from the newspaper reporting!"

After swearing the managers to utmost secrecy, the sheik confidentially revealed his sacred mission to recover Sari of Stamboul, the achingly beautiful 17-year-old daughter of "the Rockefeller of Turkey." Some months earlier, he said, stunning Sari had been spirited away from her home by a doughboy, and both her parents had dropped dead of grief, leaving her sole heiress to a $100 million fortune. A worldwide search had failed to find the missing girl. But the trail led to New York.

Upon hearing this tale, the managers instantly called the papers, precisely as Reichenbach knew they would, and the sheik decided he would speak to the press after all. "I come to this country, which to my desert-trained eyes is like the heaven promised in the Koran, to seek the betrothed of my younger brother," he solemnly announced to gathered reporters. "She is Sari, so beautiful that in all Turkey there was none like her."

Most of the sheets swallowed the yarn whole (**SHEIK HERE SEEKS $100,000,000 GIRL,** headlined The New York Times), but Boyden Sparkes of the New York Tribune smelled Harry Reichenbach's work and wrote a piece describing the affair as "a sort of thousand and second Arabian nightmare."

Reichenbach's heart sank. His stunt, he figured, was dead.

To his astonishment, the story wouldn't die. It went on for days. Newsreel crews followed the sheik as he strolled around Central Park. Nightclubs vied to get a visit. The Hippodrome Theatre offered box seats and a royal welcome, spreading a carpet from the curb to the lobby so the sheik wouldn't soil his sacred feet. On and on it all went, until poor Sari, seduced and abandoned, was found washing dishes in a hotel on Kenmare St.

Only a few carefully selected newsmen, like anyone with a pencil, were invited to meet the lost heiress in her luxury suite. They found the sheik's party on their knees around her bed as she was attended by a doctor and a nurse. Sari sobbed, Sari howled, Sari rolled from side to side in fits of delirium, but she never said a word, mainly because of her Brooklyn accent.

The happy ending was a huge news story (**ALL PRAISE TO ALLAH,** jubilated the New York American). Everyone understood that it was nothing but bunk, but nobody much cared, and "Virgin of Stamboul" was a hit when it opened a few weeks later.

BUT THIS was pretty much the end of Reichenbach's brand of press agentry. Reichenbach, after all, wasn't the only joker in the business, and hoaxes, usually involving damsels in distress, were becoming daily fare. The city finally passed a law to put the brakes on such stunts.

Also, Reichenbach's kind of shenanigan was being eclipsed by a more sophisticated form, spearheaded by one Edward Bernays, that soon would become the modern public-relations industry.

He didn't stick around to see the transformation. He died July 3, 1931, at age 49. "Harry Reichenbach, Broadway's best beloved press agent and stunt man," mourned one paper, "has pulled his last gag."

PACKING THE HOUSE
Harry Reichenbach

CULVER PICTURES

SHEIK HERE SEEKS $100,000,000 GIRL
cee of Amir of the Hedjaz
an Arabian N...

Sari, Belle of Stamboul, Found Washing Dishes on East Side
Ran Off With an American Sailor, Who Has Gone to See His Rich Uncle, the "Hadahisme...

SARI FOUND; ALL PRAISE TO ALLAH
Squalor of East Side Give...

By DAVID HINCKLEY
Daily News Staff Writer

GEORGE GERSHWIN looked like he could have ridden shotgun for the St. Valentine's Day Massacre. Ira Gershwin looked like his accountant. Growing up, they were poked like eight-balls into every pocket of immigrant New York by their lovable but bumbling father before they discovered they had a knack for melodies and lyrics, at which point they set about writing major passages for the soundtrack for the 20th century.

Sometimes apart, but mostly together, they were responsible for "The Man I Love," "Someone to Watch Over Me," "Embraceable You," "S'Wonderful," "How Long Has This Been Going On," "Nice Work If You Can Get It," "Soon," "I Got Rhythm," "Shall We Dance," "Foggy Day (In London Town)" and "Let's Call the Whole Thing Off," not to mention "Porgy and Bess."

Ira wrote words, George wrote music, and from the early 1920s to the late 1930s they were the most creative team of American brothers not named Marx.

AS GEORGE helped American popular music be taken seriously and Ira was one of the most inventive lyricists ever — a good symbol of loneliness, he once mused, was a poached egg without toast — they surely did Morris and Rose Gershovitz proud.

In the early 1890s, Morris Gershovitz of St. Petersburg, Russia, learned that the czar wanted him for 25 years of military service. So his father, Yakov, put him on a boat to America, with the address of an uncle tucked in the brim of his hat. Beholding the Statue of Liberty, Morris leaned out for a better look and the hat flew off, forcing him to spend his first days as a New Yorker walking the streets asking in Russian and Yiddish for "Greenstein the tailor."

His life never got much more successful than that, nor much less whimsical. In 1895, he married Rose Bruskin, also late of Russia, and by 1916 he and Rose had shared 28 addresses around the city, from Brooklyn to Harlem, as Morris kept getting bright business ideas — restaurants, baths, a bakery, a cigar store, a pool parlor — and they kept failing. He and Rose paused just long enough to produce children: Ira, born Dec. 6, 1896, on the lower East Side; George, born Sept. 26, 1898, in Brooklyn; Arthur, 1900, and Frances, 1906.

Taken as the fastidious Rose was with Morris' charm, she wanted a different life for her children. She insisted they have enough education to become teachers, and she arranged music lessons — though she warned them against becoming "$25-a-week piano players."

Meanwhile, Ira, as the oldest, was assigned the task of carting Rose's diamond ring to the pawnshop each time Morris' latest sure-fire moneymaker went bust. Then he would come home and sit alone, devouring every book he could find, from classics to Nick Carter mysteries.

George, conversely, loved a fight, never hard to find for the perpetual new kid on the block.

But, as early as age 6, George passed a penny arcade on 125th St., heard Rubenstein's "Melody in F" and stood transfixed. He got that same tingle from Dvorak a few years later, and when Rose bought a second-hand piano for Ira in 1910, it was George who started banging out the tunes of the day.

At 15, George quit the High School of Commerce to become a song plugger and landed a side job cutting piano rolls. He was paid $25 for six tunes, and in 1916 he got his first composition published: "When You Want 'Em, You Can't Get 'Em; When You Got 'Em, You Don't Want 'Em." He turned down an advance in favor of royalties, of which there were none.

AFTER DISCOVERING Jerome Kern, George redirected his career from concert recitals to musical theater. Ira, meanwhile, was writing songs too, such as his 1917 wedding anthem, "You

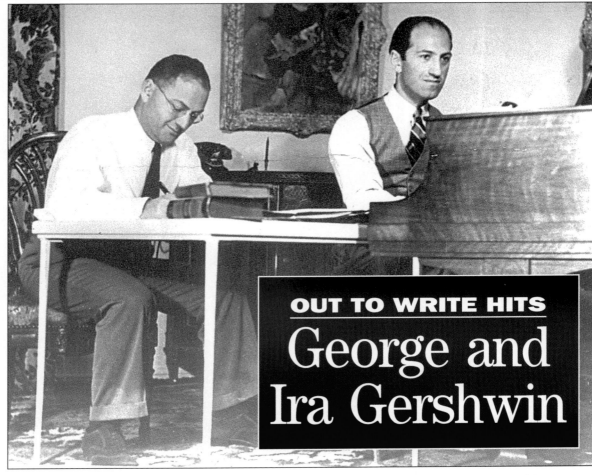

OUT TO WRITE HITS
George and Ira Gershwin

May Throw All the Rice You Desire, But Please, Friends, Throw No Shoes." That same year, the brothers completed their first major collaboration, "The Real American Folk Song," which was cut from the Nora Bayes show "Ladies First."

One night in 1919, George invited lyricist Irving Caesar to the Gershwin family's Washington Heights apartment, and in 15 minutes they wrote "Swanee," which so impressed Morris Gershovitz that he halted his poker game to join in on comb and tissue paper. A few weeks later, Al Jolson sang a more polished version in "Sinbad," and George Gershwin was on his way.

So was Ira. Opposite as the boys were in temperament, they were the closest of comrades, sharing a passion for painting, cigars, chocolate and music. They wrote together by day, and when they knocked off, Ira would go home to read a book and worry over a lyric while George headed out on the town.

He loved nightlife and company — the bigger the audience, the better the time. He dressed impeccably and had a wide enough streak of vanity to worry mightily over losing his hair.

Richard Rodgers recalled parties where George would be playing one piano and Cole Porter another for guests that included Fred and Adele Astaire, Flo Ziegfeld, Charlie Chaplin, Gertrude Lawrence and Noel Coward. On a more intimate note, when Mrs. Rodgers was struggling through a difficult pregnancy at Christmas 1934, George paid a surprise visit to play and sing the entire score of "Porgy and Bess."

After the brothers started building a reputation in the early '20s with the successful "Scandals" revues, George startled the music world at Paul Whiteman's 1924 Aeolian Hall concert by introducing "Rhapsody in Blue" and bringing jazz rhythms into classical composition. Stiff jazz, but jazz nonetheless.

By the mid-'20s, the Gershwin brothers had launched their own golden age. It started with "Oh, Lady Be Good," which featured the Astaires and tunes like "Fascinating Rhythm." The shows "Oh, Kay," "Funny Face" and "Girl Crazy" followed — the last opening on Broadway not only with "I Got Rhythm" and "Embraceable You," but with a pit band led by Red Nichols and including

Benny Goodman, Jack Teagarden and Gene Krupa.

IMPULSIVE GEORGE seemed to write brilliant melodies overnight, while methodical Ira crafted perfect, all-but-impossible rhymes like "My dear, it's four-leaf clover time / From now on, my heart's working overtime."

They wrote razor-edged political satires like "Strike Up the Band." George wrote the orchestral "Cuban Overture" before tackling "Porgy and Bess," which opened in New York on Sept. 10, 1935, to mixed notices that only hinted at its durability.

After "Porgy," they looked to film and moved West, though Hollywood feared George's symphonies and operas had taken him out of the pop music game.

"Rumors about highbrow music ridiculous," George wired an agent in California. "Am out to write hits."

The brothers landed a Fred Astaire movie that would become "Shall We Dance," and Ira found he liked California. Peace and quiet. George hated it — no action.

A month after "Shall We Dance" opened in May 1937, George started losing coordination on the keyboard and having headaches. He went to the doctor, who found a brain tumor. When he fell into a coma July 9, even the White House joined a frantic effort to find the country's top neurosurgeon.

It wasn't enough. On July 11, George Gershwin died.

IRA GERSHWIN, devastated, took some time before hooking up with other composers, including Kern. In 1954, after he and Harold Arlen wrote Judy Garland's show-stopping "The Man That Got Away" for "A Star Is Born," he finally put down his pencil.

Over a long and happy retirement, he became a patron saint for the golden age and the Gershwins' role in it. He traveled to Russia, land of his father, for the premiere of "Porgy and Bess," and on Aug. 17, 1983, drifted gently into the next life, where he no doubt found the kind of music people were no longer writing in this one.

By CLEM RICHARDSON
Daily News Staff Writer

FORWARD ON A STAR
Alain Locke

EVERYONE knew something was happening in the 10 square blocks of what was Harlem in 1925, something unique in American history.

It took Alain Leroy Locke, the nation's first black Rhodes scholar, to hang a name on this new thing.

"Harlem has become the greatest Negro community the world has known — without counterpart in the South or in Africa," Locke wrote in a seminal essay, "Harlem," that he published in a special issue of his magazine, Survey Graphic.

Harlem, Locke said, was giving birth to the "New Negro" — a Negro with his own culture and community and who had valuable contributions of music, literature and art to make to American society.

"Here in Manhattan is not merely the largest Negro community in the world, but the first concentration in history of so many diverse elements of Negro life," Locke wrote. "It has attracted the African, the West Indian, the Negro American; has brought together the Negro of the North and the Negro of the South; the man from the city and the man from the town and village; the peasant, the student, the business man, the professional man, artist, poet, musician, adventurer and worker, preacher and criminal, exploiter and social outcast.

"Each group has come with its own separate motives and for its own special ends, but their greatest experience has been the finding of one another."

Locke's essays, "Harlem" and "Enter the New Negro," both of which appeared in the March 1925 Survey Graphic, revealed to the country and to Harlem itself the dark artists of the day. That magazine, and Locke's book that followed, "The New Negro," were pivotal in getting white critics to take black artistic efforts seriously, and they united black artists under one loose banner as creators of a new esthetic.

Years later, this era would come to be called the Harlem Renaissance, and Locke — mentor, teacher and critic to many of the artists he wrote of — would be hailed as its founding father.

LOCKE KNEW THEM all: fellow intellectual W.E.B. Du Bois; poets Langston Hughes, Paul Lawrence Dunbar, James Weldon Johnson, Rosamond Johnson, Melvin B. Tolson, Angelina Grimke, Claude McKay, Countee Cullen, Jean Toomer and Eric Walrond; novelists Charles Chestnutt, Clement Woods, Walter White and Jessie Faucet; artists Henry O. Tanner, Meta Warrick and May Jackson; actors Paul Robeson, Bert Williams and George Walker; musicians Duke Ellington and Louis (Satchmo) Armstrong.

What they did just over 60 years after the end of slavery would set the tone for much of the Negro art to come. At Locke's urging, they looked to Africa for inspiration and to one another for encouragement and criticism. And by the time Wall Street crashed four years later and took their dreams of an equal society with it, they had created a culture.

Harlem in 1925 was a small nexus of the Negro world — far smaller than it would later become, extending east of Lenox Ave. and west of Seventh, running, as Locke wrote, "a mile north and south." Some 20,000 people called Harlem home, many of them Southerners who had dropped their plows to head North, but also Negroes from the Caribbean and Africa, all drawn to New York and the promise of good-paying factory jobs.

Segregation forced many into Harlem. It also created a community.

Maybe it was because so many of the earliest efforts at culture — the cakewalks and minstrel shows, for example — simply mimicked white social functions. Maybe it was because there were still many former slaves and former near-slaves among the populace. But there were serious doubts among the cultural elite of the day that Negroes were capable of creating serious art.

Until Locke explained what happened.

LOCKE'S ACCOMPLISHMENTS were many, long before his Survey Graphic articles. Born in 1886 in Philadelphia to schoolteacher parents, Locke was forced by sickness to abandon medical studies and instead concentrate on education. He graduated magna cum laude from Harvard, taking a degree in philosophy, before studying at Oxford University and the University of Berlin. He returned to Harvard, earning a doctorate in 1918, then was named head of the philosophy department at Howard University in Washington.

But Locke's spiritual home was always uptown, because he believed the artists he discovered there — he was an early supporter of Hughes, Cullen and McKay, often urging his white patrons to support them financially — were creating a culture, and culture was the tool that would prove all men were created equal.

Intellectual men and women, Locke reasoned, would gauge the depth of Negro work and realize that blacks and whites shared a common vision.

True, Locke was an elitist, and he felt culture would be found among only the most sophisticated Negroes. That did not sit well with writers like Hughes, who felt art could be found even among the most bitter of Negro stories.

Then came Locke's "Enter the New Negro."

"The Negro today wishes to be known for what he is, even in his faults and shortcomings, and scorns craven and precarious survival at the price of seeming to be what he is not," he wrote. "This deep feeling of race is at present the mainspring of Negro life. It seems to be the outcome of the reaction to proscription and prejudice; an attempt, fairly successful on the whole, to convert a defensive into an offensive position, a handicap into an incentive."

He would go on to explain the "fervent and filial appeal" of Weldon Johnson's poem:

CULVER PICTURES

O Southland, dear Southland!
Then why do you still cling
To an idle age and a musty page
To a dead and useless thing.

and the "sober query" of Johnson's "To America":

How would you have us, as we are?
Or sinking neath the load we bear,
Our eyes fixed forward on a star,
Or gazing empty at despair?

"Our poets," Locke wrote, "have now stopped speaking for the Negro, they speak as Negroes."

The Survey Graphic special issue, and then Locke's book, turned the eyes of critical New York uptown, and if Hughes and McKay and the myriad others didn't get rich, they did get noticed.

The essays also made Locke the authority on Negro culture. Though the hard times that came with the Depression derailed his dream for cultural accession of the Negro, the artists of the Harlem Renaissance defined their era and much of what was to come afterward.

"The pulse of the Negro world has begun to beat in Harlem," Locke wrote.

Locke would chair the philosophy department at Howard for 40 years. He died in New York City in 1954, just a month before the U.S. Supreme Court issued its historic Brown vs. Board of Education ruling that ended segregated schools.

By DAVID HINCKLEY
Daily News Staff Writer

I N THE deepest valley of the Depression, a man took turf where he found it, and if that meant an ex-pug and hustler like Herbert (Whitey) White had to supplement his street-gang work with a dance troupe, well, Whitey was nothing if not a pragmatist.

Frankie Manning was a pragmatist, too. But mostly he was a dancer. His association with Whitey was a matter of circumstance and mutual convenience.

Whitey was a fair dancer himself, an avocation he'd picked up at Baron Wilkins' club in the late 1920s after his first knockout convinced him boxing wasn't his future. Soon Whitey had formed the Jolly Fellows, who in short order ran almost everything between 135th and 142nd Sts., and when the Savoy Ballroom opened on his turf in 1926, Whitey took himself a job as bouncer.

By early 1927, meanwhile, the younger kids were getting bored with the same Charleston their older brothers and sisters had been doing, and they started jazzing up the steps. When a young trans-Atlantic aviator captured the country's attention that May, they borrowed his headlines and called their new moves the Lindy Hop.

Born with the short shelf life of any fad, the Lindy Hop proved durable enough that by the early '30s some practitioners were making a living at it — giving lessons, becoming gate attractions at the hipper nightspots.

None beat the Savoy, which had two bands for nonstop action, did not serve hard liquor and, unlike downtown joints such as Roseland, was integrated.

Whitey White took to scoping out the new arrivals there and inviting the most promising to join his troupe, Whitey's Lindy Hoppers, who soon became the brand name in Lindy Hop.

Turf worth holding is rarely uncontested, of course. Whitey's dancers were fresh kids like Frankie Manning and Norma Miller and Fredi Washington, whom he paid $25 a week and drilled like it was boot camp. On the other side were first-generation dancers like Leon James, Shorty Snowden, Edith Matthews and Twist Mouth George, who created the Lindy Hop and felt the prominence of these kids was due as much to promotion as skill.

And thus in late 1935 was a throwdown arranged. Three of the old-time couples vs. three of Whitey's best. Two thousand fans packed the Savoy and Frankie Manning and Fredi Washington, dancing last, figured they needed to stop the show to win.

"Shorty had a step where his partner, Big Bea, would carry him off the stage on her back, with their elbows locked together," Manning would remember. "I thought I could improve it. I'd take the girl, lock arms with her back to back and flip her all the way over."

They practiced in secret and saved the new move for last. Fredi went up and kept going. She landed on her feet and 2,000 fans went crazy.

Over the Top was born. The first "air step" of the Lindy Hop propelled Frankie Manning onto Broadway and into nightclubs with the likes of Count Basie, Billie Holiday and Duke Ellington. Whitey ran the organization, but Frankie ran the

dance as Whitey's Lindy Hoppers toured Europe, South America and Australia. Manning choreographed the best Lindy Hop scene ever filmed, in "Hellzapoppin'," as well as dance scenes in the Marx Brothers' "A Day at the Races." He danced at the 1939 World's Fair. He was featured in Life magazine.

It took nothing less than the brutish jackboots of the Axis to bust up this party.

MANNING WAS born May 26, 1914, in Jacksonville, Fla., and his family moved to Harlem when he was 2. When he was 13, walking to Sunday afternoon youth activities at the Metropolitan Baptist Church on 129th St., he rerouted himself to the Alhambra Ballroom, where he learned the gospel of Lindy Hoppers like Shorty Snowden and Stretch Jones. Soon he joined them, working his way up the Lindy ladder from the Alhambra to the Renaissance Ballroom to the Savoy.

The Savoy was where the best would gather, especially for the Sunday afternoon open challenges where the winner got the $5 prize. Manning was a familiar and unmistakable sight there, the muscles and veins on his prematurely bald head glistening with sweat. Musclehead, the regulars got to calling him. "Go, Musclehead, go!"

He borrowed Lindy Hop moves from

everywhere — the circus, the ballet. He had dancers take a long sliding split through their partners' legs. He arranged the first synchronized group steps. He added slow steps that made the fast steps seem more frenetic. More than anyone else, he turned the Lindy Hop into theater.

This dovetailed nicely with the inception in autumn 1935 of the Daily News' Harvest Moon Ball, which quickly became another Lindy Hop showcase. Ironically, the first ball didn't even have a Lindy Hop category until it became clear that many of the 150,000 spectators — a crowd that forced the first event to be postponed and relocated into Central Park — saw the ball as a showcase for just that dance. Those who called The News included, among others, Whitey White.

All this popularity surprised Manning not at all. Dance, he said, was life. People who danced together got to know each other and respect each other. Men who understood the principles of dance understood the principles of women. "The woman you are dancing with is a queen," he would say. "That's the feeling you should have. She is letting you dance with her. You should be grateful, fellas."

Also, fellas, "You have to look good. You gotta give her something to look at."

By the early '40s, however, the war clouds of Europe were darkening the dance floor. Whitey's troupe landed in Argentina on Dec. 6, 1941, and was stranded there for six months until it could catch a blackout plane to Miami. After they finally scraped up the cash to get back to New York, Whitey accused Manning of stealing his money.

Whitey was a rich man by now, with a fleet of chauffeur-driven Buicks and a club and farm in Oswego. The dancers knew they'd earned much of that money for him, and they sided with Manning. Whitey walked and Whitey's Lindy Hoppers were history.

I N 1943, Manning was drafted. He could have gone for an entertainment unit, but instead he served in the Pacific, surviving hand-to-hand combat in hellholes like New Guinea. He won some medals and stayed in the service until 1948, when he got out to find his job was gone. These new bebop rhythms? Couldn't hang a dance on them.

He formed a troupe, the Congaroo Girls, but his time was over. Rhythm and blues was already becoming rock 'n' roll. Whitey White died of a heart attack on his Oswego farm. None of his dancers attended the funeral. In 1954, Frankie Manning hung up his shoes and took a job with the post office.

For 30 years he commuted from Corona, Queens, and he was closing in on retirement when, one night in 1984, a California woman named Erin Stevens called and asked if by any chance he was Frankie Manning the famous dancer.

"I don't dance anymore," he told her after a long pause. "I just work at the post office." But she persisted — just let us come talk, just show us one step, just do one dance — and it all came back. He became the dance consultant on Spike Lee's "Malcolm X" and Debbie Allen's "Stompin' at the Savoy." He won a National Endowment for the Arts choreography grant and a Tony for the 1989 Broadway show "Black and Blue." He had more invitations than he could handle, from the U.S. and Europe, to teach and talk.

In May 1999, Norma Miller threw him an 85th birthday party at Roseland. To mark the occasion, Frankie Manning danced with 85 women.

AT THE HOP
Frankie Manning

By JAY MAEDER
Daily News Staff Writer

"You only have one body. You can't go to the store and get another one."
— Charles Atlas

ACCORDING TO the legend, it really did happen pretty much exactly like this, at Coney Island, circa 1908:

Here's the 97-pound weakling, all ribs and kneecaps, sunning himself at the shore and trying hard to make time with some pretty girl, when up struts this gorilla and literally kicks sand in his face. "Haw!" the gorilla goes. And the 97-pound weakling draws himself up and makes a ludicrously brave stab at things. "Say!" he cries. "Who do you think you…" Whereupon the gorilla gives him a flick and sends him flying about 30 feet. "That man is the biggest bully on the beach!" the kid sniffles. "Oh, don't let it *bother* you, little boy!" sneers the girl, and off she goes arm in arm with her new beau. Back in his bedroom, the spindly little fella does a few simple exercises, and 10 minutes later he looks like a United States Marine, and right away he's back at the beach clocking his tormentor. "My hero!" flutters the doll, the crimson rising brightly on her throat.

Years later, after feeble, sickly, 15-year-old Angelo Siciliano had transformed himself into Charles Atlas, the World's Most Perfectly Developed Man, a specimen who pulled railroad cars along their tracks and towed boats through New York Harbor and ran a huge mail-order business guaranteeing 97-pound weaklings everywhere that they could be he-men too, he always assured examiners such as, for example, the Federal Trade Commission that this was an absolutely true story. He had himself been that very wretch, and for several generations of half-pint lads, there was no greater man on earth than Charles Atlas, the godlike male who was going to make their muscles ripple beneath their skin like rabbits under a rug and win them flocks of admiring chickadees whenever they had occasion to take their shirts off, which you could bet would be as often as possible.

Over the course of six decades, it was said that 6 million young men came under the Charles Atlas tutelage. What was there not to believe in? If 97-pound Angelo Siciliano could do it, anybody could do it.

ANGELO SICILIANO, who had been born in Acri in Calabria in 1893 and had come to Brooklyn with his seamstress mother at age 10, lived on Front St., which was no pleasant place, and he grew up as daily pickings for every neighborhood tough. One day, smacked and humiliated and chortled at yet again, he beheld the statue of Hercules at the Brooklyn Museum. Never again, he vowed, would anyone kick sand in his face.

And, according to the legend, one day he was watching the lions at the Prospect Park Zoo, marveling at the musculature of the sleekly chiseled cats, when it struck him: Lions didn't lift weights. All they did was stretch. From this revelation did he devise a practical theory of physical development that involved pitting one set of muscles against another, or, basically, wrestling with oneself. In a year he doubled his weight. By age 19, he was a professional Coney Island strongman, tearing phone books in half and pounding nails into blocks of wood with his hands.

Sculptors discovered him, and Angelo Siciliano, now calling himself Charles Atlas, posed for many notable heroic works. George Washington of the Washington Square Arch is

Charles Atlas. So is Dawn of Glory in Prospect Park. So is Alexander Hamilton at the U.S. Treasury in Washington. Hollywood called. He could have been an early movie Tarzan. But he preferred to stay in Brooklyn.

He stood 5-feet-10, weighed 180 and had a 47-inch chest, a 32-inch waist, a 17-inch neck, 14-inch forearms and 24-inch thighs. In 1921, Physical Culture magazine staged a bodybuilding fair at Madison Square Garden and named him The World's Most Perfectly Developed Man. A year later he won the title again, and Physical Culture canceled future events on the realization that nobody but Charles Atlas was ever going to win. At this point, he understood he had something to sell. And he set up a small bodybuilding-by-mail enterprise.

This didn't go anywhere until 1929, when he partnered with an ingenious advertising man named Charles Roman, who assessed the theretofore untitled muscles-against-muscles program and christened it Dynamic Tension.

BY THE LATE 1930s, when there was no such thing as a newsstand magazine that did not have a Charles Atlas advertisement in it, 60,000 young males were tearing out comic-book coupons and ordering the $30 Dynamic Tension course every year. The loinclothed Atlas body was such a universal icon that an anthropologist traveling in Africa came across a Bantu village whose people had made a shrine of an Atlas ad torn out of

THE INSULT THAT MADE A MAN OUT OF "MAC"

Let Me PROVE I Can Make YOU A NEW MAN!

Argosy, yet the strongman was having chronic difficulties with the Federal Trade Commission, chiefly because other strongmen kept calling him a fraud.

No one, they insisted, could build a body just by stretching like an animal. Sure you could, Atlas explained to the FTC. "You take one hand and press it against the palm of the other, then you push it up in the air, with one arm resisting the other as you push it up, and then you push down, resisting the arm trying to push you down."

"Did you ever, Mr. Atlas," a lawyer sniffed, "see a dog put one paw against the other and resist it as he pushed it up in the air and push it down again?"

"My dog does that all the time," Atlas replied.

He didn't have a lot of patience with the FTC. "Is the commission saying you shouldn't exercise, or what?" he grumbled.

"I'm doing the cleanest work of any man living today." Indeed, many a boy who thought he was merely going to put a few inches on his chest found himself taking an intensively inspirational course in the Charles Atlas Way of Life. "*Avoid all dissipations and injurious habits you know to be wrong,*" sternly directed the Atlas literature. "*Think high and beautiful thoughts.*" "*A sound body and sound mind go together. They always will.*" Youngsters would make awed pilgrimages to the Atlas offices at 115 E. 23rd St., and Charles Atlas would always find a minute or two to bend a railroad spike and offer sound counsel ("*Live clean, think clean and don't go to burlesque shows*").

Cynics looking for a trace of hokum in any of this never found anything but utter sincerity. "The whole world looks up to me as the most ideal specimen of the human body," he said. "It is a great responsibility." One day the mail actually brought a coupon from India's Mahatma Gandhi. Atlas custom-designed a lesson plan for him and refused to take a dime. "Poor little chap," he clucked. "He's nothing but a bag of bones."

AT 60, HE could still bend an iron bar with his chin, and at 70 he still looked 50, ferociously walking and swimming and stretching, railing against modern dietary habits. "Dead food!" he snapped. "Everything's artificial! Not enough Vitamin A!" He blamed the moms of America for the increasingly deplorable conditions of their young. "Kids today look bad because their mothers feed them pop and crackers," he groused in 1968. "Our women are too selfish. Mothers going here and there, wearing pants like a man, showing their backsides to people. What is this? They should be home cooking real food and feeding their families instead of out showing their backsides." Interviewers who visited the old gent in his twilight years always came away with such diatribes. Sometimes he would bend a spike for them, too.

In 1972, semiretired to Point Lookout on Long Island as Charles Roman continued to run the still very prosperous business, the strongman suffered a heart attack. Refusing to believe this could ever happen to Charles Atlas, he resumed his exercise regimen at once; three days before Christmas, he was dead at 79. Mail-order sales of his Dynamic Tension course remained brisk for some few years after that, still priced at the same $30 it had always been.

By JAY MAEDER

Daily News Staff Writer

THE TWO-COLORED ball was the thing, you see. To George V. Denny Jr., the two-colored ball said everything there was to say about the American tradition of unfettered intellectual exchange in the marketplace of free ideas. The ball was black on one side and white on the other side, and if you looked at it from one direction, well, it was black, and if you looked at it from the other, why, it was white. Aha! Yes, there were *two sides to every question*, George V. Denny Jr. always said. "We could never agree on its color unless you knew my point of view and I realized that you were looking at it from another point of view," he heartily explained. "Many of our disagreements could be settled if people would only look at both sides of the ball."

That was George V. Denny Jr. for you. He had briefly been a stage actor before he became master of America's premier public-affairs radio program, and he remained sufficiently the dramatic that he was forever whipping his two-colored ball out of his pocket and genially asking what color somebody thought it was. That always got the fruitful philosophical debates going. "It is by orderly discussion that lies are unmasked!" cried George V. Denny, triumphantly returning to his pocket the admittedly thought-provoking two-colored ball.

"AMERICA'S TOWN Meeting of the Air," from the mid-1930s into the late 1940s as much a fixture of national life as The Saturday Evening Post, had its origins in 1934, when George Denny was shocked and saddened to learn that a Scarsdale neighbor of his was so violently anti-New Deal that he wouldn't listen to Franklin Roosevelt on the radio or even read about him in the newspapers. This was not what the Framers had intended, thought Denny. This was not the way of the old colonials who assembled to reason together when their bell-ringing town criers summoned them from their homes. This was not the way of Lincoln and Douglas, speaking their minds, stating their cases, each given respectful due. Why, Roosevelt had never even publicly debated Herbert Hoover, had he? The brow of George V. Denny Jr. furrowed in contemplation.

"Free speech is the most powerful and at the same time the most dangerous thing in the world," he reflected. "Implicit in free speech is the right to advocate the wrong as well as the right, the right to champion evil as well as good, to argue for slavery as well as for freedom." In the cauldron of Europe at this moment, a fellow named Hitler was mounting hypnotic, thought-eradicating mass meetings. The same could not be permitted to occur in the cauldron of America.

It happened that Denny, as chief of the lecture program at venerable Town Hall in New York City, had contacts at the National Broadcasting Co. On Memorial Day 1935, "America's Town Meeting of the Air" — a faithful re-creation of the town meeting of yore, complete with crier and bell and issues warranting discussion — made its debut on the NBC Blue Network's 120 stations. The first broadcast posed the question, "Which Way, America? Fascism, Communism, Socialism or Democracy?" Representatives of all four selections were present, speaking their minds, stating their cases, letting the people decide, as was their privilege and their duty.

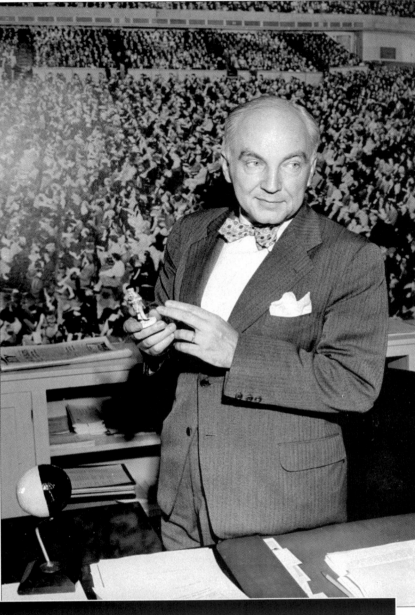

YES AND NO
George V. Denny Jr.

GREAT-SHOULDERED, graystone Town Hall was originally to have been a monument to the aspirations of the League for Political Education, a band of suffrage-minded socialites who had formed in 1894, eventually outgrown their Fifth Ave. salons and then spent years raising funds to build themselves this grand shining temple of progressive national thought. By the time the last stone was set in 1921, the ladies had, wouldn't you know, already won the vote, and their splendid neo-Federal lyceum in the heart of the Theater District became a concert hall and a vital venue for the lecturers William Jennings Bryan, Jane Addams, Booker T. Washington, Margaret Sanger and other such freethinkers. YE SHALL KNOW THE TRUTH AND THE TRUTH SHALL MAKE YOU FREE, boomed the inscription that the old girls had carved into the facade, and George Denny, for one, believed it.

Born in 1899, Denny came to New York from the University of North Carolina, where he had founded the Carolina Playmakers with, among other colleagues, a young writer named Thomas Wolfe, and proceeded to appear in several dismal flops in the 1926-27 theatrical season. Soon he decided that his true calling was lecture-bureau management. After a few years running Columbia University's programs, he became assistant to League for Political Education director Robert Erskine Ely. By 1937, when Ely retired and Denny took over as boss at what was now called Town Hall, award-winning "America's Town Meeting of the Air" was a regular Thursday night visitor in millions of American parlors.

Every large thinker of the day — congressmen, cabinet officers, columnists — came to Town Hall to debate the great grave pros and the great grave cons of inflammatory modern issues. *Do We Have a Free Press? Should Rent Ceilings Be Lifted? Is Communism Compatible With Christianity? How Should We Deal With Germany After the War? Will the Taft-Hartley Law Improve Labor Relations? How Can Peace Be Maintained in Palestine? Should the St. Lawrence Seaway Plan Be Adopted? Are We Losing Our Moral Standards? How Can We Strengthen the American Family? Have Women Failed as Homemakers?* Through years of flying fur, it was always beaming, bow-tied, shining-domed, ineluctably democratic George V. Denny Jr. — Moderator Denny, as he was civilly addressed — who could be counted on to maintain the fairest of orders, stopwatch in hand, clocking every syllable uttered, ensuring on behalf of all demagogue-hating Americans that no one stated position might tyrannically claim one minute of time more than another.

Here did Wendell Willkie become a viable presidential candidate in a single remarkable night. Here was First Lady Eleanor Roosevelt badgered into what was very nearly a screeching, hair-pulling catfight with the wife of the publisher of The Washington Post. Here did the chief of a belligerent group called the No Foreign Wars Committee offer to fistfight anyone who disagreed with him and summarily get booed off the stage. At Moderator Denny's town meeting, you rose or you fell according to what it was you had to say.

"Dictators do not permit men to think for themselves," Moderator Denny informed Americans. "The town meeting does. It played a part in the founding of this country and will continue to play a part in preserving the principles upon which the nation rests."

BY THE END of the '40s, though, while it was not wholly the case that public-affairs programs had become a dime a dozen, "Town Meeting" was no longer the novelty it had once been. It jumped from NBC to ABC; briefly and unsuccessfully it sought to reinvent itself for television. In 1951, amid some private executive dispute, Town Hall's board of trustees relieved George Denny of his presidency. The old radio show carried on without him until it quietly left the air in June 1956.

Denny moved to Connecticut, got into the shopping center business and, later in the '50s, organized a group called the People to People Foundation and took it on a goodwill tour of South America, promoting inter-American relations. He was planning yet more earnest good works when he died in November 1959.

ON THE MALL
Edwin Franko Goldman

By DAVID HINCKLEY
Daily News Staff Writer

IT WAS PAST the gloaming both for the evening of Aug. 15, 1955, and, in truth, for Edwin Franko Goldman. But the dapper, elegant Goldman showed little sign of his 77 years as he stepped to the front of the bandstand in Central Park that night and produced a white handkerchief that he waved with a flourish at the thousands of music lovers who had gathered to hear his band, the Goldman Band, play its final concert of the 1955 season.

Goldman Band concerts had been a ritual of summer in the city for decades, as reliable and refreshing as open fire hydrants, Yankee pennants and egg creams. Nineteen fifty-five was the band's 38th season, Aug. 15 its 2,146th performance, and Edwin Franko Goldman had not missed a one. He had conducted the band's first concert in 1918, at Columbia University, and he had conducted the concert this night, though in keeping with recent tradition, he had turned the baton over to his son Richard Franko Goldman for the last encore, "Auld Lang Syne."

As that wistful Scottish air wafted over Central Park, murmuring of days gone by and good times passed, thousands of New Yorkers pulled out their own handkerchiefs and waved back at the man who put this music in their summer nights.

EDWIN FRANKO Goldman was born on New Year's Day 1878 in Louisville, Ky. His father was a judge and a serious amateur musician, as were several of his aunts and uncles. His mother, Selma Franko, had toured the world in the 1860s with the Franko family singers, child prodigies who were quite the international rage.

Drawn to music from the first, Edwin took up the cornet after the family moved to New York in 1886. At 15 he won a scholarship to the National Conservatory, where he studied composition under Dvorak, and at 17 he was playing first cornet in the Metropolitan Opera orchestra.

Okay, it didn't hurt that the concertmaster of the Met was his uncle Nathan. But this was a precocious lad, and in his 10 years with the Met he played under the batons of, among others, Arturo Toscanini and Gustav Mahler.

After he left the Met, he supported himself by forming small ensembles for private engagements while he worked to form a permanent band. It was a dream rooted in his admiration for the great bandmaster John Philip Sousa and his belief that a band could play serious music as precisely and movingly as an orchestra.

In 1911, then, after seeking and receiving the blessing of the prickly Toscanini, Goldman formed the New York Military Band, a name that had marketability but barely hinted at the scope of what he had in mind.

FOR STARTERS, he envisioned free public concerts in large places on summer nights, and he immediately began raising money to launch that plan. Seven years later he had $50,000, enough to

persuade Columbia to let him use the university green.

By 1923, needing a bigger space, he moved to Central Park. But financing remained a worry until, in 1924, he met a music lover named Daniel Guggenheim, for whom money was not an issue.

Guggenheim asked Goldman what he would do if he didn't have to spend his time hustling for contributions. Goldman said he would work harder and find better music. Okay, said Guggenheim, you do that and I'll pay for it — a blank check that by 1945 had taken $2 million out of the Guggenheim fortune.

By then, the series, renamed the Daniel and Florence Guggenheim memorial concerts, was routinely drawing crowds of 20,000. By the 1950s, Goldman was up to six shows a week, four in Central Park and two in Brooklyn's Prospect Park.

AS ALL THIS might suggest, Goldman was no Harold Hill, the slick rascal whose flamboyant brass-band hustle in the Broadway hit "The Music Man" made him probably the second best-known bandleader of the 20th century, behind only Sousa.

No, Edwin Franko Goldman was a focused and fastidious man. He did not drink or smoke. He did not touch tea, coffee or cocoa, just water and buttermilk. He walked about the city obsessively to keep his 5-foot-7, 150-pound frame in fighting trim, and he ate sparingly. Among his unbreakable dietary rules: no lobster before a show.

He refused to play golf because it might tire his arms. He had a closet full of suits, a new one pressed for each show. His pajamas, like his shirts, were custom-made by a shop on Fifth Ave.

He and his wife, Adelaide, whom he married when he was 30, had two children and lived in an apartment on Riverside Drive with three baths and two maids. A chauffeur drove his Cadillac.

As for musicians, he drilled them relentlessly, focusing on such elementary detail that the standard muttering in his band was "it's like kindergarten."

To Goldman, however, disciplined practice was the only means by which bands would achieve the respect enjoyed by orchestras. A Goldman musician had to make a wind instrument sound like a string.

Goldman himself composed more than 100 band pieces. But he almost discarded his most famous, "On the Mall," thinking it mediocre until it triggered repeated calls for more.

As years went by, an "On the Mall" ritual evolved: The band would play one verse, the crowd would whistle the next.

"On the Mall" was presented only as an encore, however, because Goldman didn't put marches in the regular portion of his program. There he would focus on the likes of Bach and Liszt, to prove that bands could do anything orchestras could do. Those who came to hear "Stars and

Stripes Forever" had to wait for the encore.

Meanwhile, the new medium of radio was spreading Edwin Franko Goldman's musical vision beyond Central Park. WEAF broadcast some of the 1925 concerts to New York, and in November 1926, the Goldman Band was featured on the opening broadcast of the NBC network. For 15 years, national networks carried portions of the summer concerts live.

But for New Yorkers, the way to hear the Goldman Band was to be there: In 1955, total cumulative attendance was estimated at 40 million to 50 million.

BY THEN, Goldman was widely acknowledged as the heir to Sousa, who before his death in 1932 had become a friend as well as an idol. The first time the two met, Goldman hadn't even had the chance to declare his admiration when Sousa said he owed a great debt to Goldman's family, because his first memory of the beauty of serious music was a Franko family concert.

Goldman always took very seriously his role in preserving the band legacy, and by 1955, that was a growing challenge. While Goldman's band thrived, bandstands in many smaller corners of America were falling silent as the citizenry turned to television for its evening entertainment.

After the Aug. 15 finale, then, Goldman set to his off-season routine — lecturing at workshops around the country and composing more marches, this time for the universities of Wisconsin and Iowa.

In all likelihood, he also was making another run at the thorny "Star-Spangled Banner" problem. Over the years, Goldman had tried 15 arrangements of the national anthem and found fault with each. In particular, he was troubled that virtually all arrangements called for a diminuendo just as the song reached "the rockets' red glare, the bombs bursting in air." The 15th arrangement, which he premiered June 17, 1955, involved launching actual fireworks at that juncture in the song.

It was a problem he would not live to resolve. On Nov. 1, he fell ill and underwent an operation, from which he never fully recovered. In January 1956, he conducted a four-day clinic for school bandmasters in Minnesota, after which he returned to New York and was soon taken to Montefiore Hospital, where he died Feb. 21.

Son Richard took over until his own death in 1980, by which time the Goldman Band had become the third oldest professional musical organization in the city, behind only the Philharmonic and the Met. In 1999, it launched its 82nd season.

By JAY MAEDER
Daily News Staff Writer

FIVE THOUSAND PEOPLE couldn't get into Carnegie Hall, and they screamed in rage and crashed through the police cordons and stormed the doors as mounted cops swung their sticks and tried to hold them back. Inside, 3,500 more fought one another for standing room they'd stood in line for 13 hours to buy. Socialites spilled out of their boxes and stood on their seats and swatted off one another's hats. Mobs that had swept in through the fire escapes hung from the rafters. It was Wednesday night the 29th of April 1936, and Toscanini was making his final appearance with the New York Philharmonic-Symphony Orchestra.

The world's greatest living conductor, probably the greatest conductor of all time, certainly the greatest since Wagner, was nearly 70 years old now. He had been waving his baton for 50 years; after 429 concerts with the Philharmonic, it was time to take his last bow and go home to Milan. For his farewell he had chosen a simple program of Wagner and Beethoven. Jascha Heifetz was guest soloist. It was a cataclysmic event. Carnegie Hall was sold out weeks in advance.

At concert's end, amid shouts and whistles, as the audience rushed down the aisles to lay hands on him, frail little Toscanini nodded politely, quickly ducked out and did not reappear to acknowledge the din. He was, at last, gone.

But the world was not going to let such a giant as Toscanini withdraw simply because he was old and tired. At 70, his most magnificent years, nearly 20 more of them, were still ahead of him.

MIRACLE OF THE CANARIES
Toscanini

ARTURO TOSCANINI was a cellist who, at age 19, while touring Brazil with an Italian company, had been suddenly called in to replace an indisposed conductor because he was the only one who knew "Aida" by heart. Thereafter he was a colossus, and he had been the revered leading light at La Scala for years already when he first came to the United States in 1908 to conduct the Metropolitan Opera. A tiny storm of a man, routinely given to cyclonic furies that would leave his musicians trembling and pale, he stormed out of the Metropolitan in a fit of temper seven seasons later and refused even to discuss returning, and back to Milan he went to rejoin La Scala.

Back in New York, meanwhile, the Symphonic Society of New York, founded in 1878 by Leopold Damrosch and thereafter led for decades by his son Walter, was by the 1920s being single-handedly supported by the Standard Oil heir Harry Harkness Flagler. The rival New York Philharmonic Society — America's first symphony orchestra, whose players had doubled as ushers when they played their first concert in December 1842 and who never received salaries until 1909 — also was being kept afloat by patrons. All these deep pockets notwithstanding, it finally seemed wise to merge the two orchestras. It happened that, at exactly this time, Toscanini had fallen into Benito Mussolini's disfavor over his vigorous refusals to include the Fascist anthem in his performances. "While I conduct the Scala orchestra," he thundered, "it will remain the home of opera and never will it become a propaganda platform." So it was that in March 1928 Toscanini accepted the invitation of the reorganized New York Philharmonic-Symphony Orchestra to become its permanent conductor, marking, declared orchestra president Clarence Mackay, "an epoch in musical arts in this country."

It was more than that. In late 1930, William S. Paley, who had recently acquired control of the Columbia Broadcasting System, began broadcasting Carnegie Hall's Sunday afternoon concerts live, and Toscanini soon became a household name in every American hamlet and valley, bringing the masters into the homes of farmers and factory workers, educating the ears of an entire generation. For everyone in the land, the single majestic word — *Tos-ca-NI-ni!* — was itself identifiably synonymous with great music. "Even among the remoter fringes of the unmusical, there is a dim awareness of the momentous nature of these concerts and of what they indicate and signify," observed the New York Herald-Tribune. "Mr. Toscanini has accustomed us to revelations."

At the same time, he emerged as a powerful moral force. Touring Italy in 1931, he was beaten by Mussolini thugs when he once again refused to conduct Fascist hymns. Adolf Hitler barred his music from German radio as early as 1933. Americans admired him profoundly, this ferocious little man who, as it happened, was utterly dictatorial himself: He regularly hurled batons at his musicians, denounced them as beasts and wretches, apoplectically cursed them in three languages. Many times he stopped concerts to turn his wrath on some cougher in the audience. This was just who the man was. Everyone was really quite fond of the terrible-tempered old maestro.

EARLY IN 1937, Toscanini found that he was not going to be permitted to retire in peace. David Sarnoff, president of the Radio Corporation of America and chairman of the National Broadcasting Co., was determined to bring him back to the airwaves — so determined that he offered to create a new orchestra for him, the finest in the world, built to Toscanini's specifications. The maestro wasn't interested, and several times he rebuffed Sarnoff's importunings, but Sarnoff persisted, finally dispatching a man to Italy to appeal to him directly. Again and again, Toscanini said no.

And then Sarnoff's emissary produced a newspaper clipping he had thought to bring along with him. In Ohio, according to this clipping, a family had once been listening to one of Toscanini's radio concerts. In their cages, the family's canaries were listening as well. So enchanted were the birds by the wondrous music, the story went on, that they had all spontaneously burst into Beethoven's Ninth. Think of it, Sarnoff's man pleaded: If even canaries were so touched, think of what miracles the great maestro could work on the human heart if only he would come back again.

And this manifestly ridiculous newspaper story instantly moved Toscanini to tears; yes, he agreed, certainly he would return. All through the year, under Toscanini's imperious direction and at Sarnoff's enormous expense, Artur Rodzinski, late of the Cleveland Symphony, auditioned 700 musicians and assembled 92 of them into the NBC Symphony Orchestra. On Saturday night the 13th of November 1937, under Pierre Montaux, the NBC Symphony made its first broadcast from Studio 8H in Rockefeller Center. At 10 p.m. on Christmas night, as the largest radio audience in history tuned in, Toscanini himself conducted.

He stayed with the NBC Symphony for 17 years, one of radio's most familiar and best-loved figures. In March 1948, the orchestra came to television, and thereafter Toscanini's TV concerts were welcome Sunday evening visitors in America's living rooms.

BUT NOW he truly was an old man, and by 1954 it was evident that he could not keep going. On the 4th of April, the 86-year-old maestro conducted his last concert. No one was told it was a farewell until after he had taken his bows and gone home to his Riverdale mansion. After that, the NBC Symphony Orchestra was disbanded.

He left behind no pupils, no protégés. On New Year's Day 1957 he suffered a stroke. Fifteen days later he died in his sleep.

BIG TOWN ★ BIOGRAPHY

By CHRIS ERIKSON
Special to The News

SOME DINERS no doubt found their waiter disconcerting. Wizened little Hippolyte Havel was a rabid anarchist, and he openly despised the very paying customers he was tending. "Bourgeois pigs!" he often spat at them as he brought out their meals.

But, at Polly's restaurant, most took him in stride. The Greenwich Village of 1913 was command central for the plotting of a political, artistic and sexual revolution, a place where rabble-rousers with a thirst for new ideas and social change were making it their business to shoot down the mores of the age like so many ducks at an arcade.

Polly's was a favored haunt, both because Polly herself was an anarchist, transplanted from Illinois, who offered cheap meals and easy credit, and because her restaurant, at 137 MacDougal St., was next door to the Washington Square Bookshop, an unofficial lending library where one could pick up The Masses, Seven Arts and a dozen other radical periodicals. Upstairs was the Liberal Club, where the leading intellects-about-town gathered to discuss and debate socialism, unionism, feminism, Cubism and other issues.

In the thick of all of it was John Reed — journalist, poet, provocateur, anticapitalist visionary in general, cutting a larger-than-life swath through the stomping grounds of the new bohemians. "The Playboy of Revolution," Upton Sinclair called him; "The Wonder Boy of Greenwich Village," said Van Wyck Brooks. Opinionated, restlessly exuberant, hugely self-confident, Reed seemed to many to embody the spirit of the day. It was a spirit to which he paid homage in his own "The Day in Bohemia," a celebration of Village life:

Yet we are free who live in Washington Square,
We dare to think as Uptown wouldn't dare,
Blazing our nights with arguments uproarious;
What care we for a dull old world censorious
When each is sure he'll fashion something
glorious?

BORN IN OREGON in 1887, John Reed grew up in the lap of the bourgeoisie whose downfall he would later plot. His grandfather was a wealthy businessman; his father was a businessman as well, but a maverick of sorts who tweaked Portland's conservative elite with his embrace of Theodore Roosevelt's reform politics. At Harvard, young Jack developed a distaste for the old-money status quo and became energized by the radical new ideas in poetry, painting and theater.

Bent on literary glory, he headed after graduation for New York, where, in the summer of 1911, he took a job at American magazine and an apartment on Washington Square South.

"Within a block of my house was all the adventure of the world," he wrote. He roamed Chinatown and Little Italy, prowled the wharves and the Syrian quarter, ran with tramps on the Bowery, drank in the dives of the Tenderloin. He claimed to have once spent a night in a basket of

THE FREE OF WASHINGTON SQUARE
John Reed

squid at the Fulton Fish Market. His reputation grew as his magazine articles began appearing in Collier's and The Saturday Evening Post and eventually in The Masses, the premier journal of the radical set, his activist tendencies increasingly aroused by his forays into the city's poverty-stricken underbelly.

What really galvanized him was the 1913 silk workers' strike in Paterson, N.J. It convinced Reed that nothing less than a workers' overthrow of the capitalist system was necessary. It also introduced him to Mabel Dodge.

MABEL DODGE was the bohemian set's grande dame, hostess of weekly "evenings" held at her home at 23 Fifth Ave., freewheeling forums where writers, poets, painters, anarchists, unionists and other intellects gathered to talk, drink and argue. At any given moment one might encounter Masses editor Max Eastman, firebrand Emma Goldman, union leader Big Bill Haywood, muckraker Lincoln Steffens and feminist and free-love advocate Henrietta Rodman. Also generally present were any number of bobbed-haired, cigarette-smoking Village girls willing to put Rodman's ideas into practice.

An heiress from Buffalo, Dodge had grown up with wealth but was afflicted with terminal ennui and a revulsion for the bloodlessness of upper-class life. Married at 21, widowed with a child at 23 and remarried to a wealthy Boston architect who subsequently faded into the woodwork, she had settled in New York after a long spell in Florence and set about making herself the center of the Village's literary and artistic life.

She gave money to radical causes, posted bail for jailed activists, organized art exhibitions. Neither attractive nor well-spoken, vivacious nor witty, her main talent was "collecting people," as one acquaintance put it, "in exactly the same

spirit as she collected china dogs for her mantelpiece." Each Wednesday, she would sit swathed in a long white dress amid bouquets of lilies and welcome guests. She herself had little to say, but somehow, wrote Eastman, she created "a magnetic field in which people become polarized ... their passions become exacerbated."

She met John Reed one night when Big Bill Haywood, leader of the burgeoning Industrial Workers of the World, was bemoaning the plight of the striking Paterson workers: The trouble, he said, was that the newspapers were in the industrialists' pockets and didn't report the workers' oppression. The suggestion was offered that the workers should stage a pageant in New York to dramatize their woes; they could raise both money and awareness.

Reed jumped up, flush with enthusiasm, and volunteered to stage the show. And he did. Driving himself to exhaustion, in the following weeks he produced both "War in Paterson," a milestone of activist journalism that appeared in The Masses, and the pageant itself, where 1,000 strikers marched into Madison Square Garden to sing labor anthems for 15,000 spectators.

At left, with novelist Fannie Hurst and illustrator Boardman Robinson

CULVER PICTURES

It was a smashing success: Audiences wept, drama critics hailed a new art form, Reed was hailed as a genius. Actually, it did little for the workers, who gave up their strike shortly afterward. But it threw Reed and Dodge into the throes of a torrid romance anyway.

THE AFFAIR was the talk of the Village for a time. But while their passions were strong, so were their differences. Reed's hunger to engage the world ate at Dodge, who was rather less driven and wanted only his constant attention. She'd sit unhappily in her boudoir while he prowled through the city; once, when he persuaded her to join him one night, she insisted on traveling by limousine. Once she pretended to faint in the middle of one of his discourses; on another occasion, she took a mild overdose of Veronal. "I can't breathe," he lamented to a friend.

When Metropolitan magazine called with an assignment to cover the peasant uprising in Mexico, he jumped at the chance — and left Dodge, and New York, behind.

REED'S DISPATCHES from Mexico, where he rode with Pancho Villa, established him as one of the nation's great war correspondents. He next reported from the front lines of the European War, ruffling feathers with his insistence that it was an immoral squabble over economics. His crowning achievement was "Ten Days That Shook the World," his firsthand account of the Russian Revolution. Written in a feverish burst in an apartment on W. Fourth St., the book was a sensation, and it made Reed a hero in Russia.

That is where he died, in October 1920, at 33, of typhus, after factional infighting drove him from his efforts to build an American Communist Party. He was buried beneath the Kremlin Wall.

AS FOR DODGE, her salon fell apart with the coming of the war. So did the Village bohemians' visions of a new society. She gave up New York for New Mexico, settled in Taos, founded an art colony, married a Pueblo Indian chief and, until her death in 1962, remained "in tune with all outdoors," she happily burbled, "real at last."

By TOM ROBBINS
Daily News Staff Writer

EVEN AS A young Jewish Bundist locked in a czarist dungeon, Sidney Hillman was never one to waste an opportunity. Tossed twice into Russian prisons for his revolutionary carryings-on, young Sidney turned jail into an academy for radicalism, where he studied the classics: Marx, Kropotkin, LaSalle.

Decades later and an ocean away, critics would have pounced on that jailhouse reading list with glee, taking it as confirmation for the torrents of Red-baiting abuse they showered on Sidney Hillman after he had become one of America's most powerful labor leaders with the closest of ties to the White House.

Even without it, Sidney Hillman was typecast for shrill, right-wing brickbats. He was short, voluble, intense, with thick wire-rim glasses, carefully combed, wavy hair and a heavy Yiddish accent. And very driven. Four years after he arrived in the U.S. as a $6-a-week pants presser in 1906, he led a walkout of 50,000 clothing workers in Chicago; four years later, in New York, he formed the Amalgamated Clothing Workers of America.

Unlike his labor colleagues, such as burly mineworkers chief John Lewis, who thundered hellfire and brimstone at the capitalist bosses, Hillman was soft-spoken and unemotional.

Somehow that made Hillman even scarier to his foes. He was as practical as he was radical, as much pragmatist as socialist, willing to ally himself with gangsters, communists and even titans of capital if it helped him achieve his goals. His contracts were the first to contain the concept that shop floor disputes be submitted to arbitration, allowing cooler heads to decide and avoiding the wildcat walkouts that often erupted.

While real Reds demanded revolution, Hillman's message in the midst of Depression unemployment was simple: "Security," he argued, "is what workers want most of all."

The job of organized labor, he said, was not just to enrich its members, but to make them full partners in their communities, on and off the shop floor. And he had looked in the mirror and seen just the man for the job.

HE WAS SUPPOSED to have been a rabbi. Born March 23, 1887, in Zagare, Lithuania, a land of poor Jewish *shtetls* under constant threat of bloody pogroms, he was expected to follow in the footsteps of a famous grandfather, and by age 8 he was memorizing entire pages of Talmudic text.

But, swept up in revolutionary fervor, he joined the Bund, the Jewish socialist organization. In 1904 he was arrested at a demonstration for 10-hour work days and imprisoned for eight months, threatened with execution or exile. Released, he jumped into the doomed 1905 revolution, only to be arrested again and spend four more months in prison. Using a forged passport, he fled Russia in 1906.

He was working in Chicago as an apprentice tailor at Hart, Schaffner & Marx, the largest men's clothier in the country, when employer wage-cutting moves set off a citywide garment workers' strike. The workers were disorganized; the strike was marked by bloody clashes with police. In stepped 18-year-old Sidney Hillman, who put to use lessons learned in Russia and his own developing sense of strategy, and the strike ended in victory for the workers, as Hillman pioneered a new kind of contract that called for mediation and arbitration of disputes and regular wage increases.

His success was such that New York City labor organizers recruited him to organize the long-fractured men's garment trades into what would become the Amalgamated Clothing Workers.

He stepped carefully in New York's garment jungle, where sweatshop conditions predominated and where the 1911 fire deaths of

CONSTRUCTIVE COOPERATION
Sidney Hillman

With John L. Lewis (left), 1940

146 Triangle Shirtwaist workers — whose employers had locked the exits against union organizers — was a steady organizing incentive. He waged militant strikes against recalcitrant larger employers to set the scale for wages and hours. He also offered loans to owners who needed cash to keep them afloat.

Hillman called it "constructive cooperation." His contracts included an unheard-of benefit, unemployment insurance, to cushion members against layoffs. He had his union open its own banks to offer home and auto loans at reasonable rates to members. Then he used the banks to build workers' housing, cooperative garden apartment complexes that freed members from tenement blight.

Hailed as the first labor statesman, Hillman was still nothing if not practical. He initially turned a blind eye to the gangsters who were recruited as sluggers by some union locals to give them an extra edge on the picket line. "If I need the bar that is rusted, I'll use it," he said.

But at one point in the late 1920s, when the problem grew embarrassing, he stunned the biggest garment gangster of all, Louis (Lepke) Buchalter, by calling a one-day general strike against Buchalter shops. Briefly, Hillman found it necessary to go into hiding after Amalgamated Clothing Workers organizers in several cities were shot dead.

ALONG WITH LEWIS, Hillman in 1935 founded the upstart Congress of Industrial Organizations, which briskly began shaking up the old pie-card craft union leaders in the American Federation of Labor with sit-down strikes and mass picketing and organizing successes in auto and steel.

Along the way, he became confidant and adviser to a millionaire from New York, President Franklin Roosevelt, who called on Hillman to help shape employment programs and to serve as labor's point man in the tricky business of getting management and unions to work for a wartime economy.

In his last campaign, in 1944, Roosevelt was reported to have told an aide to "clear it with

Sidney" when the name of a potential vice presidential candidate surfaced.

Republican candidate Thomas Dewey and a Republican chorus jumped on this. Just like we always told you, they thundered: Moscow-loving Sidney Hillman and his pinko pals were the ones really calling the shots. The GOP mounted billboards with the slogan: "It's YOUR country — why let Sidney Hillman run it?"

The punch never connected, however. FDR trounced Dewey with key help from another Hillman innovation, the political-action committee. The PAC, Hillman said, as he unveiled it at a CIO meeting in 1943, would counter employers' campaign contributions with the bundled nickels and dimes of working families.

Alarmed Republicans denounced the PAC as another Red threat and said the idea violated the Corrupt Practices Act and several other federal laws. But Hillman's committee survived repeated investigations, and a few years later the Republicans and everyone else decided that PACs were useful at that.

"It was a great campaign, and nobody knows better than I how much you contributed to its success," FDR wrote Hillman.

ROOSEVELT WAS DEAD a year later, along with the national sense of common cause with Soviet Russia against the fascist foe after the end of the war. Left-leaning labor leaders with thick Jewish accents were bigger targets than ever. Hillman was still trying to adjust to the new postwar politics when he was stricken by a fatal heart attack at his family's summer bungalow at Point Lookout, L.I., on July 10, 1946. He was 59.

They laid him out in a bronze coffin blanketed with red roses in Carnegie Hall, where 3,000 people — with another 20,000 in the streets outside — heard Rabbi Stephen Wise. "His was a feeling of utmost responsibility for democracy in the full meaning of the term," the rabbi said.

The men's garment industry shut down for the day, and a 250-car funeral cortege drove down Seventh Ave., through the garment center, past a picket line at R.H. Macy & Co., then past Hillman's old office on Union Square. A few months after his death, a probate report found that Hillman had left little cash for his wife and two daughters. But he had provided for them wisely with $60,000 in insurance.

By BILL BELL
Daily News Staff Writer

BY ALL MATERIAL measure of the times, when bootleggers, plutocrats and radio stars ruled, a Catholic priest in Times Square should have lived and died with no more attention than that normally paid to a decent man's good deeds and lamented demise.

But the Rev. Francis Patrick Duffy — Fighting Father Duffy — was not just another good man in a clerical collar.

He was pastor of the Church of the Holy Cross on W. 42nd St., but he was also a battlefield legend, an Army chaplain who followed New York's famed 69th Regiment into war, a manly priest with an earthy manner that disarmed bishops and bums alike. New York City remembers him today with a small bronze plaque outside his church's entrance and with a tiny, three-sided concrete sliver called Father Duffy Square, where stands a larger-than-life statue that no longer commands much attention in the noisy bustle at Broadway and 47th St.

The words engraved on the tall Celtic cross note that Father Duffy was a lieutenant colonel, that he was born on May 2, 1871, that he died on June 26, 1932, that the U.S. awarded him a Distinguished Service Cross, that France gave him its Legion of Honor. *A Life of Service for God and Country,* the words say.

DUFFY, CANADIAN by birth, moved to New York at 22 to teach at St. Francis Xavier College. Soon he quit to enter the Catholic seminary in upstate Troy. He was ordained in 1896 and, because he was bright and likeable, he was assigned by his superiors to Catholic University for more graduate study. Two years later, he was sent to Dunwoodie, the seminary in Yonkers for priest candidates for the Archdiocese of New York, to teach psychology and logic.

Duffy combined teaching and journalism — he edited the New York Review for three years — until he was sent to the Bronx in 1912 to develop a new parish in what became the Belmont section. In his four years there, he built the Church of Our Saviour, which is still in business.

By then, he had also become chaplain for the 69th, a New York National Guard unit with a grand history.

The 69th had been organized in 1851 with volunteers, most of

them Irish, from all over the city. It got its "Fighting 69th" nickname from Gen. Robert E. Lee himself, following brave and bloody service at Gettysburg, where 988 of its men lost their lives.

The regiment later became part of the 165th Infantry, with a new designation — the 42nd Division, popularly called the Rainbow Division because of the colors of the flags of the 25 states represented in its ranks. But it forever remained the 69th to New Yorkers.

When the United States entered World War I in 1917, the 165th went to France. There, Father Duffy went into the history books.

HE WAS 46, an elderly man by warrior norms, when he saw his first combat on July 5, 1918. But nobody talked about his age when they told the tales.

He was on every battlefield, during 180 days of combat that killed 900 men, and after every battle he walked the fields, collecting metal identification tags of the dead, hearing the last words of the dying, absolving not only Catholics of sins and then helping to bury the fallen.

Once, bending over a dead soldier, he burst into

tears. An officer, Col. John Mangan, asked why. "I baptized him as a baby," Duffy said.

The biggest battle was the one at the Oureq River, which most guys in the 69th called the O'Rourke. It was there that the division's most famous member, poet Joyce Kilmer, who wrote "Trees," was killed in action.

And it was there that Duffy was so conspicuously gallant under fire that Gen. Douglas MacArthur considered promoting the chaplain to colonel and placing him in command of the division — an extraordinary idea.

It was there, too, that Duffy was decorated. "Despite constant and severe bombardment with shells and aerial bombs," his citation read, "he continued to circulate in and about two aid stations and hospitals, creating an atmosphere of cheerfulness and confidence by his courageous and inspiring example."

He was proposed for the Medal of Honor, the nation's highest award for bravery. But he dismissed the notion. "To win the Medal of Honor, a man must be an idiot," he said. "And generally dead."

The 165th returned to New York in the spring of 1919 to a rousing parade along Fifth Ave. A few months later, Duffy became pastor of the Times Square parish of Holy Cross. There he became friends with every Broadway notable from Gene Tunney to George M. Cohan.

Just before Christmas 1920, Duffy appeared in a Manhattan courtroom to plead for leniency for a 69th soldier, one Tom Mooney, who had been charged with using drugs. Mooney had been seriously wounded in combat in France, and it was Duffy who found him in a foxhole, administered first aid and took him to a hospital. During the two years it took Mooney to recover, he became addicted to painkilling cocaine. "Don't send this boy to jail," Duffy said. "Give him a chance to become a man again."

The judge freed Mooney. "If I've helped anyone become a better man and he loves me for it," the priest would say, "that's my Distinguished Service Cross."

He told everyone he would never leave Holy Cross. "I am the irremovable rector of this church," he would declare, "and they can't get me out unless they carry me out."

And that's what happened.

EARLY IN June 1932, he was admitted to St. Vincent's Medical Center for treatment of a liver infection. Nine days later, he was slipping away. His brother and sister, three priests and Col. Alex Anderson of the Fighting 69th went to his bedside.

As word of his death spread, thousands went to Holy Cross. Protestants joined Catholics in prayer on the church steps. More than 20,000 New Yorkers filed past the coffin to pay their last respects.

A military chaplain for 18 years, Father Duffy got a military funeral. The flag-draped coffin was placed on an artillery caisson, which rolled slowly along the route from Holy Cross to St. Patrick's, and behind the two-wheeled ammunition wagon marched every able-bodied member of the 165th Infantry, with Fighting 69th banners flying. Along the route, more than 50,000 stood in silence, many dropping to their knees on the sidewalk to pray.

After the service, Duffy was taken to the family plot in St. Raymond's Cemetery, in the Bronx, and interred beneath a tall cross with a grapevine motif and the simple words "Father Duffy."

His Times Square statue was unveiled in 1937.

By then, Holy Cross had a most suitable successor to Father Duffy.

He was the Rev. Joseph McCaffery, a one-time Fordham University football and track star and a decorated chaplain for the 9th Infantry Division in World War I. A few weeks after Duffy's funeral, McCaffery agreed to assume one more office — chaplain of the Fighting 69th.

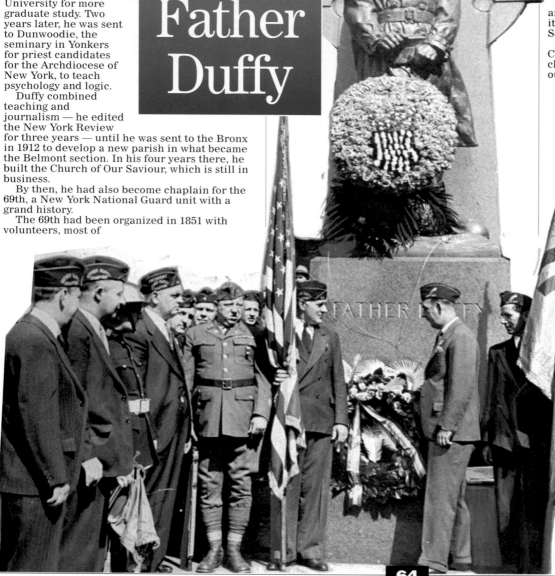

GOD AND COUNTRY
Father Duffy

By KIERAN O'LEARY
Daily News Staff Writer

ON A BITTER winter's night in 1899, the firefighters of Engine Co. 31 in lower Manhattan rushed to a blazing warehouse on West St. The fire had started in the cellar, and the Red Devil was in full fury. Led by their commanding officer, Capt. Joseph Martin, the firemen descended into hell.

Facing heavy smoke and roaring flames, they retreated, then mounted a second assault. The blaze quickly went to three alarms. Exhausted, gasping for air, man after man was driven from the unendurable basement. Thirty of them collapsed and had to be carried out.

Chief Edward F. Croker arrived to take command and ordered a head count. One man — Capt. Martin — was missing.

The firemen plunged back in, desperate to find him, fearing the worst. The conditions remained brutal and Croker ordered everyone out. Then he went back in alone.

Crawling on his hands and knees, he found Martin with a line of hose, wedged between two crates of furniture, fighting the fire by himself, barely conscious. Croker grabbed his collar and hauled him to the street.

Newspapermen crowded around. "Gentlemen," announced Croker, "this is Smoky Joe Martin, and he certainly does love it."

The reporters loved it, too. The next day's papers trumpeted the tale of the newly nicknamed hero. A New York City legend was born.

JOE MARTIN'S love affair with the Fire Department began when he was a boy. His home on E. 13th St., in the old Gashouse District, was back-to-back with Engine Co. 5 on 14th St., and he regularly ran errands for his fireman pals, and when the bells sounded and the horse-drawn wagons clattered out into the cobblestone streets, young Joe was usually running right behind, and he would watch with awe as the brave firefighters battled the lower East Side infernos and spread out nets to catch people leaping from upper floors. At 18, he tried for a time to work as a clerk, but such a life was just too boring. In January 1884, at age 22, freshly appointed fireman Joseph B. Martin reported for duty at Engine Co. 27 on Franklin St., earning $66 a month.

Promotions came quickly — to lieutenant in 1889, captain in 1893, battalion chief in 1900, deputy chief in 1907 and, in 1910, assistant chief, the department's second in command.

To many, it was a miracle that Martin had lived to make the climb up the career ladder at all. Fearless and stubborn in the face of danger, he had suffered many broken bones and serious burns on many occasions. He was on the job for 46 years, and over those years he was hauled away from fires in ambulances nearly two dozen times.

Told in 1898 that a watchman was trapped inside a burning warehouse on Walker St., he and several comrades rushed in, climbed through licking flames to the fourth floor, kicked through a door and found themselves in a room whose floor already was burning through. "That floor won't hold you, Cap," a fireman warned. But Martin went in anyway.

And indeed it did not hold, and neither did the ones below it. Martin plunged in an avalanche of burning debris 65 feet to the basement floor. There was barely a flicker of life in his broken body as he was carried away to the Hudson Street Hospital, still clutching a piece of a brass lamp he had grabbed when the floor beneath him gave way.

He came to the next day. "When can I go back to work?" he inquired. The answer was four months later.

AS ASSISTANT CHIEF, Smoky Joe was a fixture at most every big fire the city ever saw. With his aide, Daredevil Dan Healy, at the wheel, his red car showed up everywhere — at the four-day Standard Oil depot blaze in Greenpoint in September 1919, at the enormous "Greenwich Village Volcano" at Jane and W. 12th Sts. in July 1922. Two firemen died in that explosive warehouse fire, and Martin himself collapsed at the scene after working several days without sleep. A department doctor ordered him home, but Smoky Joe would have none of that. Laid out on a cot at the window of a nearby building, he continued to bark out orders, then arose and charged up to the roof to join his men again.

But the fact was that in 1922, Smoky Joe was 60 years old, and modern times were arriving. In December of that year, the City of New York retired its last remaining horse-drawn fire wagon. It fell to Martin to ceremoniously send out the alarm from Brooklyn Borough Hall and call out an Engine 205 steamer pulled by faithful Penrose, Smuggler and Bal Griffin on its last run. Then the horses, the last of their breed, were put out to pasture. Certainly Smoky Joe Martin would not be far behind them.

BY 1925, young turks in the Department were tired of waiting for its grizzled veterans to step aside. Chief John Kenlon was a 38-year man, and Joe Martin had 41 years in. A group of aldermen proposed a bill that would force Kenlon, Martin and three dozen other officers to retire. The older men survived this effort to turn them out — but the handwriting was plainly on the wall.

Smoky Joe's day of reckoning came on April 14, 1930. Fighting a midtown blaze, he suffered a heart attack. Priests from nearby St. Stephen's Church gave him the last rites, and he was carried home, presumably to die.

But he rallied again. "I hadn't changed from my winter woolens," he explained. "It was the sudden change in the weather. I wasn't dressed for it." He spent the spring and summer recuperating, then sought to return to duty, insisting he was fine.

Dr. Joseph Smith, the Department's chief medical officer, disagreed. On Oct. 2, Smith ordered Assistant Chief of Department Joseph Martin to retire, declaring him "unfit for duty."

The words hurt him more than anything the Red Devil ever had dished out. Like the old firehorses he'd loved, Smoky Joe was through.

LAST OF THE BREED

Smoky Joe Martin

'HE HAS watched the fine, big, intelligent, glossy horses, pets of the engine houses, depart one by one, to be replaced by the flashing, roaring motors," wrote the New York Sun. "He has seen the simple, crude old equipment replaced by the complicated and highly technical modern apparatus of the finest fire department in the world — bar none. He has seen the department made over and for that matter has watched all New York made over — watched it grow from a squat town of brownstone and red brick to the incredible dream city of leaping towers whose pinnacles catch the sunlight a thousand feet above the streets.

"Nobody in all New York is more typical of the town than this wise, brave, grizzled warrior with the fighting heart."

Smoky Joe's fighting heart gave out for good on Oct. 25, 1941.

By MARA BOVSUN

Special to The News

WHEN HE FOUND her, she was a snooty little gossip, forever peering through her lorgnette and tittering at jokes few could appreciate.

He dressed her in exquisite and daring new clothes, put bons mots in her mouth, introduced her to all the right people. Before long, she was an international sensation, the world's impossible dream of beauty.

She was Vogue.

He was Condé Nast, a shy, flute-playing young man from Missouri, whose pince-nez glasses made him look like an owl and whose bearing was so formal that even one of his lovers joked that he always "stood as if encased in a plaster cast from chin to toe."

But he had two things Vogue needed — ambition and a genius for selling magazines.

Starting as a $12-a-week adman, Condé Nast built a publishing empire on the notion that a magazine didn't have to have a mass audience so long as it had a class audience. Vogue was the center of that empire.

"For a generation, he was the man from whom millions of American women got most of their ideas, directly or indirectly, about the desirable American standard of living," Time magazine said on his death at age 69 in 1942.

With his carefully chosen stable of editors, Nast filled the pages of his magazines with images and articles showing women how to achieve the indefinable — style.

He turned fashion photography into an art and revolutionized magazine printing, building his own plant in Greenwich, Conn., when he decided commercial printers just weren't good enough to lay hands on Vogue.

And the man one friend described as personally having "all the vivacity of a stuffed moosehead" is credited with the birth of the ultimate in champagne-frothy nightlife — cafe society.

This happened on the night of Jan. 18, 1925, when he had a few friends in at his new 30-room duplex penthouse at 1040 Park Ave.

"A pageant of the New York theatrical and literary world," The New Yorker pronounced the event. The apartment had been arranged so hundreds could be entertained at separate dinner parties inside and at dances on the roof. Nast's dizzying kaleidoscope of Jazz Age fantasies would continue through the Depression; here did he mix the classes, the American aristocracy with politicians, theater and movie stars — George Gershwin, Josephine Baker, Groucho Marx, Mrs. Astor, F. Scott Fitzgerald. Guests were carefully categorized. Nast's secretaries knew full well which couples could not be at the same table or even in the same room.

The meticulous attention to detail was Nast's trademark, and it made him.

BORN IN New York on March 26, 1873, Condé Nast and his brother and two sisters grew up in St. Louis at the home of their maternal grandparents. It was at Georgetown University that he discovered his true calling: managing and publicizing the baseball and tennis teams, he brought fame to the school's athletics. Chum Robert J. Collier, son of New York publisher P.F. Collier, was impressed. When Nast finished law school in St. Louis, young Collier jumped in with a job offer: advertising manager at Collier's Weekly, a little offshoot of his father's burgeoning book business.

The magazine was faltering, with an ad income of about $5,600. Nast came on in 1900; in less than a decade he was bringing in ad revenues of more than $1 million, and he was earning the eye-popping salary of $50,000.

So he decided to quit.

Collier pleaded with him: "Nobody else is going to pay you that much money." Nast agreed that the money would be hard to match. But he was dead set on leaving anyway.

In 1909, with his Collier's savings and funds from his on-the-side dress pattern publishing business, the Home Pattern Co., Condé Nast bought Vogue.

AT THE TIME, the magazine was a fading weekly that catered to the upper crust. Born in 1892 and backed by a long list of Social Register types — Astors, Whitneys, Vanderbilts, Fishes — Vogue recorded who did what on whose yachts, Newport comings and goings, assorted passions and pastimes and the peculiar humor of Gilded Age high hats ("Now that the masses take baths every week, how can one ever distinguish the gentleman?"). A column called The Well Dressed Man tutored society swells on such matters as whether a tuxedo should be worn at dinner in a private residence (no, never). Another column, As Seen By Him, followed a socialite named Him through endless rounds of balls, teas, weddings and bridge games.

Editor Arthur Turnure went home ill one day in 1906 and was dead of pneumonia 48 hours later. Circulation and advertising revenues thereafter fell, and Vogue was foundering when 36-year-old Condé Nast came along.

HIS NAME first appeared on the old weekly's masthead on June 24, 1909, but for months that was the only sign he was there, as otherwise he cloistered himself in an office and planned Vogue's makeover. Nast had no interest in the common wisdom that a magazine should have a broad appeal. "If you had a tray with 2 million needles on it and only 150,000 of these had gold tips which you wanted, it would be an endless and costly process to weed them out," he reasoned. "But if you could get a magnet that would draw out only the gold ones, what a savings."

The new Vogue debuted in February 1910, suddenly a plump and lovely fortnightly packed with "notes of fashion, society, music, art, books and drama." The shift in emphasis was subtle — from fashionable magazine to magazine of fashion — but the gold-tipped-needle formula worked, and Nast was soon luring advertisers with his promise of entry into the exclusive club of his readership.

Nast biographer Caroline Seebohm reports that in 1910 Vogue had a circulation of just 30,000, compared with the Ladies' Home Journal's 1.3 million. But Vogue had 44% more advertising.

Meanwhile, what would soon become Vogue's arch rival, Harper's Bazar — the word did not become Bazaar until the 1920s — had a circulation five times Vogue's. But Vogue had three times the advertising pages.

On top of that, the price of advertising in Vogue was steep, with rates three to five times higher than that for other magazines. Yet Vogue would remain the ad leader in women's magazines for the rest of Nast's life.

With his golden flagship in full sail, Condé Nast was ready to build an armada.

COURTESY CONDE NAST PUBLICATIONS

GOLDEN NEEDLES
Condé Nast
PART ONE OF TWO

By MARA BOVSUN
Special to The News

MARCH 1936 WAS a cruel month for gentlemen of culture. It was then they discovered that their favorite urbane man about town, Vanity Fair magazine, had turned, almost overnight, into a girl — a bewitching rich girl, to be sure, dripping with diamonds, draped in furs and velvets, but a girl nevertheless.

The story went that there was turmoil in one exclusive men's club shortly after Vogue magazine swallowed her little brother. An elderly member had gone into a tizzy searching the library for Vanity Fair and had demanded assistance from an attendant. "Why, that's — that's a female magazine now, sir," the attendant explained. "We just throw it away as soon as it comes in."

In some ways, it was a fitting end. Publisher Condé Nast had started Vanity Fair in the first place to eliminate competition to Vogue from an impudent little fashion rag called Dress.

Nast's Vogue was the American symbol of chic, and Nast himself was already a legend. But he was always looking for new magnets for the gold-tipped needles, his metaphor for people who could appreciate — more important, could afford — the finer things in life.

He bought out the upstart Dress, intending to remake it into an arts journal. But somehow the name didn't fit. So in 1915 he paid $3,000 for a publication — described as a sort of "refined Police Gazette" — that had gone belly-up years earlier. He wanted only its name: Vanity Fair.

Nast struggled with his new magazine, filling it with stories provided by Vogue contributors. But the formula wasn't right. For advice, he turned to Frank Crowninshield, gentleman of letters and man about town. Crowninshield made assessments and quickly set the tone for what would become the most sophisticated magazine of its age, perhaps of any age.

"There is no magazine," he said, "that is read by the people you meet at lunches and dinners."

CROWNINSHIELD WAS hired on the spot, and, from the first, Vanity Fair not only appealed to intellectuals but also reflected the new mood of modern America — "increased devotion to pleasure," as he put it, "to happiness, to dancing, to sport, to the delights of the country, to laughter and to all forms of cheerfulness."

One of his early moves was to grab a young Vogue editor, an acid-tongued woman named Dorothy Parker. Next, he brought in a drama critic, Robert Emmet Sherwood. In 1919, he hired newspaperman Robert Benchley as managing editor.

Their time at the magazine was a thunderstorm — loud and short. For starters, they all openly sneered at the formality of the magazine's headquarters, which had been decorated by none other than their employer's wife. And then Parker wrote a theater review panning actress Billie Burke, who happened to be married to impresario Florenz Ziegfeld, who loudly complained to his

Left, with Vogue's Edna Woolman Chase and Vanity Fair's Frank Crowninshield

COURTESY CONDE NAST PUBLICATIONS

good friends Nast and Crowninshield. Publisher and editor, The New Yorker reported, together concluded that Parker, "although wildly entertaining, lacked a certain balance." She was fired. And Benchley and Sherwood immediately resigned in protest.

There was no notable dampening of the magazine's editorial verve. Crowninshield brought in crowds of his own many friends: Tallulah Bankhead, F. Scott Fitzgerald, Aldous Huxley, Noel Coward, T.S. Eliot, e.e cummings, P.G. Wodehouse. The tone became that of the

GOLDEN NEEDLES
Condé Nast
PART TWO OF TWO

wildly irreverent intellectual; a founder of the Museum of Modern Art, Crowninshield also raised eyebrows with his taste in painting and sculpture, giving many Americans their first glimpse of artistic revolutionaries. This annoyed the advertising department and terrified the proper Nast. "We were 10 years early in talking about van Gogh, Gauguin, Matisse, Picasso, etc.," Nast wrote later.

With Crowninshield always at his side, tutoring him in the finer points of culture, Condé Nast and his empire roared on into the Roaring Twenties.

Besides Vanity Fair and Vogue, and Vogue's British and French editions, Nast had also acquired House & Garden and The American Golfer. He had a penthouse, a country house, real estate holdings that included a controlling interest in the company that owned the Grand Central Palace — and his endless high-society parties.

Like the rest of the nation in the drunken last years of the '20s, he thought it would all last forever.

IN A WILD move that was uncharacteristic of him, he took a dive into the stock market. In 1927, on the urging of financial experts he knew socially, he took his company public. Then he personally borrowed $2 million to buy into Goldman Sachs Trading Corp.

"Why don't you get out of the market now?" Vogue editor Edna Woolman Chase suggested in the summer of 1929.

"I'm getting expert advice, my dear," Nast replied. "Bankers know about these things."

When the market crashed in October, he was wiped out.

CONTROL OF his magazines went to the bankers. Even his staff seemed to turn on him: one of his prize editorial princesses, Vogue-trained Carmel Snow, was stolen away by Vogue's despised Hearst rival, Harper's Bazaar, in 1932.

His fortune gone, his company in deep trouble, Nast struggled to keep going by borrowing more and more. None of his troubles stopped him from continuing to throw his gala penthouse parties; he thought nothing of ordering hundreds of gardenias to be placed one by one in flower boxes.

The parties, recalled one Vanity Fair editor, Helen Lawrenson, were "ludicrously out of tune with the era, which was that of the Depression."

Vanity Fair, too, had lost touch with the times. A perfect reflection of the surreal giddiness of the '20s, it was now falling behind the newly launched Esquire, and it was losing money.

And in March 1936, it disappeared. In its place was the beauty queen — "Vogue, Incorporating Vanity Fair."

CONDÉ NAST worked seven days a week in a desperate attempt to win back what he had lost. He got sick instead. Eventually, he had to keep an oxygen tank in his office, and staff meetings were often cut short when Nast's face would suddenly drain of color and secretaries would rush to his side.

He died on Sept. 19, 1942, leaving behind heavy business and personal debts. Vogue lived on — indeed, Edna Woolman Chase remained in charge until 1952, when, 75 years old, she retired after 38 years in her editor's chair — and so did some of the other magazines, including Glamour, added in 1939.

By 1959, Condé Nast's company was flush and fetching enough to attract a suitor, S.I. Newhouse. The new owner kept the founder's name at the top of the masthead.

By JAY MAEDER
Daily News Staff Writer

EVENTUALLY the managing editor of the fledgling New York City tabloid newspaper called the Daily News was persuaded that his enterprising proposal to kidnap a man he believed to be a murderer and drive him out to a country graveyard where reporters dressed as ghosts would jump up and rattle some chains and entreat him to come clean was basically not a great idea. For one thing, it was winter. The reporters were all going to freeze to death. Well, right, Phil Payne had to agree. So now he had to think of something else to wring a confession out of Jimmy Mills.

Okay, then, they would rent a railroad flat and turn it into a spiritualist's den, fill it full of gilt and incense and owls and snakes and crystal balls and all kinds of abracadabra. And reporter Bernadine Szold would dress up as a seer called Madame Astra and hold a séance, and Julia Harpman would go out to Jersey and sweet-talk Jimmy Mills into attending this soiree, and when Jimmy came in everybody would jabber and howl and wail, and Phil Payne and a couple of detectives would sit behind the mystical purple curtain and record Jimmy's terrified blurtings. This way they'd get the goods on Jimmy and still they'd all be indoors and nobody would freeze.

And everything went fine except that Jimmy, an unexcitable sort, didn't confess at all. So then Phil Payne dressed up Bernadine's husband Otto in a turban and harem pants and satin slippers and sent him out to knock on Jimmy's door, and Otto was supposed to scream: *You bad man! Spirits very angry!* and of course Jimmy would then blab out everything. Unfortunately, what happened here was that Jimmy put up his dukes instead and chased Otto away, so this didn't work out either.

So it was that, late in 1922, Phil Payne of the News did not exactly solve the great Hall-Mills murder case.

THERE WAS actually a quietly respectable side to Philip A. Payne. In civilian life in West New York, N.J., he was a family man who sat on the local Board of Education and helped build community libraries. Otherwise, he was a maniac, a crazed newspaper mongrel who ran gleefully amok in New York City through the rip-roaring 1920s and presided over most of the day's finest tabloid astonishers. It was Payne who first put Captain Joseph Patterson's infant News on the map; it was Payne who thereafter made William Randolph Hearst's Daily Mirror a serious rival. Whatever tabloid newspapering became in New York, for better or for worse, Phil Payne was as much the reason for it as anyone.

He had come to the News from New Jersey's Hudson Dispatch in July 1919, when Patterson's little rag was just a month old and selling barely 10,000 copies a day, 18th in a field of 18 metropolitan sheets dominated by Hearst's monarch American. Suddenly, by December, as New Yorkers discovered a paper they could read

while they were hanging from a subway strap, News circulation hit 100,000; two months later it was 200,000; by September 1920 it was 300,000; by September 1922, when the boy-wonder Payne moved up from city editor to managing editor at age 29, the 600,000-circ News was the nation's third largest daily, behind only the Chicago Tribune and the Boston Post.

Payne had presided over this entire incredible explosion, specializing in murders, society divorces and social exposés: He put an undercover reporter into the state reform school for girls and got a whopping snake-pit yarn that led to a major legislative probe; he stirred up popular fury against a rich man who had killed a poor man and got him indicted; he campaigned for the soldiers' bonus; he got several dozen city schools built in a noisy crusade against classroom overcrowding. He invented the Broadway column and hired Mark Hellinger to write it. He hired Jimmy Jemail, the News' famous original "Inquiring Photographer." He hired Julia Harpman, the first of the city's tough tabloid broads, front-page women who would sob-sister you one minute and then kill you the next. By May 1925, when the News' daily circ was 900,000 and its Sunday circ was 1.1 million, and the Mail and the Telegraph had folded, and the ancient Herald and the ancient Tribune had unthinkably been forced to merge, W.R. Hearst had every good reason to hire Payne away from Patterson and put him in charge of the volcanic new Daily Mirror.

Here now was tabloid war, as Payne took up arms against his former employer. Payne's flashy, coarse and thoroughly wonderful Mirror never came close to overtaking the News — few advertisers ever cared to dirty their hands on the thing, and even Hearst himself seemed embarrassed by it — but it was an enormous popular hit nonetheless. It was true that nobody ever mistook the News and the Mirror and the city's third tab, physical-fitness king Bernarr Macfadden's unbelievably slutty Evening Graphic, for high literature. Still, it was the middle of Prohibition, gangsters were shooting up

the whole town, exquisite scandals were breaking every day — for two or three cents, what wasn't to love?

Ever in search of headlines, the Mirror boss presently had an inspired idea: He would resurrect the old Hall-Mills killing, and this time he would solve it.

THE REV. Edward Hall, good rector of the Church of St. John the Evangelist in New Brunswick, N.J., had been found brutally slain with his choir-singer paramour Mrs. Eleanor Mills alongside a pastoral country road. This was plainly a crime of passion, and Payne figured now that the guilty party had to be the late reverend's widow, Mrs. Frances Hall. For weeks and weeks, Mirror reporters dug up all the old ghosts; headlines blared every day; finally the governor of New Jersey appointed a special prosecutor to reopen the case, and in July 1926 Mrs. Hall was charged with the murders.

Not since Harry Thaw killed Stanford White had there been such a daily courtroom sensation in the New York papers, and Payne's Mirror was right in the heart of it; it was clear to some that Mrs. Hall's ordeal was nothing but a newspaper circulation ploy. "That Mephistopheles!" the widow's lawyer screamed at Payne in court. "Four years after the murder! He and his army of reporters and photographers come marching up to this woman's home, surround her home, hiding behind trees! Then some state trooper thumps on the door and cries I arrest you for the murder of your husband four years ago! Oh yes, we'll take you to jail and we'll have you locked up! And we'll have Payne's photographers snap you while you go in! My God! What cute newspaper stuff!" Early in December, amid a furious national debate over press ethics, Widow Hall was acquitted, and even the prosecutor registered his disgust with Payne. "No newspaper should undertake to do what this sheet they call the Mirror has undertaken to do," he snapped. "To be grand jury to indict, prosecutor to prosecute, judge to sit and jury to convict."

It was true that Payne had been carried away once or twice. Sometimes the Mirror's front page had blazed with Biblical quotations such as **YOUR SIN WILL FIND YOU OUT,** and even the News and the Graphic thought this was maybe a little much. Payne was abashed only slightly by the episode, although his situation became admittedly more difficult when Mrs. Hall sued the Mirror for libel in March 1927, seeking $1.5 million for having "wickedly, maliciously, recklessly and wrongfully" ruined her life.

B Y NOW, though, there was other big news to think about. Men were undertaking to fly across the Atlantic Ocean.

DAILY MIRROR

OLD GLORY AT SEA
"Going 100 Miles an Hour; All Well," Her Own Radio

OLD GLORY ROARS TOWARD ROME AT 100 MILES AN HOUR—ALL O. K. ABOARD

CRACK AIR MAIL PILOTS WHO ARE GUIDING OLD GLORY TO ROME

2 Dead, 2 Dying in Law Office Fight

DAILY MIRROR

OLD GLORY'S HOPE
Plane Has Every Safety Device; 'Believe Her Still Up'—Densham

JAMES DE WITT HILL   PHILIP ALAN PAYNE   LLOYD WILSON BERTAUD

Liners Search Seas for Old Glory and Her Crew of Three

First Photos Show Finding of Wreckage of Old Glory at Sea

SOUGHT FLIERS

AS HOPE DIED

ALL THAT REMAINS OF OLD GLORY BEGINS THE SAD JOURNEY HOME

By JAY MAEDER
Daily News Staff Writer

CHARLES LINDBERGH, the dark-horse kid whose airplane was one of the three in the $25,000 New York-to-Paris race, suddenly received a weather report late one night in May 1927 and decided to make his flight on the spur of the instant, and of course the first newspaper editor who knew about this was Phil Payne of the tabloid Daily Mirror, who had been prescient enough to stuff cash into the mitts of every maid in Lindbergh's hotel. Mirror men, accordingly, were all over Roosevelt Field while the other newsies were still blinking. This was no particular grand coup for Payne. This was what he did. The three-year-old Mirror, circulation about 400,000, hadn't exactly driven the dreadnought Daily News into its grave just yet, but it was certainly barking its shins every day of the week.

Right away, ocean flying was all anybody wanted to read about. William Randolph Hearst's three New York newspapers, astonished when Lucky Lindy modestly rejected Hearst's half a million dollars for the rights to his life story, now charged headlong into circulation-building flying enterprises. Hearst himself all at once emerged as one of aviation's foremost patrons; that summer, when pineapple king James Dole sponsored a California-to-Hawaii race, a Hearst plane was among the entrants. Meanwhile, under Phil Payne's imaginative direction, the Daily Mirror whipped up a fabled New York-to-Rome jump in the name of American solidarity with the Italian savior Benito Mussolini. New York City Mayor James J. Walker himself would be in

Rome at Mussolini's side when the Mirror plane touched down.

Story? Story? Phil Payne was beside himself. He would go along on the Rome flight too. The New York Daily Mirror's big boss himself would fly the Atlantic and radio back exclusive dispatches every hour. Good God. What a story.

THE FACT was that by the first week of September 1927, more than a dozen ocean fliers had died since Lindbergh had hopped the Atlantic four months earlier. This was hardly a fine science. The heavily overfueled Lindbergh had been nearly 100 miles at sea before he ever climbed to much more than 50 feet off the water. He had been, as

CUTE NEWSPAPER STUFF
Phil Payne
PART TWO OF TWO

they said, lucky.

But the airplane that Phil Payne bought from Anthony Fokker for W.R. Hearst was the foremost specimen of aeronautical sophistication. Flying the ship would be famed New York-to-Cleveland mail pilot Lloyd Bertaud, a far more experienced airman than Lindbergh. Everybody wanted to be Bertaud's co-pilot on the big Mirror flight; Congressman Fiorello LaGuardia, the old World War bomber, begged to go along. In the end, LaGuardia lost the job to Bertaud's old mail-run buddy J.D. Hill. On the 31st of July, in pouring rain at Curtiss Field, the big Bristol-motored Fokker was christened Old Glory — more formally, WRHP, for William Randolph Hearst Plane.

Now Bertaud and Hill and Payne

hunkered into a long standoff against lousy weather that delayed them again and again, ultimately all through August.

In the meantime, the ill-starred Dole race to Hawaii killed off several of its entrants, including Hearst's, and Hearst finally got scared. On Sept. 2 he wired Payne from California: *I do not think Old Glory should start...In view of the recent disasters, I will not assume responsibility.*

BUT OLD GLORY was already sitting on the hard sand at Old Orchard Beach on the southern shore of Maine, awaiting a west wind as thousands of Labor Day weekenders mobbed the old resort to watch the historic takeoff. And now there were three other trans-Atlantic airplanes large in this fabulous new moment: a European princess and her crew were leaping from London to Ottawa; two Canadian ships were meanwhile warming their motors for England-bound hops. There could be no stopping now, Payne insisted. He wired Hearst assurances of success. Old Glory would depart momentarily.

By Monday the 5th, the princess and her pilots had vanished, and Hearst frantically telegraphed again:
Dear Phil. Please think of my situation. I have had one airplane lost and two fine men drowned...Give up dangerous adventure.

Hearst got Payne's reply on Tuesday afternoon:
Dear Chief...Weather ideal today and further delay ruinous to morale of pilots. Every possible precaution taken...You have been a great chief to work for. I honor and love you and I know you will forgive me any mistakes I have made. Affectionately,

Phil Payne.
Old Glory was already in the air, bound for Rome, 4,300 miles away.

THE MIRROR'S flurry of afternoon extras screamed with celebration. **COMPLETE AND AUTHENTIC ACCOUNT OF THE GREAT AERIAL VOYAGE.** At 3:54 came word that Old Glory had been sighted off Nova Scotia. **PLANE MAKING OVER ONE HUNDRED MILES PER HOUR. ALL WELL.**

And at dawn on Wednesday a Cunard liner 500 miles off Newfoundland picked up the faint call: WRHP SOS WRHP SOS.

This was the last that was ever heard from Old Glory.

SEARCHERS FANNED out across the storm-whipped sea, and for days the New York papers ran hopeful headlines. **FIGHTING CHANCE. ROME PLANE EQUIPPED WITH ALL SAFEGUARDS. STURDY SHIP, STAUNCH HEARTS CHALLENGE ATLANTIC IN CRISIS.** The wives of Bertaud and Payne refused to believe their husbands were gone. Experts promised that the three lost men were floating in a raft, had been picked up by a trawler, were possibly still in the air without a radio.

And then the Canadian airplanes disappeared too.

ALL OCEAN FLIERS DOWN, the Mirror mournfully headlined on Saturday the 10th.

'THERE IS A growing feeling," epithaphed the Daily News, Phil Payne's onetime employer, "that these transoceanic flights should be stopped. We do not agree...These present-day fliers are the rear guard of the pioneers of the air. Ocean flying yet will become comparatively safe. We bare our heads to men like these three who have so bravely tried to show us how."

On Monday the 12th, a 34-foot piece of Old Glory's port wing was retrieved from the sea. That was all of her that was ever found.

The Dawn at Curtiss Field

By JAY MAEDER
Daily News Staff Writer

NAVY VESSELS were solemnly searching the sea for three lost airplanes in the first terrible week of September 1927 when Frances Wilson Grayson of Queens announced that the fresh disasters would emphatically not interrupt her own plans to fly across the Atlantic Ocean. Nearly 20 souls had now been lost in the brave quest to follow Charles Lindbergh and Clarence Chamberlin and Richard Byrd, among them the elderly European aviation patroness Princess Anne of Lowenstein-Wertheim, who had dreamed of being the first woman to fly the sea, if only as a passenger; now it was Frances Grayson who would claim the honor. Her big, twin-motored Sikorsky amphibian was undergoing trials at College Point, she said, and she expected to hop off within three weeks, and hers was going to be a great trailblazing hop for all womankind. It was true that her pilot and navigator were men, she conceded; she had not been able to find a capable female pilot. But she was christening her historic airplane The Dawn anyway.

Little was known about Frances Grayson. She was a 35-ish divorcée who lived in Forest Hills and appeared to have real estate interests in that burgeoning community. Otherwise, some said she'd been reared by Arkansas Cherokees; some said she was a Swarthmore graduate; some said she had a godmother in Atlantic City who was a direct descendant of Francis Scott Key. Aside from that, as she made clear in her every public utterance, she was God's Chosen Aviatrix. She wore the mantle. She was the one who would lead a new generation of birdwomen into the skies. She and The Dawn were the pathfinders.

There arose a complication. From Florida at this very moment arrived young beauty queen Ruth Elder, fluttering her lashes, powdering her nose, flying a cuteheart little monoplane she called American Girl, declaring her intention to beat Frances Grayson to Europe.

The Dixie Peach, the newspapers started calling her, the Flying Flapper, and she didn't pretend for a minute that her flight was much more than a publicity stunt she hoped might break her into the movies. Indeed, she was still just a student pilot, not yet licensed; one Capt. George Haldeman was flying the airplane for her, and she prettily deferred to his judgment at all

STILL SMALL VOICE

Frances Grayson

PART ONE OF TWO

times — unlike Grayson, who never made it less than perfectly clear that she was The Dawn's commander and that pilot Wilmer Stultz and navigator Brice Goldsborough were hired hands. Ruthie Elder was just a silly little girleen, so far as Grayson was concerned. Yet here were the newsreel boys regularly falling all over her. "I wish I were a man!" the Dixie Peach would chirp. "No woman can cross the Atlantic alone! We are not strong enough!"

The brewing trans-Atlantic catfight made for swell headlines. Soon, crowds of the curious, thousands of them at a time, were flocking to Long Island's Curtiss Field to watch the two lady racers as they readied their planes and smiled daggers at each other.

ALL THROUGH September and into early October, both women regularly announced imminent departures and then postponements and then postponements again as storms lashed the coast. Autumn was approaching now; on Oct. 8, the U.S. Weather Bureau officially discontinued its ocean weather reporting and suggested that the Atlantic flying season was over till spring. Frances Grayson, undissuaded, into the darkened sky. All Copenhagen excitedly awaited her arrival. Early on Monday afternoon the 10th, Grayson and her crewmen abruptly boarded The Dawn and took off, bound for Old Orchard Beach on the southern shore of Maine.

Ruth Elder, summoned from her hotel, rushed to the airfield and found her rival gone. Grayson had won the game, the papers agreed; the Flying Flapper had been left at the post.

OLD ORCHARD BEACH in the late summer of 1927 was suddenly a focal point of world aviation. A popular oceanfront resort for generations, it boasted five miles of hard-packed sand when the tide went out, an ideal takeoff point for heavily fueled trans-Atlantic planes; Lone Eagle Charles Lindbergh had put the place on the map in July when, unable to find Portland in a fog, he had come down here instead, alongside the roller coasters and the Ferris wheels and the famous great steel pier; since then, the tiny community had become an important flying center. There were many confident expectations that it someday would be the home of North America's principal airport, when the day came that commercial

transoceanic flights would be an everyday reality.

On the evening of Oct. 10, motorcycle policemen and National Guard troops were on hand to hold back the crowds that had come to cheer the arrival of The Dawn, at the sunrise of the great trans-Atlantic age to come, these five months after Lindbergh.

Frances Grayson sniffed the wind and consulted with Goldsborough and Wild Bill Stultz. They would lay over a day or two, she decided. There was no hurry.

Early the next afternoon, she was staggered by a bulletin from New York: American Girl was in the air. Shrugging off the weather, Ruth Elder and George Haldeman had daringly roared out of Roosevelt Field and pointed their nose east. They were already hundreds of miles at sea. They were headed straight for Paris.

THEY ALMOST made it. Battered by gales, lost from contact for a night and a day as the world feared the worst, they crashed at sea some 600 miles northeast of the Azores — miraculously, right alongside a Dutch freighter that picked them up before they were in the water five minutes. Immediately, Ruth Elder was the most famous woman on Earth, her name hailed around the globe, her face on page one of every newspaper everywhere.

All this happened while Frances Grayson was still on the ground at Old Orchard Beach, waiting for the skies to clear.

Daily did the New York papers arrive in Maine, and daily did Frances Grayson seethe over the ever more breathless tales of the celebrated Ruthie Elder and her thrilling adventures. You'd have thought the little snip had actually flown the Atlantic. Well, the fact was that she hadn't, had she? And now Grayson's face was alight with grim new determination. "Nothing can stop me now," she told the assembled press. "Destiny is with me."

And on Monday the 17th, at last she was ready to fly.

Earlier, in a quietly reflective moment, the otherwise no-nonsense, strictly business Frances Grayson had sat down and composed a shy, schoolgirlish personal testament:

Who am I?
Sometimes I wonder ...
Am I a little nobody?
Or am I a great dynamic force ...
I have a God-given birthright ... a great, living, breathing power of understanding my heritage ...
Sometimes I am torn ...
Can it be that I am wrong? Wrong after these many months of hard preparations, these many months of listening to that still small voice ...
The sun is ever shining. ... It is now time for me to show my strength.
I am who or what I really am.
I will win.

This she sealed in an envelope and presented to a New York Times reporter, with instructions that it was not to be opened and read unless, she said softly, "something happens."

Then, at 9:33 a.m., The Dawn roared down the beach and lurched heavily into the air.

By JAY MAEDER
Daily News Staff Writer

THE NEW YORK newspapers on Monday morning the 17th of October 1927 were, as they had been for days on end, greatly to the annoyance of aviatrix Frances Wilson Grayson of Forest Hills, Queens, plastered with nothing but Ruth Elder, the comely young Florida flier who had not exactly crossed the Atlantic Ocean but was suddenly world-famous anyway. **RUTH'S OWN STORY. RUTH NARRATES MAGNIFICENT ADVENTURE.** At 9:33 that morning, up from the sands of Old Orchard Beach on the southern shore of Maine lifted Grayson's great flying boat The Dawn, bound at last for Denmark and the pages of history.

Exactly six minutes later, the big tub was on her way back. She was just too nose-heavy, only 20 feet off the water when pilot Wilmer Stultz dropped 260 gallons of gasoline and turned around. For an instant, Frances Grayson imagined that she could quickly refuel and get off the beach again before the tides came rolling back in, but time ran out on her. The flight of The Dawn would have to wait till another day.

HOP FLOPS, the New York papers reported Tuesday, amid the usual bunch of Ruthie Elder astonishers. **RUTH TELLS OF DANGERS. DEATH RODE WITH RUTH.**

BY SATURDAY the 22nd, when Grayson was ready to try it again, the papers were still hopelessly infatuated with the Dixie Peach — **RUTH BOARDS SHIP FOR LISBON; EUROPE AWAITS BRAVE SKY GIRL** — and The Dawn's second takeoff from Old Orchard Beach was not really an event of such spellbinding magnitude that every reporter was still paying much attention. Which was just as well, considering that this time the ship made it just about 100 yards offshore before it slapped down into the surf and forlornly taxied back.

SUNDAY SAW a third attempt, and now skies were clear and spirits were high and all seemed auspicious, and indeed The Dawn made a perfect liftoff and sailed gracefully away into the horizon.

And all went well for about 450 miles, about out to Sable Island off the tip of Nova Scotia, when rough weather came up and pilot Stultz, over Grayson's objections, decided it would be prudent to go back. What thereafter occurred in the cabin of The Dawn was a matter of some dispute. Stultz would later describe a midair fracas; a screaming Grayson, he said, had grabbed the controls and demanded that the flight continue despite the thunderheads; Grayson would firmly deny any such incident. The argument was settled anyway when the port motor blew off a piston head about this same time, and there was no longer a choice but to limp back to Old Orchard Beach, in humiliation and defeat, again.

All through the week the papers continued to follow Ruthie Elder's every step — **SPAIN GOES WILD OVER RUTH ELDER; LISBON GREETS RUTH AS FLYING PRINCESS; RUTH FLIES INTO FRENCH HEARTS; RUTH REVELS IN PARIS SHOPS** — and all through the week, on the sands of Old Orchard Beach, Frances Grayson promised reporters an imminent fourth flight even as they all started yawning in her face. "Penguin among birdwomen," the Daily News man called her, not really very politely at all. By week's end, the testiness of Grayson's relations with Wilmer Stultz was apparent to all observers, and it became generally known that he was quitting the job. On Saturday the 29th, Grayson made it official: Flying season was over and The Dawn was through.

Back in New York, Grayson publicly savaged Stultz as a coward and said she was looking for a more courageous male to fly her airplane. "It takes a stout heart to make a trip like ours," she told the press. "When I discovered that my pilot had faltered somewhat, I felt it was only fair to release him." She approached both Bernt Balchen, the Arctic flier who had been with Cmdr. Richard Byrd, and Clarence Chamberlin, who had successfully flown the Atlantic a few weeks after Charles Lindbergh did; neither male wanted anything to do with her. Wild Bill Stultz, for his part, thoroughly relieved to be out of a job, noted for the record that Frances Grayson was about the craziest woman he had ever met.

EARLY IN November, Grayson sailed for Europe to meet with her financial backers, and she was thus spared the giddy spectacle of Ruth Elder's triumphant return to the United States. Having failed to fly the Atlantic Ocean, Ruthie was met with an enormous Broadway motorcade reception, a quarter of a million dollars' worth of product endorsement offers and more Hollywood contracts than she could even think about. **MISS AMERICA OF THE AIR,** the newspapers shrieked.

MID-DECEMBER brought the very worst of the Atlantic storms feared by sailors for centuries; freighters and steamers and great passenger liners all threw out desperate signals; the whole sea heaved and quaked beneath unimaginably blinding blizzards. In New York, Frances Grayson resolved that such a thing as weather was insufficient to overcome God's Chosen Aviatrix; her newly hired pilot was a Norwegian navy man named Oskar Omdahl, long accustomed to ice on his wings; The Dawn was going to fly the ocean, she said, at Christmas, proving what a woman could do in a man's world.

Weathermen gulped. Every professional flier everywhere begged her to reconsider. Her mind was made up. Late on the afternoon of the 23rd of December, reporters were with Grayson at Long Island's Roosevelt Field as she buckled up her flying togs, slipped a revolver into her jacket pocket, rolled up her charts and walked purposefully toward her airplane. "This time there will be no turning back," she pledged to the cameras as she climbed aboard.

Old Orchard Beach

STILL SMALL VOICE
Frances Grayson
PART TWO OF TWO

At dusk, the big flying boat flew out of Roosevelt carrying Grayson, pilot Omdahl, navigator Brice Goldsborough and a hitchhiking mechanic named Fred Koehler, who planned to jump out when the ship made its first stop at Harbor Grace in Newfoundland early the next morning. That night, The Dawn was sighted over Cape Cod, northward bound.

And then morning arrived in Harbor Grace, and The Dawn did not.

HOURS OVERDUE, the papers said on Christmas Sunday morning.

And on Monday they said: **LOST.**

THE NAVY searched all week. But there was no shred of a clue. It was generally agreed that the fliers had iced up, gone down in the dark, been smashed to pieces in the brutal seas. That was the logical assumption. The New York Times at last opened the sealed envelope Frances Grayson had left with its reporter in October and published the poem therein:

I have a God-given birthright ... a great, living, breathing power of understanding my heritage. ...
Can it be that I am wrong? Wrong after these many months of hard preparations, these many months of listening to that still small voice. ...
The sun is ever shining. ... It is now time for me to show my strength.

"She was very foolish," said the unsentimental U.S. Weather Bureau chief. "The Atlantic in the winter is no place for an airplane."

AND NOW the reporters remembered that the last thing they had seen Frances Grayson do was put a gun in her pocket.

This time there will be no turning back.

HAD SHE really forced her protesting men at gunpoint to drive on into the teeth of a howling gale? No one would ever know. And not a stick of The Dawn would ever be found.

SPRING CAME, with clear skies and calm seas. Ruth Elder was in Hollywood now, far too busy to fly the Atlantic anymore, but there was still much gold to be mined from ocean aviatrices. In New York, a syndicate of businessmen went looking for a model American woman, a wholesome girl-next-door type who, purely from the marketing standpoint, might best represent the United States as its first woman across the sea. Shortly they found a young Boston social worker who met their specifications. Her name was Amelia Earhart.

By JAY MAEDER
Daily News Staff Writer

THE SOUTH Pacific search for the lost flier Amelia Earhart was slowly being abandoned late in July 1937 when her husband, New York City book publisher George Palmer Putnam, was contacted by a sailor who claimed that his tramp ship a few weeks earlier had picked up a crash-landed woman from an uncharted island. She was being held for ransom, the sailor reported; surely Putnam wouldn't object to coughing up a few thousand dollars to get his world-famous wife back.

Fleetingly, there was hope again. A down payment was made, a second meeting scheduled. But Putnam had cops waiting when his visitor returned, and the hoax fell apart at once: The sailor was just a dim Bronx janitor named Wilbur Rothar, and of course he had no idea where Amelia Earhart was.

And so it really was over. She was gone. George Palmer Putnam's finest creation was not coming back.

Fortunately, he had all her dispatches, the running log she'd been sending for weeks from the globe's far places. These were to have been collected into a quick book upon her fanfared return to America. Now he'd have to package them in some other fashion. A posthumous celebration of her memory, that would do it. "Last Flight," he'd call it.

THANKS TO Putnam and his infallible showmanship, Amelia Earhart had become the world's most honored aviatrix practically before she could fly an airplane by herself. She had gone on from that point to accomplish things on her own — setting speed and distance records, flying the Atlantic and Pacific oceans solo — but she was a Putnam-manufactured commodity before she did any of those things, and she might never have been in a position to do them at all had Putnam not so invented her in the first place.

This was merely what Putnam did. Thrills were his business. G.P. Putnam & Sons was the house that issued the adventure-packed yarns of all the day's leading explorers — Richard Byrd, William Beebe, Roy Chapman Andrews — and it was Putnam who had rushed Charles Lindbergh's "We" into print barely weeks after the Lone Eagle's May 1927 flight from Roosevelt Field to Paris. In the 1920s, the American public couldn't get enough of explorers, pathfinders, trailblazers. By early 1928, even the girl flier Ruth Elder was rich and famous, and she hadn't even made it all the way across the Atlantic. Now, marketing-wise, it was time for a woman to go the whole distance. It was time to give the world a Lady Lindy.

BORN IN RYE in 1887, Putnam was a grand-nephew of the original George Palmer Putnam, who had published Washington Irving and James Fenimore Cooper and whose firm, when Harvard man G.P. the younger joined it in 1919, was one of the nation's oldest. There were those who felt that G.P.'s taste for tales of derring-do cheapened the distinguished Putnam imprint. Still, the book-buying public gobbled up such yarns, and G.P. was a valued member of the Explorers Club. Indeed, sponsored by the American Museum of Natural History, he had personally led two steamship expeditions up the Greenland coast and had pretty much discovered Baffin Land all by himself. Such men as the Arctic conqueror Richard Byrd were his close friends. It was through Byrd that the legend of Amelia Earhart was born.

Byrd, following his successful June 1927 flight from Newfoundland to Ireland, had sold his big Fokker airplane America to one Mrs. Frederick Guest, a wealthy socialite who renamed it Friendship and announced that she was going to fly the Atlantic too. At which point her mortified husband declared that she would certainly do no such thing. Whereupon Mrs. Guest decided instead to sponsor a more likely lass in her place — a modest and decent young woman, she stipulated, a model American girl who stood for American standards and American values.

And now it fell to Cmdr. Byrd's good friend George Palmer Putnam to find her.

AMELIA EARHART was a 30-year-old Boston social worker, an enthusiastic amateur flier, though hardly experienced enough to even think about flying the Atlantic. This was irrelevant. The previous would-be ocean aviatrices had all been merely passengers; Amelia needn't be any different. And besides, there was her appearance. She was lean, tousle-haired, shyly smiling; she looked almost exactly like Charles Lindbergh. She was perfect.

On June 17, 1928, the Friendship — piloted by Wilmer Stultz, the Curtiss Field flier who the previous fall had been briefly in the employ of Frances Wilson Grayson — left Newfoundland and, 20 hours and 40 minutes later, landed in Wales. Amelia Earhart had not once at any time during the flight held the stick — as for a while she kept trying to explain to everyone, repeatedly describing herself as "just baggage" — but the entire planet went insane for her anyway.

Queen Of The Air. Lady Lindy. At long last, a female flier had crossed the sea. London feted her for two weeks. New York threw her an enormous ticker-tape parade when she came home. Putnam & Sons quickly published her book, "20 Hrs., 40 Mins." Cosmopolitan hired her as aviation editor. Lucky Strike cigarettes gave her an endorsement deal.

Stage-managing everything was G.P., her Pygmalion, who didn't trouble to stand in the shadows; there he was in every photograph, there he was making windy speeches at every appearance. Reporters despised him. The man was such a weasel.

BETWEEN THE endless lecture engagements

and her nonstop stream of magazine articles, Amelia still found time for enough sport flying to keep herself in the headlines and newsreels, and she remained a familiar national figure in her jodhpurs and boots, flying cross-country here, breaking somebody's record there, and in February 1931 it was big news when the bachelorette Lady Lindy took a husband, George Palmer Putnam, who had recently thrown over his wife of 30 years.

There were those who rather uncharitably viewed the marriage as a strictly a business deal between people who needed each other's respective skills, and indeed, soon there were Amelia Earhart clothing and luggage lines helping to finance her flying, which did not come cheap. She publicly acknowledged more than once, not unappreciatively, that she could not do what she did without G.P. behind her. In fact, she was entertaining large plans that called for his fund-raising talents. She needed a new airplane. Her first Atlantic flight had been just theater. Now she was going to fly the ocean for real. By herself.

THERE WAS nothing manufactured about Amelia Earhart's ocean hop in May 1932, on the fifth anniversary of Lindbergh's flight. Now she really was the first woman to fly the Atlantic, and, after Lindbergh, only the second human being to do it solo. "Queen of the Air" was no longer an embarrassingly empty term.

She had a new book out by now, whose publication her husband had enterprisingly timed to coincide with her return to the U.S. But aside from that, it seemed to be recognized that George Putnam was no longer essential to the partnership. The two of them began to spend more and more time apart; late in 1934, Mrs. Putnam moved to California, leaving G.P. behind in New York. In 1935, she made record-setting flights from Hawaii to San Francisco and from Mexico City to Newark. In the spring of 1937, world-acclaimed Amelia Earhart announced that she would be the first woman to fly around the globe.

On the 4th of July, amid the brass bands and live national radio hookup he had arranged to mark his wife's return, Putnam stood on the Pacific shore and stared into the sky.

But Amelia wasn't there anymore.

'LAST FLIGHT" was somewhat less than the best-seller George Putnam had hoped it might be. In 1939, he retired from publishing, remarried, moved to the California desert and opened a resort hotel. Thereafter, he made himself an expert on the geology and flora of Death Valley and wrote several books on those subjects.

He died at 63 in January 1950, long before investigators began to wonder what his phantom role may or may not have been in whatever fantastic government plot may or may not have been devised to cover up whatever spy mission Amelia Earhart may or may not have been flying when she perished at sea, or maybe didn't.

INVENTING AMELIA

George Palmer Putnam

By JAY MAEDER
Daily News Staff Writer

HE HAD NEVER really been quite himself again, not since the crash that had left him wrapped in plaster for weeks, the mishap that had cost him his grand shot at flying the North Pole legend Cmdr. Richard Byrd across the Atlantic Ocean.

Another man had flown the big Fokker in Floyd Bennett's place, and it was a still a glorious triumph for Byrd even if both Charles Lindbergh and Clarence Chamberlin had done it before he did, and New York had given the commander a rousing ticker-tape parade while the broken Bennett lay abed in St. Vincent's Hospital, mending his bones.

Now it was nearly a year later, April 1928, and 37-year-old Bennett was gingerly up and around again, looking forward to serving with Byrd on the proposed great South Pole expedition. But he was nursing a bad spring cold and he was taking it easy in his home at 239 Ocean Ave. in Brooklyn.

Then came word from the far frozen north: Two German fliers were down, crash-landed and marooned on remote Greenly Island, beyond Labrador. The New York World, with much fanfare, was sponsoring a relief plane; Floyd Bennett, the seasoned Arctic birdman, was widely viewed as the best man to fly the mercy mission. Such a man as Bennett could not say no. Against doctor's orders, he rose from his sickbed and, with fellow Byrd expeditioner Bernt Balchen co-piloting, headed for Canada.

The effort was, at last, too much for him. Once he had coolly braved the planet's most terrifying darknesses, wrapped in his skins and furs, his every breath frosting his beard; here was the man who had climbed out upon a treacherous airplane wing high above the glaciers to repair a clotted oil line; here was the man who had gone sleepless for thousands of miles and flown Byrd across the fabled North Pole itself.

Now, refueling at Quebec's Lake St. Agnes on April 20, he collapsed with double pneumonia, raging with fever, and was airlifted to Quebec City while Balchen pressed on. Byrd dropped everything to rush to his old friend's side.

The World dispatched New York's top medical experts, including the man who had invented the oxygen tent. But slowly Floyd Bennett faded, and the doctors quietly shook their heads.

As the sick man fell into a coma, Charles Lindbergh, the Lone Eagle, left New York in a fast Army plane, carrying a package of miracle serum personally provided by John D. Rockefeller Jr., and flew northward into a violent storm, racing against time to save Floyd Bennett's life.

RICHARD BYRD and Floyd Bennett owed each other pretty much everything, and the two of them were inseparable, the Annapolis officer and the faithful subordinate who stood always ready at any minute's notice to serve his chief.

Bennett was an upstate New York farm boy who had gone into airplane grease-monkeying and eventually become a Navy flier; in 1925, he was one of three petty officers detailed to accompany Byrd on the MacMillan Arctic Expedition, and here he quickly distinguished himself as the nerviest and most utterly irreplaceable fellow the senior officer had ever met. Never again, Byrd

resolved, would he embark upon any adventure without staunch Floyd Bennett at his side.

It was always Byrd who collected the headlines and the glory, and this was to be expected, for he was the commander, and this was always okay by Bennett. But the fact was that Byrd would have been dead more than once had his devoted sidekick not been there, and Byrd never failed to credit Bennett's contributions and shower him with the warmest of accolades.

High over the crags of Ellesmere Island, for example, as Byrd related many times, their airplane's oil pressure had suddenly begun to climb:

"We were sure that if the oil tank burst we should face a forced landing long before we could get back to safe country. ... Bennett let me take control. I circled, looking for a landing place that wasn't there. He then rose from his seat, gave his belt an extra yank, and slowly he began to crawl out of the cockpit onto the wing. Such a trick is not comfortable in temperate latitudes. In the Arctic, when the plane is tearing through the air that is below zero, every moment out in the open is agony. Bennett unscrewed the cap of the oil tank, relieved the pressure and so saved our lives."

This was but one of Bennett's many Arctic heroisms, and this was even before the sensational May 1926 North Pole flight itself. After that astonishing feat of primal courage and magnificent derring-do, the two men rode together up Broadway in an open limousine, cheered by all New York, the ticker-tape sailing down upon their heads, and when President Calvin Coolidge gave Byrd the Medal of Honor, no one applauded more sincerely than Floyd Bennett.

IN THE spring of 1927, naturally it was Bennett who was chosen to fly Byrd across the sea in the big tri-motor America that, weeks before anyone ever heard of the young mail pilot Lindbergh, was the early favorite in that season's storied Atlantic race.

Indeed, the Byrd plane might well have been the first across the ocean, well before latecomer Lucky Lindy entered the race at all — had not, on April 16, at Teterboro Airdrome in Hasbrouck Heights, N.J., Bennett brought America down from a trial run, busted a wheel on landing and flipped over. His injuries were severe. There would be no Atlantic flight for him.

America took weeks to repair. It was precious time lost, but if Byrd ever held his friend accountable for the long delay that probably cost him the Atlantic victory, there was never a public sign of it. In June, when Byrd took off at last, the last thing he did was telephone St. Vincent's to make sure Bennett was doing well.

Once in Europe, he immediately sent Bennett a wish-you-were-here cable. Bennett, in his hospital bed, was jubilant at his chief's success. "Gee, but that's great," he whooped.

AT 6:43 p.m. on Tuesday the 24th of April 1928, three hours and 36 minutes after he tore out of Curtiss Field and charged headlong into 450 miles of hail and sleet, Charles Lindbergh slammed aground in Quebec City and was met at once by a haggard Cmdr. Byrd. "Have you got the serum?" Byrd cried. Lindbergh handed it over, and, siren screaming, toward the hospital it went.

Miracle it might have been for another man. But Floyd Bennett was too far gone. At 10:50 Wednesday morning, he slipped away into the eternal sunshine of the isles beyond the ice. Always just a warrant officer, he was, by presidential order, given a full admiral's burial in Arlington National Cemetery.

ON JUNE 26, 1930, the one-time Commander Byrd, now Rear Adm. Byrd, who was just a week or so returned from his Antarctic expedition, formally dedicated New York's first municipal airport, Floyd Bennett Field, on Barren Island on the shores of Jamaica Bay, where it served the city until the larger LaGuardia Field was opened nine years later. The military took it over in 1942, and through the war it was a vital staging ground, a principal point from which newly built airplanes were ferried to England. Eventually, it fell into disuse. In 1972, historic Floyd Bennett Field was taken over by the National Park Service.

BYRD AND BENNETT were more fortunate than such North Pole claimants as Robert Peary and Frederick Cook, both of whom saw their boasts publicly assailed in their own lifetimes. For his part, Byrd went to his grave in 1957 still every bit the hero he'd been three decades earlier, and he was long dead before elderly Bernt Balchen alleged that the famous 1926 flight had been a lie, that the Byrd plane had never come within 150 miles of the Pole, that Bennett had confessed the fraud to him long ago. Balchen stood alone in making the charge, and Byrd's defenders have furiously rejected such an unthinkable calumny.

THE ISLES BEYOND THE ICE
Floyd Bennett

By JAY MAEDER
Daily News Staff Writer

THIS IS A small story about a long-forgotten young woman who was briefly on Broadway once upon a time, a rising star of the Ziegfeld Follies, and who perhaps might have gone on to become a Hollywood queen, as did some of the other Ziegfeld girls, or who on the other hand might just have unextraordinarily labored on in workaday show business, as did some of the others.

Helen Walsh died too young ever to know which way things were likely to break for her, which is what they said about her at the funeral — that hers was a journey interrupted at its very start, that it was not granted to her even to understand what the limitless possibilities might have been.

At 23, she was just beginning to enjoy minor notices as the 1931 Follies' most beautiful girl. That is all that Helen Walsh ever got to be before a merry summer's holiday suddenly turned into a terrifying wall of fire that took her short life away from her.

Hundreds of saddened show folk gathered at her bier to see her off. "Hark, I Hear The Angels Calling," they sang.

SHE WAS THE daughter of a New York City police lieutenant, and she lived with her sister and widowed mother in a modest frame home at Riverdale Ave. and 260th St. in the Bronx, supporting the household with her wages as a Fifth Ave. department store model. It was at the store in 1927 that a scout spotted her and broke her into chorus-line work. Since then, Walsh had appeared in "Rosalie" and "Simple Simon" and "Whoopee" and other shows, and now, in 1931, Florenz Ziegfeld had put her in the current edition of his famous Follies.

The season's show was headlined by singing star Harry Richman, and it also featured the sensational Gladys Glad, showgirl wife of the Daily Mirror's high-rolling Broadway columnist Mark Hellinger, and by and by did Helen Walsh of Riverdale Ave. become chums with all three of these very glamorous people.

In early July, Harry Richman bought himself a 36-foot motor yacht, a broad-beamed, twin-screw cruiser called Chevalier II, which he docked at Greenport, L.I., and on Sunday the 26th he took on 140 gallons of gasoline, hired a pilot and welcomed aboard a small party of friends for a sunny day of fishing off Green Hill.

The group included his lady friend of the moment, a Follies dancer named Virginia Biddle, Hellinger, Glad and Walsh. They were all making themselves comfortable as the pilot, a Capt. Samuel White, stepped aboard. Later, at the inquest, neither White nor Richman could remember which one of them had pressed the starter button.

That was when the boat exploded.

THE BLAST was heard for miles. White was blown overboard. Gladys Glad, fortunate enough to have been near the hatch, scrambled through it to safety. Virginia Biddle was pinned under debris; someone freed her and lifted her to the dock. Helen Walsh was less lucky. Deep in the smoke-filled cabin, she lay trapped beneath burning rubble, shrieking. Hellinger and Richman, their

FOLLIES BEAUTIES BURNED IN RICHMAN YACHT BLAST

2 RIVALS GET RIDES IN BEER GANG BATTLE

Helen Walsh, Virginia Biddle Hurt; Servant Saves Gladys Glad

HARRY RICHMAN YACHT EXPLODES!—Helen Walsh, beautiful Follies girl, was badly burned when Harry Richman's yacht exploded at Greenport, L. I.

Harry Richman and 6 Burned in Explosion

DAILY MIRROR
3 CENTS 3 CENTS
Vol. VIII. No. 31RP
New York, Wednesday, July 29, 1931

FOLLIES GIRL DIES From Burns On Boat

suits afire, fought their way through the flames to reach her. It was Richman who swooped her up in his arms, got her out of the inferno, threw her into the water and leaped in after her to hold her afloat. Hellinger pulled them both to the pier as Greenport firemen arrived and bystanders mobilized their automobiles and pickup trucks to rush the victims to Eastern Long Island Hospital.

"My face, my face," screamed the most beautiful girl of the 1931 Follies.

INITIALLY IT WAS felt by physicians that there was a good chance of recovery. But then the poisonous toxins that accompany burns quickly ravaged her body, and Walsh died early Monday evening.

Richman was not immediately informed, and that night he returned in bandages to his Follies role and the show went on, as shows do. Gladys Glad did not go on that night. Virginia Biddle, seriously burned, remained hospitalized for weeks.

"Hark, I Hear the Angels Calling," sang the mourners at St. Margaret's Catholic Church in Riverdale on July 30, some of Broadway's biggest names, people far more famous than dead Helen Walsh, somber stars who had turned out to grieve for one of their own: Helen Morgan, Ruth Etting, Jack Pearl, Hal LeRoy, Bobby Connolly, Gene Buck. Richman and Hellinger and Flo Ziegfeld were among the pallbearers. "She was the finest of American womanhood," said Ziegfeld.

For the benefit of the dead woman's mother, Ziegfeld scheduled a special memorial matinee performance of the Follies on Aug. 11, and the rest of this story is told by Whitney Bolton, the

CALLED BY ANGELS
Helen Walsh

theatrical critic for The Telegraph:

"There is no more impressive testimonial to the character and personality of Helen Walsh than the unanimous decision by the union stagehands and musicians of the Ziegfeld Theater to contribute their services. ... It is to be counted as a remarkable gesture, since the code in such instances has been directly opposed to gifts of work. All of us have commented on union labor in the past and the comments have not been gentle or kindly. ... Benefits have never before this enjoyed union cooperation without pay. ... It is therefore remarkable and compelling and altogether fine that without persuasion, without even hint, the stagehands and musicians responded unanimously and without pay.

"It is no less a remarkable testimony to the esteem in which Miss Walsh was held. I can think of a dozen stars, two dozen featured players and a wilderness of showgirls whose death would not affect the stagehands. ...

"It would be banal and somewhat silly to dust off that quaint old cliché that Broadway has a heart after all. I don't think this has anything to do with Broadway. Broadway, whatever that may be, has nothing whatever to do with the fact that more than 60 unionized men agreed without quibble or dissenting vote to show their affection for a girl of the show world."

LEFT UNSAID by superstitious show people were the terrible words: *The Follies Curse.* Misfortune and woe had been rained down upon so many of Florenz Ziegfeld's Glorified Girls; not even counting lives merely ruined by drink and drugs and dubious taste in men, the list of victims was considerable: Olive Thomas, who accidentally drank poison in 1920. Martha Mansfield, burned to death when a spark from a match set her dress aflame in 1923. Kay Laurell, dead of childbirth in 1927. Myrna Darby, dead of sunburn in 1929. Bobbie Storey and Allyn King, both of them suicides in 1930.

The Follies Curse would go on claiming Ziegfeld girls for years yet. This time it had chosen Helen Walsh of Riverdale Ave., dead at 23, before her life had barely even begun.

By JAY MAEDER
Daily News Staff Writer

Day by day in every way,
I am getting well (Ha!)
I am filled with health and strength,
More than I can tell (Ho!)
Now I know, I can go
All along the way (Ha!)
Growing better all the time,
And singing every day! (Ho!)
— Marching anthem by Bernarr Macfadden
(to be sung with gusto)

NOT FOR NOTHING were there those who viewed Bernarr Macfadden as perhaps something of a crackpot. Every morning he walked the 18 miles from his West Nyack home to his Broadway offices barefoot, sometimes carrying a 40-pound sandbag on his back. He presided over his executive board meetings standing on his head. For 70 years he slept on a hardwood floor. He fasted for weeks on end and otherwise appeared to live on nothing but carrots, grapes and cracked wheat. All his life he was his own doctor and dentist. He wanted to be president, though mostly what he wanted to be was the nation's secretary of health, a nonexistent post for which his many newspapers and magazines tirelessly nominated him.

However, he was nice old crackpot. The whole town was quite charmed when, on his 83rd birthday in August 1951, he parachuted from a small airplane into the Hudson River just because he felt like it. "I recommend this for everybody," he declared. "It's a damn good thing to do." He was going to jump into the Niagara Falls whirlpool too, but border authorities put a stop to that.

He was, everyone agreed, the healthiest man in America. He was the Father of Physical Culture, the man who made spa-going a way of life, the man who introduced fitness classes into public schools, the man who singlehandedly popularized whole wheat bread and orange juice. Bernarr Macfadden was the man who first proclaimed: *"You are what you eat."* Most people gorged themselves to death, he preached, no little annoyed about this disgraceful state of affairs. For his part, he fully expected to live to at least 130.

BORN A tubercular Missouri farm boy in 1868, Bernarr Macfadden was one of those sickly souls who, by dint of will and hard exercise and the fanatical embrace of mysterious physical principles divined chiefly by themselves, remade himself into a genuinely astonishing specimen.

By his late teens, he was a professional St. Louis wrestler and the developer of something called kinisitherapy. This doctrine had to do with regarding the spine as the center of all human vigor, which was why he stopped sleeping in beds, and with absorbing the planet's magnetic energy through the soles of one's feet, which was why he tried not to wear shoes. In the 1890s, there was a large market for such faddist propositions, and ere long the former consumptive wretch was a popular pamphleteer, lecturer and inventor of exercise equipment.

And by the early 1900s he was in New York, running a hugely successful magazine called Physical Culture and building sanitariums and health farms from Long Island to Michigan. For a while, he presided over a whole utopian city of his own in Pennsylvania. That particular experiment didn't last, but he still had worldwide legions of devotees, George Bernard Shaw and President William Howard Taft said to be among them, who faithfully followed his every dictate.

Doctors, he felt, were the mortal enemies of all humankind, and his crusades against the American Medical Association were long and loud; he wrote his own 3,000-page household health encyclopedia, which railed against, among other things, vaccinations, white bread and any cancer cure except milk. He was also a pioneer in the uncharted field of sexology, and his magazine's frank discussions of venereal diseases

Left: Commuting to work (circa 1910)
Below: Daily 10-mile constitutional (circa 1943)

OUT GOES THE BAD AIR
Bernarr Macfadden

finally led to his conviction on federal obscenity charges. The appeals went all the way to the U.S. Supreme Court, which ruled against him. Whereupon Taft pardoned him.

In 1919, the Father of Physical Culture diversified. His magazine featured a popular advice column that, it dawned on him, warranted a separate journal of its own. He called the new publication True Story. Bernarr Macfadden had just invented the confession magazine.

TRUE STORY sold millions of copies, such a sensation that Macfadden spun off the companion mags True Experiences and True Romances. Then he went into the crime field, introducing True Detective and Master Detective. And he launched a chain of newspapers, including, in New York, the storied Evening Graphic, a spellbindingly cheesy tabloid that liked to publish things like, for example, the late Rudolph Valentino's exclusive letters from Heaven. ("The only value ever claimed for it," one Graphic historian has noted, "was that it educated readers up to a point where they were able to understand the other tabloids.")

The Graphic folded in 1932, Macfadden's one and only business failure. Otherwise, by that time he had Photoplay and Liberty magazines in his stable as well. By 1935, in terms of total circulation, he was the nation's leading magazine publisher, personally worth about $30 million.

By that time, his health-resort empire had branched out into hotels, including the Deauville on Miami Beach, and he had his own Tennessee military academy, too. In 1936, he went after the Republican presidential nomination, quite

unsuccessfully, although four years later he actually almost got himself elected a U.S. senator from Florida. Throughout these political flirtations, he remained a dedicated champion of doing the right thing by one's body.

For some years, he presided over the annual Cracked Wheat Derby, giving his benediction as enormous crowds of Macfaddenites would go marching from New York City to, say, Cleveland, munching on raisins and grains the whole way. Observers all agreed they never saw such a happy bunch of people.

MACFADDEN ABRUPTLY sold out his publishing interests in 1941 and thereafter devoted his energies to the Macfadden Foundation and all its good works. Further political noodlings — in the early 1950s he wanted to be New York mayor — found themselves without much support. Late in his life, to the horrified disbelief of his admirers, he concluded that he'd been wrong about about some of his dietary edicts and that maybe a little meat wouldn't hurt. Thereafter he was a man who enjoyed a good beefsteak now and then.

Whether that was a contributing reason or not, he came down with jaundice one day in October 1955, sick for the first time since childhood, and three days later he was dead, at 87.

He was eulogized as "an apostle of good health whose name will one day blazon forth in the annals of civilization as a brave soul who stalked this earth in a sound, clean, vigorous body, dedicated to the furtherance of truth and enlightenment."

The Daily News, for one, was somewhat less rhapsodic, but the paper did hail Bernarr Macfadden as "a bold and rugged American individualist," a man who "deserves a large part of the credit for the fact that so many present-day Americans know the value of good health and how to keep it." Which did, of course, overlook the fact that he'd died 40 years sooner than he'd planned to.

By JAY MAEDER
Daily News Staff Writer

NOT OTHERWISE a shortsighted man, promoter Tex Rickard flatly refused to even think about bringing professional ice hockey to the New Madison Square Garden that in 1925 he was building at Eighth Ave. and 50th St. Tex had made his pile in championship fighting. That's where the money was. People were going to pay to watch some moose skate around swinging a stick? There was a laugh for you.

History records that Tex was just dead wrong. In 1925, ice hockey was sweeping America's colleges, pouring down from Canada, the most astonishing gladiator game anyone had ever witnessed, fast and brutish and primal, an overnight sensation. There were already several amateur leagues, there were hundreds of campus teams, Boston and San Francisco were building pro rinks. In New York, it was left to enthusiastic private investors to make the case. Large among these was a bluff Broadway Irishman named William V. Dwyer, who had many sporting interests.

Dwyer was a racetrack man, a nightlife man, crony of gangsters and pols and railbirds, a man who liked a good proposition. It was his $80,000 front money that purchased an entire professional Canadian team called the Hamilton Tigers and brought them to the city as the New York Americans. As it turned out, Dwyer also had to pay for New Madison Square Garden's ice-making machinery, since the entirely unconvinced Tex Rickard still didn't intend to pony up a dime for any of this.

Tex began to change his mind on Tuesday night the 15th of December, when the New Garden officially opened its doors and the Amazin' Amerks played their first game to a black-tie crowd of 20,000 in what was hailed as the social event of the season. The Amerks lost to Les Canadiens 3-1 that night, and then they kept losing game after game after that, but nobody really cared that they weren't much good.

"Professional hockey is an assured success in New York," wrote Paul Gallico of the Daily News. "Eventually the New Yorker will discover it and the thing will go over with a bang."

And so hockey came to town. Not that William V. Dwyer had long to bask in its glory. For it happened that Big Bill Dwyer, as all New York called William V. Dwyer in those days, was already in serious dutch, his federal indictment quite imminent. Hockey players, as everyone knew, were not the only things Big Bill imported from Canada.

RUM ROW, they called it, a fantastic flotilla of freighters sitting off the coast between Atlantic City and Martha's Vineyard, full of good liquor from Europe and Nova Scotia and the Bahamas, all of it shorebound aboard the great ad hoc navy of schooners and trawlers and speedboats enlisted into the noble service of quenching America's thirst in the first years of Prohibition.

By early 1923, every Tom and Dick and Harry with a fishing boat was in the offshore liquor business, and President Warren Harding ordered military blockades. Running gun battles between the federal ships and the smugglers became daily commonplaces; Coney Island beachgoers regularly cheered as motorboats came roaring past them with revenue cutters in hot pursuit. Through 1924, America's Dry Navy scored substantial victories in its war on crime,

FINAL EDITION

DAILY NEWS

NEW YORK'S ✦ PICTURE NEWSPAPER

THE LARGEST CIRCULATION IN AMERICA

Vol. 7. No. 149.   48 Pages.   ****   New York, Wednesday, December 16, 1925.   2 Cents

N. Y. LOSES HOCKEY OPENER

—Story on Page 44

This picture shows Shorty Green (center), New York wing, shooting the puck for the only score made by the New Yorkers. This took place in the first period. These two pictures are the exclusive and only action photos taken of the contest.

Randall (background) blocked by Canadiens Defense Coutu (left) and Keeper Leduc

CANADIENS BEAT NEW YORKERS IN GARDEN HOCKEY.—Before 20,000 shrieking people...

THE SPORTING LIFE
Big Bill Dwyer

frequently seizing large cargoes.

But far more got past the patrols than didn't. Much of it quickly disappeared into the uncountable hidden coves of the Long Island shore, where fleets of trucks waited for the offloading. And quite a lot of it went straight into New York Harbor, and thereafter to a marina at the East River and 132nd St.

The harbor operation was Big Bill Dwyer's. He controlled dozens of skippers and an army of landside distributors; the King of the Rum Runners, prosecutors called him, a man whose large and efficient organization, it inevitably began to appear, included about half the Coast Guard. It was not unknown for a government boat to escort a smuggler. It was not unknown for the Dry Navy to carry in a load or two of liquor itself. In May 1925, federal sleuths blew the lid off the Coast Guard's Staten Island base, implicating hundreds of sailors who had accepted liquor and women in return for their cooperation. Several of them, seeking amnesty, now began to spill everything they knew.

And in December, even as Big Bill Dwyer's New York Americans took to the ice at New Madison Square Garden, the federals made the biggest single roundup of the liquor bosses Prohibition had yet seen. On Jan. 15, 1926, Big Bill was

indicted, along with 60 other malefactors, including a young man called Frank Costello, whose name was not yet generally known to the public.

BIG BILL was convicted in July. By this time, the Amazin' Amerks were tremendously successful, and Tex Rickard had sufficiently seen the light to assemble a professional ice hockey team of his own; his New York Rangers played their first game at the Garden on Nov. 25. At Christmas, meanwhile, it was calculated that 100,000 cases of liquor were still arriving in the city every week, suggesting that Big Bill's downfall had not exactly put a measurable dent in things.

Various large federal liquor trials continued into 1927. At several points, there were broad hints that an assistant secretary of the treasury was personally in on the bootlegger take. He indignantly denied any such complicity. So, of course, did the young rum runner Frank Costello. He was convicted, though, and the treasury man wasn't.

In June, Big Bill was sentenced to two years in the Atlanta jug, expressing considerable penitence. "I wish I had never seen a case of whisky," he sighed. "I spent years in daily fear of my life, always expecting to be arrested, always dealing with crooks and double-crossers, and now look at me. My wife is heartbroken and I am worse than broke."

It got worse yet. Prison life wasn't kind to Big Bill; his health broke; there were emergency operations; in August 1928 he won an early parole and returned, pallid and thin, to his home on Beach 140th St. in Belle Harbor, Queens, publicly declaring himself to be through with the rackets.

So rehabilitated, he was just a month later elected to the board of governors of the National Hockey League. At the same time, he was named a director of the New York Hockey Club. Fellow directors were Mayor Jimmy Walker, a great hockey fan who in any case was never embarrassed about associating with ex-cons.

BY MOST public accounts, the King of the Rum Runners in fact stayed pretty much semiretired, though from time to time there did arise a suspicion or two that he might yet have a hand in this and that; he was whispered to be one of the early shadow owners, along with his old bootlegger pals Owney Madden and Big Frenchy DeMange, of a hot new joint called The Stork Club. But for the most part he lived the life of a legitimate sportsman, buying into the Brooklyn Dodgers football club, breeding horses in Jersey, always found in his Garden box whenever his Amerks played.

And here, so far as New York was concerned, the story of Big Bill Dwyer largely ended. Shortly, he became a big track man in Miami, owner of that city's popular Tropical Park, a notable figure in Florida parimutuel politics. A 1935 gambling indictment knocked him out of the game; though nothing was pinned on him, the government dogged him forevermore on one tax matter after another. He lost the Amerks in '36, six years before the team folded altogether. And then little by little he lost most everything else.

The taxman let him keep his Belle Harbor house. That's where he was quietly passing his days when he died Dec. 10, 1946, age 63, all the bright lights of Broadway just faraway memories.

By JAY MAEDER
Daily News Staff Writer

HE COULDN'T help it; he just loved Navy uniforms, the real good kind, the ones with epaulets and gold braid and medals and ribbons and doodads. He loved formal diplomatic wear too, the cutaways and the striped pants and the top hats. A striking figure did he cut as he marched into events, imperiously took charge, allowed himself to be wined and dined and feted, until, as sooner or later always happened, people began to murmur among themselves: *Say. Who is that guy?*

Why, he was Lt. Royale St. Cyr, the famed military aviator. He was Lt. Cmdr. Ethan Allan Weinberg of the Atlantic Fleet. He was Undersecretary of State Sterling Wyman. He was the consul general of Romania. He was a distinguished physician. He was screen star Pola Negri's confidential secretary. Somehow he got past gatekeepers everywhere. "Is it demotion you are seeking?" he would snap at some phalanx of secret servicemen guarding some dignitary, and the doors would fly open at once. "Who the hell are you?" some skeptical surgeon would inquire, and he would reply, "My good man, do you not read the newspapers?" and then he would go in and deliver a medical lecture. On the White House lawn, he warmly shook hands with President Warren Harding and clapped him on the back as the cameras flashed. *Who is that guy?* Harding whispered to an aide.

La, he was only Stanley Weyman of Brooklyn, impostor by trade, in and out of jails and nut wards all his days. His long-suffering wife, in 1943 petitioning once again to stick him back in Bellevue, described to the court a man who, though essentially penniless, would buy tuxedos by the dozen; he owned 80 topcoats; he owned 500 neckties. Once, he bought a huge theatrical pipe organ and attempted to knock out the walls so he could install it in his living room, despite the fact that he couldn't play a note. Once, he decided to open a zoo and came home with a truckload of monkeys.

"I get sudden enthusiasms," Stanley Weyman explained.

WELL, IT WAS true, sometimes he swindled a few bucks to keep body and soul together, sometimes he wrote a few rubber checks, but thievery was not basically the point. The point was to be anyone but entirely unimportant Stanley Weyman.

He was not yet 20 when, one day in 1910, he presented himself to city officials as the U.S. consular agent to a small African state called Port de Aubres, got a VIP welcome and spent several fact-finding weeks studying the workings of the court system until he was unmasked. Subsequently, he appointed himself a Serbian attaché. After that, he decided to represent

At right, with Princess Fatima and retinue.

NOT WHOLLY SYMMETRICAL
Stanley Weyman

Second from left, with Dr. Lorenz and City Health Commissioner Royal Copeland

Morocco for a while. Later, as Romania's top envoy, dressed in a gold-trimmed uniform and a splendidly plumed admiral's hat, he got a 21-gun salute from the U.S. Navy in New York Harbor. As Lt. Cmdr. Weinberg, he boarded the flagship Wyoming for a white-glove shakedown inspection and left its captain trembling. As Royale St. Cyr, he was inspecting the 47th Regimental Armory in Brooklyn when the law arrived to discuss his credentials.

The various incarcerations were usually short-term and were not measurably deterrent. For one thing, he'd also become a Brooklyn Democratic district leader and he was one of mayoral candidate John Hylan's campaign managers in the 1917 election. He was, for example, barely out of jail in the Royale St. Cyr matter when he got himself appointed a special assistant to the state attorney general.

IT IS GENERALLY agreed that Stanley Weyman had his finest moment in the summer of 1921, when Princess Fatima, the Sultana of Kabul, arrived in New York with her three sons, Prince Mohammed Hashim Khan, Prince Mohammed

Azim Khan and little Prince Mohammed Akbar Khan, and was immediately called on by the elegant Sterling Wyman of the State Department, who whisked her down to Washington and officially presented her to both President Harding and Secretary of State Charles Evans Hughes. The ceremonies were widely photographed, and great was the White House embarrassment when Undersecretary Wyman was revealed to be a fake. Aside from that, it did appear that he had helped the princess spend a great deal of her fortune, and in this instance, he spent several years behind bars.

Free again, he swiftly became one Dr. Clifford Weyman and attached himself to Dr. Adolf Lorenz, the revered Viennese surgeon who annually visited New York to treat crippled children. That didn't last very long. Neither did his time as Pola Negri's man, in which position he was busily orchestrating all the arrangements at Rudolph Valentino's fabulous 1926 funeral when newspaper reporters spotted him. The fact was that Stanley Weyman of Brooklyn was rather widely known by this time, and there were fewer and fewer places he could turn up unrecognized.

Which didn't keep him from being one of the official City Hall greeters during the reception for transatlantic hero Charles Lindbergh in 1927. Or from, in 1932, working as one of Judge Samuel Seabury's corruption investigators, compiling 18,000 pages of evidence against the Parole Commission before he was found out.

It was a shame he had to lose the Seabury job, he sighed when he was found out. He had rather liked it.

THIS TIME, he wasn't heard from again until 1943, when, calling himself Stephen Weinberg, he was caught by the FBI running a Times Square draft-dodging school, offering instruction in the feigning of feeble-mindedness and physical infirmity. He didn't have much of an excuse — "The pattern of life is not wholly symmetrical," he told the judge — and off he went to prison one more time.

Eight years later, the World-Telegram and Sun exposed Clifford Weyman, the London Daily Mirror's respected United Nations correspondent, as none but Stanley, and the State Department instantly revoked his press card. The Mirror was sorry to lose him. He'd been a fine reporter. "He worked like a beaver," said one of his editors.

HIS FINAL JOB — that came to public attention, anyway — was, it must be conceded, nothing but bald larceny. In June 1953, he was charged with fraudulently obtaining $8,100 in federal housing loans from two Long Island banks, for the renovations of two different homes, neither of which existed. And back to the can he went.

NEARING 70, doubtless for some profoundly psychological reason known only to himself, he took to using his real name, and it was as simple Stanley Weyman that he ended his days as a night clerk at the Dunwoodie Motel in Yonkers. That is who he was on the night of Aug. 27, 1960, when a gunman came in, shot him three times and fled with $200.

By JAY MAEDER
Daily News Staff Writer

RICHARD WHITNEY'S forebears had not actually come over on the Mayflower, but they hadn't been far behind, which was quite good enough to make the Whitneys very distinguished Old Money indeed, and at the moment of his birth in August 1888 it was already carved in stone that Richard Whitney would be schooled at Groton and Harvard, that he would establish a brokerage house, that he would be a captain of finance and a leader of men, that he would live his life, by God, as a Whitney. All these things duly came to pass. Richard Whitney bought his first seat on the New York Stock Exchange at age 23. At 28, he had his own firm and he represented J.P. Morgan. At 41, he became the exchange's president, the powerful chieftain of American brokerage, a man who self-assuredly bullied senators and presidents as he led a titanic battle to stave off federal regulation of a free marketplace. He was tall and handsome and impeccable. He had a townhouse on E. 73rd St. and a sprawling estate in New Jersey. He was treasurer of the New York Yacht Club. He was master of the Essex Fox Hounds.

At 49, ruined and shamed, he meekly asked if some accommodation might not be made for him. Perhaps this distressing little matter of the millions of dollars he had embezzled from his friends might just quietly be dropped. Public disgrace was unacceptable. Prison was unthinkable.

"After all," he protested, "I am Richard Whitney."

And for the first time in his privileged life, this was not good enough.

THE SPECTACULAR FALL of Richard Whitney in the spring of 1938 rocked high society, devastated Wall Street, led directly to the market's full surrender to the regulatory demands of the new Securities and Exchange Commission and ended the New York Stock Exchange's days as a private club operating largely for the benefit of its own patrician members. "No," gasped even Whitney's old foe President Franklin Roosevelt when he heard the news. "Not Dick Whitney."

Whitney had been a legend since Black Thursday 1929, when, amid the din of the roaring calamities that were wiping out fortunes, he strode onto the exchange floor and boomed: "205 for Steel!" With this one bold offer — U.S. Steel had plummeted to well below 205, but Whitney was a Morgan man, and thus it followed that America should be no less confident than the House of Morgan — the worst panic in 50 years briefly subsided. **HEROIC ACTION RALLIES MARKET,** the papers clamored, and Whitney was Wall Street's white knight from that moment forward. In May 1930, he was elected exchange president, marshal of 1,357 member brokers — and now, as the economy reeled, the nation's most vocal defender of their traditional interests.

As securities values continued to decline, as suspicions mounted that slick traders were responsible, as New York Congressman Fiorello LaGuardia introduced a bill requiring securities to be registered with the government, Whitney appeared many times before the Senate Banking and Finance Committee, crusading to keep the market free, denouncing his inquisitors as know-nothings. It was not the professionals who had brought on the crash, he argued, it was the greed-maddened public, the seamstresses and the bootblacks and the rest of the ignoramuses and nuisances who pumped their nickels and dimes into a marketplace best left to the better classes. Control was not to be removed from the descendants of the men who had in 1825 begun gathering at the old Wall St. buttonwood tree to transact their affairs. It would not do.

But the arrival of Roosevelt's New Deal brought still louder calls for government intervention, and increasingly Whitney was cast as the villain in the public's great war on big business, the living embodiment of the frostily conservative old-guard financial barons who controlled the nation's money. Finally, nothing could prevent the creation of the bristling New Deal watchdog called the Securities and Exchange Commission. By March 1935, even Whitney's allies agreed he had to step down from the exchange presidency to ward off any further federal incursions.

There was no appeasement. Late in November 1937, SEC chairman William O. Douglas made it plain that the stock exchange was going to be a regulated public institution. The stage was now set for epic combat between the old millionaires and FDR's Depression-stricken America.

At this precise moment, disturbing matters were coming to the attention of the stock exchange's board of governors. There seemed to be irregularities in Richard Whitney's private affairs. It, well, appeared that the eminent Richard Whitney was a crook.

HE WAS NOT a common thief, exactly, just a financially pressed man who had become accustomed to dipping into client treasuries to cover private shortfalls. Whitney had speculated badly; he was pouring millions down black holes to keep his flimsy stocks propped up; by 1937, he was furtively borrowing from Peter to pay Paul every day of his life. One day an exchange clerk realized that Whitney inappropriately was holding $1.1 million worth of pension-bond funds and reported this to his superiors. In November, even as the SEC's Douglas drew his fateful battle lines, the exchange demanded the bonds' return. Whitney had long since pledged them as collateral against bank loans. He was trapped.

This time the House of Morgan bailed him out; a check was quietly written, the bonds discreetly restored. But the rest of Whitney's world was already falling apart. The New York Yacht Club discovered that its trusted treasurer had helped himself to $150,000. It was found that Whitney had been looting his late father-in-law's estate as well. In February, an exchange auditor examined Whitney's ledgers and found them cooked. There were no more escapes.

On Saturday, March 5, Whitney met with exchange officials and humbly offered to sell his seats and disappear. In return, he proposed, there would be

NOT GOOD ENOUGH
Richard Whitney

En route to Sing Sing, April 1938

no prosecution. *I am Richard Whitney,* he said.

No, they said. On Tuesday, Whitney & Co. was suspended from the Big Board for insolvency, and Whitney was formally summoned to answer charges of "conduct apparently contrary to just and equitable principles of trade."

OFFICIALLY HE WAS $7.6 million in debt, but in the end he was prosecuted only for filching $105,000 from his wife's late father. He made no attempt to deny his improprieties. He was a gentleman, a Whitney. On Monday the 14th of March, he pleaded guilty to grand larceny in General Sessions Court. Three days later, he was expelled from the stock exchange, whose defeated officers then voted to accept the SEC's market reorganization proposals. The episode "ends any hope of relaxing government control over the Financial District," wrote one leading business columnist. "It means that the old guard is out." Market reforms were already in the wind when, on Monday, the 11th of April, Whitney stood before a judge and got five to 10 in prison.

The next morning, handcuffed to a stickup man, he was trucked to Grand Central and put aboard an upriver train to Sing Sing. "Dat guy gets five years for five million and you get thoity years for thoity bucks?" somebody in the crowd hooted at his cuff mate. The papers reported that Richard Whitney pretended not to hear.

CONVICT NO. 96835 was assigned to the overcrowded Sing Sing's oldest cell block, denounced even by Warden Lewis Lawes as unfit for human habitation. There, in the dark, he remained for the next 40 months in a foul hole that had been built the same year that the New York Stock Exchange had first begun to meet beneath the old buttonwood tree on Wall St.

He was paroled in August 1941; blinking in the sunlight, carrying his belongings in an onion sack, barred from brokering and forevermore banished from the Social Register, he stepped into a waiting car and was sped away into obscurity. For a time, he took up dairying in Massachusetts. Later, he turned to citrus ventures in Florida. He died in New Jersey in December 1974 at age 86, long vanished from the world into which he had been born a Whitney.

By JAY MAEDER
Daily News Staff Writer

FINALLY SOMEBODY drops the dime, and early one morning in February 1938 coppers come crashing into the cheap hotel room in West Philadelphia, and here at last are the fugitive New York City mob lawyer Dixie Davis and his showgirl cookie Hope Dare, worn out and broke after eight months on the run and maybe even glad the thing is over.

Dutch Schultz himself is more than two years dead now, but there's still plenty that Dixie can tell District Attorney Tom Dewey about The Dutchman's old rackets if he gets leaned on hard enough. To hear Dewey tell it, Dixie is The Dutchman's direct successor, the big boss of the city's $100-million-a-year policy game. This overstates things somewhat. Dixie is just the lawyer here. But then Dewey is district attorney in the first place because of such a God-given election issue as Dixie Davis, and this is, after all, what prosecutors do.

It is true that Dixie knows everything about everything. It is true that he is the one who kept matters organized for Dutch, the legal genius who kept him out of jail, New York's most flamboyant criminal attorney, jaunty and sleek, always found in the best nightspots. The Dutchman's right arm, sure; everybody knows this. But really, he's only the lawyer. Now Dewey's got him in the jug and he's looking at life. Dixie is beginning to feel very cooperative to begin with, and this is even before Hope Dare goes to Tammany kingpin Jimmy Hines, expecting him to stand for Dixie's bail, and instead gets herself called a name and thrown out.

This is a very bad mistake that Hines makes. Sitting in the Tombs, reflecting on the nature of things, Dixie now grasps that giving up Jimmy Hines to Dewey is his ticket out. So be it. If he's going to sing anyway, he might as well take down everything.

JUNIOR, THE Dutchman always calls him. Boy Wonder. Kid Mouthpiece. Dixie is a cutie from the beginning. Back in '28, 23 years old, he hangs up his shingle on W. 44th St. and waits for clients, of which there are none to speak of. So now he relocates to the new 12th District Magistrate's court on W. 151st St. and sets up shop in a phone booth, literally. This court is full of Harlem numbers runners, coming in, going out, and the lawyers always cost them $25 a pop. Dixie makes his own price $15, and pretty soon there are whole crowds of runners sticking their heads into the phone booth to consult with counsel and Dixie is doing very well. And before long he comes to the attention of the policy bankers and he is being introduced to Arthur Flegenheimer, aka Dutch Schultz, who has wearied of the liquor business and is seeking fresh opportunities.

And so now it is young J. Richard Davis, who has been to college, who explains to Dutch Schultz how he takes over the policy from the small operators and makes it work as a business, and The Dutchman quite genuinely and affectionately appreciates the sound advice and he starts keeping the kid at his side full time. By 1932 Dixie's got a whole 39th floor of offices at 1450 Broadway and life is good. And it goes on staying good for several years yet, at least until Sunday the 3rd of March 1935, when Dixie is sitting right there watching

With The Dutchman (left), 1935

With Hope Dare, 1938

when The Dutchman becomes enraged at some errant underling and blows his brains out, right there in front of his lawyer, and Dixie begins to figure that he might be in this deeper than he really wants to be.

MEANWHILE, DIXIE has met Hope Dare. Hope is originally Rosie Lutzinger from Iowa, but now she's a Follies chorine and her name is Hope Dare, and she and Dixie click like this and Dixie keeps her in one of his penthouses while he's upstate convincing a hayseed jury that Dutch Schultz is not guilty of tax violations. About this same time, Dixie gets called before a grand jury convened by Manhattan district attorney William Dodge, who wants to discuss the policy racket, although apparently not much. "Stupid and respectable," Jimmy Hines fondly calls Dodge, "and all mine." So

little does Dodge seem to wish to discuss anything substantive that the whole jury runs away from him and demands that Gov. Herbert Lehman appoint a special prosecutor. This is Tom Dewey, who, it fast becomes clear, does not belong to Tammany Hall or anybody else, and Dutch Schultz shortly decides that the thing to do with this nosy Dewey is just kill him.

Charlie Lucky and other such saner heads view this as an extremely bad idea, and on Wednesday night the 23rd of October 1935 The Dutchman is dining with several of his mugs at the Palace Chop House in Newark when Charlie Lucky's shooters arrive and drill the whole table. Dixie Davis starts sweating hard when he hears about this; obviously he's on the spot too, he figures, and he calls Hope Dare immediately. *Get out and get out fast,* he whispers. Then, since he has no idea it's Charlie Lucky who has ordered The Dutchman put away, he calls Charlie Lucky. *Help us,* he pleads.

Charlie Lucky, always the gentleman, sends around a car for Hope and gets her out of town right away. The cuckoo Dutchman is one thing, but Charlie has nothing against Dixie. He's a nice boy.

VANISHED NOW is Dixie from all his usual haunts, and vanished he stays until the summer of '36, when the Bar Association of the City of New York, in the first action of its kind against known mob lawyers, moves to disbar him for associating with criminals. He's been laying low with Hope Dare out West, but the bar proceedings bring him back to town, and they go on for months. Big boss of the rackets, Special Prosecutor Dewey is branding him, and at this point Dewey is running for district attorney and he's readying charges that will plainly put Dixie away for a long time. This is not lost on Dixie, who ducks out again and is already the target of a national manhunt by the time he gets named in a 13-count indictment in July 1937.

Dewey is elected DA on Nov. 2. Dixie is disbarred three days later. He and Hope are crisscrossing the land, spending nights in motor courts, eating out of cans, living like rodents. Every motorcycle cop in the country is looking for them. Meanwhile, the $5,000 reward on Dixie's head finally brings Dewey a phone call. In West Philadelphia in February 1938, the cops come crashing in.

STAR WITNESS Dixie Davis sings his heart out. District leader Jimmy Hines took $1,000 a week from Dutch Schultz for years, he testifies, in return for which Hines guaranteed protection, seeing to it that too-vigilant cops got transferred, that courts would acquit, that Dodge would not prod his rackets jury too hard. Hines' influence appears to extend to his own trial judge, who declares a mistrial as fast as he can. The dogged Dewey brings the case straight back and Dixie testifies all over again, and this time, in April 1939, Jimmy Hines goes to Sing Sing. It is the first time a politico-underworld alliance has ever been proven in court, and this makes already famous gangbuster Tom Dewey a presidential candidate. Dewey is not ungrateful. Dixie is out of jail just a few months later.

ON SUNDAY THE 6th of August, Dixie marries Hope and they head west, starting all over again on the $20,000 Dixie gets from Collier's magazine for his sensational tell-all memoirs. In 1942, the Daily News finds the loving couple in California, quietly running a carrot juice stand near Palm Springs.

Little more is heard of them until Dec. 31, 1969, when 65-year-old J. Richard Davis comes home one afternoon and discovers that bandits have invaded his house, tied up his wife and stolen cash and gems. So distressed is Dutch Schultz' old lawyer by such thuggery that he instantly suffers a heart attack and dies on his living room floor.

Presenting an apple to Mayor Abe Beame, 1976

By EDWARD T. O'DONNELL

Special to The News

H E GREW UP pretty much like any other kid in Bensonhurst, skating, going to the movies, playing ball; he sold the Brooklyn Daily Eagle down along the waterfront. One day in 1924, when he was 12, he suddenly stopped growing. Pituitary disorder. His mother dragged him to doctors all over Brooklyn, but he never grew another inch. The day he graduated high school, Johnny Roventini stood 4-foot-3.

His voice never changed either, and so, in the early 1930s, the Hotel New Yorker, across the street from Pennsylvania Station, ended up with a pint-size bellhop whose pipes pierced the walls when he paged guests to come to the phone. "The Smallest Bellboy in the World," the New Yorker starting billing its interesting little employee; his picture began showing up on hotel postcards. By 1933, Johnny was making $25 a week, which was a princely sum in the Great Depression. He might well have stayed comfortably situated at the hotel for the rest of his days.

Instead, one morning in April 1933, a man named Milton Biow dropped by, and now Johnny Roventini's voice was about to become one of the best known in America.

ADVERTISING EXECUTIVE Biow had just been hired by the Philip Morris people to create a campaign for their new cigarette, called Philip Morris, a revival of a defunct brand. This was a life-or-death effort for the company, which, like most small cigarette producers at the time, was near bankruptcy, far outsold by the Big Three — American Tobacco, R.J. Reynolds and Liggett & Myers, respectively, the makers of Lucky Strikes, Camels and Chesterfields. Now, Philip Morris execs had a survival strategy: Instead of putting out discount brands, like the other marginal firms, they would bet their company's future on a new brand with a swanky image. Fifteen cents a pack it would cost, as opposed to two-packs-for-a-

SMOKE AND MIRRORS
Johnny Roventini

quarter Camels and Luckies. It was a risky proposition. But the higher profit margin just might save them.

But how to persuade Depression-stricken Americans to buy the pricier smoke? Digging through turn-of-the-century ads for the original Philip Morris, Biow found a picture of a bellboy extending a silver tray, upon which rested a box of cigarettes and a card that read, "Call for Philip Morris." Fancy hotels. First-class service. That was exactly the pitch Biow was looking for.

What he needed now was a bellboy.

AT THE NEW Yorker, Biow called Johnny Roventini over, gave him a dollar and asked him to page Philip Morris. "Without the mister," he instructed.

And so Johnny marched through the cavernous hotel lobby, crying out four words:

Call ... for ... Philip ... Mor-reees!

That was all Biow had to hear. Days later — April 17, to be exact — Johnny made his radio debut on a Philip Morris-sponsored music program. Soon, magazine ads were matching the voice with the cherubic little man in the pillbox hat and the bright red uniform trimmed with gold.

Johnny was an overnight sensation. He made personal appearances across the country. One hundred thousand life-size cardboard cutouts of the Philip Morris bellhop went up in stores from sea to sea. Philip Morris' market share went from less than 1 percent in 1933 to 10 percent by 1940, an extraordinary 2,500 percent increase in sales.

BY THEN it was clear that radio star Johnny Roventini was no mere Philip Morris pitchman. He *was* Philip Morris. He had singlehandedly saved the company from extinction. Nobody was more aware of this than Philip Morris, which signed him to a lifetime contract that eventually hit $50,000 a year, retained a staff of doctors to look after his health and took out a $100,000

insurance policy just in case his voice suddenly changed or he started to grow. On broadcast nights (Tuesdays on WEAF and Fridays and Sundays on WABC), the company gave him a room at the Essex House. "Our living trademark," Philip Morris execs fondly called Johnny.

He went on doing radio spots and print ads for years, not to mention making cameo TV appearances on such as "I Love Lucy," but by the 1950s his fame was waning. To some extent, this reflected the age of the ad campaign, 20 years and running. It also demonstrated the growing popularity of TV over radio, the medium that had made Johnny famous.

There was another factor as well: With overall sales slipping, Philip Morris in 1954 turned its attention to another brand — again demonstrating the awesome power of advertising by reinventing what had once been an old lady's cigarette as the very embodiment of American masculinity. The Philip Morris bellhop faded away. The Marlboro Man was born.

J OHNNY, WHO never married and lived most of his life near various members of his family, eventually took to spending most of his time aboard cabin cruisers that he kept docked at Sheepshead Bay. Officially retired in 1974, and really never more than an occasional smoker, he continued to answer the call whenever Philip Morris needed him for a special event. He remained a good company man through and through: As cigarettes and cigarette manufacturers began to come under social fire late in his life, he never had a word to say about the subject.

He had spanned the rise and fall of the cigarette in the American experience. When he was born in 1912, cigarettes were held in such low repute that it was illegal in many states to smoke or sell them. Then World War I brought them into the mainstream, and advertising kept them there for 70 years and more. By the end of Johnny Roventini's days, state attorneys general across the U.S. were noisily suing the tobacco industry, charging that it had knowingly marketed a dangerous product for years.

He died at 86 on Nov. 30, 1998, a few months after Big Tobacco agreed to pay out nearly $300 billion to states seeking health-related damages.

By JAY MAEDER
Daily News Staff Writer

THE PING-PONG balls were Harry Richman's idea. If you stuffed the wings with thousands of buoyant Ping-Pong balls, Richman reasoned, the airplane wouldn't sink if it crashed at sea. Dick Merrill thought this was pretty dumb, but it was Richman's airplane. In September 1936, nine years after Lindbergh, transatlantic flights were still lovely adventurous romps, and this one was going to be the first round-trip hop, and Richman was a famous nightclub and radio crooner and his flight was making world headlines. Merrill didn't argue about the Ping-Pong balls. It was Richman's airplane and it was Richman's show.

Well, they'd been pals for years. Richman owned one of New York's swankest speakeasies, where nightly in his top hat and tails he sang his signature hits "Sunny Side of the Street" and "Puttin' On the Ritz," and Merrill had always spent a lot of time in the Club Richman back in his mail-pilot days. By now, Merrill was pretty famous himself, Eastern Air Lines' best-known captain on the New York-to-Miami run and Eastern chief Eddie Rickenbacker's hand-picked boy for a lot of special jobs, like flying 9,000 miles to the tip of South America to help search for the lost explorer Lincoln Ellsworth, and when Richman bought a $95,000 airplane and decided he wanted to cross the Atlantic both ways, there was never a question who was going to fly him. They were both of them hotshots, and the newsreel men were all over Floyd Bennett Field as they took off in their Vultee monoplane christened Lady Peace, headed for England with thousands of ridiculous Ping-Pong balls stuffed into their wings.

As it turned out, the Ping-Pong balls were irrelevant, because Lady Peace crashed not into the Atlantic but into a Newfoundland bog. This mishap occurred on Sept. 14, on the return trip, after the ocean fliers had spent a week or so being the toasts of Europe. What happened was that Richman, the amateur, had panicked in a gale and started dumping fuel at sea, and by the time Merrill could stop him they'd lost 500 gallons and they were lucky to even make the Newfoundland coast at all. Fishermen watched Lady Peace come sputtering in out of a blinding fog, circle the treetops, cough out her last and then pancake in and bust her nose. Merrill vowed never to fly with his old pal again. Richman, for his part, later decided to stamp autographs on his Ping-Pong balls and sell them for $1 apiece, and he made $400, about half of what the autograph-stamping machine cost him.

THERE WERE LESS successful Atlantic flights than this one — there were, to be sure, fatal ones — but Merrill was so mortified that he resolved to make the record-setting round-trip try again, without Richman, and of course Eddie Rickenbacker was happy to give him the time off, since in the mid-1930s the celebrated Dick Merrill could do pretty much anything he pleased.

Rickenbacker had inherited Merrill when he took over what would become Eastern Air Lines. Eastern had been Pitcairn Aviation in those days, and Merrill was the New York-Atlanta mail guy, the kind of flamboyant, cloud-hopping, blind-flying daredevil who carried a pet lion cub alongside him in his cockpit and made headlines everywhere he went. Those seat-of-the-pants times were over by 1930. It was not every mail pilot who got to live through them, but Merrill was one of those who managed to stay over the trees, and when Pitcairn fell into World War ace Rickenbacker's hands and was relaunched as a passenger line, Merrill was suddenly a senior transport captain, heading up Eastern's popular new DC-2 Florida Flier service — as identified

with the new airline as Rickenbacker himself, always in the middle of things whenever the boss figured there was a good promotional stunt to be pulled, as well-known to the public as any movie star.

So it was that on Sunday the 9th of May 1937, the whole world was watching as Merrill and co-pilot Jack Lambie climbed into a Lockheed Electra and headed out for London on the second Atlantic round-trip attempt.

This was dubbed the Coronation Flight, its nominal purpose being to return to the U.S. the first news photos of King George VI's ascension to the throne. It was the greatest aviation feat of 1937, and it won Merrill the prestigious Harmon Trophy. For all that, the two hops were relatively uneventful, and when Merrill and Lambie went to Hollywood to star as more or less themselves in a modest Monogram second feature called "Atlantic Flight," the scriptwriters had to change the details somewhat for a more exciting picture, positing a wholly fictitious beat-the-clock race across the sea to fetch a lifesaving miracle serum.

This picture didn't exactly make a matinee idol out of Merrill. On the other hand, out there in the movie colony, he met Toby Wing.

OVER THE TREES
Dick Merrill

TOBY HAD BEEN in "42nd St." and she'd made a long string of romantic comedies; publicity-wise, she was one of 1937's leading screen bombshells, all over the columns and the movie mags, courted by the likes of Maurice Chevalier, Alfred Vanderbilt and Franklin Roosevelt Jr. At 22, she still had her career in front of her. But in June 1938, she threw everything away to become Mrs. Dick Merrill, and the popular prints just swooned at the marriage of the dashing aviator and the little blondie starlet who loved him.

They settled down in a vine-covered cottage on Greenway North in Forest Hills, Queens, and the newspapers visited them from time to time. In March 1939, the city applauded as they produced a son. "I'll make a pilot of him!" Merrill boasted. In March 1940, the city mourned when the baby died in his crib. Shortly after that, the saddened Merrills resettled in Miami Beach, and their New York days were done.

Thousands of New Yorkers for years yet would not fly to Miami without calling first to establish that the legendary Dick Merrill was driving the airplane.

NOT MUCH MORE was thereafter publicly heard of the private Mr. and Mrs. Merrill. Toby Wing made a final picture in 1943 called "Come On, Marines." The captain went on dependably flying his routes, as professional captains do, making the papers again in May 1947 when he broke two speed records in a single day in one of Rickenbacker's new Constellations and again in February 1948 when his No. 3 engine exploded on him over Florida and he wrestled his burning ship to a safe emergency landing. Among the passengers who survived that day was one of John D. Rockefeller Jr.'s sons, and some years later, when Winthrop Rockefeller was elected governor of Arkansas, the Rockefeller family made a point of thanking Dick Merrill for having determined the destiny of Arkansas state politics.

Amid standing ovations from Eastern brass, Merrill retired from line service in October 1961 with more than a million miles and 38,000 hours behind him. In June 1966, he was one of several old birds who joined TV entertainer Arthur Godfrey on a round-the-world flight that once would have commanded awed headlines everywhere: Godfrey, driving a twin-jet Aero Commander, circumnavigated the globe in 57.5 hours and broke nearly two dozen speed and distance records. But in 1966, mankind was three years away from walking on the moon, and the Godfrey flight was worth just a few newspaper paragraphs and nobody cared.

Late at night, Merrill would often show up at Miami International Airport and borrow a spare 727 and jump around the sky for a while. Far below in the twinkling dark, millions of Floridians would pay no attention to the distant rumble overhead, just a happy old man playing with his toys.

H **E DIED** at 88 on Oct. 31, 1982. Toby Wing's film work was subsequently rediscovered by cultists, and in the late 1990s Miss Wing was enjoying considerable celebrity on the fan convention circuit.

By JAY MAEDER
Daily News Staff Writer

H E WAS A faceless $75-a-week Wall Street bond salesman, 38 years old, just another little gray-suited man who lived in Connecticut and took the morning train to New York, and nobody had ever heard of him before Tuesday the 20th of November 1934, when a salty ex-Marine general went before a congressional committee and charged that Gerald MacGuire of Grayson M.-P. Murphy & Co., 52 Broadway, was the point man in one of American history's most fantastic insurrectionist plots, a dark plan by dark forces to overthrow President Franklin Roosevelt and install a Fascist dictator in the White House.

Gerald MacGuire, as retired Maj. Gen. Smedley Darlington Butler told House sedition probers at the Bar Association building on W. 44th St., had come to him a year earlier with an astonishing $3 million proposition: Lead 500,000 angry World War veterans on Washington and physically remove FDR from his office. It was the only way to save American business, the American dollar and the American way from Roosevelt's ruinous New Deal, MacGuire had argued. There was a $50 million war chest available, much of it put up by Singer Sewing Machine Co. heir Robert Sterling Clark. The Remington people would supply the guns. The DuPont people would supply the ammunition. Morgan money was involved as well. Elements inside the American Legion and Roosevelt's own Democratic Party were actively abetting the planned coup.

This was Butler's story, and it was quite the page one sensation. From Europe, Clark branded the general's yarn a damnable libel. Gerald MacGuire's Wall Street boss, Col. Grayson Murphy, laughed it off as a preposterous fiction. MacGuire himself, catapulted overnight out of obscurity, stared wanly into press cameras and said he had absolutely no idea what Butler was talking about. The whole thing was just bizarre, he said.

"Gee, I'm going to catch the devil at the office for this," he mumbled.

BUTLER was not just some retired general. He was Old Gimlet Eye himself, America's best-known professional fighting man, a living legend, 30 years a warrior, hero of Cuba and the Philippines and Panama and Haiti and Nicaragua and Mexico and China. He was the man who had uttered one of the Marine Corps' most ringingly famous battlefield chest-thumpers: *If you are covered and put up your hands, you're alive. If you are covered and don't put up your hands, by God, you're Marines!* Twice Congress had tried to give him the Medal of Honor. Twice he had modestly refused it.

He was also a notoriously loose cannon. In 1931, the State Department had found it necessary to formally apologize to Benito Mussolini after Butler delivered himself of an intemperate remark about the Italian strongman.

CONSPIRACY THEORY
Gerald MacGuire

After that, he had seized upon an impulse to publicly insult the Secretary of the Navy. Retirement soon followed, and since then, he had been a loud champion of the war veterans' quest for their long-promised bonus payments, their staunchest defender when Gen. Douglas MacArthur's cavalrymen drove the Bonus Army out of Washington in July 1932. Lowell Thomas had written his biography. By 1933, he was publicly warning that World War II was inevitable.

This was the unassailable patriot Gerald MacGuire's superiors had selected as their "man on the white horse," the commander who would lead the seething Bonus soldiers against the federal government.

THE HOUSE committee's chiefs, Democrats John McCormack of Massachusetts and Samuel Dickstein of New York, initially seemed vigorous in their pursuit of Butler's hair-raising revelations. "Butler has the evidence correctly," Dickstein told the papers; MacGuire, he said, was "hanging himself" with contradictions. There seemed solid documentation: MacGuire had toured Germany and Italy and France, consulting with various right-wing groups and studying their organizations. He had met with Butler on numerous occasions. Singer's Clark was the moneyman behind a MacGuire-led group called the Committee for a Sound Dollar and a Sound Currency. Clark admitted having asked Butler to "use his influence" at the 1933 American Legion national convention to speak up for the gold standard. The national Veterans of Foreign Wars leader, James Van Zandt, came forward to support Butler's tale. So did a Philadelphia newspaper reporter with whom MacGuire had once been loose-tongued.

At the edges of the eerie story was the American Liberty League, the suddenly prominent anti-FDR federation lately founded by such out-of-power Democrats as ex-national party chief Jouette Shouse, ex-New York Gov. Al Smith, ex-U.S. Secretary of State Bainbridge Colby and unsuccessful 1924 presidential nominee John Davis. It was Davis, indeed, who had authored a speech Clark had asked Butler to make at the '33 Legion convention. Grayson Murphy was second-in-command, behind Shouse. Liberty League membership was all but a who's who of notable industrialists. Large among them was the munitions maker Irenee du Pont, who, as it happened, was in late 1934 one of those called to testify as Congress probed war profiteering. Among the things du Pont growled at his interrogators: "The only way to wage a successful war is to have an absolute monarchy. You never hear of a democracy waging a successful war." Scientist du Pont, who had developed rayon and cellophane and who was currently positing that it would be possible to create a new race of supermen with chemical injections, defended the Liberty League at some length. "The necessity for this association has become apparent in the continual gnawing at the vitals of the Constitution," he said.

But, the bombshells notwithstanding, the House committee all at once seemed to lose interest in its investigation. There were a couple of public hearings late in December, but neither Murphy nor Clark nor anyone else besides Butler and MacGuire was called to testify, and MacGuire merely repeated that he didn't know anything about anything. On Feb. 15, 1935, McCormack issued a thin report stating that there was no admissible proof of Butler's wild allegations. Dickstein, for his part, made it plain that he felt himself muzzled and that there was much more to be said.

As for Butler, he took to national radio for weeks, denouncing the committee for suppressing one of the day's most terrifying specters. Faceless, gray-suited Gerald MacGuire, he insisted, had plainly been an agent of great and far-reaching harm; why was the committee sweeping this under the rug? McCormack shrugged off his blasts. The general, he said, "must answer to his own conscience."

OLD GIMLET EYE made enough noise that he might even have forced a reopening of the investigation at some point, except for the fact that, on March 25, Gerald MacGuire mysteriously died, following what was termed a "brief illness." He left a wife and five children.

A FTER FRANKLIN Roosevelt's reelection in 1936, the American Liberty League pretty much vanished. It has long been suggested that Roosevelt personally quashed any substantive inquiry into Gen. Butler's charges, purely as a practical political matter.

Smedley Butler died at 59 in 1940, having spent his last years churning out bombastic magazine articles such as "The Peace Racket" and "How Safe Is America?"

Robert Sterling Clark died at 79 in 1956, a major benefactor of Williams College in Williamstown, Mass., a founder of that town's Sterling and Francine Clark Art Institute, a revered old philanthropist.

By JAY MAEDER
Daily News Staff Writer

BROADWAY STROLLERS gasp and scramble as the flimsy little airplane roars over their heads at barely streetlight level. At the stick is a kid named Juan Trippe, who otherwise makes a living flying sightseers around out on Rockaway Beach but who today has been hired by a newsreel man to take him up for some picture-taking. There is quite the civic uproar over this rude incident. In the early 1920s, though, there is no particular law against flying an airplane just a few feet above Broadway.

Forty years from this moment, there will stand in the heart of Manhattan the world's largest office building, and it will bear on its sides, in colossal letters for all to behold, the name of the great globe-girdling airline this young pilot will build.

THERE WOULD, in truth, be more to that than mere American pluck and luck. Juan Trippe was not the standard-issue penniless barnstormer, and this was not a rags-to-riches story. Trippe was the son of a prominent New York banker, and his chums at Yale had been lads with names like Vanderbilt and Whitney and Rockefeller. His roommate, who was named Scaife, had family ties to a man named Mellon, who was secretary of the treasury. And Trippe himself would marry a woman named Stettinius, whose brother someday would be secretary of state. It was true that such associations would prove not unuseful to Juan Trippe as he constructed an air transport empire so vast and formidable that it might as well have been an official arm of the U.S. government, which, so far as he was concerned, it was.

But it was also true that he was an authentic prophet. If fundamentally he was heir to the ruthless railroad barons of the 19th century, if he was not above crushing some struggling minor competitor when it suited him, if his company's relations with various foreign governments struck many as all too suspiciously confidential, it remained the case that he really was the one man — at a crucial point at the dawn of the commercial aviation industry the very first man — who had gazed into the skies and understood that they had no national boundaries. To this day it is unimaginable how the rivers of the 20th-century American destiny might have coursed without Juan Trippe.

HE WAS BORN in Sea Bright, N.J., in 1899, descended from English mariners. There was not a drop of Spanish blood in him; his mother had merely liked the name Juan. As it turned out, this never hurt him much over the years he spent courting Latin American presidents and generals. He was reared to join the family investment firm, but he liked flying better; fresh out of college, he bought seven cheap Navy-surplus seaplanes, set himself up as Long Island Airways and started offering rides to the beach crowds. All this was just a young man's larking. The future, Trippe divined, lay in mail routes, which by 1925 the post office was ready to privatize.

As he was not without connections, his new firm, Colonial Air Transport, was awarded the nation's first commercial air-mail run, and in July 1926 he began flying the mail between New York and Boston. Soon he decided that Colonial should expand to Miami and Havana as well. Colonial's investors failed to agree with him on this one. So

Stratocruiser, off to far places, 1949

CHOSEN INSTRUMENT
Juan Trippe

he resigned, went straight to Cuba, cordially sat down with President Gerardo Machado and, despite the fact that at this point he had no airline, proceeded to secure exclusive island landing rights.

This piece of prescience shortly paid off when a small outfit called Pan American Airways won the Florida-Cuba mail route from the post office and then discovered that it couldn't land in Havana but that Juan Trippe could. Reasonable men reasoned together. In October 1927, Trippe became Pan American's president. By January, he was offering regular Miami-Havana passenger service, and Pan Am was an international airline.

OPERATIONALLY headquartered in Miami, Trippe's Pan Am looked ever southward, fast moving into Panama, Puerto Rico, Nicaragua, Chile, Peru and Brazil, first nailing down landing rights — maybe in places that did not yet even have airstrips — and then swallowing up whatever fleabag local air services existed. By the summer of 1930, having colonized most of Central and South America every bit as much as the American fruit and sugar and mining companies had, Pan Am was the world's largest airline in terms of miles flown, 100,000 a week. Deep in the mountains and the jungles, the on-schedule Pan Am airplane became the dependable symbol of benevolent Yanqui paternalism.

This suited the U.S. government just fine. As with General Motors, what was good for Pan Am was good for the country, and through the 1930s there was little official objection to anything Pan Am cared to do. Trippe's one-man diplomacy blazed more trails and cut more deals than the State Department ever did. Many a U.S. diplomat stationed in many a banana republic over many a year came to learn that the local Pan Am man had readier access to the presidente's ministers than he ever would.

And this was only Latin America. Late in 1935, Pan Am introduced its behemoth Clippers, the mighty ocean liners of the air, and soon they were flying across the Pacific Ocean, to Honolulu, to Guam, to Manila and Macao and Hong Kong, then to New Zealand, representing the United States everywhere Pan Am wings flashed, the nation's

flag carrier, its chosen instrument.

At the same time, Trippe was readying New York City's seaplane base, the Port Washington terminal on Long Island's Manhasset Bay, for soon-to-come transatlantic flights. Bermuda came first, then mail runs to Europe. In July 1939, Trippe's Clippers inaugurated regularly scheduled passenger service between New York and England, Portugal and France.

By now, as Pan Am was locked in mortal combat with Britain's Imperial Airways and Germany's Lufthansa for global domination of the airways, there were those in Washington who increasingly had reservations about Trippe's monopoly over America's international routes. Through World War II, Trippe vigorously lobbied Congress for continued exclusivity. This time he lost; in 1945, the Civil Aeronautics Board awarded routes to several other carriers, and Pan Am's status as an unchallenged government unto itself was ended.

AFTER THE WAR, Pan Am introduced the notion of cheaper tourist-class fares to the common man. In 1958, it became the first U.S. airline to fly jetliners. In 1966, it was the first to order a fleet of futuristic jumbo jets. Trippe retired in 1968, and his company thereafter went into sharp decline, crippled by a worldwide recession, skyrocketing fuel prices and federal deregulation mandates. After selling off most of its pioneer ocean routes, America's once-great flag carrier folded in 1991, 10 years after its founder died in his Fifth Ave. home at age 81.

There remained on the New York skyline what had once been another of Trippe's legacies. Unlike many a pile thrown up as a monument to its proprietors, the Pan Am Building rising high over Grand Central Terminal had nothing initially to do with Pan Am. When first envisioned in 1958, it was going to be called Grand Central City; four years later, as its developers found themselves having to beg for a marquee tenant, Trippe agreed to move in from the Chrysler Building on the condition that the words PAN AM would be emblazoned across the new tower's sides, in colossal letters for all to behold.

So they were, and late on the eve of the 21st century, most New Yorkers looked at the Met Life Building and still instinctively called it the Pan Am Building, although, of course, within another generation or so, this habit, too, would surely pass into oblivion, as things do.

THE IN-LAWS
Brigid and Willie Hitler

By ELLIOT ROSENBERG

Special to The News

THE MATRONLY Dubliner and her handsome son were neither gifted writers nor spellbinding lecturers. But when the French liner Normandie docked at Pier 88 on the Hudson, they aspired to make their mark here as the world's preeminent sister-in-law and nephew. The date: March 30, 1939. They were Hitlers.

War neared, and the pair would call New York home for the duration and after. They had crossed the Atlantic under aliases, but anonymity vanished as reporters clamored aboard and cameras flashed.

HITLER'S HALF-IRISH NEPHEW ARRIVES WITHOUT AN O'HEIL, beamed one afternoon daily. **KIN OF HITLER, HERE, ARE COOL TO FUEHRER; NEPHEW CALLS CHANCELLOR A MENACE,** announced the town's more sedate paper of record the next morning.

Brigid Elizabeth Hitler was 47, William Patrick Hitler 28, when they brought the Hitler name to the city. She had coal-black hair, blue eyes and a rich Irish brogue; he was 6 feet tall, well-built and somewhat more elegantly mustached than was his Uncle Adolf. Mother and son took up residence at a furnished two-story house in placid Hollis, Queens, but set their gazes across the East River at bustling Madison Ave. The William Morris Agency, with a keen eye for celebrity value, had paved their financial path to New York; by June, William Patrick had published a Look magazine article titled "Why I Hate My Uncle," and the Press Alliance Syndicate was shopping around his six-part tell-all series, "My Uncle, The Third Reich and I."

Or, to put it another way, in the assessment of one newspaper editor who declined the offering: *"Discredited relative who wasn't paid off squawks."*

JUST HOW HAD Willie's mom, bred in the land of shamrocks and leprechauns, become mixed up with a family like the Schicklgrubers?

According to Brigid, she'd met Alois Hitler Jr., Adolf's older stepbrother, at a Dublin horse show in 1910. She was a naive 18, he a worldly 28.

"I won't have any foreigners in the family," her father had announced. So the lovers eloped to England. Three blustery years of marriage produced one child and four separations before Alois walked out for good.

Church strictures blocked a divorce. Years passed. Single parent Brigid settled into a threadbare existence. Then the name of a rising star in German politics began appearing in newspapers around the world. This was Adolf, her own brother-in-law. A unique financial opportunity now seemed at hand.

Hearing reports that America's Hearstpress was making offers, Adolf Hitler now summoned Brigid and her son to Bavaria for a stern lecture on family silence. Later, as chancellor, Hitler assured young Willie steady work in the thriving New Order. But after six years of humdrum jobs, mainly at the Opel auto works, Willie decided to leave the Third Reich forever. Next stop, America.

NEW YORK CITY nightlife furthered the appeal of New World freedom, and columnist Leonard Lyons picked up the tale of Willie Hitler's plan to become a U.S. citizen. As Europe blazed, his presumed cache of lurid insider material increasingly enhanced his lecture-circuit value; he could dwell at length on his personal conflicts with his uncle, general conditions in Germany, gossip about Nazi bigwigs, how he was followed by the Gestapo. If his oratorical armament fell short of achieving a wordskrieg, he toured regularly, giving it to Uncle Adolf all over the land.

Brigid, more the stay-at-home, waited for Hollywood to discover her in Hollis. One minor producer announced at one point that he was signing her for a role in "The Mad Dog of Europe," but nothing ever came of that project. Meanwhile, she began work on a memoir of her own. Its chief revelation, probably entirely fanciful: Adolf's 1912 visit to Liverpool, where, she said, he'd sponged off his in-laws for six months. He wouldn't find a job, Brigid confided, he was untidy, he slept late. "Weak and spineless," she sniffed.

The yarn might well have set Der Fuehrer to chewing the carpets at Berchtesgaden had he read it. However, her shocking typescript remained at her New York literary agent's office, unpublishable and unpublished.

BY JUNE 1941, Brigid was working as a volunteer assistant at British War Relief on Fifth Ave., and naturally that got her into the headlines too (**IN-LAW HAS CURE FOR HITLER — SLOW TORTURE, SUGGESTS MRS. BRIGID).** At the same time, Willie was heading north to try to join the Royal Canadian Air Force after kissing his mom goodbye at the Hotel Astor in front of a pack of photographers.

The Canadians eventually turned him down. So did the U.S. Army Air Forces, despite his 1-A classification. Probably the reason was the questionnaire handed all foreign applicants, the one about relatives who served in foreign armed services. Willie filled it in: *"1. Thomas J. Dowling, uncle, England, 1923-1926, Royal Air Force. 2. Adolf Hitler, uncle, Germany, 1914-1918, corporal."*

It was back to speaking engagements for Willie, at such venues as Columbia University and the Marble Collegiate Church ("The Rudolph Hess Mystery," "What About Germany and the German People?"). But he still hoped to get into the shooting war. In February 1944, he found the U.S. Navy less fussy about family genealogy. He passed his exam at the Grand Central Palace Induction Center, and, on March 6 reported to the Navy recruiting station at 88 Vanderbilt Ave. for assignment to boot camp. "I have more than one score to settle with Uncle Adolf," Willie declared to the press.

In his spare time, he promised, he would write a book, "My Uncle Adolf." But he never finished it. Fourteen months later, the war was over, and nobody much cared anymore what Willie Hitler thought about anything. Suddenly, the world's most famous nephew had lost his livelihood, relatively speaking.

WILLIAM PATRICK Hitler slipped back into anonymity. According to Hitler biographer John Toland, he remained in the New York area and changed his name. This was probably a sensible career move.

As for Brigid, she achieved literary immortality of a sort. Today, her dog-eared book, "My Brother-in-Law Adolf," shares space in the New York Public Library's Manuscript and Archive Division with George Washington's Farewell Address and Thomas Jefferson's handwritten copy of the Declaration of Independence.

BIG TOWN ★ BIOGRAPHY

LIVES AND TIMES OF THE CENTURY'S CLASSIC NEW YORKERS

By ELLIOT ROSENBERG
Special to The News

THE WAR DEPARTMENT rejected his plea for regular Army troops to man the city's ramparts. Albany similarly denied him use of city-based National Guardsmen. But Mayor Fiorello LaGuardia was not about to let enemy saboteurs set his town ablaze.

In these desperate early moments of World War II, the mayor decided he would recruit his own troops. He would put them in khaki, give them guns and send them out to secure wharves, terminals, power plants, tunnels and whatever else the foe might seek to strike. He called for 3,500 citizen volunteers. The City Patrol Corps, he christened his defense force. Everyone else called it LaGuardia's Army.

By any name, it needed an experienced field commander, and the mayor soon found one in tall, gray, ramrod-stiff Maj. Gen. Robert Melville Danford, U.S.A., Retired.

Danford, too old for the war, had just weeks earlier packed away his Army uniform after a lifetime of service that he had completed as Chief of Field Artillery. Now, the man who had been the last commander of the Army's horse-drawn guns was ready for a new challenge. Fresh in the city, he got the lay of the land and quickly noted that exposed riverfronts, multiple bridge crossings and beaches fairly invited infiltration. As a veteran artilleryman, though, he knew a thing or two about beating back an attacking force.

On the 1st of April 1942, Danford took his oath as City Patrol Corps commandant, moved into headquarters at 300 Mulberry St. and went to work whipping 1,401 freshly approved Corpsmen into a freedom-fighting unit.

"This is a military organization," he announced proudly.

ACTUALLY, AS the general little by little discovered, his overage patriots and younger 4Fs were mostly put to work as auxiliary policemen, as more and more genuine street patrolmen got scooped up weekly by the draft. The Navy, for one, never paid any attention at all to the City Patrol Corps.

But if what the city basically wanted was traffic cops, Danford intended to produce disciplined fighting men all the same. He was a 1904 West Point graduate, every inch a general, and he wanted divisions. He had five of them, each commanded by a colonel with a staff of executive, ordnance, medical and finance officers, plus a judge advocate. At the company level, there were captains, lieutenants and sergeants. And he had an official Manual of Procedure.

"When addressed by a superior officer," the manual stated, "a member of the Corps shall assume the position of attention as prescribed by the United States Army drill regulations." Training officers were to demand "exact execution and perfection in the slightest detail." The Corps, Danford declared, was a "lawful, belligerent organization under The Hague Regulations" and would "conduct its operations in accordance with the laws and usages of war."

There were a few problems. Uniforms, for one. Although the Army quartermaster agreed to supply khaki garb, Danford's overage, pot-bellied recruits often couldn't fit into them. "So small in size as to be unusable," Danford grumbled.

Guns? The Army wouldn't provide any. Pestered by the general, Police Commissioner Lewis

With Police Commissioner Lewis Valentine and Mayor Fiorello LaGuardia, accepting warriors' clubs made from pinball-machine legs

Company D, Queens Division

UNDER ARMS, SORT OF
Gen. Robert Danford

Valentine reluctantly turned over a cache of sidearms seized from local gangsters. But most Corpsmen had to make do with simpler weapons, like clubs — 2,000 of which were fashioned from the legs of confiscated pinball machines.

Also, there was the cavalry situation. It turned out that Corps mounties had to rent their horses out of their own pockets.

Still, there were actual vital installations to preserve and protect out there, and Danford's troopers walked guard many a vigilant night, successfully keeping enemy invaders at bay. The general could take pride in the reports reaching his Mulberry St. command post. One of them, from a Brooklyn waterfront unit, read: "There in the hostile and grim silence of frowning warehouses and ancient buildings was born the determination of Company A to serve."

By January 1943, some 6,000 New Yorkers were under arms, sort of, including LaGuardia's personal chauffeur, who was required to wear khakis and garrison cap when wheeling the boss around.

AS THE WAR went on, and U.S. troops advanced across North Africa, and the march toward Tokyo began, local scares receded and AWOLs became not uncommon in Danford's home-front command. In a radio address, he appealed to his men's sense of duty: Theirs was a service, he said, "in which the frail of body and

frail of heart have no place. It takes discipline and determination and loyalty to a principle to keep one on guard or patrol on a dark and lonely street in rain, cold, sleet and zero weather for hours at a stretch instead of with a good book and a comfortable chair by the fireside." Well, yes. Exactly.

Next he tried a liberal promotion policy to keep his force together. Finally, he even put aside soldierly misgivings and allowed women into the Corps. Ever hopeful, early in 1944 he called for an expansion of his command from a now much dwindled 4,300 to one 15,000 strong. "We know that there are camouflaged enemies here," he warned. "We don't know what they may be planning."

The general himself soldiered on, putting in six-day weeks at Mulberry St. and spending three nights weekly, from 8 p.m. to midnight, in the field. "I talk with them and learn who they are and why they joined the Corps," he explained to reporters. "A soldier in the front lines has got to be visited by his officers or he doesn't think much of them."

WAR'S END put LaGuardia's Army out of business. On Aug. 19, 1945, the City Patrol Corps held its final march-past for its commandant at the Bronx's 8th Regiment Armory. Demobilization and final paperwork took another month. The general reported that his troops had conducted 771,608 four-hour guard tours and undergone 324,840 hours of drill and instruction.

On the 1st of October, the elderly Danford received his own honorable discharge, handed the official Corps flag to LaGuardia and faded away. Late in his life he was occasionally feted by West Point as one of its oldest living graduates, and he was 95 when he died in Stamford, Conn., in September 1974, his duty done.

BIG TOWN BIOGRAPHY

By ELLIOT ROSENBERG

Special to The News

HITLER-LOVERS AND hatemongers around town regarded George Pagnanelli as one of their own. Hawking racist tracts, saluting local fuehrers at secret meetings, railing against Roosevelt and the Jews for dragging America into Europe's war, Pagnanelli was a reliable man.

And Pagnanelli was a joiner. Between 1939 and 1943, he bonded with the American National Socialist Party, the Anglo-Saxon Federation of America, the Paul Revere Sentinels, the Crusaders for Americanism — more than 30 outfits in all.

He was there when 1,200 brownshirts marched into Madison Square Garden in February 1939 and listened to German-American Bund leader Fritz Kuhn berate democracy beneath a portrait of George Washington flanked by giant swastikas. He joined the cheering at a Bronx rally as the screen flashed newsreel shots of Generalissimo Franco giving the straight-arm salute. He peddled Father Coughlin's anti-Semitic "Social Justice," a dime a copy.

On the court of the Midtown Sporting Club on W. 59th St. — home to "Real Americans in Action" — he drilled with the Iron Guard and won the rank of captain. He was always welcome at the Bund's tightly guarded Camp Siegfried in Yaphank, L.I.

Pagnanelli's prestige boomed among the ranks of Fascist and supernationalist faithful, thanks to his editorial talent. He began churning out his own mimeographed poison and seeing to it that it reached the elite of the farthest far right. The Christian Defender, his paper was called, designed to be one of the coarsest sheets in New York City. And the more crudely anti-Semitic it got, the more popular it became.

All of this he admitted freely — in 1943, in the pages of an explosive book titled "Under Cover," wherein "George Pagnanelli" revealed himself to be anti-Fascist crusader John Roy Carlson, a man who had spent four dark years infiltrating the city's subversive hotbeds, regularly reporting to the New York Police Department and the FBI.

JOHN ROY CARLSON named names, cited places and reproduced documents, filling 544 pages with revelations about New York's Nazi and Fascist bullies and their more genteel, behind-the-scenes moneyed backers. "Under Cover" swiftly topped nonfiction best-seller lists, energetically boosted by such people as columnist Walter Winchell, who urged Mr. and Mrs. America to read Carlson's "diary of hobnobbing with gov't wreckers" and "enjoy the way they are stripped naked." The book sold nearly 200,000 copies in a matter of weeks.

Not everyone appreciated this instant success. Newspaper publisher Frank Gannett, mentioned as founder of an anti-New Deal group called the Committee for Constitutional Government, threatened legal action against book wholesalers and retailers handling Carlson's exposé. "I don't want to suppress it," he stormed. "I want to kill it."

He failed. So did the arch-conservative Chicago

Tribune, when it sought to smear Carlson with a story that "John Roy Carlson" was every bit as fictitious as "George Pagnanelli." Carlson, the Tribune announced, was really "foreign-born" Arthur Derounian, of 34-36 93rd St., Jackson Heights, Queens. That was true enough, but authorities already knew Carlson's real name, so the Tribune report fell flat.

Neither did Montana's isolationist Sen. Burton K. Wheeler put a dent in the book's sales. Named as one of those in Congress who gave aid and comfort to the far right, overtly or covertly, Wheeler angrily threatened a full Capitol Hill investigation of the foreign-born undercover operative. It went nowhere.

ARTHUR DEROUNIAN, an Armenian born in Greece in April 1909, arrived in New York at age 12, graduated from New York University's school of journalism and began freelancing stories to magazines — small magazines, because "the big ones would not touch the kind of stuff I wrote," he said later. Those included Fortune, which had originally assigned him to investigate Fascist activity in the New York area and then killed the project. Indeed, after Derounian wrote his book, the manuscript was turned down by 18 publishers before E.P. Dutton grabbed it.

"John Roy Carlson" passed up the routine jacket photograph, marketing himself as a man whose face was already too well-known in certain now-hostile circles. When he lectured, he always surrounded himself with bodyguards to keep away press photographers, who succeeded in snapping his picture on only a few occasions.

Indeed, there were those who were out to get him. In 1944, as "Under Cover" remained a best-seller and several of its figures were soon to go to trial for sedition in Washington, one Edwin Banta, a bit player in the book, came up with a scheme to frame the author on a phony rape charge and discredit him. But the plan went awry: The attractive young woman recruited to pose as the victim changed her mind and confessed the fraud to cops. Banta went to prison.

AS THE THIRD Reich collapsed, Arthur Derounian continued to sniff about for local Fascists: Hitler was dead, but, Derounian warned, "Hitlerism in our country is a sinister and expanding reality." The result of his probings was "The Plotters," published in late

1946. For this journey into the netherworld of racists and nativist bigots, any such ethnic alias as "Pagnanelli" was out; Derounian labored mostly as the eminently Waspy "Robert Thompson Jr."

Arthur Schlesinger Jr., reviewing "The Plotters" for the Herald-Tribune, called the book an "unforgettable picture of the minds and operations of those diseased persons who would like to transform the United States into something on the model of Nazi Germany." One night in January 1947, three of those diseased persons spotted Derounian at Brooklyn's Academy of Music, where he had been taking notes at a gathering of Women for the United States of America, and beat him up outside.

'THE PLOTTERS" was only modestly successful, considerably less a sensation than "Under Cover." Derounian's focus was always on the militant right, and postwar America's nightmare in the late 1940s was no longer smoldering Fascism so much as it was dawning Red Menace. Accordingly, Arthur Derounian faded from public attention. On April 23, 1991, the old soldier died of an apparent heart attack while researching in the American Jewish Committee's library on E. 56th St. He was 82. A fresh generation of swastika-tattooed militiamen wouldn't have to worry about him.

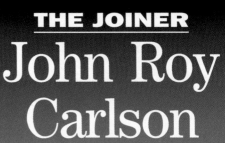

THE JOINER
John Roy Carlson

By ELLIOT ROSENBERG

Special to The News

SHOCKED BY Pearl Harbor, Americans desperately needed good news — and three days into the Pacific War, they got it, with a dazzling report from northern Luzon that one Capt. Colin Kelly had spotted and sunk the Japanese battleship Haruna. According to the popular account, the first hero of World War II had crashed his crippled Flying Fortress into the burning warship after ordering his crew to bail out. Kelly was immediately the nation's No. 1 hero, revered from his small Florida hometown to Boeing headquarters in Seattle. But in Brooklyn, the real hero was Kelly's bombardier, Meyer Levin.

The 1940s were times of unabashed references to "English stock" and "Italian stock" and "Irish stock." Meyer Levin was a Brooklyn Jew. Better than dry statistics, he shredded the old canard, revived early during the war, that Jews evaded combat. As the joke went: "Colin Kelly was first in sinking a Japanese battleship, and Hymie Kaplan was first in getting four brand-new auto tires." But there was an obvious retort to that: Colin Kelly *and* Meyer Levin had sent Haruna to the bottom.

Actually, neither one of them had. They bombed something, but the Haruna wasn't even in Philippine waters at the time. But the fog of war rolled thick in December 1941, and the War Department found the newly minted legend better for morale than facts anyway. Only Tokyo's propagandists had cause to set the record straight, and nobody in America was listening to them.

And so handsome young Colin Kelly's portrait soon ended up on a gum card treasured in every schoolyard. But every Brooklyn kid knew that it was eagle-eyed Cpl. Meyer Levin who had aimed the bombs.

HE HAD BEEN enthralled by aircraft since boyhood. Sam Levin, a tailor, sought to steer his son to the concert stage, but after he finished Brooklyn Technical High School in 1934, the lad went straight into night classes at the YMCA's Engineering School for Aviation, working as an $18-a-week stock clerk to finance the two-year course. On his 23rd birthday in June 1939, he joined the fledgling Army Air Corps, enlisting as an aviation mechanic. Two years later, he was in Hawaii.

"I'm down at Hickam Field now, going to school," he wrote his parents in June 1941. "It is of a special and secret nature. I can't tell you more about it, except that I was very fortunate in being one of the few selected for this kind of work."

That fall he teamed up with Colin Kelly. Three months before Pearl Harbor, their B-17 left Oahu for Clark Field on Luzon. The last leg of the flight, through the teeth of a typhoon, led to War Department medals for each crewman. And just a few months after that, the Haruna episode gave Levin the Distinguished Flying Cross.

Colin Kelly's Bombardier. That was his tag in the headlines that followed him through the war. The Brooklyn Eagle: **ARMY ASKS FDR, DECORATE BORO BOMBARDIER FOR KELLY.** The New York Times: **CAPT'N KELLY'S BOMBARDIER GETS ANOTHER ENEMY SHIP.** The New York Herald Tribune: **COLIN KELLY'S BOMBARDIER TELLS HOW PLANE BLASTED THE HARUNA.** The Daily News: **COLIN KELLY'S BOMBARDIER DODGES DEATH AGAIN TO GET HIS FIRST LEAVE.**

Sunday the 1st of November 1942 was officially declared Meyer Levin Day in Brooklyn, and 2,500 friends and neighbors gathered around the flag-draped porch of Sam and Leah Levin's home at 1504 E. 33rd St. An American Legion color guard was there. So were speech-making politicians. "The Butcher of Berlin must have writhed in anger," declared one of them, "to learn that his ally in the Orient was being beaten and humiliated by, of all people, a Jewish boy from the sidewalks of New York."

The bombardier's proud mother was presented with a plaque celebrating his marksmanship, and she read it aloud to a national radio audience. Then volunteers took over the Levin parlor and sold a quarter million dollars worth of war bonds to the milling throngs.

MEANWHILE, THERE was plenty of action in the South Pacific. On one occasion, after attacking and apparently sinking an enemy transport in the Coral Sea, Levin's Fortress ran out of fuel in fog; for the second time, Levin was forced to parachute from a doomed plane. He was missing in action for a while. Following rescue, he got a Silver Star. Later, he added to that an Oak Leaf Cluster.

Then, in February 1943, the terse War Department telegram arrived at the Levin home.

"I'm very proud that my boy served his country as a brave soldier," Sam Levin told reporters. "He was our only boy. But again, I say I'm proud he went as he did, fighting for his country."

Details of Levin's death in a ditching at sea Jan. 7 were pieced together from survivor debriefings. Though he had not been scheduled to fly that day, he had tagged along as a volunteer spotter. Bad weather dogged the flight, and the plane went down. "The last I saw of Levin," said one crewman, "he was standing, grasping the safety catches on the life raft inside the Fortress. He probably released the raft which saved our lives before he was knocked unconscious."

THE AMALGAMATED Clothing Workers, Sam Levin's union, raised $350,000 to buy a new bomber bearing the names of Colin Kelly and Meyer Levin. A concert raised funds for a Meyer Levin Medical Field Unit to be sent to Russia. Jewish War Veterans Post 169 of Brooklyn changed its name to the Meyer Levin Post. Eventually, the Board of Education built a school called Meyer Levin Junior High.

THE DURABLE Haruna outlived both Colin Kelly and Meyer Levin, finally falling victim to U.S. bombs while sitting in a Japanese dockyard July 28, 1945.

THE BOMBARDIER
Meyer Levin

Harry "THE HIPSTER" Gibson

Who Put the Benzedrine in Mrs. Murphy's Ovaltine?

COURTESY DELMARK RECORDS

687 delmark

FRANTIC
Harry the Hipster

By CHRIS ERIKSON
Special to The News

HE WAS THE high-living, jive-talking, piano-pounding hepcat king of 1940s Swing Street, decked out in sharp suit and pencil mustache, slamming out a rumbling boogie and mugging at the audience like a maniac, eyes rolling, eyebrows wiggling, fingers flying, suddenly jumping up and smacking the ivories with his elbows when he took a notion. He'd lay down tunes full of double-talk, cranked to the gills on reefer and pills and booze, and then he'd drive things home with his signature number:

They call him Handsome Harry the Hipster
He's the ball with all the chicks
Plays piano like mad, his singing is sad
He digs those mellow kicks.
They call him Handsome Harry the Clipster
'Cause he'll hype you for your gold
He's frantic and fanatic, with jive he's an addict
Well, I don't know, I was only told.

And every night you'll find him round the clubs
Playing and singing so wild...

BEFORE HE WAS Harry the Hipster, he was just Harry Gibson, a swing and ragtime man who worked W. 52nd St., doing intermissions and afternoon cocktail sessions. Off-hours, he'd amuse his fellow musicians by ad-libbing crazed lyrics to popular tunes or reeling off his whacked-out original numbers. "Get Your Juices at the Deuces." "Four-F Ferdinand the Frantic Freak." "While Strolling Through the Park, I Heard a Lark Bark." And his show-stopper: "Who Put the Benzedrine in Mrs. Murphy's Ovaltine?"

In 1944, it came to pass that Harry Gibson was working the Three Deuces, playing intermissions for Billie Holiday. One packed Saturday night, showtime came and Billie was nowhere to be found, and the owner asked Harry to hit the crowd with a little hipster jive to kill some time. He tore up the joint, and when he got backstage, there were a couple of squares waiting for him, reps from the Musicraft label. Did he want to make a record? Harry recruited a trio on the spot, and the next day they went in and a couple of hours later had "Boogie Woogie in Blue," which was released under the name Harry (The Hipster) Gibson.

"Two weeks later," Harry remembered years afterward, "you walk down Broadway, it's coming out of the music stores. You sit in your car, and it's coming out of the radio. Overnight, I'm a star."

AS HE WAS growing up in the Bronx, where he was born Harry Raab in 1915, the future Hipster was given a grandmotherly nudge toward what would become the two abiding passions of his life: music and mind-altering substances. A prodigy who was picking out tunes on the piano at age 3,

he was also a hyperkinetic kid who couldn't sit still. When things got tense, Grandma would take him down to the basement, seat him at the piano and break out the Manischewitz. "L'chaim, Harry!" she'd say, passing him a belt to calm him down.

By 13, he was playing dances with a little jazz band. Then he landed a job in a Jerome Ave. speakeasy owned by Dutch Schultz, playing with a Dixieland combo called the Chocolate Bars of Rhythm. His bandmates started taking him down to Harlem, where he prowled the speakeasies, studying the piano hotshots.

His favorite was a mysterious cat named Marlowe, who worked an after-hours joint on Lenox Ave. Marlowe indulged his young disciple by letting him watch his hands as he played, and eventually he started letting Harry take over when he stepped out for a spell. Thus it was that the skinny blond kid was at the piano one night when a dozen well-dressed people came in, led by a big man who stuffed a five in the kitty and called for "Honeysuckle Rose."

Harry did it up in his best Fats Waller style, and the big man was impressed. How'd the kid learn to play like that? *Fats taught me himself,* said Harry. *Me and him are tight.*

Yeah, well, maybe you can teach me something, the big man said, nudging Harry aside at the bench. Harry started steaming, but then the stranger hit a chord and right away Harry knew who he was. The big man put his hand out. *Meet your old professor,* he said.

SO IT WAS that Harry Raab got a job as Fats Waller's intermission pianist at the Yacht Club on 52nd St. And in the late 1930s, there was no better place to be on the street, where every night a string of cramped basement dives hosted a concentration of jazz talent whose like would never be seen again: Charlie Parker, Art Tatum,

Coleman Hawkins, Count Basie, Dizzy Gillespie — all the greats were there, fronting their own combos or sitting in. They'd play till closing, then head uptown to blow some more, with plenty of gin and reefer to go around.

Harry spent the next five years playing every joint on the strip, doing intermissions and afternoons for $56 a week, union scale. For a time he teamed up with a singer, Ruth Gruner, but a club owner complained that "Gruner and Raab" sounded more like a meat market than an act. So they became "The Gibsons." After the gin.

The fast life suited Harry Gibson fine. He had a wife and a brood at home by then, but he was more interested in making the scene at any jam session or after-hours party where there were women and pharmaceuticals to be had. And after his record hit, soon he was out in Hollywood, playing Billy Berg's famous swing club for a grand a week. When he came back to 52nd St., he was headlining the Onyx.

Not everybody dug the Hipster — one Los Angeles station banned his records, and in 1946 Time singled him out in an alarmist attack on "hot jazz overheated, with overdone lyrics full of bawdiness, references to narcotics and double-talk." But a few squares didn't bother him. On he went, tearing up the country's top clubs, jamming with Parker and Diz, making TV appearances, touring theaters in a stage show with Mae West.

ROCK 'N' ROLL came along, and with it a crop of entertainers whose antics rivaled Harry the Hipster's. Through the '50s, the gigs got smaller. By the '60s, Harry was driving a cab, sometimes playing strip joints. He released an occasional record, but nobody paid much attention.

He moved to a trailer in the California desert in 1986 and lived out his days as a wild-eyed old man, his dog his only companion. In 1989, at age 74, he finally went back into the studio to cut some new tunes ("I Flipped My Wig in San Francisco," "Get Hip to Shirley MacLaine," etc.). But the tapes didn't find an interested label in his lifetime. The sessions finally emerged, from Chicago's Delmark Records, five years after Harry killed himself on May 3, 1991.

HARRY THE *Hipster, former headliner, got only a small obituary in Down Beat, whose cover he had once graced, and he goes uncited in the standard jazz references. Probably he wouldn't care. "I got about everything I wanted out of life," he told an interviewer shortly before his death. "I did about everything there is to be done."*

By JAY MAEDER
Daily News Staff Writer

COCKILY SNEERING down from the lineup platform at Police Headquarters on Monday morning the 26th of November 1934 was the young punk Harry Strauss, run in for still another murder he was going to beat, and his hair was pomaded and his suit was pressed and on his head sat a snappy pearl-gray fedora and over his shoulders was draped a fine new Chesterfield overcoat with a velvet collar, and newly appointed Police Commissioner Lewis Valentine took one look at the little rodent and he exploded.

"Look at him," Valentine roared. "He's the best-dressed man in this room."

And now the new commissioner was barking fresh orders at his detectives. "When you meet men like Strauss, draw quickly and shoot accurately," he snapped. "Don't be afraid to muss 'em up. Make it disagreeable for them. Drive them out of the city. Teach them to fear arrest. Make them fear you."

Strauss blinked uneasily in the glare. "Don't be afraid to manhandle them," Valentine thundered on. "Mark 'em up and muss 'em up. Blood should be smeared all over that velvet collar."

Yes, there was a new commissioner in town. Stern and wrathful Lewis Valentine ran the New York Police Department for 11 years, top cop through the Fiorello LaGuardia years and their durable law-and-order symbol. There would come a time when his notions of old-fashioned justice would grow unfashionable among law-enforcement professionals, officially, at any rate. Readiness to use the truncheon and the meaty fist would subsequently become not so acceptable. In New York City in the 1930s, as gangsters openly ran over the whole town and had a good laugh about it, it was something you liked in a cop.

BROOKLYN-BORN Lewis Valentine became a New York policeman at age 21 in November 1903, and he spent 10 years walking a beat in Flatbush, in a day when a harness bull early learned to let his nightstick do his talking for him. All his life he would remain nostalgic about those simpler times when all a cop had to be was big and beefy, the best friend of everyone on the block except the malefactor who needed his head cracked. He was widely known to be personally incorruptible and, after he made sergeant in 1913, Inspector Honest Dan Costigan brought him into the newly formed Confidential Squad, a unit that investigated dishonest officers. If other men wanted no part of such work, Valentine had the crusader's taste for it; he genuinely hated comrades who dishonored the badge, and for several years he and Costigan were much feared by the troops.

Everyone breathed easy again after 1918, when Tammany took back City Hall from reformers and Mayor Red Mike Hylan ordered the Confidential Squad disbanded. Thereafter, Valentine's career blew this way and that along with the prevailing political winds. He had once tangled with one Lt. Richard Enright; now Enright was Hylan's police commissioner, and Valentine was banished to the sticks for years, passed over for promotion after promotion.

Under Enright, though, the department became such an army of loafers and incompetents and crooks that, by 1925, even Hylan's live-and-let-live successor Jimmy Walker realized he had to clean it up. In came a no-nonsense commissioner

With LaGuardia, 1935

named George McLaughlin, back came the Confidential Squad — and running it was Lewis Valentine, called back from exile and named a deputy inspector.

Over the next three years, Valentine's men made 1,200 investigations, gathering bombshell evidence of links between cops and politicians. Valentine was particularly energetic about raiding Tammany clubhouses and breaking up police-protected games of chance. Mayor Walker began to take heat over this, and repeatedly he tried to rein Valentine in; two police commissioners, McLaughlin and his successor, Joseph Warren, lost their jobs in part over Valentine's continued vigorous discharge of his duty. Finally Walker found a commissioner who would do City Hall's bidding; Grover Whalen's first official act, at Christmas 1928, was to bust Inspector Valentine to captain and once again dismantle the Confidential Squad.

THIS TIME HE was in exile for six years. In the meantime, Judge Samuel Seabury's corruption probe blew the town apart, Jimmy Walker resigned in disgrace and fire-breathing reformer LaGuardia became mayor. On the first day of January 1934, as LaGuardia took office, new Police Commissioner John O'Ryan ordered a huge departmental shakeup — and appointed

MANY A BLACK EYE
Lewis Valentine

Valentine, a man whose very name still struck terror into the hearts of many old-timers, his chief inspector.

"Be good or be gone," Valentine ordered his gulping commanders on that day. "The day of influence is over. There is no room in the department for parasites and drones." He wasn't kidding, and many a subordinate's life got only harder just nine months later, when O'Ryan and LaGuardia fell out and Valentine was named commissioner. If LaGuardia's man declared all-out war on the gangsters and the goons, he was just as merciless with bad eggs in his own department. By September 1938, he had personally fired 221 dirty cops, and more than 70 others had committed suicide.

THE NOTORIOUS "muss 'em up" order did not sit particularly well with the civil-libertarian community, and Valentine was condemned as a neanderthal even by many fellow police commissioners across the country. He didn't care. "There is no reason why people should tolerate one or two thousand predatory gorillas," he said. The closest he came to a retreat from his position was a poker-faced explanation that the muss-'em-up policy "must be used with great discretion." Otherwise, his additional remarks on the subject grew even more intemperate, especially after he revived the old Strong-Arm Squad in October 1935 and ordered its men to make life unendurable for miscreants at every unconstitutional opportunity. "I want the gangster to tip his hat to the cop," he said. "We want to tear the collars and dirty up the fancy shirts of a few of these mugs."

"I think a lot of them are going to 'resist arrest,' " he winked. "There'll be many a black eye in the morning."

And the fact was that many a rat fled across the Hudson River, never to return. Frank Costello picked up his slot machines and moved to New Orleans.

It is recorded that Mayor LaGuardia blew his top at Valentine only once, when fellow gangsters got to Dutch Schultz before New York police did. LaGuardia had so been looking forward to taking down The Dutchman himself.

AS THESE things are measured, the nightstick in its day proved a not altogether ineffective deterrent to criminal activity, and Valentine remained sturdily in his position. In September 1942, he became the longest-serving police commissioner in the city's history.

HE STAYED ON until September 1945, stepping down toward the end of LaGuardia's third and last term. He was such a formidable national symbol of rectitude that all three mayoral candidates pledged to keep him on if they were elected, but instead he took a job that paid him four times his $12,500 city salary; as one of America's three best-known cops, along with J. Edgar Hoover and Dick Tracy, he became host of radio's popular "Gang Busters" program.

Early in 1946, Gen. Douglas MacArthur summoned him to Occupied Japan to reorganize and modernize the shattered country's police departments. The assignment cost him his health, and he was a sick man when he returned to Brooklyn in June. He died on Dec. 16, at age 64. He was just completing his memoirs, a book titled "Nightstick."

By DAVID HINCKLEY
Daily News Staff Writer

FROM MAYBE THE summer of '41 to the summer of '53, it was said you could walk the length of the beach at Coney Island, or the length of any Brooklyn street, and never lose Red Barber's voice calling that day's Dodgers game. Blanket to blanket, window to window, The Old Redhead was there, sweet as Tupelo honey, tracking the rise of the home team from also-ran to superpower and defining the art of broadcast baseball. He understood the pace and the cadence. He knew the moment to describe all and the moment to say nothing.

He also invented a language to say it with, a mulligan stew of expressions from his native Mississippi that he somehow finessed into the everyday vocabulary of a borough that has always proudly spoken a tongue all its own.

"In the catbird seat" meant full control. It was also where Barber sat. Having a good day was "tearing up the old pea patch." A game won was "tied up in a crocus sack." An easy fly ball was "a can o' corn," and a player out of control was "as wild as a chicken hawk on a frosty morning." A bad situation was "the bottom of the pickle barrel," and at the rare moment he saw the unexpected, ol' Red would exclaim, "I'll be a suck-egg mule."

He could be whimsical — "FOB" meant the bases were "full of Brooklyns" — and every so often he'd toss a five-dollar word out to Bensonhurst just because he could. The runner advanced to third, he would solemnly say, "on the concomitant error."

But mostly he and his audience stayed in sync. When he called an argument a "rhubarb," which made no more sense than calling a compliment a turnip, so did everyone else begin to do the same.

Red Barber and Brooklyn was a blind date that worked out.

YET THOSE expecting the off-mike Barber to be the Will Rogers character they heard coming out of those Coney Island radios often found something closer to a modern-day Calvinist. He followed a rigid work ethic and tolerated no less in others. A devout Episcopalian, he read daily from The Book of Common Prayer, with some Winston Churchill on the side. He was a lay reader in the church, and in 1958 he preached a guest sermon at St. Mark's on how God was to His flock what a baseball manager was to his players.

When Dodgers owner Branch Rickey told Red in 1946 that he was going to sign Jackie Robinson as the first black major league ballplayer in the 20th century, Barber almost quit: Even broadcasting a ball game in which the races mixed, he feared, would violate God's natural order. He soon reconsidered, and in later years he not only recounted his own enlightenment but sharply criticized those who did not recognize the depth of opposition Robinson overcame in '47.

Daily News sportswriter Dick Young once described a poker game among writers on a train trip. Barber, an infrequent participant, announced that when his "dealer's choice" came up, the rule would be "last hole card wild." This was fine, except it required each player to reveal the last card he had picked up, which is not information poker players tend to share. When Young pointed this out, Barber replied: "We're all honest men, aren't we? We'll tell which card we got last." This caused such an explosion of laughter the game was suspended.

The second punch line, wrote Young, was that "Red Barber could never understand what was so funny."

In fact, this may have been precisely why Red Barber and the Borough of Brooklyn got along so well. Each was convinced he was a little better than the other.

BORN IN 1908, Walter Lanier Barber grew up the son of a school teacher and a railroad engineer. At 21, he hitchhiked to the University of Florida to become an English professor. One night, a teacher at the club where he worked as a part-time janitor asked if he'd like to make a little extra money by reading, over the campus radio station, a paper titled "Certain Aspects of Bovine Obstetrics."

Modest as this launching pad might sound, Barber was hooked and eventually became director and chief announcer of the station. In early 1934, he coaxed an offer from the Cincinnati Redlegs, and on Opening Day he broadcast the first major league baseball game he had ever seen.

In 1939, he turned down a $16,000 offer from Cincinnati to take $8,000 from Brooklyn and come to the big city. That same year, on Aug. 26, he announced the first telecast of a professional baseball game.

By 1950, he was making almost $100,000 a year — some from the Dodgers, some from CBS-TV and more than any baseball player except Joe DiMaggio. But that same year, the Dodgers were sold to Walter O'Malley, whose rule of thumb was to dislike anyone who had been in favor with previous owner Rickey. That included Barber.

Red had been getting offers from the Giants and Yankees for years, and after the 1953 season he took the Yankees up on it, making the most startling crosstown broadcast jump in New York history.

In fact, Barber had been increasingly grumpy about employment at least since 1948, when a severe ulcer attack almost killed him. He broadcast World Series games for 13 years, a job that paid an insulting $200 because sponsor Gillette knew it was the most prestigious announcing job in sports.

The 14th year, Barber said he wanted more. Gillette said forget it. After 1953, he never called another Series.

When he jumped to the Yankees, part of his deal was that he would stop going on the road and split the play-by-play at home with the other Twin Tower of New York baseball broadcasting, Mel Allen — a fellow Southerner who on the air was everything Barber was not: animated and an unapologetic "homer."

Barber's time with the Yankees ended on a cold September afternoon in 1966, when the Bombers were playing out the string on a lost season and only 413 fans showed up. Barber, calling the game on television, asked for the camera to sweep the stands because that was the real story.

Yankees management did not agree. Barber was terminated, which he said left him first startled and soon relieved. Thirty-three years, he said, was enough. Glad to have done it, glad it's over.

BARBER WENT ON to write books and become a commentator on National Public Radio. He praised baseball but made it clear that today's ballplayers, overpaid and undermotivated, didn't produce the game he knew back in his day.

He also scorned most new broadcasters, especially ex-athletes. When Phil Rizzuto said he had a pizza pie, Barber would tell him that was redundant, since "pizza" means "pie." He disdained partner Joe Garagiola as a mike hog.

Barber wanted No. 1 pencils for day games and No. 2 pencils for night games, and if an assistant got it wrong, he would throw the pencils back at him. But for other young announcers, working with Red was like learning at the feet of Plato. Vin Scully, who took over the Dodgers spot when Barber left, called Barber the best ever — a man with a love of words, the sense to use them sparingly and a wise reporter's approach to the game.

When Al Gionfriddo of the Dodgers robbed DiMaggio of a home run in the 1947 World Series — a play that drove the stoic DiMaggio to kick the dirt — the limit of Barber's emotion was his trademark "Oh-ho, DOC-tor."

When Roger Maris hit his 61st home run in 1961 and Rizzuto was yelling "Holy cow, he did it!" on the radio, Barber was on TV saying, "There it is, No. 61," then letting the crowd cheers say the rest.

When the Yankees put the Maris home run on a highlights record, they had Allen re-create the call to make it sound more exciting.

Red Barber stuck around New York barely long enough for a cup of coffee after he was fired by the Yankees. Much of his local imprint was already history, anyhow: Those radios at Coney Island now played rock 'n' roll, which Barber said "isn't music." Four years after Barber left Brooklyn, the Dodgers left Brooklyn.

But when he died in 1992, back home in the sweet sunny South, a whole lot of folks in Brooklyn were reminded that every once in a while, being a gentleman and a scholar was a little bit of all right.

With Dizzy Dean (right), 1946

ANOTHER COUNTRY
Red Barber

By DAVID HINCKLEY
Daily News Staff Writer

A S FOREMAN OF the Cadillac garage at 56th St. and 11th Ave., Ernie Brian was not unaccustomed to dealing with the whims of the owners of America's most prestigious automobile. But even Ernie wanted to make sure he'd heard correctly one day in 1950 when the welterweight champion of the world flashed a blinding flamingo pink tie at him and asked if he could whip up a batch of paint that color for a new El Dorado convertible.

Yes, confirmed Sugar Ray Robinson, he had. Every year since 1941, the first year he made money in the fight racket, Sugar Ray had bought himself a new dark blue Buick convertible. Now that he was moving up to Cadillac, he wanted his singular imprint on his fine machine.

Sugar Ray Robinson, born Walker Smith in Detroit in 1920, was 12 when he came to New York and 30 when he owned it. He ruled in the ring and he ruled from the front seat of his Cadillac. People would stop and watch as he cruised Seventh Ave., top down and radio up, in what he liked to call the Hope Diamond of Harlem. "If skinny little Walker Smith could own a car like this," he said, "maybe they could, too."

SKINNY LITTLE Walker Smith had something else other people didn't, though — maybe the finest moves ever to ennoble a boxing ring, moves that carried him to the welterweight and middleweight championships. Fellow fighter Walter Carter said Sugar Ray was the reason boxing was called the sweet science. The moves would have made Ray light-heavyweight champ, too, had it not been hotter than the fires of Hades that night against Joey Maxim in Yankee Stadium.

Ray was 5-feet-11, tall for a middleweight, with long arms to match. He understood speed, understood that a good fighter has to be limber and agile, not just strong. He liked a big ring, one that gave him room to move, and he knew how to slip punches by the crucial fraction of an inch.

He also was a natural lefty, and while he was switched to a right-handed stance by his Police Athletic League instructors, his left was deceptively ferocious. Gene Fullmer, who was built like an Army assault vehicle, had never been knocked out before May 1, 1957, when he charged forward and Sugar Ray caught him with a left he called "the most perfect punch I ever threw." Fullmer crumpled and Sugar Ray regained the middleweight title Fullmer had taken from him five months earlier.

Sugar Ray had won the middleweight title three times before. He took it from Jake LaMotta in early '51, lost it to Randy Turpin, then won it back. After he retired in 1952, he regained it from Bobo Olson in late '55. He would regain it one final time in early '58, from Carmen Basilio.

Regularly losing titles and winning them back can raise eyebrows about "arrangements" in the fight game, but while Robinson loved money dearly, his fights were not for sale. He rejected Frankie Carbo's overtures about fixing his fight with LaMotta and later walked away from a million-dollar offer to get beaten by Rocky Graziano.

He could have used the money, too. He figured he made $4 million and spent it all as he went. He bought the west side of Seventh Ave. between 123rd and 124th Sts.: Edna Mae's Lingerie for his wife, George Gainford's Golden Gloves Barber Shop for his manager, Sugar Ray's Quality Cleaning and Sugar Ray's Cafe.

Many nights Ray would tend bar himself at the

THE SWEET LIFE
Sugar Ray Robinson

cafe, whipping up a rum drink called the Sugar Ray Bolo and listening to people tell him he was the greatest. He didn't disagree. At its peak, Sugar Ray's was an uptown Toots Shor's, frequented by the likes of Joe Louis, Roy Campanella, Adam Clayton Powell, Richard Wright, Dinah Washington, Sidney Poitier, George Raft, Ruth Brown, Charlie Barnet, Paul Robeson and Ray's good pal Walter Winchell. They'd tell stories about how Ray and Winchell went to nightspots in Florida where all by themselves they violated two-thirds of the signs that said "No Negroes, Jews or Dogs."

The money rolled in, the money rolled out. Ray bought his mother a house. He was a touch for anyone $50 short on the rent. He'd give paperboys a $5 bill for early editions of the News and the Mirror. When he'd spent it all and the IRS had taken the rest, he said he had no regrets, because it all went to people who needed it.

YOUNG WALKER SMITH knew from need. His mother was raising three kids on $10 a week before the four of them hopped a bus to New York, packing cardboard suitcases and a bag of baloney sandwiches. They spent a year in Hell's Kitchen, W. 53rd St., before they moved up to 142nd. His mother scraped up the money for Walker to take dancing lessons, but while he had natural grace and a love for Bojangles Robinson, tap dancing didn't have enough action. One night he beat Samuel (Shake) Royal in a two-sewer footrace. When he declined to give Shake a rematch, a fistfight ensued and Walker gave Shake such a pounding he was signed up by Benny Bookbinder, who ran PAL boxing shows.

He had 85 amateur fights and won them all, 69 by knockout. He won the Golden Gloves featherweight title in 1939 and the lightweight title in 1940. One night way upstate in Watertown, he borrowed the name of a retired fighter to get on a card. The local sports editor called him one sweet fighter, and Walker Smith became Sugar Ray Robinson.

HE TURNED PRO in October 1940, spent the war in the Army on morale-building boxing tours, and, on Dec. 20, 1946, won the welterweight championship at the Garden by decisioning Tommy Bell.

His first defense was June 24, 1947, against a scrappy kid named Jimmy Doyle. When Doyle went down in the eighth, his head snapped against the canvas and he never woke up. Robinson fought a couple of benefits for his widow and started thinking about how long he wanted to do this.

But then he won the middleweight title from LaMotta and, on June 25, 1952, he stepped into the ring at Yankee Stadium against Joey Maxim for the light-heavyweight title.

Maxim wasn't a puncher, but Robinson was giving away 15 pounds, 160 to 175. Mostly, there was the heat. A thermometer at ringside read 104 degrees. Referee Ruby Goldstein had to be helped out after the 10th round.

Robinson swept the early rounds and in the seventh he staggered Maxim with a right. After the ninth, he told Gainford he was getting tired and he later said that was the last thing he remembered.

Robinson staggered Maxim again in the 11th. But he sprawled to the canvas after missing a punch in the 13th, and when the bell rang for the 14th, smelling salts and icepacks weren't enough. Far ahead on points, Ray couldn't stand up. Maxim could, and for the first and only time in 300 matches, Ray Robinson officially lost by knockout.

A few weeks later he announced his retirement, resumed tap-dancing and whipped up an act that he took to Vegas and Paris. Reviews said it was just okay, and Sugar Ray's Cafe faltered once its owner was only a mid-range hoofer. In October 1954 he returned to the ring, crowds returned to Sugar Ray's and this time he didn't retire until November 1965. By then he had answered the bell 202 times, with 175 wins.

L IKE HIS IDOL Joe Louis, Sugar Ray Robinson fought too many fights. And by the time he quit, the money was still gone and Sugar Ray's Cafe and the flamingo pink Cadillacs were memories. The new "greatest," Muhammad Ali, paid him $1,000 to work his corner against Zora Folley, and Ray was glad to get it.

He eventually moved to Los Angeles, where he died in April 1989. The doctors said Alzheimer's, diabetes, heart disease. Common sense said too many punches, a story writ oft and large in the postscripts of professional boxing.

But when the going was good, on a thousand warm nights in the 1950s, skinny little Walker Smith knew the crest of the wave. Black top down, hat cocked at just the right angle, Sugar Ray Robinson was as untouchable in the streets as he was in the ring.

By MARA BOVSUN
Special to The News

THERE WAS nothing so very odd about seven Christmas gifts being shipped through the Easton, Pa., post office that holiday season of 1931, nothing except that, while identical in size, shape and weight, they were all labeled as holding different contents.

That was enough to arouse the suspicions of one diligent clerk, who unwrapped one of them to see what was inside.

The blast ripped off his arms — killing him and another clerk and injuring three others.

The bombs were addressed to the leaders — the *prominenti* — of the nation's Italian-American community. They had been, the Daily News reported, "designed to wipe out" seven of Italian strongman Benito Mussolino's "most powerful supporters in the United States."

One of the addressees: Generoso Pope of New York City, wealthy owner of the Colonial Sand and Stone Co., a power in Tammany Hall politics and publisher of influential Italian-language newspapers, including the largest in the country, Il Progresso Italo-Americano.

Pope's papers, read by seven out of 10 Italians in New York, gave struggling immigrants guidance on how to become American. At the same time, he brought them the word from Italy. And in the 1920s and 1930s, the word was Fascism.

Pope's support of Mussolini was not terribly unusual in an era when many were singing the praises of Il Duce, the man who had saved Italy and made the trains run on time.

For anti-Fascists, though, Pope was one of the bull's-eyes — in large part because he was such a hero to the tired, huddled masses from his homeland, a living example of the American Dream.

True, the streets in their new country were not paved with gold. But, in New York City, many of those streets were made of something more solid: concrete, poured by an Italian-American millionaire who not so very long ago had been just like them — a nobody with nothing.

GENEROSO POPE tumbled off the S.S. Madonna onto Ellis Island on May 17, 1906, one of the 358,000 during a peak year of Italian immigration. He was 15, had $3 in his pocket and was desperate to escape his family's farm in the southern village of Arpaise.

He got a job painting pianos and was fired in four months.

He hauled water for the workers building the Pennsylvania Railroad's East River tunnel and was fired in one month.

Finally, he bounced into the sand pits, a shoveler and driver for a Long Island concrete company. This led him to Colonial Sand and Stone, where he quickly rose to superintendent and prospered.

In 1916, Colonial was on the brink of bankruptcy, and Pope made an audacious offer to the owners and creditors: If he put the company back on its feet in two years, he would become president and get half ownership.

He did it. By 1918, Pope had turned Colonial around, and within just a few more years, he ground most of his competitors to dust.

CULVER PICTURES

GOOD SOLDIER
Generoso Pope
PART ONE OF TWO

POPE'S MONEY pulled him into the inner circles of Tammany Hall. He became a close friend of Mayor Jimmy Walker, who — as Philip Cannistraro, a distinguished professor of Italian-American studies at Queens College, has documented in his forthcoming definitive Pope biography — gave his pal lucrative municipal contracts for the buildings, airports and sidewalks of New York City. It was Colonial that supplied most of the sand, gravel and concrete for those great Depression-era monuments to wealth, Rockefeller Center and Radio City Music Hall.

Meanwhile, the country's largest building materials supply company had, by 1928, made its 37-year-old owner rich enough to pay more than $2 million for the venerable, but broke, Il Progresso Italo-Americano.

The new owner immediately put a motto on the masthead of the 100,000-circulation newspaper: "The Spokesman of Italian Immigrants and American Citizens of Italian Origin."

Through Il Progresso, Generoso Pope would assume a new role: advocate for America's Italian immigrants, principal drumbeater for Italian pride.

HE SPONSORED increasingly elaborate celebrations and parades to commemorate the day in 1492 when Christopher Columbus found the New World. For years, he was the parade's grand marshal, an annual speechmaker at the explorer's monument in Columbus Circle. He played a major role in getting Columbus Day declared a national holiday.

Pope funneled thousands into charities, the Catholic Church, civic organizations, scholarships to educate young Italians. He established an anti-defamation league. He painted his fleet of cement mixers the red, green and white of the Italian flag.

Over in the Eternal City, the activities of this New York success story were being carefully watched.

IN GENEROSO Pope, Benito Mussolini had discerned a good soldier for his campaign to keep Italians tied to the apron strings of their mother country.

Il Duce had ordered all Italian citizens to remain Italian citizens, "even to the seventh generation." Pope himself, meanwhile, had become a U.S. citizen years earlier, and his newspaper encouraged immigrants to Americanize themselves swiftly, to become citizens, to learn English, to vote. Nevertheless, Mussolini felt he could use Pope to reach Italian-American hearts, minds and pocketbooks, and he began to court him with titles and awards.

Visiting Rome, Pope was feted at receptions and meetings with everyone from King Victor Emmanuel III to Pope Pius XI. During a private chat with Mussolini, says Cannistraro, Pope pledged that if the Italian government would back his intended purchase of another U.S. paper, Il Corriere d'America, he would see to it that Mussolini's policies were promoted in his editorial pages.

"Long live Italy, long live the King, long live Mussolini!" Pope cried out at the Central Opera House in 1935 as he presided over a banquet that raised $800,000 for the invasion of Ethiopia.

But as Italy drew closer to Adolf Hitler's Germany, Pope's split allegiances became increasingly uncomfortable.

At left, with Gov. Thomas Dewey and Mayor Fiorello LaGuardia, at the Columbus Day Parade, 1943

CULVER PICTURES

By MARA BOVSUN
Special to The News

'**L**ONG LIVE Italy, long live the King, long live Mussolini," cried out New York publisher Generoso Pope as Il Duce's mechanized armies rolled across Haile Selassie's Ethiopia in 1935. Italian-Americans went wild singing *"Faccietta Nera"* ("Little Black Girl"), a reassurance to an Ethiopian child that she would be safe under the Roman legions. Women sold their wedding bands to support the invasion.

But as the Italian strongman drew closer to Germany's Adolf Hitler, Pope's dual allegiances — to the Mussolini regime that supported his newspapers and to America's hopeful Italian immigrants who read them — began to give him a problem.

Fascists and anti-Fascists screamed at each other in Columbus Circle on Oct. 13, 1936, as both held rallies at once. Keynote speaker Gov. Herbert Lehman waved to the crowd, got back hundreds of fists raised in the Fascist salute and was then jeered by the anti-Fascists. An army of cops kept the two noisy groups apart. In 1937, the good soldier Pope traveled again to Rome to discuss policy with Italy's leaders.

When he got back, he informed The New York Times that he had "received the word of Mussolini that there would be no persecution of Jews in Italy, 'as long as they obey the laws.'" Within a year, Mussolini proved that his word wasn't worth much. And Generoso Pope now decided it was time to distance himself from Mussolini, if for no other reason than the very practical one that a known anti-Semite would have a tough time doing business in New York.

But he didn't move quickly enough.

AS WAR LOOMED, the FBI started hunting for the Italian fifth column — Fascist spies in New York. Pope made the list of suspects. From Washington, Assistant Secretary of State Adolf Berle sought New York mayor Fiorello LaGuardia's advice.

Among the reasons LaGuardia had not become mayor until 1933 was that the influential Pope had actively supported Jimmy Walker in the 1929 election. Now, these years later, the Little Flower publicly branded Pope a *cullo di cavallo* — horse's ass, that means — and was delighted to recommend a full inquiry.

Pope survived it unscathed, and by 1941, pro-Fascist sentiments in his newspapers were

GOOD SOLDIER
Generoso Pope
PART TWO OF TWO

pointedly fading. With Japan's attack on Pearl Harbor in December, Pope began waving the American flag with all his might.

Soon a decade of Mussolini worship in Il Progresso was all but forgotten. In 1943, the Treasury Department asked Pope to lead its Italian-American Committee to sell war bonds.
PUBLISHER WAS A DUCE MOUTHPIECE, stormed the incredulous leftist daily PM, which trotted out a 1937 photo of Pope in Italy, arm raised in Fascist salute. But Treasury shrugged off the criticisms of Pope's appointment. "We are only interested in selling bonds," an official said. "The best salesman in the Italian group is Mr. Pope."

Among the loudest attackers was anarchist Carlo Tresca, whose newspaper, Il Martello (The Hammer), for years had branded the Il Progresso publisher a gangster and a racketeer, a man with ties to the underworld, a man who used thug muscle to silence anti-Fascists and business competitors. When Tresca was assassinated in January 1943, Pope was among those at whom fingers were pointed.

But authorities could never pin the Tresca slaying on Pope — or on anyone else.

WITH THE END of the war, Pope's status continued to improve. When William O'Dwyer succeeded LaGuardia as mayor in 1945, the publisher found himself once again in tight with City Hall. He scored large points with the federal government by organizing a huge letter-writing campaign to defeat Communists in the Italian general elections of 1948. He was close to Harry Truman's White House; he and Truman were photographed marching together in the Columbus Day Parade.

On April 28, 1950, at age 59, Pope was cut down by a stroke. Thousands of mourners stood in the rain outside St. Patrick's Cathedral to pay their respects to the man whose newspaper had, its early forays into Fascism notwithstanding, taught a generation of Italian immigrants how to become Americans.

He taught them so well, in fact, that many in the next generation forgot their language and their heritage.

POPE'S SON, Generoso Pope Jr., ran Il Progresso for a while after his father's death, but, moving on to build a publishing empire of his own, eventually founded a successful weekly called The National Enquirer. Il Progresso folded in 1988, age 108.

BIG TOWN BIOGRAPHY

By JAY MAEDER
Daily News Staff Writer

SAINTED MAYOR though he later became, Fiorello LaGuardia as a 1920s Harlem congressman was sufficiently pragmatic to appreciate the services of a good flying goon squad when campaign seasons came around, and his protégé Vito Marcantonio usefully provided him with skull-crackers for a number of years — at least until LaGuardia went to City Hall in 1933 and Marcantonio succeeded him in the U.S. House of Representatives.

The poverty-stricken 18th Congressional District was fertile soil for Marcantonio's American Labor Party, and the leftist congressman kept winning reelection there for years, often without a contest. By the autumn of 1946, though, as political winds shifted in postwar America, Marcantonio found himself actually facing an opponent, Republican Frederick Van Pelt Bryan, who had come home from the war with a chestful of medals and was earnestly informing voters what a Red rat the incumbent was. And now Vito Marcantonio, suddenly fighting for his political life, once again called out the old storm troops.

The 18th District was a combat zone for weeks as hoodlums roamed the streets, smashing Bryan's sound trucks, pelting speakers with debris and socking any bystanders who objected. In late October, riot cops showed up at a Bryan rally just in time to pull a jeering mob off the candidate. On Election Day, Tuesday the 5th of November, officers were posted at every voting machine in the district, on the lookout for wolf packs. "Let them do their worst," Bryan declared.

Shortly before 6 on election morning, a 38-year-old GOP district captain named Joseph Scottoriggio kissed his wife goodbye, left his apartment in the East River Houses on 105th St. and headed for nearby Public School 168 with a list of voter challenges in his pocket. Marcantonio's brazen ghost-vote racket had been all over the newspapers for days. Hundreds of Marcantonio supporters had given as their addresses apartment buildings that had been demolished years earlier.

From her window, Cecilia Scottoriggio watched fondly as her politically active husband marched over to First Ave., duty-bound.

And then she watched as, at the corner of 104th St., four men set upon him from behind, clubbed him to the sidewalk and then stomped him until he stopped moving, and she ran screaming down the stairs.

Nationwide, as expected, the day produced a historic Republican landslide, remaking the political landscape as the GOP swept into control of both the House and the Senate. Somehow, Fred Bryan was not included in this mandate. When the polls closed, it seemed that Vito Marcantonio had defeated him rather handily. And so things went on.

THE PROBLEM, purely as a practical matter, was that Joseph Scottoriggio did not survive his beating.

He lingered, comatose, in St. Vincent's Hospital for six days. Freshly reelected Gov. Thomas Dewey visited his bedside and comforted his wife. "This is one of the most heartbreaking things I've seen in many years," Dewey said, pledging swift justice. "The most damnable of crimes," agreed Police Commissioner Arthur Wallander. **WORSE THAN MURDER!** screamed the Daily Mirror, railing against "a pre-meditated crime against the American people and their form of government." On Monday morning the 11th, the critically injured man died.

RAIN ON THE GRAVE
Joseph Scottoriggio

In his life, Joseph Scottoriggio had been no one in particular, just an ordinary, hardworking, everyday New Yorker, just your average Joe. He was a Harlem contractor's son, oldest of 11 children, a man who had dug ditches as a Works Progress Administration laborer during the Depression and then bettered himself, becoming a $4,000-a-year Federal Housing Authority accountant.

At one point, like so many working men, he had been a Marcantonio supporter. In time, like so many others who had increasingly lost their faith in the man the papers called "Stalin's little errand boy" — like, for example, an entire American Labor Party wing that broke away to become the Liberal Party — he defected. In November 1946, Scottoriggio was actively working to unseat Marcantonio. He had been warned to lay off.

And now he was New York's first Election Day murder victim in more than 40 years. "A courageous, honorable and sincere American," the defeated Bryan called the dead man. Thousands of New Yorkers who had never known him stood outside St. Lucy's Church on E. 104th St. on Saturday the 16th. *"He died so you could go on living in a democracy!"* hysterical Cecilia Scottoriggio screamed at them. *"He fought against Communism and this is what he got! Remember! Remember, every one of you!"*

In the drizzly Sunday dawn, the widow stared sleepless out her bedroom window. "It's raining on Joseph's grave," she whispered.

VITO MARCANTONIO was shocked that anyone might consider him responsible. "No violence has been connected with my campaign at any time," he announced. "The attempt on the part of certain sections of the press to connect the attack with the political campaign is outrageous." He chiefly meant the Hearst papers, the Journal-American and the Daily Mirror, which seldom lost an opportunity to savage New York's Red Congressman: **MOSCOW CALLS TUNE, MARCANTONIO DANCES. VICIOUS CRIMINALS GET OUT MARCANTONIO VOTE. CONVICTS, TRAITORS, THUGS CAMPAIGN FOR MARCANTONIO.**

For all his indignation, he was the first witness summoned by a grand jury empaneled to look into Scottoriggio's death, and the House soon sent an investigative committee of its own to New York. In Washington, the 80th Congress debated whether to seat Marcantonio at all.

Meanwhile, New York cops had jugged as their chief suspects two of the congressman's known associates. In the old days, Trigger Mike Coppola and Joey Rao had run with Prohibition gangster Mad Dog Coll; now, as the whole town knew, they oversaw Harlem's numbers racket. Lawmen never had a doubt that Joey and Trigger Mike were their men, but they stayed in jail for months and never gave up a thing. Coppola's young showgirl wife, Doris, disappeared the day her husband was arrested. Two other material witnesses also suddenly dropped out of sight.

By Christmas, the grand jury hadn't solved Scottoriggio's killing, but it had, tangentially, blown apart several flourishing Harlem dope rings and the official protections they enjoyed. Police Commissioner Wallander ripped apart the 6th Division, sacking or banishing dozens of men — notably a detective first grade who had moonlighted as Marcantonio's personal bodyguard. Marcantonio himself tirelessly continued to resent "the vicious, ruthless and dishonorable forces trying to discredit me."

MANY HAVE been the political killings never solved, and Joseph Scottoriggio's was another of them. In May 1947, the flagging investigation was briefly reenergized when one of the witnesses who had vanished the previous November, a labor party district captain, turned up floating in the river. In July, the fugitive Doris Coppola was returned to the city.

Authorities were convinced that the beating plot had been hatched in the Coppola home at 347 E. 116th St. and that she could identify the attackers, but she was loath to discuss the matter, and in November she was indicted for perjury. Trial was scheduled for the following spring, once the pregnant rackets wife had completed childbirth. On March 17, 1948, she delivered a baby girl in St. Vincent's Hospital. Eleven hours later, she was found mysteriously dead in her bed.

Eventually, the Scottoriggio probe flickered out. The grand jury was extended again and again, as meanwhile Vito Marcantonio won still another congressional term, his last one, and then ran unsuccessfully for mayor. When it was finally discharged in December 1949, it was the longest-serving jury in the city's history. "All I know," said its weary foreman, "is that we were all young men when we started out."

By JAY MAEDER
Daily News Staff Writer

"I have a delusion of grandeur. I believe myself to be Joe Gould."
—Joe Gould

DINER COUNTERMEN learned to grab up the ketchup bottles and hide them the minute The Professor stuck his head in the door. The Professor was a frugal fellow, and it was his custom whenever he could get away with it to order the cheapest possible egg sandwich, then pour out onto his plate the entire contents of every ketchup bottle in sight and then, with great grave dignity, eat up all the ketchup with a spoon. It seemed to many that The Professor kept body and soul together on mostly nothing but free diner ketchup for more than 30 years.

He was called The Professor because he was a Harvard graduate, Class of '11, and because he discoursed learnedly on many subjects in several tongues, among them Chippewa, which he had picked up one summer in North Dakota, and sea gull, a language he had learned from its native speakers during long periods of communing with them at the shore. He was an authority on modern Balkan politics. He knew a great deal about eugenics. He was versed in the works of Longfellow, some of which he had translated into sea gull.

He was toothless and gaunt and boundlessly cheerful, a besotted, ragged, mumbling, stoop-shouldered, beaming little gnome who slept on subway benches and smoked sidewalk butts and wandered cherubically through the Greenwich Village of the 1920s and '30s and '40s, the last of the original bohemians, he liked to think, a dusty relic of the lost Village of the old poets and painters and street-corner soapbox radicals. Anywhere else, he conceded, he would be considered a crazy man, or at least a crank. But this was the Village. In the Village, he was a bohemian. There weren't a lot of authentic old bohemians still around. The Professor felt there were traditions to maintain.

By the time the wry city chronicler Joseph Mitchell wrote about The Professor in the Dec. 12, 1942, issue of The New Yorker and single-handedly turned a manifestly deranged derelict into a literary celebrity, Joseph Ferdinand Gould, who was then 53 years old, had been working nonstop on his behemoth "Oral History of Our Time" for more than 25 years, day and night. The manuscript was then about 9 million words long, Joe Gould figured, about 11 times larger than the Holy Bible, and was not yet even close to being finished.

THE DUTY OF THE BOHEMIAN
Joe Gould

THE "ORAL HISTORY," Gould assured Mitchell, was the century's single most definitive social document. Since 1916 or so, he had been obsessively recording every random conversation he ever had with anyone, every thought that had ever momentarily fluttered across his mind, detailed descriptions of everything he saw on every street corner, scribbling feverishly into the notebooks he carried with him everywhere, along with his shirts and his socks.

There were now 270 of these notebooks, fat volumes crammed to their margins with tiny, scratchy, handwritten revelations that were, Mitchell noted not unkindly, mostly illegible in the first place and then frankly incomprehensible if you were able to read them at all. From time to time Gould offered his notebooks to various publishers and was routinely shown the door. No matter, he said sunnily. The "Oral History" would live as long as the English language itself.

Some years later, Mitchell would come to

suspect that most of these alleged 270 volumes were perhaps hallucinatory on Gould's part. But certainly some of them did exist, and some of them had indeed been examined by various persons of stature who spoke well of them. The poet Horace Gregory called Gould "the Samuel Pepys of the Bowery." The poet e.e. cummings, who often staked Gould to a few dollars here and there, referred to the manuscript as "a wraith's progress." William Saroyan praised The Professor as "one of the few genuine and original American writers."

Save for whatever fragments may have bobbed up in the essays and book reviews Gould occasionally contributed to the little magazines, not a syllable of the "Oral History" ever saw print, and Gould's active work on the project appears to have been largely abandoned early in World War II, when he developed a conviction that enemy bombers were approaching American soil and, as Mitchell reported, prudently buried the entire corpus on a friend's farm.

After 1942, thanks to Mitchell, Gould became semi-comfortably established as a Village tourist attraction, regularly to be found in one or another of several favored haunts, always glad to berate and insult anyone who cared to give him a sandwich or a drink or a dollar. Crashing parties, he would solemnly remove his shirt and sing "There Are No Flies on Jesus" and then throw himself into a frenzied Chippewa dance, whooping and stomping as the other guests gasped and cringed and retreated. Crashing sedate poetry readings, he would insist upon reciting his famous composition "The Sea Gull," then run around screaming and flapping his arms until he got the heave-ho. "It is the duty of the bohemian to make a spectacle of himself," he explained patiently.

JOE GOULD, who didn't live anywhere to begin with and never bothered to tell even his closer friends what he was or wasn't up to, had for years been in the habit of disappearing from the Village for weeks and months at a time to go wandering about the land like Johnny Appleseed or somebody, so nobody gave it much of a second thought when, around about 1952, it was realized that he didn't seem to be there anymore. What had happened to him, actually, was that he had been picked up sick on the street and sent to Bellevue, and after that, since he was, after all, crazy, he had been committed to the Pilgrim State Hospital in Brentwood, L.I. On Sunday the 18th of August 1957, at age 68, he died there.

None of the "Oral History," let alone anywhere near 270 volumes of it, was immediately locatable, despite efforts by The Professor's old friends to track it down for eventual publication. At the funeral, Robert de Rohan Courtenay, imperial prince of the Grand Imperial Order of Aristocratic Hoboes and heir to the throne of the Byzantine Eastern Roman Empire, pleaded with The Professor's restlessly roaming spirit to "guide us in finding it as you travel on in vast space." But The Professor wasn't much help here, really.

By JAY MAEDER
Daily News Staff Writer

BREAKFAST TIME again in New York City, and to the table come hubby and the little woman, rubbing sleep from their eyes, and sometimes they're just as lovey-dovey as they can be, like old married couples are sometimes — *Good morning, darling! Sleep well, dearest?* — and sometimes they're merely amiable, chatting over the cornflakes about the weather and the phone bill and this and that, and sometimes, of course, they get prickly about things. The little woman reminds hubby that he certainly tied one on last night, didn't he? *Oh yeah?* hubby fumes, and he snorts at the little woman that maybe she's getting a little thick around the middle these days, hey? *Is that so?* the little woman sniffs, and one thing leads to another and before long hubby is throwing down his spoon and stomping off back to bed. It's breakfast time again in New York City, just like it is in your house and in everyone else's house.

Except in this case there is a radio microphone on the table between hubby and the little woman, and they are broadcasting live to hundreds of thousands of faithful followers of this unrehearsed daily slice of, as they say, life. Ed and Pegeen Fitzgerald were New York's original Mr.-and-Mrs. radio talk team, and their program was the original show about basically nothing, pretty much what anyone talks about over breakfast, and they were on the air together for more than 40 years, off and on, as much a part of the city as the Empire State Building. If they were easy marks for comedians, who delighted in lampooning Mr. and Mrs. Fitz-Gee and the unceasing marital banalities, they went on and on and on nonetheless, and indeed only death did them part.

ED FITZGERALD and Margaret Worrall, he a film publicist, she a retail executive, met and married on the West Coast early in the Depression. By the time they left San Francisco for New York in 1936, Ed had launched a new career as a radio personality and he soon landed at WOR, hosting both a morning book-review spot and an all-night program called "Almanac de Gotham." Peg, meantime, went to work as advertising manager for the McCreery's department store, and shortly she was on WOR as well, talking fashion for the ladies. The two Fitzgeralds maintained separate broadcast schedules for several years, until one day in 1940 Peg fell ill and WOR suggested she do her "Pegeen Prefers" program from home while she recuperated.

This was fine, except Mrs. Fitzgerald did not wish her regular announcer, Henry Morgan, to see her in her bathrobe. Hubby was at this point pressed into service, and he and the little woman immediately sat down and had breakfast and began chatting, sans script, sans producer and sans engineers, just Mr. and Mrs. Fitz-Gee at home on E. 36th St. with an open mike in front of them. WOR had doubts about the formula at first. But then the fan mail began cascading in.

Pegeen understood that the listeners loved simple everyday soap opera; Ed, for his part, knew from his police reporter days that the public liked a good scrap. She was mostly saintly

FOR BETTER OR FOR WORSE
Ed and Pegeen Fitzgerald

patience, he was mostly crotchety grunt. "It isn't that she's not bright," Ed would grumble. "She's really awfully smart. But everyone has a blind side." Pegeen would explain: "He's a big show-off." Adding to what Peg termed "the charm of overheard conversation" was the charm of a houseful of cats, with names like Mrs. Dirty Nose and Fraidy Cat Plushbottom, and often the cats would come around to the microphone and purr at length, sometimes through an entire program. The audience just ate all this right up. By the time the Fitz-Gees jumped from WOR to WJZ in the spring of 1945, they were the most popular people on New York radio.

WHOLE GARDENS of other Mr.-and-Mrs. talk shows bloomed in the Fitzgeralds' wake. WOR brought in "Breakfast with Dorothy and Dick" to succeed the Fitzes, Dorothy and Dick being Journal-American nightlife columnist Dorothy Kilgallen and her actor-producer husband Richard Kollmar; in early '46, WEAF introduced "Tex and Jinx," being newsman Tex McCrary and his beauty-queen bride Jinx Falkenburg. Now the comedians had fresh material as the Mr.-and-Mrs. radio wars broke out.

Particularly with Dorothy and Dick, there was much public feuding. The Kollmars were Broadway sophisticates who openly regarded the just-folks Fitzgeralds as not their kind; what Dorothy and Dick talked about were first nights and French restaurants and things like that, whereas the Fitz-Gees never talked about much of anything but Fraidy Cat Plushbottom and some problem they were having with Con Ed. The

Fitzes just as openly viewed the Kollmars as unbearable — Dorothy and Dick got served *their* breakfasts by their *butler* — and the snipings from both sides went on for years, especially after Ed and Pegeen rejoined WOR in the late '50s to do a lunch-hour show. The station finally ordered the couples to stop talking about one another.

Tex and Jinx largely stayed out of the fray. No-nonsense Tex McCrary was a former Daily Mirror editorial writer, a one-time son-in-law of Mirror publisher Arthur Brisbane, and these days he was tight with Herald-Tribune publisher Whitelaw Reid and he was active in backroom Republican politics. His program dealt in serious public affairs, not kitties or good theater seats. He and Jinx, who provided light cover-girl counterpoint to Tex's crustiness, didn't even pretend they were eating breakfast as they mused upon Eisenhower's presidential prospects.

Dorothy and Dick and Tex and Jinx had durable radio runs, but by the early 1960s they were gone. Whereas Ed and Pegeen Fitzgerald remained New York fixtures for another 20 years after that, cats and all.

ULTIMATELY, THEY both made the grievous professional blunder of living too long. In 1973, by which time the format they had pioneered was a creaking antique, WOR tried to sack them; listeners loudly protested, and back the Fitz-Gees came, first to noons, then to evenings and finally to midnights. Ensconced in their Central Park South apartment, the familiar old microphone on the table between the two of them, hubby talked about his cancer operations and the little woman talked about animal rights and vegetarianism, and this went on until shortly before March 22, 1982, when Ed Fitzgerald died at age 89.

Pegeen carried on the program by herself for a time, but then WOR dropped it again, this time successfully. She found work again in 1983, at WNYC, and she continued to broadcast to New York City for another five years, chatting with her housekeeper and station colleagues, petting her cats. In April 1988, her health failing, she left the air for good, and she died the following Jan. 30, at age 78. To the end, she always talked about Ed in the present tense.

By JAY MAEDER
Daily News Staff Writer

THERE WERE shadings of palship, specific degrees. If Toots called you a bum, this meant he liked you a lot. If he called you a creep, this meant he liked you even better. And if he called you a creepy crumb-bum, you might as well put your money away because now you were Toots' long-lost brother. Palship was the enduring currency in Toot Shor's joint, and there were certain responsibilities. If you were Toots' pal, you were expected to call Toots regularly, even if you happened to be at the South Pole, and immediately upon your return to the city you were expected to head first for Toots' place before you even saw your wife and kids, and of course you were expected not to drink anywhere else but at Toots' bar at any time ever, and mostly you were expected to insult Toots regularly and clap his thick shoulder and call him a bum and a creep. When you reached the highest levels of crumb-bumness, there was pretty much nothing the big slob wouldn't do for you.

The insiders at Toots Shor's original saloon at 51 W. 51st St. through the 1940s and 1950s were such crumb-bums as Jackie Gleason and Phil Silvers and Pat O'Brien and Jack Dempsey and Joe DiMaggio and Yogi Berra and the sportswriters Grantland Rice and Bob Considine and Bill Corum, and sometimes Harry Truman when he wasn't otherwise busy being president, and sometimes Earl Warren when he wasn't busy being chief justice of the United States. Toots kept his place open pretty much just for his own bunch. Lesser mortals could stray in if they liked, but they'd have to wait a long time for a table. "Who sent for ya?" Toots would growl if they complained. Toots didn't care. But his personal creeps and bums, they were always royalty.

For 19 of New York City's best and most glamorous years, Toots Shor presided over one of the town's essential havens of cheery good fellowship and certainly one of its most dedicated temples of strong drink. "Whiskey helps you when you're feeling good and when you're feeling bad," Toots opined sagely. "Drinking, that's my way of praying." His own intake came to about a quart of brandy a day, and you were expected to at least halfway keep up with him. This was palship. Toots was aware that there were those who imagined such a life to be less than healthy, but he never understood the arithmetic. "There are more old bums," he reasoned, "than there are old doctors."

PHILADELPHIA-BORN Bernard Shor was a 27-year-old clothing salesman when he landed in New York City in 1930. As he was about the size of a bread truck, he quickly found work as a bouncer at Owney Madden's Five O'Clock Club on W. 54th St. and soon established himself as a bright fellow, amicable with Owney and Owney's dapper driver George Raft and the rest of the boys, with the exception of Sherman Billingsley, who managed Owney's clubs and never much cared for the newcomer.

As a result, Toots eventually moved along to

Bellying up with Yankee Lefty Gomez (right), September 1943

CULVER PICTURES

such independent spots as the Napoleon and the Maison Royale and Leon and Eddie's, and ere long he was more of a greeter than a bouncer, a familiar figure on the Stem, a favorite with the city's sports and show-business notables and particularly with the newspaper guys who wrote about them. Chief among these in the early days was the Daily Mirror's high-rolling Broadway columnist Mark Hellinger, who was largely responsible for creating the Toots Shor legend. It was Hellinger who taught Toots that money was worthless unless you spent it; Toots was, accordingly, as broke as any horseplayer at any given moment, and he made a dismal failure of things when he took over Billy La Hiff's famous old tavern in 1936. Washed up by '39, owing every supplier in town, about the only thing he could think of to do was borrow still more money from everyone he knew and build his own place.

He initially figured $50,000 would cover him, but this start-up doubled and then nearly tripled, and still all his pals kept giving him more and more money simply because they loved him so. On Tuesday night the 30th of April 1940, some $141,000 later, Toots' 51st St. joint opened for business. Dressed for dinner, he rummaged through his pockets, came up with 40 cents, his entire life savings at this point, and then flung the coins into the gutter, the better to start with a clean slate.

AND THEN EVERYBODY lived happily ever after, until everybody started dying off. Hellinger

PRAYERS FOR THE DEAD
Toots Shor

went in '47, Granny Rice in '54; after a while it was nothing but one long mournful wake after another. This was palship too. A man owed it to his pals to be sentimental. Toots was notoriously weepy when it came to passages in any case. One night George Jessel told him that President McKinley was dead, and Toots blubbered for quite a while before it dawned on him that McKinley had been dead for decades.

Sustaining him was his eternal hatred for Sherman Billingsley. There were two distinct camps in New York nightlife; either you went to Toots' place or you went to Billingsley's Stork Club; certainly you weren't a regular at both. The feud was for life. Toots finally came out ahead, after Billingsley went on TV one day in August 1955 and threw out a wisecrack about Toots' financial affairs and subsequently had to make a $50,000 slander settlement. This warmed Toots' sentimental old heart very much.

About the same time, meanwhile, he came into another windfall, $1.5 million from developer William Zeckendorf, who wanted to build a new 48-story hotel on the restaurant's site. Toots closed his doors in June 1959, and two months later the wreckers came in and demolished the historic steakhouse as Toots made plans to reopen a block away. As it turned out, Zeckendorf never built his hotel, and 51 W. 51st St. became the Sperry-Rand Building instead. As for Toots, it took longer to open a new place than he'd anticipated, and it wasn't until Christmas of '61 that he was back in business, at 33 W. 52nd St., poetically enough exactly where Leon and Eddie's had flourished a quarter of a century earlier.

AND BY NOW these were different times. The old saloon life, as anyone had known it, was disappearing. In 1963, the city's 23,000 restaurants and 400 hotels did $1.75 billion worth of business, down $100 million from the previous year. "You come to New York and it's dead," Vincent Sardi Jr. complained to a congressional delegation before which he and Toots Shor were the star witnesses. The nightlife slump got only worse through the '60s, as the famous Great White Way was allowed to turn into a sewer. "There's no such thing as late business anymore," Toots grumbled in August 1970. "People are afraid to go out ... I'd like the cops to use their clubs. Kids are running wild on Broadway today."

More specifically fatal was Madison Square Garden's move from 50th St. to 33rd St. in 1968. That put an end to any crowds Toots had left. By 1971, he had a $200,000 tax bill he couldn't pay. In April, the IRS padlocked him.

He tried one more time, in October 1972, opening a smaller place on E. 54th St., reputedly financed by Gleason, Frank Sinatra and Bob Hope. This time he lasted less than a year. He ended his days lending his name and presence to new Toots Shor restaurants operated by a corporate chain. When he died Jan. 23, 1977, there were four such Tootses in Manhattan, none of them his.

ANYWAY, A LOT of the old crumb-bums were long gone by now. *"Whatever it was that Shor did best died a long time ago,"* wrote the Daily News' Peter Coutros. *"It died when guys and gals stopped staying up late, when they stopped playing great piano at the Three Deuces and when Louis Prima disappeared from the Famous Door ... when Johnny Carson started tucking everybody in bed.*

"It died when sentiment went out the window and people stopped crying at funerals."

By MARA BOVSUN
Special to The News

WHEN THE CURTAIN rose that rainy Tuesday night of Dec. 27, 1932, in the deepest depths of the Great Depression, it was to be the greatest show in the grandest theater the world had ever seen — the premiere performance at Radio City Music Hall.

Expectations were high. The master of this spectacle was none but Samuel L. Rothafel. Roxy. The showman who turned movie joints into cathedrals, with soaring ceilings and sweet celestial choirs and a band of shapely, high-kicking angels called Roxyettes.

"Some say we are foolish to open such a place in times like these," Roxy conceded. "But I say it cannot fail."

The stupendous palace was to be devoted to elaborate variety shows, the kind Roxy had pioneered to dress up movies as they rose out of storefront nickelodeons. The stage, goggled the awestruck New Yorker magazine, "is as large as the ordinary dockyard," with room for a chorus two blocks long. The ceiling had been crafted in massive arcs to suggest a sunrise over a still ocean. The curtain was three tons of gold cloth.

As for the show, there were 500 actors, singers, dancers, comedians, the Wallendas — top stars, from grand opera to the gospel choirs of the Deep South.

More than 100,000 New Yorkers tried to get seats that opening night. Only 6,200 of the richest and most glamorous succeeded. First on the list was John D. Rockefeller Jr., who had plunked down $8 million to build the new Music Hall, the first

part of the Rockefeller Center complex to open to the public.

What they got was a disaster — a "tragic" evening, Daily News columnist Ben Gross recalled years later. Many of the glittering first-nighters ducked out long before the finale of the five-hour program. Others just fell asleep in their seats. Mayor-elect John O'Brien was one of these.

Roxy's Flop, the trades agreed. The master showman was carried out of Radio City Music Hall on a stretcher.

The fantastic visions of the shoemaker's son from the lower East Side had finally gotten the best of him.

ROXY'S FATHER had always told young Sam he had his head in the clouds. Sam could never hold a job. When Papa finally kicked him out, he went into the Marines for a while, then ended up playing for a Pennsylvania baseball team, which is where he picked up the nickname Roxy. During off-season in 1907, he was peddling books door to door when he stopped for a beer at a saloon in the coal mining town of Forest City. He took one look at Rosa, the owner's daughter, and decided to stay. After a stint tending bar, he had the birth of a notion: The saloon's back room, he thought, would make a splendid movie theater. He persuaded his boss, who was now also his father-in-law, to let him use it.

He hung up a bedsheet, borrowed 250 chairs from an undertaker, hired a local spinster to play piano and put on his first show with a hand-cranked Lubin Marvel Cineograph. Soon he added singers and violin players. He put in flashing pink and blue lights. He attached sponges dipped in rosewater to the electric fans and filled the room with floral scents. Roxy's show lit up the dull town. The place went dark only when someone died and the undertaker needed the chairs back.

The little theater's success caught the eye of vaudeville czar Benjamin Franklin Keith, who had begun to tack motion pictures to the ends of his live performances. With Keith, Roxy now transformed starving big-city vaudeville theaters into fat, happy movie houses, and his reputation spread.

In 1913, he returned to New York, to breathe new life into the Regent in Harlem. Success there led to the Strand, the Rialto, the Rivoli, each more opulent than the last — velvet curtains, white-gloved ushers, 100-piece orchestras. Reporters dubbed him "The Aladdin of the Photoplay."

Hired to rescue The White Elephant of Broadway, the Capitol Theater, Roxy wondered if radio — a new medium that had theater people worried — could be put to work boosting theater attendance instead. He decided to send Capitol performances over the airwaves, and the

first radio broadcast from a theater stage, on Nov. 19, 1922, made him a national celebrity: Overcome by the idea of so many people listening to him, he forgot his prepared closing and instead blurted out: "Good night, pleasant dreams, God bless you."

The audience loved it. There was an avalanche of mail, and the line became Roxy's signature. Radio listeners were there at WEAF every Sunday night for Roxy and his troupe of singers, actors, dancers and comics. "Roxy and His Gang" soon had millions of fans.

It was groundbreaking stuff. Until then, radio announcing had been formal, even stiff; Roxy's show was more like an evening with a bunch of buddies: lots of jokes, lots of giggling, lots of corny sentiment. Other radio voices were at first annoyed, pronouncing all this undignified, and for one week in 1925 Roxy's station tried to cut him. The blizzard of protest letters won him back his mike.

PLEASANT DREAMS
Roxy

IN 1925, at the height of his fame, Roxy left the Capitol, lured away by the offer of a lifetime — a new $11 million theater bearing his name.

The Roxy, at Seventh Ave. and 50th St., was all gold leaf, velvet and crystal. Everything was the mostest — the 60-foot Kimball organ, the 5-ton chimes, the world's largest rug in the rotunda. Elaborately uniformed ushers went through drills as rigorous as any West Point cadet's. The theater opened with great fanfare on March 11, 1927, the program starting with a solemn invocation by an actor in a monk's robe: *"O glorious, mighty hall ... thy magic and thy charm unite us all to worship at beauty's throne ... let there be light."*

Stunning as it was, the Roxy was never a financial blockbuster, and money got tighter as the country plunged into the Depression. Despite that, in January 1931, Roxy announced that he was leaving his cathedral to create an even grander showplace.

He had been dreaming about the world's largest music hall for several years. Theater man William Fox had expressed some initial interest in the big idea, but finally backed off. So Roxy aimed his sights at Rockefeller Center. With NBC president M.H. Aylesworth and David Sarnoff and Owen Young of the Radio Corp. of America, Roxy sold himself to the Rockefeller family.

He worked himself sick supervising the construction and the operations of Radio City Music Hall. By opening night, his fingerprints were all over everything, from the statues in the lobby to the massive stage to the talent picked for the 19 acts of the premiere performance.

But, with poor notices from the beginning, audiences stayed away in droves, and Radio City was soon deep in the red. Management decided to concentrate on movies, leaving the Roxyettes as one of the few remaining live acts.

Roxy had to go as well, they determined. A year after Radio City opened, he was out.

AGAINST THE advice of his doctors, he tried for a comeback, opening a theater in Philadelphia, taking his gang on tour. On Jan. 13, 1936, he went to sleep in New York's Hotel Gotham and didn't wake up. He was 53. "I'll bet even money that he died of a broken heart," wrote Daily News columnist Ed Sullivan.

The Roxy was torn down in 1960. Radio City Music Hall, meanwhile, became a New York City landmark in 1979. Twenty years later, the 67-year-old beauty got a $70 million facelift, its features restored to the way they were when Samuel Rothafel, head in the clouds, first imagined them.

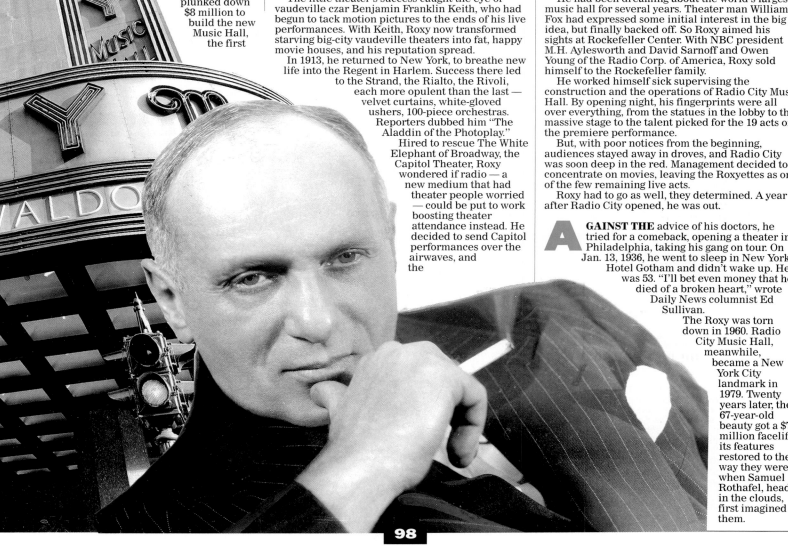

By MARA BOVSUN
Special to The News

SCIENTISTS, BEING very smart people, have invented many ways to get funding for their research. Few have been as imaginative as baby doctor Martin A. Couney, who put his tiny patients in freak shows and charged the public money to gawk at them.

For four decades, from 1903 into the early days of World War II, the "Incubator Doctor" and his premature tots were stars at Coney Island, nestled among the Lilliputian midgets, Jolly Irene the fat lady and Prince the Glass-Eyed Lion. "All the World Loves a Baby" said the sign out front, and it must have been true — Dr. Couney and his incubator infants lasted longer than any other Coney Island attraction during the amusement paradise's heyday.

Couney had dedicated himself to saving the lives of babies who had left their mothers' wombs too soon, and through his Coney Island exhibit and others he mounted at several world's fairs and other amusement parks, he was said to have saved about 6,500 of the 8,000 preemies who came under his care.

His boardwalk barkers, who included a young man named Archibald Leach, later better known as Hollywood leading man Cary Grant, shouted out spiels as they did for all the other living oddities:

Come and see them, the amazing live human infants. Don't pass the babies by!

And the crowds came by the thousands to goggle at the miniature babes in their glass cocoons.

You may talk, ladies and gentlemen, you may cough. They will not hear you. They do not even know you are here.

Childless women were the most frequent visitors. They would come day after day to monitor the progress of some favorite boy, tagged with a blue ribbon, or girl, tagged with pink. One woman came every week for 36 years.

Now this little baby came in nine days ago. It weighed only one pound,

ALL THE WORLD LOVES A BABY
Dr. Martin Couney

11 ounces, and we were afraid it might be too late. It was even bluer than that little fellow over there in the other incubator.

A LIVING INFANT that could be tucked into a pocket. It was something to see.

Premature babies were quite rare, because generally they lived for just a few minutes after entering the world. Medical literature referred to them as "weaklings." When they were born, mostly they were just wrapped in blankets and put away in a corner to die. Death certificates would say "stillborn."

In the United States at the turn of the century, there wasn't much doctors could do for them, or really wanted to. It was widely felt that these feeble infants, usually born to poor immigrant women, simply weren't meant to live.

It was a different story in France,

whose population had been devastated by the slaughter and famines of the Franco-Prussian War of 1870-71 and whose doctors desperately fought to save every child they could.

One Paris obstetrician, seeking to warm frail human infants, adapted the design of the chambers used to hatch chicken eggs. Others improved upon the contraption.

Meanwhile, as Dr. William A. Silverman reported in a 1979 issue of the medical journal Pediatrics, famed pediatrician Dr. Pierre Budin was perfecting disease-fighting methods to successfully keep the weaklings alive — and in the 1890s, young Martin A. Couney, then in his mid-20s, was in Paris, studying under Budin.

The story went that Couney was entrusted to take six incubators to the World Exposition in Berlin in 1896. He decided the display would be more captivating if the glass chambers housed actual living babies. So he borrowed a few from a Berlin hospital. He called the exhibit *Kinderbrutanstalt* — "Child Hatchery."

HIS SHOW was a phenomenal success, attracting more than 100,000 visitors in two months, becoming celebrated in music-hall songs. On he went to London, and again Couney and his babies were great hits. And now the previously supportive medical establishment began to worry that perhaps Couney was really just a carnival man at heart.

Incubator babies were all at once like "marionettes, fat women or any sort of catch-penny monstrosity," fretted the British medical journal The Lancet in 1898. "We should at once protest that human infirmities do not constitute a fit subject for the public showman to exploit."

Couney was, despite his flashiness, quite sincere in his concerns for the helpless infants and decided to carry on in technology-

smitten America. His infant incubators showed up at the 1898 Trans-Mississippi Exposition in Omaha, then bounced around to several other large fairs until they landed in the 1901 Pan-American Exposition in Buffalo.

Among those who marveled at the sight of multitudes plunking down coins to look at infants sleeping under glass and getting fed with little spoons was Luna Park impresario Fred Thompson, who lured Couney to New York and set him up as a little island of education among the freaks, dancing animals and thrill rides.

Aghast, the New York Society for the Prevention of Cruelty to Children protested as soon as Couney opened for business at Luna Park. It protested again when he moved to the grander and more glittering Dreamland. Society director John Lindsay tried to outlaw Couney's exhibit, but his efforts came to nothing. Sideshow or not, the fact was that Couney was saving the lives of children who undoubtedly would have died otherwise.

COUNEY STAYED at Coney Island for the rest of his life. Late in his career, incubator graduates would contact him with greetings, wedding announcements, progress reports in general. One of his babies grew up to be a World War I hero. One of them became a Coney Island electrician, who often came around to visit and ended up marrying one of the doctor's nurses.

By 1939, when Couney set up his incubators at the New York World's Fair, the crowds were no longer what they once had been. Back at Coney Island after the fair closed, attendance wasn't much better. Part of the problem was that mainstream medicine had by now taken up the cause of premature babies. They were no longer really oddities.

When New York Hospital opened the city's first major unit for preemies in the early 1940s, Couney called it quits. "My work is done," the old doctor said, and he retired to his home in Sea Gate, N.J., where he died in 1950 at age 80.

BIG TOWN ★ BIOGRAPHY

By DAVID HINCKLEY
Daily News Staff Writer

L IFE BEING full of stories like George Washington throwing a silver dollar across the Delaware River and such, baseball fans have shown rightful skepticism toward some of the more colorful legends of their own game, which makes it most satisfying that the one about Babe Herman doubling into a double play is true.

Ebbets Field. Aug. 15, 1926. First game of a doubleheader against the Boston Braves. Hank DeBerry was on third, Dazzy Vance on second and Chick Fewster on first when Herman sent a fly ball to deep right field.

Unsure whether it would be caught, DeBerry and Vance held up until the ball glanced off the fence. DeBerry then trotted home, but Vance, kind of a big lug, decided after rounding third that he might not make it all the way home.

So he turned around, sliding back into third as Fewster arrived from first. Meanwhile, Herman, head down and untroubled from the start by any notion the ball might be caught, kept churning until he, too, slid into third.

The Braves' third baseman promptly tagged the lot of them, figuring at least two had to be out. And as the umpire decided who that might be, Dodger teammate Rube Bressler recalled years later, Vance spoke up.

"Mr. Umpire, fellow teammates and members of the opposition," he said, "if you will carefully peruse the rules of our National Pastime, you will find there is one and only one protagonist in rightful possession of this hassock — namely yours truly, Arthur C. Vance."

He was half right.

Yes, he was safe. As the first runner to arrive, he retained the rights to third base. Fewster and Herman were out.

But no, that wasn't his name. He was born Clarence Arthur Vance, not Arthur Charles Vance. He just hated the name Clarence. Never used it. And everybody knew and nobody minded, because that was just ol' Daz and everybody loved ol' Daz because he was, well, they busted the mold after him. He was a singular character in a sport that bred oddballs like mushrooms, and not incidentally he was the best pitcher in the history of the Brooklyn Dodgers.

WHAT MADE that distinction particularly remarkable is that Dazzy Vance didn't arrive in Brooklyn until he was 31 years old. He had spent his 20s, most athletes' physical prime, passing through every bush league in America, an amiable journeyman, hanging on because pitching was easier than farming.

He came to Brooklyn, in the end, as someone's afterthought. When the Dodgers wanted to buy catcher DeBerry from the Cleveland Indians after the 1921 season, Cleveland said the Dodgers had to take Vance, too, in a $10,000 package. Dodgers owner Charles Ebbets squealed like a stuck pig but agreed.

In 1922, Dazzy won 18 games for a bad Brooklyn team, leading the National League with 134 strikeouts. The next year he won 18 games, led the league in strikeouts again and began to hear astounded comparisons to the legendary Walter Johnson of the Washington Senators.

Vance would lead the league in strikeouts his first seven seasons, a record not since approached,

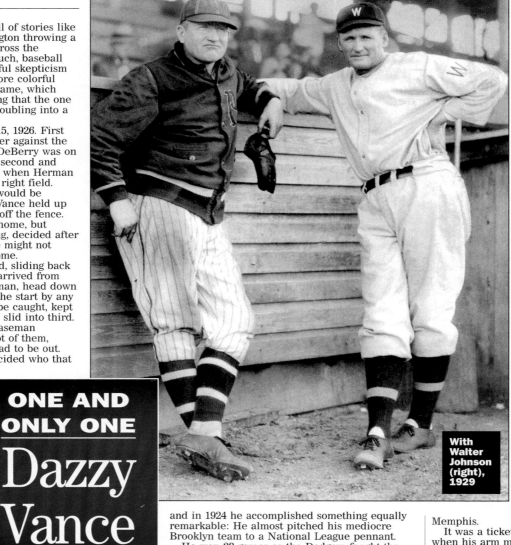

ONE AND ONLY ONE

Dazzy Vance

With Walter Johnson (right), 1929

and in 1924 he accomplished something equally remarkable: He almost pitched his mediocre Brooklyn team to a National League pennant.

He won 28 games as the Dodgers fought the Giants to the last weekend before losing the pennant by a game and a half.

That same year, Rogers Hornsby of the St. Louis Cardinals hit .424, the highest major league batting average in the 20th century — and lost out to Dazzy Vance as the league's most valuable player.

Good as he had become, though, Vance was also known as a good teammate, a valuable commodity for a team that was entering a death valley where it would go 21 years between pennants, 1920-41.

THE '20S EDITION was tagged "the Daffy Dodgers," partly for their skills and partly for their personal quirks, which Dazzy helped orchestrate and exploit. A natural schmoozer and raconteur who had spent half his life in baseball clubhouses, he was a natural leader there — though he would have stood out by appearance alone. He was 6-feet-1 and weighed about 210, with arms that spanned a huge 83 inches and a generally knobby appearance that led one sportswriter to describe him as "looking like he were assembled from spare parts."

When he pitched, he kicked his leg high in the air and leaned back as far as possible, then released either a fastball or a hard curveball with the same motion, making it next to impossible for a batter to ascertain which was bearing down on him.

He wore a chopped-up undershirt under his uniform, and its tatters would flutter as he threw. In that same spirit, his favorite day to pitch was Monday, when the housewives in the apartment houses behind Ebbets Field hung out the wash and provided one more waving white element to camouflage the ball.

For all this he was well rewarded, by the standards of the day. Before the 1925 season he signed a three-year contract for $47,500, and with that windfall he and his wife, Edyth, purchased land in Homosassa Springs, Fla., which he converted into a hunting and fishing lodge where

for the rest of his life he welcomed not only all former teammates but other adventurous sporting spirits. Dazzy's place was a regular stop for early aviators who made it to Florida in their flying machines.

Clarence Arthur Vance was born March 4, 1891, to a Scotch-Irish farm family in Orient, Iowa. When he was 5, the family moved to Hastings, Neb., where an uncle gave him the nickname Dazzy, after a cowboy who mispronounced the name "Daisy."

A strong, athletic youth, Dazzy decided early that baseball was easier than farming, and he played for local teams before signing a contract in 1912 with Superior of the Nebraska league for $100 a month.

Like many strong kids, it took him a while to control his raw pitching power, and he still hadn't really done it by 1915, when the Pittsburgh Pirates brought him up for a look.

He walked five batters in three innings and went back to St. Joseph of the Western League, where the manager figured a big strong kid like this could throw all day every day. At one point, he pitched five games in seven days, whereupon his arm began to hurt.

"Needs rest," his doctor said.

"How much?" asked Dazzy.

"About five years," said the doctor.

He pitched on. The Yankees called him up briefly at the end of 1915, and he lost three games, winning none. For the next five years, save for another brief, unsuccessful shot with the Yankees in 1918, he rode the dusty buses of the minor leagues. Toledo, Sacramento, Rochester, Memphis.

It was a ticket punched nowhere until 1921, when his arm miraculously came back to life. Five years, just like the doctor said. He had a solid year at New Orleans, Charlie Ebbets picked up his contract and the good times finally rolled. By 1932, age 41, Dazzy had won 187 games for a mostly terrible team.

He was traded to St. Louis before the 1933 season and finally pitched in a World Series in 1934, throwing an inning and a third of shutout relief. Brooklyn brought him back for a curtain call in 1935, age 44, and he won three more games for a young manager named Casey Stengel.

He then moved to Florida for good, and, while he had lost money in the crash of '29, he lived a comfortable life. He helped found the Homosassa Springs Chamber of Commerce, managed the local ball team, the Homosassa Springs Wildcats, and in his spare time fashioned driftwood carvings for his gift shop.

B EFORE THE Dodgers left Brooklyn, he would periodically return, and after he was voted into baseball's Hall of Fame in 1955, he was named the First Citizen of Brooklyn in ceremonies at Borough Hall.

On that trip, because he always stopped by Ebbets Field, he also may have met Sandy Koufax, a kid who would match him one day — but not until the Dodgers had moved to Los Angeles. If Vance did meet Koufax, he undoubtedly told him a story, because he told everyone stories, like how he was such a good hitter that opposing managers would never let their pitchers throw him a fastball, "because they'd have to buy ahtificial laigs for their outfielders after the ball whooshed by 'em, or else have to pry 'em off the outfield fence with a putty knife."

The world is full of stories, some more true than others.

On Feb. 16, 1961, two weeks short of 70 and two weeks past his last performance in an old-timers' game, Dazzy Vance died of a heart attack at his home in Homosassa Springs.

BIG TOWN ★ BIOGRAPHY

By EDWARD T. O'DONNELL
Special to The News

THERE WERE 10,173 policemen in the City of New York in 1910, and overwhelmingly they were Irish, the Police Department always having been a key source of patronage for the Irish-dominated political machine, Tammany Hall. The rest of them were mostly German and English. Despite Civil Service regulations, despite the efforts of Police Commissioner Theodore Roosevelt to open the ranks, there were relatively few Jews and relatively few Italians on the force. They were welcome to apply. But it was usually the case that a department doctor would quickly find them to be afflicted with what was called the "leaky heart."

The "leaky heart" diagnosis was common at the time, regularly handed down to subvert civil service and reserve police jobs for the more desired applicants, those with friends in high places. Many a healthy Jew and many a vigorous Italian was surprised to learn that he had heart trouble.

It went without saying that a black man, however robust, was even less likely to be deemed fit for service in New York's Irish Police Department.

Samuel Battle, however, was determined to wear the uniform. A North Carolina minister's son who worked 12-hour days as a Grand Central Terminal baggage handler, 27-year-old Battle understood what lay ahead on a trail still to be blazed. Just a handful of blacks before him had been New York policemen; the first, Wiley Overton, hired as a Brooklyn cell guard in the early 1890s, had lasted a year on the job before the open hostility of fellow officers drove him out. Now Sam Battle took the Civil Service exam and passed it. Someday he would be the city's first black police sergeant. Someday he would be its first black police lieutenant.

But now, in 1910, he was just another leaky heart.

HE WAS ENTERPRISING enough to go to two of the city's most respected cardiologists and get from them independent certificates attesting to his perfect state of health, and these he sent directly to Mayor William Gaynor. Even so, this was hardly an assurance he would win the job — so he also sought the support of one of the city's few black politicians, the prominent Republican Charles Anderson, who had held a number of appointments and who in 1905 had been named to the influential port collector's post by now-President Roosevelt. Anderson's intervention was useful. On June 28, 1911, Samuel Battle became a policeman.

And for the next 2 1/2 years, no one said a word to him.

"POLICING NEW York City is a white man's job," one cop snarled in Battle's direction on his first day at the W. 68th St. station house.

"He won't be here long," predicted another. Battle survived the silent treatment by

A visit from parole commissioner, 1941

AN OFFICER AND A GENTLEMAN

Samuel Battle

adopting a philosophy employed decades later by the civil rights movement's sitdown protesters: He refused to be baited. Denied admission to the police bunkhouse, he snoozed in a chair downstairs. He never filed a complaint. Whenever the newspapers asked him how he was getting along, he said everything was fine. By early 1914, the wall was breaking down. "Battle really took a licking," a white officer recalled years later, "but he took it like a gentleman. He was so dignified and so calm about it all that you wouldn't have suspected that anything was wrong.

"Finally we started feeling like heels."

BY NOW, a massive movement of African-Americans from the rural South to the urban and industrial North was under way. The Great Migration dramatically increased the numbers of blacks in Northern cities; by 1914, Harlem's black population topped 10,000. To Harlem went Samuel Battle, along with a handful of other black officers who had followed him to the force.

And in Harlem, he became a highly visible public fixture, a unique symbol of achievement and authority. Everyone knew him as Big Boy. In the summer of 1919, as bloody race riots swept many American cities, disorder broke out in Harlem after a black man was slain by a white policeman; quickly surrounded by raging mobs, the cop surely would have died had not Battle charged into the crowd to save his life. That act won him, unimaginably, admission into a sergeant's program, though indeed it was another nine years before he actually won the promotion.

The Police Department was not the only hurdle in Battle's life. There also was the matter of personal relations in his own community. On the one hand, he was a prominent Harlemite, a man who raised funds for charity and worked with troubled youngsters, a man who every year gave hundreds of Harlem kids a Thanksgiving

dinner. And, on the other hand, he was a policeman, wearing a uniform that many blacks simply did not trust.

IN MARCH 1935, rioting broke out in Harlem as rumors — entirely false ones — spread that police had beaten a young shoplifter to death. In fact, the lad was soon found safe at his home, but the streets already had erupted. Through the smoke and flying glass appeared Samuel Battle, a newly minted lieutenant.

"If we hadn't been able to rout Battle out of bed and get him on the street in uniform, I'd hate to think of what might have happened," another officer said. "The minute the mobs saw him, they quieted down or came over to talk to him."

But during the ensuing public investigation into the causes of the riot, Battle was forced into a difficult choice between loyalties, and his testimony in defense of the Police Department enraged many Harlem activists.

For all that, Battle remained widely respected by much of the community when he retired from the force in 1941. After 30 years as a policeman, he accepted an offer from Mayor Fiorello LaGuardia: succeeding the late Yankee legend Lou Gehrig as a member of the city's Parole Commission.

THE NEW POSITION gave Battle a substantial raise — from $4,000 to $6,000 a year — but it also gave him something he had not enjoyed as a policeman: the freedom to speak his mind. For the next 10 years, he spoke out tirelessly, criticizing the press for sidestepping racial issues, urging attention to social conditions. The Thanksgiving dinners for kids continued. He raised $95,000 for the expansion of the Harlem YMCA. "Juvenile delinquents are not born that way," he regularly declared.

He retired for good in 1951 and lived out his days as a revered Harlem elder. Asked in 1964, two years before his death, to comment on his role as a pioneer, he said only: "I'm happy to have helped break down the prejudice against my people."

Surveying his men, 1946

By TOM ROBBINS
Daily News Staff Writer

E VERY MAY, on the Saturday night nearest his birthday, Joseph P. Ryan threw himself a dazzling little party at the Commodore Hotel on E. 42nd St. Some 3,000 guests attended in 1928, including Mayor Jimmy Walker, ex-Gov. Al Smith, three district attorneys and all the big shipping executives, all celebrating the man of the hour.

He was big, broad-shouldered, heavy-jowled and often flushed of face, his rust-red hair slicked straight back. Women found him handsome, and he was given to the vanities of the wealthy. He wore camel hair coats, silk scarves, Sulka shirts, matching rings and cuff links. He sported a pince-nez when reading.

His job? Why, Joe Ryan ran the waterfront.

He was president for life of the International Longshoremen's Association, AFL, 45,000 members strong. Came up the hard way, Joe did. Born in 1884 and reared near the Chelsea docks, he worked with his hands and broad back until a load of pig iron broke his shoulder in 1913 and he took up unionism for a living.

Now he controlled the world's greatest harbor. More than 21,000 cargo carriers passed through the Narrows in 1935, stowed in their holds all the raw materials and luxuries of modern life: oil, steel and lumber; coffee, furs, caviar and Scotch whisky. All of it passed through the hands of Joe Ryan's men on the docks.

He was the town's top union man: president of the New York City Central Trades and Labor Council and chief of his own Democratic political club besides, the Joseph P. Ryan Association, firmly tied to Tammany Hall. He knew how the game worked. "I'm a machine man, and I run a machine — Tammany first and Labor afterwards," he said, and politicians and judges vied for favor.

But out on the dark, teeming docks, where longshoremen gathered in anxious clusters at dawn, baling hooks resting on their shoulders, their caps tugged down, Joe Ryan's name was muttered in quiet curses.

THEY KNEW Ryan's unionism. Other unions pushed for job security and hiring halls that gave members a fair shot at work and honored seniority. Not the ILA. It preferred the chaotic shape-up system, where old, work-worn men jostled with younger ones, shouting for the pier boss' attention when the whistle blew. Those not picked stood in rain or freezing weather, waiting for the next shape.

Work could be had — for a price. Desperate men put a toothpick behind an ear to signal that they were willing to kick back an hour's pay if hired.

On the job, the union ignored overloaded slings of cargo, tipping precariously as they were hoisted out of the hold. So, too, the short crews

QUIET CURSES
Joseph Ryan

salted with phantom workers by the pier bosses who collected their pay while the rest of the gang picked up the slack.

Such schemes were key to Joe Ryan's rogue's gallery of union leaders.

Pint-size Mickey Bowers, who had done 10 years for payroll robbery, controlled the passenger ship piers on the West Side, where Local 824 was dubbed the "Pistol Local" because the gun was the tool of choice for settling disputes.

Greenwich Village docks were under Ed McGrath, arrested twice for murder, and his brother-in-law, John (Cockeye) Dunn, who died in the chair in 1949 for killing a stevedore boss whose job he wanted.

Michael Clemente ran the East River docks, his South St. office a den of gambling, loan-sharking and dope peddling. Staten Island was ruled by ex-pug Alex (The Ox) DeBrizzi. Brooklyn was the province of Murder Inc. chief Albert Anastasia and his brothers, Anthony (Tough Tony) and Gerry (Bang Bang). Charles (Charlie the Jew) Yanowsky had the Jersey piers until a rival put

an ice pick in his eye in 1948.

Go up against Joe Ryan's boys? You'd have to be nuts. Some tried, like Peter Panto out in Brooklyn. In 1939, Panto wound up in a New Jersey lime pit.

Up in his 19th-floor office at 265 W. 14th St., where he'd had a private shower installed, Joe Ryan explained that the men liked things the way they were. He shot his French cuffs from his jacket sleeves and said: "If they wanted a hiring hall now, they'd get it. They don't."

Then the men on the docks surprised him. And themselves.

THE FIRST BIG rumbling came in the fall of 1945. Unions everywhere were pushing for big postwar raises, but Ryan agreed to a meager dime-an-hour hike and the same 44-hour week, then declared the contract unanimously approved.

The hell, said the dock men. Within a week, 30,000 of them had hit the bricks. Five thousand jammed a mass meeting at Manhattan Center on W. 34th St. "Strike! Beat Ryan! Down with the finks!" they shouted.

As his goons responded with brass knuckles and blackjacks, Ryan said he knew what was going on: "This so-called rank-and-file committee is a tool of the Communists," he declared.

It took Mayor Fiorello LaGuardia to hammer out a solution. The shaken shipping association agreed to a 25-cent raise and a 40-hour week.

In 1951, the men rose up against Ryan again, when he insisted he had 3-to-1 approval for his latest contract. Vowing to crush the 35,000 strikers, Ryan unleashed the Bowers and Anastasia gangs as cobblestones flew and fistfights raged along the waterfront.

"We will go through them and over them, but never around them," he thundered.

It lasted 25 days, paralyzing shipping along the Atlantic coast, the longest and costliest strike in maritime history, before a state fact-finding panel hatched a compromise. The men celebrated. "We won 100% by seeing Joe Ryan cringe," said wildcat leader John Dwyer.

"Ryan apparently can't control his own union," sniffed a Daily News editorial, adding ominously: "The

Port of New York is losing business."

A STATE ANTI-CRIME commission opened hearings on waterfront crime, and for weeks it was the best show in town. The panel heard how the Bowers gang forced the fabled Cunard Line to use a stevedoring firm it controlled, how Alex (The Ox) DeBrizzi kept his local's treasury in a jar at home, how Ryan had threatened a strike to force Manhattan district attorney Frank Hogan to back off a 1948 waterfront murder probe and pressured shipping firms to drop charges against gangsters caught stealing. Several employers admitted making regular cash gifts to the $20,000-a-year union boss.

That money, fumed an indignant Ryan, went into a special, confidential "anti-Communist fund" so secret he couldn't reveal its uses.

But records showed the money went for Cadillacs, country clubs, cruises, life insurance premiums and an account with a Waldorf-Astoria haberdashery.

On April 13, 1953, Ryan was indicted on charges of stealing from his union. His big shoulders sagging under a brown suit and overcoat, he walked through a drizzly rain to be booked at the Elizabeth St. station house.

F ROM THERE, it was a fast downhill slide. The AFL expelled the ILA for gangsterism. Ryan was ousted as president, albeit with a $10,000-a-year pension. He caught a break with a hung jury on the thefts, but the feds hit him with bribery charges in 1954 and a tax rap a year later.

He'd had enough. He checked in as a "mind patient" at Bellevue in November 1955, ill enough to prompt a judge to suspend his six-month sentence.

Ryan died at his home on W. 21st St. in July 1963, at age 79, following a long illness. Mass was said for him at his corner parish, Guardian Angel. A modest funeral cortege — 17 limos, four flower cars — drove past the docks.

It wasn't the first time a coffin was carried for Joe Ryan. Back in the '40s, wildcatting dockmen had held a mock funeral for "King Joe." *Here lies Joseph P. Ryan,* they wrote on the coffin, *who was both phony and finky ... never spoke the truth, and was unjust in his dealing with all union men.*

By DAVID HINCKLEY
Daily News Staff Writer

THE MAYOR OF Harlem, they called Willie Bryant in the early 1950s, back when 125th St. was just about the finest place in town to take a midnight stroll and maybe drop in on Willie himself at the Palm Cafe or the Baby Grand, where he'd be doing his live radio show over WHOM, making tracks with the wax and talking smooth about the style of the street.

In the '40s and '50s, pretty much everybody north of the park knew Willie Bryant. He was all over uptown the way Walter Winchell was all over downtown — except, with Willie, everyone liked him.

As a kid, he had worked with Bessie Smith and spent several years with the Whitman Sisters, the top act on the TOBA black-theater circuit, picking up all the tricks of the trade. Before he was 21, he was a star graduate — prepped to become a dancer, comedian, bandleader, singer, deejay, producer, movie actor, talent scout and emcee.

The only thing he couldn't become was white.

HE WAS CLOSE, with neutral features and "good" hair. But close didn't count, and he soon concluded that looking almost white was why he was almost a national star.

"Willie was a great showman," remembered Leonard Reed, who had first partnered with Bryant as a dance team in 1929. "He could do it all. But they knew he was part Negro, and they wouldn't let him work downtown. He never got the chance to work the places that, say, Bob Hope did. And Bob Hope was never as good as Willie Bryant, never in his wildest dreams."

A few black entertainers did cross the lines, Reed acknowledged. But only a few. "There was no room for, say, five. One or two, maybe." John Bubbles could outdance Fred Astaire, but the scripts went to Fred. Most of Lena Horne's movie scenes were shot so she could be snipped out if Southern theater owners didn't cotton to race-mixing.

For light-skinned blacks, the choice was this: Try to pass, living a lie for a shot at stardom, or stay home and forfeit the shot.

For a while, Bryant and the equally light-skinned Reed did pass. They did a little tap, a little soft-shoe, a little comedy. If they didn't invent the Shim Sham, tap's most famous step, they were in on it. They played the Palace.

Reed was the handsome devil, Bryant the joker. At 21, he was an elflike figure, with big teeth, soft eyes, a big nose and ears set so far back they looked pointed. Not that he was some kid who fell off a tractor. William Stevens Bryant was born in 1908 or 1909, some said in New Orleans, and grew up in Chicago, where he tended the concession stand at the Grand Theater, working up routines on everything from the merits of the popcorn to the quirks of the actors. That's where the Whitman Sisters found him, and when they offered him $30 a week to sing, dance, tell jokes and paint scenery, he was in show biz for good.

He reached New York in 1928 and spent a little time in a stock company at the Alhambra before hooking up with Reed. They worked black and white houses until 1933, when someone ratted them out. "We never worked white again," Reed said.

Reed became a producer, doing shows at the Cotton Club and the Apollo. Bryant took over

With Leonard Reed (right) at the Apollo Theatre

SOMETHING BIG
Willie Bryant

Lucky Millinder's band and later formed several others. His skill was finding sidemen: Benny Carter, Teddy Wilson, Ben Webster, Cozy Cole, Panama Francis. The first band played through the '30s, and in 1939 Bryant co-starred in the film "Keep Punching" with boxing champion Henry Armstrong. By then, Bryant was Harlem's ubiquitous man about town, his quick wit and gracious style making him a natural host for every event from the reopening of the Alhambra to Police Athletic League fund-raisers. In 1946, CBS hired him as the first black host of a network radio program, "Night Life."

It ran only five weeks, as radio's wartime flirtation with integrated programming cooled. But this powerful new black music was making an impression radio couldn't ignore, and in New York the man cashing in was "Symphony Sid" Torin, a grouchy white guy who started on WBNX in 1937 and moved to WHOM in 1940.

When Sid moved on in 1948, WHOM took the bold step of hiring a black man, Bryant, to play black music. It did hedge the bet by teaming him with Ray Carroll, a white jock who had worked with Sid.

They had an elegant old-school style, unlike some of the wild childs starting to surface on rhythm and blues radio. And soon "After Hours Swing Session," 11 p.m.-2 a.m. nightly, became a hot enough property that in the fall of 1949 CBS-TV hired Bryant to host a black musical revue titled "Uptown Jubilee."

Hampered by a low budget and reluctant sponsors, it lasted only three episodes. But the radio show soared along. In April 1950, Bryant and Carroll began working live in the front window of the Baby Grand on 125th St., where stars from the Apollo could drop in after their show.

In March 1952, the Amsterdam News decided to elect a new mayor of Harlem, filling the vacancy created when the longtime titleholder, dancer Bill Robinson, died in 1949. Ten prominent citizens were placed on a ballot and Bryant won. At the installation banquet in the Hotel Capitol, the speakers included Milton Berle, who had been one of Bryant's fellow laborers on the theater circuit before he got the full-scale, big-budget TV shot a Willie Bryant didn't.

THAT SPRING, Bryant and Carroll were hired for a second radio show, afternoons on WOV, and by 1954 Bryant smelled something big about to break: Hordes of white kids were listening to this music, and the pied pipers were black jocks like Bryant, Dr. Jive, Ramon Bruce, Hal Jackson and Jack Walker.

Bryant was right about the break. He was just wrong about who got it.

A WHITE R&B deejay from Cleveland named Alan Freed was picked up, on tape, by WNJR in Newark. In May 1954, after he sold 22,000 tickets for two R&B shows at the Armory in Newark, Freed was hired to launch a prime-time evening R&B program on WINS. He would be paid an unheard-of $75,000 a year, 10 times or more what Bryant was getting.

Black deejays called a meeting at the Harlem Y, where Bryant told WINS program director Bob Smith that any black deejay in town knew more than Freed and could do a better show. Smith blithely replied that he hadn't even known Freed was white when he hired him. Matters became sufficiently heated that Bryant several days later felt compelled to assure Billboard: "I have nothing against Freed. I am not carrying on a campaign against him."

Not that it would have made a difference. Freed only got bigger, cutting deals with record companies, starring in movies and getting his own TV show before he self-destructed in the payola scandals of 1959.

Bryant had actually cut a TV deal of his own in 1954. "Apollo Varieties" was syndicated briefly as "Showtime at the Apollo" before subscribing stations decided they still couldn't sell an all-black event. So the footage was compressed into a movie and released to theaters in an unsuccessful attempt to cash in on "Blackboard Jungle." Bryant emceed and did skits with his old partner, Reed.

In April 1955, he got another network radio show, ABC's "Rhythm on Radio." But the mayor of Harlem seemed to sense the big wave had hit the beach without him.

BRIEFLY, IN 1956, he moved to Detroit and got an ABC network TV show from the famous Flame Bar, where Jackie Wilson sang and Berry Gordy cut some of his first business deals. By year's end, he was back in New York, buying the Orchid Room in the Bronx and planning another TV show that didn't work out. A year later, he was in San Francisco, working at KSAN. A few months later, he was at KALI in Los Angeles.

"The man's mind was brilliant," said Leonard Reed. "But he was bitter and he had a right to be. He was a genius. He was one of the greats of show business who never got anywhere, because of his color."

Willie Bryant died Feb. 9, 1964, by which time much of the Harlem he had known was gone as well. The position of mayor of Harlem is currently vacant.

By JOSH MAX
Special to The News

MINNIE Schoenberg was a magician's daughter who married a very bad tailor named Sam Marx, and after they came to New York from Germany in the 1880s their lives largely revolved around one returned suit after another, endlessly brought back to Sam by irate customers come to point out some jacket sleeve or pant leg that was an inch or two longer than the other.

Accordingly, the Marxes were often on the move, dodging attachments and bill collectors and landlords. In time, they arrived at a tiny tenement on E. 93rd St., between Lexington and Third Aves., and settled down to the business of raising a family, which came to include five sons, whose names were Leonard, Adolph, Julius, Milton and Herbert.

Minnie's father was not the only show person in her life. She also had a brother named Al Shean, who was a successful vaudeville man, half of the famous Gallagher and Shean duo. Thus, early on, she was possessed of show business fever. And were not her own sons talented lads? Minnie decided she would make careers for her boys. Someday they would be famous.

And, of course, they were. That was after they abandoned their birth names and became Chico, Harpo, Groucho, Gummo and Zeppo. The Marx Brothers.

GROUCHO WAS the first to go out before the lights; Minnie put him onstage as a boy soprano in 1905, paired with a kid named Lou Levy, touring the very bottom of the vaudeville circuit. Then Gummo joined the act, which in 1907 became the Three Nightingales. When Minnie needed a fourth Nightingale a year later, Harpo was shanghaied from his pianist's job at a midtown nickelodeon. He was a horrible singer, but Minnie got around that difficulty: All he had to do was open his mouth when Groucho did, she said, and they'd make a few extra dollars. The night the curtain came up on Harpo's debut as one of the Four Nightingales, he wet his pants.

Soon a veteran stage mother, Minnie put up with crooked managers, nonexistent funds, scenery that fell apart, actors who walked out — and a set of rowdy sons who were increasingly inclined to unscripted horseplay when she wasn't around to keep them in line. One night in 1910, for example, after the Four Nightingales had taken on two new singers and become the Six Mascots, the brothers spotted a cockroach crawling across the floor. Instantly they abandoned their song, dropped to all fours and began shouting out bets on how long it would take the bug to cross the stage.

The audience loved this. So did the reviewers. And now Minnie Marx began to realize what she had on her hands.

SOON, GROUCHO and Harpo and Gummo became full-fledged Marx Brothers, on the road performing both tried-and-true vaudeville stuff and original material that combined musical numbers with the boys' insane clowning. Harpo, as terrible a speaker as he was a singer, had stopped talking entirely by now, and his harp had become a permanent part of the act. Groucho was beginning to sport his trademark cigar and greasepaint mustache. Minnie ran everything,

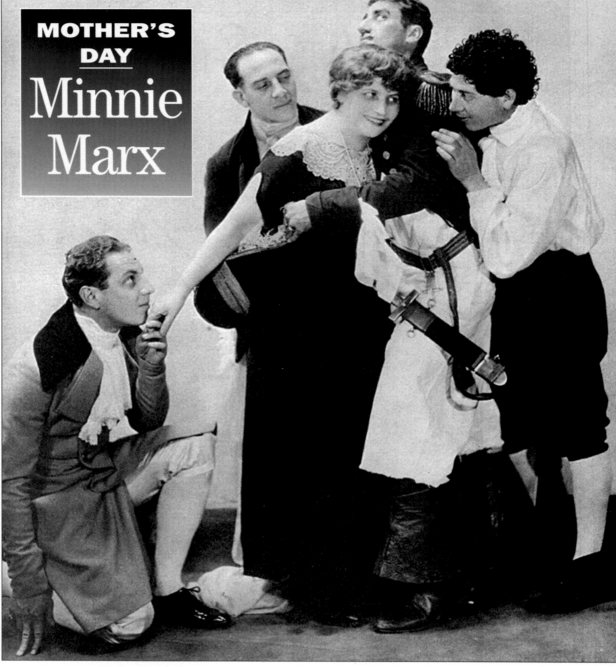

**MOTHER'S DAY
Minnie Marx**

booking and managing all the shows. It was Sam's job to sit in the audience and laugh uproariously, thus inducing the rest of the crowd to do the same.

One night in 1915, the brothers looked down into the orchestra pit of the hall they were playing and recognized the pianist. It was brother Chico. Harpo whooped and flung an orange at him. Chico caught it, flung it back, climbed onstage and started babbling in some kind of crazed Italian. This killed the audience. And Chico immediately became part of the Marx Brothers act as well.

In 1919, Gummo dropped out and was replaced by Minnie's youngest, 19-year-old Zeppo. And for a few more years the Marx Brothers and their mother were a hardworking road unit, traveling by train from town to town, fighting with club owners, chasing after bookers who tried to skip out without paying them. Finally, in 1921, the brothers went to London.

There, at the Alhambra Theatre, they were a smash. When they got back to New York, they were booked into the Palace. Minnie's sons had arrived.

And now she retired as their manager and turned them over to the William Morris Agency. Her work was done.

THE MARX BROTHERS opened their first

Broadway show, "I'll Say She Is," at the Casino Theatre on May 19, 1924. Minnie had been waiting for this moment for two decades, and it was only a slight setback when, earlier that day, as she was being fitted for her opening-night gown, she slipped off her chair and broke her leg. She had herself carried to her box in time for the show.

She saw her sons open in three smash Broadway hits. And in 1929, when their first feature film, "Cocoanuts," opened in New York, she was there as well.

ON SEPT. 15, 1929, 65-year-old Minnie Marx gathered her boys around her for a family feast at Zeppo's home in Queens. After midnight, she and Sam got into their car and headed home. Halfway across the Queensboro Bridge, she slumped against the passenger door.

Sam wheeled the car around and headed back to Zeppo's. She died there, just before 2 a.m., held tight in Harpo's arms.

'S *HE HAD DONE much more than bear her sons, bring them up and turn them into play actors. She had invented them. They were just comics she imagined for her own amusement. They amused no one more, and their reward was her smile."*
—**Alexander Woollcott in The New Yorker, 1929**

By DAVID HINCKLEY
Daily News Staff Writer

IN THE WEE small hours, after the band had finished another one-nighter and the musicians were trying to grab three or four hours' sleep, Duke Ellington and Billy Strayhorn often would find an all-night eatery that served black folks and go to work.

Fresh music was essential for the driven Ellington, America's premier composer of the 20th century, and music talk came easy between The Duke and Swee'pea, his equally impassioned protégé.

Strayhorn didn't come to New York to join Ellington until 1939, years after Duke had become an institution. But alone among Ellington collaborators, he merged his work seamlessly with that of the master.

He "cracked the code," he liked to joke, and both men said they had trouble telling who developed which part in some of Ellington's best-known work.

But before they got to music in the late-night restaurant sessions, there was first the matter of the menu. Ellington, a tall, elegant man acutely aware of the figure he cut, would often announce he was on a diet and order only shredded wheat.

Fine, Strayhorn would say. Five-foot-three with a high metabolism, thick glasses and no particular vanity, he would order a steak.

As recounted by Richard Boyer in a 1944 New Yorker profile, Duke's diet would last as long as the shredded wheat, at which point he would gaze longingly at Strayhorn's plate and order a steak of his own. Then a second steak. Then a double portion of fried potatoes, a salad, a bowl of sliced tomatoes and a lobster, followed by a medley of desserts.

Dawn now imminent, he might order ham and eggs and pancakes before returning to his diet and finishing up with a second bowl of shredded wheat.

Meanwhile, women would pass by the table, and he would pause to offer compliments. "You make that dress look so beautiful." "I never knew an angel could be so luscious."

Only when the meal and the flirtation wound down did Duke lean back and sing, "Dah dah dee dee, tah tahdle tah boom, deedle dee, deedle dee, boom."

"Why not deedle dee deedle dee, deedle dee deedle dee dee, dumtah dumtah dumtah, boom?" Billy replied.

"Not right for a trio," said Duke.

"I don't think your strain is melodic enough," said Billy.

"I think it's a nice strain," Duke said.

"It has too many notes for a trio," said Billy. "I'm looking for something small that goes up half a tone."

From exchanges like this, in hotels, diners and New York living rooms and over long-distance wires, emerged some of the most durable music stamped Duke Ellington: "The Perfume Suite," "A Drum Is a Woman," "The Far East Suite," "My People," the Sacred Concerts.

Strayhorn also arranged Ellington's small-group sessions featuring Johnny Hodges and wrote "After All," "Day Dream," "Clementine," "Raincheck" and "Take the A Train," which so enchanted Ellington that he made it the band's new theme song.

Ellington, a man sufficiently self-assured that he once said no one could pay him higher compliments than he paid himself, said Strayhorn's legacy "will never be less than the ultimate on the highest plateau of culture."

ELLINGTON KNEW that turf. He had moved to New York from Washington in 1923, aiming to become a famous musician, and a decade later he

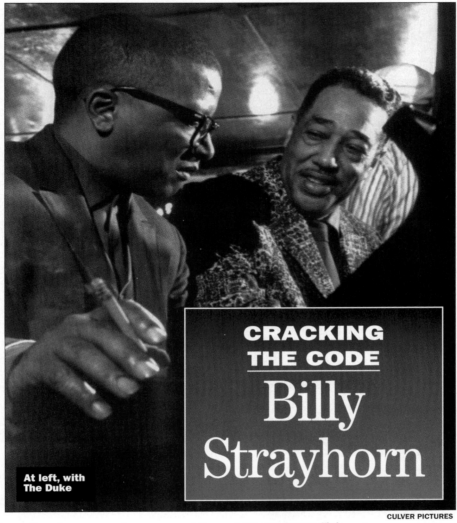

CRACKING THE CODE
Billy Strayhorn

At left, with The Duke

CULVER PICTURES

was known around the world for his Cotton Club shows and standards like "Black and Tan Fantasy," "Mood Indigo," "Sophisticated Lady" and "It Don't Mean a Thing If It Ain't Got That Swing."

Billy Strayhorn, born Nov. 29, 1915, spent those years growing up in Ohio, North Carolina and Pennsylvania with a fierce love of classical music. In grade school, he bought an upright piano with money he saved from odd jobs, and come high school he studied piano and harmony.

But he was black, and the classical music world wanted white. So he started listening to jazzmen like Art Tatum and Teddy Wilson. Unfortunately, jazz jobs weren't plentiful either in the Depression, and it didn't help that Strayhorn was gay at a time when songs like "Sissy Man Blues" were floating around in the musical currency.

So he gigged around Pittsburgh and he wrote a show called "Fantastic Rhythm" that earned $55 from a local production. Then, one night in 1934, the Ellington band came into town and he spent the evening right by the bandstand, transfixed.

Four years later, on another Ellington swing through Pittsburgh, he got up the nerve to meet the maestro and play a few songs. Duke told the kid he'd like to bring him to New York.

As Strayhorn was clerking in a drugstore at the time, this offer didn't require a lot of thought. But several months passed with no formal invitation, so Strayhorn and an arranger friend, Bill Esch, headed for New York on their own. At the Adams Theater in Newark they caught up with Ellington, who said glad to see ya, kid, I lost your address.

By this time, Strayhorn had written a classic of his own, "Lush Life," which he sat on for a dozen years until he found a singer he felt could do it justice. It eventually became a standard from a Nat King Cole recording, though Strayhorn personally felt Cole still hadn't gotten quite the nuances he was looking for.

THERE WERE NO such caveats in either the musical or personal symbiosis between Ellington and Strayhorn. They fell into what most called a

father-son relationship, though Strayhorn's close friend Lena Horne said it was more like a nonphysical love affair — creating for Strayhorn some of the same problems faced by the hundreds of women romanced by world-class lover man Ellington.

"Duke treated Billy exactly like he treated women, with all that old-fashioned chauvinism," said Horne. "Very loving and very protective, but controlling, very destructive."

From Strayhorn's perspective, whatever problems his association with Ellington may have created, it solved more. If it committed him to the twilight world of the musician — too many cigarettes, too many drinks, months on the road, no clock — it gave him something to do with his life that he was good at. Once inside the Ellington band, he never left its comfortable embrace.

He wrote lyrics, he arranged, he played piano, he led the band when Duke was spread too thin. When Duke was writing in the bathtub, his faithful valet Jonesy maintaining the water temperature, he would call out lines to Strayhorn, who would play them on the piano. If the rest of the band was around, they might pick up their cues and assemble the song on the spot.

There was some jealousy over Strayhorn's status in the band — one musician would transcribe Ellington's work, but not Strayhorn's — and some critics say Strayhorn never reached Ellington's musical level. Perhaps owing to the classical training Duke never had, Strayhorn was a bit more formal and controlled in his playing and composition.

Other critics point to "A Train" or "Lush Life" and say his work speaks for itself.

Whatever the critical assessment, Strayhorn became indispensable to Ellington, who used him to keep up with his own creativity. If Ellington needed the middle part to a suite, Strayhorn could write it. He pushed Ellington at the same time he took some of the pressure off.

He didn't always get properly thanked for this. There is evidence he helped write "Satin Doll," though only Ellington is credited. But in daily life, Ellington was appreciative and attentive: To mess with "Strays" was to mess with the Duke.

STRAYHORN EVENTUALLY did a few separate projects, and while he remained as modest as Duke was gregarious, he developed his own circle of friends, like Horne, who gave him the Swee'pea name, after the small, sweet and vulnerable character in the Popeye cartoons.

In the mid-1960s, Strayhorn was diagnosed with cancer of the esophagus. From his bed in the Hospital for Joint Diseases he wrote his last tune, "Blood Count," and Horne was at the side of that bed when he died May 31, 1967.

Ellington would live seven more years, savoring his legend and accepting the Presidential Medal of Freedom, which he viewed as partial recompense for being denied a Pulitzer Prize because the Pulitzer committee saw him as a black jazzman and felt black jazz just wasn't a worthy enough art form.

Ellington also would record a Strayhorn tribute titled "And His Mother Called Him Bill," probably the most powerful work of his later years, and he told friends that when he got the call about Strayhorn's death, he cried out loud and pounded his head against the wall.

But on the day of Billy Strayhorn's memorial service at St. Peter's Church, a composed Ellington delivered a poignant tribute and traveled across town to the Hickory House to join 20 of his comrades for dinner. He ordered a steak.

By DAVID HINCKLEY
Daily News Staff Writer

TO THE SEASONED New Yorker, Harry Smith didn't look much different from any other wild man pacing the streets.

Behind the untamed hair and the thick glasses with frames wide as 2-by-4s, he looked like the kind of guy who probably lived in the Chelsea Hotel, which he did, and drew strange pictures and scribbled odd notes to himself, which he did, and thought unseen forces were out to poison him, which from time to time he did.

Yes, Harry Smith was an odd chap. He collected gourds and painted Ukrainian Easter eggs. He collected spoons shaped like ducks, because he was fascinated by objects that looked like other objects. He was fascinated by objects in general.

"The reason for looking at objects," he informed an interviewer, "is to perfect the self."

He once put together a program of his films, describing Film 12 thusly:

"The first part depicts the heroine's toothache consequent to the loss of a very valuable watermelon, her dentistry and transportation to heaven. Next follows an elaborate exposition of the heavenly land in terms of Israel, Montreal, and the second part depicts the return to Earth from being eaten by Max Muller on the day Edward the Seventh dedicated the Great Sewer of London. Approximately 50 minutes."

To a modest cadre of students and fans of this sort of cinema, Harry Smith was a visionary. A genius, really.

To the rest of New York, well, he might have been nuts, but at least he was only shooting film, not innocent bystanders.

And the sentiment was mutual.

TO HARRY SMITH, it all connected: the spoons shaped like ducks, the Great Sewer of London, games played with string, peyote trips, Native American religions and Tarzan pop-up books.

If the masses couldn't see that, their loss. Harry saw it and so did comrades like Allen Ginsberg, at whose apartment Harry occasionally overstayed his welcome.

And so Harry Smith's life tootled along, pretty much out on the harmless fringe except for this one time and this one project called "The Anthology of American Folk Music," a three-part package released by Folkways Records in 1952 that eventually had quite the impact on popular culture.

Assembled entirely by Harry Smith, with esoteric notations and tiny weird graphics, the anthology consisted of 84 songs recorded between 1927 and 1932. Essentially, it was folk music — blues, country, gospel — in its rawest form. Charlie Patton growling "Mississippi Bo Weevil Blues" in a voice so thick he swallowed most of the words. The Rev. Sister Mary Nelson calling down "Judgment." Chubby Parker and his Old-Time Banjo whooping and hollering through "King Kong Kitchie Kitchie Ki-Me-O."

Rosemary Clooney, Percy Faith and Eddie Fisher it wasn't, and it knocked none of them off the radio. But over the next few years, it would catch the ear of many a restless musician, from Pete Seeger and the Kingston Trio to Bob Dylan and Jerry Garcia.

When the Lovin' Spoonful sang Ragtime Henry Thomas' "Fishin' Blues," or the Grateful Dead

Study in alchemy: Harry Smith turning milk into milk. Photo by Allen Ginsberg, 1985.

PERFECTING THE SELF

Harry Smith

sang Gus Cannon's "Minglewood Blues," or Dylan put Blind Lemon Jefferson's "See That My Grave Is Kept Clean" on his first record, Harry Smith was the matchmaker.

When Dylan wrote "All the railroad men/They just drink up your blood like wine," in "Memphis Blues Again," he was taking the line from song No. 63 on "The Anthology of American Folk Music," "I Wish I Was a Mole in the Ground" by Bascom Lamar Lunsford, "The Minstrel of the Appalachians."

Some young folks were so intrigued by the anthology that they drove South and tracked down artists like Mississippi John Hurt, who wondered exactly what the Sam Hill was going on.

The anthology was, critic Greil Marcus would write years later, "the founding document of the American folk revival."

The original package promised a fourth, fifth and sixth set, which Smith gathered, but never got around to annotating. He was off to other projects.

ANYHOW, HE WAS allergic to success. He refused to sell his work, despite regular generous offers, preferring to hit up friends for a few dollars whenever he was about to get evicted from one of the series of rooms and hotels where he lived with hundreds of cardboard boxes of his objects.

Harry Smith was born May 29, 1923, in Portland, Ore. He liked to tell people he was the child of Princess Anastasia, because that's who his mother sometimes said she was. In slightly more mundane truth, his parents were Freemasons and occultists. His mother taught at a Native American school, where young Harry picked up a fascination for the culture and an obsession with documentation.

He studied anthropology for a few semesters at a college in Washington, but gave it up after a trip to Berkeley on which he discovered drugs and Bohemia.

The drug and alcohol use, at times heavy, had side effects. For years, he drank only milk because he was convinced that was the only liquid the unseen poisoners could not adulterate. He

would routinely abuse both friends and strangers: He was known to order a drink, hurl it back in the waiter's face, add an expletive and storm out.

On the other hand, friends insisted no one was more intelligent or engaging, and that his snappish side stemmed mostly from his genuine concern over the condition of all life on this planet. He had a series of pet birds, and when they died, he found parting so difficult he would wrap them in foil and keep them in the freezer. He would tell friends that if they had to kill any living thing, say a cockroach, they must do it swiftly, because roaches have a different sense of time than people, so even a one- or two-second delay creates for the roach an eternity of agony.

Though Smith was of age during World War II, he was able to avoid any direct killing there. Small in stature from a childhood case of rickets, he worked in a defense plant as the little guy who could squeeze into a narrow airplane fuselage to mount the guns.

By that time, to help feed his obsession with documentation, he had begun collecting phonograph records. Considering that he lived in the urban North and was buying music targeted for the rural South, there was little competition, and he accumulated an impressive collection at closeout prices.

By 1947, he had drifted to New York and met Moses Asch, the owner of Folkways and a kindred musical spirit who was as happy to issue the anthology as Smith was to compile it.

In the postanthology years, Smith turned toward modern jazz. He was an every-night regular at Birdland and later the Five Spot, where he became friends with the likes of Ginsberg, Charlie Parker and Thelonious Monk. He worked on records with Monk and Billie Holiday and produced the first album by The Fugs, a raucous guerrilla rock band out of the East Village.

Pursuing a longtime interest, Smith set out to hand-paint a movie that would synchronize precisely with the music of Monk and Parker. He spent years on one film, then, according to legend, just rolled it away down 42nd St. one night.

Another night he almost hit Dylan. Staying at Ginsberg's place when Dylan dropped in to play a working tape of "Empire Burlesque," Smith refused to come out of his room, staying behind the door yelling at Allen and Bob to turn the music down so he could get some sleep.

He stayed with Ginsberg or other friends between longer stretches at hotels — the Earle, the Breslin, the Chelsea — where gradually most of his objects were stolen, lost or traded to some merchant for food or clothing.

If this bothered him, it didn't show. "I've lived to see my dreams realized," he said in 1991 when the Grammys honored him for the anthology. "I've seen America changed by music and music change America."

NINE MONTHS LATER, on Nov. 27, 1991, Harry Smith died in his room at the Chelsea Hotel. Friends say Ginsberg had his body stored in a freezer for 49 days, a Buddhist ritual they agreed was a nice gesture even if Harry Smith wasn't a Buddhist.

It was, after all, the thought that counts. "Our language," Smith mused shortly before his death, "wasn't built for discussing the subjects I really want to discuss."

BIG TOWN ★ BIOGRAPHY

By JAY MAEDER
Daily News Staff Writer

QUITE THE plugged-in newspaperman was the New York Daily Mirror's Walter Winchell, who on Monday the 8th of February 1932 presented this small item buried deep down in his widely syndicated "On Broadway" column:

Five planes brought dozens of machine-gats from Chicago Friday to combat The Town's Capone. … Local banditti have made one hotel a virtual arsenal and several hot-spots are ditto because Master Coll is giving them the headache. … Things are getting so tough here — a lot of us have no idea from where our next bullet is coming!

Which may have given Vincent Coll a small grim smile, but only if he had happened to pick up the Mirror's early edition when it hit the street about midnight Sunday, because by Monday sunrise, when the final came up, he was already dead, riddled with slugs as he stood in a phone booth in a drugstore at Eighth Ave. and 23rd St. A few wee-hours customers were sipping orangeade at the fountain when a machine-gunner came in at 1:10 a.m., shushed them all, blasted the booth, slipped out again and efficiently roared away in a waiting Packard. None could offer much of a description. Coll's bodyguard, for his part, had mysteriously disappeared just before the gunsmoke.

Thus concluded 23-year-old Vincent Coll's brief insurrection against Bronx beer baron Dutch Schultz, who was widely known to have put $50,000 on the young troublemaker's head. Indeed, you didn't need Walter Winchell to tell you that Coll's days were numbered. Everybody knew that. This was one boy nobody wanted walking around.

This was, after all, Coll the baby-killer. In the course of daily commerce, gunner Coll was said to have slaughtered probably three dozen men, but that was just the job. Most everyday New Yorkers even understood that. Baby-killing was another matter. You didn't kill babies.

"MAD DOG COLL" was a mostly posthumous tag, applied by the newspapers as they later assessed Vincent Coll's short, brutish career in the City of New York. In his lifetime, the underworld knew him as "Irish" or "The Mick." He was just a kid, one of the nastier customers who ever came out of Throgs Neck, a reform-school rattlesnake who decided toward the end of Prohibition that he had large designs on the business enterprises of his superiors. These, frankly, he did not deserve, nor is it likely that he could have managed them well had he prevailed. Relatively speaking, Dutch Schultz was actually the good guy here.

The Dutchman had an organization. His disaffected young ex-bodyguard had a mob of crazy upstarts. Irish Coll and his boys finally developed a specialty; what they did was kidnap The Dutchman's boys and hold them for ransom, which was a real nuisance. All through 1930 and into 1931, the two sides were bumping off each other's soldiers with numbing regularity, and in this historic season of wholesale gang carnage, New York's hapless authorities could barely distinguish this feud between the boss Jew and the maverick Mick from the simultaneously erupting wars between several different factions of ambitious Sicilians. Who knew who was killing whom, or what for?

About all New York City understood, in late July, when a little boy was machine-gunned to death in the street outside his Harlem home, was that the gangster predators, otherwise an everyday fact of life you just got used to, had gone too far.

GANG RATS SHOOT FIVE CHILDREN IN BEER WAR'S WORST OUTRAGE, screamed the Daily Mirror. At 6:33 p.m. on a sweltering Tuesday the 28th of July, as more than 100 little kids frolicked in the summer spray of an opened hydrant on 107th St. between Second and Third Aves., a sedan roared around the corner and Tommy guns chattered from behind the curtains. The specific target appeared to be Joey Rao, a Harlem hood who had been in and out of league with Dutch Schultz. Joey ducked successfully. The five kids didn't.

Dead was 5-year-old Michael Vengalli, his spine shot away. Crippled for life was his 7-year-old brother, Salvatore. The other youngsters were badly hurt. "Shoot to kill!" Police Commissioner Edward Mulrooney thundered at his force as New York resolved that it had finally had enough of the endless gang wars.

VINCENT COLL was brought up on the Harlem mayhem charges within a few weeks, and he went to trial in December, his defense in the hands of lawyer Samuel Leibowitz. Later in his days, Leibowitz would enjoy another career altogether as a respected trial judge. In December 1931, he was a mob mouthpiece. He was a good one. Three days after Christmas, Coll was acquitted, and he walked out of the Court of General Sessions a free man.

THE BABY-SHOOTER celebrated January 1932 by getting married to a somewhat older woman, a mob moll who had buried two husbands already, and then he declared war anew; cops in mid-month took credit for saving Schultz's life when they pinched Coll and a couple of associates on the eve of what was said to be a full-scale assault on The Dutchman's rackets. Three weeks later, said associates fell to a Schultz execution squad that narrowly missed catching Coll as well. It was widely observed that Coll did not seem to be a man with long-term prospects. Indeed, on Sunday the 7th of February, the Daily News headline was: **POLICE RACING SCHULTZ KILLERS.**

Irish took leave of his bride that afternoon to attend to business matters. Stories would subsequently emerge that at this moment he was holding as a ransom captive one Sherman Billingsley, pal of crime lord Owney Madden and proprietor of a hot Broadway joint called The Stork Club. It was said that Madden was the man on the other end of the line when Coll's drugstore phone call was interrupted.

So lunatic Mad Dog Coll was now out of the picture. Meanwhile, the almost equally nuts Legs Diamond was gone now as well, dispatched from this world a couple of months earlier. Surely things were going to more respectably businesslike from now on.

MAYHEM
Mad Dog Coll

HARLEM GANG GUNNERS MOW DOWN 5 CHILDREN

Fusillade From Car Misses Aim; 2 Boys May Die

Victims of Gang Guns

DOYLE DENIED STAY; OLVANY UNDER QUIZ

By J.R. COCHRAN
Daily News Staff Writer

'**B**OMBS WILL continue until the Consolidated Edison Co. is brought to justice for their dastardly deeds against me," the Mad Bomber wrote to the New York Herald Tribune in October 1951. "*I have exhausted all other means. I intend, with bombs, to cause others to cry out for justice for me.*"

He had just planted several more of his incendiary devices, he announced, including one at the Paramount Theater in Times Square. And so New York City's bomb squad was busy again.

For six frightening years, from 1951 to 1957, the Mad Bomber left his homemade "units," more than three dozen of them, at high-traffic public places across the city — Grand Central Terminal, Radio City Music Hall, the library, large theaters. His blasts injured 22 people, several of them seriously. "Potentially the most dangerous man in New York City," authorities called him.

He never wanted to harm anyone, he insisted after he was finally caught, only to air his grievances against the power company that had made him suffer so. "I was always hoping and praying no one would get hurt," he earnestly explained to the papers. "I just wanted to notify the people of New York that something was wrong."

NUT CASE, everyone had long agreed. He flooded the newspapers with letters, hundreds of them, a litany of persecutions. *My one consolation is that I can strike back for the dastardly deeds against me. ... I will bring the Con Edison to justice. They will pay ... I have dedicated my life to this task.* In the beginning, he signed his missives "Fair Play." Later he reduced that signature to just "F.P."

To the two maiden sisters with whom he lived in Waterbury, Conn., the Mad Bomber was only George Metesky, the unemployed, sickly baby brother they'd looked after ever since that awful day at the United Electric & Power Co.

He'd been a generator cleaner at United, and a model employee, even regarded as possible foreman material someday — until Sept. 5, 1931, when he was caught in a hot-gas backdraft from a boiler at the Hell Gate plant. He was flat on his back for hours, coughing blood, before anyone even noticed. "There were 12,000 Danger signs in the plant," he would bitterly recall years later. "But not even first aid was available."

United put him on paid sick leave but subsequently decided that his $37.50-a-week services were no longer needed. In January 1934, he filed a workman's compensation claim, contending that the accident had made him tubercular. That claim was rejected. So were three more.

He began writing letters to Consolidated Edison, into which United had by now merged, and he got back a form letter.

On Nov. 17, 1940, he planted his first explosive device, on a window sill of a Con Ed plant on E. 64th St.

Con Edison crooks, said the attached note. *This is for you.*

AS IT HAPPENED, that bomb proved to be a dud. So did the second one, which was found five blocks from Con Ed headquarters on Irving Place a year later.

The third one, left in a Grand Central corridor March 29, 1951, worked. So did the fourth one,

FAIR PLAY
George Metesky

deposited in a phone booth at the main branch of the New York Public Library on April 24. The bomber struck again and again, at Grand Central in August, at a 14th St. subway station in October. And by now police were on alert, tailing hundreds of known disgruntled Con Ed employees. One early suspect already had been committed to Bellevue.

On the explosions went — at a Lexington Ave. theater, at the Port Authority Bus Terminal, at Radio City, where a woman suffered minor injuries when her seat blew up beneath her. At Penn Station. At Grand Central, again and again.

George Metesky's round trip from Waterbury to New York was 180 miles. Usually he parked in White Plains, mailed off a letter or two, then caught the New York Central into Manhattan. One day a motorcycle cop checking on parked cars almost caught him, just as he was pouring smokeless shotgun powder into a pipe and wrapping a sock around the package. That scared him enough that he stopped using the train, instead driving the whole distance, taking care not to speed.

By the end of 1954, police profilers knew a few things about the Mad Bomber. They had concluded that he was a middle-age bachelor who lived a sheltered life. They knew he worked on a drill press, since the caps on his pipes were hand-turned. But that wasn't enough to find him. In 1955 he planted six more of his bombs. One of them nearly killed a Grand Central redcap.

Police stepped up the manhunt, adding 50 detectives to the Mad Bomber task force. The Veterans Administration ran down ex-servicemen trained in demolition. Con Ed combed its personnel files.

Still, Fair Play's cries for justice continued. *These same ghouls call me a psychopath — any further reference to me as such — or the like — will be dealt with — where ever a wire runs — gas or steam flows — from or to the Con Edison Co. — is now a bomb target.*

MACY'S. THE RCA Building. Rockefeller Center. Penn Station again. And the library again — the bomb left in a red Christmas stocking.

After seven people were injured in a blast at the Paramount Theater in Brooklyn, police enlisted the public's help in the search for the maniac. The Daily News began reprinting his letters, hoping some reader might recognize the phrasing. The Journal-American published three open letters to the Mad Bomber, urging him to give up, promising he would get the justice he demanded.

"Where were you people when I was asking for help?" he wrote back.

But then he was moved to write the Journal-American again — and this time he talked enough about the specific details of his old grievance that investigators at last were able to make a link to George Metesky's 1930s files.

An army of cops showed up at Metesky's Waterbury door late in January 1957. At arraignment, the prisoner carried a brown paper bag containing a change of underwear.

A 47-COUNT indictment — seven for attempted murder — was drawn up, but doctors recognized Metesky to be deranged and had him whisked off to Matteawan State Hospital.

"There is nothing wrong with me," he protested. "Someday I will be vindicated and freed."

HE WAS indeed freed, in 1973, and he was 90 when he died in 1994. In interviews late in his life, he continued to affirm that the Mad Bomber's crusade had been a matter of the highest principle.

"It was in hopes of finding a better world," he said.

"But there's no better world."

By OWEN MORITZ
Daily News Staff Writer

NEW YORK taxpayers, oppressed or otherwise, never had a truer friend than Vito Battista, a rumpled, fiery son of Brooklyn who spent most of the 1950s, '60s and '70s running for practically every public office in sight — including mayor five times. "I'd rather be right than mayor," he always said, which was good, considering he never came close to getting elected.

But the man could put on a show. A flamboyant architect with a pencil-thin mustache, a black fedora, a vivid imagination and a voice that could shatter the reveries of the laziest bureaucrat, Vito Battista was one of the great artists of New York City political theater.

Park Ave. co-op types were not his people. His were the little people — the small property owners, small landlords and civic associations in Brooklyn, Queens and Staten Island he claimed as his constituency when, in 1956, he organized his United Taxpayers Party. He made his first independent run for mayor in 1957, managing to capture 70,000 votes in what was otherwise a lackluster race.

That was the most votes he ever got for any citywide office over the next 20 years, and, recognizing that he was perhaps not really very electable, he turned his energies to comic opera, devoting himself to crazed stunts that regularly struck terror into the heart of public officialdom.

He brought an alligator to City Hall once, to illustrate the bite being taken by taxes. He strolled through midtown with a camel, warning that one more tax measure would be the straw to break the animal's back. He marched across the Brooklyn Bridge with an elephant and herded sheep through City Hall Park. He appeared on Wall St. wearing a wooden barrel.

He once delivered a black coffin filled with fake homeowner deeds to Mayor John Lindsay's office to make a point about public safety. "The only people making money in New York today are the guys who make electric locks and burglar alarms and those who train dogs," Battista shouted. He rode a horse and buggy down Broadway as the Board of Estimate debated repeal of the $15 auto-use tax: "We'll all wind up in horses and buggies," he yelled.

Politicians. They were all the same, he thundered. Government waste, bloated taxes, rent control, tax abatements, welfare, subsidized housing — the politicians were to blame for all of it. In the mid-'60s, he often made appearances with a pair of pet monkeys, named Rocky and Lindsay, after the governor and the mayor. He liked to stand outside City Hall holding up a Diogenes-style lantern and announcing to all within earshot that he was searching for an honest pol.

"You people accuse me of being a buffoon," he acknowledged to an interviewer on one occasion. "Listen, I'm liberal with *my* money — just conservative about the money City Hall spends."

No, he never seriously expected to become mayor. "I'd rather be right," he said, again. Serenely.

BATTISTA WAS born Sept. 7, 1908, in Bari, Italy, and came to Brooklyn with his family five years later. As a teenager, he studied at Brooklyn Evening High School while peddling ice during the day, very successfully; at age 18, he sold his flourishing ice company for $27,000 and used the money to pay

for an education at Carnegie Tech. Graduate degrees in architecture and planning followed at MIT and Columbia.

He was a designer of the 1939 World's Fair in Flushing Meadows. Afterward, working for the city's Department of Public Works, he helped design the Brooklyn Civic Center. Then he went into private practice and started his own architectural school in downtown Brooklyn. The Institute of Design and Construction would turn out 30,000 architects, planners and draftsmen in Battista's lifetime.

But the daily plight of the city's small property owners and "oppressed taxpayers," as he never failed to call them, became a siren song that finally drove him into politics in the mid-'50s.

He never got to be mayor, or controller, or anything else he ever ran for, until 1968, when, running as a Republican, he won the Cypress Hills-East New York Assembly seat. He served three noisy terms, mostly just annoying his fellow legislators. During one particularly do-nothing session, he suggested that everyone just go home. One colleague took umbrage: "There are millions of New Yorkers working, who would not be impressed if we adjourned at 2 p.m." Shot back Battista: "Yes, but they're accomplishing something."

In the post-Watergate elections of 1974, a Democratic challenger turned him out of Albany. One year later came New York City's fiscal crisis — and now, it appeared, everything he had ever said about bloated bureaucracies and overburdening taxes was turning out to be quite true.

FLEETINGLY HE entertained a vision that city voters might now see him a wise elder statesman. Well, no. His final race for mayor, in 1977, as an independent in a crowded field, fared not well at all.

After that wild election was won by Edward Koch, Vito Battista folded his tent and stopped running for things.

He did, though, remain an active Republican committeeman, and, in 1984, in an appointment he treasured, President Ronald Reagan named him to a federal commission on architecture and transportation for the disabled.

He died quietly in 1990, age 81.

GO FIGHT CITY HALL
Vito Battista

BIG TOWN BIOGRAPHY

By ALEX STOROZYNSKI
Special to The News

I T WAS A day that rocked the world of television, a defining moment in the inherent battle between serious programming and the advertising profit machine. Abruptly quitting his job as president of CBS News on Feb. 15, 1966, Fred Friendly said, was "the most important act of my life ... a matter of conscience."

Five days of boardroom combat had been fought over colliding visions of what TV news should be. To Friendly, television was more than just the boob tube; he wanted Americans to understand their government's involvement in the bog of the Vietnam War, and his CBS News had covered the widening conflict with a discerning eye. When Morley Safer filed a controversial report in 1965 — showing an American marine torching civilians' straw huts with his Zippo lighter — Friendly put the footage on the air.

Americans were still making up their minds about Vietnam, and Friendly wanted them to make an informed decision. When the Senate Foreign Relations Committee conducted hearings on Vietnam, Friendly ordered that they be aired live.

That interruption of commercial revenue distressed CBS chairman William Paley and President Frank Stanton. In stepped John Schneider, the network's newly appointed No. 3 man. "Housewives aren't interested in Vietnam," Schneider informed Friendly after pulling the plug on the Senate debate. So, after four days of live coverage and commentary, CBS switched to "I Love Lucy" and "The Real McCoys" reruns.

The decision, Friendly wrote his bosses, "makes a mockery" of the network's announced mission to provide the "broadest access to congressional debate." He resigned on the spot. Within 48 hours of his departure, nearly every trace of him had been eradicated from the CBS studios on W. 57th St., including the many public-service awards that bore his name.

BORN IN MANHATTAN in 1915, Fred Wachenheimer grew up in Rhode Island and, after college, got his first radio job at WEAN in Providence. There, the man who did the hiring decided: "We're going to call you Fred Friendly." As an Army sergeant during World War II, he worked for military newspapers in the Far East, then stayed on in India as a correspondent for the Columbia Broadcasting System. Back in New York in 1948, an agent introduced him to Edward R. Murrow, the legendary CBS radio reporter who had been the voice of the war for millions of Americans.

The two teamed up to produce the "I Can Hear

Left, with Edward R. Murrow

It Now" series for Columbia Records. So successful were these compilations of historic broadcasts that in late 1950 they spawned Murrow's prize-winning radio program "Hear It Now." And at this point, as fledgling TV increasingly began to displace radio, Friendly started thinking about bringing that program to the home screen.

Murrow himself was less intrigued by the idea of TV — the veteran radio man worked with words, not pictures — but Friendly's salesmanship and talent as a producer eventually won him over. "See It Now" premiered in November 1951.

The groundbreaking documentary series helped put an end to the paranoid era of Red-baiting Sen. Joseph McCarthy, early on linked cigarettes to lung cancer and brought viewers to the brink of Armageddon in "A Conversation With Dr. J. Robert Oppenheimer," father of the atomic bomb. Increasingly, sponsors became intimidated by the program's controversial material — "the most courageous documentaries in the history of an abused medium," The New York Times called the series — and CBS finally let it die in 1955.

Friendly, though discouraged, remained determined to bring serious news to TV. In 1959, he was named executive producer of a bold new venture called "CBS Reports."

BY 1960, though, even as Friendly and Murrow worked together to expose the plight of farmworkers in a startling documentary called "Harvest of Shame," Murrow's influence at CBS was waning. He soon resigned. But Friendly's star continued to rise. In 1964, he became president of CBS News, the boss to whom such newsmen as

HIGH ROAD
Fred Friendly

Walter Cronkite, Howard K. Smith and Eric Sevareid reported.

He was known as a slave driver, an aggressive boss who often drove overstressed underlings to tears. He wanted all he could get from television — "the greatest teaching tool since the printing press," he called it. But higher up in the corporate ranks, there was greater interest in advertising dollars than in public education. In his 1967 memoir, "Due to Circumstances Beyond Our Control," Friendly recalled what one-time network president James Aubrey had told him during one of their many battles over airtime:

"In this adversary system, you and I are always going to be at each other's throats. They say to me, 'Take your solid little hands, get the ratings and make as much money as you can'; they say to you, 'Take your lily-white hands, do your best, go the high road and bring us prestige.'"

Friendly's ultimate decision to leave CBS over that ceaseless battle between prestige and profit defined the rest of his life. Television, he said as he quit the wars, was being "twisted into an electronic carnival, in which showbiz wizardry and values obscure the line between entertainment and news."

A FTER DEPARTING from that twisted carnival, Friendly took a job with the Ford Foundation and taught journalism at Columbia University, where he regularly challenged students to dissect the First Amendment. As if to inhale inspiration from this "living, breathing document," he always carried in his pocket a copy of the U.S. Constitution given to him by Supreme Court Justice Hugo Black, and he used to fling smaller copies onto the desks of students and dare them to wrestle with the basics of American democracy.

Eventually, he took to public television, bringing together top figures from the government and the media to debate First Amendment issues in such provocative forums as "The Media and the Law" and "The Constitution: That Delicate Balance." When Fred Friendly died in 1998, two copies of the Constitution were buried with him.

By DAVID HINCKLEY
Daily News Staff Writer

T'S 1976 AND you're a 19-year-old guy out for a night in the city with your buddies, and someone says hey, look, there's a movie called "Linda Lovelace for President," let's go see that. Heh, heh.

It turns out this movie is someone's idea of making Linda Lovelace a semi-legit comic actress, except the product is still Linda Lovelace, so the movie is mostly sex jokes sprinkled with cameos from celebrities experiencing a career lull, like Joe E. Ross, Mickey Dolenz, Scatman Crothers and Vaughn Meader. Not to spoil it for anyone, but Meader gets the girl.

So after a while you start looking for familiar faces, in lieu of a plot, and up comes this tall guy, round face. "Oh, my God," you gasp. "That's Chuck McCann!"

And it is. The same Chuck McCann who in your formative years made gentle jokes and played out little fables with puppets every afternoon after school on TV.

And you have this brief imaginary exchange where you ask him what in the world he's doing here, and he says he was going to ask you the same thing.

CHUCK McCANN was one of the last jolly fat men who was allowed to just be jolly and not have to look like he was ashamed of his cholesterol. All through the '60s, he hosted a children's show — six years on Channel 11, 1959-1965, and then six more on Channel 5.

While the rest of the country was having a nervous breakdown, Chuck McCann was playing with puppets — Mr. McNasty, Mr. Backwards, Ace Jackson, Jonah K. Eightball, Professor Farley Fleabert, Lester. Lester was very cool. If a kid won a contest, McCann promised, "You'll get to talk with not just any puppet, you'll get to talk with Lester."

From the beginning, television realized it fascinated kids, and about five minutes later parents realized it also was a way to get kids to sit down and shut up. So it was a natural marriage, and the first-wave kids' TV shows were already, by the '60s, well-remembered cultural landmarks of youth. Howdy Doody, Captain Kangaroo, Kukla, Fran and Ollie, Captain Video. Winky-Dink and You. The Mickey Mouse Club. Shari Lewis and Lambchop.

Some of these shows attempted to include an educational component, which could range from a passing reference to the Golden Rule to the instructional work of kindly Miss Frances on "Ding-Dong School."

But most of the learning was incidental, and that was fine with the second wave of hosts who regularly made their way to the TV screen through the '50s and '60s. In New York, another star of that eccentric bunch was Sandy Becker, with Hambone, Norton Nork and the primitive animated burglar Max.

Many of the shows were low-budget, of course — built on old cartoons that could be licensed for next to nothing, with a host who didn't make much more.

"Popeye" cartoons were hosted by Captain Alan

ABSENCE OF RESTRAINT
Chuck McCann

Swift, dressed like he just stepped off one of Magellan's ships. He was replaced by Captain Jack McCarthy, who would become the annual narrator of the St. Patrick's Day parade.

Claude Kirschner hosted "Terrytoon Circus," and ended each show with the puppet Clownie telling viewers it was time to go to bed. There was that educational component again.

Officer Joe Bolton became a local star by hosting a Three Stooges show, and Soupy Sales built pies in the face and conversations with White Fang into a lucrative lifetime career.

Everything didn't always work. Comedian Morty Gunty once warmed up a live audience of pre-teens by saying, "I bought my mother-in-law a new chair. But my wife won't let me plug it in."

Chuck McCann had no such problems of context. He remembered what seemed funny back before you and your friends got old and cool.

A roomful of a man at 6-foot-3, 260 pounds, with a thousand voices and a smile that spanned the East River, McCann spun morality plays and broad slapstick comedy for his troops.

A popular recurring feature was to have his puppets lip-synch a popular song while acting it out — from "Please Mr. Custer," the most popular song ever written about the Native American victory over the Seventh Cavalry at Little Big Horn, to the Beatles' "It Won't Be Long."

During the newspaper strike of 1962-63, McCann dramatized the comic strips, donning fedora and trench coat to play Dick Tracy and a patterned dress for Little Orphan Annie.

He would do anything. No character was too outrageous or too mundane, no project too bizarre. In 1963, on a comedy LP in the character of Yogi Bear, he recorded "Yogi Bear Bossa Nova."

He came to it honestly, too, this absence of restraint.

HE WAS BORN in 1935 in Queens Village and grew up on 113th Drive. His grandfather performed in Buffalo Bill's Wild West Show and his father, Valentine, was a musician who played with

Paul Whiteman and became producer/arranger at the Roxy.

Chuck was entranced from the first time he accompanied Dad to work. By 7 he was performing for anyone who would watch, and as a teenager he was busted for running a pirate radio station. He got into every show he could at Sts. Joachim and Ann schools, then Andrew Jackson High. His idols included Charles Laughton and Laurel and Hardy — a passion that would lead him to co-found Sons of the Desert, the Laurel and Hardy appreciation society.

But that didn't pay the rent when he got out of school, and his family — practical 9-to-5ers except for Valentine — steered him to jobs that included door-to-door vacuum cleaner sales, elevator operation, department store Santa and bookkeeping for a steamship line. He eventually joined the Pasadena Playhouse, where he worked his way up to roles like Sir Toby Belch in "Twelfth Night." But he was soon back in New York, hanging out at Hanson's, working the club circuit, getting TV gigs with Steve Allen and Garry Moore and finally co-producing "Lunch Time," a Channel 5 puppet show. His break came when the station's Sandy Becker took a summer off and asked McCann to fill in for him.

On his first show, he had to do a live commercial with a talking doll. The mechanism got stuck, the doll wouldn't stop talking and he finally had to shove it in a drawer to shut it up.

N 1959, at a stage of his career when it was a coup to land a few lines as the "younger brother of the younger brother" on a "Bonanza" episode, McCann was hired by WPIX to host Laurel and Hardy films every afternoon. He brought Laurel onto the show a couple of times, not to mention a young Zacherle. But it was his dramatization of the comics that convinced 'PIX he could carry a show himself.

His own hope was to parlay all this into a legitimate grown-up acting career, and in 1968 he played Alan Arkin's friend in the Oscar-winning "The Heart is a Lonely Hunter." In 1971 he got a starring gig in "The Projectionist," a cult film about a lonely man who projects himself into the movies he shows.

But because of his distinctive size, he mostly landed character roles, and by the '70s it was clear he would have to piece together a career out of smaller parts, including TV and movie acting, voice-overs and commercials.

In the '60s he also did voices in "Cool McCool," a cartoon about a studly James Bond-type cat. In 1975-76 he cowrote and costarred with Bob Denver in the cult TV series "Far-Out Space Nuts," about two zany NASA food loaders who accidentally launch themselves.

But the general rule for a man in Chuck's position was not to be too discriminating.

He had a role in "Hamburger, the Movie." He did voices for "The Get Along Gang," a bunch of cute li'l animals like Bingo Beaver and Portia Porcupine who taught warm lessons about friendship and cooperation. He did countless TV guest shots and voice-overs. He was in the cast of "Turn-On," a comedy revue that lasted a single episode in February 1969. He made a Cocoa Puffs spot that ran for 20 years. In a semi-famous shaving cream commercial of the '70s, he looks into the mirror and says, "Hi, guy!"

In the end, the jolly fat man, like most of the kids who watched him, grew up to go to work. In 1999 he was living in Southern California, where he had a fan club, attended celebrity conventions and was available for jobs.

By PAULA M. URUBURU
Special to The News

"He left his mark upon New York City as few other men have done."
—Richard Harding Davis

"One remembers an earthquake without blaming or condemning the seismic forces."
—Evelyn Nesbit

"No man more capable was ever killed by any man less valuable in the history of homicide in the United States."
—Brooklyn Eagle

NEW YORK AT the turn of the century was a city undergoing a dramatic face-lift. In a dizzying time of con men, crusaders, conspicuous consumers and captains of industry, one magnetic man stood at the heart of this transformation.

Born in 1853, son of a noted Shakespearean scholar, Stanford White was a talented painter who was urged early to pursue architecture instead. At the suggestion of Frederick Law Olmsted, the designer of Central Park, White studied with H.H. Richardson and Charles Gambrill, then continued his studies abroad, and by 1881 he had joined Charles McKim and William Mead as the junior member of their firm.

His stamp on the city was soon everywhere. His public buildings included the Metropolitan and Century clubs, Pennsylvania Station, the Washington Square Arch, Tiffany and Co., Sherry's restaurant, the Herald Building and the Madison Square Presbyterian Church. Meanwhile, he also established himself as the purveyor of high culture for the high-living, the supreme enabler of excess for the merchant aristocracy, a favorite of the wealthy tycoons and their wives who wanted to live in castles in the upper regions of Fifth Ave.

White's clients included Joseph Pulitzer, William K. Vanderbilt Jr., Payne Whitney, Louis Comfort Tiffany and Cornelius Vanderbilt, who commissioned a $3 million replica of a 15th-century French chateau.

Sportsman and clubman, White orbited freely in all social circles, an extravagant spender whose appetite for all things gorgeous was as well known to the Bohemian artists of lower Manhattan as to the Four Hundred. And he was a familiar figure on Broadway, an insatiable patron of the Gay White Way, a man who saw "Florodora" 40 times. It was to New York's theatrical world that White left his grand ornament, the magnificent Madison Square Garden entertainment complex.

Begun in 1887, New York's second Garden boasted a row of shops, a concert hall and an arena suitable for exhibitions, balls, horse shows and boxing matches. There were more elaborate amusements as well, such as a re-creation of Venice, complete with gondolas and waterways. And, in an age when spectacle was the rule of the day, the Garden's rooftop theater, like everything White did, was electrifying and glamorous. Twinkling strands of tiny incandescent electric lights danced around the periphery of the rooftop, and luxurious potted plants were placed throughout the tables that faced the stage.

Visually stunning, its crowning glory was the Giralda tower, at the time the tallest point in the

The scene: Harry K. Thaw enters rooftop garden, shoots Stanford White, then restrains Evelyn Nesbit.

ALL THINGS GORGEOUS
Stanford White

city, and home to White's studio. Gracing the tower was the comely and controversial figure of a nude Diana, gilded goddess of chastity, sculpted by White's friend Augustus St. Gaudens. Some quipped that Madison Square Garden was merely a majestic pedestal for Diana. Others who knew the architect well hinted that Venus might have been more appropriate.

For Stanford White was a man of contradictory and ultimately fatal impulses. Like many powerful men of his day who acted outside the boundaries of accepted practice in the pursuit of profits and pleasures, White had perfected his methods of acquisition — of chorus girls as well as cultural artifacts. One of them was a frail, ethereal waif of 16, spotted by White in the "Florodora" chorus. Her name was Evelyn Nesbit. The 48-year-old White became determined to possess her like one of the many exotic objects he brought back from abroad.

AFTER THEIR initial encounter in one of his snuggeries, where Evelyn was entertained on a red velvet swing, White gained the confidence of her widowed mother and became the family's benefactor. Within a matter of months, however, he dropped his paternal mask and one night seduced a guileless and intoxicated Evelyn. She became his mistress and swiftly found herself caught up in the whirlwind of White's sphere of influence. But eventually, plagued by increasingly shaky finances and White's secretly failing health, the relationship ended.

As bad luck would have it, at this time Harry K.

Thaw, eccentric Pittsburgh heir to a $40 million fortune, began to pursue Evelyn relentlessly, and successfully. But Thaw was also ragingly obsessed with Stanford White, the man who had dishonored her.

On June 25, 1906, the newlywed Thaws were in New York, preparing for a European trip. Harry had gotten tickets for "Mamzelle Champagne," a musical opening that night at the Madison Square Garden Roof Theater. White, never one to miss an opening, especially not in his own Garden, arrived near the end of the show and sat at his private table. While the orchestra played "I Could Love a Million Girls," a demented Thaw walked up to White and fired three shots into him point-blank. "I did it because he ruined my wife!" Thaw cried. The gunpowder burned White's face beyond recognition.

By the time the "trial of the century" began in January 1907, White, unable to defend himself, was being vilified in the newspapers as a "voluptuary and pervert," and many of his wealthy old friends found it convenient to leave the country for the duration of the proceedings. But while the genteel old guard discreetly removed itself from the circuslike atmosphere of the trial, the nouveau-riche Thaws and their millions fueled it.

The fiercely ambitious District Attorney William Travers Jerome pushed Evelyn to reveal the lurid details of her affair with White, hoping to tarnish the innocent image she presented to the jury and send Thaw to the electric chair. But, dressed for effect like a prim schoolgirl, Evelyn sobbed as she made startling revelations about nude romps, mirrored rooms and drugged champagne, and by the time she was finished, Thaw's act seemed to some quite heroic.

The trial ended with a hung jury. After a second trial in 1908, Thaw was acquitted by reason of insanity and sent to Matteawan Asylum for the Criminally Insane. That was nearly two years after the body of Stanford White had been laid to rest in the small graveyard of the St. James Episcopal Church.

STANFORD WHITE, as his biographer Paul Baker wrote, was an "impresario who embodied the flamboyance of the age," a larger-than-life figure whose extraordinary achievements remain overshadowed by his scandalous death. In 1925, his fabled gift to the city, Madison Square Garden, was torn down.

By DAVID HINCKLEY
Daily News Staff Writer

AFTER THE STRIKE of 1917 collapsed and for all practical purposes the vaudeville actors who called themselves the White Rats folded their tent, some Rats turned on Variety, which had once been the Rats' strongest supporter but in the final showdown had taken the side of Edward Albee, the arrogant theatrical management lord whose philosophy was "Businessmen don't keep promises."

And so the story would spread one day in 1919 that a Rat had burst into the Variety office at 154 W. 46th St. and gunned down editor Sime Silverman at his rolltop desk.

The truth was more ragged. A drunken actor apparently did shoot out a window, and Variety advertising director Johnny O'Connor, upon being misinformed that Silverman was in the hospital, grabbed a piece of his own and marched off to a Rats watering hole to square accounts. When he learned things were jake, he settled for getting Silverman some bodyguards.

So the rubout that wasn't became one more chapter in the story of Sime Silverman, whose life generated as much drama as the theaters he spent that life covering for the sheet he built from nothing into the entertainment industry's most influential trade paper.

He was a flamboyant figure, gambler, drinker, man of the night. Like Shakespeare, he saw the world as a stage, and that included the language in which he wrote. The prose in Variety was itself theater, and Variety muggs, as reporters and reviewers were called, contributed hundreds of quirks and phrases to the English language.

It was Silverman who turned unsuspecting nouns into verbs: authored, readied, panicked. It was Variety that compressed business into biz and created or popularized words like whodunit, smash, upstage, bozo, moniker, hokum and payoff. Variety used hoofer for dancer and fold for close. Variety readers knew a headline reading "Legs Without S.A.N.G." meant "Legs without sex appeal are no good." Reporter Jack Conroy once blithely assessed an aging chorine's gams as "varicose alley." To Sime, the female of the species, including his own wife, Hattie, was a doll, twirl or skirt.

But if Sime made English teachers and feminists weep, that was nothing compared to his impact on vaudeville. From Variety's first edition Dec. 16, 1905, Sime Silverman mattered.

Early on, he rescued a young trio called Clayton, Jackson and Durante from bankruptcy when they opened a nightclub with no patrons. The night Sime walked in to check it out, the young Jimmy Durante sat down at his table in the otherwise empty club and cracked, "Let's phone the morgue for a coupla stiffs and liven up the joint." Sime stayed for the show, loved it, gave it a rave notice, nicknamed Durante Schnozzola and became his lifelong pal.

Sime also gave Walter Winchell an early break, and he was among the first to tout Al Jolson and Buster Keaton. In 1927, Mayor Jimmy Walker told Silverman the most famous midtown in the world should be renamed Sime's Square. Of course, Jimmy was one of Sime's drinking buddies.

SIME SILVERMAN was born May 19, 1873, in upstate Cortland, son of a financier who moved down to the city and in 1898 made Sime a property assessor. He was good, but when his father refused to make him a partner, he quit and got a job writing vaudeville reviews for the

fledgling Daily America at $5 a week. When that paper folded, he moved to the Morning Telegraph, where he panned a comedy act called Redford and Winchester. The team canceled its advertising and the Telegraph canceled Sime, who vowed he would never again work for a publication that would not let him call it as he saw it.

No such publication existing, he borrowed $1,500 from Hattie's father, an alderman in Syracuse, to start one. He had $40 in secondhand furniture and a room at 38th and Broadway. It would be a quarter of a century before Variety made any money.

But Silverman, an engaging and persuasive figure in brown suits, expensive shoes and bow ties, was always able to talk a bank into lending him a few thousand when his back was to the wall. Through the Roaring Twenties, red ink or black, he kept a stable of three automobiles, with two sets of chauffeurs on call around the clock, to carry him and a rotating cast of staffers and friends to the speakeasies.

If he loved the high life, however, he took the hard road getting there — because he fought every fight that came along.

WHEN SILVERMAN started Variety, the bully of the town was B.F. Keith, who owned the vaudeville circuit and thus controlled who worked and for how much. Keith and his prime henchman Albee were ruthless with competitors and performers, and Silverman hated that. So did the White Rats, who formed in 1900 as a stateside version of the British actors' association. On

paper, the Rats looked formidable, their rolls including major stars such as Eddie Foy, Lew Fields and George M. Cohan. In practice, they were easily divided and conquered.

After a couple of abortive challenges to the Keith-Albee choke hold, the Rats turned to Harry Mountford, a flamboyant hustler who merged them into the AFL in 1910, thereby turning them into something resembling a serious union.

Silverman disliked Mountford, but he disliked Albee more. Variety started giving over space to Rats news, and in 1913 Albee dropped the hammer: Any act that advertised in Variety would not work in a Keith-Albee theater, which meant not working.

His advertising lifeblood stopped and Variety's survival in grave doubt, Sime raged in print at Albee until 1915, when both sides reluctantly agreed through an intermediary to negotiate a truce. The advertising then returned — and, while Sime said no deals had been cut, Variety took management's side the next time the actors struck, in 1916. The outraged Rats screamed betrayal and sued Sime for bias, while a Federal Trade Commission complaint charged Variety was part of an illegal monopolistic collusion with the theater owners.

None of this went anywhere, largely because the 1917 collapse of the strike broke the Rats. Albee created a company union, the National Vaudeville Actors, and when the Rats declared bankruptcy, the union took over its clubhouse.

But the ship of which Albee had retained control was sinking. While he sailed into the 1920s on top, it soon became clear that the cheaper and more universal entertainment offered by radio and the movies was putting vaudeville out of business.

IF ALBEE didn't see it, Silverman did. In 1926, he moved vaudeville news to the back of Variety and motion picture news to the front. Thus did he thrive even as Albee withered, and by the late '20s, Albee was forced to sell his interests to a group that included Sime.

Even the actors got some satisfaction, because the union faded away and was replaced by the fledgling Actors Equity, which ultimately won a lot of what the Rats had fought for.

VARIETY REPORTED Black Friday on the stock market with the legendary Sime-written headline, "Wall St. Lays An Egg." A year later, in 1930, the Depression notwithstanding, Variety turned profitable. Sime passed the editorship to his son, Sid, and headed out to enjoy the bright lights, except by now he'd burned so much candle there was little wax left.

In summer 1933, he made the rounds of colleagues, including the faithful O'Connor, to say goodbye. Then he went to California and Sept. 22 died alone in his room at Los Angeles' Ambassador Hotel.

Back in New York, hundreds of the biggest names in showbiz attended his service, and for decades there was an annual memorial pilgrimage to his mausoleum in Salem Fields, Brooklyn. The regulars included Jimmy Durante.

MUGGING THE THEATER
Sime Silverman

VARIETY
WALL ST. LAYS AN EGG

VARIETY

VARIETY
SHUBERTS' NEW POLICY

By TOM ROBBINS
Daily News Staff Writer

FIRST AND foremost, struggling young poets need cheap apartments, and it was a friend's fortuitous tip that led Hart Crane in the summer of 1924 to the flat at 110 Columbia Heights in Brooklyn.

In his room, above the harbor, Crane could hear the sounds of the river echoing up to him from below.

Beshrouded wails, far strum of fog horns, he wrote at the table pushed up against the rear window. And when he lifted his head to look out and up, he saw the Gothic granite arches and soaring steel cables of the Brooklyn Bridge.

Thus was one of the city's great artistic matches made.

"I am living in the shadow of that bridge," Crane wrote excitedly to his friend, the critic Waldo Frank. "There is all the glorious dance of the river directly beyond the back window ... the ships, the harbor, the skyline of Manhattan ... it is everything from mountains to the walls of Jerusalem and Nineveh ..."

The Brooklyn Bridge, completed in 1883, was already a touchstone for artists and writers, proof that technology could be rendered in grace and beauty. But Crane, a high school dropout from Ohio in search of a theme for a poetry about America, wanted to go even further in bestowing symbolism on its architecture.

He looked out his back window — the very same window, he delightedly learned years later, from which the bridge's crippled engineer, Washington Roebling, had watched the span's construction — and saw the perfect metaphor for an epic poem to celebrate the nation.

It was an idea he could only discuss in sweeping terms. Crane's "The Bridge" was to be a "mystical synthesis" of the country, picking up where Walt Whitman had left off, peopled by the legends of Pocahontas, Columbus and Rip Van Winkle, pulled along by wagon trains, railroads, riverboats, whaling ships and subways.

It was ambitious, but the 25-year-old poet had already demonstrated a command of language rivaling the greats of his era, T.S. Eliot and Ezra Pound.

His biggest obstacle, his friends agreed, was Hart Crane.

EVEN AMONG the carefree New York literary set at the dawn of the Jazz Age, Crane was something of a handful. His writing methodology included wild bouts of drinking and carousing aimed at wrenching the words out of himself and onto the page. He would stomp about his flat, the Victrola cranked up loud, playing the same jazz record over and over, in search of "divine madness." More than once, he heaved his typewriter out the window in exasperation.

Bursting from his apartment, he would reel down the city streets, drunkenly shouting into the night: "I am Baudelaire! I am Marlowe! I am Whitman!" Crossing the great bridge by foot, he would cruise the South St. saloons, stuffing nickels into jukeboxes and casting about for a sailor for a one-night stand.

It was a life as far from his middle-class beginnings as he could find.

Harold Hart Crane was born on July 21, 1899, son of a Cleveland candy manufacturer who wanted him in the business and a domineering

FALLING SHADOWS
Hart Crane

COURTESY COLUMBIA UNIVERSITY LIBRARY

mother who wanted him always at her side. Rejecting both, he showed up in New York at 17, a burningly ambitious writer seated on the floor at the Greenwich Village literary salon of Margaret Anderson, publisher of The Little Review, which had recently unveiled Pound and Robert Frost. For a while, he lived in a garret on E. 16th St. and tried to make a living selling ads for poetry magazines. But finally, he was forced to return to Ohio and take a job in his father's candy factory after all.

Back in Cleveland, he produced a tenderly straightforward poem called "My Grandmother's Love Letters":

There are no stars tonight/ But those of memory, he wrote, cautioning himself: *Are your fingers long enough to play/ Old keys that are but echoes?*

Its acceptance by a literary magazine brought Crane racing back to New York. Chronically broke, he camped out in the living rooms of such downtown postwar intellectual friends as playwright Eugene O'Neill and photographer Walker Evans, regularly getting uninvited when his drinking got out of hand. Despite his inner tempests, he churned out a series of poems noted for their beauty. His first collection, "White Buildings," was published in 1926, shortly before he began work on "The Bridge."

He toiled on his epic for the next several years, often running out of steam, getting by on small subsidies from various art patrons. Tormented by

his demons — "caught like a rat in a trap," he moaned — he traveled to Europe. In Paris, the wealthy expatriates Harry and Caresse Crosby, whose Black Sun Press had published James Joyce, promised to publish "The Bridge" upon its completion. Instead, Crane had to flee France after a drunken brawl in a cafe.

Back in New York, he forced himself at last to finish the great poem, closing it with a description of a walk across the bridge that had inspired him:

Through the bound cable strands, the arching path
Upward, veering with light, the flight of strings,—
Taut miles of shuttling moonlight syncopate
The whispered rush, telepathy of wires.

At 60 pages, he shipped it off to the Crosbys, and in 1930 it was published. New York publisher Horace Liveright soon issued an American version. Publication brought honors and offers. "As important a poem as has been written in our time," said the New York World. Crane won the top prize from Poetry Magazine and a prestigious Guggenheim Foundation fellowship.

His work was embraced by readers with a love for the rhythm of language — as well as those who admired lives lived precariously on the edge. As time went on, devotees would include playwright Tennessee Williams, who carried Crane's slim works with him everywhere, and poet Robert Lowell, who called Crane the modern Percy Bysshe Shelley.

But "The Bridge" had sapped more of his will than Crane realized. With the Guggenheim money, he set sail for Mexico with plans for a vast new work, the story of Cortes' conquests.

IN MEXICO CITY, he rented a small villa next to the American novelist Katherine Anne Porter. Crane was charming company, she said later, except when he reached "that point of drunkenness when he cursed all things: the moon, the air we breathed, the pool of water with its two small ducks. He didn't hate us....He hated and feared himself."

There were spurts of creativity and, for the first time, he became involved with a woman, Peggy Baird, the ex-wife of an old friend, literary critic Malcolm Cowley.

But his productivity was short-lived. When David Siqueiros, the Mexican muralist, sat down to paint Crane's portrait, he said he was forced to portray the poet with eyes downcast, because otherwise there was too much desperation in his face. Crane later sliced the painting to ribbons with a razor, then drank iodine.

That suicide attempt failed. Now, in April 1932, with his fellowship funds at an end, he and Baird shipped out for the U.S. aboard the steamship Orizaba.

SOMEWHERE NORTH of Havana, in the Gulf of Mexico, Crane ventured down to the sailors' quarters and got into a fight.

The next morning, sunny and still on April 27, a passenger watched in horror as a man dressed only in pajamas and overcoat walked purposefully to the ship's stern, mounted the railing, slipped the coat from his shoulders and then threw himself into the water. A cry went up and a life preserver was thrown out, but Hart Crane quickly vanished.

His exit, friends noted later, reflected a line he had once written:

This fabulous shadow only the sea keeps.

By JAY MAEDER
Daily News Staff Writer

'**S**EE WHAT he has on his mind," an editor offhandedly directed New York Daily News reporter Joe Martin late on the afternoon of Monday the 2nd of May 1949, about 10 minutes before Martin was expecting to finish his trick and meet a girl downstairs on Second Ave., and the newsie sighed and went out to talk to the guy who had wandered up from the street with some story to tell. Well, it happened. Some people sold shoes. Some people drove buses. Some people were newspaper reporters whose job it was to talk to guys who wandered up from the street.

The guy was Frank Chisari, an ex-G.I. who was at the end of his rope. He'd been to Immigration; he'd been to the Chinese Consulate; he'd been everywhere. He'd been pounding the pavement trying to get anyone to help him, and then he'd found himself in front of the Daily News building and he'd walked in and asked to see somebody. What he got was Joe Martin, and what he had on his mind was a baby girl, a Chinese orphan, a child he'd sort of adopted four years earlier when the war was winding down, a kid who loved him, a kid he'd finally had to leave sobbing in an orphanage when he got ordered home.

He was her daddy. He had faithfully promised that he'd come back for her and bring her to live with him in the United States of America. Frank Chisari was a $70-a-week guy at the Brooklyn Navy Yard and he had two kids of his own and it had taken him four years to save up a few hundred bucks to bring the baby over. But now suddenly it was 1949, and the Reds were rampaging all over China, and the whole country was shutting down, and the waiting list was years long. He was terrified. He didn't know what to do.

Joe Martin forgot about the girl downstairs and talked to Chisari for a couple of hours. Then he went to his bosses and told them what had just walked in. In the newspaper dodge, this was called a "human interest" story. "Stay with it," barked City Editor Harry Nichols.

KUNMING, JUNE 1945. Frank Chisari, once a Golden Gloves kid from the lower East Side, is an Army corporal here, a radar technician with the OSS Far East

With Joe Martin and the U.S. Army

HUMAN INTEREST STORY
Anne Chisari

Command at the terminus of the old Burma Road. He's out driving one day and he stops at a railroad crossing as the usual train full of wretched refugees rumbles past, and then he hears a splash in the paddy and he finds a dead woman, some poor nameless peasant who has tumbled from the boxcar, and a few feet away he finds the blood-soaked little girl, maybe two years old. He picks her up and cradles her. What is he supposed to do? Just leave her to die?

But the American military doctors can't help. There are firm regs regarding treatment of natives. Sorry. So he frantically goes to a French mission, where he literally has to hold a gun to the head of a Chinese doctor to get the kid looked at, since Chinese don't care who lives or dies anyway, life and death being one and the same miserable thing out here. And after she's patched up, he takes her back to his hootch — the fuselage of a wrecked C-47 — and he names her Anne, after his wife, Antoinette, and gives her a pillow to sleep on and a crackling radio headset to keep her company and a K-9 to protect her when he has to go to work. Frank's buddies take turns looking after little Anne, too. All this is definitely against regulations.

It's November now, and it comes to pass that Frank Chisari is going home to his First Ave. tenement. What can he do? He deposits Anne with German nuns. *Daddy,* she cries out after him. *I promise,* he tells her, and then he walks away fast so she doesn't see him bawling.

NEW YORK, JUNE 1949. The story was making headlines around the world — **GI SAMARITAN WANTS CHINA TOT HE SAVED** — and Joe Martin had vowed that he was personally going to bring this baby home. It took a few phone calls to manage the impossible, but the State Department was persuaded to put little Anne's name on the list of immediate eligibles, and Madame Chiang Kai-shek was moved to communicate with her generalissimo husband and arrange for a valid passport. The condition was that Anne

had to be on U.S. soil by June 30 or else all the polite diplomatic deals would expire. On June 11, reporter Martin headed for Formosa.

And, of course, there were nothing but snafus. Baby Anne, supposed to have been awaiting the News man in Taipei, was still 1,200 miles away in a broken China overrun by both Communist troops and hill bandits. For a desperate moment or two, Martin actually tried to smuggle himself over to the mainland. The better course of action at that point was to rely on General Chiang, who, however preoccupied with his other concerns, now dispatched agents to physically remove the little girl from the orphanage and fly her out.

Amid all the sadnesses and savageries of war, a sleepy six-year-old was at last delivered to Joe Martin at Taipei, clutching all her earthly belongings, which consisted of a toothbrush, an overcoat and a packet of soda crackers.

He handed her a doll that he had brought from the States, and she smiled.

It was June 24. They had less than a week to get home.

THERE HAD initially been confirmed flight arrangements, but the unexpected delays had changed everything; air travel was thoroughly disrupted; Taipei was sealed in now; getting anywhere was a large job. And in any case, as Martin discovered to his total horror, the baby didn't even have her necessary X-ray and inoculation clearances yet.

He started banging on doors. He woke up local officials in the middle of the night and screamed at them until he got the paperwork done. Back in the U.S., the Daily News' Washington man, Jerry Greene, leaned hard on the Military Air Transport Service, got an Army plane diverted from its duties and set up an emergency airlift from Taipei to Hong Kong. Once aboard that plane, Joe Martin, himself an ex-military guy who knew his way around orders, convinced the crewmen that they wouldn't really be violating anything if they flew straight to California instead. The sweet little sleeping child was all the argument they needed anyway.

On Sunday the 26th, the MATS plane touched down at Okinawa and was welcomed by a mob of soldiers who presented tiny Anne Chisari with her very first ice cream cone. And on Wednesday the 29th, a day before the deadline, as thousands of New Yorkers flocked to LaGuardia to witness the wonderful moment, the plane arrived, and Frank and Antoinette Chisari wept as Joe Martin put the child into their arms.

IN THE BEGINNING, the little girl, knowing only orphanage ways, would creep out of her bed at night to steal bits of food and secrete them in various hiding places around the Chisari apartment. Little by little she began to realize that the refrigerator was always full. Eventually she stopped speaking Chinese. One day she came home from school and asked: "What kind of Italians are we?"

AFTER A WHILE, the Chisaris moved on to a new life in Searington, L.I. But the Daily News kept tabs on them for years and all New York watched little Anne grow up. "She is, thank God, just a normal teenage girl with nothing on her mind," her father proudly announced when she turned 13.

When she finished Herricks High in 1961, The News offered to send her on to college. She decided on marriage instead. After that, Anne and her husband and her parents all moved to Florida, vanishing from the headlines Frank Chisari had spawned one day in May 1949 as he trudged disconsolately along Second Ave. and happened to find a newspaper office.

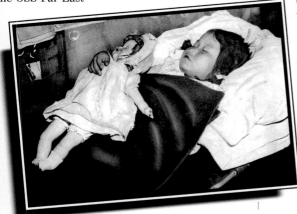

By JAY MAEDER
Daily News Staff Writer

THE ASSASSINS from New York City had done no homework at all, and they had not the remotest chance of killing the president of the United States. The assassins from New York City appeared to think that in the nation's capital in 1950, you could just walk into Harry Truman's bedroom and shoot him as he slept. Actually, there were two dozen armed guards and at least one submachine gun between the sidewalk and Harry Truman in the first place, and Oscar Collazo and Griselio Torresola were packing just two automatics and 70 bullets in the second place, and besides that, Oscar Collazo didn't know how to shoot his gun anyway. This was the situation when the assassins from New York City took the train out of Penn Station on Tuesday the 31st of October, their weapons in the pockets of the crisp new suits they had bought for the occasion.

They stayed the night in a cheap Washington hotel, and early the next afternoon they took a 40-cent cab ride over to Pennsylvania Ave. In the fall of 1950, the White House was undergoing renovations, and Truman and his family were temporarily ensconced in Blair House, the presidential guest quarters across the street. It was 2:20 p.m., and the sidewalk was crushed with tourists.

According to plan, what there was of it, the two determined attackers approached Blair House from opposite directions. Griselio Torresola paused in front of a sentry station. Oscar Collazo walked straight to the canopied steps, where a policeman was standing day duty, and he pulled out his gun and fired. There was only a click. Collazo didn't understand safeties.

In this one instant, there was now an end to any possibility that the assassins from New York City might actually get inside. Hearing the click, immediately grasping what it signified, the cop let out a yell and flung himself into the street to draw fire from the president napping upstairs. At this point, Collazo got his safety off and started shooting, but already hordes of guards were arriving from out of nowhere and down he dropped in a hail of bullets. At the same time, Torresola began blasting the sentry box. Two policemen fell, one of them forever. But as Torresola galloped toward the Blair House steps, dying officer Leslie Coffelt got off one return shot that neatly drilled his killer straight through the brain.

Suddenly, in a few explosive seconds on Wednesday the 1st of November, it was all over.

The whole thing had been insane. "No one in his right mind would have tried to carry out an assassination like that," marveled a Secret Service chief.

Indeed, the attackers were fast identified as fanatics from Puerto Rico's Nationalist Party, revolutionaries dedicated to Puerto Rican independence and the overthrow of the island's U.S.-installed government. "Puppets!" raged the wounded Collazo from his hospital bed. In San Juan at this very moment, Gov. Luis Munoz Marin's troops were rounding up nationalists who had days earlier mounted an insurrection that left dozens dead; soldiers were even now flushing party chief Pedro Albizu Campos from his stronghold. In Torresola's jacket, police found a letter from Albizu Campos appointing

Arraigned for murder

NI CON CARCEL, NI CON BALAS
Oscar Collazo

Griselio Torresola, Blair House

the dead man leader of the movement's U.S. operations.

Harry Truman was rather saddened. He liked to think he was the best friend Puerto Ricans ever had. Why would these men despise him so?

IN NEW YORK, the teeming Puerto Rican neighborhoods of East Harlem and the lower Bronx shook for days as federal agents and local police stormed the tenements in search of conspirators. It was widely imagined in Cold War 1950 that Puerto Rico's freedom fighters were Red dupes; the Communist objective, Daily Mirror columnist Victor Riesel explained, was "to divert us from Europe and the Orient and embroil us in Latin American uprisings to make us look like imperialist bandits, hated by our neighbors." Collazo, 37, who had lived in the Bronx for more than 10 years and was otherwise a quiet $71-a-week workman in a New Rochelle handbag factory, had once been a commander in the nationalist military wing; Albizu Campos himself had once lived in Collazo's Brook Ave. building.

It was true, of course, that U.S. sugar-company colonization had ravaged Puerto Rico's economy for decades and that the rabid nationalists were

not entirely without a point. Yet Truman and his man Munoz Marin were partnered in ambitious revitalization projects, and the president actively supported island self-rule, and it was not at all clear what ends Collazo and Torresola intended. On Brook Ave., it was generally observed that attacking the president really did very little to promote community interests, and neighbors began to shun Collazo's wife, Rosa, also a devoted nationalist. She made the papers for a few days, screeching party pieties — "Puerto Ricans can no longer be slaves of the U.S.!" — and then she decided to be quiet.

FOUND GUILTY in March 1951 of Coffelt's murder and swiftly sentenced to death, Oscar Collazo eagerly looked forward to martyrdom, and he was annoyed when his execution was stayed, and then he was enraged when, in June 1952, on the eve of the implementation of the new Puerto Rican constitution that Truman had pushed through Congress, the president commuted his sentence to life behind bars. By this time, Pedro Albizu Campos was serving a long prison term in Puerto Rico. By this time as well, Rosa Collazo had softened. "A grand gesture," she called Truman's clemency.

Little more was heard of the imprisoned man until the mid-1970s, when a group called Fuerzas Armadas Liberacion Nacional, or FALN, began blowing up banks and office buildings all over New York City. Among the FALN demands was the release of the hero Collazo, otherwise consigned to the pit and abyss of popular memory as the presidential assassins Guiteau and Czolgosz and Zangara.

In September 1979, following a human-rights campaign spearheaded largely by Rep. Robert Garcia of the Bronx, Collazo was pardoned by good-hearted President Jimmy Carter, over the protests of Puerto Rican Gov. Carlos Romero Barcelo, who insisted that the aging convict remained a "menace to the public safety."

Humanitarian Garcia was soon disappointed by the newly freed Collazo's immediate public embrace of FALN and warm reendorsement of political violence. "I regret the words and language that are presently being used," Garcia admitted. Fidel Castro was not so chagrined. Two months after Collazo left prison, Castro called him to Havana and showered him with medals.

"As long as the imperialists are sure that they are struggling against a divided people," Collazo shouted wherever he went, "the empire will get the better of us."

SCENE: FEDERAL
District Court, New York City, April 1980. FALN soldier Marie Haydee Beltran Torres, charged in a 1977 bombing that killed a bystander, screams that she is a prisoner of war and does not acknowledge Judge Whitman Knapp's right to try her. As Knapp rules her position legally untenable and has her removed, she raises a fist in the direction of one courtroom supporter, elderly Oscar Collazo, and shouts: "Ni con carcel, ni con balas, esta lucha no la van a apagar!" This is a bumper-sticker revolutionary slogan that means: "Not with prison, not with bullets, the struggle won't be stopped." A New York police detective who happens to be of Puerto Rican heritage smiles. "I'm glad she's taking that position," he says. "Because it means she will definitely go to jail for a long time. It makes it easier to put them in jail when they say they are prisoners of war."

OSCAR COLLAZO died in Puerto Rico in February 1994 at age 80, no particular menace to the public safety. In a December 1998 plebiscite, Puerto Ricans rejected U.S. statehood and voted to maintain their commonwealth status.

By DAVID HINCKLEY
Daily News Staff Writer

WHEN RALPH Kramden heard that Mary Monahan had passed away and that this sweet little old lady had unbeknownst to everyone been sitting on 40 million smackers and that she had left Ralph a fortune, he naturally set about planning the rest of his life.

He'd get a telephone. And a television set. Seventeen-incher. Better yet, he'd get to see the look on Alice's face. So he was never going to be more than a bus driver, eh? This'll change *your* tune, Alice. Har-dee-har-har.

It wasn't going to happen, of course. When Mary Monahan's will was read, it turned out Fortune was her pet parrot. And that's what Ralph got: Fortune, plus the handful of dust and dreams that ever seemed to define his lot in this hard old world.

Loser, they sometimes called him.

But they were wrong.

For all the things Ralph Kramden was in all the years he and Alice lived in the walkup at 328 Chauncey St. in Brooklyn, loser was never one of them. He never had much money, but that didn't make him a loser. It just made him poor. He had a wife he was crazy about, and who was crazy about him. He had Ed Norton, a pal for all seasons. And he had his dreams. No sucker punch, no sledgehammer knocked Ralph Kramden down for the count. He answered the bell for every round, dead certain his next longshot was coming in.

Besides, the important part of the Mary Monahan story isn't the money. The important part is why she included him in her will at all, which is that every day as he drove his Gotham bus along Madison Ave., he helped Mary Monahan on and off.

Without getting all weepy, the truth is that Ralph Kramden, the embodiment of irrational bluster and loud foolish overstatement, the man who pounded fist into palm and threatened to send his wife to the moon, helped little old ladies on and off his bus.

Aaah, c'mere, ya big lug.

RALPH KRAMDEN, born around 1920 in Brooklyn, entered a modest number of American homes Saturday the 22nd of July 1950 in "The Honeymooners," a sketch developed for comedian Jackie Gleason in Gleason's third week as host of the new "Cavalcade of Stars" on the DuMont television network.

DuMont, named for its creator, pioneer TV wizard Allen DuMont, was fighting with fledgling ABC to become the third major network behind well-established CBS and NBC. DuMont had a strong flagship, Channel 5 in New York, WABD, but he also had shallow pockets. In network TV's infancy, he was hustling on the cheap, betting the rent on rolls of the dice. It was the right place for Ralph Kramden.

Jackie Gleason, a veteran of B-movies and nightclubs, had already taken one shot at TV, on "The Life of Riley" in 1949. It was a mismatch, souring Gleason enough that he came close to declining the "Cavalcade of Stars" offer. But once the show started, things clicked, including the ongoing domestic saga of great-girthed Ralph Kramden and his sharp-tongued wife, Alice.

Ralph: "You're the type that would bend over and pick up a pocketbook on April Fool's Day. I wouldn't."

Alice: "You couldn't."

What the Bickersons and others had started on radio, the Kramdens picked up on television.

Part of the joke, of course, was that the Kramdens themselves didn't own a television. The Kramdens didn't own much of anything, and while they dreamed of more, they didn't count on it. They were prepared to live the way they did because that's how they'd always lived, and that's how their friends lived, and in America in the early 1950s, a lot of people knew a life in which television, or a telephone, was not a given.

THE REAL Chauncey St. was in Bushwick — Gleason had grown up there — but the Kramdens' Chauncey St. was relocated to Bensonhurst because it sounded more like Brooklyn to TV

writers. Out the front window, Ralph and Alice, who in the show's prime was played by Audrey Meadows, can see the Hong Kong Gardens and Old Man Grogan's long underwear on the line. Norton, who works in the sewers, lives one floor up with his wife, Trixie.

The Kramdens and Nortons can talk by leaning out the window and hollering. They walk into each other's apartments without knocking. Ralph makes $62 a week driving the bus, and while that's never enough, Alice does not have to work.

The bus also marks the upward mobility in Ralph's life. As a kid, he delivered groceries for the A&P and shoveled snow for the Works Progress Administration — a gag for the millions who knew the WPA's reputation for amusing make-work projects.

Though he'd been poor enough for the WPA, Ralph had dreams. He dreamed of playing the cornet. But his big score was meeting Alice Gibson, who gave up a good job at the laundry to marry him.

The strength of the Ralph-and-Alice relationship is reflected in the fact that it overshadowed the relationship between Ralph and Art Carney's Ed, which anywhere else would have been one of the great buddy dramas ever.

Ralph: "I promise you, Norton, I'm gonna learn to swallow my pride."

Norton: "That ought not to be too hard. You've learned how to swallow everything else."

That's tough to top. But this was always, first, a show about the old man and the old lady. At the start, when Pert Kelton played Alice, Norton didn't exist. Carney played a cop.

Gleason himself was a party guy, a gals-and-gams kind of nightclubber. But when the idea for Ralph developed during a session with writers Joe Bigelow and Harry Crane, Gleason rejected their initial suggestion that the sketch be called "The Beast."

"He's not a beast," said Gleason. "The guy really

HITTING THE HIGH NOTE
Ralph and Alice Kramden

loves this broad. They fight, sure. But they always end in a clinch."

And so they did. Ralph sold his brand-new bowling ball to buy a Christmas present for Alice. Alice turned down a shot at the movies to stay with Ralph and the icebox. When it all came crashing down and Ralph wondered if he had wasted his life, Alice showed him he could still hit the high note on the cornet.

It made for a timeless love story, though parts of the repertoire were decidedly of their time — like Ralph's repeated threats, which, of course, he never would have carried out, to pound Alice to a pulp. "One of these days, Alice! To the moon!" "Pow! Right in the kisser!" Those became signature Ralph lines, right next to "Har-dee-har-har" and the fat jokes and sewer jokes and money jokes.

Ralph: "Alice, I've got my pride. Before I let you go to work, I'd rather see you starve. We'll just have to live on our savings."

Alice: "That'll carry us through the night, but what'll we do in the morning?"

WITHIN TWO years, "The Honeymooners" had helped make Gleason big enough that he could jump the whole operation to CBS for a multiyear produce-and-star deal worth $11 million. It remained a segment in the Gleason show until 1955-56, when the gang did 39 stand-alone episodes, cataloging such quintessential Ralph moments as his attempt to get rich quick by making a TV infomercial for Handy Housewife Helper ("Oh, Chef of the Future …") and win big bucks on "The $99,000 Question." (He misses the jackpot when he guesses that Norton wrote "Swanee River.")

In a minor irony, those 39 episodes were preserved because they were filmed with the newfangled Electronicam, developed by Allen DuMont as part of a final effort to save his failing network.

DuMont folded anyway, in 1955. Ralph, Alice, Ed and Trixie returned periodically through the '60s and '70s for short runs and specials, and after Gleason died June 24, 1987, it was simply assumed that when the bus stopped at the Pearly Gates, Mary Monahan was there to help him off.

By OWEN MORITZ
Daily News Staff Writer

THE OLDEST OF 11 children and the first to go past high school, Junius Kellogg left the poverty of Portsmouth, Va., to play basketball at Manhattan College in 1949. A gifted, gangling 6-foot-10 center, he was 22 at the time, an Army veteran who was attending college under both a basketball scholarship and the G.I. Bill of Rights. But the kid from the backwater would make his mark — and put his life in danger doing it — busting college basketball's biggest-ever gambling scandal.

Kellogg arrived at a time when New York City was a hotbed of big-time college basketball. While the new professional team in town, the Knickerbockers, played to ho-hum crowds in the drafty, 5,000-seat 69th Regiment Armory, the city's commuter schools — City College, New York University, Long Island University, Manhattan and St. John's — drew full houses at Madison Square Garden. An irony, since the Garden owned the Knicks.

The pinnacle came in 1950. A flashy City College team led by street-smart players recruited from the city's schoolyards stunned the basketball world by sweeping both the NCAA and NIT championships — the first and only team ever to do so. In the NIT, it routed Adolph Rupp's nationally ranked Kentucky basketball machine by an incredible score of 89-50.

But the college game had a dark side. Bookies were taking huge bets from gamblers playing the point spread. Fast-talking bettors, often approaching the kids at summer basketball clinics in the mountains, had gotten to key players, offering bribes of $1,000 and $1,500 to fix games.

Point-shaving, it was called. And kids from poor families were easy targets. They weren't throwing games, just shaving points off the final score. So miss a basket here, flub a rebound there, the players were told. Perform poorly, but don't be obvious about it. And remember, it was not about who won or lost, but by how many points.

The gamblers made a big mistake. They approached Manhattan College's first black player, stringbean sophomore Junius Kellogg, and urged him to dump an upcoming game against favored DePaul University at the Garden in January 1951.

SEVERAL DAYS before the game, Kellogg was finishing up practice when Henry Poppe, co-captain and high scorer of Manhattan's previous year's team, came up to him.

"How do you think you'll do against DePaul?" Poppe asked.

"I think we'll win," Kellogg answered. "I always think we'll win."

"Well," Poppe went on, "you're picked to lose. DePaul is one of the best in the country. Are you a betting man?"

"What do you mean?" Kellogg asked naively. "Do you want to bet me?"

"No, nothing like that. This is something where you can pick up good money — a grand."

Kellogg told him to get lost, but Poppe was undaunted. "Think it over and let me know," he said.

After a sleepless night, Kellogg went to coach Ken Norton, who promptly sent him to the district attorney.

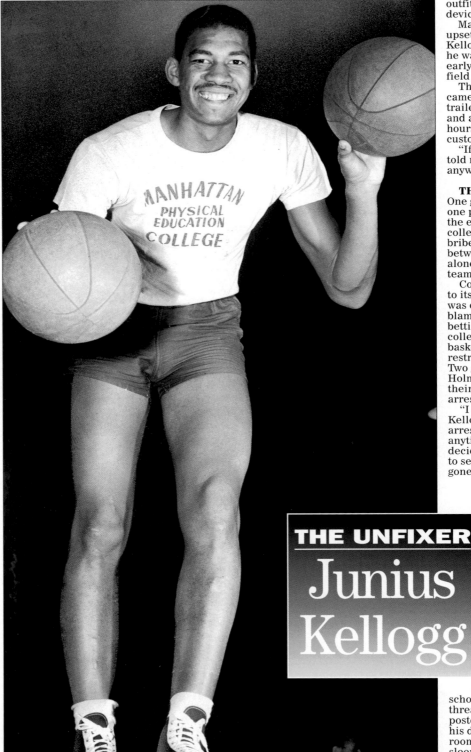

THE UNFIXER
Junius Kellogg

A FEW DAYS later, Kellogg met with Poppe as detectives watched from a discreet distance.

"This rah-rah stuff doesn't get you anything," Poppe told Kellogg over beers at a nearby bar. "I know — I have a car, and money in the bank and bonds. That's the way to do it."

Kellogg went along. "I'm willing to go for the pitch," he said.

Miss some shots, Poppe counseled him, but don't be "so bad that you stink up the joint." He added: "You're a fool if you don't go for this, because other basketball players are doing it."

The night of the DePaul game, Tuesday the 16th of January, a jittery Kellogg was warming up at one end of the Garden court when Poppe cozied up.

"It's all fixed — it's 10 points," Poppe said, referring to the projected margin of loss. He promised Kellogg the money after the game at a midtown pub where the authorities planned to

outfit Kellogg with a listening device.

Manhattan scored a stunning upset, 62-59, but not because of Kellogg. Nervous and distracted, he was taken out of the game early; his replacement hit eight field goals to key the upset.

The postgame meeting never came off. Instead, detectives trailed Poppe to his Queens home and arrested him at 3 a.m. Within hours, five gamblers were in custody.

"If it can happen here," Norton told reporters, "it can happen anywhere in the country."

THE SCANDAL mushroomed. One gambler pointed to another, one player implicated another. In the end, 32 players from seven colleges would admit to taking bribes to fix 86 games in 17 states between 1947 and 1950 — seven alone from the great City College team of 1950.

College basketball was rocked to its roots. The Garden suddenly was off limits as athletic directors blamed its management for the betting environment. Some colleges dropped big-time basketball, while the others restricted games to campus gyms. Two great coaches, CCNY's Nat Holman and LIU's Clair Bee, saw their reputations tainted by the arrests of their key players.

"I didn't want to hurt the guy," Kellogg reflected on Poppe's arrest. "But I had to do it. If anytime in the future that guy decided to tell someone he came to see me, my scholarship was gone."

KELLOGG WAS hailed nationally as "the unfixer." The New York Police Department gave him a citation. Back in Portsmouth, proud townspeople feted him with a parade and launched a Kellogg Honest Fund. When they presented him with a check for $1,000 — the amount of the bribe he rejected — he gave it to his mother.

"I didn't realize the enormity of the situation," he said later. "I was just this naive kid." Back at school, he began getting threatening letters. A guard was posted around the clock outside his dorm room. He and his roommate were instructed not to sleep near the window.

He stayed Manhattan's top scorer in 1951, then left school to go back into service for the Korean War. Upon his return, he took a double course load and graduated in 1953 with his original class. After that, he barnstormed with the Harlem Globetrotters.

But in April 1954, on tour with the Globetrotters, an Arkansas car crash damaged his spinal cord. After four years at the Kingsbridge Veterans Hospital, Kellogg regained the use of his hands and arms but remained paralyzed below the waist.

He spent the rest of his life in a wheelchair, and from 1957 to 1966 he coached the Pan Am Jets to four international championships in wheelchair basketball. After that, he held a number of New York City jobs, including director of strategic planning for the Community Development Agency. He died Sept. 16, 1998, at 71.

Among those at his Portsmouth funeral was Mayor James Holley, who had played high school basketball with him. "He set America straight about doing what was right," Holley said.

By EDWARD T. O'DONNELL

Special to The News

"Everybody talks about the weather, but nobody does anything about it."
— Mark Twain

STORMY WEATHER
Dr. Wallace Howell

T WAS *real* dry in New York in February 1950. A yearlong drought was the worst in modern memory. The upstate reservoirs had plummeted to just 45 percent of capacity. Experts warned of imminent crop failures, great fires, outbreaks of disease. Mayor William O'Dwyer closed public pools and ordered an end to car-washing and lawn-watering. A "Thirsty Thursday" campaign urged New Yorkers to cut back on bathing. The Post Office started using "Save Water" as its stamp cancellation.

But conservation alone would only postpone the inevitable crisis. It had to rain. It had to rain soon. It had to rain a lot.

From his pulpit, Francis Cardinal Spellman called upon the faithful to pray for a deluge. That couldn't hurt, O'Dwyer figured, but what was needed here was something even more miraculous.

And so New York City hired a rainmaker.

DR. WALLACE E. Howell was a man of sterling credentials in the meteorological field, but the science-fiction notion of "cloud seeding" was a very new one in 1950, and bringing him to New York was an act of last-resort desperation on New York's part.

Perhaps it was his fee that convinced city officials to take a chance on him. Howell clearly understood the cardinal rule of selling one's expertise in New York: No one takes you seriously unless you charge an outrageous per diem. He demanded a staggering $100 a day. The city, of course, gave him a one-year contract.

"Cloud seeding" had been developed just four years earlier, at the General Electric laboratory in Schenectady, where Dr. Vincent J. Schaefer had discovered that the moisture in clouds needed tiny particles of dust, soil, salt crystals, smoke and other matter to form water droplets.

Soon, the "father of weather modification" was conducting his first rain-producing experiments. His scientists flew through clouds and "seeded" them with particles of silver iodide or dry ice, promoting droplet formation and, consequently, rain.

Once perfected, its practitioners predicted, cloud seeding would usher in a new era of "weather management." Droughts would be a thing of the past. Whole new areas of the globe would be opened to cultivation.

They were confronting a problem that had plagued humanity for 10,000 years, ever since people stopped following animals and settled down to plant crops and build civilizations. Much religion, science and mathematics had developed over the millennia as mankind sought to explain and anticipate the weather. Now, at the dawn of the nuclear age, what had long been the province of witch doctors and high priests had been taken over by scientists.

Not everyone shared the optimism and enthusiasm of "$100-day Howell" and his would-be weather manipulators. A good many New Yorkers flatly refused to believe cloud seeding would work at all and berated the project as a fabulous waste of money.

Others opposed it for more philosophical reasons. Under most circumstances, they were prepared to agree, the advancements of science and technology were fine and good, but: *Wasn't this going a bit too far? Weren't Howell and his team tampering with nature itself?*

It was one thing to put scientific knowledge to use to predict the weather — and even that had been a controversial idea once upon a time — but it was quite another to use it to alter natural processes. Howell got mail from all over the world, pleading with him to leave things to God. Such concerns, of course, were not new. They had dogged Galileo and Pasteur. Howell had no trouble ignoring them.

And so, in military fashion, he established his command post on the flat top of a high hill in upstate Lakewood, near the Catskills watershed, where he had a clear view of the approaching weather and plenty of room for all his strange equipment.

BACK IN THE city, the Police Department's aviation unit stood at the ready. For weeks, parched New Yorkers waited for the work to begin. **COVER UP!** headlined the Daily News. **RAINMAKER PUNCH COMES TODAY!** The first round admittedly went to the skeptics. The first scheduled seeding, on Tuesday the 28th of March, was canceled because of — of all things — a bit of rain.

But not enough rain to call off the program. Howell began his regular seeding flights a few days later, augmented by truck-mounted generators that shot silver iodide skyward. Suddenly he was the talk of the town. Newspapers tracked his work daily. Television and radio stations competed for exclusive interviews.

"I didn't know I was going to be a celebrity," he grumbled to The New Yorker. "And I don't want to be one."

But there was no avoiding it. Particularly once the rain started to fall.

HOWELL, DERIDED by many as a quack, appeared to have mastery over the elements after all. Even the most hard-core skeptics had to rethink their positions in mid-April, when the city was hit by an unexpected snowstorm. **HOWELL'S SNOW**, the papers called it.

The emergency water restrictions were lifted a few months later, and by the time Howell's contract expired in February 1951, the reservoirs stood at 99 percent of capacity. New Yorkers were thrilled and Howell was famous: He came, he seeded, it rained. Few consultants have ever delivered results so effectively.

Well, it was true that there was another side to the story. What was a godsend for New York turned out to be a catastrophe for the Catskills. Farmers and resort owners banded together to sue Howell after their livelihoods were destroyed by never-ending rains. "I know some people up there," one man said, "that would shoot Dr. Howell on sight."

The lawsuits put Howell and his employer in an odd position: If they contended that Howell had made it rain, they would be validating the claims of the angry upstaters. On the other hand, if they argued that it would have rained anyway and that Howell had nothing to do with it, everybody would look pretty foolish. New York City, after all, paid Howell $36,500. The doctor himself made no large boasts, always referring to his New York work as an experiment. Eventually, the Catskills suits were tossed out of court.

HOWELL'S CAREER flourished after his yearlong tour of duty in New York. As a recognized cloud-seeding authority, he set up programs across the U.S. and in Canada, Cuba, Peru and the Philippines, and he went on to hold various federal weatherman positions. He was 84 when he died June 12, 1999, in California.

The scientific jury is still out on the effectiveness of cloud seeders. Most experts seem to agree that they can, in fact, produce rain. They disagree on how much control the seeders have over the process. Modern seeding programs nonetheless exist in many states, particularly in the South and West.

By OWEN MORITZ
Daily News Staff Writer

"There's a long fly … it's gonna be … I believe … THE GIANTS WIN THE PENNANT! THE GIANTS WIN THE PENNANT! THE GIANTS WIN THE PENNANT! … Bobby Thomson hits it into the lower deck of the left-field stands! The Giants win the pennant! … and they're going crazy."
— **Giants announcer Russ Hodges**

"A high fly to left field … it's a home run, the Giants have won the pennant. Now a word from Schaefer beer."
— **Dodgers announcer Red Barber**

WATCHING IT SAIL
Bobby Thomson

THE ONCE-PROUD New York Giants had become a sad-sack franchise. Not since 1937 had the Giants won a pennant; now, through much of the 1951 season, they were in dead last place. Came August, and somehow the team had climbed to second place. But they still trailed the league-leading Brooklyn Dodgers by a whopping 13 ½ games.

Then it happened. Under their Napoleonic manager, Leo Durocher, the Jints got hot while Da Bums cooled off. They won 38 of ther last 44 games — and, on the last day of the regular season, they tied the Brooklyns.

A three-game playoff followed. In game one at the mythic bandbox called Ebbets Field, they beat the Dodgers 3-1, with a key home run from Bobby Thomson. In game two, the Dodgers returned the favor, routing the Giants 10-0.

And so there was a third game, on an overcast Wednesday the 3rd of October, before 34,320 fans. In the lengthening afternoon shadows of the old Polo Grounds, hard by Coogan's Bluff and the Harlem River, the Dodgers surged to a 4-1 lead. The Giants' storybook year, it seemed, would have no happy ending.

Then, in the last moments of the ninth inning, shortstop Alvin Dark's leadoff hit slithered past the outstretched glove of Brooklyn first baseman Gil Hodges. Don Mueller followed with a skidding shot past Hodges, Dark taking third.

The tired right arm of Dodgers ace Don Newcombe induced a foul out from Giants cleanup hitter Monte Irvin, a pivotal recruit from the Newark Black Eagles. Next up was first baseman Whitey Lockman, who slammed a double into the left-field corner, scoring Dark. On the play, Mueller mangled his left ankle in a twisting safe slide at third base.

Up stepped Bobby Thomson.

As Mueller was being carried from the field, Dodgers manager Charlie Dressen signaled for a relief pitcher. His choice was first-game starter Ralph Branca, who had won 21 games as a 21-year-old rookie in 1947.

The stage was set. One out, one run in. Tying runs on base. Giants hearts pounding. As Thomson strolled to the plate, Durocher called him over.

"If you ever hit one," the little manager whispered in his ear, "hit one now."

FOR THIS MOMENT in sports history there loomed no more improbable hero than Scottish-born, Staten Island-reared Robert Brown Thomson, a Curtis High School graduate who had joined the Giants in 1946, had a couple of good years and then fallen into the ranks of the unextraordinary.

In 1950, his batting average fell to a dreadful .252. A month into the 1951 season, at 27, he lost his center-field job to prodigious 19-year-old rookie Willie Mays. Still, Durocher loved to play hunches — in 1947, he'd been suspended for a year for off-season association with gamblers — and he played a hunch with Thomson. The team lagging, Durocher installed him at third base, where he had performed poorly in the past. Suddenly, in the season's late stages, Thomson started to shine; he would finish the year .293 with 32 homers.

Now at bat, Thomson took Branca's first pitch — a high fastball on the inside part of the plate — for a strike. Branca delivered again, the pitch earmarked for the identical spot. But this time the ball veered more toward the center of the plate. Thomson swung. The ball flew off his bat and headed for the lower left-field seats.

"Right away I thought it was a home run," he would recall later. "I hit it real hard."

Then he saw it sink. No, he concluded, not a home run at all. "But I kept watching it sail as I went around the bases … I started to hyperventilate."

Fans raced onto the field as Thomson bounded around the bases. Rounding third, he could see Durocher and teammate Eddie Stankey whooping it up in a victory dance.

At home plate, Thomson vaulted into a crowd of delirious Giants. He kept running, right into the clubhouse. It was strangely silent — the newspaper boys were all chasing the dejected Branca. The dazed Brooklyns were the last to leave the field.

The Giants had won, 5-4. "The shot heard 'round the world." "The miracle of Coogan's Bluff." "The greatest baseball story ever told." The Giants had beaten arch-rival Brooklyn, wrote the Daily News' Dick Young, "in a fashion that makes pulp fiction writers look like rank conservatives."

THE WORLD SERIES started the next day, and the Giants met their Bronx neighbors, the Yankees, in a subway series. The Giants bowed in six games.

BOBBY THOMSON played two more years with the Jints, putting up more good numbers. But before the start of the 1954 season, he was traded to the Milwaukee Braves — ironically, for a pitcher, John Antonelli, who would lead the Giants to a miraculous World Series sweep of the Cleveland Indians. Thomson broke his leg during spring training, prompting the Braves to bring up a minor league outfielder named Hank Aaron, who would go on to become baseball's all-time home run king. He came back to the Giants during the 1957 season, the team's last in New York, then went elsewhere when they were hijacked to California and retired in 1960 after 14 seasons.

AFTER THAT, Thomson became an executive with a paper-products company and one of baseball's best ambassadors. He signed autographs willingly, attended countless charity functions, even teamed up with Branca in benefit golf matches. Still going strong at century's end at age 75, still signing autographs, still the solid Staten Islander, Thomson was always modest whenever someone asked him about his epic home run: "I didn't deserve to do a thing like that. Guess I must be living right."

Watching Gov. Dewey on TV, October 1953

STREAK OF LIGHT

Rudolph Halley

By OWEN MORITZ
Daily News Staff Writer

HOLLYWOOD **MOBSTER** Mickey Cohen was chafing under the relentless questioning from the steely eyed chief counsel for the crimebusters from Washington.

"Senator," an exasperated Cohen pleaded with the committee chairman, Sen. Estes Kefauver, "why can't this fellow ask questions nice, like you?"

But nice was not a word in Rudolph Halley's vocabulary.

Frank Costello's lawyer complained that Halley's questions were disrupting his client's thought processes. Accordingly, the national TV audience got to watch the sweaty hands of the Prime Minister of the Underworld, fingers nervously drumming the tabletop. Auburn-haired Virginia Hill, the mob's gal pal, shot profanities. Ex-Mayor William O'Dwyer, who had fled to Mexico as ambassador and then returned for a grilling, was left slashed and burned.

In the last months of 1950 and the first months of 1951, 30 million Americans stopped what they were doing to watch a real-life police lineup. Day after day, organized crime figures, freelance hit men and scores of crooked politicians paraded before the Senate Crime Investigating Committee, known to history as the Kefauver crime committee, as it conducted hearings at Foley Square in Manhattan.

And the public figure that Americans saw most of was the committee's brilliant, lispy, owlish counsel, Rudolph Halley, age 37.

Halley, a city kid so bright he graduated high school at 14 and had to sit out a year before college would admit him, became the first great crimebuster spawned by television.

"His investigative technique won for him a large televison audience," one newspaper reported. Indeed, Halley's weekly CBS-TV show, "Crime Syndicated," one of the new medium's early law-enforcement dramas, commanded a large local audience.

"You should run for mayor," people told him.

Halley would. But first he would run in a special election for City Council president to fill the seat

vacant since Vincent Impellitteri replaced the departing O'Dwyer as mayor.

On May 1, 1951, Kefauver's committee made public its bombshell findings — New York was a racketeering paradise, "one of the major centers of organized crime."

That day, Halley resigned. His work, he announced, was done. The jokesters had a good time: "Crime Takes a Halley Day"; "Costello Got Halley-tosis." Supporters said, watch Halley's comet. His ambition burns bright.

Within weeks, Halley announced his campaign for Council president, thundering: "I'm going to teach the political bosses a lesson." His agenda: clean up New York, sweep out crime, gangsters and Tammany Hall.

So, running on the Liberal, Fusion and Independent lines — neither the Democrats nor the Republicans were willing to endorse him — Halley stunned the political world by winning election in November 1951. He was a mere heartbeat from the mayor's office.

As he welcomed well-wishers at a victory party at his Algonquin Hotel campaign headquarters, Halley smiled when supporters shouted, "Congratulations to our next mayor."

"Just call me Rudy," he replied.

BUT POLITICAL life did not turn out quite the way Rudolph Halley had hoped.

He was a seminal New York story. His father, a dentist, died when Halley was five. His mother, working as a secretary in the Theater District, raised him alone. The child prodigy graduated elite Townsend Harris High School in Queens at 14, then bided his time taking postgraduate courses until Columbia would admit him at 16. He breezed through college and law school in four years — but still had to wait until he was 21 to practice law.

Halley came to the attention of a congressional committee headed by Sen. Harry Truman of Missouri, probing wartime waste. His tireless work, his 16-hour days, would boost Truman into the vice presidency, even as his later work for Kefauver would catapult the Tennessee senator into making a failed bid for the Democratic presidential nomination in 1952.

But his own political career foundered. Partyless, Halley found himself shut out in the Council chambers. His wild charges and investigations into city government soon were ignored by the media and public.

Crime, a hot-button topic when the Democrats were in the White House, was no longer a national issue with Dwight Eisenhower as president. America wanted to be left alone. Rudy wasn't particularly charismatic, and, as TV became less of a household novelty, his appearances lost their magic.

Then there was his clash with New York Gov. Thomas E. Dewey over charges Dewey was "ruthlessly playing politics" with state aid. Denounced for his soft campaign for president in 1948 that led to a humiliating defeat at the hands of Truman, Dewey at last took off the gloves.

Halley, Dewey roared at a press conference, was "as stupid and ignorant as he is shallow and venomous."

When the Council president vowed to go to Albany, Dewey's aides de camp ridiculed him. "He can come to Albany with a program if he wants to," said a Dewey operative, "but it won't do any good. He'll find no TV forum here."

In 1953, Rudy Halley made his bid for mayor on the Liberal ticket. He finished a distant third, well behind the Republican candidate and the Democratic winner, Robert Wagner.

Halley was crushed. "I suppose I was a young man in a hurry," he told supporters.

BACK IN PRIVATE life, Halley became an investor in a jai alai project in Puerto Rico — a perhaps unseemly decision for a man who had spent years condemning gambling.

On Nov. 19, 1956, Halley suddenly died. He was just 43.

At his funeral, the former crime buster was extolled as a genius. "His spectacular success as chief counsel for the Senate Crime Investigating Committee shook the criminal potentates and their fronting politicians from their entrenched positions and sent them where they belong," Rabbi Israel Goldstein declared. "He exposed the interlocking directorate of a national network of crime and corruption."

The cause of death was pneumonia. But friends wondered if Halley's comet hadn't just burned itself out.

By DAVID HINCKLEY
Daily News Staff Writer

AT SEVEN FEET even, with good speed, a nice one-hand push shot and a work ethic strong enough to give him a B average in pre-law, Walter Dukes was a prime cut of basketball flesh when he graduated from Seton Hall in the spring of 1953.

New York Knickerbockers coach Joe Lapchick had been waiting a year for him. Salivating as Dukes averaged 26.4 points a game in his senior year and was named most valuable player of the National Invitation Tournament, Lapchick had passed up several lesser talents just to be sure he got this prize — and the plan ticked along like clockwork until contract talks began, and the Knicks said they could go as high as $10,000 a season, and Dukes reported that he already had an offer for $25,000.

Thus did Walter Dukes, America's most sought-after college basketball player in the spring of 1953, shrug off the National Basketball Association and become a Harlem Globetrotter.

TO GENERATIONS who know the Trotters purely as a comedy ensemble, more concerned with showtime than doubling down on the weak side, it may seem unfathomable that (1) the Globetrotters could more than double an NBA team's top bid for a star, and (2) the player would take it.

But into the 1950s, when the NBA was a two-cylinder league out of towns like upstate Rochester and Fort Wayne, Ind., the Trotters could, and did, put the hurt on the best of the pros. Through the '40s, of course, it didn't hurt the recruiting that the pros wouldn't take black players and the Trotters took nothing else, with the exception of Bob Karstens, a white guy who played the 1942-43 seasons and fit in just fine.

After the NBA's color line dissolved, the Trotters lost their leverage, though they did pick up Wilt Chamberlain for a season in the late '50s.

But in the late '40s and early '50s, the Harlem Globetrotters were the big name in city pro hoops. They packed the Garden regularly as the Knickerbockers struggled to draw half that number. Small wonder they could offer 25 big ones to Walter Dukes and the Knicks could cough up only 10.

THE STORY of the Harlem Globetrotters began in 1907, when four-year-old Abraham Saperstein's family arrived in the U.S. and settled in Chicago, where Abe developed an obsession with American basketball. Far too small to have any reasonable hope of playing the game on competitive levels, he turned to coaching instead and in 1925 was offered the team at Giles Post, the largest black American Legion outfit in Chicago.

The Savoy Big Five, they were called, after the Savoy Ballroom, where they played exhibition games to draw crowds after the dancing died down. They became a fine team, but they couldn't save the ballroom and they made no money — a situation Saperstein decided to remedy in late 1926 by declaring them independent professionals.

This new stature required a newer, more impressive name, so when they made their debut on Jan. 7, 1927, in Hinckley, Ill., with 300 fans in the house and $75 in the till, the American Legion team from Chicago became the New York Globetrotters. Three years later, Saperstein

Meadowlark Lemon and, so to speak, opponent

renamed them the New York Harlem Globetrotters.

Consensus was he did this mostly to telegraph the fact that his players were black, although Saperstein himself put a more spiritual face on it. "We chose Harlem," he said, "because, well, because Harlem was to the fellows what Jerusalem was to us."

SHOWTIME IN JERUSALEM

The Harlem Globetrotters

In fact, the Trotters never played a game in Harlem itself until 1968, though they were regulars at Madison Square Garden and Saperstein set up offices in the Empire State Building.

Success came slowly. "We never missed meals, but we postponed a lot of them," Saperstein said. "The table d'hote was salami and crackers, with canned sardines for dessert."

It was 13 years before the Globetrotters broke even, and it probably isn't coincidence that this came just a year after they fell into the clown routines.

THROUGH THE early years, the Trotters played it straight and became one of the bad boys on the block. A tournament was arranged in 1940 among the best teams in the country and the Globetrotters won, making them, for all practical purposes, national champions. For years to come, into the 1960s, the Trotters regularly played college All-Star teams and racked up a 140-66

record.

Back in 1939, however, they were clobbering some poor local outfit by a score of 112-5 when, to keep themselves interested, they started doing fancy showboat dribbles and passes. The crowd loved it — and a light bulb went off in Saperstein's head.

Soon the crazy dribbling, the close-weave passing drills and the rest of the shtick became part of Globetrotter games, as much an identifier as "Sweet Georgia Brown," which became the team's entrance music in 1952 and which a lot of people never realized was ever anything else.

Showtime — which the Trotters say created the "pivot" position now standard in all of basketball — drew fans and ensured many years of prosperity.

SAPERSTEIN ALSO had the good sense to showcase individual stars, long before the NBA caught on to that same notion. At first he had Inman Jackson. Later it was Goose Tatum. Then, in 1956, he signed up the most famous Globetrotter of them all, Meadowlark Lemon.

Lemon was a magician with a basketball, and once Tatum retired in 1956, Lemon ran the show, a responsibility he took very seriously. "The team had so many prospects and so much talent," he said. "They must have had 9,000 players ready to take your place. You were scared to get hurt."

By then, the Globetrotters were in such demand that Saperstein had split them into two squads, which did create the problem of finding enough opponents. Getting humiliated by the Trotters wasn't a gig other teams fought for.

In 1953, the Trotters started bringing their own opponents, variously called the Boston Shamrocks, Atlantic City Seagulls, Washington Generals and New Jersey Reds. Their job was to lose while scoring just enough to make the night resemble a basketball game, and the Generals/Reds were good at this: In 1959, they won no games and lost 411.

THE TROTTERS played for Pope Pius XII and Nikita Khrushchev. They played Cold War Berlin. They were on "The Ed Sullivan Show." They had their own Saturday morning cartoon series. By the early '60s, they were drawing 3 million fans a year, making Abe Saperstein flush enough to think he could challenge the NBA with his own pro league. That plan failed, but he remained buoyant, saying he'd be content just to see his Globetrotters celebrate their 50th anniversary.

He didn't. On March 15, 1966, he died of a heart attack. His estate sold the Globetrotters to Potter Palmer for several million dollars, and things rolled on until 1971, when the players went on strike, claiming that as the pie got bigger, their slice got smaller — no travel expenses, no meal money, no pension, no doctor on hand.

The players also came under fire from militants in the black community, who called the Trotters a Stepin Fetchit clown show. Meadowlark Lemon, otherwise no fan of management, shot back that it was only entertainment, and they should lighten up.

After all was resolved, Palmer sold the team to media mogul John Kluge in 1976 for $11 million. The next year, it celebrated its 50th anniversary, and in 1986 it hired the first female Trotter, All-American Lynette Woodard.

She admitted she would have preferred genuine competitive basketball. But there being no female league at the time, this still made her the only woman in the United States getting paid to play the

By MICHAEL ARONSON
Special to the News

WHILE ROBERT MOSES dominated New York for decades, changing the shape of the city with his bridges and highways and parks, there was another man who was likewise never elected to anything but also held long-term power and also changed the city forever. Unlike Moses, he preferred to work quietly.

He was Austin Tobin, a Port Authority employee for 45 years, its commander for 30.

But before there was Tobin, before there was the PA, there was the port.

BLESSED WITH one of the world's best natural harbors, and connected to the Midwest by the Erie Canal, New York was always a port city, its activity by World War I centered on the vast Brooklyn docks. And that was a problem, because Brooklyn was an island, separated by the Hudson River from New Jersey, where the 12 railroads that served the harbor had their terminals.

Freight had to be barged back and forth across the harbor to connect the docks with the rail lines. The Interstate Commerce Commission, which set the shipping rates, said all firms had to charge the same. But New Jersey complained that the high cost of barging rail cars added to its costs. Thus was born the bistate Port of New York Authority on April 30, 1921, the first such public agency of its type in the country. With the power to sell bonds, condemn property and either buy or build facilities, its mission was to equalize freight rates on both sides of the harbor.

The PA set out to coordinate the 12 private railroads, and, eight months later, produced 1922's Comprehensive Plan, which called for new rail lines, terminals, highways and a rail tunnel from Brooklyn to Jersey City to finally link the docks with the rails.

When the plan was rejected by the competing railroads, the PA sought another mission. In 1924, it got the two states to okay a pair of Staten Island-New Jersey bridges. Opened in 1928, they were named for Gen. George Goethals, builder of the Panama Canal and a PA consulting engineer, and Eugenius Outerbridge, the PA's first chairman.

But traffic to and from Staten Island was minimal. Not so in the Holland Tunnel, which was making a fortune in tolls. The PA took a look and decided it wanted to get into the Hudson tunnel business — not for trains, but for cars.

The year the Holland Tunnel opened, 1927, a 24-year-old law clerk joined the fledgling agency. He would stay on for more than four decades, reshaping the great port more than any other man.

BROOKLYN-BORN Austin Tobin became the PA's assistant general counsel in 1938, and here he made his name defending the tax-exempt status of municipal bonds, the PA's lifeblood. By 1942, he was executive director. And now the PA would completely abandon its original mandate — to develop the port — and instead start collecting tolls at the Holland Tunnel, which the PA bought in 1930; the George Washington Bridge, which opened in 1931, and the Lincoln Tunnel, which opened its first tube in 1937.

It was a moneymaking enterprise — and, once he took over, Tobin formalized it, insisting that the PA not undertake any project that didn't generate funds to pay for itself. That largely ruled out rail, the agency's original concern. And so Tobin turned a public corporation, founded to support harbor trade, into a profit-making machine beyond political control.

DEPENDENT AS IT was on the bond market, Tobin's PA became tightly linked with investment circles, which in turn earned large fees underwriting PA debt. The board of commissioners he dominated was packed with bankers and brokers, insulated from such nuisances as elections. Governors and mayors would come and go, but Tobin and the PA would stay. When Tobin left office in 1972, he was earning $70,000 a year, the nation's second most highly paid public official, after the President.

At that time, the PA employed 8,000, considerably up from 1927's 300. High over the

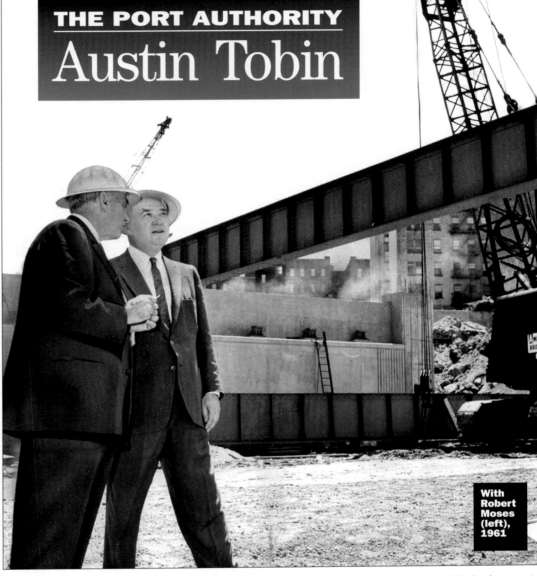

THE PORT AUTHORITY
Austin Tobin

With Robert Moses (left), 1961

city soared the gigantic new World Trade Center. Meanwhile, the port below was dying.

That rail tunnel from the Brooklyn docks to the New Jersey railheads, the original PA goal, was never built. There was no profit in it. Tobin said he couldn't put PA funds into rail because rail caused deficits, and, without taxing authority, the PA's blue-chip credit had to be maintained above all — even above the survival of the port it was supposed to preserve.

INSTEAD OF THE rail tunnel, the PA led the way in containerization, which used big cargo boxes that fit right on a truck or a rail car. The first test was at Newark on April 26, 1956; in 1962, the PA opened at Elizabeth the world's first all-containerized port. But this wouldn't work in Brooklyn, because Brooklyn wasn't linked to rail lines.

And that was the end of the New York docks. Labor peace was obtained with the Guaranteed Annual Income, providing the out-of-work longshoremen with a salary. The Manhattan docks became abandoned derelicts and later parkland; the Brooklyn docks fell quiet. Where once 30,000 Brooklyn longshoremen toiled, there were fewer than 500 by century's end.

IN THE LATE 1940s, meanwhile, the PA wrested control over the city's two airports from Moses, and, in the late '50s — ever seeking more tolls — built the George Washington Bridge's second level. Commuters found themselves betrayed: the bridge had originally been built to accommodate four rail lines across an envisioned lower level (indeed, the IND

subway has an unused spur at 178th St. that was to go across the bridge); instead, Tobin built the lower level to handle cars. Over Moses' objection, he also built the world's biggest bus terminal, which, unlike his other investments, lost money. Otherwise, teamwork with Moses was the norm. Together, through the '50s and '60s, the two men built the Throgs Neck and Verrazano bridges and miles of new roads.

Tobin was not unstoppable. He had wanted to build a giant airport twice the size of Kennedy in New Jersey's Morris County, and, in the early '60s he was held in contempt of Congress, although never jailed, for refusing to let House investigators examine internal PA documents. In another partial defeat, in 1962 he agreed to take over the struggling H&M Railroad (later the PATH train) in exchange for a permanent covenant against further rail projects and the right to build the World Trade Center; the anti-rail covenant was repealed by both states in 1974.

His end came in 1971, when both states' governors wanted the PA to undertake more rail projects. Tobin replied that the PA was considering rail links to JFK and Newark airports and a Hudson rail tunnel at 48th St. And then, in December, he resigned. Nearly three decades later, the PA would still be talking about the same unbuilt airport rail links.

In 1972, Tobin's massive harbor shift away from the dead Brooklyn docks was formally recognized when the Port of New York Authority became the Port Authority of New York and New Jersey.

Six years later, in 1978, Tobin was dead. And so was the Port of New York.

By JAY MAEDER
Daily News Staff Writer

"If we make the common man truly contemporaneous with his age, then he will be an uncommon man."

— Pat Weaver

MORE VITAL TO the American manifest destiny than even the transcontinental railroad and the automobile was the New York-to-California microwave relay system that on Tuesday the 4th of September 1951 permitted for the first time a coast-to-coast television broadcast. On that night, President Harry Truman spoke in San Francisco and was viewed live in New York. Four weeks later, Eddie Cantor began beaming his Hollywood variety program eastward over the great new net. Practicable commercial TV was thus launched on the national level. Mankind's greatest social revolution was at hand. What would it wreak?

Among those who understood that TV was more than just radio with pictures was a 43-year-old ex-radio and ex-advertising man named Sylvester "Pat" Weaver, chief of the National Broadcasting Co.'s television operations. In June 1948, when the second Louis-Walcott fight had become to fledgling TV what the 1921 Dempsey-Carpentier fight had been to fledgling radio, there had been 300,000 TV sets in America. In September 1951, there were 13 million. By May 1952, there would be 18 million; by December 1953, 27 million. This meant, Weaver knew, nothing less than a new civilization.

"With television," he said, "the average man can go anywhere and see anything...As television grows, kids will grow up with exposure to a pluralistic world. They will be face-to-face acquainted with Indians, Arabs, Chinese. Therefore, it will be more difficult for the group that has control of the child to discipline it to the we-group formula. As a result of TV, kids are already the best informed social group on the new cosmology."

Weaver talked like that. The NBC joke was that he had no job except to sit around thinking large, lofty thoughts. Colleagues called him the only man they ever knew who could reminisce about the future. It was his responsibility, he explained to Time magazine, "to see that every opportunity is used to expose people to things in which they have expressed no interest, but in which they *would* have expressed interest if they *had* been exposed to them."

ON THE 7TH of April 1927, at the Bell

Telephone laboratory on West St. in New York, as Secretary of Commerce Herbert Hoover addressed a gathering of dignitaries from a picture screen, it was grasped that television actually worked. What would be the applications? Police foresaw crime-fighting surveillance opportunities. The Navy liked pilotless seeing-eye warplanes. Showmen, meanwhile, envisioned theaters that would offer live sports events to large paying audiences. It was suggested that things called television stations might eventually be built in the nation's larger cities to service such theaters.

One confident soul was David Sarnoff of the Radio Corp. of America, whose W2XBS was licensed as an experimental station in 1928, field-testing first from the Bronx and later from atop the Empire State Building. By 1936, Sarnoff was promising that TV would be commonplace. Thousands marveled as RCA publicly demonstrated TV at the World's Fair in 1939. On Tuesday the 1st of July 1941, W2XBS became WNBT on Channel 1 with a Dodgers game and a Lowell Thomas newscast and a couple of game shows. A CBS station went on the air the same day. Commercial TV — available to 4,000 receivers in New York City — had arrived.

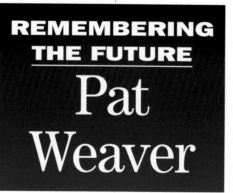

REMEMBERING THE FUTURE

Pat Weaver

World War II interrupted further development. In the Pacific, Sarnoff's son Robert met Navy skipper Pat Weaver.

AFTER THE WAR, RCA began selling a 10-inch set for $375. In January 1948, Sarnoff's NBC had stations in New York, Schenectady, Philadelphia and Washington and was looking toward Chicago. In May, Time magazine pronounced TV "inevitable." In August, NBC and CBS and DuMont covered the presidential conventions. In January 1949, 10 million Americans watched Truman's inauguration. By this time, NBC's Milton Berle owned Tuesday night in every TV household.

It was at this point that Weaver, formerly associated with comedian Fred Allen and Lucky Strike's "Your Hit Parade," moved into position, via his friend Bob Sarnoff, as postwar America's most influential TV executive. Weaver had nothing against the popular entertainments per se. The first thing he did was lure to the little blue screen such radio stars as Bob Hope, Martin and Lewis, Jimmy Durante, Red Skelton, Ed Wynn and Kate Smith. In February 1950, he launched what would become an American Saturday night institution, the 90-minute "Your Show of Shows," starring Sid Caesar and Imogene Coca. By September 1951, NBC claimed seven of TV's top 10 programs.

After that, on Monday the 14th of January 1952, Weaver invented early morning network TV with

Dave Garroway's "Today," a genial two-hour magazine that, like "Your Show of Shows," advertisers could buy pieces of but could not own outright. Over sponsors' protests that Weaver, the old Lucky Strike pitchman, was diminishing their control over programming, "Today" became a huge moneymaker, TV's biggest success, daily fare for 10 million viewers. Having won the awakening family, Weaver next went after the tykes with Miss Frances' groundbreaking "Ding Dong School" in December 1952, the housewife with Arlene Francis' afternoon "Home" in March 1954 and, finally, the night owls with Steve Allen's "Tonight" in October 1954.

At the same time, he was developing NBC's "spectaculars" — glittering specials like "Babes in Toyland" at Christmas 1954 and Mary Martin's "Peter Pan" in March 1955, and he was demanding more and more culturally ambitious material from his producers. He created the distinguished documentary series "Wide Wide World." He began to televise long conversations with such personages as architect Frank Lloyd Wright.

And in the end, he proved too elegant for a practical business that increasingly found itself confronting too much evidence that the freshly minted uncommon man, for all his new cosmology, really did prefer, say, "Gunsmoke" over, say, Frank Lloyd Wright. In September 1956, Weaver and NBC parted company.

BACK IN ADVERTISING, Weaver nonetheless remained the TV industry's principal conscience. In 1962, a year after Federal Communications Commission chief Newton Minow famously scathed TV as a "vast wasteland," he predicted that new UHF stations carrying blue-chip programs would someday smother the networks. "If you don't keep the elite audience, the medium is going to be devalued," he warned. Soon, in California, he was running the nation's first pay TV service, offering the Bolshoi Ballet and the Vienna Philharmonic. "We are not in the discipline of the big-audience, flow-of-audience, length-of-viewing-time equation," he said, Weaveresquely. "Either this is the time for this to happen or it isn't."

It wasn't. Theater owners with political pull lobbied hard, and in November 1964 voters outlawed pay TV, shutting down what Weaver mourned as "the greatest communications innovation of our lifetime." Two years later, the California Supreme Court ruled the '64 referendum unconstitutional. But by then the pay service was broke.

ESSAYING FOR The New York Times in September 1976, sneering at the season's TV offerings, the father of modern television stubbornly clung to his heretical notion that someday there would be dozens of interest-specific channels in every home. "The air belongs to us," he wrote. "The temporary franchises will not hold when the public finds that better television is available to them under new arrangements."

By BILL BELL
Daily News Staff Writer

THE BIG MOMENT of the fifth annual Emmy Awards program in Los Angeles in February 1953 was the crowning of television's Most Outstanding Personality of the year, and of course the favorite was Lucille Ball, whose "I Love Lucy" was America's No. 1 program. Other candidates were Arthur Godfrey, Jimmy Durante, Edward R. Murrow, Donald O'Connor, Adlai Stevenson — and Fulton J. Sheen.

Sheen, the New York priest who starred in the unlikeliest of TV hits, a folksy, inspirational, weekly 30-minute prime-time program called "Life Is Worth Living," beat out Lucy and all the other big stars. "I want to pay tribute to my writers," he said. "Matthew, Mark, Luke and John."

At 57, Bishop Sheen had been a New York favorite for years, preaching a Lent sermon every year at St. Patrick's majestic cathedral, and for several years, the Good Friday service at St. Agnes Church in midtown Manhattan. There, he was so popular that E. 43rd St. between Third and Lexington Aves. was closed by thousands who listened over outside loudspeakers. Now TV had made him a household name from coast to coast.

For five seasons, starting in 1952, Sheen hosted "Life," a one-man, no-frills show with an unchanging format — Sheen seated at a desk, dressed in priestly garb, a blackboard behind him, telling little jokes and calling for a return to religious values. "God love you," he would always conclude.

He started on the old DuMont network, then moved to ABC and every year competed against the other networks' biggest draws — Ball, Groucho Marx, Gene Autry, Red Skelton and Milton Berle.

"Uncle Fultie" even inspired a memorable crack by "Uncle Miltie," who was sponsored by the Texaco petroleum company. "We both work for the same sponsor — Sky Chief," Berle said.

Sheen's program never ranked among any season's top 25, but it attracted its share of viewers and even beat Berle on a couple of occasions. At its peak, it was carried on 123 TV ABC stations and more than 300 ABC radio stations.

The secret, if there was one, was the simplicity of Sheen's message, and its contrast to the slapstick and corn on rival channels. Sheen was dramatic, with deep, hypnotic eyes, dark hair combed straight back from a high forehead, and a speaking style honed by years of practice and elocution lessons.

The show was an extension of his job as national director of the Society for the Propagation of the Faith, the chief Vatican fund-raiser for overseas missions. He never appealed for money on the air, but money poured in anyway — from viewers and sponsors, including the appliance giant Admiral Corp., which paid the society $16,500 a week for his services.

Sheen already was the star of a weekly national network radio show, "The Catholic Hour," with a following of millions, when he arrived in New York in 1950 to become an auxiliary (assistant) bishop to Francis Cardinal Spellman.

Spellman's decision to bring Sheen to New York surprised a lot of people who thought the cardinal could not work with the popular, articulate priest, and it indeed was a wary relationship. Eventually, the two men clashed over Sheen's image and control of the missions' treasury. Their dispute became so heated that Sheen reportedly argued his case in Rome, and won.

Sheen was no stranger in New York. In 1926, he preached the Good Friday sermon at St. Agnes Church for the first time, and created a sensation. In 1940, he led the first televised religious service.

Over the years, as "The Catholic Hour" and his own reputation grew, he became celebrated for his high-profile conversions to Catholicism of, among others, playwright Clare Boothe Luce, columnist Heywood Broun, Henry Ford II, and perhaps most

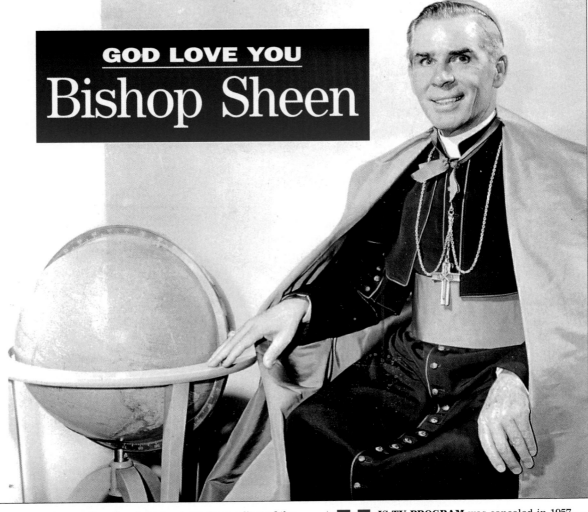

GOD LOVE YOU

Bishop Sheen

sensationally of all, Louis Budenz, editor of the Daily Worker, the newspaper of the American Communist Party.

Sheen's life was charmed, and he knew it.

HE WAS BORN Peter Sheen in El Paso, Ill., son of a well-to-do farmer. At age 12, he added John to his name at his coming-of-age Confirmation rite, and subsequently adopted his mother's maiden name, Fulton, as his own.

He never thought of any career but the priesthood. After graduating with an arts degree from St. Viator's College in Kankakee, Ill., he entered the seminary and was ordained in 1919.

His superiors, singling him out for bigger things, sent him to Catholic University, in Washington, then to Belgium and Rome for further study. One early honor came at the University of Louvain, Belgium, where he received the Cardinal Mercier Prize for philosophy, the first time that the prize went to an American.

Sheen had set out to improve his speaking skills while at Catholic University by signing up for off-campus courses in elocution. A class in "voice culture" required him to practice speaking in various styles — one moment chatty, the next thunderous or dramatic and tremulous.

But he did not start speaking outside the pulpit until 1925, when he was assigned to a church in a rundown neighborhood in London. There, he began a series of debates with European philosophy teachers, and his abilities were quickly noted back home.

A year later, he was summoned to Peoria, Ill., to work in a parish church. His superiors, it turned out, had plans for Sheen, but first they wanted to test his humility by taking him out of the spotlight.

The parish appointment lasted one year. Then his bishop told him that he had been appointed a philosophy teacher at his old alma mater, Catholic U. It was a job that permitted him to return to Europe every summer for lectures, a schedule that he kept until the outbreak of war in 1939.

HIS TV PROGRAM was canceled in 1957 — by now, he was competing with Danny Thomas and the "Twenty-One" quiz show — but he returned four years later with his syndicated "The Bishop Sheen Program," which lasted until 1966.

That year, at Spellman's urging, the Vatican appointed Sheen bishop of the relatively obscure upstate diocese of Rochester — a stunning move that removed him from the national spotlight for the first time in more than 30 years.

He was almost immediately embroiled in controversies, starting with a dispute involving the Eastman Kodak Co.'s racial and ethnic-minority hiring practices. Sheen sided with black community leaders demanding more jobs. Another firestorm came when he offered to give a church and its rectory to the government as a home for the poor. With even his priests opposing the move, he withdrew the offer.

"I do not follow traditional methods," he said, "except in the faith."

In 1969, the Vatican announced that Sheen was retiring. It also named him an archbishop, but placed him in honorary charge of a fictional diocese — the long-inactive see of Newport, Wales.

Sheen returned to New York, where he resumed his preaching and writing. He turned down a TV offer on grounds it would involve too much travel. His final major address was the Good Friday service at St. Agnes in 1979.

When the newly elected Pope John Paul visited New York that fall, he said he wanted to meet Sheen, and the two men embraced at St. Patrick's Cathedral. Weeks later, Sheen was dead, apparently of a heart attack, in his three-room East Side apartment.

Five cardinals, 56 bishops, 90 priests and more than 2,000 mourners, among them evangelist Billy Graham, Gov. Hugh Carey and Mayor Ed Koch, attended the funeral Mass at St. Pat's.

Then his body was interred in the cathedral's crypt. He was only the eighth person laid to rest there, and the only one who was not a New York bishop or cathedral rector.

By RICHARD E. MOONEY
Special to The News

WILLIAM GRIFFITH WILSON was born Nov. 26, 1895, in — was it fate? — a room behind the bar at his family's inn in East Dorset, Vt. Countless gallons of booze later, as "Bill W.," he and a fellow alcoholic would start Alcoholics Anonymous — but not before he got so falling-down drunk one night that he couldn't put the key in the lock on the front door of his house in Brooklyn. His long-suffering wife, Lois, found him when she left for work in the morning, out cold in the basement entryway, bleeding from a gash in his head.

Bill hadn't had a drink for five weeks, but couldn't resist a bartender's offer of a free Scotch on that Armistice Day in 1934.

"I went back to drinking," he said later, "one, two, three bottles of gin a day. I could not stop, and I knew it."

So, for the fourth time in a year, he entered the Towns Hospital on Central Park West, where John Barrymore and other notables dried out and where doctors told Lois "I was hopeless."

But one night in the hospital something happened, a spiritual experience.

"Suddenly, the room lit up with a great white light," he said. "I was caught up into an ecstasy which there are no words to describe."

A lifelong agnostic, he left the hospital on Dec. 18, joined a nondenominational Christian movement called the Oxford Group and never drank again.

Five months later he came perilously close. He was in Akron, Ohio, for a business deal that collapsed. Alone, pacing the hotel lobby on Saturday afternoon, hearing giggles and the clink of ice in the bar, he craved the solace of a drink. Instead, he found the name of a minister and phoned him.

The minister referred him to Henrietta Seiberling, of the Goodyear Tire Seiberlings, who was active in the Oxford Group. She told him to come right over, then rang up Dr. Robert Smith, a friend whose heavy drinking worried her. The doctor had passed out. He couldn't come until the next day. But when they met on Sunday — Mother's Day 1935 — Bill W. and Dr. Bob talked for hours.

The doctor drank his last on June 10. To this day, recovering alcoholics celebrate it as the day AA began.

NAN ROBERTSON, in her book, "Getting Better: Inside Alcoholics Anonymous," observes that "there had to be two [founders], because the essence of the process is one person telling his story to another as honestly as he knows how." Starting with those two middle-age men, membership has grown to something like 2 million — men and women, young and old, pursuing recovery through AA's 12-step program in about 150 countries.

As a young man, Bill already had developed an unhealthy appetite for fame and applause. He fantasized he would make a great industrialist. But drink determined differently. He drank to excess from the start — as a newly commissioned second lieutenant about to sail for Europe during World War I.

Waiting for orders in New Bedford, Mass., he went to a social affair for young officers. Robert Thomsen's book "Bill W." describes the scene. Bill wasn't a drinker and was so uncomfortable that he was about to slip out the door when a hostess handed him a glass and lifted hers in a toast.

"This is something new," she said. "A Bronx cocktail."

"I felt so self-conscious that I simply had to take that drink," Bill would recall. "So I took it. And another. And then — the miracle! That strange barrier between me and everyone else seemed to vanish. What rare magic those first three or four drinks produced!"

Back home after the war, he launched into business in the big city, lured by visions of riches on Wall Street. Puzzled by people who put money in the market blindly — it was the 1920s — he set out on his own after a few years, on a Harley-Davidson, with Lois in the sidecar, a tent and a set of Moody's manuals. He investigated companies from New York to Florida for a year, and sold his findings to investors for a good price. One reason Lois went along was to get Bill away from bars. Lois herself was later a co-founder of Al-Anon, for the wives of alcoholics — a program similar to but wholly separate from AA.

Returning to New York, he made his mark as a margin trader.

"For the next few years, fortune threw applause my way. I had arrived."

But the '29 crash wiped him out. Lois went to work at Macy's, and Bill picked up jobs around Wall Street, then drank himself out of each one

He was finally steered to sobriety by the combined influence of a friend who had sobered up in the Oxford Group and a doctor at the Towns Hospital who thought alcoholism was an obsessive disease — and finally that moment when "the room lit up." His obsessiveness then propelled him into lecturing other drunks, but he failed to persuade a single sot until he found Dr. Bob.

Two lanky 6-footers, Bill would be the idea man, the talker, the booster, while Dr. Bob provided stability, a check on Bill's grandiose schemes. They were no overnight sensation. After two years, they counted only 40 successes, but that was good enough. It was 40 lives rescued, proving the program worked.

FOR FOUR YEARS they were nameless. "Alcoholics Anonymous" came from the title of the first of four books Bill wrote about their program, published in 1939. Bill had considered titling it "The Wilson Movement" — his irrepressible ego again. AAs know it as as the Big Book, 500-plus pages of how the program works, with more than three dozen real-life stories about people who hit bottom and came back — some as sloppy as Bowery bums, like Bill, and others more fastidious but nevertheless compulsive.

The book sold slowly until 1941, when a cover story about the program in the popular Saturday Evening Post magazine put AA on the map. Membership leaped to 8,000 from 1,500 in one year. The Big Book, which goes for $6, is in its third edition and 67th printing. More than 15 million copies have been sold.

AA was thriving, but the Wilsons were not. They scraped by on Lois' department-store salaries while living in her family's house at 182 Clinton St. in Brooklyn Heights. Just when the Big Book came out, the bank foreclosed on their mortgage.

"We didn't even have enough to pay the movers," Bill wrote in one of his books.

Their furniture went into hock while they bounced from friend to friend. When AA got its first clubhouse on W. 24th St., they squeezed into rooms upstairs.

Then a woman whose husband had been an alcoholic offered them a house she had fixed up in suburban Bedford Hills — for $6,500 and monthly payments of $40. They dubbed it Stepping Stones and lived there the rest of their lives. It is now a historic site and home of the Stepping Stones Foundation.

Bill finally had income from book sales. While the books were published anonymously, he shed his personal anonymity for lectures and newspaper interviews. But he shunned Yale's offer of an honorary degree and a Time magazine offer to put him on the cover, showing the back of his head.

When he died of emphysema in 1971, there were memorial services all over the world. At the Cathedral of St. John the Divine, one speaker alluded to the fact that hundreds, maybe thousands of churches provided space for recovering alcoholics to share their "experience, strength and hope" at AA meetings. "Bill believed the wisdom of AA came out of church basements," he said, "not from the pulpit."

GREAT WHITE LIGHT
Bill W.

By PETER GRANT
Daily News Staff Writer

BETTER HOMES AND GARDENS
Sam LeFrak

SAM LEFRAK built not grand Manhattan spires but stodgy mid-rise apartment buildings in Queens and Brooklyn, and he built them faster and more efficiently than anyone else when the city desperately needed them. For middle-class New Yorkers who suffered through the acute housing shortages of the 1950s and 1960s, volume mattered more than appearance, architecture or height. They needed homes — and Sam LeFrak churned out tens of thousands of them, in places like Bay Ridge, Kings Bay, Forest Hills and Far Rockaway. With an assembly-line approach to building, he developed huge tracts of land, permanently changing the city's landscape, dozens of neighborhoods and the lives of hundreds of thousands of people.

In his signature project, he bought a 40-acre parcel of swampy land along the Long Island Expressway from the Astor estate. On that site, from which once had sprouted Quonset huts for G.I.s returning from World War II, he developed a sprawling complex of 18-story buildings with 5,000 units. Opened in 1961, Lefrak City was New York's largest privately built housing project.

But it was not only his buildings that began to pierce the New York skyline; his feisty, in-your-face personality began to penetrate the city's political, social and media circles as well. Thirty years before a brash young developer named Donald Trump became synonymous with hyperbole, LeFrak was the city's leading expert at the outrageous comment, the grandiose claim, the bold marketing effort.

He said so many times that one in 16 New Yorkers lived in his buildings that this came to be accepted as fact, though there have never been any specifics to back the claim up. When inflation was a worry, he drove his competitors crazy by promising not to raise rents, forcing them to explain why they wouldn't do the same. Reporters could always count on him to ridicule a politician, attack a government program or grandstand for the housing needs of New York's working stiffs.

When the city was hysterical about the loss of the Dodgers, LeFrak offered to help the team stay by building it a low-cost stadium. That proposal didn't work out, but it kept his name in the headlines and his buildings filled.

REAL ESTATE was a natural career choice for him. Like Lewis Rudin, Seymour Durst, Daniel Rose and the other big developers of the postwar years, he came from a family of builders, born Sam small-f Lefrak in 1918. His father, Harry, had started a successful apartment-building business after emigrating to New York in 1900 from Palestine, at the age of 15, with just $4 in his pocket. Young Sam could read blueprints at age eight. He put up his first apartment building, a 120-unit project at 1440 E. 14th St. in the Midwood section of Brooklyn, when he was just 20. Ten years later, in 1948, his father called him into his office and handed him the reins of the Lefrak Organization.

His genius was in mass production, turning out apartment buildings the way Detroit turned out cars. He kept his costs down by buying land and materials in huge quantities. He spent little on architecture, concentrating instead on giving his tenants the most space for the least money. The simple virtue of his units, he liked to explain: "The windows opened and closed. You opened them in the summer and closed them in the winter. Middle-class New Yorkers could afford to live in them and raise families."

This philosophy meshed perfectly with the postwar years. Tens of thousands of discharged soldiers were going to college on the G.I. Bill, starting families and looking for places to live. They wanted something better than the lives they had known in the crowded tenements of the South Bronx, East Harlem and the lower East Side. Now, thanks to their service savings, they could afford it. And, thanks to automobiles that were increasingly available to the masses, they had mobility.

But they had few places to go. The city housing industry had virtually ground to a halt during the Depression. Space was so tight after the war that New York City was one of the few places to maintain wartime rent regulations as they were phased out in the rest of the country. A 1955 report by a blue-ribbon panel appointed by Mayor Robert Wagner declared that shoddy and insufficient housing was the city's most serious physical problem, responsible for a wide range of other social ailments, and called for subsidies and government housing programs.

But with his no-frills philosophy, Sam LeFrak was able to build without any government assistance. His projects mushroomed throughout the 1950s and 1960s, mostly in Brooklyn and Queens, but also in Staten Island, the Bronx, Westchester, Long Island and New Jersey, and he filled them as fast as they went up. Lines often began forming the night before his rental units became available; by the end of the next day, they would all be taken.

His formula made him one of the richest men in America, with a net worth surpassing $2 billion by the 1990s, and a gentleman as well, a collector of fine art and an extraordinary number of plaques and medals and honorary degrees. In the early '70s, he changed his name from Lefrak to LeFrak. After he was knighted Commander of the Royal Norwegian Order of Merit, he enjoyed referring to himself as Dr. Samuel LeFrak and Sir Samuel LeFrak.

BUT FOR ALL his honors and wealth, LeFrak had difficulty changing with the times. In 1970, his company was slapped with a U.S. Justice Department lawsuit alleging that Lefrak City discriminated against blacks; he eventually settled the case by agreeing not to discriminate. He had an even harder time dealing with the neighborhood opposition and bureaucratic red tape that began slowing down his real estate juggernaut.

By the '70s, community groups were becoming skilled at blocking the zoning changes and permits LeFrak needed to have for his high-volume strategy to work. He had to go to the U.S. Supreme Court to build one 400-unit middle-income project on the border of Kew Gardens and Forest Hills. One of his opponents was a young community lawyer named Mario Cuomo.

LEFRAK'S BIGGEST disappointment always remained his inability to break into big-time development in Manhattan. Most of the other real estate dynasties succeeded in moving across the river from the boroughs. But LeFrak's only office building project was the unremarkable Squibb Building at 40 W. 57th St., built in 1972. He came close to buying a huge portfolio of office buildings that had been developed by the Uris family. But in the end he was outbid by Olympia & York, a Canadian company that went on to become one of the biggest owners of commercial property in the 1980s.

LeFrak had hoped to leave his mark in Manhattan as the lead developer of Battery Park City. But that plan also crumbled. He helped create the 100-acre site out of landfill and built the first apartment buildings on it. But he had a falling out with the Battery Park City Authority in the early 1980s, forcing him to leave the rest of the site to other developers. The fight was partly over building philosophy. LeFrak wanted to stick to his strategy of building for the masses. Authority officials preferred a more upscale development.

Frustrated with his setbacks in New York, he turned his attention to a 400-acre site of decaying railheads and warehouses on the New Jersey side of the Hudson River. Late in the '80s, he announced to the world that he would spend $10 billion to build Newport, a mini-city rivaling Battery Park City.

By 1999, he was well on his way toward achieving that goal. Six apartment towers and three office buildings were close to full occupancy, mostly with tenants who came from Manhattan, and work was under way on a hotel and another office building. At 81, Sam LeFrak was still going strong, and with his son and grandson in the business, there was no reason to think that LeFraks would not continue to build

By DAVID HINCKLEY
Daily News Staff Writer

TOWARD THE END, which everybody figured was the end although of course you couldn't come right out and say it, Mickey Mantle sat patiently and answered all the questions no one ever would have asked him when he was filling their summer afternoons with the soaring arc of baseballs he hit harder and farther than any man since Babe Ruth.

Those days were a quarter of a century gone by the early 1990s, and Mickey Mantle was behind microphones, saying he had checked into the Betty Ford Center because he realized he had a problem with alcohol. He drank too much of it. And with this realization came related contemplations and regrets about how he had lived his life and how he didn't see enough of his children and so on.

No longer was the world arguing whether Mantle of the Yankees was a better center fielder than Mays of the Giants or Snider of the Dodgers, but whether it was right that he be jumped to the top of the list for a liver transplant because he was famous when nonfamous people were just as sure to die without a new one.

And the more the discussion continued, the greater became the distance between this aging, ailing man and the man of whom teammate Jack Reed had once said: "Good night, ole Moses, there was one fine-looking ballplayer. He was so young, so strong, and he looked immaculate in that white Yankee uniform, like he was born to wear it. It always seemed like he could run as fast as he wanted. He could do almost anything he wanted."

The Yankees felt that way too in 1951, when they made him the first player they ever jumped from Class C, deep in the minors, right to the Big Club. Sportswriter Tom Meany watched him in spring training and cracked, "Let's skip the career and send him right to Cooperstown."

He had that effect. Once upon a time, "Mickey Mantle" meant baseball the way "Albert Einstein" meant smart.

"Ah, who d'ya think y'are, Mickey Mantle?"
Even the name was perfect.

FROM 1951 through the last year Mantle was really good, 1964, the Yankees won 12 pennants and seven World Series. He was the best and most glamorous player on the best and most glamorous team.

In 1956 he won the Triple Crown, batting .353 with 52 home runs and 130 runs batted in. In 1957, he batted .365. From 1955 to 1962, he never hit fewer than 30 homers, plus 18 more in the World Series.

He also would, every so often, hit a ball that made the whole sport stop and marvel. A home run he hit in 1953 off Chuck Stobbs of the Washington Senators traveled 565 feet. He twice came within inches of hitting a fair ball out of Yankee Stadium — a feat accomplished by no one, including Ruth.

New York baseball never got better than it got in the early '50s. The Giants were good, the Dodgers were very good and the Yankees were always just a little bit better — except of course in '55. Baseball had not yet been seriously challenged by football or basketball, putting a Jackie Robinson, Willie Mays or Mickey Mantle in the center of the sports stage.

With Casey Stengel, 1954

SO YOUNG, SO STRONG
Mickey Mantle

Hundreds of thousands of little boys from Pearl River to Toms River, from Newark to New Haven, from Fordham Road to Forest Hills, grew up pretending they were Mickey Mantle. Or, in Flatbush, they grew up pretending to strike him out.

Mickey Charles Mantle was born Oct. 20, 1931, in Spavinaw, Okla., to a family whose menfolk worked the zinc and lead mines and dreamed of playing ball. Mick's father Mutt and his grandfather Charles played semipro, and Mickey became their project. Mutt would pitch to him right-handed. Then grandpa would throw to him left-handed. This turned a reluctant Mickey into a switch-hitter, one of the best ever.

By the time he reached high school, he was a solid knot of muscle on his way to 5-feet-11, 185 pounds, with blond hair and an aw-shucks grin.

In high school, he also played basketball and football, where he racked up the first in a lifetime of serious leg injuries. That's why Mutt didn't think he should play football, though the truth was that Mickey never shared his father's exclusionary passion for baseball. As late as his rookie year in the majors, discouraged by a slump, Mickey told Mutt he wanted to quit and had to be shamed out of it.

To the end, Mickey never became obsessive about baseball. His off-season workouts were conducted in a golf cart, which made pulled muscles an annual ritual of his spring training.

But he was known on the Yankees as a good teammate — lots of after-hours fun with running buddies like Whitey Ford and Billy Martin, stoic about pain. Tony Kubek recalled that they'd go to a restaurant and Mantle would need help getting out of the cab. If Mantle didn't start out loving the game, he grew to do so, or at least grew to feel it was part of his life. If he didn't study the game, he learned to play it very well.

In the famous seventh game of the 1960 World Series, Pittsburgh Pirate Bill Mazeroski would never have had to hit his game-winning home run in the last of the ninth were it not for some quick thinking by Mantle in the top of that inning.

The Yankees were trailing by a run with one out, Mantle on first and Gil McDougald on third, when Yogi Berra hit a ground ball to Pittsburgh first baseman Rocky Nelson. Had Nelson thrown to second, then taken the relay back to first, it would have been a double play and Pittsburgh would have won right there. But Nelson stepped on first, meaning Mantle could take the unusual but legal step of returning to first himself — which he did, ducking in safely by an eyelash as the tying run scored.

By the standards of the times, which were not high, Mantle was moderately well compensated. The year he won the Triple Crown, he earned $30,000 from the Yankees and $59,000 from endorsements and appearances — a good haul in the days when an endorsement fee was often a free sample.

Mantle was paid $5,000 for endorsing Batter Up pancake mix. He was paid $2,000 by Wheaties and $2,500 by Viceroy. He was paid $1,000 to appear on the Perry Como show and $2,000 to be interviewed by Jack Lescoulie. He sold the TV rights to his life story to Kraft Foods for $15,000, and he was paid $2,000 to speak a few lines on a silly Teresa Brewer tune called "I Love Mickey."

This didn't make him a financial genius: His investments did poorly enough that one reason he kept playing until 1968 was that he needed the $100,000 the Yankees were finally paying him. It did confirm the mystique of his name.

That mystique was cemented for good by a competition he neither solicited nor won. In 1961, he and teammate Roger Maris were challenging Ruth's record of 60 home runs in a season. Maris, less accustomed than Mantle to the daily spotlight, started to shy away from the press, which responded by painting him as a churl, making Mantle the fair-haired fellow.

Mantle got injured and Maris broke the record. But for the rest of his career, Mantle was cheered pretty much everywhere by pretty much everyone, giving him the legend and the power that went with it. When former teammate Jim Bouton's best-seller, "Ball Four," noted some of Mantle's road pastimes — mild naughty-kid stuff like ogling women and enjoying a drink — Mantle let it be known the Yankees should not invite Bouton to their annual Old-Timers' Day if they wanted Mantle.

They did, of course, and Bouton was out, although by this time it was an accepted part of the Mantle legend — whispered in awe, not condemnation — that several of his 536 career home runs were hit at moments when he could not have passed a Breathalyzer test.

AFTER HE RETIRED, Mantle did a little coaching and broadcasting. He played much golf, and he finally got paid well just for being Mickey Mantle — speaking, shaking hands, signing autographs. He still liked hanging around with pals like Martin, and it was Martin's death in a 1989 car crash, Mantle said, that persuaded him to go for rehab and sobriety.

Soon he was ringing up guys like Bouton, in a kind of fence-mending tour, and confessing to interviewers that he often had behaved with abandon because no male Mantle had lived past 40 and he was convinced he had to cram in his whole life before then.

With that as a goal, he did a pretty fine job. He made it all the way to 63 — and when he died, on Aug. 12, 1995, he took with him many more youths than his own.

By CHRIS ERIKSON
Special to The News

ABOUT THEIR neighbor in Apartment 502, the residents of 252 Fulton St. agreed — Emil Goldfus was a right guy. Like many who lived in this downtown Brooklyn building, Goldfus was an artist; not a great one, maybe, but he filled his $35-a-month studio with his cityscapes, and some of them showed real promise. A slight, soft-spoken fellow with thinning hair and a beaklike nose, he took an interest in his neighbors' work and liked to chat about art world trends and the latest exhibitions.

Not that art was his only field of expertise. Goldfus was a man of many talents. By trade he was a photographer, and he dabbled in radio repair. He was a classical guitarist of some skill and a bookworm who read Einstein for relaxation and was fluent in a number of languages. On a few occasions, when the building's tired old elevator broke down, he pitched in to help super Harry MacMullin fix it, and MacMullin reported that Goldfus knew as much as most engineers.

One tenant, Burt Silverman, became particularly fond of Goldfus. A fellow artist, Silverman found him good-humored and erudite, if a bit reticent, and when Silverman got married he was touched when Goldfus surprised him with a gift.

Everyone was very surprised when, in August 1957, some three years after he had moved in, 55-year-old Goldfus was hauled into the Brooklyn Federal Courthouse, a mere 100 yards from 252 Fulton. He was not Emil Goldfus at all. His name was Rudolf Ivanovich Abel, he was a colonel in the Soviet State Security Service and he was now under indictment for having masterminded an espionage ring from the very building where he had so charmed his neighbors.

FROM HIS STUDIO, the government charged, Abel had served as the hub of a Cold War network of operatives who pilfered U.S. military secrets and delivered them to Moscow. The Kremlin communicated with him via a shortwave radio concealed in his apartment, and he in turn passed along messages to his subordinates using a complex system of codes, couriers and secret drops. The court heard details of covert meetings in Prospect Park in Brooklyn, Fort Tryon Park in upper Manhattan and Penn Station in Newark.

Tales emerged of marks chalked in subway stations, microfilm deposited under park lampposts, notes left in phone booths, large sums of cash buried in the ground for later retrieval. In Abel's apartment, amid the clutter of oil paints and scientific texts, were the tools of his furtive trade: maps, codebooks, the short-wave, hollowed-out cufflinks and coins.

Rudolf Abel was the highest-ranking Soviet spy ever captured in the United States. "This is as professional and intricate an operation as we have ever worked on," said federal prosecutor William Tompkins. Abel's ring, he said, posed "a threat to the whole free world, to civilization and the American people."

THAT RING had begun to come apart the previous May 4, when a man named Reino Hayhanen walked into the U.S. Embassy in Paris with a fantastic yarn.

For five years, Hayhanen announced, he had been a Soviet agent in the United States. His superior was a man he knew only as Mark, with whom he had met regularly in New York, until Mark became displeased with Hayhanen's disturbing appetite for liquor and his attention-drawing disputes with his wife. When Moscow sent word that Hayhanen was to return home, the errant spy wasn't overly eager to go. Duly, he had sailed for France — then headed for the American Embassy instead of traveling on.

The FBI listened with great interest, and soon agents were hot on Mark's trail. Through Hayhanen's information, they tracked their quarry to Brooklyn and then to 252 Fulton. By that time, Emil Goldfus had informed super MacMullin that he was going south for a spell to treat a sinus condition. Actually, he'd only gone across the river, to a cheap hotel room on E. 28th St. There, near daybreak June 21, the FBI closed in and arrested Mark, aka Emil Goldfus, aka Rudolf Ivanovich Abel, master spy.

ABEL WAS held initially as an illegal alien, and he freely admitted having entered the U.S. in 1948 with false documents; Emil Goldfus, it turned out, was a Manhattan child who had died in 1902. Otherwise, he steadfastly refused to answer questions throughout days of interrogation. It later developed that the CIA made a bid at this time to turn him into a double agent, but he didn't want to discuss that either. Of the self-possessed prisoner, CIA Director Allen Dulles said: "I wish we had three or four like him inside Moscow right now."

The trial was fairly quick work. The Soviet Embassy disavowed any knowledge of Abel, so the court appointed lawyer James Donovan to represent him. But, in accordance with Abel's wishes, little in the way of a defense was presented during the nine-day proceedings. No witnesses were called. Abel did not take the stand. With Hayhanen as the star prosecution witness, it took a jury less than four hours to find the defendant guilty. Abel showed no emotion as he was sentenced to 30 years in prison.

BEHIND BARS, Abel passed his time quietly: reading, painting, playing Bach on his guitar. Then, in May 1960, an American U-2 pilot, Francis Gary Powers, was shot down over Russia while on a reconnaissance mission and sentenced to 10 years for spying.

At the prodding of Powers' family, Washington quietly made a barter proposal: a spy for a spy. Donovan was called in to negotiate. And so it was that in February 1962, Donovan accompanied Abel to West Berlin. There, the Russian colonel set out across a bridge connecting West to East — passing Powers midway. As the American flier was reunited with his countrymen, Rudolf Abel disappeared behind the Iron Curtain.

HE LIVED OUT his days in Russia, highly decorated, a people's hero. In 1966, five years before he died of lung cancer, he wrote of his experiences for a Communist youth magazine. "Clean hands, a cool head and a warm heart" were what one needed to be a successful agent, he advised his young readers.

A few months after Abel's release, a Russian courier arrived at the Berlin Wall's Checkpoint Charlie and delivered a package to be sent on to Donovan. Inside were two rare 15th-century German law books, inscribed by Abel to his lawyer: "Please accept them as a mark of my gratitude for all you have done for me." Donovan sent back a gift of his own, a copy of "Strangers on a Bridge," the book he wrote about his encounter with the Soviet spy.

"An intellectual and a gentleman," he called Abel in the book. "As a man, you could not help but like him."

Burt Silverman, the Fulton St. artist, likewise could not erase the warm feelings he held for his former neighbor, even if he had been a threat to the national security. "He was the enemy," Silverman said, "but he was also my friend."

**THE SPY NEXT DOOR
Rudolf Abel**

Pinched by the FBI, August 1957

By JERE HESTER
Daily News Staff Writer

IT WASN'T LONG after the Dodgers and Giants played their last games at Ebbets Field and the Polo Grounds in 1957 that New Yorkers began to feel a nagging emptiness.

Dodger and Giant fans, of course, were predictably forever crushed that the scoundrels Walter O'Malley and Horace Stoneham had uprooted their teams and moved West, leaving the city without a National League club.

But even people who didn't much care for baseball — for that matter, even Yankee fans — sensed something was terribly wrong.

"It used to be," noted Bill Shea, politically connected lawyer and hemophiliac bleeder of Dodger blue, "that the elevator man in my office building couldn't wait for me to arrive every morning. He's a Yankee rooter, and he'd get all over me on some comparison or another. Now, with the Dodgers gone, I don't get a word out of him. He just sulks. It's awful."

Unlike most sulking New Yorkers, Shea was in a position to do something about this situation. Mayor Robert Wagner was worried about his reelection prospects — and Shea was the man Wagner instructed to bring the city another National League team, by any means possible.

So Shea, a strapping, friendly fellow who moved as easily among politicians and millionaires as among elevator men, set out to get the job done — whether that meant swiping a team from another town, fighting owners in Congress or even starting his own league.

Never mind Wagner's political future. Shea understood that what was at stake was a piece of the heart of New York.

"A lot of people don't think sports are important," he said. "I think it's the lifeblood of a city. The teams here are the only thing we agree upon."

WILLIAM ALFRED Shea's own best sport had been basketball. Born in Manhattan on June 21, 1907, he was a standout at George Washington High School and, later, NYU. With a Georgetown law degree in hand, Shea returned to New York, settled in Brooklyn and became a disciple of Democratic leader George McLaughlin, earning a reputation as a lawyer who rarely saw the inside of a courtroom but knew how to work the corridors of power. Among those he advised was Wagner, who didn't need anyone to tell him what a huge blow it was for two teams to suddenly skip town after nearly three-quarters of a century.

The Dodgers were the soul of Brooklyn, and after years of "Wait till next year," had only just won their first World Series in 1955, beating the hated Yankees. The Giants had captured their last championship in 1954, led by Willie Mays, who was shaping up to be possibly the greatest all-around player ever — maybe even the best center fielder in New York, it was posited during streetcorner debates.

Still, O'Malley found Los Angeles real estate too lucrative a prospect to pass up, and Stoneham followed the same dollar trail to San Francisco. By then, Shea was already a behind-the-scenes player in the baseball business, thanks to his

relationship with McLaughlin, who had been the one-time administrator of the Dodgers and had waged a secret, last-ditch effort to buy the Giants for $2 million.

During the negotiations with Stoneham, Shea had met with Parks Commissioner Robert Moses to discuss moving the Giants to a new ballpark Moses had unsuccessfully dangled before O'Malley: a state-of-the-art stadium to be built on landfill in Flushing, Queens, near the site of the 1939 World's Fair and the upcoming 1964 edition.

With his mandate from Wagner, Shea's first course of action was to attempt to lure a National League club to New York. Initially, he focused on the struggling Philadelphia Phillies, the Pittsburgh Pirates and the Cincinnati Reds — then abandoned these efforts after deciding that transplanting an out-of-town team would be "a terrible thing."

Expansion, so far as National League President Warren Giles was concerned, was out. There had been eight clubs in each league since 1900, and, postwar boom or not, it was going to stay that way.

Besides, Giles had been a big cheerleader behind the Dodgers' and Giants' defections. "Who needs New York?" he chuckled.

This attitude did not sit well with fans. A nice old lady cornered Giles in a hotel lobby one day and gave him hell. "I don't like you," she shouted at the flabbergasted baseball man. "You took the Giants and Dodgers out of New York and put them in dirty old California."

Shea's response to Giles and the baseball establishment was no less blunt: If you don't want us, he said, we'll create a league of our own. "We cannot wait any longer," he declared in late 1958. "We are convinced New York cannot get along without another major league baseball team.

"This country has grown too big for the entire framework of the major leagues to consist of 16 franchises, just as it did 58 years ago," he said. "How tight can a monopoly be?"

He was about to find out.

SOON SHEA LINED up about $100 million from rich folks all over the country; in New York, racing heiress Joan Payson signed on as a backer.

The new Continental League was to be headed by beloved old Branch Rickey, the man who had made history by signing Jackie Robinson for the Dodgers. Baseball owners agreed publicly to work with Shea, but it turned out they didn't much mean it.

So, in the summer of 1959, Shea went to Sen. Estes Kefauver of Tennessee, who headed the antitrust subcommittee, and at this point the owners started to worry. Thanks to a 1922 U.S. Supreme Court decision, the National Pastime had been exempt from antitrust laws. This propped up the so-called reserve clause, allowing owners to trade players at will and forbid them from becoming free agents. But now Shea was talking war.

"I don't believe they'd dare sue us if we raided them for players," he said. "They know they wouldn't have a leg to stand on. The reserve clause in a player's contract isn't worth the paper it's written on."

In May 1960, Kefauver upped the ante with a bill that would limit each team to control over a mere 100 players. Three months later, the owners gave up: The major leagues would absorb four teams from the Continental League — including the New York Metropolitan Baseball Club, nicknamed the Mets.

SHEA NOW SET out to build a stadium on the former Corona Dumps, calling for a grandiose ballpark with an unheard-of retractable dome. "If I have my way, it will be the finest in the world," he said. The Board of Estimate approved the new $27 million stadium in January 1962. Shea didn't get the dome he wanted, but, at Wagner's insistence, he got the park named after him. "There would have never been a stadium if it hadn't been for Bill," Wagner said. "It would probably still be a parking lot."

In April, the Mets moved into the Polo Grounds and began playing some of the worst baseball ever exhibited. The fans didn't seem to mind.

On April 16, 1964, Shea baptized Shea Stadium, ceremoniously pouring onto the infield one bottle of water from the Harlem River and another from Brooklyn's fetid Gowanus Canal. "You couldn't see the Gowanus from Ebbets Field, but you could always smell it," he said.

The next day, a crowd of 50,312 watched the Mets play their first game at the House That Shea Built. While the adults grumbled about the record traffic jam and the Mets' loss, younger eyes — many of which had never witnessed the Dodgers or Giants — saw only a field of dreams.

"Oh, daddy, daddy, it's beautiful," one little boy cried.

BILL SHEA continued his Opening Day tradition of presenting a horseshoe floral arrangement to the Mets' manager until he was felled by a stroke in the late 1980s. He died in his sleep at age 84 on Oct. 3, 1991, three days before the end of the Mets' 30th season.

In 1997, Mets management announced plans for a new stadium — complete with a retractable dome and modeled after Ebbets Field. While there were calls to name the park after Jackie Robinson, it appeared likely that the naming rights eventually would go to the highest corporate bidder.

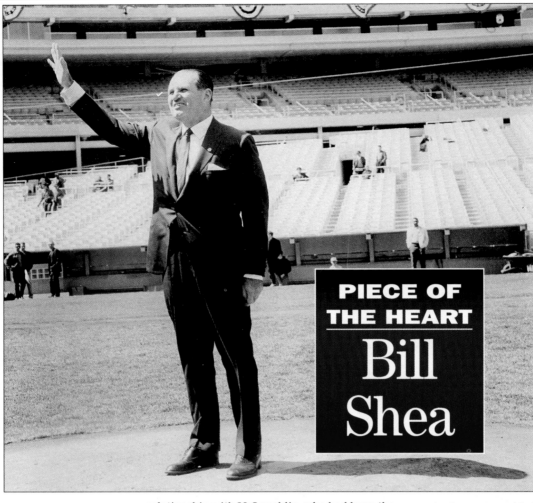

PIECE OF THE HEART
Bill Shea

By DAVID HINCKLEY
Daily News Staff Writer

"I would say I wouldn't know, but I would say the reason why they'd want it passed is to keep baseball going as the highest baseball sport that has gone into baseball, and from the baseball angle — I'm not going to speak of any other sports, I'm not in here to argue about other sports, I'm in the baseball business — it's been cleaner than any baseball business that was ever put out in the hundred years at the present time."
— **Casey Stengel, explaining to the U.S. Senate anti-trust subcommittee why baseball's anti-trust exemption should be continued, July 9, 1958**

WHEN PITTSBURGH Pirates second baseman Bill Mazeroski hit a baseball out of Forbes Field late on the afternoon of Oct. 13, 1960, winning the decisive Game 7 of the World Series for the Pirates over the New York Yankees, it left 70-year-old Yankee manager Charles Dillon (Casey) Stengel with seven world championships in 12 years. This was a record deemed extraordinary by all but Yankee management, which for reasons mildly unclear, seized the aftermath of Mazeroski's home run as an opportunity to put the old gent out to pasture.

They arranged a press conference at which Stengel was to announce his voluntary departure, suggesting that between his baseball achievements and his oil and real estate investments, he was ready to savor the kind of well-deserved retirement ordinarily associated with champion racehorses. Instead, Stengel, gnarled and stooped, stepped to the microphone and said he'd been fired.

"I was told my services would not be desired any longer with this ball club," he said. "I had not much of an argument." This pretty much killed any chance of a ceremonial position with the Yankee organization. It also tipped the last domino in the personal Stengel legend. Two years later, when the Mets came to New York, a still-irritated Stengel signed on to manage them, well aware that he was moving from one of the finest baseball teams ever to one of the worst.

In truth, the original Mets were barely even *that* good — memorable in baseball history mostly for the things an exasperated Stengel said about them. ("Can't anybody here play this game?") Still, misery somehow rendered both manager and team ever more lovable, and Stengel stayed in the dugout until he broke a hip in July 1965 and retired for real — making the Mets the bookend for his 53 years in Major League Baseball.

He played his first game in 1912 as an outfielder with the Brooklyn Robins, who finished 58-95, 46 games out of first place. His 1965 Mets finished 50-112, 47 games out of first place. So in 53 years, he had slipped only one game. As Stengel could have said, some guys lose two games in a day, if they play a doubleheader.

CASEY STENGEL may or may not have been a great baseball mind. Joe DiMaggio and Mickey Mantle thought so. Others did. What all agreed is that he was a great baseball character — and unlike, say, Yogi Berra, he was entirely self-designed. Casey Stengel wrote his own material.

"Greg Goosen is a fine young man who's 19, and in 10 years he has a chance to be 29," Stengel said of one Mets prospect.

"He looks like the greatest hitter in the world,"

April 1962: Waiting for the Mets to win something, anything

THE BASEBALL ANGLE
Casey Stengel

Stengel said of Yankee infielder Jerry Lumpe, "until you send him up to bat."

If issuing this type of public performance review didn't always ingratiate him with his players, he had a line for that, too: "The secret to good managing is to keep the five guys who hate you away from the five guys who are undecided."

Charles Stengel was born in Kansas City, Mo., in 1890 and went on to become a respectable major leaguer, racking up a .284 average over a 14-year career and hitting two game-winning home runs in the 1923 World Series. He also racked up a reputation for a hot temper — after he started a fight against the Phillies one afternoon, police had to escort him off the field — and the more useful reputation for colorful conversation.

He would later refine this into Stengelese, a unique blend of contorted syntax and impenetrable references that established him as baseball's resident grandpa, the old codger who seemed to be speaking in tongues right up until the very last word, when it became clear he knew exactly where he was going all along and all that gibberish actually made sense if you could just crack the code.

There wasn't much anyone could say, though, about his first two major league managing jobs in the 1930s: three years and three second-division finishes in Brooklyn, six years and six more second-division finishes in Boston.

Instead, he honed his skills at diversion. When writers got tired of reporting on his inept pitchers, he gave them better stories that would become cornerstones of the Stengel mythos. In his first game back in Ebbets Field after the Dodgers traded him in 1918, he lifted his cap and a sparrow fluttered out.

Since the average baseball player had trouble with words of more than one syllable, grateful writers helped keep Stengel on the baseball screen while he spent the 1940s managing in the minors. He won three championships there, but when the Yankees tapped him in 1949 to manage the best team in baseball, it was still an act widely seen as roughly the equivalent of Groucho Marx getting a major-party nomination for president.

It was also widely seen as payback. When Stengel was knocking around Worcester of the Eastern League in the early '30s, he struck up a friendship with baseball executive George Weiss. Come 1949, Weiss was president of the Yankees — a fact Stengel, in his first press conference, testily called pure coincidence: "I didn't get this job through friendship. They don't hand out jobs like this because they like your company."

The ranks of the doubters had diminished 12 seasons later, after those seven world championships and 10 American League pennants. Even those who didn't think Stengel had mystic insight agreed he had a passion for the game and that, unlike many managers, he was unintimidated by the fact his players were good. This was, after all, a guy who had played against Ty Cobb, Babe Ruth and Walter Johnson.

"So what if DiMaggio doesn't talk to me," Stengel said around 1950. "He doesn't get paid to talk to me, and I don't either."

THAT ANSWER also illustrated his ability to sidestep whatever question a sportswriter was really asking — though Stengel often said things just because he appreciated a good one-liner. When he went to the mound one time to remove a Yankee pitcher from a game and the pitcher asked why, Casey swept his arm toward the stands and said, "Up there, people are beginning to talk."

So it all worked out. Casey Stengel did with the Yankees what he would have done with other teams if he'd had the horses: He shuffled them in and out to take advantage of each player's strength, oblivious to their complaints. By jabbing at the players with his sharp tongue, he took heat off the Yankees' famously cheap front office. His crusty old codger act even softened the rock-hard and stone-cold image of the hated Yankees.

Stengel said he thought about baseball 24 hours a day. Evidence suggests that's not entirely true: He was shrewd enough at business that, after the Yankees fired him, he was given a directorship at a California bank.

Presumably he did not speak Stengelese at bank board meetings. But then, the great ones pick their spots. If Stengel didn't like a TV reporter, he would politely answer that reporter's question right up until he got to his point, when he would insert a rank obscenity that rendered the footage unusable.

Casey Stengel died in 1975, after a good and full 85-year run, and while the private Casey may not have been as wise or lovable as his public persona, few had the heart or saw any need for a reassessment of his life and work, which pretty much spoke for themselves.

By C.J. SULLIVAN
Special to The News

ON WARM summer nights, the kid would stroll up Crotona Ave., and in the hum of the traffic he would hear the song of the city. Buying mortadella and peppers at Joe's Grocery, he heard the tarantellas of Italy. In Tally's pool hall, the old janitor taught him the blues of Big Bill Broonzy. All over the radio there were Hank Williams and Fats Domino. Outside Crazy Tony's candy store on 187th St., he watched the older kids combing their hair and laying down doo-wop harmonies.

Flash forward: Feb. 2, 1959, Clear Lake, Iowa. The barnstorming rock 'n' roll tour is called The Winter Dance Party, and the four finger-popping boys from the Bronx, wearing pimp boots and nylon shirts and slick suits like these heartland kids have never seen before, are fourth on the bill behind Buddy Holly, Richie Valens and The Big Bopper. Dion and the Belmonts, they're called; they've had a couple of hit records, but they're not yet so big that the lead singer, 19-year-old Dion DiMucci, is really sure he wants to come up with the $35 when Holly asks if he wants to come along on a charter flight to the next show. Thirty-five dollars is the monthly rent Dion's folks pay for their second-story walkup back home at 749 E. 183rd St.

Dion and the Belmonts take the bus to North Dakota. Buddy and Richie and the Bopper board the plane and disappear into the sky.

Warm summer nights in the Bronx. The kid had a hock-shop guitar, and he was singing in bars like Ermondo's on Fordham Road across from Bronx Park, Hank and Fats and Little Richard; later he added doo-wop to the act, Flamingos, Moonglows, Five Satins, and on 187th St. he was watching three of the best harmonizers in the neighborhood. Carlo Mastrangelo, Fred Milano and Angelo D'Aleo called themselves the Belmonts, after Belmont Ave., and Dion would jump in and join them on their stoop and the crowds would gather around beneath the stars, and the warm summer nights seemed like they'd never end.

IN THOSE DAYS, particularly when it came to rock 'n' roll, which was cheap and easy, it didn't take much to sign a singer or produce a record. In 1957, Dion met a kid named Phil Noto, who was trying to make it as a songwriter in the city. Noto introduced him to Bob and Gene Schwartz, a couple of crew-cut, bow-tied accountants who had just started a company called Mohawk Records.

The brothers were so square that they bought a Brill Building tune called "The Chosen Few," which was scored by Hugo Montenegro, and they had Dion sing it with a barbershop group called the Timberlanes. It became a small hit in Boston, but Dion now had a better idea: Why didn't he bring down the Belmonts and let the Schwartzes hear what the real deal of Bronx doo-wop

Fred, Carlo, Dion, Angelo

PURE BRONX SOUL

Dion and The Belmonts

sounded like?

The next day, Dion and the Belmont Ave. guys crashed into the Mohawk offices with a bag of sandwiches, chowed down, wiped the crumbs off their mouths and kicked into their street-corner act. The astonished Schwartzes signed them on the spot, then found them a song. The new group practiced it everywhere — on the corner, on rooftops, in hallways, on the downtown D train. They always loved the D train. It had great bass acoustics.

In the spring of '58, backed by session musicians from the Apollo Theatre's house band, Dion and the Belmonts cut one of rock 'n' roll's classic singles, "I Wonder Why," in three takes at the Allegro studios. It was two minutes and 14 seconds of pure Bronx soul, and it stayed on the charts for three months, almost making the Top 20.

The Bronx kids were elated, spraying "The Belmonts" across the backs of their black leather jackets, running up the street kicking and screaming. Other people in the neighborhood weren't all that impressed. It seemed to them that the boys had done the song better on the corner.

AFTER THAT, there was a bigger hit, called "No One Knows," and then, in the spring of '59, a smash million-seller, "A Teenager In Love." Dion bought a White Plains home for his folks and a silver T-bird for himself, and he would drive his car to the White Castle and acknowledge the cheers. The one-time Fordham Daggers gang kid had made good. His picture was all over the teen magazines.

But he was getting itchy already. He'd always

been the group's driving force; he'd always had to force the Belmonts to get out of bed to rehearse. They were just knock-around neighborhood guys, he was deciding, guys who got lucky and didn't aspire to much more than enjoying the ride. Yokels, he figured. Spaghetti eaters. Tomato sauce on their shirts. Dion planned on being a star, a big one. In early 1960, the group's remake of the old ballad "Where or When" hit No. 3 on the charts. Then and ever since, that record has been widely considered a masterpiece, but Dion hated the thing.

Mohawk was Laurie Records now, and all the company wanted from Dion and the Belmonts were ballads — "When You Wish Upon a Star," "In the Still of the Night." Dion was fed up with the label's small-time outlook, sick of the Belmonts' simple ways. He was ready to move on, in the world he continued to live in once fate decreed that he would not board an airplane with Buddy and Richie and The Big Bopper.

LATE IN 1960, Dion went solo — sticking with Laurie for a while, later jumping to a $5 million deal with Columbia — and began a series of attempts to kick a heroin habit that had been part of his life for several years. On their own, the Belmonts continued a modestly successful career for a time; Dion himself, with huge hits like "Runaround Sue" and "The Wanderer" and "Ruby Baby," turned into one of the hottest acts of the early '60s. The roaring machismo of his best stuff was exactly what every Bronx kid wanted to believe he felt. Bobby Darin told Dion he was creating a whole new sound, Bronx Blues.

By '64, particularly given the heroin, the best of those early days were pretty much over for Dion. Clean again, he had another hit in 1968, "Abraham, Martin and John," as his career took folkier directions, and in June 1972 he reunited with the original Belmonts for a memorable concert at Madison Square Garden. *Din din din din din din.* For an instant it was 1958 all over again, a warm summer night in New York City.

By DAVID HINCKLEY
Daily News Staff Writer

T IS PERHAPS assumed by some that because their lives were never the same after they saw the Beatles on Ed Sullivan's television show in February 1964, the night must have had a similar effect on Sullivan, the campy old-timer whose role was to book them, introduce them and dive for cover as history roared past.

In fact, Sullivan's attitude that night — after a truly bad week in which all his show preparation routines had been knocked silly by the commotion surrounding these fine young lads — was better reflected by an exchange close to showtime with Beatles manager Brian Epstein.

Said Epstein: "I would like to know the exact wording of your introduction."

Replied Ed: "I would like you to go away."

Ed Sullivan had seen bigger than the Beatles and tougher than Epstein, and while he enjoyed a niche in history as much as the next man, he knew his legacy did not depend on the Beatles any more than it had depended on Elvis Presley, for whom 80% of TV-owning Americans tuned in CBS in the fall of '56.

No, Ed's legacy was the show, because it was the show that went on, and so, for 23 years, he kept alive one of the grandest legacies of American entertainment, the true variety pack, and along the way he helped make television an entity on which America came to depend.

From June 20, 1948, to June 6, 1971, through the Red Scare, the space race, the assassination of a president, the fall of the Edsel, the civil rights movement and the Dodgers leaving Brooklyn, Daily News columnist Ed Sullivan was on television at 8 o'clock every Sunday night.

Whoever was hot that week, the show went on. If you didn't like the bear riding the unicycle or the acrobat with the flaming torch or Gogi Grant waving her hands to "The Wayward Wind," wait five minutes and Ed would bring out a Russian folk troupe or the cast of "South Pacific."

Sonny Liston, who had just demolished Floyd Patterson for the heavyweight title, came on to skip rope. Charles Laughton read the Bible. Irving Berlin and Walt Disney made their TV debuts on the Sullivan show, which began as "Toast of the Town" and by public consent became "The Ed Sullivan Show" in September 1955.

While Ed insisted fiercely that his show was not vaudeville, his signature guests included ventriloquist Señor Wences, with the box that held the puppet that said *"S'alright,"* and Topo Gigio, the Italian puppet-mouse. Señor Wences was on the bill with Elvis. Topo was on the bill with the Beatles.

On paper, this shouldn't have worked for an Elks Club Christmas party. But then, little about this show should have worked, starting with Ed.

A tall ex-athlete whose thick neck made him look perpetually hunched over, he had a wooden gait to match his wooden tones. While most early TV host spots went to the likes of Jack Benny and Arthur Godfrey, proven radio entertainers, Ed had been forgettable on radio. He also suffered from ulcers, for which he took the pain

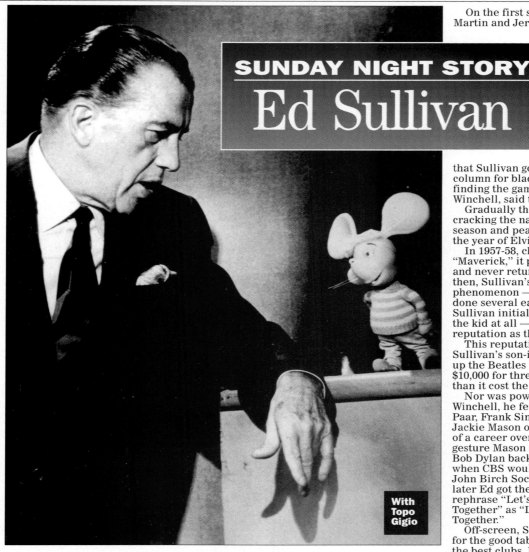

SUNDAY NIGHT STORY
Ed Sullivan

With Topo Gigio

medication belladonna, which dilates the pupils and makes it impossible to read cue cards.

Of course, that still doesn't fully explain "World War II" coming out as "World War One One" or the introduction of Jose Feliciano as "He's blind — and he's Puerto Rican!"

ED SULLIVAN was Irish, born Sept. 28, 1902, on E. 114th St. After his twin brother, Dan, and a sister died, his parents moved the family to Port Chester, where Ed won 10 varsity letters in high school. At 16, he landed a job writing sports for the Port Chester Daily Item, making $10 a week.

He then hopped to a series of jobs at newspapers that kept folding: the Hartford Post, the Philadelphia Ledger, New York's Evening Mail. After the Mail died in 1923, Sullivan jumped to Bernarr Macfadden's zany Evening Graphic, where he became sports editor and, among other things, started a feud with Graphic columnist Walter Winchell.

When Winchell jumped to William Randolph Hearst's Daily Mirror, Sullivan became the Graphic's Broadway columnist, fuming that Winchell had also become a national radio star by now.

The Graphic folded in July 1932, and Sullivan was looking at the relief line until he got a call from Daily News publisher Capt. Joseph Patterson. "I have a job for you," the captain said, and soon this cocky lad with the slick part in the center of his hair settled in for a 42-year run writing the column "Little Old New York."

He became the second-most influential Broadway columnist in town, after Winchell. True, a 1947 Esquire survey of Broadway writers curtly noted about Sullivan: "Accuracy of items low." But his column gave him contacts and personal cachet, and he emceed events like The News' annual Harvest Moon Ball. It was at the '47 Ball, they say, that a CBS exec decided he'd be perfect for "Toast of the Town."

On the first show, he introduced Dean Martin and Jerry Lewis, who were paid $100 each. That ate up more than half the $375 talent budget, so he talked Richard Rodgers and Oscar Hammerstein into performing for free. For two years Sullivan didn't take a salary, spending the show's whole budget on guests.

Winchell sniped that Sullivan got talent by using his column for blackmail. Sullivan, gleeful at finding the game where he could beat Winchell, said that was sour grapes, pal.

Gradually the show came together, cracking the national top 10 in the 1954-55 season and peaking at No. 2 for 1956-57, the year of Elvis.

In 1957-58, challenged by ABC's "Maverick," it plunged out of the top 25 and never returned to the top 10. But by then, Sullivan's association with the Elvis phenomenon — even though Presley had done several earlier TV shows and Sullivan initially had vowed not to book the kid at all — had secured his show's reputation as the place to be seen.

This reputation was so strong that when Sullivan's son-in-law Bob Precht signed up the Beatles in late 1963, he paid $10,000 for three shows — $50,000 less than it cost the Beatles just to get here.

Nor was power lost on Ed. Besides Winchell, he feuded publicly with Jack Paar, Frank Sinatra and others. He threw Jackie Mason off his show and almost out of a career over an allegedly obscene gesture Mason swore was a mutual joke. Bob Dylan backed out of a 1964 show when CBS wouldn't let him sing "Talkin' John Birch Society Blues," but three years later Ed got the Rolling Stones to rephrase "Let's Spend the Night Together" as "Let's Spend Some Time Together."

Off-screen, Sullivan never lost his taste for the good tables his stature gave him at the best clubs. But he was no playboy: He married Sylvia Weinberg in 1930, and that was it. In the mid-'50s, he even bought a 60-acre farm in Connecticut, where Ed was duly photographed talking to the animals and firing up a chain saw. Years later he said he couldn't get out of there fast enough: "I hated the rustling of leaves. I'm a city slicker."

They moved to the Delmonico Hotel, where Ed kept a Broadway columnist's hours, crawling into bed at dawn and sleeping until afternoon while his longtime assistant, Carmine Santullo, would get the column under way.

As early as '36, Ed and Sylvie had traveled to Europe on the Normandie with Capt. Patterson, the Jack Bennys and Marlene Dietrich. They attended Lyndon Johnson's dinner parties at the White House and John F. Kennedy's 1962 New York birthday party. They traveled around the world, for the show and for fun, though Sullivan vowed that after his farm experience he'd never leave New York more than briefly again.

O NE SIDE EFFECT of that vow, his pal Walter Cronkite mused later, was that Sullivan helped "recapture television for the East Coast."

But by the late '60s, Sullivan was finding it harder to sell a family-style variety show to a country increasingly agitated and fragmented. Though he had signed a 20-year deal with CBS in 1955, the network cashed him out in June 1971.

He hung around only a little longer. He died of cancer Oct. 13, 1974, which was, of course, a Sunday night. His final "Little Old New York" column, prepared with the faithful Santullo, ran Monday the 14th and included 48 short items that ranged from Russian military purchases to the everyday affairs of showbiz life: Sinatra was making $2 million, Quincy Jones was having surgery. There were birthdays, weddings, separations, openings, closings. The show would go on.

By JERE HESTER
Daily News Staff Writer

AS J. RAYMOND Jones usually told the story, his personal turning point came in 1921, when he was a novice volunteer delivering voter registration books to the brownstone Harlem headquarters of the Cayuga Democratic Club, which had an upstairs clubhouse for whites and one in the basement for blacks. Young Jones went upstairs. A doorman immediately informed him that he had come to the wrong place.

"I think I became dedicated right there," he would recall years later. "I had no appreciation for history at that moment, but I was filled with resentment. The contrast was too much for my stomach, and I was really hooked."

"If anybody got hooked, it was that doorman," remembered a Jones colleague, adding to the story. "Solid left hook, too."

So began a political career that would span half a century. Reaching into largely untapped black political power in New York, Jones launched his own clubhouse and began a decades-long climb to the top of the city's Democratic Party. He had gentlemanly charm, wily smarts, persistence — and an uncanny ability to pick winners. In time, he would come to be called the Harlem Fox.

While resentment sparked the fire in his belly, it never ruled his head, as he worked the system from the inside to help folks on the outside. Along the way, he paved the groundwork for a generation or two of political leaders. He would live long enough to see one of his many protégés become the first black mayor of the biggest city in America.

"We all stand on somebody's shoulder," David Dinkins would say.

WHEN JOHN Raymond Jones of St. Thomas, Virgin Islands, hopped a freighter to New York shortly after World War I, just 1,000 of the city's 150,000 blacks had municipal jobs, and mostly menial ones at that. Tammany Hall, the otherwise dependable dispenser of patronage, had in 1898 established the offshoot United Colored Democracy but otherwise had paid little attention to the fast-growing numbers of blacks. But things were beginning to happen above 125th St.

In 1917, Harlem Republican Edward Johnson became the first black elected to the state legislature. Marcus Garvey had created the Universal Negro Improvement Association, the vehicle for his briefly popular back-to-Africa movement. And Harlem was brimming with what would come to be called a renaissance, a politically charged explosion of black ideas, energy and talent.

The Depression, though, dealt a crippling blow, leaving half of New York's blacks — as well as a quarter of its whites — jobless. In 1932, black voters for the first time went Democratic, breaking with the party of Abraham Lincoln to put Franklin Roosevelt in the White House.

None of this was lost on Jones, who established the Carver Democratic Club at Amsterdam Ave. and 145th St. and made himself the man to see in Harlem, whether you needed advice, a favor or a job. And he hooked up with the Rev. Adam Clayton Powell Jr., the fiery pastor of Harlem's Abyssinian Baptist Church, who had led Depression boycotts of white-owned businesses on 125th St. to end employment discrimination.

With Powell ascending to the City Council and then to Congress, the quieter Jones won the behind-the-scenes Democratic district leader spot in 1944, becoming the man to see, even for those who lived well below 125th St. — like Tammany-bashing mayor William O'Dwyer, with whom he struck an alliance in the late '40s.

Meanwhile, into the second-floor Carver clubhouse trod a long line of young men and women, educated and ambitious and hardworking. David Dinkins, Charles Rangel, Percy Sutton and Basil Paterson would all seek wisdom from the tall, courtly man they respectfully called the Emperor Jones.

"A flick of a cigar made you understand he was the master and you were the subject," Sutton would remember.

"There is no better way than by starting low and climbing the ladder," the Fox would repeatedly tell his disciples. "Every newcomer group has learned that lesson."

THE STUDENTS also learned just by watching him operate. When Tammany in 1958 sought to oust Powell for having backed Republican Dwight Eisenhower's presidential reelection two years earlier, Jones risked all to keep his friend and sometime rival in office. In 1961, when Democratic mayor Robert Wagner broke with Tammany and joined the successful movement to boot party boss Carmine DeSapio, Jones defied both the machine and Powell and backed Wagner.

That paid off in 1964, when Wagner installed Jones as Tammany chief, making him the machine's first black boss and highest-ranking black party official in the nation. At age 65, Jones was at the top.

"It's possible some of the ancient sachems of Tammany Hall might be turning over in their graves," he mused.

THERE WERE those, Powell among them, who openly felt that, so far as black leadership went, Jones was not enough of a boat-rocker.

Some suggested that Jones' frequent clashes with Powell, over everything from politics to dubious real estate deals, were manufactured, that perhaps the two of them were the good cop and bad cop of black politics. Jones, indeed, explained once that good politics required a Mr. Inside and a Mr. Outside. "When they think you are going to hit them from the inside, you do it from the outside. Then when they think you are coming from the outside, you hit them from the inside."

But genuine conflicts were clear. The increasingly erratic Powell, who had all but disappeared from Congress amid legal woes, wasn't invited to the 1963 March on Washington. He blamed Jones for this slight, branding him a "traitor to the black revolution," and unsuccessfully tried to oust him from the City Council.

When Powell stood with Malcolm X, belittling white civil rights groups, Jones struck back: "We cannot call for integration while advocating segregation."

It was a balancing act he would teach his protégés.

Black politicians, he said, "must be militant. Yet they must also continue to identify with the major political parties. We discovered years ago in New York that it is impractical for blacks to go their own route.

"When all is said and done, the eventual effectiveness of the Negroes now in office depends on how long they can stay there."

JONES' END, in large part, came from a seemingly unlikely source: New York Sen. Robert F. Kennedy.

In 1966, Jones handpicked a candidate for a judgeship over a candidate who happened to be managed by an RFK brother-in-law, and Kennedy griped that there was a "suspicion of corruption" surrounding the nomination. Jones was incensed. A year later he quit. "A Tammany leader is of no importance unless he is recognized as such or honored as such by elected officials," he said.

He remained in the city until 1970, when Charles Rangel ousted Powell from Congress. Then he returned to St. Thomas — for good, he said.

He came back 20 years later, to check into the Greater Harlem Nursing home, where he died of heart failure June 9, 1991.

Later that month, about 200 members of the old Jones Gang — among them Mayor Dinkins, Rep. Rangel, ex-borough president Sutton and former New York secretary of state Paterson — gathered for a memorial service at Convent Ave. Baptist Church, about a block from the Carver clubhouse that had reared them.

"Build men and women," the Harlem Fox had once defined his Carver mission. *"Fit them and support them where they could do the most good."*

INSIDE OUTSIDE

J. Raymond Jones

By SIDNEY ZION
Special to The News

ROY COHN was the Picasso of the inside fix. It's his true legacy, overshadowing his infamous years with Sen. Joe McCarthy, his prosecution of the Rosenbergs, his feud with Bobby Kennedy, his gay life in the New York limelight at Studio 54, his seat at the side of George Steinbrenner in Yankee Stadium, even his deathbed disbarment at the hands of longtime political enemies.

Thirteen years after his death, still the mantra lived on: *"It's days like this I miss Roy Cohn."* From pols, judges, Mafia bosses, tycoons, reporters, husbands, wives, mistresses — everybody out there who's trying to get a wire in, wanting something done nobody else can get done, needing to find out what nobody else can find out.

Jeez, they say, *do I need Roy Cohn today.*

This about a man who never held public office, never ran a political party, never published a newspaper, never owned a TV station, never controlled a crime family, never built a building, never even owned one.

And yet today, a consensus as big as Trump Tower holds that if Roy Cohn was there for Bill Clinton, Monica Lewinsky would have been oceans away from Kenneth Starr's subpoena. Starr could have hired 40 more prosecutors, but if they worked 40 more years they'd never discover just how come Monica managed to become a part owner of a Tokyo baseball team or the public relations director of a hotel on the Riviera or a TV producer in London.

How would Cohn have done it? He'd never tell, and he'd leave no fingerprints. How could he have done it? Ask Michael Jordan how he could jam from the foul line, ask Louis Armstrong how he hit high C, ask Babe Ruth anything.

Art never explains, it just delivers. Roy Cohn delivered contracts like the Babe delivered homers. The difference was that in Cohn's world it had to be behind curtains.

HE WAS THE only son of Albert Cohn, lieutenant of Tammany Hall's Ed Flynn, who was a confidant of President Franklin Roosevelt and perhaps the most powerful boss in the country. Al Cohn was a respected judge of the Appellate Division, and his clout enabled Roy to become the youngest assistant U.S. attorney in history, in 1948, at age 21.

Cohn had scored brilliantly at Columbia Law School and now quickly moved up the ladder in the U.S. attorney's office. After playing a lead role in the atom-spy trial of Julius and Ethel Rosenberg, he caught the eye of Joe McCarthy, who hired him as chief counsel to the Senate's anti-Communist committee.

Cohn got the job against the toughest competitor imaginable: Robert F. Kennedy, son of Joe Kennedy, McCarthy's chief financial and ideological supporter. What won the day for Cohn was McCarthy's need for a Jew. Accused of anti-Semitism, the last thing he needed as his top counsel was the son of Joe Kennedy, the former ambassador to England, a notorious anti-Semite. It didn't hurt that Roy had the support

NO FINGERPRINTS
Roy Cohn

of George Sokolsky, the powerful right-wing columnist, and the Hearst papers, or that his best friend was Si Newhouse, whose father owned another newspaper empire.

But the "win" made Roy Cohn one of the most hated men in America, his name indelibly linked to Tail Gunner Joe, the man who smeared the Democrats as the party of treason and destroyed innumerable lives with his witch hunts. The picture of Cohn whispering in Joe's ear during the 1954 Army-McCarthy hearings — an early political TV event — defined him as a modern-day Iago.

Bobby Kennedy didn't know how lucky he was to lose out to Cohn. Imagine the difference in American history had a Kennedy been at Joe McCarthy's right arm. Bobby wound up as the Democratic minority counsel to the committee — which saved his political career and probably his brother Jack's as well.

BOBBY DIDN'T show his appreciation for this historic break

— to say the least. He hated Roy, and when Bobby became attorney general in 1961, Cohn called Jim Juliana, who had worked for him on the McCarthy committee and later for Bobby on the Senate committee that went after Teamster boss James Hoffa.

"Jim," Cohn said, "I don't want to bother you with this, I haven't spoken to Bobby in years, I can't imagine he's sitting around thinking about me. But just between us, Jim, what's his attitude toward me?"

Jim Juliana said: "Hoffa's No. 1. You're No. 2." As it turned out, the only difference was that Bobby was able to convict Hoffa. Cohn, indicted three times by Manhattan U.S. Attorney Robert Morgenthau for a variety of alleged swindles, beat every rap, most famously when his lawyer mysteriously took ill and Roy, who never took the stand, wowed the jury with a summation that is still talked about where barristers congregate.

But the multiple trials of the mid-'60s and early '70s busted him financially. You wouldn't know it from the way he lived. He turned up in Palm Beach and Acapulco. He was a fixture at 21. But he was broke. He lived on credit, which worked only because he was feared — nobody wanted to call the cards on him.

When things got to breakpoint, in the late 1960s, he called on Samuel Newhouse, father of Si. "How much do you need?" Newhouse asked. Roy told him $250,000. Sam Newhouse smiled and wrote out a check. "I don't know if I can pay it back," Roy said. "You've already paid me back with friendship," Newhouse said.

Ironically, all the trials accomplished — "the vendetta," Roy Cohn called them — was to create a mystique of infallibility. Big-shot clients lined up at Cohn's East Side townhouse, everybody from Aristotle Onassis to Fat Tony Salerno. Esquire magazine ran his picture on the cover under the title "Legal Executioner." Roy bought 500 copies, sent them all over the country and the world. Of course, his practice exploded — who doesn't want an executioner? The editors scratched their heads while scratch rolled into Roy Marcus Cohn, Esq.

Even before Esquire, Cohn was the power broker par excellence in New York's Democratic Party. Nationally he was a right-wing Republican — he bragged to me on the record that he handed five grand in cash to Richard Nixon at the Waldorf Towers in 1968 — but he remained a Democrat in New York.

In the spring of 1973, Cohn changed the course of New York City politics. He did it with one turn of the stiletto — and no fingerprints.

MARIO BIAGGI, an ex-cop who parlayed heroism on the force to a seat in Congress, looked like a cinch to become mayor after eight years of Republican John Lindsay. In the polls, Biaggi was running 20 points over Abe Beame, the candidate of the Democratic bosses.

The problem was clear: Biaggi was the candidate of Queens boss Matty Troy, who would wire the city if Biaggi won. Nobody had done this since Tammany's Charlie Murphy, before World War I. Ever since, a duchy system had prevailed, wherein power resided in the various county leaders, who basically respected territorial limits.

Now Matty Troy, through Biaggi, was about to kill the duchies. He was all over town, claiming he would "wipe out" Brooklyn boss Meade Esposito, that he'd "put away" deposed but still influential Manhattan boss Carmine DeSapio's frontman Frank Rossetti. Matty Troy was the Bugsy Siegel of New York politics, and he had to go. But who could pull the trigger?

Only Roy Cohn, because only Roy Cohn knew that Biaggi had taken the Fifth Amendment before a federal grand jury in Manhattan. It had to do with immigration, but what worried Biaggi was a question about his daughter. The feds thought she had a pad job. Against Roy's advice, Biaggi took the Fifth.

Cohn told this story to Meade Esposito — and then advised Biaggi to run for City Council instead, on a ticket with Beame as mayor.

Biaggi laughed it off. The next thing he knew, a story about his Fifth Amendment claim appeared on the front page of The New York Times.

It finished Biaggi. After Cohn died of AIDS in August 1986, I ran into Biaggi in Elaine's and told him the story. Biaggi reeled. "But I loved him," he blinked.

The last thing Roy Cohn told me — I was his biographer — was this: "I love Mario Biaggi."

By BRIAN KATES
Special to The News

BONGOS BEAT in the background, the scent of espresso wafts through the smoky air and a drunk taunts the poets at a reading of their work. "What are you trying to prove?" he shouts. "Nakedness!" a bespectacled bard retorts, ripping off his shirt and hurling it at the heckler. Stepping out of his pants, he throws them, too. Then, clad only in audacity, the poet shouts: "Stand naked before the people! The poet always stands naked before the world!"

Behold Allen Ginsberg, poet laureate of the beatniks, original flower child, acid-dropping Vietnam War resister, pansexual Zen philosopher, mantra-chanting gadfly. A balding, bushy-bearded Buddha with Coke-bottle glasses, Ginsberg was not a man anyone would go out of his way to see unclothed. But metaphorically, at least, he did stand naked before the world from the moment his protean poem "Howl" gave voice to the Beat Generation. The year was 1956, and Ginsberg was barely 30.

I saw the best minds of my generation destroyed by madness, starving, hysterical naked. A frenzied, scatological, sexually explicit bebop riff, "Howl" shocked staid Eisenhower America and catapulted Ginsberg into instant notoriety. He said it was inspired by "an extreme, rhapsodic wail I once heard in a madhouse." He was stoned on peyote when he wrote it, he said.

The appearance in print of "Howl" triggered the swift arrest of Ginsberg and its publisher, San Francisco poet Lawrence Ferlinghetti, on obscenity charges. Federal authorities banned it from being read on the airwaves, and the case wended its way through the courts for years. Four decades later, it is considered one of the most important poems of the second half of the 20th century, and Ginsberg is revered as the second coming of Walt Whitman.

His poetry — described by one critic as "outsized, darkly prophetic, part exuberance, part prayer, part rant," created a bridge of words between the angry postwar existentialists and the dreamy flower children of the '60s. It influenced the music of Bob Dylan, Yoko Ono and Patti Smith and provided a model for the political antics of such '60s radicals as Abbie Hoffman.

Irwin Allen Ginsberg was, to quote his poem "Methedrine Vision," "born in 1926 in Newark, New Jersey, under the sign of sweet Gemini." An awkward Jewish misfit, his father was a high school teacher and poet and his mother a Russian émigré who died the year "Howl" was published after years in a mental hospital. In "Kaddish for Naomi Ginsberg," written in the style of a Hebraic lament and considered by some critics to be his most powerful work, Ginsberg recalls his horror at watching her deteriorate: "... small broken woman — the ashen indoor eyes of hospitals, ward grayness on skin."

The fledgling poet went to Columbia University on a scholarship to study law; he quickly switched to literature. But it was in the off-campus

GONE DITHYRAMBS
Allen Ginsberg

apartment of a Columbia dropout named Jack Kerouac — whose bop novel "On the Road" would officially give birth to the Beat Generation a decade later — that Ginsberg in the late 1940s honed his philosophy and developed his style. His pals back then included underground writers like William ("Naked Lunch") Burroughs and such hipsters-at-large as Neal Cassady and Herbert Hunke, who fenced stolen goods out of Kerouac's cluttered flat.

After earning a bachelor's degree in '48, Ginsberg experienced, without benefit of drugs, a series of what he described as "mystical visions" and landed in a mental hospital. There, his friendship with a fellow patient opened his eyes, he said, to the power of poetry as a weapon of political dissent. He would come to wield that weapon with stunning force.

FIRST, HE WOULD struggle to be a respectable man in a respectable career. This was market research consultant in a buttoned-down Manhattan ad agency. Five years into the job, he found himself taking part in a project to determine which word consumers preferred to describe ideal teeth: "glamorous" or "sparkling." "We already knew people associate diamonds with 'sparkling' and furs with 'glamorous,' " he would recall. "We spent $150,000 to learn that most people didn't want furry teeth."

It was the last straw. On the advice of his shrink, Ginsberg quit to "devote myself to writing and contemplation, to Blake and smoking pot and doing whatever I wanted."

Great work would follow — "America," "Kaddish," "The Change" and others — and Ginsberg would come to be celebrated as much for his outrageous lifestyle as the phenomenon of his poetry. As one writer put it, "Allen lived like someone running a poetic medicine show" — dropping acid with Timothy Leary, chanting mantras with Indian gurus and trotting the globe as, to use his own description, "a bearded American fairy dope poet."

Ginsberg coined the term "flower power" to describe his special brand of passive resistance. And powerful it was. In 1965, Hell's Angels were putting the muscle on antiwar demonstrators; tripping on LSD and chanting a mantra, Ginsberg

strolled into the motorcycle gang's California headquarters and began passing out bouquets. To everyone's amazement but his own, he converted the tough gang members to his cause. The stunt made him the first-ever flower child and an instant icon of the antiwar movement.

Thereafter he was a ubiquitous presence at counterculture love-ins and be-ins — decked out in love beads, clinking finger cymbals. He was carted off in handcuffs at protests on both coasts and was clubbed and tear-gassed by cops in the riots accompanying the 1968 Democratic National Convention. In the '70s, he protested CIA involvement in the Third World and railed against the shah of Iran. The '80s saw him banging heads with Jesse Helms and other right-wing foes of the First Amendment.

Indeed, one old friend noted, the only radical event of his era Ginsberg was not part of was the Stonewall gay uprising. And he did show up the next day to offer his support.

FBI director J. Edgar Hoover branded Ginsberg a "dangerous subversive" — the same label he pinned on the Rev. Martin Luther King Jr. — and larded his thick dossier with hundreds of allegations. One dark charge: "Ginsberg chanted unintelligible poems in Grant Park on Aug. 28, 1968."

But Ginsberg was no knee-jerk pinko. Fidel Castro kicked him out of Cuba after he called Che Guevara "cute" and urged the dictator to grant rights to homosexuals. And Czech officials banished him from Prague after he challenged Communist police.

All the while he was on the cutting edge of controversy, Ginsberg continued to write poetry from the cluttered East Village apartment he shared with his longtime lover, Peter Orlovsky, and to teach at Brooklyn College. He published more than 40 books and produced 11 albums of poetry and music. His CDs still sell well. His honors included a National Book Award for poetry, a Guggenheim Foundation Fellowship and a National Arts Club Medal. He toured with Bob Dylan and performed onstage with the punk rock band The Clash.

Ginsberg lived his life to the hilt and celebrated it, to use his words, "in one gone dithyramb after another." It ended April 5, 1997, at age 70, as a result of liver cancer.

The trick to writing poetry, Ginsberg once advised, is to be "a stenographer of your own mind."

BIG TOWN ☆ BIOGRAPHY™

LIVES AND TIMES OF THE CENTURY'S CLASSIC NEW YORKERS

By BRIAN KATES
Special to The News

WHEN JAZZ LEGEND Thelonious Monk stumbled backward off the high bandstand at The Village Gate one memorable night in the 1960s, a grandfatherly man in a black suit and turned-around collar was there to help him to the hospital.

And that was why the Rev. John Garcia Gensel was put on this Earth: to minister to fallen musicians.

Gensel was a fixture in the city's jazz clubs through the '60s and '70s, sitting near the stage, sucking down diet sodas, bobbing his balding head in time to the music. He was one unlikely hipster. Soft-spoken and a congenitally nice guy, he didn't play an instrument, sing or read music. He just showed up to dig the scene and keep the beat of the Lord.

An ordained Lutheran minister, Gensel eventually came to be revered as New York's Jazz Pastor. Drummer Max Roach called him "our spiritual guru, our psychiatrist and the greatest booster of American music," and Duke Ellington wrote one of his strongest tone poems, "The Shepherd Who Watches Over the Night Flock," specifically for him.

But for a long time, Gensel was considered more than a little suspect in an orthodoxy where many think the devil hides behind the syncopation.

BORN JUAN Garcia Velez in Manti, Puerto Rico, in 1917, he was sent by his impoverished parents to live with an aunt, Josephine Gensel, in the farming town of Catawissa, Pa. Catawissa was not exactly a hotbed of hipitude, and John Gensel was in his teens before he heard any jazz. But what he heard was about as good as it got: the Duke Ellington Orchestra, playing a dance in Berwick, holding forth with "It Don't Mean a Thing (If It Ain't Got That Swing)."

Recalled Gensel later: "I flipped."

But he was determined to give his life to God, not to music, and jazz remained on a back burner through college and graduate work at Union Theological Seminary. Then it was off for a stint in Guam as a Navy chaplain and on to Ohio, where he ran a chapel-on-wheels ministry for defense workers and was known as The Atomic Pastor.

In 1956, he landed in New York, assigned to the Church of the Advent at Broadway and 93rd St. It was the height of the bebop revolution, and 52nd St. was swinging.

Inspired by Marshall Stearn's seminal "The Story of Jazz," Gensel took Stearn's course at The New School on the influence of jazz in modern culture and eagerly attended class field trips to haunts like the Half Note, Cafe Bohemia and the Five Spot. He would stay long after closing time, talking with the musicians, listening to their troubles, offering them a bit of sanctuary.

One night, Max Roach approached him. "It is

The Pastor and the Duke

NIGHT FLOCK
The Rev. John Gensel

your responsibility," the great drummer told him, "to seek us out and teach us the moral values that can save us. We need a moral code to save us from all the enticing things that confront young men in the clubs."

Gensel took it to heart. His clubbing evolved into a quasi-official night ministry.

By 1960, he was spending three or four nights a week in jazz joints. "A jazz musician can be a lonely guy at four o'clock in the morning," Gensel told one reporter.

BUT THOSE 4 a.m. counseling gigs were putting a strain on the pastor's day job.

Gensel appealed to the Lutheran Church hierarchy to make his night ministry official. After a lengthy hearing — musicians and a psychiatrist testified on his behalf — he was given permission to devote half his time ministering to jazz musicians. Five years later, as Gensel's reputation spread nationwide, the church named him the official pastor to the jazz community and made the job full time. That was a giant step for a church that otherwise grooved to "A Mighty Fortress Is Our God."

Still, Gensel insisted: "Jazz is probably the best music for worship, because it speaks to the existential situation of a human being."

To musicians, he put it a different way: "If Jesus were making the scene, he'd have dug Zoot Sims."

Creating the new ministry was "an obvious thing to do," music critic Dan Morgenstern would later say. "Except for their union, there is no organization to serve musicians and their families. John Gensel was the man who realized the need."

Himself, Gensel was a bit stumped about just what a jazz pastor was supposed to do. By then assigned to St. Peter's Church, he doubted that night-working musicians would flock to his 11 a.m. service. He seriously considered holding formal services in nightclubs. But Ruth Ellington, the Duke's sister, set him straight. She suggested that if there were "beautiful surroundings," musicians would come.

To Gensel, beautiful meant jazz.

Thus began, with Joe Newman on trumpet and Randy Weston on piano, the Jazz Vespers services that became the hallmark of Gensel's ministry. At first, jazzmen, for so long regarded as playing godless music, were wary. But, Gensel told them, "Music is neither secular nor religious. You can play 'Jumping at the Savoy' and call it, 'Jesus at the Cross.' Because you called it that, does it make it holy?"

Anyway, he added: "You wouldn't let the devil have the best times, would you?"

The services were held at the merciful hour of 5 p.m., and for more than three decades they have attracted some of the hottest musicians in the the city — and, of course, a congregation of jazz worshipers.

OVER THE years, Gensel performed weddings for a galaxy of jazz stars — Herbie Mann, Bill Evans and Rashid Ali among them — and, as the great originators passed on, he buried more than a few of them, too. He was in the room when Duke Ellington died. He officiated at the Duke's funeral and buried or eulogized John Coltrane, Coleman Hawkins, Billy Strayhorn, Thelonious Monk, Erroll Garner, Philly Joe Jones and many others.

Most of the sendoffs were loosely planned jam sessions. Typical were the preparations for the Dixieland memorial service for cornetist Wild Bill Davison. At one point, the bandleader of the Grove Street Stompers asked Gensel how many numbers the band should play. "It's a worship service," the minister replied. "You play four spots. We pray, you play."

While the celebrity of Ellington and other well-known performers helped shed a spotlight on Gensel's ministry, it was his quiet decency with the down-and-out — imprisoned, homeless, destitute, drug-and-booze-besotted musicians — that gave his unique calling credibility.

Trumpeter Jimmy Owens worked with Gensel on a committee to help care for indigent jazzmen. Said Owens: "Pastor Gensel is a very special human being. He has managed to pull the jazz community together to do something they don't do too often — and that is to worship among friends."

On New Year's Eve 1994, Gensel, 76 years old, bade goodbye to his congregation. He returned to the wooded hills of his childhood Pennsylvania home, puttering in his garden until his death Feb. 6, 1998.

The Jazz Vespers live on every Sunday at St. Peter's Church on Lexington Ave.

He'd been asked once if he was concerned that jazz might attract a wayward, nightclubbing crowd to St. Peter's. "That's the kind we want," he replied. "The good ones can stay home."

By JAY MAEDER
Daily News Staff Writer

BLACKWELLS ISLAND was by 1921 such a grim, gray place of crumbling old bedlams for hopeless charity cases suffering from smallpox and syphilis and dementia that the city just sighed and outright renamed it Welfare Island, and by 1935 it was so gray and grim that even prisoners were moved out to an island called Rikers. Three decades after that, the two-mile-long rock jutting up from the East River between the United Nations and Long Island City was a mostly abandoned junk pile, populated principally by rats. And it was here, on Welfare Island's moldering southern tip, directly off E. 49th St., that George T. Delacorte — "delightfully eccentric philanthropist," the papers called him — chose to build his great geyser, a spectacular, 400-foot, night-lighted spray of water rivaling the Jet d'Eau in Switzerland's Lake Geneva.

"What good is it?" people wondered.

"What good is the Eiffel Tower?" George Delacorte shrugged.

CIVIC LEADERS were beside themselves in the summer of 1969. Delacorte's money had built a Central Park home for the New York Shakespeare Festival. He had given the park its whimsical Alice in Wonderland sculpture, he had given the park the Delacorte Clock at the Children's Zoo, he had built the fountain in Columbus Circle. He was a splendid old gentleman who had done splendid things. But $400,000 for a geyser? Plus thousands a month to maintain it? When people were hungry? When hospitals needed beds? The editorialist elders of The New York Times clucked themselves into a dither: Delacorte, they said, was "the Wrong-Way Corrigan of New York philanthropy." Why could he not do something more socially useful with his millions?

"It's my money," he replied serenely. "I'll do anything I want with it."

But people were *poor,* bleated the civic leaders, wringing their hands.

"People are poor," he snapped, "because they're dumb or because they're lazy."

NEITHER OF which ever applied to George Thomas Delacorte Jr., born a New York lawyer's son in 1893, graduated from Columbia in 1913, from the 1920s to the 1970s a leading publisher of popular newsstand magazines and paperback novels and finally, in the last decades of his extraordinarily long and vital life, a man dedicated to the ideal of funding lovely things, whether they had any severely useful purposes or not. Well, so far as that went, what good *was* the Eiffel Tower? "Not everything has to have a practical function," he said. "What do we remember about Rome? We remember the fountains and the statues. There has to be a place in life for the eye's pleasure."

He had previously put in a career successfully "guessing what the lowbrows want," as the publishing trade described his particular business genius. He invented or perfected movie, horoscope and crossword-puzzle magazines; he was a pioneer publisher of comic books; he very early got into the paperback game. In the '30s, he was the first to grasp that the Dionne quintuplets were celebrities, and he instantly deluged the newsstands with Dionne photo scrapbooks; in 1960, he understood at once that Jacqueline Kennedy was a new cultural icon and flooded the land with Jackie albums. He made a bad call or two — one of his editors had to quit to launch True magazine on his own after Delacorte gave it a thumbs-down — but the Dell Publishing Co. ran prosperous journals for years: Modern Romances, Modern Screen, Inside Detective, Ingenue, many more. Dell's humor mag Ballyhoo was a sensation of the early '30s. Dell's pulp-fiction stable covered the genres: All Detective, All Western, War Birds, Sky Riders, Navy Stories, Public Enemy, Federal Agent. The paperback line, launched in 1942, was long a major producer of romances, mysteries and Westerns. Dell's wonderful comic books were known to every American kid of the 1940s and 1950s — all the famous Disney and Warner Bros. cartoon characters, Dick Tracy and Smilin' Jack and other Sunday-funnies stars, most of the cowboy heroes from Roy Rogers and Gene Autry and The Lone Ranger to Rex Allen and Wild Bill Elliott, plus Tarzan and Little Lulu and Jungle Jim and Sergeant Preston of the Yukon and Francis the Talking Mule. Dell sold literally billions of comics.

In the late '50s, as newsstand economics were changing and Dell became more interested in books than in magazines, very rich George Delacorte turned over his company's daily details to his editors and dedicated his life to giving curious little gifts to the people of New York City. A man who died wealthy, he believed, was a disgraceful man. For years he had been giving his money to hospitals and foundations and other such worthy things to which rich people give their money, and he had never seen a single specific thing his money had bought other than letters of acknowledgment. This was not going to be the case much longer.

HIS FIRST wife had liked to sit in one of Central Park's more unusually bucolic spots, and at this very site in May 1959, near the Conservatory Pond, he dedicated Jose de Creeft's sculptures of Alice and the Mad Hatter and the Dormouse. For most all the rest of his life, he enjoyed sitting quietly on a nearby bench and watching children joyously clamber all over them. Sometimes he liked to climb up into Alice's big bronze lap himself.

In January 1961, he gave a 2,500-seat amphitheater to the Shakespeare Festival, theretofore performing on truckbeds. In June 1965, the Andrea Spadini animals of the Delacorte Clock began piping their carousel nursery tunes. Four months later, the illuminated Columbus Circle fountain was turned on. Late in his life, Delacorte would still sometimes come around to personally pick trash out of his fountain and sadly shake his head. Some dirtball actually threw a mattress into it once.

THE WELFARE Island geyser, truth to tell, was always a folly. "My greatest landmark," he insisted. "A majestic addition, matching the Empire State Building and Radio City." But for once the city was not overwhelmingly grateful. Switched on in December 1969, Delacorte's magnificent jet did nothing but spew filthy river water onto passing boats, and the Health Department finally stepped in to demand chlorination machinery. The thing seldom worked properly in any case. By 1971, when he decided he wanted to put up a 125-foot stainless-steel obelisk on Park Ave. at 68th St., a good many citizens mobilized against all his unceasing monuments. "Delacorte is the modern-day equivalent of the pharaohs who built pyramids to memorialize themselves," snarled the chairman of Community Board 8. "Why doesn't he spend his money on improving classrooms?"

Under fire, the City Art Commission rejected the gleaming Park Ave. tower. "I'm sore as hell," grumbled the 78-year-old benefactor. His fond dream of building a grand fountain in Times Square was never realized either. Late in the '70s, he did install fountains at Bowling Green and in City Hall Park and was hailed for his devotion to civic beauty. "George T. Delacorte is to the City of New York what Lorenzo de Medici was to the city of Florence," Mayor Edward Koch warmly proclaimed in 1979. But these were Delacorte's last public gifts.

BY 1976, when he sold Dell to Doubleday & Co. for $35 million, he was an eminently respectable hardcover man who published Kurt Vonnegut, Irwin Shaw and James Jones, and his Modern Screen, Federal Agent and Roy Rogers days were long behind him. In his final years he showered his money upon Columbia, establishing both the George T. Delacorte Center for Magazine Journalism and the Delacorte Professorship in the Humanities. He even gave the university a set of iron gates. He got an honorary doctorate in return.

One cold morning in December 1985, as 92-year-old George Delacorte strolled with his wife through Central Park, en route to visit his beloved Alice, a couple of teenage punks, dumb and lazy, knocked the couple down and ran off with Mrs. Delacorte's mink coat. They went unapprehended, and the old man was never quite so vigorous again. He died in his sleep at his Fifth Ave. home May 4, 1991, age 97.

PHARAOH IN WONDERLAND
George Delacorte

By BRIAN KATES
Special to The News

HE LOOKED LIKE an old Norseman in need of a decent tailor. Or a refugee from a third-rate production of "Gotterdammerung." Six-foot-something and clad from head to foot in patched-together pieces of leather, thonged cowhide foot covers, a long, flowing cape and — the *pièce de éce résistance* — the magnificent horned headgear that covered his sightless eyes. Also, he carried a long iron spear.

He called himself Moondog, and through the 1950s and '60s you could see him every day at the corner of Sixth Ave. and 54th St. — summer and winter, rain and shine — standing stock-still for hours on end, gathering alms in a hollowed-out moose foot.

So immobile was he, the story went, that one summer day in 1965, a leggy young woman stepped from a cab, saw him and took him for a mannequin. She threw her arms around the leather-clad figure, hiked up her skirt seductively, and chirped: "Somebody take a picture." The statue was motionless no longer. Moondog squeezed back. "Let's go, baby," he said.

The girl dined on the experience for years. But, obviously, she was a tourist. Most real New Yorkers knew Moondog on sight. Or sound. He didn't talk much, but he sure did like to beat on his homemade drums. Made quite a racket. A regular musical Eric the Red.

He got into the rhythm of the thing, he said, "back in '48, when I visited the Blackfoot tribe in Idaho and realized I was one of them at heart. I would sit down at the big sundance tom-tom and we would play together. I felt a community of spirit."

When he wasn't standing guard outside the ABC studios in midtown, you could see Moondog striding around town, his moose foot swinging from a rope around his waist, his spear at the ready. At a time when street eccentrics were common — a drag queen on roller skates in the Village, an opera singer in combat gear at Bryant Park, a guy who played three saxophones at once in Times Square — Moondog managed to achieve a certain urban celebrity.

His name — or rather his moniker, for few knew who he actually was — appeared in newspaper columns, his stark presence even noted in some of the hipper New York City guidebooks. But most New Yorkers knew nothing of the man inside the leather suit.

Most didn't want to know. The mystery was half the fun. Moondog was rumored to be doing penance for a variety of sins, crimes or unrequited loves. Or, some thought, he was an escaped mental patient. Or maybe just another blind beggar with a pretty slick racket.

The truth is more compelling.

MOONDOG WAS born Louis (he pronounced it Louie) Hardin in 1916, the son of an itinerant Episcopal minister from Maryville, Kan. He was blinded at age 16 when a dynamite blasting cap exploded in his hands. A year or so later, he began studying stringed instruments and the organ at the Iowa School for the Blind. That's where he decided he wanted to be a composer. So in 1943, he left the sticks and headed for New

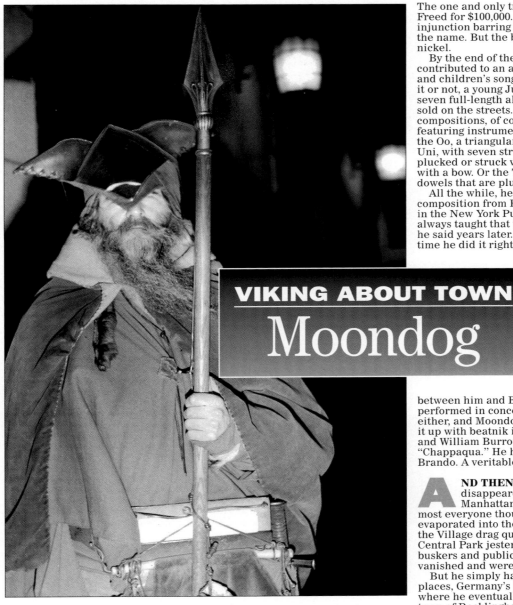

VIKING ABOUT TOWN
Moondog

York. He arrived with $60 in his pocket and took up residence in an attic on W. 56th St., bunked in a homemade sleeping bag, subsisted mostly on raw vegetables, fruit and black bread and composed music on a tiny organ.

It didn't take New Yorkers long to notice him. He had taken to haunting Carnegie Hall, where New York Philharmonic conductor Artur Rodzinski took a liking to him and let him sit quietly in a back row during rehearsals, and a columnist for the newspaper PM spotted him there and gave him a write-up. "The solitary listener might have stepped out of the pages of the Bible," the item noted. "His face was long, pale, ascetic...We asked the Philharmonic's press agent who this man was. She replied that he was a mysterious music lover."

Mysterious indeed. By 1949, Louis Hardin had fashioned his Viking getup and renamed himself Moondog. "It's an Indian name," he told one reporter. "When I took it, it just meant a dog that howls at the moon. Later I learned it means an Arctic rainbow."

Back in the early 1950s, when R&B was struggling to become rock 'n' roll, a musicologist was so stunned by Moondog's idiosyncratic sounds that he made field recordings of them for the Folkways label. Moondog called it "snake time music." One critic called it "the sweetest music this side of faulty radiators." Which was why for decades, though he made numerous recordings, the bulk of his income came from whatever strangers dropped into his moose foot.

In 1954, Moondog took umbrage when legendary rock 'n' roll disk jockey Alan Freed named his radio program the "Moondog Show."

The one and only true Moondog sued Freed for $100,000. The judge granted an injunction barring the deejay from using the name. But the blind Viking never got a nickel.

By the end of the '50s, he had contributed to an album of nursery rhymes and children's songs — along with, believe it or not, a young Julie Andrews — and cut seven full-length albums, some of which he sold on the streets. All his own compositions, of course, and many featuring instruments he invented. Like the Oo, a triangular stringed gizmo. Or the Uni, with seven strings that could be plucked or struck with a mallet or played with a bow. Or the Tuji, a board with dowels that are plucked.

All the while, he was studying composition from Braille books he found in the New York Public Library. "I was always taught that the model was Bach," he said years later. "But...about half the time he did it right, and half the time he made terrible mistakes. I think he didn't analyze his work. He wrote so many pieces and had so many children to support he just didn't have the time."

That Moondog had no kids was not the only difference between him and Bach. Bach never performed in concert with Tiny Tim, either, and Moondog did. He also hammed it up with beatnik icons Allen Ginsberg and William Burroughs in the film "Chappaqua." He hobnobbed with Marlon Brando. A veritable Viking about town.

AND THEN, in 1974, Moondog disappeared from the streets of Manhattan. Years went by and most everyone thought he had just evaporated into the ether, like Rollarina the Village drag queen or Pegasus the Central Park jester or any number of other buskers and public eccentrics who vanished and were never seen again.

But he simply had relocated — to, of all places, Germany's industrial Ruhr Valley, where he eventually turned up in the little town of Recklinghausen.

He was still decked out in full regalia, selling his poems on the street. Tolerant villagers thought he was an out-of-work actor, and a young woman named Ilona Goebel was so enchanted by him that she took him home to Mama and Papa and transformed herself from a geology student into the blind musician's transcriber, publisher and booking agent. They remained together ever after.

Off came the helmet, out went the spear, gone was the moose foot. "The persuasion of a woman is unbeatable," Moondog confessed.

Recording contracts and invitations to conduct European orchestras followed. In 1989, he returned to New York to conduct the Brooklyn Philharmonic in a 30-minute suite of his compositions. The performance consisted of him sitting to the side of the orchestra and keeping the beat on a drum. "In my music," he explained, "they don't have to worry about time changes. If I start in four-four, I end in four-four. All they have to do is count straight."

And then he went back to Germany, where he composed "Sax Pax for a Sax," which was issued by Atlantic Records in 1994, sort of '40s-style swing featuring, well, saxophones, lots of them, and little else. Moondog played bass drum.

At his death in September 1999, at age 83, he was still going strong, orchestrating a contrapuntal symphony titled "Overtone Tree." Said the composer: "I've been working on overtones for 20 years, and I discovered they're really a secret code. If there is a God — I call him Megamind — He's relaying a message through the overtones to us."

Can you hear it?

By JAY MAEDER
Daily News Staff Writer

"Since the professors do not educate the students, the students will have to educate the professors."

— Upton Sinclair, 1905

MARTIN LUTHER KING was 17 days dead, and the riots that had rocked America's cities had only tentatively subsided. There was heavy fighting outside Saigon; bombers were hammering the A Shau Valley; North Vietnam was accusing the U.S. of stalling peace talks. President Lyndon Johnson had declared himself a lame duck. Robert F. Kennedy, Hubert Humphrey, Eugene McCarthy, Nelson Rockefeller, Ronald Reagan and Richard Nixon were all rushing to succeed him. Across the U.S. and Europe and Latin America and the Far East, colleges were erupting into melees. This was the temper of the time in the last week of April 1968, as, in New York City, on a small piece of Morningside Park, Columbia University proceeded with a plan to build a gymnasium.

At the time, the uprising seemed to be spontaneous; later, it appeared more likely that it had been planned for months, that the gym issue itself was merely a convenient flashpoint. Campus rabble-rousers deemed the gym racist, an arrogant theft of parkland from neighborhood kids. Actually, the site was a known muggers' paradise, and some Harlem community leaders didn't understand what the fuss was about. On Tuesday afternoon the 23rd, co-led by the Student Afro-American Society and Students for a Democratic Society, several hundred protesters took over Hamilton Hall, barricaded it and held acting dean Henry Coleman prisoner in his own office.

They freed him the next day, but by then other squads had taken over Low Library, the Mathematics building and several other halls. President Grayson Kirk's office was looted. Classes shut down as mobs of fist-shaking student rebels laid siege to their school.

They were, as the expression had it, a tiny minority, but the Columbia administration didn't seem to want to do anything about them but bluster. "We can't let a small group get their way," fumed Kirk. Yet the days went on, and the rebels held their captive buildings even after the university called off work on the gym and cops were held back from removing them. "Campus chickenry," sneered the Daily News, no champion of student unrest. "How much of these disruptions and distractions by Reds and their kooky dupes do the solid students have to stand for?"

Indeed, many nonprotesters were deeply annoyed by this interruption of their education and banded together to charge the hostage buildings themselves, but the administration held them back, too. "You'll see plenty more Columbias," predicted one disgusted policeman. "They've been getting away with it."

SO IT WAS that 20-year-old Mark Rudd briefly became a leading spokesman for one segment of his generation.

The president of the local Students for a Democratic Society chapter was all but a walking lampoon of the standard-issue campus radical: a middle-class white kid from Maplewood, N.J., who had never known a day of privation in his life, an unformed college boy who had read a little Herbert Marcuse and Che Guevara and decided he was a revolutionary. He had visited Cuba, and he wrote rhapsodic pieces about Fidel Castro's "extremely humanistic" government for the Columbia Daily Spectator. He'd won a few spurs by getting arrested at this rally and that. His rhetoric was straight out of bad folk rock: "We will take control of your world, your corporation, your university and attempt to mold a world in which we and other people can live as human beings," he wrote Kirk. "Your power is directly threatened, since we will have to destroy that power before we take over."

Suddenly, in the tumult and the din of the American spring of 1968, Mark Rudd was a national figure. The New York Times appeared to

THE CHILDREN'S CRUSADE
Mark Rudd

think he was Tom Paine (**STUDENTS RUN COLUMBIA PROTEST ALONG PRINCIPLES OF DEMOCRACY**), and so did such faculty elders as Margaret Mead and Lionel Trilling, who declared that Columbia was stuck in the Stone Age and needed a good shake. "Rebelliousness among young people occasionally is not a bad thing," agreed presidential aspirant Bobby Kennedy.

The somewhat crustier News continued to figure Rudd for just a noisy little snot. "He's a combination of a revolutionary and an adolescent having a temper tantrum," agreed Columbia vice president David Truman. Even Rudd's SDS colleagues more and more began to find him quite the totalitarian. It was seen by the more moderate that what mattered to him was the confrontation, not the reform. He didn't seem to have any genuine political convictions at all. He just liked to break things.

ONCE MAYOR JOHN Lindsay grasped that the kid gloves were probably not going to redound to his political credit, 1,000 New York City cops, before dawn on Tuesday the 30th of April, crashed the occupied buildings and carried out 500 screaming strikers. By then, the protest had gathered considerably more student strength, and Columbia remained shut down for another five weeks.

Charged with inciting to riot, Rudd was suspended by Columbia. This cost him his student draft exemption. In November, when he was reclassified 1-A, he actually sought an occupational deferment on grounds that he was a professional revolutionist. "My occupation is vital to the national interest," he contended. When it became clear that the argument was not impressing his draft board, he held a press conference to announce that he would accept induction and then devote himself to organizing fellow soldiers; he would, he vowed, "smash the arbitrary and brutal power of officers in our armed forces."

The charming prospect of what your average drill instructor would have done with Pvt. Mark

Rudd became moot when, after he took his physical, the Army decided it didn't want him anyway.

LINDSAY WENT ON to be reelected. Kirk, meanwhile, resigned in the wake of Rudd's strike. As for Rudd himself, by the summer of 1969, repudiated by much of the rest of SDS and branded "adventurous, diversionary and alienating to the working people," he had spun off his own faction, the Revolutionary Youth Movement, also known as The Weatherman.

This grimly radical bunch initially specialized in trying to shut down high schools and recruit youngsters into their New Red Army; subsequently, they started plotting to bomb police stations. Weatherman pretty much went out of business in March 1970, when several fumbling young bomb builders blew themselves up inside a Greenwich Village townhouse. Under indictment in Chicago and New York, Mark Rudd now disappeared deep underground.

SEVEN YEARS LATER he quietly reappeared and surrendered, along with a few other once-shrill revolutionaries from a vanished time — "a figure from out of the past," The News said, "like Thomas Dewey or Eli Whitney." By now, all the old charges were gone or reduced, and Rudd left court basically a free man and moved to New Mexico to teach school.

In April 1988, on the 20th anniversary of the Columbia strike, Rudd and several other principals reunited in New York to reminisce and to assess what, if anything, they had wrought. Well, they had, after all, successfully stopped the gym. And they had measurably reformed university governance, bringing more students into the process. Some remained proudly certain that they had personally ended the Vietnam War.

Rudd himself seemed not so sure. Maybe it had been no real revolution at all, he conceded. "I bought into a fantasy," he said.

There was a moment of silence for the comrades who had died in the Village blast. And a letter was read from another brother, David Gilbert, who was serving a life sentence for heisting an armored car and killing a policeman. "The struggle has turned out to be much longer, more difficult and complex than we had imagined," Gilbert wrote, and there was certainly no argument there.

BIG TOWN ★ BIOGRAPHY ™

LIVES AND TIMES OF THE CENTURY'S CLASSIC NEW YORKERS

By DAVID HINCKLEY
Daily News Staff Writer

THEY HAILED from military stock, Tom and Dick Smothers, their father having died a Japanese prisoner in World War II, and now come the late 1960s, with Vietnam raising domestic adrenalin to battle levels, you looked at the boys and you'd have bet the ranch they'd be telling the long-haired hippie peace creeps to go back to Russia if they didn't like the way we did things here in America.

And you'd have lost the ranch, because by 1967 the clean-cut, short-haired Smothers Brothers suddenly found themselves, not entirely by design, two of the most visible stop-the-war voices in the land.

They didn't get there by chanting, "Ho, Ho, Ho Chi Minh, Viet Cong is gonna win!" They simply had something other antiwar protesters could only dream about: an hour every Sunday night on CBS television. Location, location, location.

Rather than singing ballads off the back of a flatbed truck, like Joan Baez or Phil Ochs, the Smothers boys could sign up veteran com-symp Pete Seeger to sing "Waist Deep in the Big Muddy" for 30 million CBS viewers.

"Waist Deep" was written from the point of view of a World War II soldier whose sergeant insists on marching his men through a deadly stream — too bull-headed to realize a 100% mortality rate adversely affects any long-term objective. Seeger added a sixth verse that never mentioned Vietnam by name but which CBS snipped out anyway when he sang it on the Smotherses' first show of the 1967-68 season.

After months of heavy memo combat, Tom Smothers persuaded the network to let Seeger do the whole song Feb. 25, 1968. A few days later, viewer Irene Walker of Queens wrote to the Daily News, "The Smothers Brothers make me sick. If they lived in a Communist or fascist country, they'd be shot."

WALKER DID NOT stand alone. With hundreds of G.I.s dying every week in Vietnam, those who opposed the war were widely seen as betraying America, and that was the dilemma the Smothers Brothers presented to a network that already took flak every time Walter Cronkite dropped so much as a hint of bad news.

The Smotherses were recruited specifically to help CBS appeal to The Young People. But when they started to use words Young People used, like "mind-blowing," well, CBS wasn't about to let a word like that on the air when nobody at CBS was sure what it meant.

When the brothers signed up guests who reflected the antiwar sentiments of some Young People — Seeger and Baez, Dr. Benjamin Spock — CBS didn't want to look as if it were disrespecting those who did believe, or were already serving. When Baez dedicated a song to her husband, David Harris, a jailed draft evader, CBS cut it. Twice the brothers interviewed antiwar activist Spock, and twice CBS would not let the interview run.

In hindsight, the Smotherses' political commentary would seem mild, just baby steps past NBC's 1964-65 satire "That Was The Week That Was." But when America's internal divisions ran so deep they were forcing Lyndon Johnson out of the presidency, it was considered radical when Dick mentioned that Johnson had tightened

Tom (left) and Dick

worldwide travel restrictions and Tom turned to the camera and said, "Okay, all you guys in Vietnam, come home now."

On April 3, 1969, shortly after Richard Nixon had become President with a promise to end the war, CBS announced the Smotherses' program terminated.

Though it had become the first CBS show ever to nibble into NBC's "Bonanza," it was simply too much trouble. CBS was tired of getting, say, a tape of Harry Belafonte singing "Lord, Lord, Don't Stop the Carnival" over news footage of the 1968 Democratic convention.

CBS solved that one by killing the segment and selling a five-minute ad spot to then-candidate Nixon. But the problems ran deeper. Comedian Jackie Mason compared sex to a concert. Snip. A sketch had Nanette Fabray asking, "Did you get that girl in trouble?" Snip. Elaine May and Tom Smothers wrote a long sketch in which two censors solemnly change the phrase "My heart beats wildly in my breast whenever you're near" to "My pulse beats wildly in my wrist." Snip.

No, in the end CBS decided it would be better off with "Hee Haw." The move was "wise, determined and wholly justified," wrote TV Guide, because in the end, CBS' highest responsibility was to the American public.

CBS said it got 16,000 letters, 10,000 saying right on. "There's a line of responsibility we all must recognize," wrote one TV critic. "Tommy and Dickie reflect this generation's inability to know where to draw that line."

THE SMOTHERS Brothers went on to respectable lives and careers. But their brightest moment had passed.

Tom Smothers was born Feb. 2, 1937, his brother, Dick, Nov. 20, 1939, in a military hospital on Governors Island. Their father was transferred to the Philippines a year later, and when he died after being captured at Bataan, Ruth Smothers

took a job and raised her two boys and their two sisters.

The brothers showed little interest in school or discipline, though Tom began to develop a knack for performance. He formed a folk-style group called the Casual Quintet, with himself on guitar and Dick on bass.

Having neither a large repertoire nor the kind of deep reverence for folk songs that characterized the serious followers of that movement in the late '50s, the brothers developed an on-stage patter that, in part, satirized folk singers and their ponderous commentary. "In Uruguay every June 3, they hold camel races," Tom would deadpan before "Tzena, Tzena, Tzena."

Many folk singers found them appalling, but audiences warmed up fast to Tom as the goofy space cadet and Dick as the straight man. They turned a two-week run into 36 at the Purple Onion in San Francisco, and that led them to the Village's Blue Angel, where in 1962 they caught the eye of Jack Paar, who thought they'd be swell on television.

They were, it turned out, doing some 65 guest spots on various shows over the next few years and parlaying that exposure into lucrative tours and a pair of well-received 1964 concerts at Carnegie Hall.

CBS then signed them up for a 1965 sitcom. It proved terrible, so CBS suggested "The Smothers Brothers Comedy Hour," which premiered Feb. 5, 1967.

When that show became a topic of conversation, Tom emerged as the brother who did the talking. Though he and Dick shared antiwar sentiments, Dick preferred to spend his time with his family and his racing cars.

After the cancellation, Tom kept talking, at one point hooking up with John Lennon and Yoko Ono to discuss how the views of youth on peace and brotherhood could find a forum on international TV.

"Sometimes," confessed Tom, "it feels like we've been dropped in the ocean 800 miles from land and told to swim to shore."

"We should pray for a porpoise," said Lennon.

A YEAR AFTER the cancellation, ABC gave the brothers a summer replacement show. But the show flopped, as did a 1975 comeback on NBC.

In 1976, they broke up, though for the next decade they did sporadic shows together as well as solo. Both had squirreled away enough money to buy estates, and Dick for a time ran a winery. He also passed Tom in marriages, three to two, and they both said the time apart was good.

"Our relationship gets a little testy," is how Tom put it, though it was never clear where the on-stage shtick about sibling rivalry ended and real-life irritation over bookings and missed cues kicked in.

By the late '80s, they were back together, doing anniversary specials, playing Atlantic City, promoting yo-yos. If they got another regular TV show tomorrow, Tom said, they would offend just as many politicians and moralists as they did in the bad old days.

LINE OF RESPONSIBILITY

The Smothers Brothers

By JAY MAEDER
Daily News Staff Writer

UNEARTHLY WASN'T even the word. The principal professional singing voice of Herbie Khaury of Washington Heights was like nothing any human had ever imagined, a ghastly falsetto screech that could peel paint off walls. He had several other voices, including a not unpleasant tenor, but it was the falsetto he favored and it was the falsetto that, for one brief and shining moment in the late 1960s, catapulted him into preposterous, impossible worldwide fame.

HAD HE NOT been so ungainly and clumsy, he would really rather have been a ballplayer, but Herbie was one of these big galoots who tripped over his feet when he walked. At George Washington High School, he was a figure of ridicule. At home in the West 160s, mom Tillie and dad Boutros sighed and shook their heads as Herbie decided he was going to be a glamorous show-business legend someday, like Rudolph Valentino or maybe Carmen Miranda.

This was an old-fashioned immigrants' home Herbie grew up in, and in the late 1940s the parlor entertainment remained a windup Victrola and stacks of ancient 78s that had entranced Herbie since he was a small child, Aeolian Vocalions and Victor Red Seals and Columbia Bluebirds, hundreds upon hundreds of the popular hits of a musty earlier day: "Beautiful Ohio" and "Pony Boy" and "On the Old Front Porch" and "Keep Away From the Fellow Who Owns an Automobile" and "The Good Ship Lollipop" and so on and so forth. Plunking away at his ukulele, he could summon up credible impersonations of those tinny

With Dick Martin, "Laugh-In"

THE VOICES WITHIN
Tiny Tim

gramophone voices from a time long since flickered away: Henry Burr, Arthur Fields, Eddie Morton, Jeanette MacDonald, Irving Kaufman, Gene Austin, Ruth Etting, Annette Hanshawe, Walter J. Van Brunt. In 1950, at age 20, Herbie took his music on the road, playing amateur contests and sidewalks and subway platforms and Times Square freak shows and getting shoes thrown at him everywhere he went. Muggers used to change their minds in mid-mug and give him their own money, he was so pathetic.

For fully a dozen years, Herbie tried to click, wandering the city like a village idiot, packing his ukulele and cosmetics and his Old Testament in a shopping bag, singing for supper at any bar that would have him, usually getting pitched into the street instead. Around about 1954, God appeared before him and commanded him to grow his hair long and stringy, paint his face white and sing falsetto. "Now he's a sissy," groaned old Boutros Khaury back home in Washington Heights.

Herbie went through several names at the time: Emmett Swink, Darry Dover, Vernon Castle, Dollie Dell. In 1962, calling himself Larry Love, he landed his first paying jobs, on the Greenwich Village lesbian bar circuit, and shortly the big vampire scarecrow — a singularly striking figure even amid the emerging period weirdness — began to develop a cult following.

At this point, a manager took hold of Larry Love and sought to rename him Sir Timothy Thames. Herbie didn't like that much. Eventually, the two settled on Tiny Tim.

IN 1965, following the shutdown of his chief Village venue, a bar called Page Three, Tiny Tim wandered up to midtown and got himself installed as a house regular at a happening disco called The Scene, which is where Mo Ostin of Reprise Records heard him in late 1967 and, there at the dawning of the Age of Aquarius, signed him to a recording contract on the spot.

At exactly that moment, a zany new TV comedy show called "Laugh-In" was looking for guest talent, the more bizarre the better. In early 1968, Tiny Tim got a couple of bookings on the fledgling program, and host comics Dan Rowan and Dick Martin, to their astonishment, discovered that their unknown guest was suddenly about the biggest star since, well, Rudolph Valentino and Carmen Miranda.

And now Herbie Khaury and Planet Earth converged at last.

FLUTTERING, GIGGLING, curtseying, blowing kisses, Tiny Tim was an overnight sensation. "Laugh-In" led to appearances on Johnny Carson and Ed Sullivan; the record album "God Bless Tiny Tim" was on the charts most of the year; the trilling single "Tiptoe Through the Tulips," which had been an enormous hit for one Nick Lucas in 1929, was once again a smash.

"Ageless envoy of the 1920s," Newsweek called Tiny. Audiences regularly burst into guffaws at the first sight of him, then quickly found themselves quite enchanted by the man's manifest sweetness. Tiny, said his new agent, Roy Silver, "has the virtue of being so kind and harmless that everyone around him becomes kind and harmless."

Many were the cynics who suspected that this swooning Victorian ragbag was not entirely real, and there was perhaps a little something to this. "He likes he should be a little bit mysterious," agreed mom Tillie back home in Washington Heights. "People say he dresses and wears his hair like a meshuggener, but they don't know show business. If you are not meshuggener in show business these days, with these hippie-dippies and these hoppy-poppies, you are going to starve."

Still, this was a man who bathed six times a day and turned crimson whenever he was asked if he liked girls. "Women must not be touched before marriage," he trembled. "Sometimes it's difficult, but I have learned to resist temptation. My Bible is always with me, protecting me from the temptation of dear, sweet 17-year-old girls. My mother, my dear parents, taught me to be so careful of s-e-x."

"One of these swinger girls gets hold of him,"

scowled Tillie of her 38-year-old son, "right away he is cooked."

TINY TIM sold out the Fillmore in San Francisco. He sold out the Royal Albert Hall in London, where Beatles and Rolling Stones came to hear his concert. He was boffo in Las Vegas. In 1968, he made nearly $1 million. And he signed to write a book of Tiny observations called "Beautiful Thoughts." In June 1969, at a book signing in Philadelphia, he looked up to see a dear, sweet 17-year-old girl waiting in line for his autograph.

He proposed almost at once. Victoria May Budinger of Haddonfield, N.J., accepted. For the next six months, a spellbound nation followed the chaste love affair between the swain and his girl-child princess. Tiny Tim and Miss Vicki, as he never called her anything but, were doing the Carson show one autumn night when the subject of a wedding came up and an impromptu decision was made to air the nuptials on the Carson show itself.

On the night of Dec. 17, 1969, as an estimated 35 million Americans watched, Tiny Tim and Miss Vicki became husband and wife. Carson got a Nielsen rating of nearly 40 that night, twice his usual. In New York, Con Edison had to throw on extra power to handle the overload. The event remains one of the most-watched in television history.

AND AFTER THAT, the phenomenon that was Tiny Tim fairly abruptly vanished. He never had another hit record. Miss Vicki walked out after a while. For a long time he worked the fringes of the business. Toward the end, his career picked up again; rediscovered, he was a modest hit on the state-fair and casino circuits and he was recording anew. On Nov. 30, 1996, at age 64, he was entertaining the Women's Club of Minneapolis, and he had just finished singing "Tiptoe Through the Tulips" when a heart attack killed him.

Voices of the past live within me, he had always loved to say. *I'm just the instrument that brings them to life.* Upon Herbie Khaury's death, assessments were being made that he was one of the greatest musicologists of the century, a remarkable performer, probably even sort of a genius.

By JAY MAEDER
Daily News Staff Writer

"People who make a lot of money off my boy, they are very rich. What my boy got? Just a grave."
— Freddie's mom

JOHNNY CARSON had never laughed so hard. A lot of times the hopeful young guest comics who got positioned somewhere in the middle of the Carson show were, you know, not necessarily all that drop-dead hilarious, and the camera would cut over to Johnny at his desk during some labored routine and he would be nodding pleasantly, maybe chuckling politely. But tonight was palpably different, tonight was magical and everybody could see it — this unknown Puerto Rican kid on the stage was the most spectacularly funny human being alive, and Johnny Carson was falling out of his chair, holding his sides, roaring.

December 1973. No first-time tryout comic ever got invited to sit down with Johnny Carson once the bit was over, it just never happened. But Freddie Prinze did, and the king of late-night TV told him he could come back anytime, and the kid did that, again and again, and just six months later Freddie Prinze from Washington Heights was the hottest young star in America.

Live fast, die young. That's the way Freddie wanted it to be. He always said he'd never live to 30. In fact, he didn't make 23, and after he died of a self-inflicted gunshot wound, maybe deliberate, maybe a Russian-roulette accident, those around him searched for a cautionary tale somewhere in his short and unhappy life, some kind of message. But there wasn't one.

RICAN WAS what he knew. Rican was what he did. New York City Rican is where the material came from. You try to get the super to fix the sink: *Ees not my yob.* You're bopping on the corner, trying to pick up gorls: *Ey ey, psss psss...Ey, honey baby, mi negrita...What's the matter, I no good enough for you?* The cockroaches are as big as buses and they menace you all night: *Ey, Freddie, where you going, man? You don' bring back some potato chips, we shut the door on you, man.* He couldn't be bothered with the older, more timid souls who worried that his stuff rocked the boat for no good reason they could see. *Puerto Ricans don't know there's land on the other side of the Washington Bridge.* He sneered at the young, bank-bombing FALN revolutionaries who thought they were entitled to scold him. *What kind of schmuck blows up money?*

"Sure, I stereotype Puerto Ricans," he said after he got famous. "And if that gets some of them angry enough to stop baby-crying and make things better for themselves, good."

Well, actually, he was only half-Rican, on his mother's side. The other side was Hungarian Jewish, and the family name was Preutzel, but he grew up more or less Rican at Broadway and 157th St., and he stole quarters from washing machines and he spray-painted graffiti and he ran with a gang called the Royal Lords — or at least he liked to tell people he did — and his world was plenty full of winos and junkies he had to step over every day of his life on his way to school.

What he always knew, since he was a kid, was that someday he was going to get out of the miserable hood.

A lot of kids dream that. Freddie did it. One day he's working alongside his mom at the El Greco Leather Products factory in Brooklyn, putting labels inside shoes; suddenly he's crashing the midnight shows at every comedy-club dump in town, perfecting his repertoire of outrageous voices, shrieking Hispanics, mumbling black hipsters, corny old Jewish comics he used to watch on the Sullivan show, Nelson Rockefeller. And just as suddenly he's working the Improv and Catch a Rising Star and a big-time agent spots him, and the next thing he knows he's doing the Jack Paar show and ...

... And now he's doing Carson, December 1973, and Johnny is falling off his chair, holding his sides, and one of those who's watching is a TV producer named Jimmy Komack, who is casting a new sitcom called "Chico and the Man," and Komack gets in touch with the uproarious kid right away. A month later, Freddie Prinze lands in Hollywood. He's not yet 20 years old.

Hollywood is cool. Hollywood is amazing. *Even the junkies have suntans,* Freddie thinks.

FREDDIE WAS all over Carson and Merv Griffin and Mike Douglas for months, and he was already a shooting-star show business legend before "Chico" came to NBC-TV on Sept. 13, 1974. He played a smartass-yet-warm Mexican kid who became pals with a cranky East Los Angeles old-white-guy barrio garage owner played by Jack Albertson. And notwithstanding critical carpings that the show wasn't much more than a flaccid knockoff of Redd Foxx's "Sanford and Son," which it followed on Friday nights, and also despite early indignant howls from Mexican-American activists that a New York Rican was playing an L.A. Chicano, the show was Top Five all season.

Forty million people laughed at Freddie every week. When shooting concluded in the spring of '75, he went on the road, playing Caesars Palace in Vegas, the Westbury Music Fair on Long Island, Playboy Clubs here and there, pulling down a quarter of a million a year, driving a Corvette Stingray.

He had already moved his family from Washington Heights to California. That was the important thing to him, getting his mom off 157th St. "I got no ties back there, no regrets," he said. He did make one brief visit back to the block, and what he found was a bunch of street cats all staring at him sullenly and suspiciously as he came around. "You on *tee-vee* now," some kid spat at him. "What the hell," Freddie snapped. "I'm not gonna move back here and work in the post office so these guys will dig me again."

EVERYTHING IN THE WORLD
Freddie Prinze

WHETHER IT WAS Hollywood that did it to him or Freddie that did it to himself, he fast turned into a very bad doper. In those days, anybody with any sense of reason would judiciously cut a Quaalude in half; it was nothing for Freddie to swallow six or eight ludes a day and wash them down with wine. By all accounts, this never once affected his stone-pro work on the "Chico" set. Otherwise, everybody around Freddie Prinze sadly understood that he was out of control. He liked guns. He liked to wave them around. He liked to fire them into his walls. He liked to put them in his mouth. He made his friends hysterical again and again.

On Jan. 19, 1977, America's most famous and best-loved Puerto Rican celebrity performed at Jimmy Carter's pre-inaugural gala in Washington — *Ey, I had to park cars for an hour outside before they'd let me in,* and everyone held their sides and roared — and then he flew back to California and, about a week later, bouncing off the ceiling, 22-year-old Freddie Prinze fired a .32-caliber bullet into his left temple. He lingered for 33 hours. A nurse was pounding on his chest, screaming, "Don't give up!" when the machines went flatline on the afternoon of the 29th.

"The kid had everything in the world to live for," mourned Jack Albertson. "The only thing we can do now is say a kind word for him, a prayer, that's all we can do."

'BEING POOR** doesn't hurt as much as people say," his mother wept. "We had love, a family, we had laughs. Hollywood killed him. He went to Hollywood, and, yes, he made it big, then what happens? He became a product, a piece of merchandise."

Back on 157th St., there was mostly just quiet anger. "Everybody that lives here wants to get out," one girl said. "He made it. He was the first half-Puerto Rican comic, and he threw it away."

By HOWARD KISSEL and JAY MAEDER
Daily News Staff Writers

"I feel better when I lose Tonys than when I win them. When I win, I become part of that Broadway thing. When I lose, it makes me feel clean."
— **Joe Papp**

THE TORRENT
Joe Papp

I N THE SPRING of 1959, at 71, three decades into his seldom challenged reign as the city's most powerful man, imperious Robert Moses crossed swords with a volcanic 37-year-old showman named Joseph Papp and discovered to his horror that he had suddenly been made a laughingstock, the man who was petulantly refusing to let New Yorkers continue to enjoy free Shakespeare in Central Park for a third season of warm summer nights.

Playgoers were trampling the grass, Moses had grumbled, and his Parks Department had ordered Papp's New York Shakespeare Festival to start charging admission to offset the caretaking expenses. Press-savvy Papp had taken this edict straight to the papers, and the whole town was jeering old Moses' crotchety determination to remove Shakespeare from the reach of the commoners. City Council members and borough presidents rallied behind Papp. Mayor Robert Wagner openly urged his Parks Commissioner to reconsider.

Moses had many times backed down Wagner, and mayors before him. Early in May, the two men lunched at the Players Club — apparently oblivious to the delicious irony that the club had been founded by Edwin Booth, the foremost Shakespearean of his day — and Moses laid down the law. "We must back the Parks Commissioner," Wagner announced feebly, making it plain to all who really worked for whom. As civic indignation came to a boil, Papp went to court.

The state Supreme Court on June 2 agreed that the Shakespeare Festival was "a bright constellation in New York's firmament" but deemed itself powerless to intervene. It took the Appellate Division to rule Moses "arbitrary" and "capricious" and "unreasonable" and "irrational." Thus upheld, Papp in August mounted a triumphant and critically acclaimed "Julius Caesar" on his flatbed trailers at Belvedere Lake, and never again was there any suggestion to charge anyone so much as a dime.

The episode left Moses badly damaged. As for Papp, the populist firebrand who wanted only to bring culture to the masses, it left him a hero, holding moral and political capital he banked on for the rest of his career. At his death 32 years later, by which time he had become the dominant figure of the modern American stage — producer of more than 350 plays, the man behind "Hair" and "A Chorus Line" and other smash money-makers, as well as the foremost champion of serious experimental drama and nurturer of an entire generation of fresh playwriting talent, the winner of three Pulitzer Prizes and more than 100 Tonys and Obies — Papp could reflect that he was what he was largely because Robert Moses had been fussy about his lawns.

JOE PAPP LIKED to say he had never actually seen Shakespeare until he started producing it, but he had loved it since his childhood in Williamsburg, Brooklyn, when it was the Bard who in no small measure had helped the son of a Polish-Lithuanian family learn English. Embracing the theater through a poverty-stricken youth otherwise spent laboring as telegraph messenger, laundry deliveryman and chicken plucker, Yosl Papirovsky got his first real brush

with show business by staging programs aboard an aircraft carrier during World War II service in the Navy. Back in New York after studying on the G.I. Bill and managing the radical Actors' Laboratory in California, Joseph Papp was working as a CBS-TV stage manager when he created his visionary workshop dedicated to the proposition of a readily accessible public theater.

The Shakespeare Festival, chartered as a nonprofit organization by the state Education Department, began its life in 1954 in a small church on E. Sixth St., an on-the-cheap enterprise that salvaged lights and equipment from junk piles and paid next to nothing to struggling unknown actors as Papp energetically cajoled funding from patrons of the arts and indeed was known to pass the hat after performances.

New Yorkers of every class and stripe cherished the festival from the beginning and in 1956 followed it to East River Park when Robert Moses, an enthusiastic Papp benefactor at the time, made an old amphitheater available as a new home. By the summer of 1957, when the festival moved to Central Park with Moses' blessing, it was a civic institution. In 1958, as the festival faced financial collapse — particularly after Papp lost his CBS job when he refused to answer congressional inquiries into his one-time flirtations with the Communist Party — citizens opened their pocketbooks to keep it alive.

After the Parks Department fracas in the summer of '59, patrons and foundations and the city itself began to subsidize Joe Papp and William Shakespeare on a regular basis. Even Moses, who was, after all, arbitrary and capricious, decided to spearhead a drive for a permanent park amphitheater that eventually was completed by and named for publisher George

Delacorte. Through the '60s, Shakespeare flourished in Central Park as the festival made stars out of, for example, George C. Scott and James Earl Jones. Many nights, thousands of New Yorkers were turned away after they had stood in line for hours for first-come, first-served free seats.

Then, in 1967, Papp made a major leap. He acquired the old Astor Library on Lafayette St., converted it into a beehive of five stages and announced the creation of the Public Theater. His first production there was a musical imported from Texas, called "Hair."

AT THIS POINT there began to emerge two notably distinct Joe Papps — one of them committed to upsetting all extant theatrical conventions by producing works by, for example, David Mamet and John Guare and Sam Shepard and Vaclav Havel, the other a canny commercial impresario ever in search of a hit he could send on to Broadway to subsidize the smaller properties — a "Two Gentlemen of Verona" to support a "Sticks and Bones."

He openly sneered at commercial theater: "No content at all," he would snap; "Money is all that matters on Broadway. It's a distorted and watered-down Broadway, one that has lost its audience for serious plays, a Broadway which has priced out its potential audience and turned away serious writers." Through the '70s he was nonetheless Broadway's biggest earner; some seasons he mounted as many as a dozen shows. One smash was 1972's "That Championship Season"; more celebrated and lucrative yet was the astonishingly successful "A Chorus Line," which opened in 1975 and remained for years a primary source of the Public's income.

Papp seemed to be everywhere. He had the Public and the Delacorte; for a time he had the Booth, meaning that the man who never stopped railing against Broadway controlled both ends of it. The Booth didn't work out. Neither did the Vivian Beaumont at Lincoln Center, which he ran from 1973 to 1977 in an ill-starred venture that lost millions. "You can't experiment there," he sighed. "And you definitely can't afford to fail."

In his 60s, it was observed, he remained an Angry Young Man. He was endlessly explosive, possessed of mighty passions and furies, "a torrential man in a difficult business," said playwright Albert Innaurato. He carried on legendary feuds with critics Walter Kerr and John Simon — Simon termed him "uncivilized" and "lowbrow" — and antagonized authors who had been his protégés; he once nearly came to public blows with David Rabe, and Shepard furiously vowed never to work with him again.

For all that, Papp approached the end of his life widely viewed as courageous and important. "He's one of the major reasons we still have a theater today," Bernard Jacobs, head of the Shubert Organization, hailed Papp as New York feted him in 1985.

'A CHORUS LINE" closed in April 1990, after 6,137 performances, the longest-running show in Broadway history (until 1997, when "Cats" broke that record). By that time, Papp's health was failing, and he was turning the fortunes of the Public and the festival over to successors. Among his last official acts was noisily refusing a grant from the National Endowment for the Arts, which he found increasingly repressive under the political thumb of Sen. Jesse Helms.

Broadway dimmed its lights when he died at 70 on Oct. 31, 1991. Cultural observers wondered what would become of the Papp empire. It had always been a strictly one-man show. How could it live on without him?

By DAVID HINCKLEY
Daily News Staff Writer

IT TOOK 180 years after the convening of the first Congress for a black woman to become a representative, and when Brooklyn schoolteacher Shirley Chisholm did, the fellows who ran things realized that this was just what they'd been afraid of.

"Some of these politicians think I'm crazy," the 12th District Democrat observed soon after she arrived in Washington in January 1969. "Good. Let them think that."

Now if a black woman in Congress was an unusual sight in 1969, Chisholm's path to that seat had been straight and narrow. Congressional lines had been redrawn in Brooklyn to insure another black representative, and as a veteran activist in local politics, albeit the reform wing, she simply took the next step on a ladder she'd been climbing for years.

In her campaign, nobody disagreed much on the issues — expand the war on poverty, shrink the war in Vietnam — only on who should do it. Her Republican opponent, civil rights veteran James Farmer, said big issues needed a man's voice and underscored that message by campaigning with burly men pounding manly drums.

But Brooklynites listened instead to tiny Shirley Chisholm, who took 70% of the district vote on an Election Day that made Richard Nixon the nation's president.

Once in Washington, Chisholm made it plain she wasn't going to get along with even her own party leaders — informing them at once that it was lunacy to assign her to the Agriculture Committee when her district had fewer farmers than it had tropical reefs.

House Majority Leader John McCormack of Massachusetts told her to be a good soldier. She refused, and made enough noise to get herself reassigned to the Veterans Affairs Committee. Some of her peers felt this was a modest victory won at a terrible cost. Shirley Chisholm wouldn't get a bill passed if she stayed in the House until she was 130, it was said.

Oh, fiddle-dee-dee, she replied. With only nine blacks in all of Congress, it was incumbent on the system to maximize their influence.

Two years passed, and after the election of 1970, young black Rep. John Conyers of Michigan decided to take black political power for a test drive by challenging Hale Boggs of Louisiana to succeed McCormack as majority leader.

Chisholm promptly endorsed Boggs, not exactly the solidarity gesture her fellow black lawmakers had hoped for. Nothing against Conyers, she shrugged; she just figured Boggs was going to win, and sure enough, after he did, she got a seat on the far more desirable Education and Labor Committee.

In case anyone hadn't noticed, Shirley Chisholm wasn't defying the system at all. She was playing it.

MAKING ALLIANCES, Chisholm always contended, was the highest political art. She raised many eyebrows when she paid Alabama firebrand George Wallace a get-well visit after he was shot in 1972, but she later insisted it was because of that gesture that Wallace convinced dubious Southern congressmen to support her bill extending minimum wage coverage to domestics, giving it the margin to pass.

Chisholm was, in fact, a hybrid of old-fashioned hardball and equal-opportunity skepticism, a maverick politician who eventually positioned herself outside almost every established group, including most black groups, by breaking alliances as fast as she forged them. She was quite capable of appearing at a Black Panthers fund-raiser one night, then denouncing militants as "woolly heads" and "spear carriers" if they challenged her on another issue the next.

Born Barbadian-Guyanese in New York in 1924, Chisholm had been reared by grandparents in Barbados, where school standards were high and motivation was corporal punishment, and she was a disciplined, orderly child when she came back to the U.S. at age 10. After graduating from Brooklyn College, she went into teaching, the only profession readily open to bright black women. Eventually, she ran child care centers, took a husband, learned to play backroom politics and went to Albany as an assemblywoman.

Come 1968, she rode a Reform Democrat surge to the 12th District nomination — and then, months later, abandoned the Democrats' colorless old-line mayoral candidate, Mario Procaccino, to back John Lindsay, who was seeking reelection as a Liberal.

Three years later, as she quite audaciously ran for president of the United States, now-Democrat Lindsay suggested she would cut into his vote and asked her to withdraw. Chisholm curtly replied that if he really wanted someone to drop out, he should go flip a coin with George McGovern.

"I DARE TO run," she announced to cheers from minorities and the poor and the disenfranchised when she made it known in late 1971 she would go after the presidency. She never seriously thought she would win. "I do not have a chance," she conceded. Her poverty-row campaign was haphazard at best, consistently ill-organized outside New York, and pundits wondered aloud exactly why she was doing it.

But she began surprising the professionals early on: In February 1972, she already had a third of the black independent and black Democrat vote, and the Harris Poll termed her a "distinct threat" to such inhabitants of the Democratic left wing as Lindsay, McGovern and Eugene McCarthy. Hubert Humphrey, for one, was deeply concerned about Chisholm's party-splitting potential. In the end, in Miami in August, she had a voice on the convention floor and several dozen delegates she handed off to McGovern.

If she sensed at the time she had found her political ceiling, she didn't phrase it that way; she had, she declared, made her statement.

SHE WAS, of course, still Shirley Chisholm. "Unbought and Unbossed" went her slogan, and a truism it was. When Manhattan Borough president Percy Sutton, who had put her name in nomination at the 1972 convention, ran for New York mayor in 1977, Chisholm supported Edward Koch instead. By now, her bridges to fellow black political leaders were pretty much small piles of ashes.

Sutton wrote her off in 1978: "She had a potential for real leadership, which, I'm afraid, she'll never realize because of her unwillingness to share with others. She remains a loner and will not assume the role of leader."

Added Brooklyn Democratic rival Major Owens: "Chisholm would like to be known as a great leader, but the commitment is not there. She ends up acting as a conspirator with the white power structure. She'll make a pact with anyone."

Chisholm's reply: Riding alone was what served her constituents best. And, while her major legislative successes were largely nothing more than endorsements of general liberal programs for education and the like, those constituents seemed to agree, consistently giving her three-quarters or more of their vote. If she didn't turn Bed-Stuy into Strivers' Row, she made its residents feel they had a voice that was heard.

In the end, she said it was the solitude of Washington that wore her down. She divorced her longtime husband, remarried and then, in 1982, shrugged off another reelection cakewalk and quit Congress. No one, she said, understood the art of making alliances any more.

CHISHOLM FLIRTED *with a New York mayoral run in 1989, finally deferring to David Dinkins' candidacy. In 1992, she was one of several running-mate possibilities considered by independent presidential candidate Ross Perot. In 1993, citing failing eyesight, she declined President Clinton's offer of the ambassadorship to Jamaica.*

RIDING ALONE
Shirley Chisholm

By PAUL SCHWARTZMAN
Daily News Staff Writer

THERE WAS A moment in 1969 when New York's otherwise fickle heart settled on a man whose taste for shag rugs, expensive whiskey and flinty blondes was matched only by his talent for throwing a football 60 yards into the outstretched hands of a teammate streaking for glory.

Joe Namath embodied all the excess and absurdity of that period when he rose to become not only the New York Jets' star quarterback but a singularly outlandish personality named Broadway Joe.

His face could be found everywhere — in the smoky mirror on the ceiling over his bed, in the TV ad in which he was paid $10,000 to shave off his Fu Manchu mustache. In the pantyhose commercial. In the cheesy motorcycle movie in which he co-starred with Ann-Margret. "The Brady Bunch." Sonny & Cher.

Teammates favored Marine-style buzz cuts. Namath grew his hair collar-long. He wore slick white cleats and sprinkled his conversation with words like "chicks" and "foxes" and "cool." When most athletes praised only God, country and their mothers, he celebrated himself.

"I like my girls blonde and my Johnnie Walker Red," he announced in his 1969 autobiography, an unabashed chronicle of his sweet life called "I Can't Wait 'til Tomorrow ... 'Cause I Get Better Looking Every Day."

The book, with chapters such as "I Never Drink at Halftime" and "They Probably Would Have Told Our Lord to Cut His Hair," describes his childhood in Beaver Falls, Pa., his strict Hungarian parents (" 'Til I was 13, I thought my name was shut up"), how he stole golf balls to help pay the rent, how the Jets offered him an unprecedented $427,000 to sign his first contract.

Its most intriguing passage may have been his account of bedding a woman he didn't know on the night before he led the Jets to what many still regard as the most startling upset in football history.

In those days, athletes lived under a monastic 11th commandment: Thou shalt not booze or canoodle on the night before a game. But Joe Namath wasn't about commandments.

It was nearly a blasphemy in the football world when he predicted — no, guaranteed — that the Jets would knock off the Baltimore Colts in the 1969 Super Bowl. The Colts were football's version of IBM. Dominant. Reliable. Ironbound by tradition. Their injured star quarterback, Johnny Unitas, was the very crew-cut model of the American dream, Gary Cooper and John Wayne, all the other monosyllabic heroes whose greatness was measured not in words but in deeds.

Namath was the new generation, the antihero, cool, cocky, ironic. His rebellion was based not on politics or philosophy, but on style, which meant that he not only was sure he'd win the biggest game of his career, but he'd also have a damn good time doing it.

BEAVER FALLS was a steel town 30 miles from Pittsburgh. Joe Namath's father and grandfather were both steelworkers, and when Joe was born on May 31, 1943, it was taken for granted that he

would be a steelworker, too.

Instead, he developed an aptitude for sports, which was a way out of life in the mills. Actually, his game was baseball, and he was good enough to get bonus offers from half a dozen major league teams. But a talent for football was emerging. In his senior year of high school, he led Beaver Falls to nine straight wins on its way to a championship. And 52 colleges and universities offered him football scholarships.

His dream was to attend the University of Maryland, which he somehow thought was located in the South. But he scored too low on the college boards and wound up at the University of Alabama — under the tutelage of one of college football's most formidable coaches, Paul (Bear) Bryant.

Namath's record on the field was impressive. One year he completed an unheard-of 64% of his passes. "The greatest athlete I've ever coached," Bryant called him.

NO COMMANDMENTS
Joe Namath

JETS OWNER Sonny Werblin earned millions as a showbiz agent, handling the likes of Jack Benny and Ed Sullivan, and he could recognize star power. Joe Namath, the hawk-nosed kid with the infectious grin, had it. In 1965, Werblin offered him $427,000 to join the Jets, in a package that included a new Lincoln Continental and scouting jobs for Namath's two brothers and brother-in-law.

The Jets' fortunes, floundering before Namath joined the team, began improving almost immediately. So did New York's nightlife. "Booze and broads, what else?" was his explanation after he threw four interceptions against Houston.

He seemed to live every bachelor's fantasy, drinking with Sinatra at Jilly's, or escorting a parade of blondes — always blondes — to the Copa or the Pussycat. His East Side apartment became a conversation piece, with visiting reporters breathlessly describing the Victorian night tables, the marble fireplace, the six-inch-

thick llama rug.

If his lifestyle reflected the freewheeling tone of the times, Namath remained mute on the more substantial issues that weighed on other sports figures, such as Cassius Clay, whose opposition to the Vietnam war cost him three years of his boxing career.

"I don't speak out on politics or religion," Namath told an interviewer. "I have complete confidence in our government. I've got to believe they know what they're doing — that they know a lot more about running a country than I do."

He did have one outspoken moment in 1969, when Commissioner Pete Rozelle demanded that he sell his interest in a nightclub that was believed to be frequented by gamblers, and he publicly threatened to quit instead. In the end, his lawyers calculated how much money Broadway Joe would lose without the Jets and negotiated a compromise.

HIS PRIVATE LIFE made it easy to forget that Namath was an accomplished quarterback, known not only for his passing arm but his ability to step up to the line of scrimmage and, in a moment's notice, call a new play to take advantage of a weakness he had spotted in an opponent's defense.

In 1967, he threw for an astounding 4,007 yards, all on a pair of gimpy knees that would require four operations before his career ended. He was elected to the Pro Football Hall of Fame in 1985, capping a 13-year career in which he spent all but one season with the Jets. His golden season was 1968, when the Jets ended up in the Super Bowl against the Colts.

Baltimore was favored by more than two touchdowns, not only because it had lost only two games in two years, but because it belonged to the long-established National Football League. The Jets and their relatively young American Football League were considered lightweights.

None of that mattered to Namath, who stood up two days before the game and announced: "The Jets will win it Sunday. I guarantee it."

He was right. New York won 16-7. For Joe Namath, the locker room celebration was missing one essential element: champagne. Rest assured. He made sure there was plenty when he got home.

By CHRIS ERIKSON
Special to The News

HERBERT LEVIN typically made his collections twice a week for the boss, wheeling a steamer trunk down W. 42nd St. Navigating the sidewalks of the nation's most notorious Smut Row, a strip respectable citizens avoided like the plague, Levin carried with him a scale as he discharged his duties, stopping in one by one at the adult bookstores that lined the street. The scale was needed to divide the bounty — quarters collected from the peep-show machines that colonized the rear of the shops, offering two steaming minutes of entertainment for each coin. The piles were split 50-50, half left to the store owner, half dumped into Levin's trunk.

Then the trunk was wheeled to the Chemical Bank at 42nd St. and Eighth Ave. There were a lot of quarters, sometimes $10,000 a day. During the first two months of 1969, it was estimated that 85% of the quarters shipped to Chemical's main branch came from Levin's peep-show collections.

After a while, Chemical began to chafe at the onslaught. Levin's boss was Martin Hodas, the peep show king of Times Square, a man who ruled a porn empire so vast that his very name was synonymous with sleaze, and Chemical finally sued to close the Hodas accounts, arguing that it could "expose itself to community disapproval" by doing business with such a person. Chemical lost the case, and Hodas continued to deposit his quarters here. In time, the bank left the corner, and the site became home to Show World, the biggest peep emporium of them all.

BROOKLYN-REARED Martin Hodas was in the jukebox business. In 1966, at age 35, he had a wife and four children and a route with 60 jukes. One day a repairman suggested that maybe Hodas could do something with a bunch of old nickelodeons lying around the shop.

Inspiration struck. Hodas bought 13 of the machines, threaded them with short stag films and started shopping them around to the shady little stores sprouting up on 42nd St., places offering girlie photos, decks of French playing cards and other such fare. Fear of legal repercussions made the machines a tough sell at first, but finally one shopkeeper took the chance. More followed, and then more after that. By the end of 1968, Hodas was running hundreds of machines in dozens of locations. "Even the successful porno book industry has been dwarfed by the phenomenon," the Daily News reported.

At home in Lawrence, L.I., Hodas was a good neighbor and a devoted dad who was active in the Little League and took local kids on fishing trips on his 40-foot cabin cruiser. To New York City's moral and civic leaders, he was the King of Porno. Authorities were slackjawed at the tidal wave of sleaze that had engulfed Times Square, much of it connected to the peep magnate. He had bookstores now, model studios, a string of massage parlors, all

NAKED CITY
Martin Hodas

pulling in some $40,000 a week. If it wriggled, Martin Hodas had a piece of it. "An open sewer running through the heart of the city," declared a shaken Rev. Billy Graham after he toured the Deuce. The greatest danger facing America, Graham said, was not communism but "deteriorating morality."

THE CROSSROADS OF the World had been hearing all this for years already. It had been decades since the Depression dimmed the lights of the great theaters once graced by Eddie Cantor and Will Rogers and the dance halls and penny arcades and the Minsky Brothers' racy burlesque shows moved in. "Cesspools of indecency and vice," crusaders called the flashy new establishments. Heeding their call, Mayor Fiorello LaGuardia began cracking down on burlesque in 1937, and three years later he banned it entirely.

But there was no turning the tide. World War II slowed down the theaters even more, and by 1948 the City Planning Commission was studying complaints that Times Square had become "a honky-tonk playground." One cleanup campaign after another was launched. None had the slightest effect. By the late 1960s — emboldened by the sexual revolution and a landmark Supreme Court ruling that made obscenity cases difficult to prosecute — Martin Hodas and his ilk were blanketing the Crossroads with peep emporiums, triple-X theaters, live sex shows and massage parlors. Prostitutes and hustlers filled the streets. Crime rates skyrocketed.

The peep show king contended he was just offering a service. His clients, he explained, were "normal American men" who happened to admire nude women. "Show me a man who doesn't admire a nude beautiful woman," he told a reporter in 1969, "and I'll show you a degenerate."

BUT IT WAS not easy being the Porno King of Times Square. Between the cops and the mob, it could be downright murderous.

Soon after business took off, Hodas began finding it necessary to make weekly payments to Colombo family capo John (Sonny) Franzese. And after Joe Colombo was slain in 1971 and a gangland turf war ensued, Hodas found himself in the middle of it. He was shot at in his office by visiting thugs. His massage parlors were hit with a rash of firebombings. His own house burned down. A fellow porn magnate was rubbed out.

Meanwhile, the city began to dog him, too. Machines were padlocked, clerks arrested, fire-code violations issued, licenses denied. In 1971, Hodas was arrested on wholesale pornography charges; a year later he was charged with bribery after police said he tried to pay off a sergeant. Rattled, he complained to one reporter that life was a nightmare. "I wish I could sell out," he said. "But with all this heat, nobody wants to buy."

Things got worse. In 1973, he was implicated in the firebombing of a rival massage parlor. His gun permit was revoked and later he was charged with illegal possession of a firearm. Then, in 1975, he was convicted of income tax evasion. Despite his testimony that the profits he was alleged to have pocketed had all been paid out in protection money, he went to prison for 10 months. At sentencing, his attorney told the judge that Hodas' wife had suffered a nervous breakdown; he had witnessed, the lawyer said, "the virtual destruction of this man and his family."

Hodas went to jail again in 1984, this time after pleading guilty to transporting videotapes across state lines and into Canada. Following his plea, which cost him a year behind bars, he began selling off his empire. "I don't want to have anything to do ever again with the porn business," he said. "It's shown me nothing but misery."

HE DIDN'T EXACTLY stay true to this vow; in 1994 it was reported that he was back in midtown with an interest in three adult businesses. But his timing was as bad then as it had been perfect a quarter of a century earlier. With Walt Disney moving in and new zoning laws taking effect, it just wasn't the same old Slime Square anymore.

By GENE MUSTAIN
Daily News Staff Writer

FRANK SERPICO was dead. He looked it, anyway, lying there in that forlorn hallway, his blood puddling on the grimy floor outside the dope dealer's den.

He felt it, too. The dealer's bullet had burrowed in below the left eye and rattled around before spewing fragments that lodged close to his brain.

They got me. Just like they said they would. My so-called brothers in blue set me up. What a way to check out. Dead on a two-bit hophead bust in Brooklyn.

Make that nearly dead. Someone in the building — not his backups in the hallway — dialed for help, and an ambulance came to 778 Driggs Ave. in Williamsburg on that night in February 1971 and took the city's most famous and most despised cop to a hospital.

He was famous and despised for the same reason. He had blown the whistle on crooked cops in the Bronx, and then unloaded to The New York Times about all the other crookedness he'd seen in the NYPD during 10 years on the job.

That would have been enough to earn the enmity of even many honest cops, but there was more: Serpico didn't look, act or think like the average cop. He loved ballet and opera, quoted poetry and lived in Greenwich Village with his pet cricket. With his beard and long hair, some cops thought he looked like Jesus Christ. Commissioner Howard Leary openly called him a psycho.

"He was the kind of cop who, if you put him on a prostitution detail, would question the meaning of love," his lawyer once said.

It was touch and go, but the 34-year-old Serpico survived. He lost hearing in his left ear, and the bullet fragments that stayed buried in his head would always cause him migraines. A few months later, the bosses gave him a gold shield. But Detective Serpico, whose revelations had caused many downtown heads to roll, had finally had it with the NYPD.

Truth be told, he'd had it with New York, too, and the country and the whole silly culture.

Late in 1971, he testified before a commission that had been formed a year earlier, after he first spoke out. Then, in 1972, after also testifying against the drug dealer who shot him — and still believing that brother blues were behind it — he retired on a $12,000 annual pension and exiled himself to Europe.

Over the next decade, he roamed here and there, often in a mobile camper, accompanied by his sheepdog Alfie and pet mouse Obelix.

In 1974, a reporter found him in a Dutch cafe, tugging on the gold hoop in his good ear and sipping gin. He said he'd had time to contemplate the ruckus he had raised in New York City and was sure the problem was bigger than corrupt cops.

"The whole system is rotten," he said. "America has become the land of the big ripoff. Rip off others before they rip you off."

Still, he was worrying now more about animals than people. Specifically, he worried about the swans in Holland's polluted canals, and had taken to feeding them whole-wheat bread "instead of that white-flour slop." He was toting a movie camera around, for a film contrasting animal and human behavior.

"I don't look beyond tomorrow," he added. "The way my head is now, I don't think I'll be around very long. Who wants to live forever?"

Back home, his life was churned through the book-movie-TV show cycle. The very word "Serpico" became synonymous with "honest cop."

BROTHERS IN BLUE
Frank Serpico

Briefly visiting New York for the premiere of the Al Pacino movie, he endorsed his lawyer Ramsey Clark's bid for a U.S. Senate nomination from New York.

Serpico told reporters who clamored around that he had left the seclusion of a Swiss chalet because Clark's candidacy meant so much to poor people.

"My being here is a matter of dealing with my conscience," he added. "I can't sit in the Swiss Alps while people are sitting here and suffering."

That was the extent of Serpico's political career. He returned to Europe and resumed the vagabond life.

THE SUDDENLY famous, disaffected exile had grown up humbly in Brooklyn, the son of an immigrant shoemaker who raised canaries from right out of the egg and taught his son to be truthful and strong. One day he watched in horror

as a cop sauntered into his father's shoe shop for a shine and departed without paying.

But that incident didn't sour him on police work for himself someday. In 1951, at age 14, he wrote in one of his school papers that he wanted to be a cop.

He got his wish in 1960. He soon saw there were many cops like the one who had come into his father's shop — and that many more were worse.

There was small-time graft and there were big-time payoffs — all of it immune to change because cops were not supposed to rat out other cops.

Initially, Serpico just looked the other way and steered his own course, refusing to take even free meals in the different Brooklyn precincts he worked. In time, dishonest cops who regarded his honesty as a threat decided to set him up.

One day, a cop stuffed an envelope into his hand and ran off. It contained $300. Serpico had two choices — keep the cash and become part of the system, or report the event to a boss and get branded a traitor.

He reported it. The sergeant he told kept the money for himself. And Frank Serpico's troubles in the NYPD were on.

WARNED BY cops in a particularly dirty Brooklyn plainclothes unit that he ought to be careful, in 1966 he asked for and got a transfer to the Bronx. But it was the same old story. Gamblers, bookmakers and prostitutes had to give regularly to "the pad" — the cops' dirty payroll — to stay in business. One day, Serpico learned that his name had been placed on the pad, and that his partner was secretly pocketing his cut.

He decided to talk to NYPD higher-ups. For two years, he was bounced around the brass bureaucracy; he tried the mayor's office; he tried the Department of Investigation. Finally, Bronx District Attorney Burton Roberts paid attention to him, and put together a case against eight cops.

To Serpico, it seemed like a small response to a big problem. And it was.

HE'D MET some other cops along the way who shared his indignation over the crooked system. These included a friend, Sgt. David Durk, and a former boss, Capt. Paul Delise. In the fall of 1969, joined by Durk and Delise, Serpico poured it all out for David Burnham of The New York Times.

The headlines forced Police Commissioner Leary to quit. Mayor John Lindsay appointed a special commission to probe the long-neglected sickness inside the NYPD. He picked a former assistant Manhattan district attorney who had entered private practice on Wall Street, Whitman Knapp, to lead it.

The Knapp Commission hired some cops who thought like Serpico, including one Detective Robert Leuci, to work undercover against fellow officers. Leuci's work led to another book-and-movie cycle, "Prince of the City." The commission also wanted to hear testimony from Detective Serpico, and it did, in the fall of 1971, soon after he recovered from being shot in the face.

Looking like a shaggy young professor at an antiwar meeting, Serpico told the commission about the pad. He said the NYPD must create a new atmosphere — one in which dishonest cops feared honest cops, and not the other way around.

The NYPD closed ranks against him even as its dirtiest ranks were cleaned out; he had violated the code, the one about never speaking out against a brother cop, an oath that placed cops above the law. The damage to his body was healed. The wound to his spirit was not.

SERPICO RETURNED to the U.S. in the early '80s, eventually retiring to a little cabin in the woods upstate. Every so often, he would make himself available for a few quotes about whatever police scandal was lately breaking.

"They say I am running away from life," he said during one of those occasions. "Of course I'm bitter, but maybe I have a right to be."

BIG TOWN ★ BIOGRAPHY

By JAY MAEDER
Daily News Staff Writer

ORIGINALLY, HE was not known to his fellow man as Crazy Joe. Originally, he was called Joey the Blond. This was before his fellow man realized that he was crazy. Paranoid schizophrenic, to be precise, so diagnosed by doctors at Kings County Hospital as early as 1950, when Joseph Gallo of Brooklyn was just another barely postjuvenile hoodlum. But that word never got out much, and eight years later, when he was a big enough jukebox racketeer that he had to go to Washington to take the Fifth before Bobby Kennedy and the Senate crime committee, he was still mostly just Joey the Blond.

Nice carpet you got here, he cracked when he first walked into Kennedy's office. *Good for a crap game.* Kennedy blinked at this guy, who looked exactly like Richard Widmark in "Kiss of Death," like he was New York City's flashiest gangster since Legs Diamond. Actually, Joey the Blond was just a nickel-and-dime enforcer for a mobbed-up Teamster local, but it is conventionally said of paranoiacs that delusionalism per se doesn't necessarily mean that nobody is trying to get you, and Joey was born late enough that by the time he was coming up in the world there were federal racket squads climbing all over guys like him.

Joey had it figured that large forces were marshaled against him; big labor, he divined, wanted to make Kennedy's senator brother John the President, and this is what he got for being a legit Teamster. The jukebox king wasn't about to let Bobby Kennedy break him. Toughest hood he'd ever met, Kennedy later recalled. *Nice carpet.*

Back home in Brooklyn, more famous now after he'd sneered down the U.S. Senate, Joey got shrunk again, one day in May 1959 he held a knife to the throat of a candy shop owner who didn't want a pinball machine, and this time the doctors decided that he might be sane after all. Disturbed, maybe. Joey laughed out loud to reporters about the ink-blot pictures the doctors kept showing him. Pictures like that could make a man crazy, he said.

THE CHRONICLE OF New York mob warfare is full of crafty, cunning and occasionally brilliant insurrectionary strategists. Joey Gallo was one of the more frankly unsubtle of the lot, a man whose plan of action chiefly involved just ignoring the dons and taking over their rackets for himself. Not cops, not dons, not street soldiers could believe how nuts he was as he singlehandedly touched off gangland wars such as the city had not seen for 30 years.

It was said of Joey Gallo that he had been one of the shooters called upon to do ganglord Albert

DEAD MAN WALKING
Crazy Joey Gallo

Anastasia in the barber's chair in October 1957 after Vito Genovese cut a deal with Anastasia's ambitious underboss Carlo Gambino and the job went to Joe Profaci's family. It was said that Joey had expected some career reward for this service. It was said that he was moved to turn on his elders when no such reward forthcame.

There was no reason a young man such as himself should be taking orders from the ancient olive oil king Profaci, he decided. By early 1961, Joey and his brothers Albert and Larry were openly leading a small mob of equally disgruntled breakaway Profacis, blatantly moving in on rackets that didn't belong to them. The old boss finally decided they were real nuisances and they had to go. At which point, in a show of rebel bravado, the Gallos kidnaped Profaci's brother, brother-in-law and a couple of other guys and held them hostage for a while.

Lawmen dropped their jaws at this insanity. The episode plainly portended a gangland bloodbath. The Gallos were obviously walking dead men. War, in fact, swiftly followed. The payback began with the quiet disappearance of Gallo man Joe Jelly, whose coat was delivered to his comrades wrapped around a fish, signaling that Joe was now at the bottom of Sheepshead Bay. A few days later, on Sunday afternoon the 20th of August

1961, a couple of Brooklyn policemen made a check of a Utica Ave. bar called the Sahara Club and found 33-year-old Larry Gallo getting himself strangled inside the place. One cop was shot in the subsequent fracas that saved Larry's life, and the Gallo-Profaci war was now very public.

Gunfire blazed for months, and hoods dropped left and right, but mostly the ridiculously outmanned and outgunned Gallo mob kept themselves holed up in their headquarters at 51 President St. in Brooklyn, and their revolution was essentially already over. It was, at any rate, interrupted in November, when Crazy Joey had to stand trial on an old charge of trying to muscle in on a check-cashing service. In December, convicted of extortion, he was sentenced to seven to 14 in prison and his insurgents were left leaderless.

By now, what was left of Gallo Inc. was under police protection, which was pretty embarrassing to begin with. Meanwhile, the newspapers were having a wonderful time writing about these Poverty Row hoodlums who had imagined that they were going to knock over the syndicate. "Hillbillies," one sheet hooted at them. "Poor slobs," chortled another. Gravely opined the Daily News: "What this mob needs is not a lot of harassment by big tough cops, but a weekly check from the welfare department."

INSIDE THE BIG house, Joe Gallo was quietly carving out new territory. In an unheard-of business move, he was crossing the color line, making Italian alliances with black cons, building a new mob for modern times. At one point he went public with a blast against Ku Klux Klan influence inside state prisons. Suddenly Crazy Joey was a noted civil rights spokesman. When racial uprisings broke out in East New York in the summer of 1966, the New York City Youth Board — to the disgust of police and prosecutors — actually deputized the Gallo family to mediate.

By the time Joey got out in early 1971, it was said that he had under his command a powerful black gangster army and that he was readying a fresh assault against the former Profaci family, now Joseph Colombo's family since Profaci's death a few years earlier. Certainly there were these rumors to consider when a black gunman showed up at the Italian Unity Day rally in Columbus Circle in June and gunned Colombo down.

Lawmen again braced for bloody war in the New York underworld. Nobody would put a nickel on Joey Gallo's life now.

BUT HE DIDN'T appear to want to act like a man with an open contract on his head. At this point a celebrity, thanks to the recent film that had been made of Jimmy Breslin's book "The Gang That Couldn't Shoot Straight," he got himself adopted by show business and literary types and became a welcome guest at the parties of swells, kind of everybody's pet mobster.

Shortly after 5 a.m. on April 7, 1972, celebrating his 43rd birthday with his new bride and his bodyguard and several other merrymakers, he stopped off in Little Italy, at a place called Umberto's. A few minutes later, a team of shooters burst in and blew him away over scungilli and mussels, and he lived just long enough to crash through a plate-glass door and drop in the middle of Mulberry St. Cops could never figure why he had kept doing the town night after night, seemingly so unconcerned about stalkers. It was like he was crazy or something.

By CORKY SIEMASZKO
Daily News Staff Writer

I N AN ERA of loosening marital bonds and anything-goes sexuality, New York Yankee pitchers Mike Kekich and Fritz Peterson charted new territory nonetheless in October 1972 by trading everything — wives, children, addresses, even family dogs.

They had seemed so normal. These were doting parents, residents of the New Jersey suburbs, where what people customarily traded were garden tools and recipes.

"Don't make anything sordid out of this," Peterson pleaded with the press when the arrangement became public knowledge.

"We didn't swap wives," Kekich explained. "We swapped lives."

LIFE IN The Show for professional baseball players means living in the spotlight. There's always someone to carry your bags. There's always an adoring fan begging for an autograph. And while the players are on the road for at least half the season, they always fly first class.

It's a different story for baseball wives. They are the ones left behind to tend to the children, pay the bills and keep the household running while their men are away. If they are lucky, they'll have to move only half a dozen times before their husbands hang up their cleats for good.

They do, however, get primo seats for the home games, where, as often as not, they can be seen commiserating with the other baseball wives. And thus did Marilyn Peterson and Susanne Kekich became fast friends.

Both appeared to have come to terms with their lives. "Being separated from your husband for a week or more at a time during the season is something you learn to live with," Marilyn said. Their kids were about the same age. They would all pile in the Peterson station wagon with picnic lunches and head for the park or the Jersey shore or the Bronx Zoo; when the Yankees played a home stand, the wagon would head over to the Stadium, and they'd all root for the boys, who were close pals themselves in the 1972 season.

At some point, Fritz fell for Susanne and Mike fell for Marilyn, and by midsummer the four of them had reached what they subsequently described as "a tremendous amount of affection and compatibility."

And by the time the Yankees closed out a so-so season in fourth place in the American League East Division, Fritz and Mike had gotten to first base with each other's wife. On Oct. 1, Fritz moved in with Susanne and Mike moved in with Marilyn.

All winter long, Susanne's Franklin Lakes neighbors kept asking her how Mike was, and she kept telling them just fine. The cat didn't get out of the bag until February, when she filed for divorce and custody of the two tiny Kekich daughters.

Shortly after that, Mike countersued — admitting in court papers that his end of the marital experiment hadn't worked out quite so well as had his teammate's. Mike and Marilyn, he confessed, had struck out.

At this same time, a blustering Florida shipbuilder named George Steinbrenner was buying the Yankees from CBS — and, at the end of March, the club traded Mike Kekich to the Cleveland Indians.

And so, while Fritz and Susanne were living in their happy little Franklin Lakes home, Marilyn and her two sons were living with her parents in Illinois. And Mike was stuck in Cleveland, by himself. Strike two.

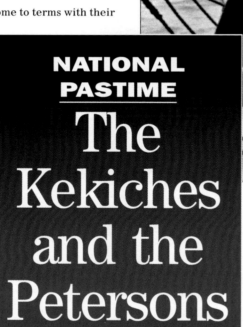

Marilyn and Mike and Susanne and Fritz.

NATIONAL PASTIME

The Kekiches and the Petersons

AND NOW, as rumors flew everywhere, the two pitchers decided to go public with their story.

Facing incredulous sportswriters at spring training in Fort Lauderdale, they calmly described their tradeoff, originally envisioned as a two-month trial run to see how things might work out. Fritz said his pal Mike wanted Marilyn because she had "more education and zest." As for himself, he said, "Susanne is the perfect person for me...She's what I always wanted in a wife, a person and a mother. Before, we both felt dominated. Now, we have free minds."

Mike, meanwhile, told of what he initially had regarded as "a love far greater than I had ever known," until Marilyn had second thoughts about the whole arrangement. Everything was fine between Fritz and Susanne, he noted, but "all of a sudden Marilyn and I were left out in the cold." Fritz acknowledged he had some regrets, "for my kids...If Mike and Marilyn don't get together, they'll be without a father. That eats me up. But I won't go back. I'll never go back."

Their teammates supportively rallied around the two southpaws. But the barons of baseball — still aghast over Jim Bouton's best-selling book "Ball Four," which painted the Yankees as a bunch of randy Peeping Toms — were far less forgiving. "It is not possible for an administrator of sports to reach the private lives of people like these," thundered baseball commissioner Bowie Kuhn. "But this isn't to say it is not a regrettable situation."

Everyday fans were also dismayed. "Every kid in

America looks up to these players," fumed John Santana, a married postal worker from the Bronx. "It's not right for them to do this." Agreed Santana's co-worker Larry Williams: "These people should consider their children...Celebrities can't live any way they want."

Dr. Joyce Brothers was called on for her view of things, and she predicted that the switch would end in disaster. "It's very rare that a four-way sweep ever works," she said.

Mike Kekich caught hell from the fans every time he mounted the mound. "Hey, Kekich, let your wife pitch," one guy shouted.

Fritz Peterson didn't get quite the fan roasting that Mike did, but then he was widely regarded as a better pitcher.

Susanne regularly scolded the press for its prying and at the same time admitted that she'd be "dying of curiosity" herself if she weren't part of the story. "You have to admit there are some funny aspects about this," she said.

A FTER THEIR divorces, Fritz and Susanne married and had four children of their own. A few seasons later, Fritz also was traded to Cleveland and wrapped up his career in Texas. The Petersons moved to the Chicago suburbs, where Fritz worked in real estate for a time, then found religion and became an evangelist.

Marilyn, who never said a public word about the episode, disappeared into Midwestern obscurity.

Mike pitched in Japan, Mexico and Venezuela before signing up for medical school in the Dominican Republic. He remarried, fathered another daughter and later went to work as an insurance adjuster in New Mexico.

"Neither Fritz Peterson nor I will ever make it into the Hall of Fame," he observed in 1992.

By JERE HESTER
Daily News Staff Writer

LIKE A FOOTBALL team's offensive line, former Miss America Bess Myerson, renowned architect Philip Johnson and a gangly Greenwich Village congressman named Ed Koch marched, hands outstretched, across 42nd St. on the morning of Jan. 30, 1975, halting cars, trucks and buses to clear a path for a woman whose name alone was enough to stop traffic: Jacqueline Bouvier Kennedy Onassis.

Jackie O, perhaps the most famous woman in the world, was following her VIP blockers to another treasured symbol of the city, Grand Central Terminal, which was in imminent danger of desecration at best and destruction at worst. A state Supreme Court decision nine days earlier had paved the way for a developer to plop an addition up to 59 stories tall atop the 1913 Beaux Arts landmark and potentially raze its stunning facade.

Grand Central's historic old clock, surrounded by statues of Minerva, Mercury and Hercules, ticked away precious seconds as news photographers snapped picture after picture of the elusive former First Lady, who patiently posed and smiled.

"Only Jackie Onassis can save us now," Johnson declared.

Onassis, who long had avoided the press with an almost Garbo-like intensity, gamely addressed the throngs of reporters who jammed the Oyster Bar for the rare audience.

"If we don't care about our past, we cannot hope for our future," she said, her soft voice competing against the kitchen clatter.

"I care desperately about saving old buildings."

JACKIE BOUVIER had surely passed by the grand old railroad station hundreds of times as a young girl. Born in Southampton on July 28, 1929, the daughter of banker Black Jack Bouvier split her time between Long Island and Park Ave. before moving to E. 82nd St. as a teen following her parents' divorce.

She had displayed her love of old buildings as John F. Kennedy's First Lady, overseeing the refurbishment of the White House, filling it with antiques she proudly displayed during a 1962 televised tour.

After JFK's assassination in November 1963, she and her children briefly moved to Georgetown, but the tourists flocking to her doorstep quickly proved too much to bear. So the young widow returned to the only place where she believed she, Caroline and John Jr. had any shot at a normal life: New York.

For $200,000, she bought a 15-room, 15th-floor apartment on Fifth Ave., overlooking Central Park. Even after ensconcing the kids in local schools, in truth, Jackie barely had time to really settle in, what with her jet-set romance and marriage to Greek shipping magnate Aristotle Onassis. But after his death in early 1975, she made New York her permanent headquarters, estates in New Jersey and Martha's Vineyard aside.

For the first time, Jackie was determined, she would establish an identity not as a powerful man's wife or widow, but as a mother and a New Yorker. Her life in the city would become her own personal Camelot.

BEHIND HER trademark dark glasses, Jackie attempted to lose herself in the crowds. She was, to be sure, sometimes known to drop tens of thousands of dollars at Bloomingdale's, but she also was seen inspecting the shmattes at the local thrift shop, squeezing produce at Gristede's and praying at the tiny Church of St. Thomas More on E. 89th St.

"My life is very dull right now," she insisted to a reporter in Central Park one day. "I'm doing just very ordinary, everyday things. Really, my life at the moment would make very uninteresting reading. Do you think it would be of much interest for anyone to know that I go shopping at the local A&P?"

Her foray into the Grand Central fight aside, Onassis was becoming a little bored in the months after the Greek tycoon's death. At the urging of pals, she notched in September 1975 an editor's post at Viking Press, her first job since she'd been an inquiring camera girl for the Washington Times-Herald in the early 1950s.

Her positions at Viking and later Doubleday edged her back into the nightlife. She would be seen at Elaine's and P.J. Clarke's on the arms of bandleader Peter Duchin or director Mike Nichols, and her stable of authors included such bold-face names as Diana Vreeland and Michael Jackson.

While stalkers and paparazzi were a constant worry — she famously had secured a restraining order against celebrity shutterbug Ron Galella — she managed to get around without limos and was a favorite fare of cabbies, who fondly recalled their brushes with Jackie O.

Once she got into a taxi with a box of tangerines and offered one to the hack. "Eat it," she insisted. "It's good for you."

"So I did," the driver recalled. "And we got into this long conversation. She told me what she ate. Things like tangerines. Other fruit. I told her what I ate. It was a very interesting talk."

Her common touch, regal charm and aura of mystery launched Onassis to heights of popularity not seen since her White House days — even

With Myerson, Johnson and Koch

EVERYDAY THINGS

Jacqueline Kennedy Onassis

sparking talk in 1976 that she would run for U.S. Senate.

"I'd win, of course," she told friends privately.

BUT HER BIGGEST political cause would be the Grand Central Terminal battle, which by 1978 wound its way to the U.S. Supreme Court.

The city argued that its landmarks law — enacted in 1966 after the demolition of Penn Station, the staggering blow that spurred the powerful preservation movement — was necessary to keep Gotham's most precious structures from meeting the wrecking ball. The bankrupt Penn Central Transportation Co. contended that the city Landmarks Preservation Commission's kibosh on selling lucrative development rights over the station represented an unconstitutional seizure of property.

The stakes were high: The court could nix the city's landmarks law, potentially exposing countless architectural gems in New York — and around the country — to destruction.

On the eve of oral arguments, Jacqueline Onassis led a mobile menagerie of 300 clowns, banjo players, mimes, fire eaters and preservationists on an old-fashioned, rollicking whistlestop rail ride from New York to Washington, hoping the nine men in black robes were listening.

Stopping only to munch on hamburgers and crackers, she strolled through the eight-car chartered Landmark Express, glad-handing supporters and making speeches at stops in Philadelphia and Baltimore.

"If Grand Central Station goes, all of the landmarks in this country will go as well," she warned. "If that happens, we'll live in a world of steel and glass."

Singing a pep song to the tune of "Tipperary" — *Let's make a grand stand to save Grand Central, the greatest landmark site of all* — the crew arrived in Washington, greeted by a brass band. Whether all the hoopla really helped was unclear, but two months later the court rejected Penn Central's arguments 6 to 3. The station had been saved.

"The old dame has been in town for as long as any of us can remember, and now we can be sure that she'll be around long after we're gone," wrote Daily News columnist Pete Hamill. "The wreckers have been defeated."

EARLY IN 1994, Jackie was diagnosed with non-Hodgkin's lymphoma, and on May 15 she took her last walk through Central Park, clutching her longtime companion, diamond merchant Maurice Tempelsman.

Four days later, she died, surrounded by family, in her apartment. On the morning of her funeral Mass, thousands of ordinary New Yorkers lined up along Park Ave., across from St. Ignatius Loyola Church, to mourn one of their own.

On Oct. 1, 1998, thousands flooded Grand Central's main concourse to celebrate a $200 million restoration that would take the terminal well into the next century. An orchestra played as eyes turned upward to the glistening constellations of the soaring, newly cleaned ceiling. Then all eyes turned to John F. Kennedy Jr., who accepted a plaque in Jackie's memory.

"My mother would be very happy today," he said.

By JERE HESTER
Daily News Staff Writer

I've been sloughed way down,
But I'll slow drag up again.
When that big day arrives,
Remember my name.

FROM THE MOMENT frail old Alberta Hunter stepped onto the stage of the Cookery on Oct. 10, 1977, and saw that the small Greenwich Village jazz club was packed, it was clear that no one had forgotten her name.

Still, there was room for worry. It had been nearly a quarter of a century since she had quit show business cold and become a practical nurse, selflessly bathing and feeding the infirm and dying in a hospital on the dank human dumping ground called Welfare Island.

And it had been some 50 years since her heyday as the toast of Broadway, London's Drury Lane and the Folies Bergère in Paris, where she strutted the streets, clad in diamonds, with pals Josephine Baker and Mabel Mercer.

Now, Hunter's fanciest accoutrement was a pair of oversize gold hoop earrings that loomed even larger on her 82-year-old frame. But as the band began to play, she reached back and found the powerful voice.

It's hard to love someone,
When that someone don't love you.
I'm so disgusted, heartbroken, too,
I've got the down hearted blues.

OLD VIOLINS
Alberta Hunter

Hunter smiled, snapped her long fingers and slapped her hips as grown men brushed away tears, knowing they were witness to what Cookery owner Barney Josephson called the greatest comeback in the history of music.

"She can still swing, God bless her," one stirred soul couldn't help but say aloud.

The audience wouldn't let her leave the stage. The applause, she said after her final encore, "was food for a hungry person."

From here on, all of Alberta Hunter's days would be big days.

SHE WAS BORN in April 1895 and reared in Memphis, on legendary Beale St., brimming with prostitutes, gamblers and blues musicians. Her mother, a brothel maid, strived to shield her from the seedier elements.

But at 16, the spirited girl ran away from home, hopping a train for Chicago, where, she had been told, one could make $10 a week singing.

By day, she peeled potatoes for $6 a week, sending $2 home to her mother. By night, she haunted a honky-tonk called Dago Frank's, begging for a chance to entertain the hookers, pimps and gangsters who frequented the joint for business and pleasure. Finally, the owner gave her a shot, and Hunter wowed the crowd with "Where the River Shannon Flows," notching a $5-a-week job.

Eventually, she won a following as the South Side's Sweetheart and went on to Chicago's famed Dreamland Ballroom, where her fans included Eddie Cantor, Al Jolson and Sophie Tucker, who made her piano player write down every note Hunter sang.

It was here that she honed her repertoire, singing everything from ballads to show tunes to raunchy blues, working with the likes of Fats Waller, Eubie Blake and Louis Armstrong. She also became a songwriter, penning "Down Hearted Blues," Bessie Smith's first big hit.

In 1923, Hunter decided it was time to blow out of the Windy City. Five days after she landed in New York, she was in an all-black Broadway musical called "How Come?" The public prints were enthusiastic. "Those girls and boys strut their stuff," noted the Evening Journal. "Yes suh!"

SHE SETTLED IN Harlem and became a hot

act, bouncing from clubs to vaudeville theaters to Europe, where she played opposite Paul Robeson in the London production of "Show Boat" and replaced Josephine Baker at the Casino de Paris. Her shows drew repeat visits from English royalty, Cole Porter and Noel Coward, who wrote the ballad "I Travel Alone" for her. "There is a real class to this girl," The New York Times observed in 1929.

Even through the Depression, Hunter, who lived clean and was tight with a buck, made a decent living, cutting records and doing radio. She went on to join the USO, entertaining overseas troops during World War II and the Korean War. As she approached 60, it seemed like Alberta Hunter would go on singing forever.

But on Jan. 17, 1954, Hunter's beloved mother, who had come to live with her years earlier, died at 77. Suddenly, performing was no longer important. From now on, she decided, she wanted only to "help humanity."

THE DAY AFTER her mother was buried, Hunter marched into the Harlem YWCA and signed up for nursing school, shaving 12 years off her age on her application. After graduating, she began work at Goldwater Memorial Hospital on grim Welfare Island.

She seldom breathed a word of her past and never opened her mouth to sing. "There was no hummin' or singin' there," she said years later. "I just wanted to cuddle 'em and make 'em comfortable. If my patient was restless, I'd stay there and try to soothe my patient to sleep, no matter how long it took. Then, when they went to sleep, I'd go on home."

Still, when a colleague once told Hunter how she loved Bessie Smith, she couldn't help but open her purse and show off a royalty check for "Down Hearted Blues."

By the mid-1970s, with the city in a fiscal crisis, Hunter's hospital bosses increasingly began to wonder how old she was. She kept fudging, but finally they decided she had to be at least 70, which was the mandatory retirement age, and she lost her $220-a-week job.

"I don't think I've ever been more hurt," she lamented later. "That hurt me to my heart."

ELDERLY, JOBLESS and bored, a few months later Hunter attended a party for her old friend Mabel Mercer at Bobby Short's apartment and, prodded by guests, belted out "Down Hearted Blues." At this point she was introduced to Barney Josephson, who invited her to the Cookery — where she was a instant hit and played three shows a night, six days a week.

She sang some ballads and gospel, but her trademark was bawdy blues — mostly her own compositions — full of sly double entendres delivered with a wink.

I got a man,
He's kinda old and thin.
But there are many good tunes left
In an old violin ...

Between songs, she dispensed motherly advice. "God Almighty and the dollar are your best friends," she would inform the crowds. "Call your parents! On Saturdays, Sundays and holidays, you can call for practically nothing!"

Not only was Hunter once again a formidable star, she was a big story. She did "Today," "Good Morning America," "60 Minutes." In 1979, she sang for President Jimmy Carter, not troubling to spare the religious First Family her most risqué material: *I want him to grab me/ And tear off all my clothes/ Just to let me know who's boss... .* First Lady Rosalynn Carter dropped her jaw in amazement. The president, for his part, insisted on half an hour of encores.

Hunter toured the U.S., played Europe and South America, recorded several albums. "Honey, I could stand in one spot and sing all night," she'd say. "Hard work, courage and stamina. That's what keeps me going. I'm going out with my shoes on."

BUT IN the summer of 1984, an ailing Hunter had to cut short a performance in Denver. She was 89, and her comeback was over. On Oct. 17, she died in her Riverside Drive apartment. Three months later, the city renamed the building where she had worked as a nurse, on what had by now been renamed Roosevelt Island, the Alberta Hunter Memorial Building. Her name would be remembered after all.

BIG TOWN ★ BIOGRAPHY

By JERE HESTER
Daily News Staff Writer

CLARA HALE, by her own admission, couldn't much carry a tune. But that didn't keep her from singing night after night to the babies she walked up and down the hallways of her Harlem brownstone, cradling them in her frail arms as they shook and cried from the cravings in their veins for drugs.

"Amazing grace, how sweet the sound ..."

"Sometimes my singing is so bad, I can see them starting to laugh, and I just look at them and I tell them, 'All right, I can't sing, but I'm gonna keep on singing,' " the white-haired woman called Mother Hale would tell visitors to her Hale House.

Clara Hale, who had toiled anonymously for years, taking in children nobody wanted, would keep on singing even after praise from President Ronald Reagan earned her national acclaim in 1985, at age 79. Even after the dual scourges of crack and AIDS left hundreds more tiny souls on her doorstep. Even after City Hall tried to put her out of the business of saving lives barely begun.

No one and nothing would keep Mother Hale from her mission.

"I love children and I love caring for them," she would say. "That is what the good Lord meant me to do."

LEFT WIDOWED at 27 with three children, she had cleaned houses by day and Loews theaters by night until, frustrated by the lack of good day-care facilities, she started taking the children of other domestics into her walkup apartment on W. 146th St. She had a way with the little ones. "The kids must have liked it, because once they got there, they didn't want to go home," Mother Hale would recall.

She eventually began welcoming foster children into her home for $2 a week. In 1968, at age 63, having reared the last of 40 foster kids, she called it quits and decided to kick back and enjoy retirement.

That all changed one day a year later, when her daughter Lorraine encountered a heroin addict on a park bench, a 2-month-old slipping out of her nodding mother's arms.

"I said what I always say: 'Take it to mother,'" Lorraine Hale remembered.

When the junkie arrived at her door, Clara Hale was dubious. After all, she hadn't raised her daughter to consort with drug addicts. She went inside to call Lorraine to verify the woman's story. When she returned, the woman was gone and the baby was on the doorstep.

Two months later, 22 drug-addicted infants were packed into her five-room apartment. Mother Hale didn't know how to say no.

"Before I knew it, every pregnant addict in Harlem knew about the crazy lady who would give her baby a home," she said.

SHE DIDN'T KNOW much about drugs, but she knew children, and she knew the value of tough love. There were rules: No fixes — not even aspirin — no matter how much a baby cried. Mothers would have to go into rehab and would be required to visit their children once a week. Ninety percent of the time, she was able to reunite a cleaned-up child with a cleaned-up mom.

But this didn't impress city officials, who, once they began hearing about Mother Hale, promptly ordered her to return the infants to their mothers or relinquish them to child welfare authorities.

She turned to Manhattan Borough president Percy Sutton, who got the city to lay off — and, more important, got her some government funding and helped secure a W. 122nd St. brownstone that in 1975 became Hale House.

As word of the operation expanded, tales of Mother Hale's good works began to trickle downtown. One day in 1979, she got a call from an Englishman looking for the "old lady of Harlem."

"He told me he had been trying for two years to

find me," Hale said. John Lennon gave her a $20,000 check and celebrated the last Christmas of his life by sending food and presents to Hale House.

Word eventually made it as far south as Washington, where the White House was eager to trot out Mother Hale as a shining example of private charity and self-reliance during Reagan's fifth State of the Union address.

No Reagan fan, she tried to beg off, citing health problems. But the White House was insistent — and so, on Feb. 6, 1985, Mother Hale sat next to First Lady Nancy Reagan as the president declared Hale to be a "true American hero." Amid a standing ovation, the old lady of Harlem mouthed a simple "Thank you."

WERE LIFE A movie, the credits would have rolled there and then, and everyone would have left the theater teary-eyed and happy.

In real life, though the publicity had helped spur fresh donations, Hale House faced new crises. An alarming number of infants born with the AIDS virus were languishing in hospitals — so-called boarder babies, a moniker that smacked of hopelessness. By 1987, there were hundreds of such kids in New York, many of them cradled in Mother Hale's arms.

"These children are so pathetic," she lamented. "We know some of them will die."

At the same time, there were several thousand crack-addicted babies. Even the patient Mother Hale betrayed hints of exasperation. "Mothers on crack are not like the mothers of old," she noted. "It used to be that mothers would be rehabilitated and would return to claim their children. But mothers on crack sometimes simply disappear."

By Mother Hale's 85th birthday, with an increasing number of children in need of her unique, if unorthodox, services, the city suddenly decided to cut her off cold. Past administrations had benignly ignored her flouting of regulations barring group care for children under 5. But David Dinkins' City Hall, deciding that the crack menace had peaked and welfare officials were doing a satisfactory job of placing troubled

infants in foster families, stopped sending babies to Hale House — meaning a $360,000 annual loss in funding.

Mother Hale responded as any mom would: By turning into a lioness.

"He's a dummy," she said of the mayor. He had been cowed, she charged, by white-owned child care agencies that long had wanted her shut down. "This is what happens when they give a black man a job. He does what the white man tells him to do."

Dinkins wouldn't back down, even as aides conceded they had a public relations disaster on their hands. "It's like trying to tell Mother Teresa that a vaccine for leprosy has been discovered, so she should find a new line of business," one official sighed.

Private donations began to pour in from other sources — churches, regular folks and the likes of Donald Trump, Lena Horne and Tony Bennett. "She's a giver," Bennett explained.

HALE HOUSE went on and so did Mother Hale, sleeping only when the babies napped. In her 87th year, when she somehow found the time to earn her general equivalency diploma, she suffered a stroke — and, on Dec. 18, 1992, she died, having cared for nearly 1,000 children no one else wanted.

There would be no expensive coffin or flowers at her funeral. "Use that money for the children," she had ordered. A crowd that included Sutton, Dinkins, Sen. Alfonse D'Amato and Yoko Ono laid red roses on her simple pine coffin at Riverside Church.

Sutton hailed her as "Our Lady of Inner-City Royalty." The Rev. Carolyn Knight said: "She touched children no one else would touch. She showed us that what children really need is a hug and a kiss and a smile."

And a song.

As Harlem bade a final goodbye, the church filled with her favorite hymn.

Amazing grace, how sweet the sound, that saved a wretch like me. I once was lost, but now I'm found. Was blind but now I see.

AMAZING GRACE
Mother Hale

By HOWARD KISSEL
Daily News Staff Writer

JONATHAN LARSON was sitting in the tiny New York Theater Workshop on E. Fourth St. on Jan. 21, 1996, watching one of the last rehearsals of a musical he had written. Suddenly he experienced chest pains, dizziness, shortness of breath. An ambulance was called, and he was rushed to Cabrini Medical Center. Food poisoning, it was decided. Larson's stomach was pumped, he was given a painkiller and he was sent on his way.

Two days later, still in pain and running a fever, the young playwright went to the emergency room of St. Vincent's Medical Center. There he was given a chest X ray and an electrocardiogram. Viral syndrome, it was decided. He was sent home again.

Two days after that, feeling no better, he left his show's final dress rehearsal around midnight and went back to his Greenwich Village apartment. At 3:30 in the morning, his roommate, Brian Carmody, found him lying dead on the kitchen floor. A gas flame on the stove burned under a scorched teakettle.

Aortic aneurysm, the autopsy concluded.

His show opened a few weeks later. It was called "Rent."

NOT SINCE the legendary director-choreographer Gower Champion died the day his "42nd Street" opened in 1980 and producer David Merrick announced it from the stage of the Winter Garden during the opening night curtain calls had the New York theater seen anything so melodramatic.

By the time "Rent" opened Feb. 13 at the 150-seat Theater Workshop, it was already impossible to discuss the show without referring to the tragic story of its creator.

"Rent" won almost unanimous rave reviews and a few months later moved to Broadway, where it won numerous Tonys, including Best Musical. It also won the Pulitzer Prize, the seventh musical in 80 years to do so.

And Bloomingdale's opened a Rent Boutique to sell East Village clothes at upper East Side prices.

LARSON HAD worked on "Rent" for seven years. The idea — an updated version of Puccini's "La Boheme" set in Alphabet City — had come up while he was sitting on the roof of his rundown apartment building on Greenwich St., in the far West Village, with playwright friend Billy Aronson. Larson was not a happy man at the time, supporting himself as a waiter while he sought the break that would enable him to devote himself

LA VIE BOHEME
Jonathan Larson

to writing. He'd recently had a futuristic rock musical, "Superbia," presented in workshop at Playwrights Horizons. Theater people praised it highly, but no one with money wanted to move it to a commercial venue.

Aronson's idea of a "La Boheme" rewrite excited Larson. Here was potentially a "Hair" for the MTV generation of the '90s. Aronson dropped out of the project in 1991, and Larson continued on his own, developing ideas from his own life and the bohemian world in which he lived.

Like several of the characters in "Rent," he had grown up in middle-class comfort in Westchester. As a boy in White Plains, he had taken piano lessons and played tuba in the high school band. He played Tevye in his high school's production of "Fiddler on the Roof." At Adelphi University, where he majored in acting, he began writing songs for college cabaret revues.

In 1990, he performed "Tick ... Tick ... Boom," a rock monologue at The Village Gate. It was the rant of a man who had just turned 30 and found his ambitions frustrated, a fictional conceit not far removed from his own situation; the anger was tempered, however, by the conclusion, in which he explored his feelings on discovering that one of his closest friends had been diagnosed as HIV-positive. This was part of Larson's experience as well. He was a straight man, but many of his friends, as part of New York's theater community,

were gay, and in the early 1990s AIDS was taking an enormous toll on that community. Larson wanted his show to reflect that loss.

In March 1993, a staged reading of the work was presented under the direction of Michael Greiff, who would continue as director until the show reached Broadway. Later that year, Larson submitted his material to the Richard Rodgers Studio Production award competition, a prestigious and lucrative contest whose chief judge was Stephen Sondheim.

Sondheim, generous to young composers despite his reputation for being an intimidating figure, had seen "Superbia" and admired it. What Sondheim found interesting was how versed Larson was in pop music — gospel, rock, rhythm and blues. Most theater composers know only theater music; Sondheim liked the fact that Larson was grounded in the music of his time. And so, Larson won the $45,000 award, which enabled the New York Theater Workshop to mount a workshop production of "Rent."

That production was seen by producers Alan Gordon, Kevin McCollum and Jeffrey Sellers. For $60,000, half of what it would cost for the workshop to mount a full-scale production, they got the right to move the show to Broadway. The production went into rehearsal in early January 1996, and there was buzz from the beginning, even as Jonathan Larson's heart was giving out on him.

'RENT" WAS a media event from the day it opened and has remained so ever since, through openings across the country and in London. Its profits enabled Larson's parents to establish a foundation to assist young writers struggling as their son had done.

The two hospitals that misdiagnosed Larson were fined a total of $16,000. In late 1999, his parents had malpractice suits pending against them.

In 1998, Larson's former Village apartment was advertised for rent. Only minor improvements had been made since the days when a young playwright could live there on a waiter's earnings. The floorboards were still rotting, the sink still rusty. Given the fame of the former tenant, the landlord now wanted $3,000 a month.

By DAVID HINCKLEY
Daily News Staff Writer

IT'S PERHAPS a trifle harsh to say Tony Bennett's whole career was built on a lie. After all, the guy won seven Grammy Awards, sold millions of records, sung his songs for the whole second half of the 20th century. When someone once asked Frank Sinatra to name his favorite singer, he said Tony Bennett got more out of a song than anyone he could think of.

Still, there remains the matter of "I Left My Heart in San Francisco," which for the casual listener remains the song most associated with Tony Bennett.

Recorded in 1962, "San Francisco" was a pleasant enough ditty. Joe DiMaggio could have sung it. From the lips of Tony Bennett, well, that's another story. Bennett's real "city by the bay" was Astoria. He grew up around 32nd St. The bay was Flushing Bay. After Astoria, he lived in Riverdale. Then he moved to Manhattan. To blow Tony Bennett out of New York would take a blast stronger than rock 'n' roll, which tried to wreck his career for 30 years, only to find he was still standing.

No, he was born in New York, still lives in New York, paints in New York, plays tennis in New York. He sings songs written by New Yorkers like Irving Berlin and George Gershwin.

The only place outside New York he ever came close to leaving his heart in was Moe's Main Street Tavern in Cleveland, where he was singing in April 1951 when he met a girl in the audience named Patricia Beach. She became his wife. The marriage had a good run, 19 years and two children, D'Andrea and Daegal. But still, as soon as things got serious, Tony persuaded Pat to move to New York, where she got a job on Wall Street. The wedding was at St. Patrick's Cathedral.

San Francisco? Right. The only thing Tony Bennett left in San Francisco was his room key, when he checked out and came home.

What he brought to the table in New York, meanwhile, was one of the more buoyant musical careers of the 20th century.

IT WAS A career that for a long time didn't look like it would happen at all, back when he was a kid out of the High School of Industrial Arts and the Army — infantry, Europe — who developed the kind of hunger for showbiz that made him work tables as a singing waiter at the Pheasant Tavern in Astoria and run elevators in the Park Sheraton while he studied bel canto singing.

In 1949, he got a shot on "Arthur Godfrey's Talent Scouts." He finished second to Rosemary Clooney, but impressed Jan Murray enough that Murray signed them both for his own TV show, "Songs for Sale."

There are several versions of what happened next, the simplest being that Pearl Bailey saw Bennett and got him a gig where Bob Hope saw him and gave him a guest spot on his show.

It is generally agreed that Hope suggested the young singer stop calling himself Joe Bari and start using Tony Bennett, which was closer to Anthony Dominick Benedetto, the name under which he was born Aug. 3, 1926. His father, John, an immigrant tailor and grocer with a beautiful voice, died when Tony was 8, after which his mother, Anna, supported three children as a seamstress.

So it was Tony Bennett who, in March 1950, was signed to a contract with Columbia Records by Mitch Miller, the label's musical gatekeeper, who liked the way the kid sang "Boulevard of Broken Dreams." As a single, that song didn't sell too well, but the follow-up, "Because of You," went to No. 1, and Cash Box magazine voted Bennett the outstanding male vocalist of 1951.

It was a good time to be a hot young male crooner: Sinatra was in his doldrums, and many of the top pop voices were women. But that didn't guarantee good notices. After Bennett scored another No. 1 with Hank Williams' "Cold Cold Heart," he later recalled, ol' Hank rang him up and asked him why he ruined the song.

Actually, Bennett said he'd never heard Williams' version. Still, he waited until Hank was dead, in 1954, to record another Williams tune.

Such caution did not mollify critic Harriet Van Horne, who wrote that Bennett's live performance "was so overwrought as to make an audience look away in polite embarrassment. Stiff-legged, wildly off-key, eyes in a fine frenzy rolling. And those top notes! Pure screaming agony."

In fact, Bennett was working under a handicap in those first years: Miller, whose belief that the public craved lightweight pop caused him to steer all Columbia artists in that direction.

Sinatra eventually walked. But Bennett stayed, quietly holding his own against Miller and an even weirder beast called rock 'n' roll.

NO ROCK fan, Tony Bennett. Asked about it, he would quote the line often attributed to Jimmy Durante that rock 'n' roll consists of three chords — and two of them are wrong.

For a long time, rock 'n' roll seemed to be getting the last laugh. Though Bennett recorded regularly into the early 1960s, records often served as an adjunct to his thriving concert career.

Fortunately, "I Left My Heart in San Francisco" made him, in Columbia's mind, an evergreen. The album stayed on the charts for almost three years and led to a flurry of albums that solidified his brand name and guided him back toward the music he'd really wanted to sing all along — the golden-age popular standards of the big bands that, alas, were gone when he got back from the war.

After 1967, when top 40 radio tossed out the last vintage pop singers — Bennett, Sinatra, Dean Martin — Bennett's sales shriveled further. He had recorded more than 50 albums for Columbia, but now he was back to the worst of the Mitch Miller days: The material he was being asked to record, he said, made him feel like Anna Benedetto felt when she was handed a cheap dress. It made her feel cheap too.

Bennett wouldn't give in. He was not going to sing the songs of Iron Butterfly. He held to Gershwin, and inevitably something had to give.

In 1971, he was divorced from both Patricia and Columbia, and he would not record for a major label for 15 years.

Furthermore, his son Danny had a rock band. Et tu, D'Andrea?

But Bennett didn't give up. He kept singing, kept going with the live shows until he and Ralph Sharon, his musical arranger, were like a single instrument. He kept painting and eventually would exhibit all over the country. He married Sandra Grant, and they had two daughters, Joanna and Antonia.

Without recording, he made a good living, and come the '80s, he figured that's just how it would be. But he didn't figure on the ambitions of his new manager, son Danny, who had given up the rock band because Tony Bennett was the most promising property he knew.

Keep doing what you do, Danny said. Let me talk to some people.

AND SO, in 1986, Tony Bennett returned to Columbia and recorded an album pointedly titled "The Art of Excellence." He would follow that with albums themed to the songs of Sinatra, the songs of Berlin and Gershwin, and darned if he wasn't in the right place at the right time. They weren't all million-sellers, but he became a steady presence — a respected and admired symbol for the best of his era. He also won five more Grammy Awards.

It helped that, with a nudge from Danny, he decided to work with rock 'n' roll instead of against it. He still didn't sing it, but he played an "MTV Unplugged" concert of Tony Bennett songs — the recording became one of his Grammy winners — and he was a regular at awards shows and other celebrity affairs, cheerfully sharing podiums with fellow artists as goofy as the Red Hot Chili Peppers.

I'm still not a rock 'n' roller, he would say. But live and let live. There's room for everybody. Besides, life is more fun this way.

As the century came to a close, then, Tony Bennett was living in midtown Manhattan, painting, singing the great songs, enjoying his family. It's the American Dream, the dream of the immigrant's son, and he probably could have done it in San Francisco.

But he didn't. He did it in New York.

DOING WHAT YOU DO
Tony Bennett

By JON KALISH
Special to The News

"A man should know how to use a knife and a spoon, and he should know how to use a handkerchief."

— Ab Cahan

HE COULD HAVE stayed in Russia and faced prison along with other such young revolutionary agitators as himself. He could have joined other expatriate radicals in France or Switzerland. The third alternative was America. Abraham Cahan arrived in New York in June 1882, and he went straightaway to work inciting the lower East Side proletariat. In August, the 22-year-old firebrand ranted for two hours in a German anarchist saloon on E. Sixth St., delivering the first socialist speech in Yiddish on American soil. By September, he was urging workers to take up axes and march on the homes of the Fifth Ave. millionaires.

Of those fine early days, he later wrote: *"I felt America's freedom every minute. I breathed freer than I had ever breathed before."*

AB CAHAN'S axe-swinging fervor subsided, but he remained a dedicated socialist, speaking at rallies across the Northeast, writing for the Yiddish press, reflecting the tumultuous passions of New York's new immigrant floods and increasingly positioning himself as their voice. By the late 1880s he had founded two socialist newspapers, the Neue Zeit and the New York Arbeiter Zeitung, and in 1895 he became editor of a third, the Zukunft. In 1896, his novel "Yekl" — hailed as the first authentic novel of immigrant life in New York, the story of a Jew who left his wife and baby in Russia and came to the city to toil in a sweatshop — made him famous overnight.

When, in 1897, a group of peddlers, tailors and cigar makers in the Socialist Labor Party got together $800 to start another newspaper, Ab Cahan was their choice for editor.

THE NEW broadsheet was called the Jewish Daily Forward, and it debuted with the slogan *Workers of the World, Unite!* on its masthead and tedious doctrinaire socialist dogma in its pages. After just eight months, the editor decided the paper was nothing more than a party organ, and he left.

By that time, Lincoln Steffens was city editor at the Commercial Advertiser, the oldest paper in the city, affectionately known as "Grandma." Steffens took on Cahan as a reporter, and at the turn of the century Cahan was a leading portraitist of the humor and pathos of daily life in the lower East Side tenements. What he mostly saw all around him was profound ignorance. "The immigrant Jews here were not educated," he would recall years later.

"Most of them had learned to read the Bible in Hebrew, but they were ignorant of geography and of events going on around them." When, in 1902, the failing Forward urged him to come back, he agreed to do so, with the stipulation that he could edit a useful household journal instead of a dry political screed.

So it was that Abraham Cahan became a father figure to several generations of New York City's humbler Jews, the most influential man in their lives — occupying, said The New York Times at his death many years later, "a unique position among the poor and laboring classes of his own people, contributing profoundly to their Americanization."

"IN THE GREAT daily," Cahan said, "an editor is exactly an editor. On the East Side, he is an editor, a rabbi, a sympathizer and a friend."

The Daily Forward carried on as an ardent unionist, active in organizing the needle trades and crusading against brutal sweatshop conditions, and workers regularly

CLEAN NOSES
Ab Cahan

concluded their strikes by parading triumphantly toward the Forward's East Broadway offices. But Cahan was equally energetic as he undertook to educate and elevate his immigrant readers. Among his newspaper's many pet projects was its insistent campaign for the use of handkerchiefs. When critics protested this as trivial, Cahan replied: "Since when is socialism opposed to clean noses?"

He was not particularly a likable man, even his admirers agreed; he was cranky and imperious, convinced of the infallibility of his own judgments. But he was possessed of an ear "attuned to the aches and aspirations in his readers' hearts," as his biographer Moses Rischin puts it. Or, as Cahan put it himself: "I knew whom we were writing for and we wrote so they could understand." It was this obsession with the human drama that led Cahan in 1906 to establish the Forward's famed advice column, the Bintel Brief, the "bundle of letters."

The first letter was from a man who had abandoned his wife and son; when the family was reunited at the Forward building, readers jammed East Broadway for the happy event. The Bintel Brief would continue for more than 60 years, dispensing domestic counsel and etiquette lessons, finding lost relatives, an essential member of every immigrant family. By the early 1920s, the Forward had a circulation of nearly a quarter of a million.

THE SOCIAL WORK aside, Cahan remained a leading political voice. Though the Forward editor was initially an apologist for Russia's Bolshevik regime, he began to retreat from his support of Communism in the early '20s; in 1927 he toured Russia for six months and came back to call Josef Stalin "the Richard Croker of Russia" and the Communist system "a rope of sand." Thereafter he fought vigorously against Red influences in New York's garment unions. "The Forward was no *nuchshlepper* tagging along after false messiahs," longtime Forward staffer Gus Tyler recalled in a memoir.

Cahan's positions led to a long-running split with many fellow socialists, who now deemed him anti-labor. In the mid-'30s he infuriated many of his old comrades when he threw the Forward's support to New Dealer Franklin Roosevelt instead of the socialist presidential candidate Norman Thomas.

Later, the Forward exposed slave labor in the Soviet Union, provided early word of the Hitler-Stalin pact and aggressively covered the Holocaust. Cahan, in the assessment of Seth Lipsky, current editor of the Forward's English-language edition, "probably broke the three greatest stories of his time."

RETIRED FROM his editorship for several years, Cahan died at 91 on Aug. 31, 1951. Ten thousand people gathered in the streets outside the Forward building, listening to the funeral service on loudspeakers — an astonishing turnout, considering that most Jews had left the lower East Side by then. Indeed, at Cahan's death, the Forward's circulation had fallen to 83,226 daily, 94,390 Sunday.

That in itself could be counted as a victory. Wrote Time magazine: "Cahan's own measurement of success was the rapidity with which Jewish immigrants were absorbed into American life and turned to non-Yiddish papers. In effect, the paper's success could be measured by its drop in circulation."

By DAVID HINCKLEY
Daily News Staff Writer

HIS THRONE WAS a ragged chair in a shopworn living room in a nondescript house on a blue-collar street in Queens, but that didn't matter: When Archie Bunker arrived home from work at the Prendergast Tool and Die Company, he was a king.

And a good thing, too, because away from his chair, Archie was tormented at every step. If it wasn't the spics or the sheenies or the jungle bunnies, it was the fairies or the freaks or the liberals.

Not by coincidence was Archie named Bunker. His living room was his last stand, Archie's Alamo, the one place where a man who just wanted things to be the way they always used to be had any shot at holding off a world that kept wanting to change them.

ARCHIE BUNKER hit the American television set Jan. 12, 1971, the dawn of the '70s, as the angry protagonist of a situation comedy called "All in the Family." Conceived by 1960s liberals to show the true colors of the closed mind, the bigoted buffoon Archie quickly became a lot more complex than that.

As the linchpin of TV's most popular show between 1971 and 1976, drawing 50 million to 60 million viewers a week, Archie for starters attracted more than a few fans who simply thought he was right on target.

On the other end were critics who argued that the program's socially conscious creator, Norman Lear, sabotaged his own goal by pulling Archie's punches. If Lear was serious about shoving a real-life bigot into America's face, they said, why did Archie rail about "spades" and "Hebes" when everyone knew that real-life bigots used N-words and K-words?

But that sort of academic analysis had little to do with daily life at 704 Houser St. in Corona, where Archie lived with his good-natured, slightly slow-witted wife, Edith, their mildly liberal daughter, Gloria, and her aggressively liberal husband, Mike, an unemployed student customarily addressed by Archie as Meathead.

This was the station in life to which Archie had risen, not because it was his choice, but because it was his lot.

One day, Mike, temporarily exhausted by Archie's abuse, fled to the kitchen to ask Edith why Archie mistreated him so.

"Do you wanna know why Archie yells at you?" softly explained the woman regularly called Dingbat by her husband. "Archie is jealous of you. You're going to college. Archie had to quit school to support his family. He ain't never going to be no more than he is right now.

"Now you think that over," she said.

And maybe Mike did. Archie probably didn't.

ARCHIE ON the Nixon presidency: "I'll tell you one thing about Nixon. He keeps Pat home. Which was where Roosevelt should have kept Eleanor. Instead, he

let her run around loose until one day she discovered the colored. We never knew they were there. She told them they were getting the short end of the stick and we've been having trouble ever since."

Archie on, more specifically, the colored: "Their systems is geared a little slower than ours."

In the good old days, the ones in Archie Bunker's mind, such remarks wouldn't have raised a murmur. Mississippi, 1924, no problem. Queens, 1924, no problem. Archie's problem was that he lived in Queens, 1971, with an integrated crew at the plant and a black family right next door: the Jeffersons.

It happened that George Jefferson was not so unlike Archie that all the bull-headedness was entirely on Archie's side of the scale. George, for example, habitually referred to white folks as "honkies." One time he asked a guest if, for drinks, he wanted a White Mule. "What's that?" the guest asked. "A Honky Donkey!" replied George, who thought that was pretty hilarious. But Archie's side of the scale was where things fell when the real-life Sammy Davis Jr. dropped in.

Davis — himself a huge "All in the Family" fan — was talking with Mike about Archie, and Mike was saying Archie really wasn't the kind of guy who'd, say, burn a cross on your lawn.

"No," said Davis. "But he might stop to toast a marshmallow."

Moments later, when Archie asked directly if Davis thought he was prejudiced, Davis replied: "You prejudiced, Mr. Bunker? Why, if you were prejudiced, you would have called me nigger or coon or something. Not you. You came right out and called me colored."

Archie's face lit up with vindication. So, presumably, did Norman Lear's — as he had now managed to get the N-word onto the show without having his white character say it.

CARROLL O'CONNOR'S
Archie Bunker was begot by at least two distinct TV ancestors. One was Jackie Gleason's blustering Ralph Kramden, though the difference between Ralph and Archie, ethnic slurs aside, was that Ralph never stopped thinking he was going to beat the system, that one day his ship would come in. When Archie came along 20 years later, the '50s had become the '70s and that dream had somehow dissolved. If Archie ever had it, he had lost it, leaving him with a sour undertone that was never a part of Ralph Kramden. The other side of Archie's family was a mid-'60s British couple, Alf and Else Garnett, whose "Till Death Do Us

Part" series portrayed two folks simply old, bitter and nasty. But the idea caught Lear's eye, and after several years and turndowns he sold it to CBS, which saw youth culture all around, looked at a schedule that included "Green Acres" and "Hee Haw" and worried it would become as extinct as Mitch Miller if it didn't get something hipper and more daring onto the air fast.

Even after the '60s lowered the bar for acceptable public expression, it was hard not to notice a fat white guy sitting in his chair, cigar in hand, ranting about the polacks, chinks, micks, japs and pinkos.

Moreover — not unlike, say, your own Uncle Fred, who told great dinner-table stories even though you had to admit he was a frightful racist — Archie was entertaining. It was, after all, a sitcom.

Mostly a sitcom. Part of Archie's dilemma, of course, was that he had to face dramatic crises more often than the average blue-collar bigot:

Gloria talks Mike into a vasectomy. Mike becomes impotent. Archie almost has an affair. Edith leaves him. Edith is attacked by a rapist. A Jewish activist is blown up in front of their house by a car bomb.

Gloria has a miscarriage. Edith renounces God. Archie has a gambling problem. Gloria poses nude. A relative turns out to be a lesbian. Gloria has a baby. Edith goes through menopause.

The menopause episode did underscore the catholic nature of Archie's distress: He had no more time for Edith's problem than he did for the problem of segregated lunch counters. "If you're gonna have your change of life, have it right now," he bellowed. "You got exactly 30 seconds. Change!"

That was the short form of the discomfort spread over an episode that found Archie trapped in an elevator with a black businessman and a Puerto Rican couple about to have a baby. The baby was born while the other two men first helped and then marveled. Archie didn't even turn around to look. He simply didn't want to be there.

BUT THERE HE was all the same, and he soldiered on, because that was his lot. He saw Richard Nixon resign, saw the Commies win the war. He saw long hair on men, sure sign of a queer, become stylishly fashionable. He saw equal-opportunity legislation blossom like poison ivy.

And still Archie Bunker kept reloading and firing, defending his ragged throne as if it were the last chair in the world, his own last best hope.

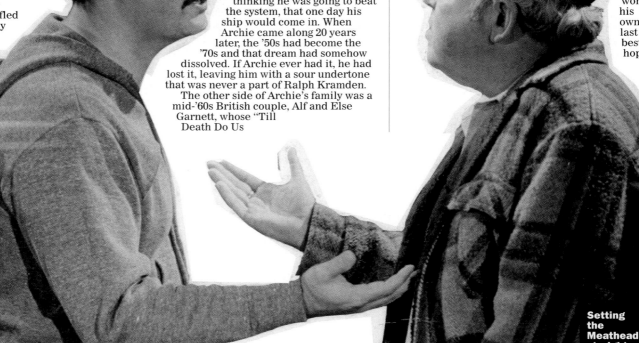

Setting the Meathead straight on things

CHANGE OF LIFE
Archie Bunker

BIG TOWN BIOGRAPHY

By EDWARD T. O'DONNELL
Special to The News

WHEN MADISON Grant, a wealthy and privileged descendant of Scots who had been in New York for a century, was born in 1865, the city was being flooded by thousands of Irish and German immigrants, and what had once been a metropolis of mostly American-born Protestants was now 60 percent foreign-born and 50 percent Catholic.

As it turned out, this was only the beginning. More than 5 million newcomers arrived on U.S. shores in the 1880s alone, and by the time Grant received his law degree from Columbia in 1890, the immigration matter was a constant thread running through a tumultuous period of enormous social change: the industrial revolution, urban expansion, rising class tensions. And still the huddled masses came, and came, and came — a minimum of more than 800,000 every year between 1900 and 1914.

The truth is that New York, the great melting pot, the embodiment of ethnic and racial diversity, has always been full of strong anti-immigrant voices. Traditionally they have focused on the new arrivals' "alien" religions and languages, their negative effect on American wages, their associations with poverty and crime and unclean habits. In the early 20th century, though, many of those who advocated the closing of the Golden Door turned to the pseudo-science of "eugenics" to argue that the period's particular crop of immigrants were racially inferior peoples whose genes were simply unacceptable in such a land as America. Few men did more to popularize the argument than Madison Grant, himself sprung from unassailably good stock.

EUGENICS, ONE OF the great intellectual fads of the early century, held that humanity was composed of many races of varying qualities and abilities. So long as they remained separate, the civilization of the higher races was secure. Intermingling, however, of the higher races of northern Europe ("Teutons") with the lesser southern Europeans ("Mediterraneans") amounted to "race suicide" — the inevitable pulling down of the higher races to the level of the lower ones.

Madison Grant was a distinguished and useful gentleman of his time. He was an energetic naturalist and conservationist who helped establish Yellowstone National Park, the Save the Redwoods League and the Bison Society. With Theodore Roosevelt and others, he was a co-founder in 1895 of the New York Zoological Society and he was its longtime president. He was a prime force in lobbying for the construction of the Bronx River Parkway, which was built largely to improve public access to the Society's splendid Bronx Zoo. He also was a devotee of eugenics, and in 1916 he published an influential book titled "The Passing of the Great Race," a manifesto positing that, by accepting ever-growing numbers of southern and eastern Europeans, America was committing race suicide.

COURTESY DEPT. OF LIBRARY SERVICES, AMERICAN MUSEUM OF NATURAL HISTORY

"The only way to handle it."

ALL ALONG THE WATCHTOWER
Madison Grant

The new immigration ... contained a large and increasing number of the weak, the broken, and mentally crippled of all races drawn from the lower stratum of the Mediterranean basin and the Balkans, together with hordes of the wretched, submerged populations of the Polish Ghettos. Our jails, insane asylums and almshouses are filled with this human flotsam and the whole tone of American life, social, moral and political, has been lowered and vulgarized by them.

"The Passing of the Great Race" was an immediate best-seller, with new editions in 1918, 1920 and 1921 and translations into many languages. It was read by presidents, industrialists, reformers, scientists and everyday Americans. Reviews, both scholarly and popular, were positive. The Saturday Evening Post recommended the book to every American who "wishes to understand the full gravity of our present immigration problem."

Grant's growing anthropological stature won him a medal from the National Institute of Social Sciences. He was treasurer of the Second Eugenics Congress, held in 1921 at New York's American Museum of Natural History, an event whose honored guests included Herbert Hoover, Alexander Graham Bell and Charles Darwin's son Leonard. Grant's opinions and judgments were sought out by many members of the U.S. Congress, who quoted from his book during floor debates as the subject of immigration restriction gained momentum in the early 1920s.

Greatly moved indeed was Congressman Hiram Johnson, the chief sponsor of what came to be known as the National Origins Act:

Our capacity to maintain our cherished institutions stands diluted by a stream of alien blood, with all its inherited misconceptions respecting the relationships of the governing power to the governed.... It is no wonder, therefore, that the myth of the melting pot has been discredited.... The United States is our land.... We intend to maintain it so. The day of unalloyed welcome to all peoples, the day of indiscriminate acceptance of all races, has definitely ended.

When the law took effect in 1924, it dramatically cut back immigrants to 150,000 per year. More significantly, it assigned specific quotas to each nation. Favored "races" like the English got more than 50,000 annual slots — more than they ever used — while unwanted "races" such as Italians and Russians got fewer than 3,000, a small fraction of the number seeking admission.

The law led to profound changes in the nation's immigrant capital, New York City. The influx of the city's two largest immigrant groups, Jews and Italians, practically screeched to a halt. Immigrant neighborhoods like the lower East Side lost population for the first time in a century. In 1954, the ultimate symbol of mass immigration, Ellis Island, closed its doors. These changes were offset somewhat by increased migrations of Puerto Ricans and of blacks from the American South. But it is still possible to argue that Madison Grant's influence on New York City's social makeup was equal to Robert Moses' influence over its structure.

Grant died in 1937, doubtless secure in the knowledge that, even though he had failed to close the nation's gate entirely, he had successfully kept out many, many thousands of his racial inferiors. And yet there was a certain irony in his death: The man who had devoted so much of his life to preserving the white race died childless.

HISTORY EVENTUALLY overtook the eugenics movement. Adolf Hitler came to power in Germany in 1933, the same year that Grant's last book, "Conquest of a Continent," was published, and the similarities between Grant's "racial history" of the United States and the ideologies of Nazism were unmistakable. Noted one reviewer: "Substitute Aryan for Nordic and a good deal of Mr. Grant's argument would lend itself without much difficulty to the support of some recent pronouncements in Germany." The coming of World War II effectively relegated eugenics to the intellectual scrap heap. Congress reopened America's gate in 1965.

A few remnants of eugenicist thought persist to this day, as evidenced by the publication of "The Bell Curve" a few years ago and, more recently, studies suggesting that legalized abortion has contributed to the declining crime rate. But the philosophy that ultimately triumphed was that espoused by another writer in the same year "The Passing of the Great Race" was published. Writing for The Atlantic Monthly, Randolph Bourne offered one of the earliest and most poetic assertions of the multicultural ideal:

America is already the world-federation in miniature, the continent where for the first time in history has been achieved that miracle of hope, the peaceful living side by side, with character substantially preserved, of the most heterogeneous peoples under the sun.

As America enters the 21st century, it is clear whose vision prevailed.

ALPHABETICAL LIST OF BIOGRAPHIES

Abel, Rudolph...129
Atlas, Charles...58
Barber, Red...90
Battista, Vito...109
Battle, Samuel...101
Bennett, Floyd...73
Bennett, Tony...155
Bowes, Major...29
Broderick, Johnny...12
Bryant, Willie...103
Bunker, Archie...157
Cahan, Ab...156
Carlson, John Roy...86
Chapin, Charles...35
Chisari, Anne...115
Chisholm, Shirley...145
Cohn, Roy...135
Coll, Mad Dog...107
Collazo, Oscar...116
Comstock, Anthony...20
Cook, Dr. Frederick...21
Couney, Dr. Martin...99
Crane, Hart...114
Danford, Gen. Robert...85
Davis, Dixie...79
Dead End Kids...17
Delacorte, George...138
Denny, George V. Jr...59
Diamond, Alice...49
Dion and the Belmonts...132
Divine, Father...28
Duffy, Father...64
Dwyer, Big Bill...76
Eastman, Monk...36
Elliott, Robert...39
Fitzgerald, Ed and Pegeen...96
Fitzgerald, Zelda...50
Frick, Henry Clay...16
Friendly, Fred...110
Gallo, Crazy Joey...149
Gensel, The Rev. John...137
Gershwin, George and Ira...55
Ginsberg, Allen...136
Goldberg, Molly...26
Goldman, Edwin Franko...60
Gordon, Vivian...11
Gould, Joe...95
Grant, Madison...158
Grayson, Frances...70, 71

Green, Hetty...33
Guinan, Texas...14
Hale, Mother...153
Halley, Rudolph...121
Hammond, John...41
Handwerker, Nathan...27
Harlem Globetrotters...122
Harry the Hipster...88
Hillman, Sidney...63
Hitler, Brigid and Willie...84
Hodas, Martin...147
Holland, Clifford...44
Howell, Dr. Wallace...119
Hunter, Alberta...152
Jafsie...31
Jolson, Al...51
Jones, J. Raymond...134
Kekiches and the Petersons...150
Kellogg, Junius...118

Kelly, Shipwreck...48
Kid Dropper...37
Kramden, Ralph and Alice...117
Larson, Jonathan...154
LeFrak, Sam...127
Leone, Mamma...32
Levin, Meyer...87
Locke, Alain...56
Lonergan, Anna...19
Macfadden, Bernarr...75
MacGuire, Gerald...82
Manning, Frankie...57
Mantle, Mickey...128
Martin, Smoky Joe...65
Marx, Minnie...104
Masterson, Bat...34
McCann, Chuck...111
Merrill, Dick...81
Metesky, George...108
Mitchel, John Purroy...22, 23
Mock Duck...45, 46, 47
Moondog...139
Namath, Joe...146
Nast, Condé...66, 67
Onassis, Jacqueline Kennedy...151
Outcault, R.F...53
Papp, Joe...144
Payne, Phil...68, 69
Pope, Generoso...92,93
Prinze, Freddie...143
Putnam, George Palmer...72
Randolph, A. Philip...24
Reed, John...62
Reichenbach, Harry...54
Rhinelander, Kip and Alice...18
Robinson, Sugar Ray...91
Rockefeller, John D. Jr....25

Rothstein, Arnold...13
Roventini, Johnny...80
Roxy...98
Rudd, Mark...140
Ruppert, Jacob...30
Ryan, Joseph...102
Schomburg, Arthur...40
Scottoriggio, Joseph...94
Serpico, Frank...148
Shea, Bill...130
Sheen, Bishop...125
Shor, Toots...97
Silverman, Sime...113
Smith, Harry...106
Smothers Brothers...141
Stengel, Casey...131
Straus, Nathan...42
Strayhorn, Billy...105
Sullivan, Big Tim...52
Sullivan, Ed...133
Tesla, Nikola...38
Thomson, Bobby...120
Tiny Tim...142
Tobin, Austin...123
Toscanini...61
Trippe, Juan...83
Tunney, Gene...15
Valentine, Lewis...89
Vance, Dazzy...100
W., Bill...126
Walsh, Helen...74
Wanamaker, Rodman...43
Weaver, Pat...124
Weyman, Stanley...77
White, Stanford...112
Whitney, Richard...78